OXFORD CLASSICAL MONOGRAPHS

Published under the supervision of a Committee of the
Faculty of Literae Humaniores in the University of Oxford

OXFORD CLASSICAL MONOGRAPHS

The aim of the Oxford Classical Monographs series (which replaces the Oxford Classical and Philosophical Monographs) is to publish outstanding revised theses on Greek and Latin literature, ancient history, and ancient philosophy examined by the faculty board of Literae Humaniores.

'Virgins of God'

THE MAKING OF ASCETICISM
IN LATE ANTIQUITY

Susanna Elm

CLARENDON PRESS · OXFORD
1994

BV
5023
.E45
1994

Oxford University Press, Walton Street, Oxford OX2 6DP
Oxford New York Toronto
Delhi Bombay Calcutta Madras Karachi
Kuala Lumpur Singapore Hong Kong Tokyo
Nairobi Dar es Salaam Cape Town
Melbourne Auckland Madrid
and associated companies in
Berlin Ibadan

Oxford is a trade mark of Oxford University Press

Published in the United States
by Oxford University Press Inc., New York

British Library Cataloguing in Publication Data
Data available

Library of Congress Cataloging in Publication Data
Virgins of God: the making of asceticism in late antiquity, Susanna Elm.
(Oxford classical monographs)
Includes bibliographical references and index.
1. Asceticism—History—Early church. ca. 30-600. 2. Monasticism and
religious orders for women—Turkey—History. 3. Monasticism and religious
orders for women—Egypt—History. 4. Women in Christianity—History—Early
church. ca. 30-600. I. Title. II. Series.
BV5023.E45 1994 271'.9'0009015—dc20 93-36710
ISBN 0-19-814920-4

1 3 5 7 9 10 8 6 4 2

Typeset by Best-set Typesetter Ltd., Hong Kong
Printed in Great Britain on acid-free paper by
Biddles Ltd., Guildford and King's Lynn

Nah ist
Und schwer zu fassen der Gott.
Wo aber Gefahr ist, wächst
Das Rettende auch.

                    F. Hölderlin, Patmos

Meiner Mutter
11. 2. 1930, Prag–23. 8. 1992, Berlin

PREFACE

THE following is a study about institutions, their genesis, their function, the means by which they endure, but also the means through which they regulate, control, and select. It originated in a very different context, in an area of study seemingly remote: a period that witnessed the complete breakdown of political and social structures under a totalitarian regime, but also, at the same time, the durability of certain institutional models. It is thus a study deeply influenced by the knowledge that institutions are also human beings, not just abstract entities, and that it therefore behoves us, as human beings, to understand how institutions think, how they remember and forget.

One institutional model of great durability is the Catholic Church. For example, in Germany between 1933 and 1945 it alone through a series of moral compromises, was not *gleichgeschaltet*, not incorporated as an institution into the National-socialist system. As a hierarchically organized institution, the Catholic Church is one of the oldest, if not the oldest, extant multinational institutions in the Western world. How did it accomplish this feat of longevity under constantly changing external conditions? How did an institution of such durability originate?

An attempt to answer these questions suggests a step back in time, not only to the Middle Ages but further, to the fourth century when Christianity became legitimate. When such a step is made, it becomes evident that one of the factors instrumental in the Church's durability is its adaptability. This adaptability seems to have been facilitated, if not made possible, by a constant creation of subsystems, more agile and thus more responsive to the internal and external challenges at hand, and as a consequence also more capable of incorporating a great variety of cultural, social, and economic diversity. Among the most successful of these subsystems are monasticism and the religious orders.

Asceticism and monasticism as phenomena are well known in most cultures. In the Western tradition they have assumed a high degree of differentiated organization: monks belong to orders and live in monasteries that are organized on the basis of specific rules. These rules constitute a standard ('orthodoxy') according to which all religious orders can be classified. As a consequence, whatever is not encompassed by these rules is regarded as ephemeral, and is relegated to the miscellaneous category of 'other'. The Benedictine rule in particular has defined the term monasticism at least since the ninth century, and monastic reform and innovation used to be judged according to what was considered a correct interpretation of this norm, that is, the *regulae rectitudo*. Similarly, throughout the high and late Middle Ages the rule of St Augustine, that of the Templars, and the constitutions of the Dominicans became the blueprint for almost all canonical, military, and mendicant orders. As a consequence, forms of religious life that rejected these rules, or did not a priori conform to their concepts, had to struggle for their right to exist or were relegated to the precarious existence of the heretical. This phenomenon is observable not only in the periods after Benedict but even during those prior to him, when the norm was established by men considered to be his direct precursors, such as Basil of Caesarea, Pachomius, and Antony. This phenomenon is particularly relevant for a special subcategory of ascetics and monks: women.

My study is concerned with a group thus relegated to the margins. It has two tasks. The lesser one is to re-evaluate critically the historiographical conception that takes Benedictine monasticism as its point of reference. The second and larger task is to reconstruct how the monastic norm did evolve and change. Here the role of women becomes crucial. It becomes clear that fourth-century women ascetics adopted organizational patterns and forged institutions via a complex process involving both the transformation of the given model of the family and a reaction against that very model. Moreover, women did so in concert with men. An initial focus on female asceticism thus provides an ideal point of leverage not only for prying apart the historiographical boundaries erected in the wake of monasticism, but also for revealing the great variety of organizational forms against which an 'orthodox' norm was created.

By the end of the third and the beginning of the fourth century AD ascetic communities had developed in urban centres and gained an important voice in ecclesiastical decisions and doctrinal disputes. These communities consisted of male and female ascetics who cohabited. To put it differently, monasticism originated as an urban phenomenon and consisted largely of men and women living together. This symbiosis not only conforms to the structural model of the household, which also comprises men and women; it further represents a stringent interpretation of scriptural precepts. If the ascetic life transforms humans into angels, if angels neither marry nor are given in marriage (Matt. 22: 30), and if there is neither male nor female in Jesus Christ, then the symbiosis of male and female ascetics represents the highest form of ascetic perfection. If through asceticism a woman achieves 'male' virtue (*aretē*), and is thereby transformed into a 'manly woman', then she has not only achieved true equality with her male counterparts, but has been transformed into an ideal, complete human being.

On examining the early history of asceticism in two regions of the Roman Empire, Asia Minor and Egypt, it becomes evident that Basil of Caesarea, Pachomius, Athanasius of Alexandria, and other ascetic and monastic 'innovators' were much less innovators than *reformers*. As reformers they replaced already existing organizational models of ascetic life with others, better suited to the demands of contemporary society. One aspect of this adaptation was the attempt to segregate the sexes. In theory, men and women as ascetics were equal. However, this equality was increasingly projected inwards: only the soul of an ascetic woman may 'become male', and none of these male qualities may find an external expression. Poverty became a personal matter rather than an absolute goal to be pursued by the ascetic community as such. And withdrawal from the world was to be effected by a move to the countryside (the *desertum*), by a removal from the urban scene of politics, rather than solely as a personal choice of life-style. In Egypt the dialectical interaction between norms which increasingly stress the advantages of ascetic life in the desert and an urban ascetic audience becomes even more evident, as highlighted by the tensions between Alexandria and the *koinē*.

Throughout all these processes concepts of orthodoxy and heresy, as well as the doctrinal struggles to define the notion of the Trinity, were fundamental to the creation and selection of ascetic models. After Theodosius' accession in the year 379, in a clear reversal of historic development, existing ascetic communities of long standing found themselves branded as 'heretical innovations', while newly developed notions of ascetic life in common were heralded as traditional and 'orthodox'. In this process the relation between the true import, the actual practical value of an organizational concept, and the merely fortuitous doctrinal alliances of ascetic leaders perforce remains unclear.

My study focuses on female asceticism and its organization to demonstrate that the conventional picture of asceticism and of its making in the fourth century needs to be revised. This revision entails a new attention to the dynamic process by which the past is shaped into a 'tradition', reaching the present only refashioned according to contemporary norms.

A project of this duration necessarily incurs many debts of gratitude. Dumbarton Oaks, the National Humanities Center, and the National Endowment for the Humanities provided me with the funds and leisure without which the completion of this book would have been very difficult indeed. To them, and that means in particular to the staff at both Dumbarton Oaks and the National Humanities Center, I remain deeply indebted. Special thanks are also due to Robin Lane Fox, who sparked the idea of 'virgins', and to John Matthews, who guided me throughout all stages of the dissertation from which this study developed; I can only say that he was the best supervisor I could have hoped for. I should further like to thank my colleagues in the History Department at Berkeley, who have contributed much not only in the way of intellectual stimulation, but perhaps more importantly by making me feel at home in California. I am especially grateful to William Bouwsma, Robert Brentano, Gerard Caspary, Robin Einhorn, Carla Hesse, Geoffrey Koziol, Thomas Laqueur, and Peter Sahlins. Thomas Brady and Erich Gruen were true mentors, offering advice in many matters, both small and not so small. Their insights and guidance extended well beyond the substantial portions of the manuscript they have read.

Over the years many friends have given me ideas, insights, and encouragement, in conversations and through their work, among them Joseph Alchermes, Peter Brown, Alessandra Casella, Elizabeth Clark, Kaspar Elm, Marcella Forlin Patrucco, Hartmut

Galsterer, Elena Giannarelli, Linda Gregerson, Robert Gregg, Joan Gruen, George Lawless, Barbara Levick, Stephan zur Lippe, Rita Lizzi, Rebecca Lyman, Johann Michael Möller, Steven Mullaney, Jeffrey Schnapp, Eve Sedgwick, Ramon Teja, and Simon Wallis. Lennard Sundelin helped me a great deal with the footnotes in Part I, and I am very grateful to William North not only for compiling the index, but, more importantly, for all his comments, corrections, and ideas. Linda Morgan and Karen Carroll accomplished feats on the keyboard and prevented many a typing error. My very special thanks are due to Lucy Gasson and Hilary O'Shea, my editors at Oxford University Press, and to copy-editor Julian Ward. All errors remaining after the cumulative effort of all these friends are exclusively my own.

Finally, I wish to give special thanks to Theodore Correl, who made me happy, and, above all, to my parents. Over the years, they have given me support, courage, opportunities for many a lively discussion, and a constant sense of belonging. This book, however, is dedicated to the memory of my mother, to her strength and courage in the face of the inevitable.

University of California at Berkeley   S.E.
September 1992

CONTENTS

LIST OF MAPS

ABBREVIATIONS

AnBoll	*Analecta Bollandiana*
ANRW	J. Vogt and H. Temporini (eds.), *Aufstieg und Niedergang der römischen Welt* (Berlin, 1972–)
ARW	*Archiv für Religionswissenschaften*
Aubineau, *Virginité*	Grégoire de Nysse, *Traité de la virginité*, ed. M. Aubineau (SC 119; Paris, 1966).
ByZ	*Byzantinische Zeitschrift*
CH	*Church History*
CIL	*Corpus Inscriptionum Latinarum* (Berlin, 1862–)
Courtonne, *Lettres*	Basile de Césarée, *Lettres*, ed. Y. Courtonne, 3 vols. (Paris, 1957–66)
CSCO	Corpus Scriptorum Christianorum Orientalium (Louvain, 1903–)
CSEL	Corpus Scriptorum Ecclesiasticorum Latinorum (Vienna, 1866–)
DACL	*Dictionnaire d'archéologie chrétienne et de liturgie*
DB	*Dictionnaire de la Bible*
DHGE	*Dictionnaire d'histoire et de géographie ecclésiastique*
DIP	*Dizionario degli Istituti di Perfezione*
DOP	*Dumbarton Oaks Papers*
DSp	*Dictionnaire de spiritualité*
EtCarm	*Études carmélitaines*
Eusebius, *HE*	Eusèbe de Césarée, *Histoire ecclésiastique et les martyrs en Palestine*, ed. G. Bardy (SC 31, 41, 55, 73; Paris, 1952–60)
Gallay, *Lettres*	Grégoire de Nazianze, *Lettres*, ed. P. Gallay, 2 vols. (Paris, 1964)
GCS	Die griechischen christlichen Schrifsteller der ersten drei Jahrhunderte (Berlin, 1897–)
GN	*Gregorii Nysseni Opera*, ed. W. Jaeger, 10 vols. (Leiden, 1952–90)
GR	*Greece and Rome*
Hauser-Meury	M.-M. Hauser-Meury, *Prosopographie zu den Schriften Gregors von Nazianz* (Bonn, 1960)

Hefele– Leclercq	*Histoire des Conciles d'après les documents ori- ginaux*, ed. C. J. Hefele and H. Leclercq, 2 vols. (Paris, 1907)
JAC	*Jahrbuch für Antike und Christentum*
JEH	*Journal of Ecclesiastical History*
JÖB	*Jahrbuch der österreichischen Byzantinistik*
JRS	*Journal of Roman Studies*
JThS	*Journal of Theological Studies*
Lampe	*A Patristic Greek Lexicon*, ed. G. W. H. Lampe (Oxford, 1961)
LSJ	H. G. Liddell, R. Scott, and H. Stuart Jones, *A Greek–English Lexicon* (Oxford, 1940^9)
MAMA	*Monumenta Asiae Minoris Antiqua*, ed. W. M. Calder and J. M. R. Cormack, 8 vols. (Publications of the American Society for Archeological Re- search in Asia Minor; Manchester, 1928–62)
Mansi	*Sacrorum conciliorum nova et amplissima collectio*, ed. J. D. Mansi, 31 vols. (Florence–Venice, 1757– 98)
Maraval, *Macrine*	Grégoire de Nysse, *Vie de Sainte Macrine*, ed. P. Maraval (SC 178; Paris, 1971)
Mommsen– Meyer	*Theodosiani Libri XVI (Codex) cum constitutioni- bus Sirmondianis et leges novellae ad Theodosianum pertinentes*, ed. T. Mommsen and P. Meyer, 2 vols. (Berlin, 1954^2)
ODCC	*Oxford Dictionary of the Christian Church*, ed. F. Cross and E. Livingstone (Oxford, 1974^2)
OrChrA	Orientalia Christiana Analecta
OrChrP	*Orientalia Christiana Periodica*
Patrucco, *Lettere*	Basilio di Cesarea, *Le Lettere*, i, ed. M. Forlin Patrucco (Corona Patrum 11; Turin, 1983)
PG	Patrologia Graeca, ed. J. P. Migne *et al.* (Paris, 1857–)
PL	Patrologia Latina, ed. J. P. Migne *et al.* (Paris, 1844–)
PLRE	*The Prosopography of the Later Roman Empire*, ed. A. H. M. Jones, J. R. Martindale, and J. Morris, 2 vols. (Cambridge, 1971–80)
RAC	*Reallexikon für Antike und Christentum*
RAM	*Revue d'ascétique et de mystique*

RBén	*Revue Bénédictine*
RE	*Paulys Real-Encyclopädie der classischen Alterthumswissenschaft* (Stuttgart, 1893–)
REA	*Revue des études anciennes*
REG	*Revue des études grecques*
RevSR	*Revue des sciences religieuses*
RH	*Revue historique*
RHE	*Revue d'histoire ecclésiastique*
RHR	*Revue de l'histoire des religions*
RSR	*Recherches de science religieuse*
SC	Sources Chrétiennes (Paris, 1942–)
SP	*Studia Patristica*
StT	Studi e testi
ThZ	*Theologische Zeitschrift*
TIB	*Tabula Imperii Byzantini*, vols. ii and iv, ed. F. Hild and M. Restle (Österreichische Akademie der Wissenschaften, phil.-hist. Klasse 149, 172; Vienna, 1981, 1984)
Tillemont, *Mémoires*	S. Lenain de Tillemont, *Mémoires pour servir à l'histoire ecclésiastique des six premier siècles*, 16 vols. (Paris, 1693–1712)
TRE	*Theologische Realenzyklopädie*
TU	Texte und Untersuchungen zur Geschichte der altchristlichen Literatur (Leipzig, 1882–)
VigChr	*Vigiliae Christianae*
ZKG	*Zeitschrift für Kirchengeschichte*
ZNW	*Zeitschrift für die neutestamentliche Wissenschaft*
ZPE	*Zeitschrift für Papyrologie und Epigraphik*

Introduction

askēsis: exercise, practice, training, profession, mode of life.
anachōrēsis: retirement, retreat (e.g. from battle, public life, the world).
monachos: unique, singular, solitary.[1]

The disciple of Apa Sisoes said to him, 'Father, you have grown old. Let us move a little closer to the settled land.' The Old Man said, 'Where there is no woman, that is where we should go.' The disciple said to him, 'What other place is there that has no woman, if not the desert?' The Old Man said to him, 'Take me to the desert.'[2]

Asceticism appears to many as a strange and peculiar phenomenon, perhaps even an affliction. It evokes solitary men driven by their quest for God into the *desertum*, the barren wilderness of remote countrysides, far removed from the world, and in particular far removed from women. The great champions of the movement, revered as its originators—Paul of Thebes, Symeon the Stylite, and, most importantly, Antony the Great—all embody these essential characteristics, and their victories over physical afflication and demonic temptation have fuelled the imagination for centuries.[3] Monasticism, the 'higher evolution' of asceticism, is likewise clearly defined by our commonplace notions. By moderating the physical extremes of the ascetic life, monasticism emphasizes order, work, prayer, obedience, stability—all within the monastic family. This monastic family, again located mostly in the *desertum*, the countryside, is organized into communities of either monks or nuns, who, under the guidance of an abbot or abbess, follow a specific rule.[4] Like asceticism, monasticism also

---

[1] According to the definitions given in LSJ s.vv.

[2] Sisoes 3 (J.-C. Guy, *Les Apophtegmes des Pères du Désert, série alphabétique*, Textes de Spiritualité Orientale 1; Begrolles, 1968), 276; here in the trans. by P. R. L. Brown, *The Body and Society: Men, Women, and Sexual Renunciation in Early Christianity* (New York, 1988), 242.

[3] G. Penco, 'Il ricordo dell'ascetismo Orientale nella tradizione monastica del Medioevo europeo', *Studi Medievali* 3 (1963), 571–8.

[4] D. Knowles, *Christian Monasticism* (London, 1969); J. Gobry, *Les Moines en Occident*, 3 vols. (Paris, 1985–7).

has its heroes and founding fathers: Pachomius, Basil of Caesarea, Augustine of Hippo, Benedict of Nursia, and later Francis of Assisi, men whose names, not by coincidence, are also associated with the most influential monastic rules.

The history, more precisely the historiography of monasticism, has essentially been that of its 'originators' and 'founders' and, as a consequence, that of the normative writings associated with them.[5] The question of the origin, and by implication that of the role and function of monasticism, has been a central aspect of Church history since the early fifth century.[6] Whenever theological concepts were in fierce competition, monasticism became one of the principal tools that could be marshalled to legitimize one's own and to dismantle one's opponent's doctrinal position. Thus in 1521 Martin Luther chose Antony the Great as one of his primary weapons in attacking the monastic orders of his day, arguing that, in stark contrast to the Catholic orders, Antony's life was truly in accord with the Gospel.[7] Philipp Melanchthon adopted a similar line of argument in his *Apology for the Augsburg*

[5] A. S. Cua, 'Morality and the Paradigmatic Individuals', *American Philosophical Quarterly* 6 (1969), 324–9; J. Dubois and G. Renaud, 'Influence de Saints sur le développement des institutions', in *Hagiographie, cultures et sociétés, IVe–XIIe siècle. Centre de Recherches sur l'Antiquité tardive et la Haut Moyen Age. Université de Paris X. Actes du Colloque organisé à Nanterre et à Paris, 2–5 Mai 1979* (Paris, 1983), 491–513; J. P. Gilmont, 'Paternité et médiation du fondateur d'ordre', *Revue d'ascétique et de mystique* 40 (1964), 393–426; J. M. Lozano, *Foundresses, Founders, and their Religious Families* (Chicago, 1983); U. Ranke-Heinemann, 'Das Motiv der Nachfolge im frühen Mönchtum', *Erbe und Auftrag* 36 (1960), 353–47.

[6] W. Nigg, *Kirchengeschichtsschreibung: Grundzüge ihrer historischen Entwicklung* (Munich, 1934); P. Meinhold, *Geschichte der kirchlichen Historiographie*, 3 vols. (Orbis Academicus. Problemgeschichten der Wissenschaft in Dokumenten und Darstellungen; Freiburg i.B., 1962); G. Penco, 'La storiografia del monachesimo nel quadro e negli sviluppi della storiografia ecclesiastica', *Studia monastica* 22 (1980), 15–28.

[7] M. Luther, *De votis monasticis* (Weimarer Ausgabe 8; Weimar, 1889), 573–669, here 578: 'Sanctus Antonius, ipsissimus monachorum pater et monasticae vitae princeps, sapientissime et Christianissime censuit et docuit, nihil prorsus esse tentandum, quod auctoritatem Scripturae non haberet'; Ger. trans., ed. J. G. Walsch, *Dr. Martin Luther's sämtliche Schriften*, xix (St Louis, 1889), 1500–1665, here 1509; B. Lohse, *Mönchtum und Reformation: Luthers Auseinandersetzung mit dem Mönchsideal des Mittelalters* (Forschungen zur Dogmengeschichte 12; Göttingen, 1963); H. M. Stamm, *Luthers Stellung zum Ordensleben* (Wiesbaden, 1980).

Confessions, where he attributed the withdrawal of Antony, Dominic, and Francis to their true adherence to the teachings of the Bible, and emphasized that they all had valued pure faith higher than monastic works or vows.[8] Luther and Melanchthon were less concerned with historical investigation than with theological argumentation. Yet, invoking as it did the names of 'founders', their argument created precisely that: a historical concern. Was Paul of Thebes or Antony the Great the first true monk? Were the monks the direct successors of the Apostles? Or was there an interim stage? If indeed monasticism originated in the fourth century AD, then how was it possible that all the excellent Fathers of the Church flourishing at the same time did not prevent the emergence of such an unbiblical deviation?[9]

Rodolphus Hospinianus published the first comprehensive discussion of the Protestant point of view in 1588, declaring that Apostles and monks had been separated by an interim period; a repudiation came in the same year with Caesarius Baronius' Catholic *Annales Ecclesiastici*, which argued for uninterrupted continuity from John the Baptist via Antony and Benedict to contemporary monastic orders.[10] The now crucially important quest for the true origins of monasticism produced, especially in the Catholic camp, a flood of new textual editions centring around the originators: the *Life of Antony* in 1611, the *Vitae Patrum* in 1613, the first volumes of the great collections of the Bollandists in 1634, L. Holstenius' *Codex Regularum* of Benedict of Aniane in 1661, and the great enterprise of the Maurists in 1675.[11] While providing the basis for subsequent scientific

---

[8] Ph. Melanchthon, *Apologia Confessionis Augustanae*, iii, ed. G. Rechenberg (Würzburg, 1978), 99. E. P. Meijering, *Melanchthon and Patristic Thought* (Studies in the History of Christian Thought 32; Leiden, 1983), 19–93.

[9] K. Heussi, *Der Ursprung des Mönchtums* (Tübingen, 1936), 2–10; F. Wulf, 'Die Stellung des Protestantismus zu Askese und Mönchtum in Geschichte und Gegenwart', in *Geistliches Leben in der heutigen Welt* (Freiburg i.B., 1960), 194–218.

[10] C. Baronius, *Annales Ecclesiastici*, 12 vols. (Rome, 1590); R. Hospinianus, *De Monachis: hoc est, De Origine et Progressu Monachatus ac Ordinum Monasticorum Equitumque Militarium tam sacrorum quam secularium omnium libri 7* (Zurich, 1609²).

[11] L. Holstenius, *Codex Regularum, quas sancti Patres Monachis et Virginibus Sanctimonialibus servandas praescripsere, collectus olim a s. Benedicto Anianensi Abbate* (Rome, 1661); cf. J. Neufville, 'Les Éditeurs des "Regulae Patrum": Saint

investigation, the nature and selection of these editions underlined the cental point. The history of monasticism was not a historical issue (however rudimentary) but a doctrinal one, and it was told by means of and as being identical with its key figures. To choose one example: when the Maurist Jean Mabillon wrote the first comprehensive history of Western monasticism between 1703 and 1707, he gave it the title *Annales Ordinis Sancti Benedicti*.[12] In other words, according to Mabillon, the history of Latin monasticism (and, indeed, *non minima*, that of the Latin Church) was identical to that of the order of Benedict. Anything else, prior or contemporary, was, if seen at all, either 'proto-benedictine' or 'extra-benedictine'.

Even the new methods of scientific analysis developed in the eighteenth, nineteenth, and early twentieth centuries were slow to effect significant change with regard to these fundamental axioms of monasticism.[13] Beyond doubt, in the early 1900s the work of Adolf von Harnack, Walter Bauer, and Max Weber dramatically changed the nature of Patristic studies as a whole, with profound consequences that continue to this day.[14]

Harnack emphasized that Christianity was not a homogeneous

Benoît d'Aniane et Lukas Holste', *RBén* 76 (1966), 327–43; D. Knowles, *Great Historical Enterprises* (London, 1963); P. Peeters, *L'Œuvre des Bollandistes* (Mémoires de l'Académie Royale de Belgique, cl. des sciences. mem. coll. 8, 2nd ser., 54: 5; Brussels, 1960[2]).

[12] J. Mabillon, *Annales Ordinis s. Benedicti occidentalium monachorum patriarchae. In quibus non modo res monasticae, sed etiam ecclesiasticae historiae non minima pars continetur*, 6 vols. (Paris, 1703–39); H. Leclercq, *Mabillon*, 2 vols. (Paris, 1957).

[13] In the 18th cent. J. L. v. Mosheim, in his *De rebus Christianorum ante Constantinum Magnum commentarii* (Helmstedt, 1753) (see K. Heussi, *Die Kirchengeschichtsschreibung Joh. Lorenz v. Mosheims* (Geschichtliche Unter-suchungen 4; Gotha, 1904), 60 f.), introduced basic methods of comparative religious study into the discussion of the origins of monasticism; E. Gibbon on the other hand, in his *History of the Decline and Fall of the Roman Empire* (London, 1776–88), was not interested in the origins of monasticism *per se*, but considered it a subversive power, and a principal cause for Rome's decline (see A. Demandt, *Der Fall Roms: Die Auflösung des römischen Reiches im Urteil der Nachwelt* (Munich, 1984), 264–73). W. J. Mangold, in his *De monachatus originibus et causis* (Marburg, 1852), stressed the non-Christian and heretical origins of mon-asticism, which then, according to him, infiltrated Catholicism.

[14] See E. A. Clark, 'The State and Future of Historical Theology: Patristic Studies', in ead. *Ascetic Piety and Women's Faith: Essays on Late Ancient Christianity* (Studies in Women and Religion 20; Lewiston, 1986), 3–19.

entity, but a constantly evolving system of beliefs, at every stage shaped by the forces of its surroundings: by culture, society, economy, and politics. Christian dogma did not 'create' itself, but had its source 'in the individual living man and nowhere else', and, as Harnack affirmed, it was the scholar's task to take the conditions of this individual's life seriously, whether or not he belonged to the orthodox 'mainstream'.[15] Bauer's work contested the belief that orthodoxy was always the chronologically prior tradition and heresy therefore a deviant innovation, by proving that more often than not the reverse was the case. In so doing he further drew attention to the fact that early Christianity was characterized by significant regional and geographical diversity.[16] Using Harnack's typologies of early Christianity as a basis, Max Weber then developed a sociological analysis, which has remained an intellectual challenge to this day.[17]

The effect of these and similar works was profound. They set the course of scholarship for the subsequent decades, not least by prompting a host of new critical editions of the relevant texts. Scholars began to use the methods of anthropology and psychology,[18] the techniques of numismatics, papyrology, and

[15] A. v. Harnack, *Dogmengeschichte* (Grundriß der theologischen Wissenschaften 4: 3; Tübingen, 1922[6]); trans. N. Buchanan, *History of Dogma*, i (New York, 1958[2]), esp. 12; see also his very illuminating lecture, 'Was hat die Historie an fester Erkenntnis zur Deutung des Weltgeschehens zu bieten?', in A. Harnack-v. Zahn, and A. v. Harnack, (eds.), *Adolf von Harnack: Ausgewählte Reden und Aufsätze* (Berlin, 1951), 181–204, esp. 187f.; A. v. Harnack, *Das Mönchtum, seine Ideale und seine Geschichte* (Giessen, 1901[5]).

[16] W. Bauer, *Rechtgläubigkeit und Ketzerei im ältesten Christentum* (Beiträge zur historischen Theologie 10; Tübingen, 1934); Eng. trans. R. A. Kraft and G. Krodel, *Orthodoxy and Heresy in Earliest Christianity* (Philadelphia, 1971).

[17] M. Weber, *Economy and Society*, 3 vols., ed. G. Roth and C. Wittich (i: Berkeley, 1978[2], ii–iii New York, 1968), esp. 'The Sociology of Religion', here i. 399–634; id. *Gesammelte Aufsätze zur Religionssoziologie*, 3 vols. (Tübingen, 1972[6]), esp. 'Die protestantische Ethik und der Geist des Kapitalismus', i. 17–206.

[18] Especially works such as M. Douglas, *Purity and Danger* (London, 1966); C. Geertz, 'Centers, Kings and Charisma: Reflections on the Symbolics of Power', in J. Ben-David and T. Nichols Clark (eds.), *Culture and Its Creators: Essays in Honor of Edward Shils* (Chicago, 1977), 150–71; J. Goody, 'Religion, Social Change and the Sociology of Conversion', in id. (ed.), *Changing Social Structure in Ghana* (London, 1975); also very influential is psychologically based work such as N. Chodorow, 'Family Structure and Feminine Personality', in M. Zimbalist Rosaldo, and L. Lamphere (eds.), *Woman, Culture, and Society* (Stanford, Calif., 1974), 43–66.

archaeology, and sought to investigate regions of Christianity well beyond the Greek and Latin boundaries.[19] New methodological approaches also shifted attention away from the more traditional, theologically influenced concerns, primarily those of doctrine, to new subjects such as social stratification, urban versus rural developments, poverty and wealth.[20]

With the advent of twentieth-century feminism, an additional dimension was added to the scholarly discourse. Women certainly had been discussed in earlier scholarly work, but while they had remained a somewhat marginal concern, they were now beginning to become the focus of study.[21] Virginity, misogyny, aspects specific to female asceticism, the position of women in the Church, and the theological and social underpinnings of these issues became central to a discourse[22] which was, however, often

[19] To name but one outstanding example: A. Vööbus, *History of Asceticism in the Syrian Orient*, 2 vols. (CSCO 184, 197; Louvain, 1958, 1960).

[20] See especially the fundamental work by G. Dagron, *Naissance d'une capitale: Constantinople et ses institutions de 330 à 451* (Bibliothèque byzantine. Études 7; Paris, 1974); id. 'Le Christianisme dans la ville byzantine', *DOP* 31 (1977), 3–25; P. Garnsey, *Social Status and Legal Privilege in the Roman Empire* (Oxford, 1970); also in particular E. Patlagean, *Pauvreté économique et pauvreté sociale à Byzance (4ᵉ–7ᵉ siècles)*, (Civilisations et Sociétés 48; Paris, 1977).

[21] H. Achelis, *Virgines Subintroductae: Ein Beitrag zum VII. Kapitel des I. Korintherbriefes* (Leipzig, 1902); D. Kirsch, A. Hagel and T. Hillenkamp (eds.), *Characterbilder der katholischen Frauenwelt: Aus der Zeit der Kirchenväter* (Paderborn, 1911); H. Koch, 'Virgines Christi: Das Gelübde der gottgeweihten Jungfrauen in den ersten drei Jahrhunderten' (TU 31; Berlin, 1907), 59–112; id. *Virgo Eva, Virgo Maria: Neue Untersuchungen über die Lehre von der Jungfrauenschaft und der Ehe Mariens in der ältesten Kirche* (Berlin, 1932); M. R. Nugent, *Portrait of the Consecrated Women in Greek Christian Literature of the First Four Centuries* (Washington, 1941); F. de B. Vizmanos, *Las Virgenes cristianas de la Iglesia primitiva* (Madrid, 1949); J. Wilpert, *Die gottgeweihten Jungfrauen in den ersten Jahrhunderten der Kirche nach patristischen Quellen und den Grabdenkmälern dargestellt* (Freiburg i.B., 1892); L. Zscharnack, *Der Dienst der Frau in den ersten Jahrhunderten der christlichen Kirche* (Göttingen, 1902).

[22] To name but a few examples: J. Anson, 'The Female Transvestite in Early Monasticism: the Origin and Development of a Motif', *Viator* 5 (1974), 1–32; F. Bourassa, 'La virginité dans l'état d'innocence', *Sciences ecclésiastiques* 6 (1954), 249–57; T. Camelot, *Virgines Christi: La Virginité aux premiers siècles de l'Église* (Paris, 1944); id. 'Les Traités "De Virginitate" au IVᵉ siècle', *Et Carm* 31 (1952), 273–92; of particular significance here is the work of Elizabeth A. Clark, 'John Chrysostom and the Subintroductae', *CH* 46 (1977), 171–85; ead. *Jerome, Chrysostom, and Friends* (New York, 1979); and esp. ead. *Ascetic Piety and Women's Faith*; F. E. Consolino, 'Modelli di santità femminile nelle più antiche

dominated by the notion that women were mere victims of patriarchal suppression.[23] More recently, in part as a direct result of feminist concerns, but mainly under the influence of new theoretical approaches, in particular those of Paul Veyne and Michel Foucault, much of early Christianity has been reconceptualized once more, now in terms of the body and sexuality.[24]

As a result of these studies asceticism and monasticism underwent a profound re-evaluation.[25] Yet, even in the work of the

---

Passioni romane', *Augustinianum* 24 (1984), 83–113; ead. 'Modelli di comportamento e modi di santificazione per l'aristocrazia femminile d'Occidente', in A. Giardina (ed.), *Società romana e impero tardoantico, i: Instituzioni, ceti, economie* (Bari, 1986), 273–306; E. Giannarelli, *La tipologia femminile nella biografia e nell'autobiografia cristiana del IV° secolo* (Istituto storico Italiano per il Medioevo. Studi Storici 127; Rome, 1980); E. Patlagean, 'L'Histoire de la femme déguisée en moine et l'évolution de la sainteté féminine à Byzance', *Studi Medievali* 17 (1976), 597–623; G. Scharffenorth and K. Thraede (eds.), *"Freunde in Christus werden..."* (Kennzeichen 1; Berlin, 1977); C. Tibiletti, *Verginità e matrimonio in antichi scrittori cristiani* (Atti della Facoltà di Lettere e Filosofia della Università degli Studi di Macerata 2; Macerata, 1969), 10–217.

[23] E. S. Fiorenza, 'Word, Spirit and Power: Women in Early Christian Communities,' in R. R. Ruether and E. McLaughlin (eds.), *Women of Spirit: Female Leadership in the Jewish and Christian Traditions* (New York, 1979), 29–70; S. L. Davies, *The Revolt of the Widows: The Social World of the Apocryphal Acts* (London, 1980); A. E. Hickey, *Women of the Roman Aristocracy as Christian Monastics* (Studies in Religion 1; Ann Arbor, 1987); R. Kraemer, 'Ecstatics and Ascetics: Studies in the Functions of Religious Activities for Women in the Greco-Roman World', Diss. (Princeton, NJ, 1976); E. Kaehler, *Die Frau in den paulinischen Briefen unter besonderer Berücksichtigung der Unterordnung* (Zurich, 1960); R. R. Ruether, 'Mothers of the Church: Ascetic Women in the Late Patristic Age', in *Women of Spirit*, 71–98; ead. 'Misogynism and Virginal Feminism in the Fathers of the Church,' in ead. (ed.), *Religion and Sexism: Images of Woman in the Jewish and Christian Tradition* (New York, 1974), 150–83; A. Yarbrough, 'Christianization in the Fourth Century: The Example of Roman Women', *CH* 45 (1976), 149–65.

[24] P. Ariès, and G. Duby (eds.), *A History of Private Life*, i: *From Pagan Rome to Byzantium*, ed. P. Veyne (Cambridge, Mass. 1987); Brown, *The Body and Society*; M. Foucault, *The History of Sexuality*, i: *An Introduction*; iii: *The Care of the Self*, trans. R. Hurley (New York, 1978, 1986); R. Lane Fox, *Pagans and Christians* (New York, 1987); P. Veyne, 'La Famille et l'amour sous l'Haut-empire romain', *Annales E.S.C.* 33 (1978), 35–63.

[25] See especially the seminal articles by P. R. L. Brown, 'The Rise and Function of the Holy Man in Late Antiquity', *JRS* 61 (1971), 80–101, and G. Dagron, 'Les Moines et la ville: Le Monachisme à Constantinople jusqu'au Concile de Chalcédoine (451)', *Travaux et Mémoires* 4 (1970), 229–76; cf. also

last two decades, asceticism has again been used selectively to further arguments in contemporary debates. And the study of monasticism itself, especially the institutional aspects of monasticism, have remained strangely untouched by these new approaches. To be sure, there has been an ever-increasing quantity of specialized studies focusing, for instance, on individual monastic personalities, specific locations, the relationship between monasticism and society at large, and various typological questions. New results have wrought profound changes with regard to our knowledge of 'heresies', and brought increasing insights into the relationship between Eastern and Western monasticism. Yet, despite (and even within) this flood of new research, Benedict, his rules, and Benedictine monasticism, have remained the centre of historiographical attention.[26] In the East a similarly prominent position is held by Basil of Caesarea, quoted in the Benedictine rule itself as one of its immediate precursors.

Thus, the fact remains that the historiography of monasticism continues to be overwhelmingly concerned with its founding figures and their normative writings. As a direct consequence, it remains dominated by the institutions which created these norms and were in turn regulated by them. More specifically, the historiography of monasticism as a whole, regarding its history both before and after Benedict, remains dominated and deeply influenced by the notions exemplified by Benedictine monasticism and its related concerns. Or, to put it another way: the notions here broadly defined as Benedictine monasticism continue to be the privileged vantage point from which everything else is defined as liminal.[27] If this is so, then any attempt to focus again on the

the critical new study of Italian asceticism and monasticism by G. Jenal, *Italia ascetica ac monastica: Das Asketen- und Mönchtum in Italien von den Anfängen bis zur Zeit der Langobarden (ca. 150/250–604)*, 3 vols. (Monographien zur Geschichte des Mittelalters; Stuttgart, 1994), here referred to in the typescript manuscript, i. 1–52, esp. 11.

[26] Cf. especially G. Penco, *Il monachesimo fra spiritualità e cultura* (Milan, 1991); A. de Vogüé, *Histoire littéraire du mouvement monastique dans l'antiquité*, i: *Le Monachisme latin* (Paris, 1991).

[27] Cf. e.g. V. and E. Turner, *Image and Pilgrimage in Christian Culture: Anthropological Perspectives* (New York, 1978); and the perceptive critique by C. Walker Bynum, 'Women's Stories, Women's Symbols: A Critique of Victor Turner's Theory of Liminality', repr. in ead. *Fragmentation and Redemption: Essays on Gender and the Human Body in Medieval Religion* (New York, 1991),

history of monasticism, especially that history prior to Benedict, must ask why certain writings are considered normative and others not. On what grounds, for what purpose, and by whom are such distinctions being made? Moreover, it must be asked: what is thereby revealed about the nature of the excluded writings and the organizational models and institutions addressed by them? How do insights gained by investigating excluded forms reflect upon the role and function of the norm? And, finally, on a more fundamental level, what is thereby revealed with regard to the processes leading to the formulation of any normative canon and the institutions that both formulate norms and are regulated by them?

'Institutions create shadowed places in which nothing can be seen and no questions asked.'[28] Benedict of Nursia was a man and the order devoted to obeying his rule primarily male. It follows that in the case of asceticism and monasticism, what is immediately placed in the shadows are the models of religious life adopted by women, models that fall outside the Benedictine mould, and, up to a certain point, developments in the Greek East, which all too often is seen as distinct and separate from the Latin West of the Roman Empire long before the actual separation had taken place. Indeed, there is to my knowledge no comprehensive study that attempts to reconstruct the models of ascetic life chosen by women from the point of view of their institutionalization.[29] More precisely, there has been no attempt to place the organizational development of female asceticism in its historical context, that is, in the context of the institutional development of male monasticism, and that means of monasticism as such.[30] If, as Mabillon thought, the history of monasticism is indeed essential to that of

27–51; I would like to mention that the citations in the following do not exhaust the influence C. Walker Bynum has had upon my work.

[28] M. Douglas, *How Institutions Think* (Syracuse, 1986), 69.

[29] See S. Elm, 'The Organization and Institutionalization of Female Asceticism in Fourth Century Cappadocia and Egypt', Diss. (Oxford, 1987).

[30] What has been said, has remained largely focused on women alone, and has mostly been based on Latin sources; cf. e.g. J. A. McNamara, 'Muffled Voices: The Lives of Consecrated Women in the Fourth Century', in J. A. Nichols and L. T. Shank, *Medieval Religious Women*, i: *Distant Echoes* (Cistercian Studies Series 71; Kalamazoo, 1984), 11–29.

the Church, then to redress this evident omission should not only shed some light on what has remained in the darkness, but should also place what is in the light in a more appropriate place on the colour scheme: it should alter our understanding not only of the making of asceticism and monasticism but of the making of the early Church.

The task is not an easy one. Darkness is not monochromatic. Darkness, or in our case 'ignorance', is not 'a single Manichaean, aboriginal maw', but there exists indeed a 'plethora of ignorances', and 'these ignorances . . . are produced by and correspond to particular knowledges and circulate as part of particular regimes of truth'.[31] Further, what is in the light does not necessarily have its direct antithesis in the darkness: the inferior is not the exact reverse of the superior.[32]

The road leading into that darkness, into these ignorances, is thus by necessity a circuitous one. First, most of our sources were preserved only because they fit the orthodox canon. Secondly, all our texts were written by men and are for the most part addressed to men. Almost all these men belonged to the same social class: an élite with common aristocratic notions of proper comportment, ethical behaviour, and rhetorical skill, firmly anchored in stoic-platonic traditions. These notions underlie the Church Fathers' understanding and thus their shaping of Christianity, and influence much of what they considered the appropriate ascetic life. Thus, when these Fathers describe and attempt to regulate the ascetic life of women or those they call heretics, their writings reflect their own preoccupations and fears. They are often motivated by a desire to persuade or even coerce an essentially like-minded addressee, rather than by a wish to provide accurate descriptions of what women and heretics actually did or thought. In other words, we have to be constantly aware of the fact that what we are reading are rhetorical masterpieces exchanged between members of a homogeneous élite: masterpieces that portray a historical reality 'as it should be', but not 'as it truly was'. But before resigning ourselves to the notion that we may know nothing about what women and others did, we may find some consolation in the fact that almost all the protagonists, whether men or women, orthodox or heretical, belonged to the

---

[31] E. K. Sedgwick, *Epistemology of the Closet* (Berkeley, 1990), 8.
[32] Bynum, 'Women's Stories', 33.

same culture, used the same rhetorical techniques, and sought to fulfil the same ideals—those of the Gospel. And with some patience and investigative spirit enough fragments can be gathered to piece together an adequate mosaic of what lies behind our sources—their subtext, what it was that they were written over and against—and thereby reconstruct the intentions and practices of women and so-called 'heretics'.

In such an attempt, as in all attempts to study processes of institutionalization, the work of Max Weber remains fundamental, though his insights and methods will, in our case, not be exhaustive. Thus, I shall in what follows consider the issues raised and discussed by Weber, such as the 'routinization' of a charismatic movement; the emergence and legitimization of a hierarchy; the translation of an idea into an organized form, of religious inspiration into well-defined norms, rules, and laws. Three general areas will be examined: 1. factors with normative impact on the life of the individual, such as existing laws, precepts, and customs; specific formalities, economic conditions, and an individual's position within the hierarchy of society as such; 2. existing models of community and their specific function for both the indicidual and society; 3. the sets of ideas, doctrines, concepts—in short, the theology—which constitute a religion.[33]

---

[33] The theoretical framework is not only crucial but also very complex, and thus difficult to relate adequately in the space appropriate here; much of my thinking has also been influenced by works such as K. G. Faber, *Theorie der Geschichtswissenschaft* (Munich, 1982⁵); L. Fleck, *The Genesis and Development of a Scientific Fact* (Chicago, 1979); N. Luhmann, *Religious Dogmatics and the Evolution of Societies*, trans. P. Beyer (Studies in Religion and Society 9; New York, 1984); id. *Zweckbegriff und Systemrationalität: Über die Funktion von Zwecken in sozialen Systemen* (Soziale Forschung und Praxis 25; Tübingen, 1986); G. Melville (ed.), *Institutionen und Geschichte: Theoretische Aspekte und mittelalterliche Befunde* (Cologne, 1992); G. Scarvaglieri, 'Problematica sociologica dell'obbedienza', in G. Tamburrino (ed.), *Autorità e obbedienza nella vita religiosa* (Milan, 1978), 189–227; G. Schneller, *Religiöse Gruppen und sozialwissenschaftliche Typologie: Möglichkeiten der Analyse religiöser Orden* (Sozialwissenschaftliche Abhandlungen der Görres-Gesellschaft 3; Berlin, 1979); J. Séguy, 'Une sociologie des sociétés imaginées: Monachisme et utopie', *Annales ESC* 26 (1971), 328–54; E. Servais and F. Hambye, 'Structure et signification: Problème de méthode en sociologie des organisations claustrales', *Social Compass* 18 (1971), 21–44; E. Shils, *Center and Periphery: Essays in Macrosociology* (Chicago, 1975), esp. 111–303, discussing 'Charisma, Ritual, and Consensus' and 'Status and Order'; E. Troeltsch, 'Die Sozialehren der christlichen Kirchen und Gruppen', in id. *Gesammelte Schriften*, i (Tübingen, 1912), 226–38, 358–93.

In other words, much of the following study revolves around such questions as: how did the status of the individual female ascetic, the virgin, develop? How was it made distinct from that of the clergy and the laity? How was that difference symbolized? If an increase in institutionalization implies a progressive separation from familiar social models, then how did this occur in the case of women? How does a woman distance herself from family, marriage, and the congregation? What alternative models arise and how are they constituted? Would they be based on a common way of life, on a common legal status, on common property, or on some combination of all the above? What was the internal organization, and how did it relate to existing models of community and institutions? And how were these phenomena and processes viewed by others?

This said, much of what has to be analysed and described in the following pages belongs to a realm which is prima facie precisely the antithesis of 'institution', the antithesis of what Weber defines as authority, power, law, or norm. Therefore categories and modes of description have to be employed which take this into account. These methods are perhaps best described in words used by Michel Foucault to characterize what he defines as power/knowledge, and which he coined specifically to describe phenomena outside a strictly 'legal-institutional' framework:

power must be understood . . . as the multiplicity of force relations immanent in the sphere in which they operate and which constitute their own organization; . . . [It] must not be sought in the primary existence of one unique central point, in a unique source of sovereignty from which secondary and descendent forms would emanate; it is the moving substrate of force relations which, by virtue of their inequality, constantly engender states of power, but the latter are always local and unstable.[34]

This description is particularly appropriate because I am attempting to describe a historical process, a state of flux, where

[34] Foucault, *History of Sexuality*, 92 f. I would like to emphasize that what I am using here is a descriptive terminology; I am decidedly not engaging in a discourse on the philosophical implications and normative quality of Foucault's use and understanding of power/knowledge, which is explicitly 'modern' and indeed 'postmodern', but, I feel, nevertheless methodologically applicable to a pre-enlightenment period; cf. e.g. N. Fraser, *Unruly Practices: Power, Discourse, and Gender in Contemporary Social Theory* (Minneapolis, 1989), 17–54, esp. 18–25; cf. also the very penetrating article by A. Cameron, 'Redrawing the Map: Early Christian Territory after Foucault', *JRS* 76 (1986), 266–71.

very little, even on the theoretical level, had as yet attained any definitive form.

From a practical point of view this approach requires the suspension, as far as possible,[35] of a number of prior assumptions and categorizations, in particular convenient dyads such as orthodox/ heretical; asceticism/monasticism; normative writings/other writings; public/private; and male/female. In keeping with a synchronistic method, it also requires limitation to a well-circumscribed historical period and a focus on specific geographical regions, in this case fourth-century Asia Minor and Egypt.

The heuristic value of suspending the distinction between orthodox and heretical has been recognized at the very least since A. von Harnack, was significantly advanced by G. Volpe, H. Grundmann, and others, albeit with regard to medieval history, and requires no further elaboration.[36] As far as the distinction between 'asceticism' and 'monasticism' is concerned, the need for such a suspension may be slightly less obvious.

As is evident in its etymology, asceticism is essentially a *discipline*. Based on distinct stoic-platonic notions, it is a systematic method to achieve self-control, a way to channel and counteract 'passions', which range from the appetitive passions for food and sexual pleasure to emotions such as anger, jealousy, avarice, and hubris. As understood quite clearly by Weber, asceticism is thus not primarily a dualistic phenomenon, which considers the body as evil in opposition to a soul which is good (and thus has far less of the masochistic or self-torturing notions often associated with it). As method or discipline, asceticism is not an end in itself, but

[35] That is, as a conscious attempt, conscious of all the inescapable caveats, as discussed (among many others) by H. Gadamer, *Gesammelte Werke. Hermeneutik*, ii: *Wahrheit und Methode* (Tübingen, 1986): 'Wie weit schreibt Sprache das Denken vor?', 199–206; 'Text und Interpretation', 330–60; 'Destruktion und Dekonstruktion', 361–72; 'Hermeneutik und Historismus', 387–424.

[36] H. Grundmann, *Religiöse Bewegungen im Mittelalter: Untersuchungen über die geschichtlichen Zusammenhänge zwischen der Ketzerei, den Bettelorden und der religiösen Frauenbewegung im 12. und 13. Jhd. und Über geschichtliche Grundlagen deutscher Mystik* (Historische Studien 276; Berlin, 1935; repr. Darmstadt, 1970); id. *Ausgewählte Aufsätze*, 3 vols. (Schriften der Monumenta Germaniae Historica 25: 1/3; Stuttgart, 1967); G. Volpe, *Movimenti religiosi e sette ereticali nella società medievale italiana secoli xi–xiv* (Florence, 1961), and cf. J. Cervelli, 'G. Volpe e la storiografia italiana ed europea fra Otto e Novecento', *La Cultura* 8 (1970), 250–61.

aspires to a higher good: namely, to transform the practitioner
into a pure vessel of divine will, and so to create the possibility
for communication with the divine through some form of *unio
mystica*. This does not necessarily require 'a flight from the world'
in the practical sense, but can be decidedly 'innerworldly'. The
ascetic may well remain involved in his or her community, par-
taking in ordinary economic endeavours, acts of charity, and the
like.[37] Even *anachōrēsis* or retreat does not necessarily require a
physical removal from the community of a village or town. As a
method of retreat from the world (i.e. transformation into a 'holy
vessel'), asceticism can thus be practised with equal success in
the middle of a city or in the countryside, while living alone
(*monachos*), or in groups. Our sources call such groups in effect
anything from 'communal household' (*synoikia*), brotherhood
(*adelphōtes*), community (*koinōnion*)—echoing pagan religious
associations called *koinon*[38]—to, eventually, 'community of
solitaries' (*monastērion*), the term most widely used by the fifth
century. To be sure, communal forms of asceticism, in other
words monasticism, have always been judged to be an evolution,
the 'higher form' of asceticism. But since this is clearly a value
judgement made consciously by later sources, the methodological
distinction between asceticism and monasticism is not only unnecessary but anachronistic, and thus counter-productive when
examining the very early forms of the movement.[39]

The same is true for distinctions between writings defined as
'canons' or rules and all other literary genres addressing questions
of *askēsis*. In particular the then developing genre of the treatise
On Virginity, as well as the hagiographical writings or *Lives*,
both usually classified by the authors themselves as 'letters', are
eminently normative in nature. They as well as numerous 'actual'
letters were written with the sole and clearly stated intention of
regulating and 'normalizing', and were understood as such by

[37] Bynum, *Fragmentation and Redemption*, 53–78, esp. 66–74; B. Lohse,
Askese und Mönchtum in der Antike und in der alten Kirche (Religion und Kultur
der alten Mittelmeerwelt in Parallelforschungen 1; Munich, 1969); Weber,
Economy and Society, i. 541–51; id. *Gesammelte Aufsätze zur Religionssoziologie*,
i: 'Die protestantische Ethik', esp. 106–21.

[38] A. Strobel, *Das heilige Land der Montanisten: Eine religionsgeographische
Untersuchung* (Religionsgeschichtliche Versuche und Vorarbeiten 37; Berlin,
1980), 273.

[39] See also Jenal (n. 25 above), *Italia ascetica*, esp. 18.

their addressees. More to the point, the 'monastic rule' as a literary genre and as a regulatory device is a later development and must not, therefore, be used retroactively to account for the evolution of monasticism.[40] Thus, the following study is founded upon the broadest base of available sources, ranging from ecclesiastical canons and imperial laws to inscriptions and papyri.

When one is attempting to define the position and radius of action available to women in Late Antiquity, categories such as 'private' and 'public' may at first glance appear to be useful. This form of distinction between the private household or *oikos* on the one hand and the public sphere of the state or *polis* on the other, suggests itself in part because it is the very distinction introduced by Aristotle and has ever since remained fundamental to political discourse.[41] Beyond doubt, the separation of the household or private sphere as the primary female domain from the state or public sphere as the primary male one, and the expression of this separation not only in the juridical treatment of women but in almost all ideological discussion of the male and the female, was (and remains) fundamental to ancient society. Yet it is this very pervasiveness of the metaphor that must lead us to extreme caution when using it as a category of inquiry. To literalize the ideological underpinnings of the gender-specific rhetoric employed in the texts is to short-circuit a lengthy, complex, and contested process. Or, to put it differently, if we set out to examine the role of women and take as our basis the assumptions of those theorizing about this same role, our own insights must by definition be limited by the very assumptions we are setting out to investigate.[42] Thus, rather than asking whether a woman's role

[40] The problem of the formation of norms, rules, canons, and laws is of course fundamental and one of the main themes of my study; I have discussed some of its aspects further in 'The *Sententiae ad Virginem* by Evagrius Ponticus and the Problem of Early Monastic Rules', *Augustinianum* 30 (1990), 393–404 and in 'Evagrius Ponticus' *Sententiae ad Virginem*', DOP 45 (1991), 97–120.

[41] Aristotle, *Politics*, Book I, esp. I. 5 and I. I. 2–7; see also M. Foucault, *The Use of Pleasure*, trans R. Hurley (New York, 1985), 143–84.

[42] This acquires further relevance given that we are inevitably influenced by the modern understanding of the categories 'private/public' in today's political discourse. For some aspects of the contemporary public/private debate, especially in the law, see C. MacKinnon, *Toward a Feminist Theory of the State* (Cambridge, Mass., 1989), *passim*; N. Taub and E. M. Schneider, 'Perspectives on Women's Subordination and the Role of Law', in D. Kairys (ed.), *The Politics of Law: A Progressive Critique* (New York, 1982), 117–39.

was 'public' or 'private,' the primary question should rather be along the lines of: just how 'private' is or was what we consider private and just how 'public' was what we today consider public? Do conceptual pairings such as private/public, and that means *de facto* mainly male/female, have any actual correlation to gender? To give two examples: first, is an aristocratic lady, who endows the see of Constantinople with substantial sums of money, and thereby openly, i.e. publicly, controls its occupant, a senatorial bishop, exercising 'public' or 'private' power? Secondly, the notion that women were disproportionately represented in heretical and marginalized movements has led to an intense debate over whether women were attracted to such marginalized movements because they seem to have given them a greater degree of 'public' participation, or whether these movements were marginalized as a result of that 'public' participation. While factually accurate— women appear to have constituted a significant presence in those movements—the focus of the debate obscures the role played by women in orthodox, i.e. central, movements. This point has been raised by Grundmann, who noted that women were over-represented in both orthodox and heretical, central and marginal movements. What, then, does that say about the public/private nature of their presence?[43] While in no way questioning the significance of the classic distinction between the public/male and private/female sphere both in theory and practice, I would argue, again, that its use as a theoretical category tends to limit the potential scope of the inquiry.

This is particularly true for the last of the categories mentioned, that of male versus female, which is, of course, intrinsically linked to that of public versus private. First and foremost, while it is necessary and indeed crucial to reconstruct the organizational models developed for (and presumably by) women, it is—to repeat what I have already stated above—equally necessary and crucial to be aware that this did not occur in a vacuum. Aristotle and those following his basic distinction (in other words most authors until Rousseau) understand the notion of the *oikos* and

---

[43] Grundmann, *Religiöse Bewegungen, passim*; cf. also K. Elm, 'Die Stellung der Frau in Ordenswesen, Semireligiosentum und Häresie zur Zeit der Elisabeth', in *Sankt Elisabeth: Fürstin, Dienerin, Heilige: Aufsätze, Dokumentation, Katalog* (Sigmaringen, 1981), 7–28; but cf. also G. Koch, *Frauenfrage und Ketzertum im Mittelalter* (Berlin, 1962), *passim*.

the *polis* with its female and male characteristics as intrinsically linked and use each as a device to explain the other, and thus the whole. This has direct consequences for the way in which the individual parts have to be seen. In concentrating solely on the female with all its accompanying notions such as 'inferior, indoors, stationary, natural, weak, receptive, porous'—descriptive categories in use well into the Patristic age—one might easily conclude, as has often been the case, that women lived in a constant and indeed existential state of suppression within a patriarchal system. But this implies a binary opposition to one 'unique source' of power, and as such it all too easily overlooks the potential extent of the interaction between these two models.

For example, when a celibate bishop writes about marriage, and in so doing elaborates upon the wife's weakness and inferiority, one might easily read this as an example of misogyny. But, when this same exposé on marriage is addressed to a public official of higher social standing, to what degree is the wife's inferiority really at issue? Is the subject the wife, or rather the fact that the bishop, as a public figure and a celibate, is of a higher, more manly rank than the *de facto* higher-ranking addressee, since the latter's public persona (and consequently his position) has been 'diluted' because of the mere presence of his private realm, i.e. the wife?[44] In other words, is this discourse about female weakness truly about a woman or rather one concerning two men?

A too rigid view of a binary opposition also misses a crucial point. It denies the women in question imagination, creativity, and thus the potential, as a 'marginal and disadvantaged [group] in a society, to appropriate that society's dominant symbols and ideas in ways that revise and undercut them'. It neglects to register the extent to which 'no voice—past or present—is more than partially empowered or partially distinctive . . . women in every age speak in a variety of accents.'[45] Notions of maleness and femaleness, their appropriation and revision, were precisely one of those ways in which a *de facto* unequal situation could nevertheless be made fruitful. We have thus to be careful not to let modern conceptualizations of gender, and modern meanings

[44] See in particular K. Cooper, 'Insinuations of Womanly Influence: An Aspect of the Christianization of the Roman Aristocracy', *JRS* 82 (1992), 150–64.

[45] Bynum, *Fragmentation*, 17–19.

and applications of 'male' and 'female' interfere with the richness of the texts, thus diminishing the 'lost voices' we are purporting to reconstruct.[46]

Central to my method is the comparison of two distinct geographical regions within the Roman Empire during a fairly limited period.[47] This study is restricted to the fourth century, a period of crucial transition, during which Christianity became the dominant religion, and the Roman Empire underwent fundamental changes in its administration, economy, and the composition and structure of its society, which led eventually to its division into a Western and an Eastern part.[48] The choice of Asia Minor and Egypt is based on several key factors. Both regions were of central significance in the fourth century for secular as well as religious reasons. Asia Minor was the see of the new capital, Constantinople, as well as a border province with extensive military in-

---

[46] See in particular the critique by J. W. Scott, 'Gender: A Useful Category of Historical Analysis', *American Historical Review* 91: 5 (1986), 1053–75; also interesting is J. Butler, *Gender Trouble: Feminism and the Subversion of Identity* (New York, 1990), esp. 147, 'I have tried to suggest that the identity categories often presumed to be foundational to feminist politics . . . simultaneously work to limit and constrain in advance the very cultural positions that feminism is supposed to open up.'

[47] Syria, Palestine, North Africa, Italy, Southern France, and Spain also have a tradition of ascetic movements by the fourth century. Consequently, they have been studied to a greater or lesser degree; cf. for example S. Brock and S. Ashbrook Harvey (eds.), *Holy Women of the Syrian Orient* (Berkeley, 1987); Clark, *Jerome, Chrysostom, and Friends, passim*; J. M. Fiey, 'Cénobitisme féminin ancien dans les églises syriennes orientale et occidentale', *L'Oriens Syrien* 10 (1965), 281–310; G. Folliet, 'Aux origines de l'ascétisme et du cénobitisme africain', *Studia Anselmiana* 46 (1961), 25–44; J. J. Gavigan, *De Vita Monastica in Africa Septentrionali* (Rome, 1962); R. Metz, *La Consécration des vierges dans l'Église Romaine: Étude d'histoire de la liturgie* (Bibliothèque de l'Institut du Droit Canonique de l'Université de Strasbourg 4; Paris, 1954); Vööbus, *History of Asceticism, passim*.

[48] P. R. L. Brown, *The World of Late Antiquity, A.D. 150–750* (New York, 1971), 34–111; T. S. Miller, *The Birth of the Hospital in the Byzantine Empire* (Baltimore, 1985), 68–74; G. Ostrogorsky, *Geschichte des byzantinischen Staates Handbuch der Altertumswissenschaften, Byzantinisches Handbuch.* i. 2; Munich, 1963³), 19–57; Patlagean, *Pauvreté économique*, 156–81, 301–40; A. M. Ritter, *Das Konzil von Konstantinopel und sein Symbol: Studien zur Geschichte und Theologie des II. Ökumenischen Konzils* (Forschungen zur Kirchen- und Dogmengeschichte 15; Göttingen, 1965), 21–33.

stallations, protecting the capital against eastern invasions. Egypt always held a distinct position in the Empire, largely because of its importance as the leading supplier of grain for Rome and then Constantinople.[49]

Both regions became centres of religious debate early on, and in both regions the theoretical discussion of 'asceticism' reached a peak during the fourth century. In Asia Minor the three Cappadocian Fathers, Basil of Caesarea, Gregory of Nazianzus, and Gregory of Nyssa, laid the foundations of Eastern monasticism. In Egypt the same is true for Pachomius, Shenoute, and above all, Athanasius. But both regions also were characterized by an indigenous religious culture prone to what one may call religious enthusiasm. Though Asia Minor does not provide us with many inscriptions, it was the scene of the most important ecclesiastical synods. Egypt offers a unique category of sources with its papyri.[50] The relative availability of the source material stimulated a more intense historiographical discussion of monasticism in these two regions than was the case for other areas of the Empire.

The choice of two regions rather than one emphasizes the importance of regional diversity, while affording us greater insight into the relation between regional factors and unifying and centralizing tendencies.[51] Both Asia Minor and Egypt were united by their common history as part of the Roman Empire and by their early exposure to Christianity. At the same time, each had fundamentally distinct geographies, climates, and social, political, and economic structures.[52] Asia Minor is a varied region, com-

---

[49] A. Johnson and L. West, *Byzantine Egypt: Economic Studies* (Princeton, NJ, 1949), 4.

[50] M. and N. Thierry, 'Les Enseignements historiques de l'archéologie Cappadocienne', *Travaux et Mémoires* 8 (1981), 501–19.

[51] Regionalism was a factor of far greater importance in Late Antiquity than has long been assumed, and it increased with the decline of the capability of the central government to enforce its dictates throughout the Empire; cf. E. Demougeot, *De l'unité à la division de l'émpire romain, 395–410* (Paris, 1951), 530–2; J. Matthews, *Western Aristocracies and the Imperial Court, AD 364–425* (Oxford, 1975), 88–145.

[52] The 4th and subsequent cents. did not, therefore, witness the formation of 'Roman Christianity', but the rise of many varied strands which only gradually came to adhere to a Roman or Greek Orthodox canon. The same is true for asceticism, which also arose in several different centres; C. W. Griggs, *Early*

prising both coastal areas and the central plateau, today's Anatolia, roughly identical with ancient Cappadocia. This plateau, bordered by highlands in the north which separate it from the Black Sea coast, and limited by the Taurus range in the south and east, consists of undulating hills interspersed with marshy basins and volcanic cones, and has a distinctly continental climate with very harsh winters and hot summers.[53] Cities were few and concentrated in the more clement areas like the basin formed by the river Halys, while the economic foundation of the region lay in its vast tracts of open countryside.[54] Cappadocia's main products were agricultural, and both the geography and the nature of the economy favoured large-scale utilization.[55] Thus most of the land was owned by *possessores* (private landowners), by the state, i.e. the imperial household, and originally by large temple estates and then by the Church.[56] In accordance with their wealth, these

---

Egyptian Christianity from its Origins to 451 C. E. (Coptic Studies 2; Leiden, 1990), esp. 13–78; C. D. Müller, *Grundzüge des christlich-islamischen Ägyptens von der Ptolemäerzeit zur Gegenwart* (Darmstadt, 1969), 89–93; R. C. Teja, 'Die römische Provinz Kappadokien in der Prinzipatszeit', *ANRW* 2. 7. 2, 1083–1124.

[53] W. B. Fisher, *The Middle East: A Physical, Social, and Regional Geography* (London, 1979[6]), 302–15.

[54] J. G. Anderson, 'The Road System of Eastern Asia Minor', *Journal of Historical Studies* 17 (1897), 22–44; *TIB* ii 41–70, 124–7, 149; S. Mitchell, 'Population and the Land in Roman Galatia', *ANRW* 2. 7. 2, 1053–81.

[55] Primarily horses for the imperial army, sheep, and grain, but slaves were also an export commodity; Strabo, *Geogr.* 12. 2. 7–10 3. 32–40 (Strabon, *Géographie*, ix, ed. F. Lasserre, Paris, 1981), 56–59, 99–109; L. Frank, 'Sources classiques concernant la Cappadoce', *Revue hittite et asianique* 24 (1966), 5–122, here 67–72, 78–81, 114f.; R. C. Teja, *Organización economica y social de Capadocia en el siglo IV, según los Padres Capadocios* (Salamanca, 1974), 24–31 with 24 n. 5.

[56] The exact extent of private *latifundia* remains unclear, but was considerable. By the 4th cent. more land belonged to the imperial household than to the cities. This was partially brought about by the annexation of temple property after Constantine's conversion. These domains, used primarily to raise army horses, were concentrated in what in 372 became *Cappadocia Prima*, and were administered by the *comes domorum divinarum*, directly responsible to the emperor; M. Forlin Patrucco, 'Domum Divinam per Cappadociam', *Rivista di filologia e d'istruzione classica* 100 (1972), 328–33; A. H. M. Jones, *The Cities of the Eastern Roman Provinces* (Oxford, 1971[2]), 184–8. The Church holdings had increased progressively since 312, either through private donations or annexation of former temple estates; *CTh* 16. 2. 4 Mommsen–Meyer, i.2, 836; *TIB* ii. 112–15. Most of these land-holdings were maintained by *coloni* and a few free peasants; Patlagean,

possessores—the three Cappadocian Fathers were among them—were also the principal political authority.[57]

The inhabited area of Egypt is essentially the narrow Nile valley, although in Roman times its territory extended to the eastern highlands as well as to the western deserts with their deep saline basins and some inhabited oases. Egypt enjoys a fairly uniform climate with hot summers and mild winters.[58] The inhabited areas were densely populated, and the nature of the agriculture—based on intense irrigation after the annual flooding—made a centralized government a necessity for high productivity.[59] The principal landholders were the crown and the priests, but from the beginning of the fourth century the number of private owners increased, partially as a result of the dismantling of temple estates. This trend did not, however, result in the vast *latifundia* of the Western Mediterranean.[60] Church property likewise increased only slowly, either through trade or donation; and donated land was often of lesser value.[61] Thus Egypt's social composition differed markedly from that of Asia Minor. The number of small landowners was considerable and despite certain communal tax responsibilities, which curbed migration from village to town, the individual was not bound to the soil. However, by the end of the third and beginning of the fourth century, a decrease in the efficiency of irrigation, high inflation, and mounting taxation forced many to abandon their villages for the

Pauvreté économique, 236–52; M. Rostovtzeff, 'Studien zur Geschichte des römischen Kolonates', *Archiv für Papyrusforschung. Beiheft* 1 (1910), 283–312; Teja, *Organización*, 34–43, 67–74, 196–201.

[57] Ibid. 79–96.

[58] The Nile valley itself is approximately 800 km. long and on average 10 km. wide, the river's width being on average 1 km.; the summer temperature averages *c*. 30°C; Fisher, *The Middle East*, 482–8.

[59] The larger landowners as a rule subleased to small tenants; Johnson and West, *Byzantine Egypt*, 4–6, 8–13.

[60] H. I. Bell, *Egypt from Alexander the Great to the Arab Conquest* (Oxford, 1948), 117–19; A. K. Bowman, 'The Economy of Egypt in the Early Fourth Century', in *Imperial Revenue, Expenditure and Monetary Policy in the Fourth Century* AD. *The Fifth Oxford Symposium on Coinage and Monetary History* (British Archeological Reports, Int. Ser. 76; Oxford, 1980), 23–40; Johnson and West, *Byzantine Egypt*, 7–10, 13–20; A. Johnson, *Egypt and the Roman Empire* (Ann Arbor, 1951), 67, 78–85.

[61] E. Wipszycka, *Les Ressources et les activités économiques des églises en Égypte du IVᵉ au VIIIᵉ siècle* (Papyrologia Bruxellensia 10; Brussels, 1972).

desert (*anachōrēsis*) to avoid debt-bondage.[62] Alexandria (often
called 'Alexandria ad Aegyptum') the Greek-speaking com-
mercial, intellectual, and ecclesiastical centre, played a role apart
from its mainly Coptic-speaking hinterland, the *koinē*. It was
oriented towards the West and its Graeco-Roman influence
gradually decreased the further south one went. This distinction
between Alexandria and the *koinē* is also reflected in the relationship between the indigenous Egyptians in the Nile valley and the
'Hellenistic' upper class, which never gained the same political
influence as its counterpart in Asia Minor.[63]

These are, roughly, the external contours of the lives of the men
and women we are about to encounter. But, more than any
theory or geographical description, it will be the texts themselves
which will bring the voices of these men, and mediated through
them the voices of these women, back to life. It will also be these
texts—in much of the following they speak for themselves—that
will have to perform the hardest task facing a historian: that of
bringing to life, from beneath and in spite of the layers of critical
analysis, the fervour of the believers, the intensity of their devotion, the depth of what it meant to them to struggle for the
perfect life, the perfect imitation of Christ—be they orthodox or
heretical, ascetics or monks, male or female.

[62] A. E. Boak, 'The Population of Roman and Byzantine Karanis', *Historia* 4
(1955), 157; H. Braunert, *Die Binnenwanderung: Studien zur Sozialgeschichte
Ägyptens in der Ptolemäer- und Kaiserzeit* (Bonner historische Forschungen 26;
Bonn, 1964), 314 f.
[63] Braunert, Die *Binnenwanderung*, 291 f., 294–8, 320–33; M. Krause, 'Das
christliche Alexandrien und seine Beziehungen zum koptischen Ägypten', in G.
Grimm (ed.), *Alexandrien: Kulturbegegnungen dreier Jahrtausende im Schmelztie-
gel einer mediterranen Großstadt* (Aegyptiaca Treverensia 1; Mainz, 1981), 53–62;
J. A. Timbie, 'Dualism and the Concept of Orthodoxy in the Thought of the
Monks of Upper Egypt' Diss. (Philadelphia, 1979), 4–22.

I   Asia Minor

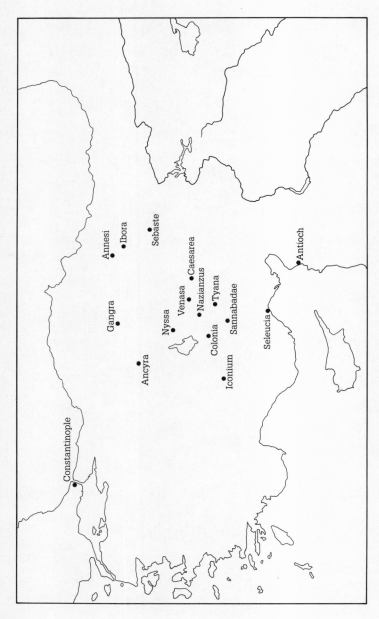

MAP 1. Locations of female ascetics in Cappadocia

I

'Virgins of God': Variations of Female Ascetic Life

VIRGO DEO DICATA

In the year 314, just two years after Constantine had accepted Christianity as a *religio licita*, an official religion, bishops and priests from Galatia, Cappadocia, and Pontus met in Ancyra, today's Ankara in Turkey, to discuss various practical issues which in the past had caused controversies and required official regulation.[1] As a result of their efforts the Fathers issued several orders or canons, one of which, canon 19, reads as follows:

Those, men or women, who have proclaimed (ἐπαγγελόμενοι) virginity, and then revoked their proclamation shall be subjected to the regulation concerning those who married for a second time (τῶν διγάμων). We prohibit those, who live together with men (συνερχομένας) as if they were their sisters, from doing so.[2]

---

[1] For the date of the council see, 'Ancyra, Council of', *ODCC* 51; R. B. Rackham, 'The Text of the Canons of Ancyra', *Studia Biblica et ecclesiastica* 3 (1891), 139–216. For the chronology of the struggle between Constantine, Galerius, Maximinus Daia, and Licinius, and its impact on the toleration vs. repression of Christianity in the East and the West, cf. Eusebius, *HE* 9. 2. 1, 9. 10. 7–12; Lactantius, *De mortibus persecutorum*, 35 (*Lactance: De la mort des persécuteurs*, ed. J. Moreau (SC 39; Paris, 1954), 118); H. Castritius, *Studien zu Maximinus Daia* (Frankfurter Althistorische Studien 2; Kallmünz, 1969), 63–70; F. Millar, *The Emperor in the Roman World* (Ithaca, NY, 1977), 445 f.; J. Vogt, *Constantin der Große* (Munich, 1949), 154–71.

[2] Ὅσοι παρθενίαν ἐπαγγελόμενοι ἀθετοῦσι τὴν ἐπαγγελίαν, τὸν τῶν διγάμων ὅρον ἐκπληρούτωσαν. τὰς μέντοι συνερχομένας παρθένος τισὶν ὡς ἀδελφὰς ἐκωλύσαμεν (Mansi, ii. 519 f.); Hefele–Leclercq, i.1, 321. Citations are from the Eng. trans. of Hefele by W. R. Clark (*A History of the Christian Councils*, 2 vols. (Edinburgh, 1871)); the Lat. trans. by Dionysius Exiguus, here canon 18, reads: 'quotquot virginitatem promittentes, irritam faciunt sponsionem, inter bigamos censeantur. Virgines autem quae conveniunt cum aliquibus, tanquam sorores, habitare prohibemus'

Eight years earlier, in 306, very similar matters had arisen in a different region of the Roman Empire, the Iberian peninsula, today's Spain. Iberian bishops had congregated in Elvira, and declared in canon 13 of their final regulations:

It has been decided that virgins who dedicated themselves to God must not be given communion, not even on their death-bed, if they have broken their promise (*pactum*) of virginity, and have given in to their desire, not being aware of what they were losing. However, those women who have only once been persuaded and led astray through the fall of their weak body, if they repent all their lives by abstaining from sexual intercourse, so that the truly lost ones become through that all the more recognisable, they should be allowed to receive the communion at the end of their lives.[3]

What is at stake in these two canons, pronounced at virtually the same time, yet in two provinces as distinct as Iberia and Asia Minor? In both regions men, but more frequently women, 'dedicated themselves to God' through a public profession of their intention to preserve their virginity. Both sources employ terms, which imply a quasi-legal obligation—proclamation (*epangelia* in the Greek East) and contract (*pactum* in the Latin West). It remains open whether the proclamation or contract was a simple vow, what kind of public was present, and whether pre-

(Mansi, ii. 526); R. Cacitti, 'L'etica sessuale nella canonistica del cristianesimo primitivo: Aspetti di istituzionalizzazione ecclesiastica nel III secolo', in R. Cantalamessa (ed.), *Etica sessuale e matrimonio nel cristianesimo delle origini* (Studia Patristica Mediolanensia 5; Milan, 1976), 69–157, esp. 100–24. (Greek words and phrases throughout the text are quoted as they appear in the original, except where I thought corrections to be necessary; the English translations also follow mainly those cited in the Bibliography, except where I felt changes to be appropriate.)

[3] 'Virgines, quae se Deo dicaverunt, si pactum perdiderint virginitatis, atque eidem libidini servierint, non intelligentes quid admiserint, placuit nec in finem eis dandam esse communionem. Quod si semel persuasae aut infirmi corporis lapsu vitiatae omni tempore vitae suae huiusmodi faeminae egerint penitentiam, ut abstineant se a coitu, eo quod lapsae potius videantur, placuit eas in finem communionem accipere debere' (Mansi, ii. 8); Hefele–Leclercq, i.1, 229; for the date see 'Elvira, Council of', *ODCC*, 454; S. Laeuchli, *Power and Sexuality: The Emergence of Canon Law at the Synod of Elvira* (Philadelphia, 1972), 3–55, 97–113; L. Sybel, 'Zur Synode von Elvira', *ZKG* 42 (1923), 243–7.

conditions other than virginity were required.[4] The Fathers at Elvira further give no clue as to how such a person, identified as a virgin, was supposed to have lived. The Ancyran Fathers only tell us what they disapprove of: apparently some of these 'virgins of God' lived together with men 'as if they were their sisters'.

The issue at stake, as to be expected from regulations, is violation of the principal precondition: the loss of virginity and its consequences. Those who renounced their profession, like the Ancyrans, or broke their contract, like the Elvirans, were to be punished accordingly.[5] However, these violations were not judged with the same severity. The Fathers at Ancyra simply mentioned the offence and then pronounced their sentence, while the Elvirans took the possibility of repentance into consideration and varied their punishment accordingly.

In Ancyra 'virgins of God' who had failed to keep their publicly proclaimed intentions were seen as equal to widows and widowers who married for a second time. In Christian circles *bigamoi*, or 'those who marry twice', were traditionally held in low esteem, but hardly ever actually punished since their numbers were so considerable.[6] The council of Neocaesarea, which took place

---

[4] Methodius, *Symposium*, 3. 11 (*Méthode d'Olympe: Le Banquet*, ed. H. Musurilloc (SC 95, Paris, 1963), 114); Origen, *Contra Celsum*, 3. 46 (PG 11. 981); id. *Hom. in Jer.* 9. 1 (PG 13. 349); ἐπαγγελία is translated as 'profession, declaration' in LSJ s.v.; but the word did not originate in a religious context; Methodius uses it with ἐγκράτεια and Origen in the context of chaste devotion to the *logos*; cf. Lampe, s.v. 'epangelia'; J. Schniewind and G. Friedrich, 'epaggello', *Theologisches Wörterbuch zum Neuen Testament*, ii, ed. G. Kittel (Stuttgart, 1935), 573–83.

[5] Elvira's canon 13 clearly addresses women; Ancyra's canon 19 uses ὅσοι or οἱ, in Latin *soi*, and *ii*, i.e. it addresses both men and women; B. Kötting, and B. Kaiser, 'Gelübde', *RAC* ix. 1055–99 (esp. 1088).

[6] For the use of δίγαμοι cf. 1 Cor. 7: 8–9, 39–40; 1 Tim. 5: 3–13 (the translation of the New Testament used in the following is *The New Oxford Annotated Bible* (New York, 1971²)); Clement of Alexandria, *Strom.* 3. 1 (PG 8. 1104); Brown, *The Body and Society*, 147, 206; J. Mayer (ed.), *Monumenta de viduis diaconissis virginibusque tractantia* (Florilegium Patristicum 42; Bonn, 1938), 5–6; Y. Courtonne, *Un témoin du IVᵉ siècle oriental: Saint Basile et son temps d'après sa correspondance* (Paris, 1973), 494 n. 1; J. Grotz, *Die Entwicklung des Bußstufenwesens in der vornicänischen Kirche* (Freiburg i.B., 1955), 414–36; A. G. Martimort, *Les Diaconesses: Essai historique* (Bibliotheca Ephemerides Liturgicae, Subsidiae 24; Rome, 1982), 19–21; I. de la Potterie, 'Mari d'une seule femme: Le

sometime between 314 and 325, merely declared that presbyters ought not to attend weddings of *bigamoi*, and suggested some form of punishment for those who married more than twice.[7] Spanish virgins who failed to keep their promises suffered more severe consequences. Hardened offenders were *de facto* excommunicated, but even those who had trespassed just once received communion only on their death-bed.[8]

Who was the partner in this contract; who was the addressee of the proclamation, that its violation was punished so harshly? The Fathers at Ancyra may provide the answer. Since they considered those who broke their promises as *bigamoi*, a woman's initial profession must have been the equivalent of a marriage vow, a lifelong commitment on an individual and personal level, yet with its own legal consequences. This marriage was not an ordinary one; any actual 'consummation' led to its 'dissolution'. Even if a man and a woman who had contracted such a marriage lived like 'brothers and sisters', they had still forfeited the very terms of their contract.[9]

In the case of the Spanish virgins, nothing reminiscent of a marriage is mentioned. On the contrary, if those who had dedicated themselves to God transgressed, the Church itself rejected them in response. Here, a much more 'abstract' partner of the contract appears to be implied: the congregation, that is the assembled Church itself. Perhaps these differences are simply a matter of terminology, yet the punishments could reflect actual differences. In Iberia virgins occupied a more visible position within their congregation and received, therefore, a more severe punishment: complete exclusion.

Around the beginning of the fourth century, before the official toleration of Christianity, a phenomenon had appeared in

sens théologique d'une formule Paulinienne', *Paul de Tarse, Apôtre du notre temps* (Rome, 1979), 619–38; M. Lightman and W. Zeisel, '*Univira*: An Example of Continuity and Change in Roman Society', *CH* 46 (1977), 19–32.

[7] Can. 7 (Mansi, ii. 539 f.); the punishment was exclusion from worship, reduced in case of conversion and sound faith. For the date see 'Neocaesarea, Council of', *ODCC*, 959. Hefele–Leclercq, i.1, 328 f; Gr. Naz. *Or.* 39. 18 (PG 36. 357) prohibits second marriages.

[8] However, only the Synod of Chalcedon (*c.* AD 451) legalized the excommunication of fallen virgins (can. 16: Mansi, vi. 1169).

[9] Textual variations confirm that both sexes were implied.

Christian congregations as far apart as Iberia and Asia Minor, and required the attention of two local synods. Men, but most of all women, declared publicly that they henceforth intended to lead a life of 'virginity'. Their number was quite significant and they enjoyed considerable standing within the congregation: those who reneged on their promises suffered official retribution.

Like most other forms of regulation, canons reflect but a single aspect of the issue. Arising *ex post facto*, they address deviations from the norm while shaping it at the same time by the tacit assumption that the norm itself is widely known and accepted. But from which norm had the 'fallen ones' deviated? Who were those men and women, those *virgines Deo dicatae*? What lives did they lead? The canons of Ancyra and Elvira confirm the existence and importance of men as well as women called *Deo dicatae* in Asia Minor and in Iberia by the end of the third and the beginning of the fourth century. However, traces, any traces at all, of these virgins, their circumstances, and what motivated their rather extraordinary decisions have to be sought elsewhere. The fact that in attempting to do so we are going back, to a time when Christianity was still, or had barely emerged from being, a *religio illicita*, does not help our task. Sources are scarce, a sentence here, a fragment there, and only through a painstaking process of reassembling disparate parts will a clearer picture emerge—much like the mosaics of the time where empty spaces far outnumber the actual images, leaving much to the spectator's imagination.

A RELIGIOUS WOMAN AND A PROPHETESS

In 419 or 420, almost precisely one hundred years after the Fathers had assembled at Ancyra, Palladius, a fellow Galatian, wrote an account of his most formative years, the *Historia Lausiaca*. Here he tells us that one day, while browsing through a very old book, he found that Origen, the great Alexandrian theologian and his own spiritual mentor, had found this book 'with the virgin Juliana in Caesarea when I was hidden in her house'.[10] An intriguing remark! What makes it more intriguing

---

[10] Palladius, *HL* 64 (*The Lausiac History of Palladius*, ii, ed. C. Butler (Texts and Studies 6: 2; Cambridge, 1904; repr. Hildesheim, 1967), 160).

is another incident recorded in Eusebius' *Historia Ecclesiastica*. When Origen attempted to master the writings of the Old and New Testament, he collected all available translations, especially those by Symmachus, the foremost translator of his time. He acquired some of these translations 'from a woman called Juliana, on whom . . . Symmachus had himself bestowed them'.[11] Almost two hundered years later Palladius held one of these books in his hands. More important than the fate of the book is that of the person to whom it was dedicated, the 'virgin Juliana'.

Following the election of Firmilian as bishop in 230, Caesarea in Cappadocia evolved into one of the principal theological centres of the time. Firmilian himself was a highly learned man, and the close friend of several leading theologians, in particular Dionysius and Origen of Alexandria, and Cyprian of Carthage.[12] For Origen this friendship became of vital importance: in 235 the Egyptian Christians suffered under persecution, and, as pressure was mounting, Firmilian invited his friends to weather the storm in Caesarea.[13] Origen accepted, and spent two years in Caesarea 'hidden in the house of the virgin Juliana'.

But rather than finding peaceful times, Origen brought turmoil with him. Precisely at the time of his arrival an earthquake triggered a wave of spontaneous and cruel persecutions in and around Caesarea. Christians were in a state of terror; many had left their homes to seek refuge in neighbouring provinces. Suddenly, according to bishop Firmilian in a letter to Cyprian, a certain woman appeared, 'who pretended in a state of ecstasy to be a prophetess, and behaved as if she were full of the Holy Spirit'.[14] When she was in a trance, she would predict the future

[11] Eus. *HE* 6. 17; Origen, *Comm. in Ps.* 4 (PG 12. 1145); Jerome, *De viris illustribus* 54 (ed. E. C. Richardson (TU 14; Leipzig, 1896), 32).

[12] A. v. Harnack, *Geschichte der altchristlichen Literatur bis Eusebius* (Leipzig, 1893), 407–9; id. *Die Mission und Ausbreitung des Christentums* (Leipzig, 1902), 469 f.; Teja, 'Die römische Provinz Kappadokien', 1121 f.

[13] H. Crouzel ('Origène s'est-il retiré en Cappadoce pendant la persécution de Maximin le Thrace?', *Bulletin de littérature ecclésiastique* 64 (1963), 195–203) prefers an earlier date (215), during the reign of Caracalla. According to Teja ('Die römische Provinz Kappadokien', 1122) Origen came to Cappadocia after 235; cf. Harnack, *Geschichte der altchristlichen Literatur*, 209 f.; E. Kirsten, 'Cappadocia', *RAC* ii. 861–91 (here 881).

[14] 'emersit istic subito quaedam mulier quae in extasin constituta propheten se praeferret et quasi sancto spiritu plena sic ageret' (Cyprian, *Ep.* 75. 10, ed.

and perform miracles, such as walking barefoot in the snow without discomfort, and before long she had caught 'the minds of certain devotees to her sway that they gave her their obedience and would follow her wherever she directed and led'.[15]

Among her closest followers were a *presbyterus rusticus* and a *diaconus*, who, as Firmilian is quick to point out, carried their obedience only too far. Despite such 'scandalous' behaviour, the woman attracted a large following not only through her countless miracles but mainly because she 'pretend[ed] to sanctify the bread and celebrate the Eucharist. . . . and she would baptize many also . . . and all this she did in such a way that she appeared to deviate in no particular way from ecclesiastical discipline.' Only an exorcist could finally subdue this evil spirit and terminate her career.

Firmilian is clearly outraged by what he perceives as the 'principalium daemoniorum impetu'. Reducing his account to the mere facts, we are faced with a woman who, perhaps in response to the natural disaster she had witnessed, felt called by the Holy Spirit to challenge and change her fellow Christians. She encouraged them to leave house and home and to follow her wherever she led them. Yet, the woman's wanderings were not entirely random. She claimed that she 'must be off to Judaea and Jerusalem, giving the false impression that she came from there'.[16]

This reference to Judaea and Jerusalem as both the beginning and end of her journeys adds an interesting dimension: the woman understood herself as a prophetess, enraptured by the Holy Spirit and entitled to preside over the Eucharist with the aid of a *presbyter rusticus* and a *diaconus*. She justified this in part through the fact that she came from 'Jerusalem', whither she intended to return.

Around 160 a certain 'Montanus and his women', Maximilla and Priscilla, appeared in the region of Phrygia, near the town

---

G. Hartel (CSEL 3: 2 (Vienna, 1871), 817); *Saint Cyprien: Correspondance*, ii. ed. L. de Bayard (Paris, 1961²), 289–308; Harnack, *Geschichte der altchristlichen Literatur*, 407–9; C. Saumagne, *Saint Cyprien: Evêque de Carthage, 'pape' d'Afrique (248–58)* (Paris, 1975), 35–40.

[15] 'mentes singulorum ut sibi oboedirent et quocumque praeciperet et duceret sequerentur' (*EP*. 75. 10).

[16] 'diceret etiam se in Iudaeam et Hierosolymam festinare, fingens tamquam inde venisset' (*Ep*. 75. 10).

Ardabau.[17] Montanus and his women predicted 'in a kind of trance and unnatural ecstasy' the imminent end of the world, and declared two small towns in Phrygia, Pepuza and Tymion, to be the site of the Lord's Second Coming. These two towns were the 'New Jerusalem', they would witness the Lord's return, and 'people [from] every district [gathered] there'.[18] Montanus' adherents called his message 'the Prophecy', his adversaries 'the New Prophecy', 'the Phrygian Heresy', and eventually simply 'Montanism'.

Evidently Firmilian's prophetess was a member of this movement founded some sixty years earlier in Phrygia. Indeed, to quote Kurt Aland: 'if the letter did not quite clearly indicate 235 as the time during which these events took place, one would be tempted to regard the document as a description of the earliest Montanist prophetesses'.[19] It is possible that the extraordinary distress caused by a series of natural disasters led to the resurgence of this eschatological movement. Clearly, the woman's teachings, which predicted the near end of the world, were powerful enough to attract a large following, including members of the clergy, and to force the authorities to exorcize her, branding her as possessed.

Here, then, are two examples of women who, at a first glance, have very little in common except that they both lived in and around Caesarea at the same time. On the one hand, there is Juliana, an erudite Christian lady of prominence, who was in

---

[17] Epiph. *Haer.* 48. 1 (Epiphanius, *Panarion Haereses*, ii, ed. K. Holl (GCS 31; Berlin, 1980²), 219); Eus. *HE* 5. 16–17. Eusebius and Epiphanius differ in their chronology of Montanus' emergence. I am following here, together with most modern scholars, Epiphanius, who proposes more precisely 'the nineteenth year of Antoninus Pius', i.e. AD 156/7; K. Aland, 'Bemerkungen zum Montanismus und zur frühchristlichen Eschatologie' and 'Augustin und der Montanismus', *Kirchengeschichtliche Entwürfe* (Gütersloh, 1960), 105–64; H. Bacht, 'Montanisme', *DSp* x. 1670–6; H. Kraft, 'Die altkirchliche Prophetie und die Entstehung des Montanismus', *ThZ* 11 (1955), 249–71; Strobel, *Das heilige Land der Montanisten*, 34–64, 274–7.

[18] Eus. *HE* 5. 18. 2; S. Elm, 'Perceptions of Jerusalem Pilgrimage as Reflected in Two Early Sources on Female Pilgrimage (3rd and 4th century AD)', *SP* 20 (1989), 219–23.

[19] 'Bemerkungen', 117 (translation my own). Aland suggests a possible identification of this prophetess with Quintilla, mentioned by Epiphanius in *Haer.* 48. 14–49. 2 (2 GCS 31. 238–43).

close touch with the leading members of her congregation, as well as with such figures as Origen and Symmachus. Then there is the prophetess: neither her name nor her origins are known; she was stigmatized as demoniac, and finally exorcized. Yet the two women are linked by a common denominator. They represent the extremes of an entire range of possibilities for women to express one common sentiment: their intense religious feelings.

Juliana lived alone. Her husband is never mentioned—if he was alive such an omission would have been inexcusable, unless he was purposely ignored as a pagan—and she is not identified as a widow. Yet the fact that she shared her house with Origen 'as if she was his sister' did not raise eyebrows. Her reputation was above suspicion. In Palladius' understanding Juliana was a *parthenos*, a virgin, one of those who had dedicated their lives to God. If so, her dedication did not significantly affect the circumstances of her daily life. She remained firmly a part of society, leading a life no different from that of any other lady of equally sufficient means—Juliana must have been quite wealthy, as not only her erudition but also her hospitality prove—with the sole exception of being without a husband.

The prophetess, like Juliana, had also dedicated her life to God, but she had chosen a very different path. Her understanding of this dedication altered her way of life significantly: she had left home and perhaps family to wander around the countryside, accompanied by a deacon and a presbyter; she was dedicated only to her divine message, without consideration for herself and her well-being, much less for marriage and procreation. Her conduct, her way of expressing religious ideas, was popular, but not appreciated by the clergy. She was condemned as heretical and possessed. Interestingly, the most inflammatory of her activities seems to have been her presiding over liturgical acts, in clear defiance of Paul's prescriptions: 'for I do not allow women to teach, or to exercise authority over men' (1 Tim. 2: 11–13).

Between the option chosen by Juliana, the lady who conversed with leading theologians, and who was praised long after she had died, and that chosen by the prophetess, the outcast and demon incarnate, women found other ways to lead lives dedicated to God.

PARTHENOI WITHIN THEIR FAMILY

The prophetess, guided by religious enthusiasm, left her home
and thus all confines of society to wander around the country
preaching. Juliana, on the other hand, remained in her own
house in Caesarea, while at the same time leading a life apart,
as a single, presumably unmarried, woman who had 'dedicated
herself to God'. Two essential prerequisites must have been fulfilled to allow her to do so: financial and personal independence
made possible by mature age. Without these, a woman's options
in realizing her religious intentions were considerably narrowed.
There was, in fact, only one place for a young and financially
dependent woman to cultivate a religious life apart: paradoxically,
in her own family.

In 1953 D. Amand and M.-Ch. Moons published an anonymous
Greek text in an article entitled 'Une curieuse homélie grecque
inédite sur la virginité adressée aux pères de famille'.[20] The lack
of an author's name makes it difficult to ascertain the homily's
date and provenance. On the basis of internal evidence the editors
dated it prior to the council of Nicaea in 325,[21] with a region of
origin in Syria or neighbouring areas, including Asia Minor.

Since each of us has received from God the [gift of] free will, everyone
has, as Paul says in his first letter to the Corinthians, 'the freedom of his
own will. Whoever has decided in his heart to keep his daughter as a
virgin has done well, in the sense', says he, 'that he who marries his
daughter acts well, but he who keeps her as a virgin', says he, 'does
better' (1. 1–2).[22]

Marriage and virginity are the homily's central themes and its

---

[20] *RBén* 63 (1953) , 18–69, 211–38.

[21] Relevant for the dating is the absence of references to Trinitarian questions
and the archaic description of Christ as 'child of God'; if written later, the author
was at least tending towards an Arian position; the location was established by a
comparison with two homilies by Eusebius of Emesa. Amand and Moons, 'Une
curieuse homélie', 236–8; D. Amand de Mendieta, 'La Virginité chez Eusèbe
d'Émèse et l'ascétisme familial dans la première moitié du IVe siècle', *RHE*
50 (1955), 777–820 (here 818); A. Vööbus ('Syrische Herkunft der Pseudo-
Basilianischen Homilie über die Jungfräulichkeit', *Oriens Christianus* 40 (1956),
69–77) argues likewise for the homily's Syriac origin. Though the homily does not
necessarily derive from Asia Minor itself, it illustrates a custom supported by later
evidence from Asia Minor proper.

[22] The text varies considerably from the NT original (1 Cor. 7: 37–8), as noted
by Amand and Moons, 'Une curieuse homélie', 35 n. 4.

very title, *Peri Parthenias*, indicates the author's preference. The homily aims exclusively at persuading parents that their children should keep themselves 'pure for Christ', and that parents should not have the audacity to impede in any way those 'who desire with fervour to practise virginity, be they a son or a daughter, a servant or a maid' (2. 10–11).

At the same time the author never condemns marriage. Created by God, marriage is sanctified through procreation, but those who marry can only achieve salvation by remaining continent (once they have fulfilled their procreative duty), as if they were 'brother and sister' (1. 3–9). The advantages of preserving a child's virginity are self-evident, and no parent, 'glued to earthly matters', ought to dissuade his child if he or she shows even the faintest trace of a favourable disposition (2. 13, 8. 99, 111–12).

Parents (the homily addresses fathers in particular, while the role of the mother remains more obscure) ought to rejoice if their child expresses the wish to cultivate virginity, but must not consent lightly to the proposed undertaking. The task awaiting both father and daughter—and again, the homily stresses this relationship in particular—is a heavy one. The father becomes the 'priest of the high temple', and he is responsible that 'nothing evil approaches the pure temple' (2. 18–20), that nothing corrupts what has been entrusted to him (παραθήκην). First of all, he has to ascertain his daughter's capacity to lead the life of a virgin of God: her comportment (ἴχνη) has to be measured, her gestures regulated, her eyes respectful. He ought to be conscious of her thoughts, her love for all matters human and divine, her endurance in fasting, and her works of Christian charity. Only if he is certain that she possesses these qualities, may a father allow his daughter to adopt a virgin's life (2. 15–18).

Now his duties as 'priest of the temple' begin. He must keep his daughter in absolute seclusion like a prisoner (*sic*). No man must come near her, not even under the pretext of religion. Dangers lurk on all fronts. The daughter cannot visit the church at night, for fear that 'she may lose the lamp of chastity while lighting that of the night vigil (ἀγρυπνία)',[23] and she may not

---

[23] 'De virg.' 2. 34–6. In this context ἀγρυπνία has become a Christian *terminus technicus*, the night-long liturgical vigil or παννυχισμός; cf. ἀγρυπνία, *Thesaurus linguae graecae* i.1, ed. H. Stephanus (Paris, 1831), 506 f.; LSJ s.v. does not mention this sense; Amand and Moons, 'Une curieuse homélie', 42 n. 2.

attend funerals. Her father must constantly guard her bed (even in his own house!); he must control her laughter, anger, and words, in short all her passions and desires. He may not concede anything, because the enemy is everywhere (2. 27–40).

Difficult and unforgiving as they may seem, it is not sufficient merely to fulfil all these external prescriptions.

If you are a virgin for Christ, you must not be so according to your own wishes (θέλεις), but according to the wishes of Him, for whose sake you are virgin . . . 'no athlete has been crowned [with the laurel of victory] who has not competed according to the rules' (7. 81–5).[24]

The 'rules' discussed so far have addressed only external circumstances. Yet, more important than her actions are a girl's thoughts. 'You must not wish for the same as those who have worldly thoughts (τοῖς τὰ κόσμου). . . . [Because] one needs virgins who are . . . sincere in their moral behaviour' (7. 82–94). To achieve such sincerity the father should collect 'a bouquet of aphorisms from the divine Scriptures' with thoughts such as: 'Better a life bereft of children, but rich in virtue.' Constant meditation on such thoughts will strengthen his daughter's devotion to matters divine (2. 43–4).

Never be negligent in guarding her. . . . Even if your daughter suffers [under this kind of life], it is better that she should suffer for Christ. And it cannot be without killing one's child that it will be taught perfection: one is not brought to that by anger but by a father's tenderness for his beloved child (2. 22–5).

A surprising conception of fatherly love, to be sure. But to what end would any father want to subject both himself and his daughter to such rigour, while bearing at the same time all the material disadvantages of keeping an unmarried child, and devoting considerable effort to the supervision of her stern regime?

. . . So that [your daughter] will progress with generosity towards the immaculate bridal chamber of Christ, where she will dwell in the company of the wise virgins, so that you, who guided her as well will be admitted to the bridal chamber of the heavenly kingdom, and that she, on her part, will receive the crown of immortality (2. 44).

---

[24] Cf. 2 Tim. 2: 5.

To dedicate one's life to God is a betrothal with Jesus Christ. The life of virginity is a period of preparation in anticipation of the wedding night with the heavenly bridegroom, strict and at times miserable on earth, but leading to a blissful eternity.

The virgin has illustrious models to follow: the five wise virgins of the Gospel of Matthew, Mary, and the famous Thecla, heroine of the *Apocryphal Acts* of Paul.[25] Moreover, her bridegroom is not swayed by superficialities: 'Are you bereft of parents? You are not bereft of God. Come then, whether you are very rich or little known, whether you are poor or living from the work of your hands. Have courage, because the bridegroom Christ does not regard fading beauty . . . whether you are short or tall' (8. 105–9).

With such future rewards, a father also stands to gain immensely. He is now guardian of a heavenly bride, a pure temple, a prize possession. Even his most mundane preoccupations might now be viewed with complacency: no dowry had to be paid; and it no longer mattered if a girl was no beauty, or of low class, or disadvantaged in any respect.

The call of Christ, however, was by no means restricted to women. Sons were called as well. The father of a son who remains a virgin is compared to Abraham who offered his son as a sacrifice to God—perhaps an indication that in a son's decision to dedicate his life to God the idea of 'sacrifice' played a greater role than that of the engagement to Christ.

The homily *On Virginity* was written at about the same time as the Fathers at Ancyra drafted their canon 19. Although it does not necessarily originate from Asia Minor itself, it brings into sharper focus many aspects of a virgin's life that canon 19 only alluded to. Like the canon, the homily addresses throughout offspring of both sexes, and reflects on the consequences of their decision to 'dedicate their lives to God', to become engaged to Christ.[26] This engagement was preceded by a brief period of

---

[25] Matt. 25: 1–13; 'De virg.' 8. 100–1 (Amand and Moons, 'Une curieuse homélie', 61, cf. 60 n. 2). According to the editors, the author knew the *Acts of Paul* and considered them canonical; the text of these *Acts* has been edited by e.g. L. Vouaux, *Les Actes de Paul et ses lettres apocryphes* (Paris, 1922); E. Hennecke and F. Schneemelcher (eds.), *Neutestamentliche Apokryphen*, ii (Tübingen, 1964³), 177–90.

[26] 'De virg.' 4. 58–5. 66 (Amand and Moons, 49–55).

close observation, to make sure of the candidate's capabilities. The precise form of the engagement itself remains unclear. It appears to have been a private, personal declaration, made within the family under the auspices of the *paterfamilias*.[27] The private character of this declaration is emphasized by the fact that: 'If [the daughter] does not want to remain virgin, no one must constrain her by force, no one must blame her' (3. 45–46). Although the tenor of the homily leaves no doubt that the engagement was definite and binding, the girl could change her mind without official punishment. Reproach and remonstration belong completely to her own conscience, once she is faced with all the disadvantages of marriage, the pains of childbirth, the sufferings of losing children and husband, the remorse at opportunities lost.

In a manner similar to the decision reached at Ancyra, the homily stresses the personal character of a girl's decision. It is not seen as legally binding and official as a marriage vow, and thus a recantation was viewed more leniently, without diminishing the 'moral' demand for a lifelong obligation.

Another aspect of the homily is even more striking: young women as well as young men who decided to 'become virgins', remained an integral part of their families.[28] The same is true for male and female slaves. It is therefore conceivable that within a single family sons and daughters, and male and female slaves alike would have engaged in a life 'dedicated to God', while even the parents lived 'as if they were brother and sister'—all under the authority of the *paterfamilias* and materially provided for by the family's means.

Whereas the homily of uncertain origin and anonymous authorship was primarily concerned with young women and men, a situation similar to such a theoretical model can indeed be reconstructed from another source, written much later and belonging to an entirely different literary genre. Here as well the protagonist begins her life as a virgin of God in her family, yet we observe a gradual process whereby more and more members of the original family *became virgins*—in short, where the original household was slowly transformed into an 'ascetic household', and then an ascetic community. For the present the protagonist's early years

---

[27] Ibid. 225.
[28] 'De virg.' 1. 1–2. 44 (Amand and Moons 35–45).

will be the focus, since they afford a much more personal perspective on a young woman's decision to remain a virgin.

FROM THE INDIVIDUAL *PARTHENOS* TO THE ASCETIC FAMILY: MACRINA

Between the years 380 and 383 Gregory of Nyssa wrote what he called a *Letter about the Life of Saint Macrina*,[29] conceding at once that: 'you might think that [this work] is a letter, but its sheer volume . . . exceeds any letter's dimension.' The subject of his letter is none other than Gregory's elder sister Macrina and, following the rules of the classic biography, Gregory presents Macrina as the perfect example of a truly philosophical life.[30] Accordingly, Macrina's life is conceived as a homogeneous unity reflecting the heroine's continuous progress from earliest childhood towards her perfection. In Macrina's case, perfection carried a very specific sense: her destiny, the ideal towards which she progressed, was that of a saint. *The Life of Saint Macrina* constitutes both biography and hagiography; here, Gregory constructs our first image of the perfect Christian woman.[31]

---

[29] Gregory of Nyssa, *Vita Sanctae Macrinae (VSM)*, ed. P. Maraval (SC 178; Paris, 1971), 136–266; for background, see esp. 21–34, 67, 136–8; an English translation of the *VSM* is available in V. W. Callahan, *Saint Gregory of Nyssa: Ascetical Works* (The Fathers of the Church: A New Translation 58; Washington, DC, 1967), 163–91. Other sources for Macrina's life include Gr. Nyss. *De anima et resurrectione* (PG 46. 12–160); id. *Ep.* 19, ed. G. Pasquali (in *Gregorii Nysseni opera (GN)* viii.2, ed. W. Jaeger (Leiden, 1959), 62–8 (see esp. §§ 6–10, pp. 64 f.)); and Gregory of Nazianzus, *Epigr.* 163, ed. H. Beckby (*Anthologia graeca*, ii (Munich 1957), 528). R. Albrecht (*Das Leben der heiligen Makrina auf dem Hintergrund der Thekla-Traditionen* (Göttingen, 1986)) has independently reached similar conclusions, to which I shall not always refer specifically in the following.

[30] 'Biographie . . . [ist] überall dort zu greifen, wo sich das Interesse an einer unverwechselbaren Persönlichkeit nicht in der bloßen Deskription ihres Wesens, . . . ausspricht, sondern wo das Wesen dieser Persönlichkeit durch die als Einheit aufgefaßte Gesamtheit ihrer Handlungen und Schicksale, kurz durch ihren Lebenslauf, erfaßt und ausgedrückt wird', A. Dihle, *Studien zur griechischen Biographie* (Abhandlungen der wissenschaftlichen Akademie in Göttingen, phil.-hist. Kl. 3: 37; Göttingen, 1956), 11; cf. H. Delehaye, *Les Passions des martyrs et les genres littéraires* (Brussels, 1966²), 143; R. Reitzenstein, *Des Athanasius Werk über das Leben des Antonius* (Sitzungsberichte der Heidelberger Akademie der Wissenschaften, phil.-hist. Kl. 5; Heidelberg, 1914), *passim*.

[31] W. K. L. Clarke, *The Life of Macrina* (London, 1916), 12; P. Cox, *Biography in Late Antiquity* (Berkeley, 1983), 45–65, 134–49; A. J. Festugière, 'Lieux

To demonstrate the sanctity of Macrina's life thus emphatically underlies and shapes the entire account. Events are stylized to emphasize early signs of the heroine's destiny, and Gregory employed those topoi that generally form part of the 'Life' of a θεῖος ἀνήρ, a 'divine human being'—in particular, dreams, visions, and miracles. Gregory's rhetorical craft and his intention in compiling the *Life* have always to be kept in mind when attempting an interpretation.[32] Nevertheless, his account is unquestionably based on authentic historical detail and thus represents an extremely valuable source, illustrating the way in which *a known individual*, one specific young woman, chose to express and realize her dedication to God.[33]

Macrina was born about 327, the eldest of the nine children of Basil the Elder and Emmelia. No document relates the place of her birth. She could have been born in Pontus, where her father enjoyed a considerable reputation as teacher of rhetoric, or in Cappadocia, the home of her mother's family.[34] Macrina 'was well born and came of a good family'.[35] Her father's income was vast, and the landholdings owned by the family were dispersed over three Asian provinces. While it is not clear that Macrina's

communs littéraires et thèmes de folk-lore dans l'hagiographie primitive', *Wiener Studien* 73 (1960), 123–52. The works of K. Holl ('Die schriftstellerische Form des griechischen Heiligenlebens', *Neue Jahrbücher für das klassische Altertum, Geschichte und deutsche Literatur* 29 (1912), 406–27) and F. Leo (*Die griechisch-römische Biographie nach ihrer literarischen Form* (Leipzig, 1901)) are classic discussions of the literary form of both biography and hagiography; F. Loofs, 'Makrina, die Jüngere', *Realencyklopädie für protestantische Theologie und Kirche*, xii (Leipzig, 1903), 93 f.; U. Mattioli, 'Macrina e Monica', in P. S. Zanetti, (ed.), *In verbis verum amare* (Miscellanea dell'Istituto di Filologia Latina e Medioevale, Università di Bologna; Florence, 1980), 165–203; H. Mertel, *Die biographische Form der griechischen Heiligenlegenden* (Munich, 1909), *passim*; A. Momigliano, 'The Life of St. Macrina by Gregory of Nyssa', in J. W. Eadie and J. Ober (eds.), *The Craft of the Ancient Historian: Essays in Honor of C. G. Starr* (Lanham, Md., 1985), 443–58.

[32] L. Bieler, Θεῖος Ἀνήρ: *Das Bild des 'göttlichen Menschen' in Spätantike und Frühchristentum*, i (Vienna, 1935/6; repr. Darmstadt, 1967), 1–134, 141–50.

[33] Loofs, 'Makrina, die Jüngere', 93 f.

[34] Gr. Nyss. *VSM* 21. 9–14; Gr. Naz. *Or.* 43. 3, 12 (PG 36. 497 C, 509 A–B); Aubineau, *Virginité* 33–5; P. J. Fedwick, *The Church and the Charisma of Leadership in Basil of Caesarea* (Toronto, 1979), 133; Patrucco, *Lettere*, 28 f.; Maraval, *Macrine*, 37 f., 48. Regarding the profession of rhetorician cf. P. Wolf, *Vom Schulwesen der Spätantike* (Baden-Baden, 1952), *passim*.

[35] Gr. Nyss. *VSM* 21. 8–9.

family actually belonged to the senatorial class, it is certain that her father was one of those provincial landowners 'from whom not only the curials in the cities but even new members of the senatorial order were chosen'.[36] Unlike many families of this class, that of Basil and his wife Emmelia was noted for its long association with the Christian faith: Macrina's grandmother, Macrina the Elder, had defended her beliefs during the persecutions of Maximinus Daia and, according to Gregory, shortly before Macrina's birth her mother Emmelia was blessed by a vision of the holy Thecla, the ideal of virginity already mentioned in the context of the homily addressed to fathers.[37]

Despite her family's Christian affinities, Macrina's early life was spent much as may be expected of a young lady of her rank. She was, as Gregory emphasizes, a gifted girl who learned easily, and her talents soon became obvious. In accordance with traditions that favoured educated children—including girls—Macrina received a sound education.[38] The syllabus generally taught is well known. It included the works of Homer, Plato, Demosthenes, and, to a lesser extent, Greek tragedies. As far as girls are concerned we are less well informed.[39] Judging from

[36] These provinces were Pontus Ptolemaicus, Helenopontus (cf. Gr. Nyss. VSM 8. 13–16, 21. 11–14), and Cappadocia (cf. Gr. Naz. Or. 43. 3 (Grégoire de Nazianze: Discours funèbres en l'honneur de son frère Césaire et de Basile de Césarée, ed. F. Boulenger (Paris, 1908), 64); Gr. Naz. Ep. 2 (Gallay, Lettres, i. 1 f.); Maraval, Macrine, 160 n. 1. For Basil the Elder's social rank see B. Treucker, 'A Note on Basil's Letters of Recommendation', in P. J. Fedwick (ed.), Basil of Caesarea: Christian, Humanist, Ascetic, i (Toronto, 1981), 405–10 (here 409); Gr. Nyss. VSM 2. 12–20; Aubineau, Virginité, 33 f.; Patrucco, Lettere, 26–8, with a discussion of the controversy concerning Basil's social background; S. Giet, 'Basile était-il sénateur?', RHE 60 (1965), 429–44.

[37] Gr. Nyss. VSM 2. 1–12, 2. 23–30; Aubineau, Virginité, 33; Patrucco, Lettere, 25–8.

[38] Gr. Nyss. VSM 3. 1–20; G. Bardy, 'L'Église et l'enseignement au IVᵉ siècle', RevSR 14 (1934), 525–49, here 525–41; A. J. Festugière, Antioche païenne et chrétienne (Paris, 1959), 211–40; H.-I. Marrou, Μουσικὸς 'Ανήρ: Étude sur les scènes de la vie intellectuelle figurant sur les monuments funéraires romains (Grenoble, 1938), 197–207. L. Robert (Hellenica 13 (Paris, 1965), 47–52) mentions two girls, one aged 10, described as φιλόλογοι and φιλογράμματοι in inscriptions from Greece.

[39] Festugière (Antioche païenne, 216) considers Libanius to be representative of the standard education. H.-I. Marrou (Histoire de l'éducation dans l'Antiquité (Paris, 1965⁶)) hardly mentions girls apart from a few hints (e.g. concerning Stilicho's daughter, p. 445); W. M. Ramsay ('A Noble Anatolian Family of the

Gregory's account, their syllabus was virtually identical to that of boys, though he insists that Macrina never studied tragedies nor, of course, comedies or Homer and his myths. The inevitable harm caused to impressionable souls by the indecencies alluded to in pagan authors (an argument proposed by many Christian writers[40]) accounts for his insistence in this matter. But Gregory's argument assuredly did not reflect his own experience. He and his brothers had received a sound classical education, and considering their father's fame as a master of 'sophistics', it is highly unlikely that Macrina grew up without any notion of classical learning or profane culture.[41]

Even if much of Macrina's education differed little from what was considered appropriate for any young lady, it is characteristic that she was educated at home by her mother and kept secluded from outside influence. Private education was no rarity; in fact it was fairly common throughout Antiquity, but society's hostile attitude towards their faith had made it almost a necessity for Christian children. Gregory's emphasis on the fact that the mother herself was devoted to the daughter's education is quite striking.[42] What may have been a novelty at the time was soon considered

Fourth Century', *Classical Review* 33 (1919), 1–9, here 5–9) discusses an epitaph obviously composed by an educated lady; S. Pomeroy ('*Technikai kai Mousikai*: The Education of Women in the Fourth Century and the Hellenistic Period', *American Journal of Ancient History* 2 (1977), 51–68) is too early, but interesting.

[40] Festugière, *Antioche païenne*, 225–9, esp. 225; even in his day Plato did not entirely approve of these authors as standard reading, cf. Pl. *Republic* 377a–392b; H. Fuchs, 'Enkyklios Paideia', *RAC* v. 365–98.

[41] Gr. Nyss. *VSM* 21. 12; a suggestion supported by Gregory's own account in *De anima et resurrectione* (PG 46. 21); cf. id. *Ep.* 13. 4–6 (*GN* viii.2, 45 f.); Basil, *Homilia 22: Sermo de legendis libris gentilium. Ad adolescentes* (PG 31. 563–90), esp. § 5 (575–9); Basil was possibly a disciple of Libanius; cf. Festugière, *Antioche païenne*, 409. According to Eusebius (*HE* 6. 21), Origen taught Julia Mammaea; regarding educated women cf. also Eunapius, *Lives of the Philosophers and Sophists*, 466–70 (ed. W. C. Wright (Loeb; London, 1922), 398–416).

[42] Marrou (Μουσικὸς Ἀνήρ, 41) describes a sarcophagus depicting a female figure, apparently not the mother, instructing a girl. He points out (pp. 198 f.) that while parents took an interest in their children's education, professional tutors were standard for girls as well as boys; a girl aged 15 was 'eruditae omnis artibus' (p. 202; *CIL* 6: 4: 1, no. 25808 (Berlin, 1894), 2574; cf. *CTh.* 9. 8 (4 April 326) (Mommsen–Meyer, i.2, 450); Festugière *Antioche païenne*, 106–8, refers to students who lived as lodgers; T. A. Goggin, *The Times of Saint Gregory of Nyssa as Reflected in the Letters and the Contra Eunomium* (Washington, DC, 1947), 97; Marrou, *Histoire de l'éducation*, 440, 444 f., 451 ff.

beneficial and therefore exemplary for future generations. When Gregory wrote his *Life of Macrina* the practice had become a staple of pastoral advice. In 393/4 John Chrysostom devoted an entire treatise to Christian fathers as teachers of their sons, and mothers of their daughters.[43]

The exemplary character of Macrina's education is quite obvious. Under her mother's guidance, in the seclusion of her house, she studied 'all those parts of the Scriptures inspired by God, which seem most accessible to early age . . . , first and foremost the Wisdom of Solomon, and here in particular that which contributes to the formation of a sound moral life. . . . She further knew the Psalms very well. . . .'[44] Macrina, in short, fulfilled a Christian writer's educational ideal, though her education may in fact not have differed all that much from current practice.[45]

In accordance with fourth-century mores, at the age of 12, 'when the flower of youth begins to flourish in particular splendour of beauty', Macrina was engaged to a young man, then approximately 25 years of age, 'who had just completed his studies', and was selected by her father because of his excellent family background and character. During the engagement—Macrina had to wait two years to reach the legal age for marriage—the young man suddenly died. This occurred about the year 340.[46]

---

[43] John Chrysostom, *De inani gloria et de educandis a parentibus liberis*, 90 (*Jean Chrysostome: Sur la vaine gloire et l'éducation des enfants*, ed. A.-M. Malingrey (SC 188, Paris, 1972), 196; see 46 f. for the date of the work); cf. id. *In Epistolam ad Colossenses commentarius*, 10. 5 (PG 62. 374); Albrecht, *Das Leben der heiligen Makrina*, 75–8; J. Grosdidier de Matons, 'La Femme dans l'Empire byzantin', *Histoire mondiale de la femme*, iii, ed. P. Grimal (Paris, 1967), 11–43.

[44] Gr. Nyss. *VSM* 3. 15–20.

[45] Basil, Jerome, and John Chrysostom considered exactly this kind of education to be the essential preparation for the monastic life and recommended the same syllabus to younger members of monastic communities; Gr. Nyss. *VSM* 12. 9–14; Basil, *Regulae fusius tractatae*, 15. 3 (PG 31. 953); Gr. Nyss. *In inscriptionis Psalmorum*, 1. 1–1. 2, ed. J. McDonough (*GN* v. 24–9; Jerome, *Ep.* 107. 4, 12 (CSEL 55 (Vienna, 1912), 294, 302 f.); H. Bacht, *Das Vermächtnis des Ursprungs* (Würzburg, 1972), 194.

[46] Gr. Nyss. *VSM* 4. 3–24; id. *De virginitate*, 20. 4 (SC 119. 498–502). The engagement was most probably a preliminary contract, an *engyesis*, see LSJ s.v. κατεγγυᾶν; M. Collignon, 'Matrimonium', *Dictionnaire des antiquités grecques et romaines*, iii.2 (Paris, 1904), 1639–63, here 1643; for nubile age cf. *CTh.* 3. 5. 11 (17 June 380) (137), which allows marriage at 10 (cf. W. M. Calder, (ed.), *MAMA* vii. 56, no. 258; C. De Clercq, 'Mariage dans le droit de l'église Orientale',

Macrina's reaction to her personal tragedy contravened every social custom. Instead of consenting to a second engagement as her parents suggested, she decided, in open opposition to their expressed will, to remain unmarried.

The young girl knew the decision of her father well, but, once death had destroyed that which had been decided for her, she now called her father's [original] decision a marriage, as if that which had been arranged had indeed taken place, and she was firmly determined to live from now on 'by herself' (ἐφ᾽ ἑαυτῆς).[47]

With a firmness 'surprising in someone of her age' Macrina defended her position against repeated entreaties by her parents; she regarded her first engagement as a bona fide marriage, contracted once and for all time. All attempts to deny this she declared absurd and illegitimate; in her understanding her fiancé's untimely death left her widowed. It was on this basis that she chose, as Gregory emphasizes, with complete freedom and in opposition to her parents' wish, to remain 'by herself'.

The phrase Gregory used here, to live ἐφ᾽ ἑαυτῆς, is highly significant. Of Platonic origin, it had by that time become the technical term to express an individual's choice to lead a solitary life.[48] Macrina's decision to remain unmarried is clearly represented as the equivalent of dedicating her life to God, but is expressed by a term that evokes the concept of a 'philosophical life'.[49] By the middle of the fourth century φιλόσοφος βίος, a

Dictionnaire de droit canonique, vi. (Paris, 1935), 787–802, here 790; H. Leclercq, 'Mariage', *DACL* x.2, 1843–1982, esp. 1967; for the age of the fiancé see Maraval, *Macrine*, 44 f.

[47] Gr. Nyss. *VSM* 5. 1–16.

[48] Gr. Nyss. *VSM* 5. 4; cf. id. *Vita Moysis*, 2. 18 (*Grégoire de Nysse: Vie de Moïse*, ed. J. Daniélou (SC 1bis; Paris, 1987⁴), 116); ἐφ᾽ ἑαυτοῦ in id. *In laudem fratris Basilii* (PG 46. 809 B). The expression καθ᾽ ἑαυτόν derives from Platonic usage (e.g. *Phaedo* 65) and indicates the search for a perfect life, a 'philosophical life'; Aubineau, *Virginité*, 146–9.

[49] Gr. Nyss. *VSM* 1. 28–9. In *VSM* 8. 13 Gregory uses the same expression as Basil in *Ep.* 2 (Courtonne, *Lettres*, i. 13). A. Dihle, 'Das Problem der Entscheidungsfreiheit in frühchristlicher Zeit', *Gnadenwahl und Entscheidungsfreiheit in der Theologie der Alten Kirche* (*Oikonomia* 9; Erlangen, 1980) 9–31, 90–4; K. S. Frank, *Angelikos Bios* (Münster, 1964), 136–9; P. Hadot, *Exercices spirituels et philosophie antique* (Études Augustiniennes; Paris, 1981), 59–74; J. Leclercq, 'Pour l'histoire de l'expression "philosophie chrétienne"', *Mélanges de science religieuse* 9 (1952), 221–6; A.-M. Malingrey, "*Philosophia*." *Étude d'un groupe*

philosophical life, understood in the Christian sense, meant nothing less than a life devoted to the fulfilment of the highest Christian ideals, a life of virginity.[50] In Macrina's case the decision 'to remain by herself' had, Gregory tells us, clear consequences. Claiming socially and legally the position of a *widow*, and hence of a social role long familiar to herself and those around her, Macrina now began to lead the life of a 'virgin dedicated to God'.[51] At scarcely 12 years of age she was determined to merge two mutually contradictory and exclusive concepts, that of an unmarried girl and a widow, into a new social role: the virgin widow. And 'she judged that there was only one way for her to safeguard this noble decision, never to leave the side of her mother, not even for a single instant.'[52]

Even as 'virgin widow' Macrina remained within her family. An outside observer would have noticed hardly any difference in her life-style; rejected suitors might have been puzzled. Only intimate acquaintances could have noticed slight changes in her life, perhaps observed a new routine, but Macrina's decision had

---

de mots dans la littérature grecque des présocratiques au IVᵉ siècle après J.C. (Paris, 1961), 207–61; Maraval, *Macrine*, 90–103; G. Penco, 'La vita ascetica come "filosofia" nell'antica tradizione monastica', *Studia monastica* 2 (1960), 79–93.

[50] Since the 2nd cent. the Apologists, in particular Justin Martyr, had proclaimed Christ's teachings to be the 'true philosophy'. Within Christianity the notion that Christ's revelation alone, the λόγος ἀληθείας, guaranteed man's true ethical and moral education became almost a universal topos. 'True philosophy' was for many a synonym for 'Christianity', or as Clement of Alexandria (*Paedagogus*, 3. 11. 75 (ed. O. Stählin (GCS 12; Berlin, 1972³) 279)) phrased it: 'How can you love God and your neighbour, if you do not practise *the* philosophy?'; Justin Martyr, *Apologia II pro Christianis*, 13 (PG 6. 465–8); id. *Dialogus cum Tryphone Judaeo*, 8 (PG 6. 492 f.); cf. Clem. Alex. *Strom.* 1. 5. 32, 1. 13 (ed. O. Stählin (GCS 52; Berlin, 1960³) 21 f., 36 f.); the word gains a more technical meaning in the specific usage of the Cappadocians, cf. Malingrey, "*Philosophia*", 207–61.

[51] Bas. *Ep.* 199. 24; R. Albrecht ('Asketinnen im 4. und 5. Jahrhundert in Kleinasien', *JÖB* 32: 2 (1982), 517–24, here 519 f.) fails to note this development; Davies, *Revolt of the Widows, passim*; R. Gryson, *Le Ministère des femmes dans l'Église ancienne* (Gembloux, 1972), 31–3; A. Kalsbach, *Die altkirchliche Einrichtung der Diakonissen bis zu ihrem Erlöschen* (Römische Quartalschrift, Suppl. 22; Freiburg i.B., 1926), 11–16; Martimort, *Les Diaconesses*, 19–21; Mayer, *Monumenta de viduis*, 3–12, 55 f.; for the disregard of second marriages see, 1 Cor. 7: 39 and above, p. 27.

[52] Gr. Nyss. *VSM* 5. 18–20.

a purely private character. She began to pray and recite the Psalms at regular intervals: in the morning, before and after her work, before and after meals, before going to sleep and during the night.[53] Regular prayer and manual work—she 'exercised her hand mainly in working wool'—were, however, occupations associated with the life of any Christian girl. Only one feature, albeit small and seemingly insignificant, indicated that Macrina's life had taken a new turn: she began to bake her mother's bread with her own hands.[54]

By the mere quality of this work, even if its quantity may have been negligible, Macrina took a conscious step to humble herself considerably before those who were in a position to observe her, and perhaps most of all in her estimation of herself. By baking her mother's bread she engaged in work strictly reserved for slaves.[55] This act of servitude, though it may appear small enough to us, must have had a significant impact on those who knew her. By undertaking a service task Macrina consciously overstepped the rigid boundaries set by her rank and social class, and introduced a new dimension into her life. Whereas her entire life had previously been circumscribed by the limits of her social status, this personal act of humility signifies her first breaking away, her first tangible rupture with the conventions of the time. It was indicative of what was to come.

For now, it suffices to underline the fact that the years after the death of her fiancé in 340 witnessed the earliest stages of Macrina's turn towards individual asceticism. Her ascetic life remained in all its phases intrinsically interwoven with that of her family, and even the social model she chose for herself, that of a

[53] Ibid. 4. 2; 3. 19–26.
[54] Ibid. 5. 30; cf. Maraval, *Macrine*, 49 n. 1; Xenophon (*Oeconomicus*, 10. 10–11) advises young ladies to make dough as well as to sew. See also Jer. *Ep.* 107. 10 (CSEL 55. 300 f.).
[55] Bas. *Ep.* 37; Gr. Nyss. *In ecclesiasten homiliae*, 4 (*GN* v. 334–53); Jer. *Ep.* 108 (CSEL 55. 308). Textile work was generally the only form of manual labour acceptable for free women; for Roman evidence see Plutarch, *Quaestiones Romanae*, 284 F; *Vita Romuli*, 15. 5. H. Gülzow, *Christentum und Sklaverei* (Bonn, 1969) 175, on class distinction; A. Hadjinicolaou-Marava, *Recherches sur la vie des esclaves dans le monde byzantin* (Athens, 1950), 32 f.; Teja, *Organización*, 127; W. L. Westermann, *The Slave Systems of Greek and Roman Antiquity* (Philadelphia, 1955), 126 f.; H. Wallon, *Histoire de l'esclavage dans l'antiquité*, ii (Paris, 1847), 108–14.

widow, was a well-known and time-honoured element of her environment. Her personal claim to be a widow without ever actually having been married was the only open indication of a new life-style, one that could exist strictly within the confines of society without losing any of its own integrity.

However stylized and subject to rhetorical conventions it is, the account of Macrina's earliest years is the first in which we encounter a virgin 'dedicated to God' with the recognizable features of an individual. For the first time we can get a glimpse of the person behind the *virgo Dei dicata*; we can imagine circumstances, such as the death of a fiancé, that may have acted as the catalyst for a woman already disposed towards a religious life, prompting her to take a further step that would transform her from pious daughter and dutiful wife into someone else: a 'virgin of God'. Macrina exemplifies the tensions such a decision may have caused within the most Christian of families; even she had to justify her decision on the basis of an already existing social model, the widow. External pressure, so it seems, forced her to create a new social concept. Small wonder that her brother Gregory was impressed, even in retrospect, by her will-power and determination.

THE PSEUDO-MARRIAGE OF MALE AND FEMALE ASCETICS: *SYNEISAKTES*

Juliana, the young Macrina, and the daughters who were the subject of the anonymous early fourth-century homily *On Virginity* were all women, separated by almost a century, who had chosen an unconventional path by deciding to spend their lives 'by themselves', as virgins. However, when we compare their course to that chosen by the prophetess, it becomes clear that they are linked by a common denominator: all sought to realize their unconventional religious inclinations within the traditional framework of society; all remained in their own homes, and within their families. To 'become a virgin' did not necessitate any obvious and dramatic change; there were no prerequisites other than chastity and a specific daily regime. Anomalies appear only upon close observation; only then do we detect a sense of experimentation. An erudite woman living alone can be a solicitous hostess to an unmarried man for two years; daughters are engaged to a fiancé who is no ordinary mortal but Christ himself, and are on this account 'imprisoned' and subjected to rigours that may result in bodily harm; a 12-year-old girl, though never married, declares herself to be a 'virgin widow'. That 'virgins' are not always women, has also become clear. Grammatically, the Greek term *parthenos* (παρθένος) is of neuter gender, as long as it is not accompanied by an article. The canon of Ancyra as well as the homily referred to leave little doubt that men as well as women dedicated themselves to a life of virginity.

Canon 19 issued at Ancyra consists of two parts. The second part reads: 'We prohibit those who live together with men as if they were their sisters, from doing so.' In Greek 'those who live together' is rendered by one phrase: τὰς συνερχομένας. It derives from the verb συνέρχεσθαι, 'to come together, to be united or bonded together', suggesting a firmly established union.[56] Judging from canon 27 issued by the Iberian Fathers at Elvira, the Fathers in Asia Minor were not alone in their pronouncement: 'It has been decided that a bishop, or any other member of the clergy, may only have his sister, or his daughter, if she is a 'virgin dedicated to God', living with him; he may not live with a stranger.'[57]

Ten years later, in 325, the famous council of Nicaea issued yet another canon: 'The great Synod absolutely forbids, and it cannot be permitted to either bishop, presbyter, deacon, or any other cleric, to have in his house a woman συνείσακτος, with the exception of his mother, sister, aunt, or other such persons as are free from all suspicions.'[58] All three canons address more or less the same custom. The canon of Ancyra simply mentions men and women 'who lived together as if they were brother and sister'. But the context implies that such women had previously pro-

---

[56] Mansi, ii. 520; Ignatius, *Ad Smyrnaeos*, 13. 1 (PG 5. 857), mentions παρθένοι; LSJ s.v. συνέρχεσθαι; Achelis, *Virgines subintroductae*, 1–7, 68–70; see also Heussi, *Ursprung*, 30, who refers to *Didache* 11: 11.

[57] 'Episcopus, vel quilibet alius clericus, aut sororem, aut filiam virginem dicatam Deo, tantum secum habeat; extraneam nequaquam habere placuit' (Mansi, ii. 10).

[58] Can. 3, Ἀπηγόρευσεν καθόλου ἡ μεγάλη σύνοδος μήτε ἐπισκόπῳ μήτε πρεσβυτέρῳ μήτε διακόνῳ μήτε ὅλως τινὶ τῶν ἐν τῷ κλήρῳ ἐξεῖναι συνείσακτον ἔχειν, πλὴν εἰ μὴ ἄρα μητέρα ἢ ἀδελφὴν ἢ θείαν, ἢ ἃ μόνα πρόσωπα πᾶσαν ὑποψίαν διαπέφευγε; (Mansi, ii. 669); LSJ s.v. συνάγω; Achelis, *Virgines subintroductae*, 33–5.

claimed their virginity. The Fathers at Elvira were more specific. Here, members of the clergy only are explicitly forbidden to live together with women other than their sisters or those daughters who wished to remain virgins. In like manner Nicaea addresses exclusively members of the clergy, stating quite clearly that only the closest family members—interestingly enough, daughters are no longer mentioned—with the sole exception of persons entirely beyond suspicion, are at all acceptable as living companions for a cleric. No other woman, defined as *syneisaktē*, is permissible.

The Ancyran women, who lived with men as if they were their sisters were called *synerchomenai*, 'those united with them'; in Nicaea they are described as *syneisaktes*, women who are 'brought in or introduced into a house'.[59] Both terms imply continuity, an element of permanence, rather than intermittent visits. The original Greek vocabulary further implies a certain passivity on the part of the women concerned. The women were selected and invited by the men, not the other way round. What kind of living arrangements were operative, especially with male clerics? What was it in such distant areas of the Roman Empire as Asia Minor and the Iberian peninsula that so aroused their clerical colleagues to legislate immediately in these matters?[60]

The history of the term *syneisaktē* offers further clarification. In the year 268 several bishops, among them Firmilian of Caesarea, gathered in Syrian Antioch to decide whether the teachings of the local bishop, Paul of Samosata, were doctrinally sound and within the boundaries of orthodoxy.[61] In the course of the investigation it not only transpired that this was not so, but that he and members of his clergy lived with young women described as *syneisaktes*. Indeed, Paul himself lived not only with one but two such women, both in the flower of their youth and beauty; he provided generously for their material needs and they accompanied him wherever he went.

Yet, even in the eyes of his adversaries, Paul's association with these young women was not considered to be an incriminating factor. His conduct could have set a detrimental example for

[59] Ibid. 68–70.

[60] Achelis (ibid. 12) mentions the example of Juliana and Origen, but Origen's stay was certainly temporary. The unions in question here appear to have been permanent.

[61] Eus. *HE* 7. 30. 12–15; Achelis, *Virgines subintroductae*, 9–11.

others, but the Fathers explicitly state that the *subintroductae*
were neither the occasion nor reason for Paul's excommunication.
The entirely platonic nature of their relationship is never questioned. In fact, the association of Paul and his two girls possessed
many of the features of a charitable institution: Paul clearly
offered his *syneisaktes* material and perhaps social protection.[62]

The situation at Antioch, described by Eusebius without any
implied criticism, apparently reflects circumstances similar to
those banned subsequently by the various canons. Members of
the clergy, from the bishop on downwards, lived together with
women to whom they were not related by any family ties. Unfortunately, early sources illustrating these peculiar living conditions
in greater detail are rare, especially in Asia Minor. A treatise
written between 336 and 358 by the then bishop of Ancyra, Basil,
attests to the inefficiency of legislation, in this case ecclesiastical
legislation, when faced with an apparently popular custom.[63]

In chapter 43 of his treatise Basil writes: 'It is absurd that those
who lead a virginal life (παρθενικὸν βίον διώκοντας) are stupidly
involved in the imitation of a marriage (τῶν γάμων μιμήμασιν)'—
adding that those who purportedly care for their heavenly spouse
only, become the companion of men as caretakers. Virgins, according to Basil, should prefer to live naked on the pavement, in
any kind of poverty conceivable, rather than forgo divine love by
living comfortably together (συμβιοῦν) with men who look after
their earthly needs, all under the pretext of charity.[64]

Basil's words provide some explanation. In a fashion that
resembled a marriage in every respect but one (albeit a fundamental one), men, members of the clergy in particular, cohabited
with women who had professed their intention of remaining virgin.
The men provided for the women's financial and social needs; the
women in return took care of the men's household chores.

The obvious practicality of this custom, banned so adamantly,

---

[62] Eusebius of Emesa, *Homilia* 7. 20 (ed. É. M. Buytaert (Spicilegium sacrum
Lovaniense 26; Louvain, 1953), 188 f.), confirms the continuity of this practice
in Syrian Antioch until *c*. 330–50, condemning it as a marriage under false
pretences; cf. Amand, 'La Virginité', 801–3.

[63] Bas. Anc. *De virginitate* (PG 30. 669–810); cf. F. Cavallera, 'Le "De
Virginitate" de Basile d'Ancyre', *RHE* 6 (1905), 5–14; not to be confused with
his better known namesake Basil of Caesarea.

[64] Bas. Anc. *De virg.* 43 (PG 30. 753–6).

suffices to explain its popularity. Both parties benefited. Both Eusebius' account of Paul of Samosata's young women and Basil of Ancyra's words indicate the motive that induced a woman to become a cleric's *syneisaktē*: plain economic need. A woman who wanted to lead a 'virginal life', but did not come from a family which could afford to support a single girl, or a woman without any family at all, had in fact no means of supporting herself other than living with a man in a 'pseudo-marriage'. She became a 'married virgin'. For the men involved the advantages of this arrangement are equally obvious. Without forfeiting their bid for salvation, they could nevertheless enjoy almost all earthly comforts. Not only did women 'beyond all suspicion' care for them, but the men performed a constant act of charity, which in the early days at least was regarded favourably and, further, if they were clerics, was implicitly supported by the congregation as a whole, which provided for the clergy.

That the first legal restriction of the custom coincides with the first occurrence in a canon of *virgines Deo dicatae* is significant. It is tempting to suggest that so unusual a convention, the cohabitation of unrelated men and women, developed simultaneously with the concept of the *virgo Deo dicata* for a specific reason: it was an alternative to the family in providing these newly emerging types of women with economic and social support. Such a 'pseudo-marriage' has additional significance from a purely organizational point of view. The women described thus far had begun to reinterpret familial roles in response to their religious calling: as virgin fiancée or as virgin widow. All these roles are variations of the one paramount role of any woman: to be a wife and mother. Yet none of the patterns traced thus far—with the sole exception of the prophetess—involved a *de facto* rupture with the natural family, as a bona fide marriage would have done. Only in this last role, as a 'virgin wife', did a woman actually leave her family to live 'as if she was his sister' in a 'spiritual marriage' with a man to whom she was not related.

PROTOTYPES OF ASCETIC COMMUNITIES: THE LIFE OF THEODOTUS

When Maximinus Daia during the years 311 and 312 sought to strengthen his position in the provinces of Asia Minor by forcibly effecting, alongside other, harsher measures, a revival of paganism, he promoted a certain Theotecnus to the governorship of Galatia Prima. Theotecnus had already earned a well-established reputation as an anti-Christian while he was the *curator* of Syrian Antioch. Panic erupted when the news of his impending arrival reached his new headquarters at Ancyra, and many Christians fled to the countryside and the mountains. Some who remained were forced into hiding, others had to die for their faith.[65]

In 1901 the Italian scholar Pio Franchi de' Cavalieri published a new edition of the *Lives* of two Anatolian martyrs, St Theodotus of Ancyra and St Ariadne of Prymnessus. Both *Lives* subsequently attracted scholarly attention, and their historical value was gradually confirmed beyond dispute.[66] After the discovery of a chapel dedicated to St Theodotus, Stephen Mitchell re-examined the *Martyrdom of Saint Theodotus of Ancyra*, emphasizing again its historical accuracy and suggesting an even earlier date for its composition, between the years 360 and 363.[67] The events themselves, described by a certain Nilus, took place in Ancyra and at a lake outside the city, and date back to the years 312 or 313.[68]

In fact *The Martyrdom of Saint Theodotus of Ancyra* is only

[65] Eus. *HE* 9. 2–4, 5. 1, 9a. 4, 10. 7–12, 11. 5–6; 'Theotecnus', in *PLRE* i. 908; Millar, *Emperor in the Roman World*, 445 f.

[66] Cf. the text of Theodotus' *Life* in P. Franchi de' Cavalieri, *I martirii di S. Teodoto e di S. Ariadne con un'appendice sul testo originale del martirio di S. Eleuterio* (*StT* 6; Rome, 1901), 61–87; a second *Life* of Ariadne in *Ancora del martiro di S. Ariadne* (StT 8; Rome, 1902), 3–21, reviewed by A. v. Harnack in *Theologische Literaturzeitung* 27 (1902), 358–61; S. Mitchell, 'The Life of Saint Theodotus of Ancyra', *Anatolian Studies* 32 (1982), 93–113. The text is also discussed by H. Delehaye ('La passion de S. Théodote d'Ancyre', *AnBoll* 22 (1903), 320–8), who argues that it is largely fictitious, and by H. Grégoire and P. Orgels ('La passion de S. Théodote, œuvre du Pseudo-Nil, et son noyeau montaniste', *ByZ* 44 (1951), 165–84), who maintain its historical authenticity.

[67] Mitchell ('Life of St Theodotus', 93, 111–13) based this date on the description of Theodotus as προστάτης τῶν Γαλιλαίων (c. 31), a pejorative term in vogue during the reign of Julian the Apostate; Grégoire and Orgels, 'La passion de S. Théodote', 178–84; L. Robert, *A travers l'Asie Mineure* (Paris, 1980), 244–56; Franchi de' Cavalieri, '*I martirii di S. Teodoto*', 22 f.; S. Scicolone, 'Le accezioni dell'appellativo "Galilei" in Giuliano', *Aevum* 56 (1982), 71–80.

[68] Identified with the lakes Mohan göl and Emir göl near Dilimnia (at or near modern Gölbaşi); Mitchell, 'Life of St Theodotus', 94 f., 105, 107–13; Grégoire and Orgels, 'La passion de S. Théodote', 178.

part of the title. It reads in full: . . . *and the Seven Virgins with him.*[69] Theodotus, a shopkeeper, was a well-known and zealous supporter of the Christian community at Ancyra (cc. 1–3). When Theotecnus' persecutions set in his shop became for many the last place of refuge (4–9). At a certain point Theodotus went to a small town called Malos to collect the remains of a martyr whose corpse had been thrown into the nearby river Halys. At Malos Theodotus met the local priest, Fronto, and several other Christians. Their reunion occasioned a 'picnic' during which Theodotus selected a pleasant spot as the potential site of a chapel dedicated to a future martyr (10–12). Meanwhile, at Ancyra, seven Christian ladies had been seized and put to death by Theotecnus. Encouraged by a vision, Theodotus recovered the dead bodies and buried them (13–19). As a result he himself was arrested. Just before being led away he asked his companions to bury his remains, if possible, near Malos. When confronted by the governor, Theodotus refused an offer to become priest of Apollo; instead, he delivered an inflammatory speech in defence of Christianity and was predictably tortured and put to death (20–31). Just before his body was burned, the priest Fronto arrived, carrying some of the wine for which Malos is famous. The guards could not resist a generous tasting, and were soon inebriated enough for Fronto to retrieve Theodotus' body and place it on a donkey cart. The donkey, without any guidance, then carried the body to Malos, to the spot where Theodotus had envisaged a site for a martyr's chapel, and there his remains were duly buried (32–36).

The discovery of the site of St Theodotus' chapel at Malos, now Kaleçik, reinforced the historical accuracy of the sections of the *Martyrdom* concerned with Theodotus, and lent additional authority to the central part of the entire work, the account of the martyrdom of the seven Christian ladies (13 ff.).[70]

---

[69] See also Delehaye, 'La passion de S. Théodote d'Ancyre', 320–2.

[70] Delehaye ('La passion de S. Théodote d'Ancyre', 327) considers this part a later addition intended to enliven the somewhat uninspired account of Theodotus' own martyrdom; he points to a similar story regarding Amisus in the *Synaxarium ecclesiae Constantinopolitanae* (ed. H. Delehaye (Brussels, 1902), 546). Grégoire and Orgels ('La passion de S. Théodote', 174 ff.) and, following them, Mitchell ('Life of St Theodotus', 101 f.) all argue strongly for its organic link. I adopt their arguments.

These seven Christian ladies were among the first victims of Theotecnus' persecution. After their arrest they were sentenced to be raped, but the pleas of one of them, Tekousa, succeeded in delivering them all from this fate. When the young men recruited to perform the deed approached them, she tore off her veil, revealed her white hair, and pointed to her wasted body. How could young men rape such old women? Tekousa herself was over 70 at the time, and the others had reached an equally mature age. Indeed, the youths proved incapable of executing the punishment. Theotecnus then ordered the women to be ordained as priestesses of the virgin goddesses Artemis and Athena. It was the time of year when these two deities were honoured with a procession to a nearby lake, where their statues were being cleansed in an act of ritual purification. The seven ladies were ordered to participate in this procession: stripped naked they were placed on the carts carrying the statues, and, accompanied by female dancers and musicians, were led through the city amidst the jeers of the entire population. Once the procession had reached the lake, the ladies refused to accept the white robes of the priestesses, and were drowned far from the shore, with stones tied round their necks. Later in the night a terrible storm exposed the drowned bodies, allowing Theodotus and a few companions to reclaim and bury them beside the church of the Patriarchs.[71]

Who were these seven Christian ladies? The narrative focuses on their martyrdom; references to their previous life are merely incidental. However, chapter 13 begins: 'They were seven virgins, from their earliest age trained in abstinence (ἀσκούμεναι), each of them educated to esteem continence (τὴν σωφροσύνην) above all and to have the fear of God always in their minds.' Throughout the text, they are referred to as *parthenoi* (or virgins) in a manner

---

[71] cc. 13–19. The description of the procession in honour of Artemis conforms precisely to accounts of the *lavatio* of Cybele and Attis; cf. Mitchell, 'Life of St Theodotus', 107; H. Hepding, *Attis, seine Mythen und sein Kult* (Religionsgeschichtliche Versuche und Vorarbeiten 1; Giessen, 1903), 172 f. Virgins received similar treatment in Alexandria during the Arian controversies, as recorded by Theodoret, *HE* 4. 22. 2–5 (*Theodorets Kirchengeschichte*, ed. L. Parmentier and F. Scheidweiler (GCS 44; Berlin, 1954²), 249–51). Here, they are paraded naked through the town and humiliated by the masses. The account could thus indicate a topos, apart from the possibility that people just had similar ideas about how to treat virgins of opposing creeds; cf. L. Duchesne, *Histoire ancienne de l'Église*, ii (Paris, 1910), 389 f.

that bears the characteristics of a title rather than simply reflecting their physical integrity. Furthermore, all 'seven virgins' are always mentioned together. Does this indicate that these women formed an established group?

Only one lady is frequently mentioned by name, and thus bears some individual traits, the πρεσβυτέρα Τέκουσα. The adjective *presbytera* (the elder) reflects her age, but age alone does not convey the full weight and significance of this designation. Tekousa, although used relatively frequently as a proper name, in fact means 'Mother'.[72] Could this name reflect a deliberate choice? When faced with the rapists Tekousa approaches one of them and persuades him to abstain from his intention. She appears to Theodotus in a dream, exhorting him to recover the drowned bodies. In short, the *presbytera parthenos Tekousa* is characterized throughout as the leader of the seven women. Her name (literally, 'elder virgin Mother') indicates quite possibly a title, emphasizing her position of authority.[73] In fact, there can be little doubt that Tekousa was 'the spiritual mother', the leader of the seven virgins, both in experience and years. Nor was her authority limited to the virgins alone. This is clear from her appeal to Theodotus, whom she calls 'child' (τέκνον), and whom she reminds of the fact that she had guided him towards the Christian life, introducing him in his earliest years to ἄσκησις.

---

[72] Aorist participle of τίκτω; cf. LSJ s.v. I 5b (e.g. Aeschylus, *Sept.* 928); Grégoire and Orgels, 'La passion de S. Théodote', 174 f.; L. Robert (*Hellenica* 13, 217) mentions two occurrences in *MAMA* vii: nos. 80 (Laodicea) and 418 (Kerpişli), pp. 15, 94; L. Robert *Noms indigènes dans l'Asie-Mineure gréco-romaine* i (Bibliothèque archéologique et historique de l'institut français d'archéologie d'Istanbul 13; Paris, 1963), 71 n. 6; S. Mitchell (ed.), *Regional Epigraphic Catalogues of Asia Minor*, v. 2: *The Ankara District. The Inscriptions of North Galatia* (British Institute of Archaeology at Ankara Monograph 4 (British Archaeological Reports, Int. Ser. 135); Oxford, 1982), nos. 179, 185, 284, 381; Mitchell ('Life of St Theodotus', 103 n. 46) does not accept the interpretation of Tekousa as spiritual mother.

[73] Tekousa is not the only 'virgin mother' we know of. W. M. Calder ('The Epigraphy of the Anatolian Heresies', in W. H. Buckler and W. M. Calder (eds.), *Anatolian Studies Presented to Sir W. M. Ramsay* (Manchester, 1923), 59–91, here no. 10 (Ladik, Laodicea Combusta), pp. 88–90 (= *MAMA*. i. no. 176, 94 f.)) discovered an inscription dating from the second half of the 6th cent. in nearby Ladik, containing the words ... καὶ παρθένῳ μητρί ... ; H. Grégoire, *Recueil des inscriptions grecques chrétiennes d'Asie Mineure*, i (Paris, 1922), 10, no. 23: ἡ ὁσία μ(ήτ)ηρ.

He indeed used to honour her as if she were his mother (ὡς μητέρα)—again, a mother in spirit (16).

Evidently, the seven virgins formed a distinct, coherent group under the guidance of an elder member, and exercised a discernible influence over those associated with them. However, it is not entirely clear how closely these ladies were linked, what precisely formed the basis for their community. Did they actually live together or did they maintain their family ties, coming together only on special occasions? What position and functions did they have within their community?

Tekousa's main achievement in Theodotus' education was to instil in him a zeal for *askēsis* (literally, 'disciplined training'), ἐγκράτεια (self-control), and καρτερία (endurance). He was a known teacher of 'dignity and piety' (διδάσκαλος δὲ πρὸς ἀρέτην ... μετ᾽ εὐσεβείας ἀσκουμένοις), and when he was persecuted Theodotus proved to be a staunch fighter against paganism (ἀθλήτης πρὸς ἀντίπαλον) (cc. 1, 2, 6). When faced with her prospective rapists Tekousa draws attention to her body, destroyed by 'age, fasting, illness, and tortures'. The opening sentence of chapter 13 emphasized that from their earliest youth the virgins had been accustomed to *askēsis* and *sōphrosynē*, and a single sentence in chapter 19 attracts immediate attention, a list of the virgins' names: 'Tekousa, Alexandreia, Phaeine ('the Apotaktikai' claim that these belong to them, but in truth they are ⟨ . . . ⟩), Klaudia, Euphrasia, Martona, and Joulitta.'[74]

Epiphanius of Salamis, the famous cataloguer of heresies, described these Apotactites, who apparently had a certain claim on the first three virgins, as an 'offshoot of the doctrines of Tatianus, the Encratites, the Tatiani, and the Cathari, all of whom reject the Law'. With its centres in Phrygia, Cilicia and Pamphylia, and a large following throughout Pisidia, Isauria, and Galatia, this group emphasized a rigorous regime that rejected

---

[74] Τέκοῦσα, Ἀλεξανδρεία, Φαεινή (ταύτας οἱ ἀποτακτῆται λέγουσιν ἰδίας εἶναι, κατὰ ἀλήθειαν δὲ ⟨ . . . ⟩ εἰσιν), Κλαυδία, Ἐυφρασία, Ματρῶνα καὶ Ἰουλίττα. This list was of course immediately subjected to scholarly investigation, made difficult by the lacuna concealing the virgins' true affiliation; Franchi de' Cavalieri's explanation ('*I martirii*', 38) is based on D. Papebroch (ed.) (*Acta Sanctorum*, '*maii 4*' (Paris, 1866), 147–64, here 157), P. Allard (*La Persécution de Dioclétien et le triomphe de l'Église*, i (Paris, 1890), 321–38, here 325 n. 2), and S. L. de Tillemont (*Mémoires*, v. 189–98, and see esp. 661 f.); cf. Grégoire and Orgels, 'La passion de S. Théodote', 172–4; Mitchell, 'Life of St Theodotus', 103.

second marriages and all attachment to worldly goods, and refused to readmit people who had lapsed during persecutions.[75]

On the strength of these considerations, it is probable that Theodotus, the seven virgins, and their community had close ties with 'a rigorist, heretical and probably Montanist milieu'. Such an association is further suggested by two additional sources.[76] According to Tertullian, Montanus himself had exhorted his followers actively to seek martyrdom; Theodotus had followed these exhortations to the letter.[77] More importantly, in the fullest extant account of Montanist practices, Epiphanius' *Panarion* 49 dating from 374, we read:

Often, in their own church, a group of seven virgins enters, carrying torches and clad in white robes, and they go out from there to prophesy to the people. They put on a kind of enthusiasm and dupe the assembled people; they cause them to weep, as though they were inducing the mourning of repentance, shedding tears and bewailing, by a sort of pretence, the life of men.

Epiphanius then adds: 'In their community they have *female bishops* and *female presbyters* and others.'[78]

The significance of these passages for the interpretation of the *Martyrdom* is evident. Besides Tekousa, Fronto is the only person addressed as *presbyteros*, as one bearing a clerical rank. The *Martyrdom* mentions no other 'orthodox' hierarchical term.[79]

[75] Epiph. *Haer.* Pr. 1. 6 (1 GCS 25. 160); cf. Julian, *Or.* 7. 224a–b (*L'empereur Julien: Œuvres complètes*, ii.1, ed. G. Rochefort (Paris, 1963), 70); Bas. *Ep.* 199. 47; Basil's letters, which will be referred to frequently, are available in English translation by R. J. Deferrari, *St. Basil: The Letters*, 4 vols (Loeb; London, repr. 1986; Cambridge, Mass., 1951 and 1955); Calder, 'The Epigraphy of the Anatolian Heresies', 84–6; Mitchell, 'Life of St Theodotus', 103.

[76] Grégoire and Orgels, 'La passion de S. Théodote', 172–8; quotation, Mitchell, 'Life of St Theodotus', 104.

[77] Tertullian, *De fuga in persecutione*, 9 (PL 2. 111 f.); cf. id. *De anima*, 55 (PL 2. 742–4); cf. Mitchell, 'Life of St Theodotus', 102 n. 41.

[78] Ἐπίσκοποί τε παρ' αὐτοῖς γυναῖκες καὶ πρεσβύτεροι γυναῖκες καὶ τὰ ἄλλα; Epiph. *Haer.* 49. 2 (2 GCS 31. 242 f.); cf. Mitchell, 'Life of St Theodotus', 102 f.

[79] Interestingly, the virgins are also buried near a 'Church of the Patriarchs' (cf. Mitchell, 'Life of St Theodotus', 107). According to Jerome, *Ep.* 41. 3 (CSEL 54 (Vienna, 1910), 313), 'patriarch' was the highest rank in the Montanist church, followed by the *koinoni* and bishops; cf. E. Gibson, *The 'Christians for Christians' Inscriptions of Phrygia* (Ann Arbor, 1978), 136 f.; H. Grégoire, 'Notes épigraphiques', *Byzantion* 8 (1933), 49–88, here 69–76; Mitchell, 'Life of St Theodotus', 104 f.

Moreover, both sources refer to seven women; both sources stress that the women in question were virgins. In both sources these women played a significant public role in their respective communities, certainly comparable to that usually attributed to a member of the clergy, and, accordingly, Tekousa enjoys the title of a *presbyteros*.

The *Martyrdom* does not refer to 'white robes', except when the virgins are pressed to become priestesses of Artemis and Athena, but as the episode preceding the intended rape implies, the seven virgins were all veiled. Now, in the Greek-speaking part of the Roman Empire the veil was part of the common attire of a married woman.[80] According to the account of Apollonius (noted in the context of the prophetess, p. 32 above), Maximilla and Priscilla, the earliest Montanist prophetesses, had 'deserted their husbands'. In other words, at the time they felt the call to profess Montanus' beliefs, they were married and may, at least legally, have remained so even afterwards.[81] All seven virgins were of mature age, veiled, and one of them is called 'elder virgin mother'—an address which also appears on an inscription originating from the same region—and at least some Montanist prophetesses were married, despite their 'virginal' way of life.[82]

Several explanations regarding the seven virgins' social status and their actual way of life are therefore feasible. They could have been widowed, or still married, or they could have been virgins since their earliest years, as stated explicitly in the *Martyrdom*, and spent their lives 'engaged' (if not, as indicated by the veil, 'married') to Christ. While they could have lived as celibates in their families, a different solution is more likely: the women had formed their own community, where they practised a

---

[80] Though the scarcity of sources and secondary literature makes it extremely difficult to generalize. Cf. Plutarch, *Qu. Rom.* 267 A–C; Dio Chrys. *Or.* 33. 48 (ed. H. L. Crosby (Loeb; London, 1940), 318); Eus. *De mart. Pal.* 4. 15 (long recension) (*Eusèbe de Césarée: Histoire ecclésiastique et les martyrs en Palestine*, ed. G. Bardy (SC 55), 135 f.); R. MacMullen, 'Woman in Public in the Roman Empire', *Historia* 29 (1980), 208–18, here 208 f. 217 f.; Tert. *De virg. vel.* 2. 1 (ed. E. Schulz-Flügel (Göttingen, 1977), 25–33 nn. 176–9).

[81] Eus. *HE* 5. 18. 3.

[82] Calder, 'The Epigraphy of the Anatolian Heresies', 88; *MAMA* i. 94 f., no. 176; cf. Davies (*Revolt of the Widows*, 74, and *passim*) for communities of continent women calling themselves 'widows' although some had living husbands.

life of abstinence and untold mortifications under the guidance of a leader, the 'presbyter virgin mother' Tekousa.

About sixty years divide the first references to the virgin Juliana and the exorcism of the prophetess from the *Martyrdom of St Theodotus and the Seven Virgins*. During this period women who wished to devote their lives to the service of God found two fundamentally distinct ways to fulfil their intentions. Either they remained, rigorously secluded, within their own families, or they severed all family ties. Especially in the first case, they may have lived in the company of male relatives with the same intentions, but non-related ascetics of both sexes also lived together. Neither male nor female virgins had any apparent function within the ecclesiastical framework or the congregation other than the self-imposed obligation to live according to their status as 'brides of Christ'. Alternatively, we find women who practise their intense religious life completely alone or as members of a group with a definite public role of more than mere ceremonial character. All followed very similar principles of self-control, fasting, and continence. It is worth noting that both of the sources which indicate a more public role played by 'virgins' (including an active part in ceremony, as teachers of ascetic virtues, and as bearers of clerical titles such as presbyter and even bishop) have to be associated with a 'heretical' milieu (in both instances Montanist).

2

Basil of Caesarea: The Classic Model

In the autumn of the year 355 a young man of 25 or 26 returned from his studies in Athens to Caesarea in Cappadocia. Following in his late father's footsteps, he intended to turn his extraordinary talents to a career as a rhetor.[1] However, the initial attraction to the glamours of that profession was short-lived. His years as a student had already been marked by what he calls the search for 'a more perfect life' (βίου τελεωτέρου). Within the year, in 356, he was baptized by the local bishop, Dianios of Caesarea. Dianios, well aware of the young man's potential, immediately began to draw him more and more into the affairs of the Church.[2]

Yet the young man was not satisfied. He had left Athens attracted by 'the fame of the philosophy of disregard of the things of this world', a philosophy taught by a certain Eustathius, also a native of Asia Minor. Ever since his sojourn in Athens he had attempted to meet 'Eustathius, the philosopher'—unfortunately, to no avail. Upon his return to Caesarea the young man had fallen sick and missed Eustathius, who in the mean time had left for an extended journey. This did not deter the eager young man.

---

[1] Bas. *Ep.* 210. 2; Gr. Naz. *In laudem Basilii Magni* (*Or.* 43), 25 (Boulenger, 112 f.). An English translation of *In laud. Bas.* is available in L. P. McCauley, *et al.*, *Funeral Orations by St. Gregory Nazianzen and St. Ambrose* (The Fathers of the Church 22; Washington, 1968[2]), 27–99. J. Gribomont ('Eustathe le Philosophe et les voyages du jeune Basile de Césarée', *RHE* 54 (1959), 115–24, here 121), argues against Basil having actually taught (almost all of Gribomont's articles used in the following have been reprinted in J. Gribomont, *Saint Basile: Évangile et Église*, 2 vols. (Spiritualité orientale 36–7; Bellefontaine, 1984); I quote the first editions); however, Fedwick (*Church and Charisma*, 135) and Aubineau (*Virginité*, 54 f.) argue convincingly in favour.

[2] Gr. Naz. *In laud. Bas.* 24 (Boulenger, 110). Basil had known Dianios, who had been bishop since 341, from his earliest youth; cf. Bas. *Ep.* 51. 1. It is generally accepted that Basil was not baptized until after his return from Athens; Bas. *De Spiritu Sancto*, 29 (*Basile de Césarée: Traité du Saint-Esprit*, ed. B. Pruche (SC 17; Paris, 1945), 246); Gr. Naz. *In laud. Bas.* 27 (Boulenger, 118).

He followed the elusive philosopher first to Syria, then on to Mesopotamia, Palestine, and Egypt, where he stayed briefly in Alexandria. All in vain; he never actually caught up with the famous philosopher.[3]

The young man in question was, of course, none other than 'the grand Basil', son of Basil the Elder and Emmelia, and eldest brother of Gregory of Nyssa and Macrina, later to be bishop of Caesarea and one of the famous Cappadocian Fathers of the Church, 'eclipsing with his reputation all those who distinguished themselves by their virtue'.[4]

It is the same Basil of Caesarea, who—in the eyes of his contemporaries and followers—became the founder of monasticism in Asia Minor; who brought order into the chaos of experimentation by creating 'communities of ascetics and written precepts' that were to set the standards for generations to come.[5] Basil's efforts turned Cappadocia and Pontus into a fertile garden of monastic communities, called *koinōnia*;[6] his 'written precepts' were copied and emulated in both East and West. When Benedict of Nursia wrote his own rule it was guided by 'the rules of our

---

[3] As he reports in *Ep.* 1, written in 357 and addressed to 'Eustathius the Philosopher'; cf. also *Epp.* 223, 244. Dom Gribomont identified Eustathius of Sebaste as the recipient of this letter in his above-mentioned article, 'Eustathe le Philosophe'; for dating, cf. P. Maran (*Vita S. Basilii*, PG 29, pp. xiii–xv), who places the journey in 356, and P. J. Fedwick ('A Chronology of the Life and Works of Basil of Caesarea', in id. (ed.), *Basil of Caesarea: Christian, Humanist, Ascetic*, 2 vols. (Toronto, 1981), i. 3–19, here 6, who dates it prior to 357.

[4] Gr. Nyss. *VSM* 6. 15–16; for a bibliography of Basil of Caesarea cf. Fedwick, *Basil of Caesarea*, ii. 654–99; and Patrucco, *Lettere*, 19 f., 249 f.; J. Gribomont, 'Notes biographiques sur s. Basile le Grand', in Fedwick, op.cit. i. 21–48, here 21–4; K. G. Bonis, 'Basilios von Caesarea und die Organisation der christlichen Kirche im vierten Jahrhundert', ibid. 281–335, esp. 300; Fedwick, *Church and Charisma*, 129–32, 156–65.

[5] οἱ παρθενῶνες, καὶ τὰ ἔγγραφα διατάγματα, Gr. Naz. *In laud. Bas.* 62 (Boulenger, 186).

[6] 'Basilius Ponti urbes et rura circumiens, . . . in unum coire, monasteria construere . . . ita brevi permutata est totius provinciae facies, ut in arido et squalenti campo videretur seges fecunda . . .' (Rufinus, *HE* 2. 9 (PL 21. 518)); Rufinus of Aquileia, just returned from the East in 397, sent Basil's rules to Urseius, abbot of Pinetum near Ravenna, in response to the latter's request for a description of the Eastern monasteries; cf. id. *Praefatio in regulam S. Basilii* (PL 103. 485), trans. W. K. L. Clarke, *The Ascetic Works of St. Basil* (London, 1925), 29; id. *St. Basil the Great: A Study in Monasticism* (Cambridge, 1913), 56.

Holy Father Basil', a model for the true monastic life in obedience and virtue.[7]

Basil's position as ascetic innovator and ecclesiastical leader, shared by his friend Gregory of Nazianzus and his brother, Gregory of Nyssa, is such that any attempt to reconstruct the development of asceticism in Asia Minor virtually amounts to a reconstruction of the history of Basil's ascetic concepts.[8] Such a task, unfortunately, is not as easy as it might appear at first sight. Basil left a substantial literary *œuvre*. However, contrary to what one might expect from a man considered one of the principal founders of monasticism, Basil's work is not primarily concerned with matters of monastic organization. Indeed, references to strictly structural and organizational aspects of the ascetic life occur only sporadically.[9] Even his principal ascetical works, the 'written precepts' known as the *Ascetica*, fundamental for his position as ascetic innovator, contain surprisingly few concrete details.[10] An attempt to reconstruct the organizational structure

[7] 'sed et regula sancti patris nostri Basilii quid aliud sunt nisi bene viventium et obedientium monachorum instrumenta virtutum?' *Regula Benedicti*, 73. 5–6, (ed. R. Hanslik (CSEL 75; Vienna, 1960), 164 f.).

[8] Of course, much has already been done on this subject; for a bibliography, cf. J. Quasten, *Patrology*, iii (Utrecht, 1960), 207, 211–14, 221 f., 235 f. Most works are concerned with Basil's spirituality and his ascetic doctrine, less so with organizational principles. The most fundamental works here are D. Amand, *L'Ascèse monastique de saint Basile: Essai historique* (Maredsous, 1949); A. de Vogüé, 'Les Grandes Règles de saint Basile: Un survol', *Collectanea Cisterciensia* 41 (1979), 201–26; E. L. Fellechner, *Askese und Charitas bei den drei Kappadokiern*, Diss. (Heidelberg, 1979); G. Lombardo, 'Il monachesimo basiliano', *Quaderni Medievali* 9 (1980), 217–22; M. Mazza, 'Monachesimo basiliano: Modelli spirituali e tendenze economico-sociali nell'impero del IV secolo', *Studi Storici* 21 (1980), 31–60; T. Špidlík, 'L'Idéal du monachisme basilien', in Fedwick, *Basil of Caesarea*, i. 361–74.

[9] Clarke, *St. Basil the Great*, 43 f. 59; for references to letters, Patrucco, *Lettere*, 37–54; B. Gain, *L'Église de Cappadoce au IVe siècle d'après la correspondance de Basile de Césarée (330–379)* (OrChrA 225; Rome, 1985), 123–7.

[10] The *Ascetica*, which will be discussed more fully below, have also attracted much scholarly attention; cf. Clarke, *St. Basil the Great*, 63–79; D. Amand, 'Essai d'une histoire critique des éditions générales grecques et gréco-latines de s. Basile de Césarée', *RBén* 52 (1940), 141–61; 53 (1941), 119–51; 54 (1942), 124–44; 56 (1945/6), 126–73; id. 'L'Authenticité de la lettre 45 de la correspondance de Basile de Césarée', *SP* 10 (1970), 44–53; and, in particular, J. Gribomont, *Histoire du texte des Ascétiques de S. Basile* (Bibliothèque du Muséon

of Basil's communities, even such mundane matters as, for example, the number or actual location of the communities involved, is quite a complex undertaking. In addition, the majority of our information regarding the development of Basil's ascetic ideals stems from his earlier years, a period during which he could afford to pay undivided attention to his ascetic interests; though a notable exception is the part of the *Ascetica* known as the *Regulae fusius tractatae*, or the *Longer Rules* (*RF*).[11]

After returning from his futile search for Eustathius the Philosopher in 357/8, Basil decided to retire to Annesi, a προάστειον or country mansion on his family's estate near Ibora in Pontus (see Map 2).[12] This retirement was of a very specific nature: a 'withdrawal from the entire world, . . . to break all the links that bind the soul to the body, that is, to be without city, without house, without personal property, without particular friendships, without possessions, without means of livelihood. . . .'[13] Upon arriving at Annesi, Basil remained only briefly at the family mansion. Almost immediately, he began to search for a μονή, a secluded spot far from human habitation. He found it on the opposite side of the river Iris, not too far away from Annesi.[14] In a letter inviting his friend and fellow student, Gregory of Nazianzus, to join him in this new life, Basil gives a vivid descrip-

---

32; Louvain, 1953). Out of a total of over 350 letters, only 44 deal with aspects of ascetic life, mostly in brief passages and often at best tangentially to organizational matters. For dates, cf. notes on individual letters in Courtonne, *Lettres*, i–iii; for questions of authenticity I follow Fedwick, 'A Chronology', 3–19; for abbreviations, cf. id. *Basil of Caesarea*, i. pp. xix–xxxi.

[11] The primary biographies are Tillemont, *Mémoires*, ix. 1–304, and Maran, *Vita S. Basilii*, PG 29, pp. v–clxxvii; Patrucco (*Lettere*, 21–54, esp. 22 n. 4) is the most recent summary.

[12] Modern Sonusa; Bas. *Ep.* 3. 2; Gr. Nyss. *In quadraginta martyres* (PG 46. 784); id. *VSM* 34. 15–18; P. Gallay, *La vie de Saint Grégoire de Nazianze* (Paris, 1943), 249; E. Honigmann, 'Un itinéraire arabe à travers le Pont', *Annuaire de l'institut de philologie et d'histoire orientales et slaves* 4 (1936), 261–71, here 264 f.; G. de Jerphanion, 'Ibora—Gazioura? Étude de géographie pontique', *Mélanges de la faculté orientale de l'université Saint Joseph* 5 (1911), 333–54; H. Leclercq, 'Ibora', *DACL* vii. 1, 4–9; Maraval, *Macrine*, 38–44.

[13] Bas. *Epp.* 2, 223. 2.

[14] Bas. *Epp.* 2. 2, 14; Patrucco, *Lettere*, 255–8, 313–16; Fedwick, 'A Chronology', 6.

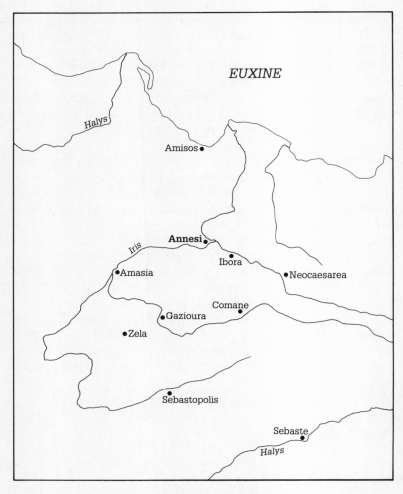

MAP 2. The region of Annesi

tion of this 'solitude'. For him, it was a 'place for meditation' (φροντιστήριον), a μοναστήριον and a 'school'.[15]

[15] The words are actually those used by Gregory of Nazianzus in a letter written after his stay; Gr. Naz. *Ep.* 4. 3; LSJ s.v. translates φροντιστήριον as 'place for meditation, thinking shop'; cf. the description of Socrates' school in Aristophanes' *Nubes* (ll. 94, 128); Gregory uses the word here in an ironical sense.

Gregory accepted and spent the winter of 357–8 with Basil at Annesi.[16] In his description, the place sounds much less inviting. It was dark, cold, and inaccessible; the only shelter against the harsh climate was a hut which Gregory calls a 'rat-hole' (μνωξία). If it had not been for the regular food supply from the estate, the two friends would have starved to death.[17] Nevertheless, the place must have encouraged meditation. During Gregory's stay the two friends acquainted themselves with the work of Origen, and assembled a collection of excerpts, the so-called *Philocalia*.[18]

One observation, though, is of fundamental importance: even without Gregory present, Basil did not live alone in his *monē*. Others had already gathered at the same spot. Gregory's letters especially leave no doubt that in 358 Basil had joined an already existing group: he mentions 'brothers' united in their souls by prayers and meditation (συμφυίαν καὶ συμψυχίαν) and guided in their zealous pursuit of virtue by 'written rules and canons' (ὅροις γραπτοῖς καὶ κανόσιν).[19] The brothers chanted psalms together, observed vigils, worked in the woods (apparently to build more permanent dwellings), planted gardens, and maintained at the same time a strict fast.[20]

By the time of Basil's arrival, it appears that these brothers were already following a certain routine and living in accordance with

---

[16] Gregory agreed in principle to share Basil's life, but would have preferred a place closer to his home since he had to care for his elderly parents. He therefore suggested a part-time solution, spending half the time at Annesi, half at Tiberine, a suggestion Basil did not accept; Gr. Naz. *Epp.* 1, 2; Clarke, *St. Basil the Great*, 44 f. Forlin Patrucco (*Lettere*, 31 n. 62) interprets *Ep.* 14 as indicating that Basil stayed briefly at Tiberine, the area around Arianzus (AD 357/8); *TIB* ii. 150 f. 295.

[17] Letters 4 and 5, written after his return to Tiberine in 358 and in reply to Basil's *Ep.* 14; two dates for Gregory's sojourns at Annesi are certain: 358 (cf. Gr. Naz. *Ep.* 115) and 362 (cf. Patrucco, *Lettere*, 31 n 63).

[18] Gr. Naz. *Epp.* 6, 115; Clarke, *St. Basil the Great*, 55; Fedwick, 'A Chronology', 6; J. Gribomont, *L'Origenisme de S. Basile* (Mélanges H. de Lubac, i; Paris, 1963), 281–94; J. A. Robinson, *The Philocalia of Origen* (Cambridge, 1893) *passim*.

[19] *Ep.* 6; Gregory is alluding to Basil's *Ep.* 2 which was written in 358; Clarke, *St. Basil the Great*, 49 n. 1, 51; Gr. Naz., *Ep.* 4, also mentions several ascetics chanting psalms in the φροντιστήριον.

[20] The content of these 'rules' has to be extrapolated from Gregory's *Ep.* 6; the assumption of an organization present from the very beginning is confirmed by Basil's *Ep.* 2.

specific principles. However, it was Basil, who, as early as 358, formulated these principles into ὅροις γραπτοῖς καὶ κανόσιν.[21]

Basil's Letter 2, addressed to Gregory of Nazianzus, reflects the content of these regulations and canons.[22] Beginning with a brief description of those aspects of the world that led to his withdrawal, Basil then specifies how such a withdrawal should be accomplished in practice: through solitude and continuous *askēsis*.

Askēsis signifies 'the great route, which will lead to the discovery of the duty, [based on] the meditation of the Scripture. It is there that one finds the precepts for the right conduct. . . .' 'Right conduct', in turn, consists, first, of regular prayers, beginning at sunrise, and heightened by the reading of appropriate scriptural passages (each biblical personage represents in fact a model (εἰκών), to which the ascetic ought to aspire); secondly, silence (no one ought to utter a word without first considering whether it would be appropriate in the presence of the Lord); thirdly, a profound sense of humility and self-abasement. These dispositions find their external expression through downcast eyes; by neglecting one's appearance—the dress serves only to cover and protect the body against the elements; by reducing the hours of sleep to avoid undesirable dreams; and by strict limitation of all nutrition to the minimum necessary for survival: bread, water, and vegetables. The goal of this 'right conduct' is the conquest of one's emotions. All desires and passions, anxieties and aggravations have to be overcome before the divine can be contemplated in tranquillity (ἡσυχία). Letter 2 contains the essence of Basil's ascetic concepts. Influenced by Stoic and Platonic anthropological teachings, these concepts reflect an understanding of asceticism which was rigorously individual and yet adapted at the same time to ascetic life in common.[23]

Basil's stay at Annesi was, however, short-lived. Towards the end of 359 he left his ascetic companions to attend the council of Constantinople in the company of Dianios of Caesarea. Although he had by then been appointed a 'reader', this was a lowly rank in the clerical hierarchy, and his role at the council was accordingly quite negligible. By 360 Basil had returned to Caesarea; two

---

[21] Gr. Naz. *Ep.* 6. 4.

[22] Bas. *Ep.* 2.

[23] Hadot, *Exercices spirituels*, 13–74; also Elm, 'Evagrius Ponticus' *Sententiae ad Virginem*', 97–120, here 107–11; Patrucco, *Lettere*, 256 f.

years later he was ordained presbyter. As a priest, he could not refrain from involvement in ecclesiastical affairs, nor could he enjoy the tranquillity he may have desired; his sojourns at Annesi became more and more infrequent.[24]

In fact, in the year of his ordination as presbyter, a disagreement arose between Basil and Dianios' successor to the episcopal chair, Eusebius. By that time, as a result of his aristocratic origins as well as his personal achievements, Basil had gained considerable standing within the Caesarean congregation, among one group in particular. Gregory of Nazianzus characterizes this group as 'all the more select and wiser members of the Church; since they are wiser than the multitude they have separated themselves from the world and consecrated themselves to God, ... [they are] the Nazarites.'[25] This highly intriguing group had opposed Eusebius' election and, preferring Basil as a more worthy leader, they threatened to split the congregation between Basil and Eusebius. Basil suffered the consequences. In order to avoid open schism, he returned once again to Annesi and his *phrontistērion* in the *erēmos*. This time he stayed until 365.[26]

During the following years Basil composed 'some memorable regulations', the *Moralia*, a collection of precepts intended for all Christians,[27] and also found the time to visit other ascetics, whom he advised as a priest and ascetic himself. Eventually, he gave these consultations permanence in the form of twenty questions and answers, the *Small Asceticon*.[28]

---

[24] Bas. *Epp.* 9. 3, 51; Gr. Naz. *In laud. Bas.* 27 (Boulenger, 118); Rufinus, *HE* 2. 9 (PL 21. 518 f.); Clarke, *St. Basil the Great*, 51 f.; Patrucco, *Lettere*, 32 f.; Fedwick, 'A Chronology', 7 n. 26; Tillemont, *Mémoires*, ix. 63 f.

[25] εἴπερ σοφώτεροι τῶν πολλῶν, οἱ κόσμου χωρίσαντες ἑαυτοὺς καὶ τῷ Θεῷ τὸν βίον καθιερώσαντες. λέγω δὲ τοὺς καθ᾽ ἡμᾶς Ναζιραίους ..., Gr. Naz. *In laud. Bas.* 28 (Boulenger, 120); Clarke, *St. Basil the Great*, 52; Patrucco, *Lettere*, 33–5.

[26] Gr. Naz. *In laud. Bas.* 29 (Boulenger, 122).

[27] The *Moralia* are essentially an arrangement of 1,500 quotations from the New Testament; Bas. *Moralia* = PG 31. 692–869; also edited under the direction of K. G. Bonis, in *Bibliotheke Hellenon Pateron*, liii (Athens, 1976), 13–131; Gribomont, *Histoire du texte des Ascétiques*, 277 f., 287–9, and *passim*.

[28] Not extant in Greek; see Gribomont, *Histoire du texte des Ascétiques*, 109, who refers to an important subscript in a 5/6th-cent. Syriac MS (British Museum, Additional 14544); the *Asceticon* has survived in a Syriac MS and in a Latin translation by Rufinus in 203 *interrogationes* (PL 103. 483–554); J. T. Lienhard, 'St. Basil's *Asceticon parvum* and the *Regula Benedicti*', *Studia Monastica* 22 (1980), 231–42.

In 370 Basil was elected bishop of Caesarea.[29] The obligations connected with this new office explain the decrease of references to the ascetic life in his later correspondence. From now on, the task of regulating the day-to-day affairs of his diocese and his involvement in dogmatic controversies occupied the greater part of his time.[30] Basil's new duties had, however, one fortunate consequence: they forced him to communicate with his ascetic brothers at Annesi by means of the written word. The result is the vast body of rules known as the *Great Asceticon*, which consists of the so-called *Longer (RF)* and *Shorter Rules (RB)*, once again in a question and answer format.[31]

THE ORGANIZATION OF BASIL'S FEMALE COMMUNITY

Of the available sources the *Great Asceticon* is the most helpful in any attempt to reconstruct the organization of Basil's community or, indeed, communities. Rather than repeat the results of many detailed studies, however, I have limited the following to Basil's concepts for ascetic women—more precisely, to the structures he devised for their organization.[32] Only a fraction of Basil's

---

[29] Gr. Naz. *In laud. Bas.* 28 (Boulenger, 118–20); for the date of the episcopate (370), cf. ibid. 37 (Boulenger, 138); Clarke, *St. Basil the Great*, 58–60; J. Gribomont, 'Un aristocrate révolutionnaire, évêque et moine: s. Basile', *Augustinianum* 17 (1977), 179–91; Maran, *Vita S. Basilii*, pp. li–lix; Tillemont, *Mémoires*, ix. 103–5, 654; M. Simonetti, *La crisi ariana nel IV secolo* (Studia Ephemeridis Augustinianum 11; Rome, 1975), 405–18. Shortly before his election Basil wrote Letter 22 ('concerning the perfection of the monastic life'), a concise collection of fifty maxims containing again the essence of his ascetic convictions; J. Gribomont, 'Les Règles épistolaires de s. Basile: Lettres 173 et 22', *Antonianum* 54 (1979), 255–87; de Vogüé, 'Les Grandes Règles', 202.

[30] Clarke, *St. Basil the Great*, 43 f.

[31] *Regulae fusius tractatae (RF)* = PG 31. 889–1052; *Regulae brevius tractatae (RB)* = PG 31. 1080–1305; references to *RF* and *RB* in the notes below are accompanied by the col. nos. in PG 31; English translations of both are available in W. K. L. Clarke's *The Ascetic Works of St. Basil*, 145–351; Gribomont, *Histoire du texte des Ascétiques*, 323–6; de Vogüé, 'Les Grandes Règles', 201–4. Their dates of composition are uncertain, but the *RB* is later than the *RF*.

[32] Of course, all Basil's ascetic writings, and in particular their interdependence, are crucial in reconstructing his organizational concepts; but the *Great Asceticon* contains the quintessence of his regulations. For a reconstruction of the development of Basil's thought, the relationship between the *Great* and the *Small Asceticon* would be particularly revealing. Many of the relevant aspects have been dealt with in the works of Doms Gribomont and de Vogüé referred to above, esp. de Vogüé, 'Les Grandes Règles', 202–4 and Gribomont's *Histoire du texte des Ascétiques*.

Asceticon magnum deals explicitly with women, for out of more than 400 'questions' dealing with all aspects of ascetic life, only thirteen address matters relating to women, who are called sisters or ἀδέλφαι. These 'questions' fall into two distinct categories: those that deal with the 'right order' (εὐταξία) of the ascetic community as a whole; and those that specify the duties and conduct required of the superiors. All other features of the organization of a female community have therefore to be reconstructed by analogy with those of the male ones.[33]

Basil's communities, described in the early letters as *monastērion* or *phrontistērion*, and later on generally as 'brotherhoods' or ἀδελφότες, consisted of two 'general divisions' of brothers: 'those who are entrusted with leadership and those whose duty it is to follow and to obey'.[34] Foremost among those entrusted with leadership was the so-called 'superior', or προεστώς.[35] The superior held a position of pre-eminent authority, though firmly based on the New Testament notion that 'any man among you [who] would be first, let him be last of all and servant of all'.[36] As such, the superior of the brotherhood is expected to be a model, representing all the spiritual principles which guide 'our discipline', the ascetic life. He ought to be 'able to look ahead, well-equipped with utterance, sober, compassionate, one who seeks

---

[33] As pointed out by de Vogüé ('Les Grandes Règles', 204), the *RF* are divided into seven main sections: (Prol. 1–7) obedience to the Ten Commandments; and two fundamental precepts, to love God and one's neighbour; (8–15) renunciation of the world; (16–23) control of one's desires; (24–36) the correct order of the community (ταξία); (37–42) work; (43–54) the duty of the superiors; (55) the use of medicine. Ταξία, the 'good order' of life in common, is of primary importance. The overall structure of Basil's rules and several direct references to the equality of men and women (e.g. *RF* 15, 33 (PG 31. 952, 997–1000); cf. Bas. *Ep.* 207. 2) indicate analogous organizational principles for both the male and female communities; cf. also Gribomont, *Histoire du texte des Ascétiques*, 54, 222, and other references in the index s.v. 'monastères doubles'; Clarke, *The Ascetic Works of St. Basil*, 37–9; Fedwick, *Church and Charisma*, 4 f., 12–26, 161–5; L. Vischer, *Basilius der Große*, Diss. (Basle, 1953), 167 f.

[34] For the terminological change, cf. *RF* and *RB*, *passim*; Gr. Naz. *Ep.* 4; Bas. *RB* 235 (1240).

[35] This is the title most frequently used and it appears repeatedly throughout the *RF* and *RB*; other titles include: ὁ ἐφεστώς (*RF* 24 (984 B)), ὁ προιστάμενος (*RF* 43. 2 (1028 C)), ὁ προκαθιστῶν (*RF* 44. 1 (1029 C)), and ὁ προέχων (*RF* 49 (1037 D)); Fedwick, *Church and Charisma*, 41 n. 22, 47; id. 'The Function of the Proestos in the Earliest Christian Koinonia', *Recherches de théologie ancienne et médiévale* 48 (1981), 5–13.

[36] Bas. *RF* 30 (992 f.); cf. Matt. 20: 26–7; Mark 9: 35; 10: 43.

the ordinances of God with perfect heart', and most of all he ought to be humble (*RF* 35). Blessed (it is hoped) by these characteristics, the superior is responsible for all transactions with the outside world and for all matters of discipline inside the community, including the pastoral care of the brothers. However, the superior's power, if absolute during the early stages of Basil's ascetic experiment, did not remain exclusive. *RF* 45 reveals the existence of an 'able brother', who acts as the superior's representative or proxy in his absence. This representative or 'second-in-command' is chosen by the *proestōs* and by a committee of προεχῶντες or πρεσβύτεροι (elders) acting in conjunction with the leader of the community.[37]

The selection of the representative was but one function of these elders. This committee of 'experienced and counselling brothers', 'in charge (προέχουσι) because of their age and wisdom', acted as the superior's control, and assisted him with advice—for instance, in the distribution of tasks to individual brothers.[38] Some brothers entrusted with special duties may also have formed part of the group of elders, including those responsible for the 'care of the weak' (*RF* 26), for the οἰκονομία or practical administration of the community, and for the distribution of food. Besides those offices the *Rules* mention a cellarer, a distributor of alms, several overseers of work, and a tutor responsible for the education of the youngest members.[39]

Personal poverty, prayer at regular intervals day and night, and work (chiefly of an agrarian nature) formed the basis of the brotherhood's life in common. Admission to the community required prior settlement of one's personal affairs. Family members had to consent and to be provided for, arrears of taxes had to be paid, and all personal property had to be disposed of. In practice,

---

[37] In *RF* 31 (993) Basil speaks of προεχόντες. Here used in the plural, *proechontes* could be a general term for leadership. However, in most cases where Basil is addressing several leaders he refers to them as προεστῶτοι rather than as *proechontes* (e.g. *RF* 30, 43, 54 (992 c, 1028 a, 1044 a); *RB* 96, 160 (1149 a, 1188 a)). The most convincing interpretation of the term *proechontes* is as a separate body of authority. In several places Basil uses *presbyteros* also as synonymous with τελειότερος, and in *RB* 110 and 111 (1157) and, most notably, 103 (1153), for a position of authority.

[38] *RF* 27, 48 (988, 1037); *RB* 104 (1153–6).

[39] *RF* 34 (1000); *RB* 100, 141, 142, 148, 149, 152, 156 (cols. 1152, 1177, 1180 f., 1184 f.); *RF* 15 (956).

this could mean that certain members of the brotherhood continued to receive income, though any such funds had to be entrusted to a member of the local clergy to avoid discord between wealthier and poorer members of the community.[40] Full admission followed a period of trial, a form of noviciate, and required the consensus of the entire community.[41] Some were accepted as full members at no more than 16 years of age, and the very young brothers attended the schools attached to the communities. According to *RF* 15, the brotherhoods accepted young children, both boys and girls, who were either orphaned or brought to the brothers by their parents.[42] These children occupied separate houses within the precinct, and the greatest care was taken to educate them in an exemplary Christian manner; in fact the curriculum was virtually identical to the one followed by the young Macrina.[43] A specially appointed teacher supervised the academic side and the superior himself dealt with matters of discipline.

Once a member, the new brother became one of 'those who obey', also called the 'inferiors'.[44] This group of 'obeying brothers' was by no means homogeneous. Some brothers were more religious (εὐλαβέστερος), others were slower of learning, some came from a wealthy, others from a poor background. All ought, however, to be treated according to their individual character, without undue preference being given to some at the expense of others. Nevertheless, religious calling alone did not suffice to gain acceptance into the brotherhood. Escaped slaves, for example, were returned to their masters, unless the latter were of exceptional cruelty. Even in those cases, a slave was accepted only if all attempts at persuading him to endure his God-given fate had failed. Once a former slave had become a brother, however, the community was prepared to bear all potential legal and financial consequences. Married applicants, as has been indicated,

---

[40] *RB* 187 (1208); the percentage of wealthy members, as well as the type of work performed, affected the prosperity of each brotherhood, so that some of them were wealthier than others; cf. *RB* 181 (1204).

[41] *RF* 10, 15 (944–8, 952–7).

[42] In the case of children delivered by their parents, acceptance was witnessed by officials in order to avoid subsequent complications (*RF* 15 (952 B)). The children's vow of continence made upon reaching maturity was also witnessed, specifically by Church authorities (*RF* 15 (956 B)).

[43] Cf. above pp. 41–43.

[44] ὁ ἐλάττων, e.g. *RB* 171 (1193).

needed the prior consent of their spouses before being admitted. In their case, however, opposition by family members could always be overruled on the basis of Luke 14: 26, from which it was clear that divine calling possessed greater authority than mortal bonds.[45] Admission to the community implied a lifelong commitment, and change from one community to another was not encouraged, much like the later, medieval concept of *stabilitas loci*.

The female communities followed the same guiding principles. As we have noted above, very few regulations address matters specifically relating to the sisters. The primary concern of these regulations is the nature of any contact between the male and the female community; an aspect crucial for the 'good order' (εὐταξις) between all communities. As a consequence many aspects of the internal workings of the female community remain unspecified, and received later clarification in the *Shorter Rules* only in a few instances. Basil occasionally addresses both communities at the same time, for instance when dealing with the education of children or discussing the committee of elders. It is worth noting that several later manuscripts eliminated all references to female communities simply by changing the addressees from 'sisters' to 'brothers'.[46]

Like its male counterpart, the female community, or sisterhood, was guided by a leader. She was identified as a προεστῶσα, 'the one who leads, protects, and cares for the ones in her keeping', a title obviously created by analogy with its male equivalent.[47]

However, this observation is not without its intricacies: as in the case of the brotherhood, Basil is not always consistent in his choice of titles. Thus, *RB* 110 and 111 speak of a πρεσβυτέρα', again in the context of leadership. It is probable, therefore, that the *proestōsa* as well was assisted by a 'committee of able elder sisters'. *RB* 104, for example, disscusses whether it should be solely the supervisor's responsibility to assign various duties or whether this should be done by vote of the brethren: 'and likewise in the sisterhood'—ὁμοίως δὲ καὶ ἐν ταῖς ἀδελφαῖς. Basil replies that these questions ought to be submitted to the judge-

---

[45] *RF* 11, 12 (948f.).

[46] *RF* 15 (952); *RB* 104 (1153); Gribomont, *L'Histoire du texte des Ascétiques*, 54, 222, and other references in the index s.v. 'monastères doubles'.

[47] Cf. *RB* 108 (1156); προΐστημι, LSJ s.v. B II 1.; Clarke, *The Ascetic Works of St. Basil*, 40–2.

ment of those 'who have aptitude for this', and who have previously demonstrated their capabilities to supervise: the selected elder brothers. Apparently, the same practice ought to be employed in the female community, a suggestion corroborated by *RF* 33.

RF 33 provides the most detailed regulation of the relationships between the two communities. Basil begins by pointing out that those who have forgone marriage in order to be liberated from all that so distracts the married man, should indeed maintain this state of liberation. Otherwise, they incur the risk of becoming 'men-pleasers' (Ps. 53: 5). Therefore, a brother should never meet another man by himself 'in order to please him', only for those services 'every man has a right to expect from his neighbour'. A meeting has to be previously arranged, and take place in the presence of at least one but no more than two other persons on either side. Such precautions eliminate even the shadow of a suspicion.

In the same vein, should any member of the brotherhood have a private message for a sister or vice versa, this may not be given in person. All such negotiations have to be carried out by selected elder brothers (*presbyteroi*) who will meet with selected elder sisters (*presbyterai*). Clearly, these intermediaries were selected because of one pre-eminent factor: age. Moral integrity obviously played a part, but as the titles *presbyteros* and *presbytera* indicate, in this particular context age was the critical qualification.

Contact between the two communities was not limited to occasional exchanges between brothers and sisters. 'Certain other brethren' were dispatched on a regular basis to assist the sisters in caring for their physical needs. Again, these brothers had to be of a certain age, 'grave in demeanour and character', and were chosen after careful examination. *RB* 154 suggests that these assistants, who apparently carried out various kinds of manual labour, actually lived within the female community, or spent at least the majority of time with the sisters. The female community was thus largely dependent on its male counterpart for economic subsistence. The sisters had their own income, derived perhaps from donations, but mainly from textile work. *RB* 153 mentions a sister who is responsible for keeping wool and distributing the appropriate work to each sister. Yet the daily support provided by the male community and the work of the brothers was essential.

The relationship between the male superior, the *proestōs*, and his female counterpart, the *proestōsa*, reflects this economic dependence. Judging solely from the terminology, both superiors should have had the same degree of authority within their own community, being assisted and controlled by the committee of elders.[48] *RB* III clearly conveys this impression: 'If the elder has ordered something to be done among the sisters without the knowledge of the senior sister, is the senior sister justified in being angry? By all means, yes.'[49]

Yet the relationship between the male and the female communities, embodied by their respective superiors, was far more complex. *RB* III was written in response to later developments. Evidently, male superiors had begun to interfere in the internal affairs of the female community, only to be sternly rebuked. The reasons why a male superior might have felt justified in his intervention are implied in *RB* IIo:

When a sister confesses to the elder, should the senior sister be present too? Confession to the elder, who is able to prescribe the manner of repentance and correction with due knowledge, will take place more fittingly and discreetly in the presence of the senior sister.[50]

While the female superior was certainly the undisputed authority within her own community, spiritual guidance and, as a matter of course, the administration of sacraments were the prerogative of the male superior and the selected elder brothers. This spiritual authority held by the male superior over his female counterpart led on occasion to an assumption of prerogatives beyond those defined by 'spiritual guidance'. *RB* 108 again concerns a male superior dealing with individual sisters without the presence of the female superior (*proestōsa*), and stresses that even if these dealings are purely spiritual the male superior may not act without the female superior's prior consent.

Judging from the scanty information of the *RB*, Basil seems to have felt an increasing need to curb the male superiors' infringement of the authority of the female superior. This required considerable delicacy, rendered all the more complicated because the

---

[48] *RB* 82 (1141) speaks of elder women who are honoured as mothers, and deals with the difficult task of disciplining them. The superior appears to be included in this discussion.

[49] Translation by Clarke, *The Ascetic Works of St. Basil*, 271.

[50] Ibid.

situation was certainly ambiguous. On the one hand, female communities were largely dependent on male communities for their economic support and male superiors also provided all the spiritual guidance. Yet any attempt to exploit this *de facto* imbalance of power was frowned upon. The authority of the female superior, based on her position as an ascetic in her own right, had to be respected. It was essential to ensure a relationship of mutual respect and regular consultation between *proestōs* and *proestōsa*. So *RB* 109: 'May the male superior speak frequently with the female superior, especially if some of the brethren are offended thereby? Yes.'[51]

Basil's female communities were thus closely linked to their male counterparts. Both followed essentially the regulations which guided the life in the *brotherhood*. Although the sexes were clearly segregated, this segregation was by no means enforced to the exclusion of all contact between the communities. Regular, if supervised, contacts between 'brothers' and 'sisters' were possible, made necessary because many of the members were blood relations.[52] Also, selected brothers either lived or spent a great deal of time among the sisters to help them. Consultations between the superiors were frequent. In short, it appears that Basil considered the sisterhood to be essentially of the same standing as the brotherhood, certainly in so far as the sisters' ascetic qualities were concerned.

This equality on an ascetic level did not affect the women's attire, work, and general bearing, which (as far as can be discerned) retained their essentially 'female' characteristics. In *RB* 210 Basil emphasizes that women even as ascetics ought to wear clothes befitting their sex, and their work was likewise 'female', chiefly the production of textiles. Spiritual matters and their supervision remained an exclusively male domain. Possibly teaching was the sole exception to this rule: it appears reasonable to assume that a sister was specially appointed to teach young girls.[53]

*

[51] Ibid. 270.

[52] *RF* 32 (993–7).

[53] *RF* 15 (952–7) mentions the acceptance of boys and girls into the schools, but without referring to a female teacher. This could suggest that boys and girls were, at least initially, educated together by a male teacher. The later *RB* 292 (1288) refers only to boys; cf. Gr. Nyss. *VSM* 12. 13; 19. 6; 26. 9; 28. 6.

It becomes clear that it was Basil's achievement as an ascetic innovator to furnish a structure and a blueprint for a way of life that was then new, experimental, and as a consequence, highly diversified. His concept of ascetic life in common, *koinōnia*, has been reduced here to its barest organizational implications, laying aside its highly complex philosophical and theological undercurrents. Several features of Basil's model are worth pointing out. Most importantly, he advocates ascetic life in common over and above ascetic life pursued individually, and his rejection of ascetic life as a solitary became more pronounced in time.[54] Was this exaltation of communal ascetic life Basil's own invention, inspired solely by scriptural models such as the earliest Christian *koinōnia* in Jerusalem?[55]

To organize this life Basil began virtually immediately to express his ideas in writing, thus creating a constantly increasing body of normative texts. His precepts reveal, again virtually from the outset, a tendency to emphasize moderation.[56] Letter 22, for example, already prescribes an increased amount of food, prohibits strict fasting, and suggests that living accommodations had improved.[57]

Basil's communities of men and women were hierarchically organized brotherhoods and sisterhoods, 'brother' and 'sister' having long since become honoured forms of address within Christian circles. They were segregated by sex, and appear to have been located primarily in the countryside. Both male and female superiors had authority within their own communities, but

[54] Bas. *Ep.* 199. 19; id. *RF* 7 (928–33); he eventually condemns individual asceticism altogether; cf. *RF* 36 and *RB* 102 (1008 f., 1153) regarding monks who want to leave the community; Amand, *L'Ascèse monastique de saint Basile*, 118–28; Fedwick, *Church and Charisma*, 12–23; J. Gribomont, 'Le Renoncement au monde dans l'idéal ascétique de saint Basile', *Irénikon* 31 (1958), 282–307, 460–75; id. 'Saint Basile', *Théologie de la vie monastique* (Paris, 1961), 99–113, here 106 f.; id. 'Obéissance et Évangile selon s. Basile le Grand' (*La Vie Spirituelle*, Suppl. 21; 1952), 191–215; A. M. Ritter, 'Statt einer Zusammenfassung', in Fedwick, *Basil of Caesarea*, i. 411–36.

[55] Acts 2: 44; 4: 32; *RF* 35 (1004–8).

[56] Gr. Naz. *In laud. Bas.* 61 (Boulenger, 184); Gr. Nyss. *In laudem fratris Basilii* (PG 46. 789–92); *RF* 18, 19, 20, 37 (965, 968 f., 969–76, 1009–16); Clarke, *St. Basil the Great*, 54 f.

[57] Bas. *Ep.* 22; Patrucco, *Lettere*, 337 f.; Fedwick ('A Chronology', 8 n. 29) dates *Ep.* 22 to the period 363–70 against Gribomont ('Les Règles épistolaires', 266, 284–6), who argues for a later date.

the relation between brothers and sisters was ambiguous and complex. On a formal, organizational, and theoretical level, as ascetics *per se*, brothers and sisters were apparently considered to be equals. Yet economically and spiritually, more precisely as far as any involvement with sacraments or any other potentially clerical function was concerned, the sisters were not in the least on an equal standing with the brothers. What caused such a peculiar balance of power? Why was Basil so concerned with maintaining it? And why did he feel the need to stress the sisters' duty to wear a 'female' dress?

A number of other observations are appropriate. Basil was not a creator *ex nihilo*. Men and women had been practising ascetic life long before him. We recall that his first *monē* or place of solitude was shared by 'brothers' who were already established there when he arrived. Furthermore, his second retreat to Annesi was occasioned by conflicts with the newly elected bishop of Caesarea, and in particular by his involvement with the Nazarite group there (see p. 67 and n. 25 above). Who were these men and what does their advocacy of Basil as prospective bishop signify? And who was Eustathius the Philosopher?

Basil's ascetic innovation cannot be fully appreciated for what it was unless it is placed within its historical context. Unless we are familiar with, or at least attempt to examine, the nature of the 'ascetic landscape' at the moment of Basil's arrival on the scene, the true significance of his innovation will be lost. Conversely, too narrow a concentration on this great Father of the Church alone distorts our vision and causes us to lose sight of the potential which such a new social movement, the ascetic movement, possessed.

3

In the Background: Macrina and Naucratius

Basil the Elder died sometime between the years 341 and 345. Predictably, his death had several profound consequences for the entire family, most noticeably of course for his widow.[1] It was now Emmelia's task to arrange marriages for her younger daughters and to ensure careers for her sons. However, once she had made all the necessary arrangements, nothing compelled her to remain in Neocaesarea, the late Basil's professional seat. Together with her eldest daughter Macrina, Emmelia thus decided to transfer the household to their country estate.

Annesi must have been an idyllic spot: high, pristine mountains, forests dense with trees of variegated species, brooks with clear, rushing water, gently sloping plains, a small village on the banks of the river Iris opposite the mansion inhabited by the family itself—in short, a spot ideally suited to those seeking tranquillity (ἡσυχία), solitude (ἐσχατιά), and escape from the tumults of the world.

The move itself must have been quite an undertaking, but even more considerable must have been the contrast between the ladies' former life-style in Neocaesarea and their new life in the country. Given such a remarkable change, it is striking that Gregory of Nyssa, as author of the *Life of Macrina*, never mentioned the precise moment when the move took place; apparently, he considered it nothing out of the ordinary. Indeed, many members of the Cappadocian gentry preferred the quiet beauty of their country estates to the discomfort of life in towns and cities.[2]

---

[1] Aubineau, *Virginité*, 34; J. Gribomont, 'Le Panégyrique de la virginité, œuvre de jeunesse de Grégoire de Nysse', *RAM* 43 (1967), 249–66; Maraval, *Macrine*, 48 n. 2.

[2] Gr. Nyss. *VSM* 6. 1–2; Gr. Naz. *Or.* 43. 13 (PG 36. 512); id. *Ep.* 11; Maraval, *Macrine*, 46 f.; id. 'Encore les frères et les sœurs de Grégoire de Nysse', *Revue d'histoire et de philosophie religieuses* 60 (1980), 161–6; J. E. Pfister, 'A Biographical Note: The Brothers and Sisters of St. Gregory of Nyssa', *VigChr* 18

Macrina and Emmelia's move to Annesi has frequently been interpreted as a conscious retreat into solitude, as the essential step initiating a life of monastic contemplation. But the *Life of Macrina*, our principal source, furnishes no evidence in support of such a view. More importantly, Macrina and her mother were by no means on their own at Annesi. The area owned by the family was vast, ranging over three provinces, and after her husband's death Emmelia apparently managed her affairs very successfully. In all this she was assisted by Macrina.[3] Under her management, so Gregory tells us, the estate increased ninefold— an astonishing success even allowing for her son's rhetoric.[4] If this increase was perhaps extraordinary, the fact that women managed their own estates was not, as Emmelia's contemporaries, Simplicia, Thecla, and Seleukia exemplify—all are identified not only as landowners but also as successful managers.[5] But involvement in such duties need not imply a privileged position for women in Asia Minor; it was only natural, and certainly common, that a widow and her daughter should look after their own

(1964), 108–13. For Annesi cf. the description by Bas. *Epp.* 3. 2, 14; Gr. Nyss. *In quad. mart.* (PG 46. 784); id. *VSM* 34. 15–18; Gallay, *La Vie de Saint Grégoire*, 249; Honigmann, 'Un itinéraire', 264 f.; Jerphanion, 'Ibora—Gazioura?', 333–54; Leclercq, 'Ibora', *DACL* vii.1, 4–9; Maraval, *Macrine*, 38–44. For the estate cf. Gr. Nyss. *In quad. mart.* (PG 46. 784 (dating from 10 Mar. 383)); id. *Hom. in Eccles.* 3 (PG 44. 653–6); Bas. *Hom. in div.* 2 (PG 31. 284 f.); cf. J. Daniélou, 'La chronologie des sermons de Grégoire de Nysse', *RevSR* 29 (1955), 346–72, here 362 f.; M. M. Fox, *The Life and Times of St. Basil the Great as Revealed in his Works* (Washington, DC, 1939), 25–31; A. H. M. Jones, *The Later Roman Empire*, ii (Oxford, 1964), 795–808; Kirsten, 'Cappadocia', 867–71; Mitchell, 'Population and the Land in Roman Galatia', 1073–81; E. Stein, *Histoire du Bas-Empire*, i (Bruges, 1959), 14–16; Teja, *Organización*, 35–7; B. Treucker, *Politische und sozialgeschichtliche Studien zu den Basiliusbriefen* (Munich, 1961), 13–16.

[3] Tillemont (*Mémoires*, ix. 6) assumed the provinces to be Pontus, Cappadocia, and Armenia, whereas J. Daniélou ('Bulletin d'histoire des origines chrétiennes', *RSR* 51 (1963), 112–63, here 148, speaks of two Pontus provinces, Cappadocia, and Armenia Minor; Maraval (*Macrine*, 160 n. 1) suggests Helenopontus, Pontus Ptolemonaicus, and Cappadocia.

[4] Gr. Nyss. *VSM* 20. 16–20.

[5] Gr. Naz. *Epp.* 57, 79, 72; Bas. *Ep.* 321; John Chrys. *Ep.* 9. 2 (*Jean Chrysostome: Lettres à Olympias et Vie anonyme d'Olympias*, ed. A.-M. Malingrey (SC 13bis; Paris, 1968), 226); Hauser-Meury, 154 f. ('Simplicia I'), 159 f. ('Thecla III'); W. M. Ramsay, *The Church in the Roman Empire Before A.D. 170* (Grand Rapids, 1954⁵), 160–2.

affairs.[6] Emmelia's refuge at Annesi probably resembled those of other rich *possessores*, who were censured by Gregory and his brother for their mansions decorated with multicoloured marbles, exotic woods, precious inlays, mosaics, paintings, and sculptures.[7] Emmelia and Macrina's household included numerous servants and slaves, as well as the youngest son Peter, and the mother, at least, lived like any *grande dame* of her time.[8]

Emmelia, Macrina, and Peter were not the only members of the family who lived at Annesi. Yet another of Emmelia's children, her third child Naucratius, had also chosen this remote area.[9] Born about 330, Naucratius resembled his elder sister Macrina as an exceptionally talented child. According to Gregory, his exemplary character was matched by an outstanding physique and an impressive intellect: when he was 21 he gave such a magnificent exhibition of rhetorical skill that the entire audience remained virtually spellbound. At this pristine moment of scholarly success and public recognition, Naucratius suddenly decided to 'turn to a life of solitude and poverty, taking nothing with him but himself' (μεθ' ἑαυτοῦ πλὴν ἑαυτόν).[10] Accompanied by a single slave, Chrysaphius, who followed him as a friend as much as out of desire to lead a similar kind of life, Naucratius retired around the year 352 'by himself' to an isolated spot (καθ' ἑαυτὸν ἐσχατιάν) in the forests near the river Iris. Here, hidden in a mountain hollow, he pursued a life 'far from the noise of the city, military activities, and the business of rhetoric in the law courts'. Free from 'worldly' considerations, he cared 'with his own hands' for some ailing and destitute old men who lived in the vicinity, sustaining them and himself with the spoils of his hunting. Thus mastering his physical desires through

---

[6] Goggin (*The Times of Saint Gregory of Nyssa*, 36) emphasizes the privileged position of women in Asia Minor citing no other source than H. Leclercq, 'Femme', *DACL* v.1, 1300–53; Leclercq himself (p. 1319) cites P. Paris, *Quatenus feminae res publicas in Asia Minore Romanis imperantibus attigerint* (Paris, 1891); Goggin is then referred to by Maraval, *Macrine*, 160 n. 1; cf. MacMullen, 'Woman in Public', 213–18.

[7] Bas. *Hom. in div.* 2 (PG 31. 284 f.); Gr. Nyss. *Hom. in Eccles.* 2 (PG 44. 653–6); Fox, *Life and Times of St. Basil the Great*, 25–31; Teja, *Organización*, 83–6.

[8] Gr. Nyss. *VSM* 7. 2–5.

[9] Ibid. 8. 13–14.

[10] Ibid. 8. 8–10.

fatiguing labour, he exercised his mind by scrupulously obeying his mother's every wish. In other words, he sought to lead what Gregory calls 'the philosophical life'.[11]

Five years after Naucratius' withdrawal from the world, as we noted in the preceding chapter, in the autumn of 357, his elder brother Basil likewise decided to forgo fame as a rhetor, 'to break all the links that bind the soul to the body', and to seek a new life of solitude at Annesi.

Basil's renown as an ascetic and theologian, like that of the other two Cappadocian Fathers, his friend Gregory of Nazianzus and his brother Gregory of Nyssa, needs no further emphasis. Virtually uncontested is the judgement that finds its echo not only in contemporary sources, but also in subsequent historical analysis: Basil 'eclipsed in reputation all those who were conspicuous by their virtue'.[12]

Some of those who were thus eclipsed were undoubtedly Basil's siblings, in particular his sister Macrina. Indeed, much of the secondary literature still conveys the impression that asceticism in fourth-century Asia Minor is essentially synonymous with Basil. All later ascetic developments are seen as if through his eyes. More importantly, even those forms of ascetic life that may have existed before him, and may have continued to exist while he was formulating his own concepts, are seen as homogeneous developments culminating in Basil, and thus are judged *ex post facto*. Basil appears to function virtually as a lens, filtering not only our vision of what came after him, but also what came before.

Thus, it appears a foregone conclusion that 'Macrina founded a monastery for women on their estate at Annesi, where Basil had already founded a monastery for men. . . . Macrina was not the head of the community of the women.'[13] Or, 'some kind of association between men and women was inevitable at first, for women ascetics could not stand alone . . . . For the actual form which the association took in Cappadocia and Pontus, Basil

[11] Ibid. 8. 13–14; 8. 22–9. 5; Gr. Naz. Epigrams 156–8 (*Anth. graeca*, ii. 526); unfortunately A. Hamman (*Guide pratique des Pères de l'Église* (Bruges, 1967), 182) is representative of much of the writing on Naucratius; Hauser-Meury, 'Naucratius', 125 f.; Marrou, *Histoire de l'éducation*, 303–6.

[12] Gr. Nyss. *VSM* 6. 15–16.

[13] J. LaPorte, *The Role of Women in Early Christianity* (New York, 1982), 86.

seems to have been responsible. . . . His own early experience provided a model for subsequent arrangements.'[14] These and similar representations leave little doubt as to the relative influence the parties concerned exercised on each other. In part, this results from certain ambiguities within our sources themselves.

Basil never mentions his sister by name in any of his writings. He attributes his choice of the ascetic life directly to the influence of 'Eustathius the Philosopher'. This Eustathius, on the other hand, is never mentioned in Gregory's *Life of Macrina*. According to Gregory, it was Macrina who 'attracted [Basil] rapidly to the ideal of philosophy', thus instigating his 'conversion'. This statement has usually been interpreted as an attempt on Gregory's part to inflate the role played by Macrina, the protagonist of his work, which in turn was intended to present her as a saint.[15] Most authors, therefore, accord Macrina at best the role of a mediator.

However, some basic observations can hardly be ignored. Macrina and Emmelia arrived at Annesi some ten years before Basil, and were followed in second place by Naucratius. At the end, we are confronted with two ascetic communities, one male, one female. First, therefore, it is crucial to reconstruct Macrina's personal ascetic development, as only this illustrates the nature and sequence of the changes which eventually transformed an √ordinary household into an ascetic household and then into an ascetic community. Secondly, this will further enable us to clarify and calibrate the relative influence exercised by all the parties involved in Basil of Caesarea's early ascetic years. As a direct result of the personalities in question—Basil, Macrina, Naucratius, and the elusive philosopher Eustathius—this development thirdly sheds light on one of the most important periods in the making of fourth-century asceticism.

When Basil arrived in Annesi in 357 or 358, he was confronted with two models of ascetic life, which at first glance appear almost diametrically opposed. His elder sister Macrina adhered to an ascetic regimen consisting of prayer, frugal nourishment,

[14] Clarke, *Ascetic Works of St. Basil*, 37 f.; cf. Albrecht, *Das Leben der heiligen Makrina*, 47–51.
[15] Maraval, *Macrine*, 52 f., 162 n. 4; Gribomont, 'Eustathe le Philosophe', 115–24.

and manual labour which included a nominal, yet highly significant, amount of work ordinarily reserved for slaves. Yet she remained firmly a member of Emmelia's household, which embraced her brother Peter as well as male and female slaves. Their brother Naucratius, in the mean time, attempted to achieve ascetic perfection by living in a *monē* at some distance from his mother's dwelling, together with a slave and several old men.[16] However, around the time of Basil's arrival, an event occurred which was to have profound consequences for all the family.

Sometime in 357 Naucratius and his companion Chrysaphius died in a hunting accident three days away from home.[17] Emmelia's shock and distress were great. 'Her soul faltered, speechless and breathless, her reason (λογισμοῦ) giving way to pain (πάθει); under the impact of the terrible news she sank to the ground, she, an athlete of the noble race, felled by an unforeseen blow.'[18] Yet she never displayed anything 'ignoble and womanish' (δυσγενές τι καὶ γυναικεῖον).[19] Macrina, on the other hand, maintained a stoic calm. She is represented as a true example of virtue (ἀρετή). 'Setting reason against pain, she, ... through her firmness and unyielding spirit, educated her mother's soul to be courageous (lit. manly)' (πρὸς ἀνδρείαν παιδοτριβήσασα).[20]

Naucratius died in the same year that Basil arrived at Annesi. After a brief stay at the family mansion Basil moved to his *monē*, a dwelling of the roughest kind on the opposite side of the river but within walking distance of his mother's home. Here, he adhered to a strict ascetic regimen in the company of several others. The facts are compelling. Basil's choice of an ascetic lifestyle was strongly influenced by the example of Naucratius; he

---

[16] The exact location of Naucratius' retreat is unknown. It must have been quite close to Annesi since Nacratius' contact with his mother never ceased; cf. Maraval, *Macrine*, 41, 167 n. 3; Gribomont, 'Le Panégyrique', 251.

[17] The information concerning Chrysaphius is slightly ambiguous, but it seems that he died with his former master. Gregory of Nazianzus implies that it was a fishing rather than a hunting accident (Epigr. 156 (*Anth. graeca*, ii. 526)). According to D. Gorce (*Les Voyages, l'hospitalité et le port des lettres dans le monde chrétien des IVe et Ve siècles* (Paris, 1925), 76), the average distance covered by an ancient traveller was around 30 km. a day, making it probable that Naucratius' accident occurred 75–90 km. away from Annesi.

[18] Gr. Nyss. *VSM* 9. 18–22.

[19] δυσγενές means literally 'of low birth'.

[20] Gr. Nyss. *VSM* 10. 1–6.

picked up where his brother had so recently left off. His earliest companions were in fact those of the late Naucratius, who now found a new leader in Basil. Continuity was maintained. The estate still accommodated both a family-household with attendant slaves where one member had for ten years been following an ascetic regimen, and a five-year-old *monē* inhabited by several brothers.[21]

In a chapter of the *Life of Macrina* placed between the account of Basil's move to Annesi and Naucratius' death, Gregory describes the following:[22] Macrina, long since liberated from the burdens of material life, persuaded her mother to 'renounce the way of life she had been accustomed to and her manners of a great lady', and 'instead of receiving the services of her servants, to adopt the feeling of community and to partake in the life of the virgins around her, after having made them from the slaves and servants they were, into sisters and equals.'[23]

Here Gregory interrupts the narrative to insert, as he himself says, 'in a short parenthesis', the tragic fate of Naucratius. He then continues in chapter 11:

When the mother was freed from the worries of rearing her children . . . and when most of the material resources were divided among the children . . . the life of [Macrina] became the symbol for her mother of the 'philosophical life' . . . [guiding] her mother to the same degree of humility, after having persuaded her to place herself on the same level as the group of virgins to share with them one table, one lodging, and all the necessities of life, like an equal, all differences of rank having been removed from their lives.[24]

What does this change signify? Chapters 7 and 11 clearly refer to two occurrences, both highly significant in themselves as well as in regard to their chronological sequence: Emmelia abolished all difference of status between herself and her slaves, and she subdivided her possessions among her children.

[21] It is equally possible that Basil set up his *monē* while Naucratius was still alive, so that for a brief period all three establishments may have coexisted side by side. Cf. Gribomont, 'Eustathe le Philosophe', 115–24; id. 'Eustathe de Sébaste', in *DSp* iv.2, 1708–12; Maraval, *Macrine*, 52.

[22] Events to be dated between 356 and 357.

[23] μεθ᾽ ἑαυτῆς ἐκ δουλίδων καὶ ὑποχειρίων ἀδελφὰς καὶ ὁμοτίμους ποιησαμένη: Gr. Nyss. *VSM* 7. 2–8.

[24] Ibid. 11. 1–13.

The material concerning the slaves suggests manumission of all domestic servants, at least those closest to Emmelia and Macrina. This manumission could have occurred in two ways, either as a *manumissio in ecclesia* or as a *manumissio inter amicos*.[25] *Manumissio in ecclesia*, promulgated by two Constantinian edicts dating from 316 and 323, authorized Christian congregations to free their own slaves. The procedure was highly formalized and involved a declaration in the presence of the bishop or his representative and the entire congregation. A slave thus freed became a full citizen and *persona sui iuris*.[26] *Manumissio inter amicos*, on the other hand, was far less complicated. A master simply declared a slave to be his friend, expressing this either by letter (*per epistulam*) or by inviting him to dine at the same table (*per mensam*). In contrast to the other forms of manumission, *manumissio inter amicos* did not result in full citizenship, a slave thus freed merely becoming Latinized.[27]

The events in Emmelia's household presumably took the latter form of manumission, *inter amicos*, more precisely *per mensam*.[28] If this was the case, Emmelia's former slaves thus continued to be of a lesser rank than their former masters, not merely in social,

---

[25] The interesting technicalities of this process have never, to my knowledge, been clarified, and none of the relevant discussions use the *VSM*; cf. J. Gaudemet, *Institutions de l'Antiquité* (Paris, 1967), 718 f.; Hadjinicolaou-Marava, *Recherches sur la vie des esclaves*, 101–13; J. Imbert, 'Réflexions sur le christianisme et l'esclavage en droit romain', *Revue internationale des droits de l'antiquité* 2 (1949), 445–76, here 466 f.; E. J. Jonkers, 'De l'influence du Christianisme sur la législation relative à l'esclavage dans l'antiquité', *Mnemosyne*, 3rd ser., 1 (1933/4), 241–80, here 252–75; J. Karayannopoulos, 'St. Basil's Social Activity', in Fedwick, *Basil of Caesarea*, i. 375–91, here 385 f.; C. G. Mor, 'La manumissio in ecclesia', *Rivista di storia del diritto italiano* 1 (1928), 80–150; Westermann, *Slave Systems*, 154 f.; R. Teja, 'San Basilio y la esclavitud', in Fedwick, *Basil of Caesarea*, i. 393–403.

[26] *Codex Justinianus* 1. 13 (*Corpus Juris Civilis*, ii, ed. P. Krüger (Berlin, 1959[12]), 67); *CTh.* 4. 7. 1 (Mommsen–Meyer i.2, 179); F. Fabbrini, *La manumissio in ecclesia* (Milan, 1965), *passim*; J. Gaudemet, 'La Législation religieuse de Constantin', *Revue d'histoire de l'église de France* 33 (1947), 25–61, here 38–41; Jonkers, 'De l'influence du Christianisme', 265; Mor, 'La manumissio', 92 f.

[27] Gaudemet, *Institutions de l'Antiquité*, 718–20.

[28] A suggestion further supported by the slow spread of the first type of manumission (*in ecclesia*); cf. Westermann, *Slave Systems*, 155.

but also in legal terms. Yet Macrina and her mother treated them as equals, regardless of status and rank.[29]

The significance of such a step can only be evaluated in the light of the contemporary social and psychological barriers which separated masters from their slaves. Given the scarcity of sources, the then prevailing opinions regarding the treatment of slaves are difficult to assess.[30] While most scholars agree that the number of slaves declined during the fourth century, they disagree strongly as to the causes of this decline. Some attribute it primarily to the cessation of offensive Roman warfare; others to the increasing transformation of free citizens into *coloni* (dependent tenants), or to the beneficent influence of Christianity. Whatever the causes, the decline in number led to a rise in the costs of slave-labour, which in turn led to a gradual amelioration of the lot of individual slaves. In Asia Minor, for instance, slaves were utilized chiefly for less physically demanding housework—they are accordingly described as *oikētoi*—and were assigned duties which included a wide range of specialized crafts, for example baking.[31] This amelioration was supported on an intellectual level by the teachings of both the Stoa and Christianity, which emphasized the ultimate equality of human beings.[32] While these factors may have prompted a more favourable treatment of individuals, actual acts of liberation increased only fractionally. Despite the theoretical claims, the spread of Christianity had scarcely any consequences for the lot of this sector of society, as is perhaps best summarized by Imbert: 'l'Église, si elle considère comme égaux à ses yeux l'esclave et le libre, si elle protège le *servus* contre son maître, ne touche pas au lien de subordination qui

---

[29] Gr. Nyss. *VSM* 11. 8–13.

[30] Cf. Westermann, *Slave Systems*, 128–33, for a discussion of contemporary literature; Teja, *Organización*, 130–2.

[31] M. Rostovtzeff, *The Social and Economic History of the Roman Empire*, i. (Oxford, 1957²), 522–31; Gaudemet, *Institutions de l'Antiquité*, 715–18; Westermann, *Slave Systems*, 120, 126 f., 133, 145 f.; Hadjinicolaou-Marava, *Recherches sur la vie des esclaves*, 32 f.; Teja, *Organización*, 126–36.

[32] F. Bömer, *Untersuchungen über die Religion der Sklaven in Griechenland und Rom*, i (Abhandlungen der Akademie der Wissenschaften und der Literatur (Mainz) 7; Mainz, 1957), 757 f. (repr. in Forschungen zur Antiken Sklaverei 14: 1 (Wiesbaden, 1981), here 179, 182 f., and *passim*); Imbert, 'Réflexions', 452–6; Karayannopoulos, 'St. Basil's Social Activity', 385 f.; Westermann, *Slave Systems*, 149 f.

unit l'un à l'autre: chacun reste socialement dans sa situation, bien que, spirituellement, tous deux aient la même destinée.'[33] The foundations of slavery as such were never seriously challenged. Indeed, the Church relied increasingly on its own slaves, which contributed to the preservation of barriers between slaves and masters.[34]

This short excursus—far more general than is desirable—at least brings into focus Macrina and Emmelia's action. As may be recalled, Macrina's ascetic evolution proceeded gradually, each step marking a slight deviation from the norms which governed the life of a lady of her rank. At the age of 12, she considered herself to be a widow without ever having been married. She then began to dress plainly and to take on a limited range of domestic chores, in particular tasks usually reserved exclusively for slaves. All these initiatives, with the possible exception of the last, remained—at least from the viewpoint of an outside observer—within the framework of convention.

But now some profound changes occurred in rapid succession. Basil returned to Annesi and Macrina 'attracted [him] rapidly to the ideal of philosophy'.[35] Naucratius died either shortly before or after Basil's return. Throughout the ensuing upheaval, only Macrina is depicted as maintaining calm and courage. In this moment of crisis the traditional roles of mother and daughter are virtually reversed. After her father's death Macrina had already assumed a substantial portion of her mother's managerial burdens. At the same time she also became a 'mother' to her youngest brother Peter. 'She was all for the child: father, teacher, pedagogue, mother, counseller of all which is good' (πατήρ, διδάσκαλος, παιδαγωγός, μήτηρ, ἀγαθοῦ παντὸς σύμβουλος).[36]

Now Macrina becomes 'father, teacher, pedagogue, mother' to her own mother. She assumes the role of the head of the household, displaying for all to witness the true 'manliness' of her

---

[33] 'Réflexions', 465.

[34] Westermann (*Slave Systems*, 157 f., following H. C. Lea, *Studies in Church History* (Philadelphia, 1883), 523–76, here 537–40) even suggests that the notion of slaves being the spiritual equals of their masters declined from the 4th cent. onwards; Jonkers, 'De l'influence du Christianisme', 252–75.

[35] Gr. Nyss. *VSM* 6. 8–10.

[36] Ibid. 12. 1–15; Peter's birth in one of the years between 341 and 345 was overshadowed by his father's death in the same year.

character, fortified by the strength gained from her philosophy. At that point Gregory portrays Macrina as introducing her mother Emmelia to the ascetic, that is to say, the 'philosophical' life. 'Macrina persuaded her mother to renounce her customary way of life . . . [and] to become of the same status (ὁμοτιμόν) as the many (τοῖς πολλοῖς) and to share the same life as the virgins.'[37]

Who were the virgins in Emmelia's company? Are these *parthenoi* to be identified with the former slaves? Had Macrina already gathered several other virgins of unknown provenance around her, and did Emmelia and the newly freed slaves now merely join them? Or is Gregory implying a gradual development?[38]

While the initiative belongs to the daughter, who prompted her mother's first public attestation of ascetic designs, both Macrina and Emmelia had broken a societal barrier of formidable strength. The abasement to the level of former slaves, Latinized freedmen, signifies a break with social conventions equal to Naucratius' and then Basil's rejection of a worldly career; it had the same value as their physical retreat into the wilderness. However, whereas both men declared their new psychological disposition immediately, openly, in an unmistakable fashion by physical withdrawal, for Macrina, a woman, such a step appears to have been impossible. Her transformation occurred gradually, always within the structures of the family, and signified by unobtrusive modifications of her daily life.[39] Only now, by descending to the level of *hoi polloi*, does the first public break with the norms of society and the structures of convention occur. In the case of both women, however, the medium of the rupture is a social rather than a physical retreat.

[37] *VSM* 7. 2–8.

[38] Maraval's introductory comment (*Macrine*, 53) unfortunately leaves the sequence of events ambiguous; Gregory's arrangement of the relevant passages indicates that the servants had been freed shortly before Emmelia decided to participate fully in Macrina's ascetic regime (*VSM* 7. 2–8, 11. 8–13). Ch. 6 contains Basil's return from Athens (just after Emmelia had arranged suitable settlements for her other children) and his conversion to the ascetic life. Ch. 7 and 8 describe changes in the household, ch. 9 and 10 deal with Naucratius and his death in 357, and ch. 11 resumes the description of the newly formed community.

[39] Maraval, *Macrine*, 100; A. Strobel, 'Der Begriff des "Hauses" im griechischen und römischen Privatrecht', *ZNW* 56 (1965), 91–100.

This act further represents the first step towards the transformation of an ascetic household into an ascetic institution. At first, only members of the immediate family joined the ascetic life: Naucratius and Basil in a more public manner outside the family; Macrina, then Emmelia, both privately, within its confines. Finally, other members of the *oikos*, the extended household, became symbolically elevated to full membership of the family. They became 'sisters and equals'.

During the same period the organization of the household changed fundamentally. Both women, Macrina and Emmelia, had rearranged their financial matters. In chapter 20 of the *Life* Macrina briefly reflects upon her family's financial situation: when the parents' property was divided among the nine children, each received a portion larger than the original fortune of the parents, thus marking out the family as one of the wealthiest of the time.[40] Chapter 11 refers to the same division of property.[41]

Emmelia had already disposed of much of her property before 356 or 357 and her acceptance of personal poverty. Macrina had given away all her money as soon as she had received it. The terms of this disposal are as interesting as is its early date. Neither Macrina nor Emmelia were inclined to give their religious feelings priority over the family's financial affairs: Emmelia distributed her fortune in equal parts to her children; Macrina entrusted her portion, undoubtedly a considerable sum, to the priest of the local church, who administered it as *oikonomos*.[42] This may have taken the form of a permanent gift to the local church, or of a temporary trust fund where the property would revert to the family after Macrina's death. In both cases the use of the funds was subject to certain obligations; the money had to be spent for charitable means—for instance to

---

[40] Gr. Nyss. *VSM* 20. 14–20; Maraval, *Macrine*, 207 n. 3; concerning the number of Macrina's siblings, cf. Pfister, 'A Biographical Note', 108–13; Aubineau, *Virginité*, 71; Maraval, 'Encore les frères et sœurs', 161–6.

[41] Gr. Nyss. *VSM* 11. 1–5; 20. 20–3.

[42] P. Landvogt, *Epigraphische Untersuchungen über den "oikonomos": Ein Beitrag zum hellenistischen Beamtenwesen*, Diss. (Strasburg, 1908); G. Theissen, 'Soziale Schichtung in der korinthischen Gemeinde', *Studien zur Soziologie des Urchristentums* (Wissenschaftliche Untersuchungen zum Neuen Testament 19; Tübingen, 1979), 238–45; R. van Bremen, 'Women and Wealth', in A. Cameron and A. Kuhrt (eds.), *Images of Women in Antiquity* (Detroit, 1983), 223–42.

alleviate the recurrent periods of famine which affected the entire region.[43]

After Macrina and her mother had reduced their personal share of the family fortune, Basil did the same. When he renounced his position as rhetorician he also renounced a substantial share of his possessions, which meant in effect that he was no longer officially a member of the senatorial class; he had placed himself in a far lower census category. The gesture seems to have been of symbolic rather than enduring significance—Basil had to make five attempts to divest himself of his fortune. But the symbolic power of this gesture cannot be overestimated; like Emmelia and Macrina, Basil had publicly repudiated his social rank and lowered himself to a much inferior position.[44] Neither Basil, Naucratius, nor Macrina, however, adopted such measures in a fashion that could have posed any threat to the fortune of their brothers and sisters.

Naucratius' death seems to have been the event that prompted Emmelia's decision to join her daughter as well as Basil's decision to settle in the *monē*. Both had already entertained the notion of leading a philosophical life, Basil more so than Emmelia, but it seems that at least in Emmelia's case Naucratius' death acted as a catalyst. And although this is nowhere specified, his brother's death seems to have strengthened Basil's resolve to follow in his footsteps. The years between 356 and 357 thus witnessed important changes at Annesi.

Apart from the untimely death of Naucratius, had there been

---

[43] Note the allusion to Acts 4: 35; J. Gaudemet, *L'Église dans l'Empire Romain (IVe–Ve siècles)*, (Histoire du Droit et des Institutions de l'Église en Occident 3; Paris, 1958), 288, 291–315. Gaudemet states with respect to private donations, 'Techniquement le droit le permettait, par la précaire, de durée brève, mais pratiquement renouvelable.... Il est d'ailleurs probable que ... la donation était souvent faite avec réserve d'usufruit.... Une variété particulière de donation est représentée par la dotation ... le plus souvent en terres, dont les revenus servaient aux besoins de l'Église' (294 f.). Bishops were obliged to administer donations for charitable aims, as indicated by can. 25 of Antioch (Mansi, ii. 1319); at times they delegated their obligations to an οἰκόνομος; cf. Gangra can. 7 (Mansi, ii. 1107); for other examples of charity, cf. *VSM* 20. 28–9; 37–8; regarding the famine in 368/9, cf. *VSM* 26. 31–3; Maraval, *Macrine*, 54 n. 1, 55 n. 1–2.

[44] Garnsey, *Social Status and Legal Privilege*, 221–76; Treucker, *Politische und sozialgeschichtliche Studien*, 26.

another driving force behind these changes? So far it appears that Basil and Emmelia at least were reacting to events rather than initiating them.

By declaring herself a widow and by renouncing marriage Macrina was the first to adopt an ascetic lifestyle. Naucratius followed suit by turning his back upon the world in 352. In 356 or 357 Emmelia renounced her personal luxuries and freed all her slaves; in 357 or early 358 Basil renounced his worldly possessions, taking his cue from Naucratius' example.[45]

Naucratius' death only accentuated an ascetic life-style, which had by that time been realized in virtually two diametrically opposite ways.[46] The men, Naucratius and then Basil, retreated physically into the wilderness; the women, notably Macrina, transformed their household into an ascetic community.

This transformation of the household was accompanied and symbolized by a transformation of the roles played by its individual members, men as well as women.[47] Macrina, from the 'virgin daughter' she once was, is transformed progressively into a 'virgin widow', then a 'virgin mother', and finally into what Gregory calls a 'manly virgin'. Through asceticism she became a woman who was 'father, teacher (*didaskalos*), pedagogue, mother', and counsellor for her own mother, her brother Peter, and all around her.

[45] In his introduction to the *VSM* (p. 52) Maraval makes this misleading statement based on Gribomont: 'la rude vie de "gentil-homme campagnard" du frère puîné de Basile . . . s'apparentait bien plutôt à l'ascétisme eustathien qu'au monachisme basilien, déjà beaucoup plus organisé.' While there can hardly be any doubt concerning the first assertion, the second statement is mistaken. Maraval himself writes at a later stage: 'Sa [Naucratius'] retraite aurait duré jusqu'en 357 environ, un peu avant que Basile vienne prendre sa succession au bord de l'Iris (en 358)' (*Macrine*, 165 n. 3). Cf. Gribomont, 'Eustathe le Philosophe', 123 f.; id. 'Le Panégyrique', 251.

[46] Basil's reluctance to join Gregory of Nazianzus may also have been caused by his brother's death.

[47] Initially, no strict segregation of the sexes was practised. Macrina's brother Peter continued to live in the house for some time, as well as other male dependents; Gr. Nyss. *VSM* 12; Maraval, *Macrine*, 182 n. 1. Interesting is Emmelia's insistence on calling a male doctor when Macrina is suffering from cancer, though his assistance significantly is made unnecessary by a miracle; Gr. Nyss. *VSM* 31. 14–37; P. Devos, 'Années d'épiscopat de S. Pierre II de Sébastée', *AnBoll* 79 (1961). 359 f.

THE ORGANIZATION OF MACRINA'S COMMUNITY

By the time that Basil of Caesarea initiated his personal ascetic experiments, Macrina and Naucratius had already taken some advanced steps towards the cultivation of an ascetic life. Chronology alone, however, does not suffice to explain the importance and relative influence of all the parties involved in the subsequent developments. A comparison of the evolution of both Basil's *monē* and Macrina's ascetic household clarifies the degree to which the brother and sister influenced each other and their followers.[48] At the same time, it reveals the changes which constitute and then crystallize the transformation of a family into an ascetic community.

Macrina and her mother's new way of life soon attracted wider attention. Gregory tells us that several 'virgins' gathered around Macrina and Emmelia as early as 357. Whenever he refers to the household after that time, he identifies it as a group or a *choros* of *parthenoi* (τῆς παρθενίας χορὸς). While some of these virgins may have been the former domestic slaves, the ascetic household at Annesi soon attracted new, unrelated members: an ascetic community began to emerge.[49] In Chapter 26 of the *Life* Gregory describes Macrina's death, which devastated all those who were close to her. 'Some who called her mother and nurse were even more seriously distraught than the others. These were those she had nursed and reared after finding them wandering along the roads in the time of famine, and she led them to the pure and uncorrupted life.'[50] Cappadocia and Pontus had been ravaged by severe famine in the years 368 and 369. At that time Macrina adopted girls orphaned by the disaster into her community,[51] eventually giving them the opportunity to 'become virgins'.

Thus, in 368/9 the social composition of the household changed dramatically for a second time: Macrina again accepted a con-

---

[48] The difficulties encountered result primarily from the fact that Gregory mentions organizational details only rarely and in retrospect (he was writing of course after Macrina's death (19 July 380) and anyway had been absent from Annesi during the period between 357 and 380); Maraval, *Macrine*, 57–67.

[49] Gr. Nyss. *VSM* 11. 9; 16. 5; 26. 1–2; 29. 1; 32. 4; 33. 15; 34. 24; *Ep.* 19. 7 (*GN* viii.2, 64).

[50] *VSM* 26. 29–34.

[51] Ibid. 12. 30–5.

siderable number of new members from a low stratum of society, and made them into 'sisters and equals'.[52] This signifies a further step towards the institutionalization of an ascetic community. If the former slaves had been part of Macrina's *oikia* these new members certainly had no such previous connection. Their incorporation into the household was an adoption into a newly constituted family, on the basis of Christian principles alone: they became members of an ascetic family, which by virtue of their inclusion was becoming an ascetic community.

But not all new members came from the lower strata of society. One such individual was Vetiana. Like Macrina, Vetiana was of noble birth, extremely wealthy, and had in her youth been an acclaimed beauty.[53] The daughter of the senator Araxios, she was married as a young girl to Agilo, a man of equal distinction. Many years her senior, the Alaman Agilo had risen rapidly under Constantius to the post of commander of the infantry, a position he maintained under four emperors: Constantius, Julian, Procopius, and Valens.[54] Indeed, thanks to his influence, Vetiana's father, Araxios, became praetorian prefect under the usurper Procopius and, more significantly, was spared execution after Procopius' demise.[55] Agilo's marriage to Vetiana was apparently short-lived. He must have died some time after 366,[56] and, with her father now in exile, Vetiana must have found herself in a difficult situation. On her own, she took refuge with Macrina as

---

[52] Regarding the date of the famine cf. Bas. *Epp.* 27 and 31; id. *Homilia dicta tempore famis et siccitatis* (PG 31. 304–28); Maraval, *Macrine*, 184 n. 1; Basil's *Ep.* 315 is intriguing, mentioning a female relative of his who is in charge of orphans or an orphanage. Could it be an indirect reference to Macrina?

[53] Gr. Nyss. *VSM* 28. 1–10.

[54] Cf. Jones, 'Agilo', *PLRE* i. 28 f.; Seeck, 'Agilo', *RE* i. 1, 809.

[55] Amm. Marc. *Res gestae* 26. 7. 6, 9. 7; Socrates, *HE* 4. 5 (PG 67. 469). Agilo had changed sides in the decisive battle between Procopius and Valens in 366, a move which sealed the usurper's fate. This sudden reversal saved Araxios who, through Agilo's intercession, was only sent into exile from which he returned soon thereafter (Amm. Marc. *Res gestae* 26. 10. 7). Cf. Jones, 'Araxius', *PLRE* i. 94; Maraval suggests an identification of Araxios with the addressee of Libanius' letters, but with caution (*Macrine*, 235 n. 2); J. Matthews, *The Roman Empire of Ammianus* (Baltimore, 1989) 194–203, 270, 316.

[56] Agilo's final fate is unknown (cf. Gr. Nyss. *VSM* 28; Jones ('Agilo', *PLRE* i. 28 f.) doubts that Agilo was executed after 366, but unfortunately does not elaborate further.

her 'guardian and teacher', perhaps to avoid a second marriage.[57] She spent 'the majority of time in the company of the virgins to learn from them the virtuous life'.[58]

Vetiana was present at Macrina's death-bed and was consulted with regard to the funeral arrangements, together with the 'deaconess Lampadion'. Like Vetiana, Lampadion was also a lady of means as well as a widow.[59] Neither belonged to Emmelia and Macrina's original family; they had joined a community created and held together by ascetic aspirations.

Significantly, all those women whom Gregory identifies by name and who thus emerge as individuals possess an elevated social background. Without extrapolating too much, it seems evident that both Macrina and Gregory remained fully conscious of the social distinctions that separate those who are noble from those who are not. Their ascetic aspirations prompted them to negate the practical effects of class distinction, but in no instance the notion of distinction itself.

Another factor is worthy of note: Emmelia and Vetiana were certainly, and Lampadion was most probably, widowed; Macrina had always regarded herself as a widow. All four women were therefore absolved from the paramount female obligation: procreation.[60] The mere fact that at least two of the women had been *de facto* married, and one had borne children, highlights another factor: to be a *parthenos*, a virgin, need not indicate a physical condition. The term describes a way of life. By entering

---

[57] According to Gregory of Nazianzus (*In laud. Bas.* 56 (Boulenger, 170)), a certain widow appealed to Basil in 370 to protect her against a second marriage. Maraval (*Macrine*, 234 n. 1) suggests caution in identifying this widow with Vetiana, following Tillemont (*Mémoires*, ix. 667) against Baronius.

[58] Gr. Nyss. *VSM* 28. 5–8. Vetiana's relationship with Macrina's community was not necessarily as straightforward as it may at first appear: she spent 'most of the time' (τὰ πολλά) within the community. This could mean 'most of her life', but also 'most of her time', as if she had a part-time arrangement. Vetiana—like Gregory of Nazianzus—may have visited Annesi for extended periods while keeping a residence in the capital. Cf. Gr. Nyss. *VSM* 28. 7–8; other passages where τὰ πολλά means 'often, most of the time' include *VSM* 3. 2 and 8, and 31. 18.

[59] Gr. Nyss. *VSM* 29. 2; the origin and development of the title 'deaconess' will be discussed below, pp. 170 ff.

[60] Consolino, 'Modelli di comportamento e modi di santificazione per l'aristocrazia femminile d'Occidente', 273–306.

Macrina's community the women chose a new way of life; no longer widows, wives, and mothers they were now 'virgins'. The designation *parthenos* conferred a new social status that transcended not only the mere physical condition of intactness, but also the notions of biological function and predetermination as expressed by childbearing and motherhood.

Sheer numerical expansion of the household during its transformation into an ascetic community required some form of internal organization. Macrina, the founder, guided the community and was recognized as ἡ καθηγουμένη, the leader.[61] What precise functions did this position entail? One aspect of Macrina's position is encapsulated in her characterization as 'mother', 'father', *paidagogos*, and *didaskalos*.[62] She was the sole and final authority in all matters. The nature of this authority is best illustrated in chapter 26 of the *Life*. When Macrina was dying all the virgins made almost superhuman efforts to contain their grief and sorrow, to maintain silence. Though their souls were tormented as if by fire, they still fought, at times in vain, to suppress their laments. They knew that any display of emotion would displease Macrina, 'causing their teacher (ἡ διδάσκαλος) distress'. But after she had died, all restraint was abandoned. The virgins gave free rein to their sorrow, knowing what they had lost:

the light of our eyes is extinguished, the lamp guiding the path of our souls is gone; the safety of our lives has been destroyed; the seal of our incorruptibility has been removed; the bond of our union demolished; the support of the feeble has been shattered; the care of the weak has been taken away.

---

[61] Gr. Nyss. *VSM* 16. 10; cf. LSJ, s.vv. καθηγεμών and καθηγέομαι; e.g. Philodemus Philosophus, *Volumina rhetorica* B 23. 23–4 (ed. S. Sudhaus (Leipzig, 1892), 49). The term's clear connotations of leadership facilitated its rapid development into a *terminus technicus* for leadership of a religious community. Gregory's use here is an important step in that direction. At the end of the 4th cent. the term is still only rarely used in the sense of leading a religious community. The first writer to use it in that sense is Athanasius in his *Vita S. Antonii* 54 (PG 26. 921 B); it also appears in Bas. *Sermo asceticus* 1. 5, 2. 2 (PG 31. 877 D, 888 B); cf. Lampe, s.v. καθηγέομαι (4 b); Maraval, *Macrine*, 195 n. 5; Martimort, *Les Diaconesses*, 133–7.

[62] Gr. Nyss. *VSM* 10. 5–6, 20–1; 11. 5–8; 26. 9; 28. 5–7; *Ep.* 19. 7 (*GN* viii.2, 64).

Despite such admirable qualities Macrina did not preside in splendid isolation. As chapter 27 suggests, she had gathered an inner core of special friends around her, 'those from whom she had always voluntarily accepted help throughout her life'. Among these close friends were Vetiana and Lampadion, who appear to have been in charge of specific tasks.[63] Lampadion, for example, 'presided over the χορός of virgins'.[64] This *choros* could, indeed, have been simply a choir, but it is likely that it had more than a ceremonial function: the term is used regularly to describe the community as a whole (which may of course also have sung together as a choir). As leader of the *choros* of virgins, Lampadion could best be depicted as Macrina's proxy, a role which explains her involvement in the arrangements following Macrina's death and funeral; her title of 'deaconess' corresponds to the importance of such a position.[65]

The young girls adopted in 368/9 formed another distinct group. The very fact that they were younger and in need of education implies that they were treated differently from older members, although it is impossible to reconstruct the precise nature of this treatment.[66] As Gregory's use of the term both in the *Life* and elsewhere attests, all members together constituted the χορὸς τῶν παρθένων.[67]

The *choros* inhabited the family's mansion (*proasteion*), which was spacious enough to accommodate a substantial number of people.[68] It was situated 'on the other side of the river' from

[63] Gr. Nyss. *VSM* 28–9.

[64] Ibid. 29. 1–2; J. Quasten, *Musik und Gesang in den Kulten der heidnischen Antike und christlichen Frühzeit* (Münster, 1930), 229; Maraval, *Macrine*, 236 n. 1.

[65] The discussion of Lampadion's role will be resumed in greater detail in the context of 'deaconesses' (see below, pp. 177–8).

[66] Gr. Nyss. *VSM* 26. 29–34.

[67] The same expression used in: Gr. Nyss. *VSM* 16. 5; 33. 15; id. *Ep.* 19. 7 (*GN* viii.2, 64); id. *De virg.* 4. 2. 7, 23. 6. 11 (SC 119. 306, 544); id. *De instituto Christiano* (*GN* viii.1, 41).

[68] Gr. Nyss. *Hom. in Eccles.* 3 (PG 44. 653–6); Bas. *Hom. in div.* 2 (PG 31. 284 f.); when visiting Macrina, Gregory is guided into the house; at another point he refers to a vestibule or *proaulion* (*VSM* 16. 11; 33. 5); Maraval (*Macrine*, 248 n. 2) points to the use of *proaulion* to describe the vestibule of a church; cf. J. Kollwitz, 'Bestattung', in *RAC* ii. 194–219, here 211; A. C. Rush, *Death and Burial in Christian Antiquity* (Catholic University of America Studies in Christian Antiquity 1; Washington, 1941), 160, 171 f; Treucker, *Politische und sozialgeschichtliche Studien*, 12; Teja, *Organización*, 84–6.

Annesi, a village which was owned exclusively by Macrina's family until long after her death.[69] Gregory also describes the community's dwelling as the παρθενών and γυναικωνῖτις, or φροντιστήριον, and, in a very general fashion, as the ἐσχατιά.[70] This choice of terms, oscillating between the 'gender-neutral' *phrontistērion* and 'solitude' on the one hand and the 'women's quarters' on the other, could suggest another development.

Initially at least, Macrina's younger brother Peter remained in his mother's house as a member of the family. And almost certainly, though this is never explicitly stated, the household also included male as well as female servants. Peter continued to live at Annesi until well past the time when Macrina and, afterwards, Emmelia decided to adopt an ascetic life, for, in 356/7, when Naucratius died and Basil moved to Annesi, he was still a boy, somewhere between 12 and 17 years old. His biography for the ensuing years is somewhat sketchy, but we know that he had been ordained as a priest and was elected bishop of Sebaste in 380.[71] Until then Peter remained at Annesi. In other words, Gregory's usage of the gender-neutral terms

[69] Bas. *Epp.* 3. 2, 223. 5 (Courtonne rejects this part of *Ep.* 223); Gr. Nyss. *In quad. mart.* (PG 46. 784); Maraval, *Macrine*, 41–4.

[70] The last two terms were also used by Gregory of Nazianzus to describe Basil's refuge. Gr. Nyss. *VSM* 12. 32; 15. 23; 33. 21; 34. 16; 37. 2, 12, 15, 30; one possible source for Gregory of Nazianzus' use of the term *phrontistērion* in an ascetic context is Philostratus, *Vita Apollonii*, 3. 50 (*Philostratus: The Life of Apollonius of Tyana*, i. ed. F. C. Conybeare (Loeb; London, repr. 1989), 334); LSJ, s.v. *Gynaikonitis* traditionally denotes the women's quarters of a house. From the beginning of the 5th cent. it takes on the technical meaning of 'convent', as well as denoting the section of the church reserved for women. Lampe (s.v.) lists Theodoret, *Historia Religiosa* 9. 12. 4 (*Théodoret de Cyr: Histoire des Moines de Syrie*, i. ed. P. Canivet and A. Leroy-Molinghen (SC 234; Paris, 1977), 428), a later work, as the first use of the term to mean 'convent' which places *VSM* 37. 30 among the first occurrences. The term *parthenōn*, originally the area of the house inhabited by young girls, is used as early as the middle of the 4th cent. to denote a community of women leading an ascetic life. Athanasius' use at *V. Ant.* 3 (PG 26. 844 A) is the best known example, but, as demonstrated by G. Garritte ('Un couvent de femmes au IIIᵉ siècle? Note sur un passage de la Vie grecque de saint Antoine', in *Scrinium Lovaniense: Mélanges historiques E. van Cauwenberg* (Louvain, 1961), 150–9, here 157 f.), it is based on a corrupt reading, see below, p. 227 n. 2; Gr. Naz. *In laud. Bas.* 62 (Boulenger, 186); Epiph. *Haer.* 58. 3, 5 (2 GCS 31. 361); Lampe, s.v. παρθενών.

[71] P. Devos, 'S. Pierre Iᵉʳ évêque de Sébastée dans une lettre de s. Grégoire de Nazianze', *AnBoll* 79 (1961), 346–60, here 347–56, 359 f.; Maraval, *Macrine*, 182 n. 1.

could well reflect a historic reality: far from being an exclusively female community throughout, Macrina's ascetic household included, at least in its initial stages, men as well as women.

In chapters 36–8 of the *VSM*, in the context of a miracle performed by Macrina, Gregory informs us that at one point prior to 380 the commander or *hēgemōn* of the local garrison at Sebastopolis, a close friend and relative of the family, visited Macrina's *phrontistērion*. He was accompanied by his wife and little daughter, who suffered from an infectious eye disease. 'Once we entered this holy place, we separated, my wife and I . . . for I went to the men's quarters where your brother Peter was superior, and she went to the *parthenōn* to be with the holy one.'[72] Quite clearly, then, two distinct communities had been formed: one for women under the exclusive guidance of Macrina, the other for men under the supervision of Peter.[73] At some point during the years between 357 and 380 the sexes had been segregated.

The decision to join Macrina's community was, in each case, personal. No public ceremony, vow, or proclamation is mentioned. Acceptance seems to have been based solely on Macrina's consent. Yet the decision to become a virgin was clearly marked by a new external appearance. Macrina, Emmelia, and consequently all virgins wore a distinctive dress, consisting of 'a coat, a veil, and shoes', the coat being 'of sombre colour'.[74] In close adherence to Matt. 10: 9–10 Macrina owned only one set of these clothes; they continued to emphasize her femininity, however, as well as her status as a 'virgin widow'.[75] Only on her death-bed, once she had (presumably) risen to the everlasting kingdom of heaven, was Macrina clad in a white robe; only then did she wear the robes of the virginal bride awaiting the heavenly spouse.[76]

---

[72] Gr. Nyss. *VSM* 37. 8–13.

[73] *VSM* 37 suggests that the male and female communities were very close to one another; *eschatia* should be interpreted metaphorically rather than as a precise geographical statement.

[74] ἰδοὺ τὸ ἱμάτιον, ἰδοὺ τῆς κεφαλῆς ἡ καλύπτρα, τὰ τετριμμένα τῶν ποδῶν ὑποδήματα (*VSM* 29. 15–16); cf. the description of Emmelia's coat in *VSM* 32. 5.

[75] See Franchi de' Cavalieri, *Martyrium S. Theodoti*, 13, 69.

[76] Gr. Nyss. *VSM* 30; 32. 3.

Garments constitute clear symbols expressing the virgins' understanding of themselves. Simplicity represents a single, fundamental aspect: personal poverty. The concept of personal poverty, despite *de facto* wealth, is further accentuated by manual labour, consisting primarily of textile work and the preparation of food. These tasks serve as a reminder of humility, which requires obedience, and this is ensured in turn by the fact that all members serve each other. In close imitation of Matt. 20: 27 Macrina is portrayed throughout the *Life* as a servant. She personally serves not only her mother, but also her youngest brother and the members of her community who in turn serve her.[77] Similar emphasis upon service is also fundamental to an understanding of Naucratius' ascetic practice.[78]

Enkrateia, control of the physical and emotional self to the point where one remains untouched by 'worldly' passions and concerns, is the true aim, achieved through continence and fasting. However, even self-control and all the other disciplines practised so meticulously—poverty, humility, obedience, manual labour, and mutual service—are nothing but tools (πάρεργα). They are merely preparatory, heightening the virgin's readiness to concentrate on her genuine occupation: constant prayer and uninterrupted contemplation of the Divine by day and night.[79]

Compared to the daily routine developed by Macrina during the earliest years of her ascetic life, the basics of the ascetic regimen have not changed. Yet Macrina was no longer the sole member of an otherwise ordinary household who adhered to a specific *horarium*. Now, many virgins worked together, served each other, and prayed together. Differences in age and social background had to be bridged, those who were well-born (εὐγενής) had to be persuaded not to take advantage of their status, while those who came from inferior (δυσγενής) backgrounds had at all times to be treated as true equals. Although the increase in numbers alone must have resulted in more elaborate organizational measures, it was not Gregory's concern to present a detailed account of the inner workings of Macrina's community. We can only expect to find occasional insights into

[77] Ibid. 5. 23–35; 27. 13–15.
[78] Ibid 8. 22–34.
[79] Ibid 11. 27–33; 1 Thess. 5: 17.

day-to-day arrangements or the changes that presumably occurred as the community matured.

Chapter 16, for example, speaks of a church in the village, attended regularly by the members of Macrina's community; evening prayer included specific hymns chanted by a choir; and a rudimentary Eucharist was celebrated at Macrina's sick-bed.[80] The spiritual life within the community became more institutionalized, and in the process more directly interwoven with the already existing structures of the local church. As noted earlier, the local priest was the trustee or *oikonomos* of Macrina's fortune; at least two members of the ascetic communities were clerics, Basil and Peter. Although Macrina was supreme in all matters within her community, spiritual direction seems to have been the prerogative of the official clergy. They in turn fully sanctioned Macrina's ascetic experiment: the local bishop Araxios and his entire clergy attended Macrina's funeral; he himself together with Gregory and two clerics 'of elevated rank' carried her bier.[81]

The transformation of Macrina's immediate family into an ascetic community proceeded in successive stages, which can be viewed as the gradual dissolution of the traditional family structure and its reconstitution on a spiritual basis: personal poverty; the manumission of slaves and their treatment as equals; the widening of the inner circle to include those slaves; and finally, the reception of members without any relationship to the original household into the newly created ascetic community, which now, interestingly, reflected the social composition of society at large, with the majority of its members from a low stratum of society, and the leaders, including Macrina herself, from the highest.[82] All these stages further reflect an increasing rupture with the norms and traditions of Macrina's social background, although never carried to an extreme. The requirement of poverty, for example, was not absolute; personal poverty never led to poverty of the

[80] Gr. Nyss. *VSM* 16. 5; 22. 3–4; 11. 29–32; 25.

[81] Ibid. 33. 22–34. 6; presumably Araxios was bishop of Ibora; see Gr. Nyss. *In quad. mart.* (PG 46. 784 B).

[82] Gr. Nyss. *VSM* 21. 7–9; the interest in Macrina's community displayed by members of the upper class (e.g. the *hēgemōn* mentioned earlier) confirms that her experiment found widespread approval.

community as such, which was alway able to support itself and others through extensive charity.[83]

Each stage was accompanied by a modification and increasing complexity of Macrina's role. Her first explicit expression of her desire to live ἐφ' ἑαυτῆς (albeit as the constant companion of her mother) resulted in her request to be considered a virgin widow; each subsequent stage in her ascetic development was likewise symbolized by an increasingly intricate combination of essentially incompatible, indeed paradoxical, notions. Upon the death of her father and posthumous birth of her brother Peter, Macrina is represented as her brother's mother, her own mother's equal, but further as Peter's teacher, educator, and counsellor.[84] The virgin widow assumed not only the role of a mother, the person representing authority within the household, but also quintessentially male roles which conveyed the notion of public authority both on a practical as well as an intellectual level.

While Macrina fulfilled these functions initially only privately (for her youngest brother), her responsibilities gradually increased. At the crucial time of Naucratius' death she became her own mother's teacher and guide, thus reversing the original hierarchy. At that point Gregory portrays her in traditional male terminology. She displays courage, that is 'manliness' (ἀνδρεία), steadfastness, and self-control: all characteristics of the Stoic philosopher, the truly wise man. Macrina is no longer only female, but her character is further enhanced by maleness, she becomes a 'manly woman' or γυνὴ ἀνδρεία. Yet all of these changes occur internally, on a purely spiritual and intellectual level. Macrina's outward appearance remains female. It is only her soul that, as her asceticism progresses, adopts the qualities of a sage, an exemplary man. In their capacity as ascetics, both Macrina and her mother Emmelia are then also represented as athletes, fighters who compete victoriously in the race towards the eternal life.

---

[83] The aforementioned famine attracted crowds of the hungry, transforming Annesi into a town; see Gr. Nyss. *VSM* 12. 30–4. Four possible sources of the community's income come to mind: revenues from Emmelia's property; inheritances from other family members, e.g. Naucratius; donations made by wealthy members such as Vetiana; and last but not least the fruits of manual labour.

[84] Gr. Nyss. *VSM* 12. 12–15.

The radius of this highly complex array of functions and roles expanded along with Macrina's community and assumed an increasingly public quality. She is progressively portrayed as the mother, father, teacher, and guide of all members of her community. As her ascetic strength and thus her 'manliness' grow, she becomes a healer and wonderworker for outsiders too, such as the army commander and his wife. Towards the end of her life, at the peak of her ascetic perfection, Macrina's complex roles and functions also reach their zenith: she has become the virginal bride of the heavenly groom, a virgin widow, a virgin mother, a *didaskalos* and *paidagogos*, an athlete, leader, healer.

Thus in the *Life of Macrina* Gregory, and presumably Macrina herself, created a new, composite role. This role not only combined and transformed traditionally female roles in unconventional ways, but also incorporated aspects of traditionally male ones, thereby according her both private and public functions, simply by merging female and male roles. Macrina, through asceticism, became a *gynē andreia*, a 'man and a woman', a new kind of human being who combined in herself all that was most female with all that was quintessentially male. Gregory created in her an *exemplum* for a complete human being through the creation of a new female image: that of the ascetic, the 'virgin of God', in short, that of a true saint, who, on her way to God, had progressed beyond male and female.[85]

THE RELATIONSHIP BETWEEN MACRINA AND BASIL

The developments thus far described did not occur in isolation. At the same time, and in close geographic proximity, Macrina's brother Basil articulated his concepts concerning both the spiritual and practical foundations of ascetic life. It is reasonable to suggest that Basil and Macrina developed their ideas in continuous exchanges, although we do not possess a single source by her alone.[86]

[85] See the fundamental study by Giannarelli, *La tipologia femminile*, 9–28, and esp. 16 f., for the Aristotelian origins of the notion; C. Walker Bynum, ' ". . . And Woman His Humanity": Female Imagery in the Religious Writing of the Later Middle Ages', in C. Walker Bynum, S. Harrell, and P. Richman (eds.), *Gender and Religion: On the Complexity of Symbols* (Boston, 1986), 257–88.

[86] Maraval, *Macrine*, 272 f.

One obvious point for comparison is the attitude of Basil and Macrina towards slaves. Like Macrina, Basil accepted slaves as members of his community, but only after he had received official authorization from their masters, presumably after manumission (*RF* 11). However, unlike Macrina, and unlike his younger brother Gregory of Nyssa and his friend Gregory of Nazianzus, Basil never questioned the institution of slavery as such.[87] He argued, on the contrary, that slavery reflects the God-given order of mankind; a slave obediently carrying his burden had thus a greater opportunity to reach perfection than one who rebelliously attempted to change his place, even if he wanted to embrace the ascetic life.[88] Basil, therefore, assumed a moderate stance, which reconciled the more radical position taken up by Macrina and Naucratius with a more conservative attitude. Such a tendency towards compromise and moderation is consistent with other aspects of Basil's ascetic organization. He promoted life in a stable and settled community, consisting of members of one sex only, with an attitude towards work and communal property very similar to that in Macrina's community. Basil consistently emphasized the value of marriage; prospective members who were married had to have their spouse's prior consent. All these aspects underline the same search for a model that combined the demands of an ascetic life 'outside the world' with the acceptance of the world's continued existence along with *its* inevitable demands.

Basil fashioned an ascetic role for women by following the same pattern. He never questioned their capacity to lead an ascetic life, or their prospect of achieving salvation. Women

[87] The two Gregorys denounced the institution of slavery, describing it as unnatural and a tyranny, but in practice neither one maintained their own laudable standards, for both owned slaves; see Gr. Naz. *De pauperum amore* (*Or.* 14), 25–6 (PG 35. 892); id. *De se ipso*, 69–82 (PG 37. 975 f.); Gr. Nyss. *Hom. in Eccles.* 4 (PG 44. 664 f.); id. *VSM* 30. 3–4; Gregory of Nazianzus did grant liberty to his slaves in his will (PG 37. 392); concerning Gregory of Nyssa and Basil see Teja, 'San Basilio y la esclavitud', 397–9; Westermann, *Slave Systems*, 160.

[88] Some of Basil's passing remarks on the subject of slaves reveal a surprising amount of the customary contempt felt by rich owners towards their servants. In this respect Basil is very much a man of his times. See Bas. *Homilia in Psalmum XXXII*, 5 (PG 29. 336); id. *De Spiritu Sancto*, 20 (SC 17*bis*. 204); Hadjinicolaou-Marava, *Recherches sur la vie des esclaves*, 15 f.; Karayannopoulos, 'St. Basil's Social Activity', 358 f.; Teja, 'San Basilio y la esclavitud', 393–403.

had the same potential for an ascetic life as men, but their sex precluded them from exercising any 'spiritual guidance', for the Gospel had excluded them from teaching and, by implication, from ordination and thus the administration of sacraments. Even so, the sisters in a Basilian *koinōnion* enjoyed a high degree of autonomy which was firmly rooted in the *Rules*. This aspect could well attest to the influence of Macrina, who was after all 27 or 28 years of age by the time Basil moved to Annesi, and could draw on fifteen years of ascetic experimentation.

It has, of course, been suggested that Basil's rules regarding women were intended for Macrina's community, demonstrating once more Basil's influence as an ascetic teacher. Macrina is viewed by some as merely a component of Basil's monastic programme, which consisted of a double monastery under Basil's guidance, with his sister as an aide.[89] Nothing in Basil's writings suggests such an interpretation.[90] Indeed, because of her significantly earlier experience and her uninterrupted presence, Macrina may well have been the dominant figure at Annesi; her share in developing what is known as Basilian monasticism ought not to be underrated. However, Macrina and her ascetic household were not the only possible models for Basil's fledgling ascetic system. The fate of his younger brother Naucratius was no less decisive.[91]

Basil's early ascetic initiatives were a virtual 'action-replay' of those undertaken by Naucratius. Like Naucratius, Basil abandoned a promising career as a rhetor to retire into solitude, devoting himself to a 'philosophical life' consisting of manual labour, service to others, and obedience to the demands of the

---

[89] Bonis, 'Basilios von Caesarea und die Organisation der christlichen Kirche im vierten Jahrhundert', in Fedwick, *Basil of Caesarea*, i. 292 f., 297.

[90] If anything, Basil seems to have considered Macrina's community as model; even down to details such as the singing of psalms; Bas. *RB* 281 (PG 31. 1230); *Ep.* 207.

[91] Graffiti in the surroundings of Ibora suggest a continuous presence of solitary ascetics, male and female; see J. G. Anderson, F. Cumont, and H. Grégoire (eds.), *Recueil des inscriptions grecques et latines du Pont et de l'Arménie* (Studia Pontica 3; Brussels, 1910), 254 f. no. 278, esp. 278d; no. 134 (ibid. p. 146), found near Amasia in Pontus and dating from the 5th or 6th cent. AD, mentions a Μα[ρ]ίας ἀσκ[η]τρίας στυλίτισας: a female stylite in other words, which in itself is an exciting find and worthy of further investigation.

Scriptures.[92] But even Naucratius had not been entirely alone, not the first to settle in this remote spot; others, 'old men', had preceded him there, and Basil likewise had immediately a number of companions in this 'philosophical life' apart from the world. Another observation is of interest. Naucratius had experienced his conversion while still living in the city, presumably in Neocaesarea. There he first came into contact with the concepts that induced him to change his life. Indeed, we have read above of men in cities, in this case Caesarea, who 'have separated themselves from the world and consecrated themselves to God', the Nazarites.[93] In other words, the notion of a 'philosophical life' apart from this world was already circulating in several cities in Asia Minor, and had already taken its effect by the time Basil returned to his native country.

At least one potential source for these notions has been mentioned on several occasions: the elusive Eustathius, the philosopher whose fame had already reached Basil in Athens and had motivated him to undertake the strenuous journey to Egypt.

[92] Gr. Nyss. *VSM* 8. 8–20, 22–34; 9. 1–5; Gr. Naz. Epigr. 156–8 (*Anth. graeca* ii. 526).
[93] Gr. Naz. *In laud. Bas.* 28 (Boulenger, 120).

4

Homoiousian Asceticism

In the year 340 or 341 thirteen bishops under the leadership of one Eusebius decided to meet in Gangra, the metropolis of the province of Paphlagonia, 'on account of certain necessities of the Church, and for the investigation of the affair of Eustathius; and having found that many improprieties had been committed by the Eustathians, [they] therefore sought to remove the evils occasioned by him, Eustathius.'[1] These improprieties were of such a magnitude that they raised concerns far beyond the boundaries of Paphlagonia itself. The bishop presiding at Gangra, Eusebius, was at the time bishop of Constantinople,[2] and the assembled Fathers not only issued twenty canons, but also sent a warning letter to their colleagues in the neighbouring province of Armenia.

Who was this Eustathius? He was born sometime before 300, the son of Eulalius, bishop of Sebaste in Armenia. At approximately the age of 25, Eustathius left his home town after a conflict with his father; Eulalius had subjected him to public penance because 'he was not wearing a habit becoming to a

---

[1] Cf. Mansi, ii. 1106f.; H.T. Bruns, *Bibliotheca ecclesiastica*, i (Berlin, 1839), 106; Hefele–Leclercq, i.2, 1029–45, here 1031; the episcopal sees of the participants are not mentioned, which makes their identification virtually impossible; Dagron, 'Les Moines et la ville', 249f.; J. Gribomont, 'Le Monachisme au IVe siècle en Asie Mineure: De Gangres au Messalianisme', *SP* 2 (TU 64; Berlin, 1957), 400–15, here 401; id. 'Saint Basile et le monachisme enthousiaste', *Irénikon* 53 (1980) 123–44, here 129; W. D. Hauschild, 'Eustathius', in *TRE* x (Berlin, 1982), 547–50; for the date of the council cf. Fedwick, 'A Chronology', 4 n. 14, 14 n. 81; other possible dates are the 360s or 380s.

[2] The identification of Eusebius with the well-known bishop of Nicomedia and then Constantinople depends, of course, on the accepted dating of the synod. Those supporting a later date assume the bishop in question to have been Basil of Caesarea's predecessor, Eusebius, bishop 362–70; Hefele–Leclercq, i.2, 1029 n. 1.

priest'.[3] Eustathius then sought to become a member of the clergy in Antioch, but the local bishop did not accept him. His whereabouts until 330 are not known with certainty, though Athanasius' *Historia Arianorum* tells us (no doubt polemically so) that he spent these years in Alexandria as a disciple of Arius.[4] After 330 Eustathius became a member of the clergy at Caesarea in Cappadocia; he left Caesarea again sometime before 338 to serve under our Eusebius in Constantinople, only to return virtually within the year to Armenia and Pontus. Here, around 339, he was officially condemned for the first time by a synod in Neocaesarea—in the same year in which Macrina, also in Neocaesarea, decided to become a 'virgin widow'. Then, in 340 or 341 he was condemned for a second time at Gangra.

Eustathius was a controversial figure. Repeated turning points in his life as sketched so far reflect constant tensions resulting in migrations from one congregation to another, and are exemplified by the public rupture with his own father. Yet he also had a sizeable number of supporters and admirers, as demonstrated by his renewed clerical appointments. What caused such diametrically opposed reactions? The Church historian Sozomen probably provides the answer: 'It is said that Eustathius, who governed the church of Sebaste in Armenia, founded a society of monks in Armenia, Paphlagonia, and Pontus, and became the author of a monastic philosophy'[5]—a 'philosophy' that appears to have been at the root of his frequent conflicts with other authorities in the Church.

We do not possess an account of this philosophy or 'discipline', or of its consequences, in Eustathius' own words. Any reconstruction of his convictions has to be unravelled from other sources, mainly a few allusions in Basil of Caesarea's later writings, and

---

[3] Soc. *HE* 2. 43 (PG 67. 352).

[4] Ath. *Historia Arianorum*, 4. 2 (PG 25. 697); Bas. *Epp.* 263. 3, 244. 9; G. Blond, 'Hérésie éncratite vers la fin du IVe siécle', *RSR* 32 (1944), 157–210, here 159; Gribomont, 'Le Monachisme', 400 n. 1; Hauschild, 'Eustathius', 547; id. *Die Pneumatomachen: Eine Untersuchung zur Dogmengeschichte des vierten Jahrhunderts*, Diss. (Hamburg, 1967), 217 f.; F. Loofs, *Eustathius von Sebaste und die Chronologie der Basilius-Briefe* (Halle, 1898), 54–6, 79.

[5] Ἀρμενίοις δὲ καὶ Παφλαγόσι καὶ τοῖς πρὸς τῷ Πόντῳ οἰκοῦσι λέγεται Εὐστάθιος ὁ τὴν ἐν Σεβαστείᾳ τῆς Ἀρμενίας ἐκκλησίαν ἐπιτροπεύσας μοναχικῆς φιλοσοφίας ἄρξαι; Sozomen, *Historia Ecclesiastica*, 3. 14, 31 (*Sozomenus: Kirchengeschichte*, ed. J. Bidez (GCS 50; Berlin, 1960) 123).

the twenty canons issued by the Fathers at Gangra, who hardly strove to represent an historically accurate, unbiased picture.[6]

Their letter to the Armenian bishops summarizes the improprieties committed by Eustathius and his supporters:

As the Eustathians condemn marriage, and maintain that no married person has hope with God, they have dissolved many marriages; and as those separated lacked the gift of continence, they have given occasion to adultery. They caused many to forsake the public assemblies for divine services, and to organize private conventicles. They despise the ordinary dress, and introduce a new dress. The first-fruits which are given to the Church they claim for themselves as being *par excellence* the saints. Slaves run away from their masters and despise them, presuming upon their new dress. Women now assume men's clothes, and think themselves thereby justified; nay, many shave their heads under the pretext of piety. They fast on Sundays, but eat on the fast-days of the Church. Some forbid all animal food. . . . They despise married priests and do not take part in their worship. They despise the services in honour of the martyrs, as well as those who join in them. They maintain that the rich who do not forsake all have no hope of being saved.

Of the many issues raised by this first summary, it is striking that Eustathius' teachings addressed two groups in particular— women and slaves—and encouraged them to change their present condition on the basis of 'the dress'. Accordingly, three of the twenty canons deal explicitly with women.[7] Canon 14 reads: 'If a woman leaves her husband, despising marriage to practise anachoresis, she will be anathematized'; canon 13: 'If under the pretence of asceticism a woman changes her clothes and, instead of wearing female ones as she should, wears male clothes, she will be anathematized'; and canon 17: 'If under the pretence of asceticism, women cut off their hair, which God has given them to remind them of their subordination, in order to defy that subordination, they will be anathematized.'

Prima facie, Eustathius taught women to abandon their husbands, wear men's clothes, and cut their hair short, behaviour which even by itself could give rise to amazement, but which becomes even more bizarre when justified by what the Fathers describe as 'the pretence of asceticism'.

[6] Gribomont, 'Le Monachisme', 400–3; Dagron, 'Les Moines et la ville', 247; T. Kopecek, *A History of Neo-Arianism*, ii (Patristic Monograph Series 8; Philadelphia, 1979), 299–303.

[7] Hefele–Leclercq, i.2, 1031 f., 1038 f., 1040.

Paul's First Letter to the Corinthians contains a passage which anticipates the wording of canon 17:

Every woman praying or prophesying with her head uncovered disgraces her head, for it is the same as if it were shaven. But if it is a disgrace for a woman to have her hair cut off or her head shaved, therefore let her cover her head. A man indeed ought not to cover his head, because he is the image and glory of God. But woman is the glory of man. This is why the woman ought to have a sign of authority over her head, because of the angels. . . . (1 Cor. 11: 5–16).

Long hair is a God-given symbol of woman's subordination to man, and the acknowledgement that she is not God's image. If then a woman shaves her head, she not only denies this subordination, but she assumes a position as man's equal, and may further express this by wearing a man's dress.[8] If she has thus become—at least externally—a man, she ought to be, like a man, God's image and glory. It appears that the women who followed Eustathius did not simply cast aside their female clothes and exchange them for male attire, but assumed an entirely new role.[9] The factor instrumental in this transformation was evidently

---

[8] A practice already banned in the Old Testament, Deut 5: 22; cf. also Bas. Anc. *De virg.* 34 (PG 30. 737); 1 Cor. 11: 10; J. Hurley, 'Did Paul Require Veils or the Silence of Women? A Consideration of 1 Cor 11: 2–16 and 1 Cor 14: 33b–36', *Westminster Theological Journal* 35 (1973), 190–220; B. Kötting ('Haar', in *RAC* xiii. 175–203, here 195) points to the prostitutes' habit of cutting their hair short (without sources); he also suggests (p. 199) that swearing the vow of virginity required tonsure; I have found no evidence in support of this, apart from his quotation of Jerome.

[9] Cf. also the Gospel of Thomas, 114 (E. Hennecke and F. Schneemelcher (eds.), *Neutestamentliche Apokryphen*, i (Tübingen, 1959³), 216): 'Simon Peter said to them, "Let Mary depart from us for women are not worthy of life." Jesus said, "Behold, I shall guide her myself in order to make her male so that she herself may become a living spirit ($\pi\nu\epsilon\tilde{\nu}\mu\alpha$) like you males, for every woman who makes herself male shall enter the kingdom of the heavens"'; Clem. Alex. *Strom.* 3. 6. 45, 13. 92 (GCS 52 (15), 217, 238); Anson, 'The Female Transvestite in Early Monasticism', 1–32; R. A. Baer, *Philo's Use of the Categories Male and Female* (Arbeiten zur Literatur und Geschichte des hellenistischen Judentums 3; Leiden, 1970), 45–55, and *passim*; E. Bellini, 'La posizione dei monachi e dei vergini nella Chiesa secondo Gregorio Nazianzeno', *Scuola Cattolica* 99 (1971), 452–66, here 455; A. Cameron, 'Neither Male nor Female', *GR* 27 (1980), 60–7; Giannarelli, *La tipologia femminile*, 13–25, 86–88; on the development of the notion 'religious transvestite' see Patlagean, 'L'Histoire de la femme déguisée', 597–623.

'the pretence of *askēsis*', which in turn seems to be intrinsically linked to the dress in question.

In canon 12 the Fathers anathematize men who, again under the pretext of *askēsis*, wore a so-called *peribolaion*, and felt by this mere fact justified to despise all others who wore ordinary clothes. It will be remembered that Eustathius' dress had been a point of contention. His own father had imposed a public penance for 'not wearing a habit becoming to a priest', and his condemnation and excommunication at Neocaesarea were also linked to the way he dressed.[10] The garment in question could only have been the περιβόλαιον, a wide, simple overcoat usually worn by philosophers as a token of their disdain for mundane vanities. Indeed, Socrates reports in his *Historia Ecclesiastica* that Eustathius adopted 'a philosopher's dress'[11] as an external expression of his convictions.

These convictions—according to the Fathers at Gangra—included the rejection of property ownership, especially by the Church; the refusal to pay a 'church tax'; rejection of certain liturgical practices; disdain for married clergy; annulment of traditional marriage; and, finally, equality of slaves and women on a par with men, perhaps the most important feature:[12] 'to practise *anachōrēsis*' constitutes the basis and justification for these teachings. The Greek term ἀναχορέω, 'to withdraw', expresses the abdication of all responsibilities connected with the world, and the binding of oneself by a new and overwhelming obligation towards *askēsis*.[13]

Judging from the canons issued at Gangra, Eustathius' followers, men and women, were condemned because they had severed all ties with their natural families, questioned the legitimacy of the clergy, and disregarded distinctions considered fundamental by

[10] Gribomont, 'Le Monachisme', 403; Hauschild, 'Eustathius', 548 f.; Loofs, *Eustathius und die Chronologie*, 1–3, 54.

[11] φιλοσόφου σχῆμα φορῶν, Soc. *HE* 2. 43 (PG 67. 353); Bas. *Ep*. 223. 3; Tert. *De Pallio* 5. 1–5 (ed. S. Costanza (Collana di Studi Classici 3; Naples, 1968), 68–72); LSJ s.v. περιβόλαιον; Gribomont, 'Eustathe de Sebaste', 1709; P. Oppenheim, *Das Mönchskleid im christlichen Altertum* (Theologische Quartalschrift, Suppl. 28; Tübingen, 1931), 218–24; Patlagean, *Pauvreté économique*, 137 f.

[12] Canons 4, 19, 2, 8, 3; Hefele–Leclercq, i.2, 1033–41; Dagron, 'Les Moines et la ville', 251; Gribomont, 'Le Monachisme', 404–7; id. 'Le Monachisme enthousiaste', 131–5.

[13] LSJ s.vv. ἄσκησις and ἀσκέω; Lampe, s.v.

society, such as that between slaves and their masters. Men had abandoned their wives, women their husbands, and children their parents. Women had assumed the appearance of men, thus obliterating sexual distinctions and becoming 'male women': all 'under the pretence of asceticism'. These events were taking place in Asia Minor, more precisely in Neocaesarea and its environs, at just the time when Basil the Elder's children were growing up—when Macrina became a 'widow', Naucratius 'left the world', and Basil as a student in Athens was attracted to the teachings of Eustathius the Philosopher.

MACEDONIUS AND MARATHONIUS

Bishop Eusebius of Constantinople, better known by his former see of Nicomedia, died shortly after the Fathers had anathematized Eustathius' followers. His death gave rise to a fierce battle for succession to perhaps the most influential episcopal see in the Empire. The contenders were Paul, the candidate of the so-called 'Nicaean party', and Macedonius, who was supported by the 'Arians' and had been characterized by their predecessor Alexander as 'conversant with public affairs and with the council of rulers'. At some point between 344 and 350 the 'Arians' carried the day. Macedonius was officially installed as bishop after a long and at times exceedingly bloody struggle, which cost the lives of thousands, and was only settled through the intervention of the emperor Constantius II. However, in addition to the imperial support, both Socrates and Sozomen stress one other factor as instrumental in Macedonius' final success.[14]

In seizing power Macedonius found support 'among several monasteries that he had founded at Constantinople' (μοναστηρίοις πολλοῖς ἃ συνεστήσατο κατὰ τὴν Κωνσταντινούπολιν). Though founded by Macedonius, these monasteries were actually guided by a certain Marathonius whom Macedonius had ordained as deacon, 'a zealous superintendent of the hospices of the poor and the monastic dwellings inhabited by men and women' (σπουδαῖον ἐπί-

---

[14] Soz. *HE* 3. 3 (GCS 50. 104); Soc. *HE* 2. 6 (PG 67. 192). The controversies involving Paul and Macedonius date back to the death of Bishop Alexander in 337/8; the disputes concerning his succession then were also settled by imperial intervention leading to Eusebius' election. Eusebius' death in 341 led to the renewal of the conflict as discussed here. Dagron, *Naissance d'une capitale*, 419–25, 431–3.

τρόπον πτωχείων τε καὶ μοναχικῶν συνοικιῶν ἀνδρῶν τε καὶ γυναικῶν).
Socrates likewise attests that Marathonius—eventually appointed
bishop of Nicomedia—was himself 'zealous in founding monasteries of men and women' (σπουδαῖος δὲ περὶ τὸ συστήσασθαι ἀνδρῶν
τε καὶ γυναικῶν μοναστήρια).[15] Neither Sozomen nor Socrates
discuss these 'synoikia of men and women' in greater detail, but
chapter 27 of Sozomen's Book 4 contains an interesting nuance.

The lives of Macedonius and Marathonius greatly impressed
many in Constantinople, Bithynia, Thrace, and round the Hellespont. Both men displayed great 'gravity of manner' and adopted
what the later historians describe as a life similar to that of
monks. Marathonius in particular epitomized this life-style. He
had originally held a high-ranking position in the army, and
had managed to amass a sizeable fortune. Then he suddenly
abandoned the military service, becoming at first 'superintendent
of the synoikia of the sick and the poor', and shortly thereafter
adopting the 'ascetic life' (ἀσκητικὸν βίον) and founding συνοικία
μοναχῶν in Constantinople. He was inspired to do so by Eustathius
of Sebaste.[16]

Far from being the leader of a group of mere outcasts, Eustathius
of Sebaste had apparently won the admiration of both a wealthy
army officer and a contender for the bishopric of Constantinople.
Both these men adopted what is descibed as an 'ascetic life',
displayed a new seriousness in their conduct, and, at least in the
case of Marathonius, parted with their fortunes. Moreover, in
response to their new calling, Macedonius and Marathonius
founded an institution resembling a hospital as well as ascetic
communities for men and women. The support of these men and
women 'who had left the world' played a significant part in
assuring Macedonius' election as bishop of Constantinople against
his opponent Paul.

[15] Soz. *HE* 4. 2. 3, 20. 2 (GCS 50. 141, 170); Soc. *HE* 2. 38 (PG 67. 324);
Socrates and Sozomen leave no doubt that Macedonius and Marathonius had
introduced these establishments to Constantinople during the reign of Constantius
II, a date which, unlike some other attempts at predating Constantinopolitan
events, has withstood the scrutiny of modern scholarship; cf. also Soz. *HE* 4. 20,
27 (GCS 50. 169–71, 183–4); for Constantius II cf. Jones, 'Flavius Julius Constantius 8', *PLRE* i. 226; Dagron, 'Les Moines et la ville', 239, 245; id. *Naissance
d'une capitale*, 439.
[16] Presumably during the latter's stay in Constantinople before 356; Soz. *HE* 4.
27. 4 (GCS 50. 184).

BASIL OF ANCYRA

One can observe many followers of our bridegroom Christ, who have been left with bleeding wounds by their heavenly love for the contemplation of the good; and others in the Church, who cultivate other forms of virtue. Some sing the hymn of virginity, others the praise (ἐγκώμια) of torturing the body through fasting and sleeping on the bare ground; yet others write grandiose words of admiration for the magnanimity of those who abandon their entire fortune for the sake of the Lord; ... I, however, dear Letoios, my soul-mate (ὁμόψυχε) amongst the bishops, have tried my utmost to present to you ... not the praise of virginity, nor a eulogy (ἐγκώμιον) of selling one's fortune, nor a sermon about mortifying the body through fasting, but about those things which are necessary to achieve true virtue ... so that you and I together may guide all those who are governed by you ... and all those who will read this, to the true beauty of virginity.

These words introduce a treatise *On the True Integrity of Virginity to Letoios, Bishop of Melitene*, composed only a decade or two after the anonymous homily *On Virginity* discussed in Chapter 1.[17] This remarkable work—despite its apparent contemporary popularity[18]—has never to my knowledge been adequately discussed, and will therefore receive particular attention here, though by no means as much as it deserves. Basil, bishop of Ancyra between 336 and 358, is its author.[19] The rank of both sender and recipient gives an indication of the scope of the work: rather than instructing the head of a family, it is

[17] PG 30. 669–809.

[18] F. J. Leroy ('La Tradition manuscrite du "de virginitate" de Basile d'Ancyre', *OrChrP* 38 (1972), 195–208, here 197) points to the far wider distribution of the treatise than that of the ones written by Gregory of Nyssa and John Chrysostom on the same subject.

[19] Identified in 1905 by F. Cavallera ('Le "De virginitate" de Basile d'Ancyre', *RHE* 6 (1905), 5–14). The absence of a detailed discussion may be caused by the lack of a critical edition; according to the *Clavis Patrum Graecum* (1974), F. J. Leroy is in the process of preparing a new edition, which to my knowledge has not yet appeared (there exists, however, an edition of an old Slavonic version by A. Vaillant, *De Virginitate de Saint Basile (texte vieux-slave)*, (Paris, 1943)). The treatise is mentioned briefly by T. Camelot ('Les Traités "De Virginitate" au IVᵉ siècle', 290 f.) and by F. de B. Vizmanos (*Las Virgenes cristianas de la Iglesia primitiva*, 11 f.); it received further consideration by J. Ianini Cuesta ('Dieta y Virginidad: Basilio de Ancira y san Gregorio de Nisa', *Miscelánea Comillas* 14 (1950), 187–97) and M. Aubineau (*Virginité*, 137–42), in both latter cases in reference to Gregory of Nyssa's work.

designed to help a bishop, the leader of his entire congregation, to guide some selected men and women to the 'true practice of virginity'.

Basil was originally trained as a medical doctor. Large sections of his treatise, written in a somewhat clumsy style replete with rhetorical figures and frequent repetitions, bear testimony to his former profession.[20] For unlike other authors, Basil devotes much attention to the anatomical and physiological implications of a continent life, and his frankness in certain respects—for which he frequently excuses himself—may have contributed to 'une sorte de conspiration du silence, [qui] avait enveloppé ces pages. . . .'[21]

Basil's 'medical' approach to 'the beauty of virginity' leads him to begin with a discourse on the creation of the world and the nature of all beings: God created all life out of a few seeds, but he created everything in male and female form, so that all might 'grow and multiply and fill the earth' (Gen. 1: 28). The strongest and most natural urge in all beings, including of course humans, is therefore that of the male and female to 'become out of two one again'. Nature in her wisdom supported these urges in creating the female soft, 'tender, and inviting to the touch', so that she might attract, receive, and duly channel the strong, dynamic urges of the male.[22] Given these natural forces, virginity is an unnatural state and its maintenance requires unceasing efforts: nature itself has to be conquered. A virgin—the following section addresses mainly, but by no means exclusively, women—must therefore overcome all those natural instincts in herself which 'force' her to seek male attention; she must suppress and, finally, eradicate all urges towards the other sex. She may achieve both ends by carefully controlling the roots of

---

[20] Jer. *De vir. ill.* 89 (TU 14. 45): 'Basilius Ancyranus episcopus, artis medicinae, scripsit Contra Marcellum et De Virginitate librum . . .'; R. Janin, 'Basile', in *DHGE* vi. 1104–7. J. Schladebach, *Basilius von Ancyra: Eine historisch-philosophische Studie*, Diss. (Leipzig, 1898), written before Basil's identification as the author of the *De virg.*, is the only full-length treatment of Basil of Ancyra that I am aware of; I have not seen Theresa Shaw's forthcoming dissertation, Duke University.

[21] Aubineau, *Virginité*, 137 f.

[22] Bas. Anc. *De virg.* 3 (PG 30. 675).

all evil, namely her senses: taste, vision, hearing, touch, and all her bodily movements.

To facilitate the control of her senses, the virgin must pay special attention to her food. Of course, she should never fall into gluttony or γαστριμαργία. However, it is not enough to limit the quantity of food; its quality is equally important. Thus, a person 'exercising virtue', an ascetic, cannot just replace meat with an over-abundance of any other food. Most vegetables, fruit, and other dishes are beneficial, but their choice must be made with care and in accordance to the individual's physical disposition. If a person is 'hot', he or she must eat 'cold' food, and vice versa; an older, 'cold' person may even consume such 'hot' foods as wine. Bread is highly recommended: a 'dry' food, it counteracts 'wetness', the cause of all sexual desires.[23] Some ascetics, however, fall into grave errors. Out of mistaken enthusiasm they eat excessive quantities of salt with their bread; deceived by its 'pure' appearance, they are unaware that salt incites internal fires more than any other food. The golden rule is to eat so as to be always in harmony with the four elements of the universe—earth, fire, water, air—and never to be excessive by eating too little or too much. To weaken the body through excessive fasting is as mistaken as it is to indulge the body by gluttony.

The same principle applies to each of the other senses: a virgin's eye must not see images that could adversely affect her soul, she must not listen to any utterance she has not carefully examined and, most importantly, she must be careful whom and what she touches, because touch is the sense most directly linked to libidinous desires.

In short, as emphasized by traditional Greek wisdom, man was created with a logical upper and an illogical lower part, like the Centaurs, half man, half horse. The logical upper part must rule the lower, not vice versa. But—one cannot stress the point too often—such rule must be benevolent. The body is the servant of the soul; and no master would voluntarily kill his servant. Thus, no ascetic should excessively mortify his or her body. To be over-

---

[23] Cf. also A. Festugière, *Hippocrate et l'Ancienne Médécine* (Paris, 1948), pp. xx–xxvii.

concerned with the physical aspects of virginity is, indeed, to confuse its true beauty with a false image. A virgin might have the perfect virginal body, but without the perfect virginal soul it will avail nothing.[24]

Virginity allows humans to resemble God. In this lies its greatness: virginity renders the soul (though not the body) incorruptible. Physical continence and self-control are only tools to achieve the true virginity, that of the soul. A virginal soul, liberated from all desires, reflects God's incorruptible image like a clear mirror, in constant contemplation of the Scriptures. Unfortunately, many male as well as female ascetics pay mistaken attention to the name of virginity only, that is, to its physical aspects, and by neglecting true virginity, they labour all their lives in vain.

Basil therefore repeats time and again that the sole aim of controlling one's bodily desires is to achieve purity of the soul. A virgin must remain at home primarily to avoid hearing and seeing things which may disturb this purity. If she must leave the house then she may do so prudently only in the company of a female companion and at a suitable time. Virgins who 'are gadding about from house to house, who wander around the villages', cannot maintain the preconditions for true virginity, cannot be a pure sanctuary, a silent and tranquil temple of Christ.

Virginity has to be achieved steadily and quietly, not by leaps and bounds: even if one sails over vast seas and travels through distant countries, covering enormous distances in search of virginity, one can only find it inside oneself.[25] Yet concentration on the purity of the soul must not lead, as so often happens, to such a fear of the body that it is almost killed as a result of fasting and austerities. Such practices do not necessarily elevate the soul to its true beauty, because it may still be corrupted by anger (ὀργή), rage (θυμός), hypocrisy (ὑπόκρισις), and envy (ζῆλος). Peace not warfare must reign between body and soul; both must be in complete harmony and only the middle way will lead to true virtue.[26]

'Ne enim declines, inquit, ad dexteram aut ad sinistram'[27]—

---

[24] *De virg.* 5–13 (680–93).   [25] Ibid. 59 (788).

[26] Ibid. 47–8 (760–5).

[27] Μὴ ἐκκλίνῃς γὰρ, φησὶν, εἰς τὰ δεξιὰ ἢ εἰς τὰ ἀριστερά (Deut. 5:32); *De virg.* 5 (684 D).

Basil's emphasis on the middle way, on moderation, is his leitmotif. He paints marriage in the darkest colours, a form of death on earth; yet God created marriage for a beneficial reason, and married people ought to remain united, whatever their ascetic inclinations.[28] He emphatically praises the many advantages of virginity; yet he is adamant that no general law prescribes virginity for everyone, no divine commandment requires it. On the contrary, Mosaic Law sanctifies marriage, which makes virginity a state above the Law reserved for a chosen few.[29] But then he writes:

he who loves the Lord truly, . . . must not only condemn money and wealth, . . . but also disregard even the necessary food and sleep, the clothing, and all those considerations, which corrupt this world. . . . He must leave the walls of the family and the paternal home and merely pass through this transient world; given the opportunity, he must seek the swords of martyrdom, and if he spends his life dressed as is customary, he will not participate in the divine love; but he must prefer the pauper's dress and a life frowned upon by many.

It was to those, called away from the world, that the Lord said: 'Leave your land, and your family and your father's house and come into the land I will show you' (Gen. 12: 1).[30] Yet Basil also explicitly criticizes those who give away their entire fortunes. He repeatedly stresses the importance of stability as a condition for virginal life—ideally, a virgin should not even leave her house.

In chapter 39 Basil introduces another theme:

In the same way in which a young girl does not leave her father's house before she is legitimately bound to her future husband, publicly acknowledging him as her lord and master of her life, and only then steps out of her father's house bearing the name of the man, who has been selected for her; in the same way does a virgin leave her father's house, and appear in public as the bride promised to her legitimate husband under whose dominance she now belongs. All who witness this procession are indeed the witnesses of the one to whom she is now

---

[28] The discourse on the negative aspects of marriage contains many features which became topoi; cf. e.g. Gr. Nyss. *De virg.* 12. 2–14 (SC 119. 398–45); also T. H. van Eijk, 'Marriage and Virginity, Death and Immortality', in J. Fontaine and Ch. Kannengiesser (eds.), *Epektasis: Mélanges patristiques offerts au Cardinal J. Daniélou* (Beauchesne, 1972), 209–35, here 224–7, 230–5.

[29] Bas. Anc. *De virg.* 55 (778).

[30] Ibid. 25 (721 C, D).

joined, and whose promised wife she is, and for whose sake she left her paternal dwelling in a public procession.

A virgin is the earthly spouse of the heavenly bridegroom Jesus Christ, with whom she will be united in a 'mystical wedding' (τὴν μυστικὴν νυμφαγωγίαν) in heaven—a wedding in the presence of God the Father, solemnized by Christ's favourite servant, John, surrounded by angels who will chant the *epithalamium*, the wedding song.[31]

The fact that a virgin dedicated to God was already on earth a heavenly spouse was not without its consequences. As a woman 'married' to Christ, a virgin must never touch a man; never even think about another man, 'because the divine law judges our thoughts, not our deeds';[32] never consciously solicit any man's attention. She must always behave prudently and with decency. Prudence is required 'even when she is alone in her house, only in the presence of women and servant girls'; and under no circumstances must a virgin undress herself carelessly, not even when it seems that she is completely alone for a virgin is never alone.[33]

Her heavenly bridegroom watches over all her thoughts and movements, and his angels are always with her. It is because of these angels, 'because of the power over their heads', that God gave all women long hair, so that their head may never be exposed. Thus, a virgin's head and her entire body must be covered at all times (1 Cor. 11: 10).[34]

But then, in chapter 36, Basil says:

A virgin, who in her mind, movement, appearance, and dress, alone or with others, soberly (ὑγιῶς) contemplates only what pleases the Lord, may speak chastely (καθαρῶς) with the friends of the bridegroom. We do not lock her away so that we may induce her to hatred of men (μισανθρωπίαν), but that we may lead her prudently to the house-mates (οἰκείους) of the faith; the body covered from head to toe in clothing, like an image of God, so that . . . she may profit from their conversation. She must, therefore, I say, talk with the servants of the bridegroom like a true bride, . . . simple like a dove and prudent like a serpent.

---

[31] Ibid. 50 (768 and *passim*).
[32] Ibid. 61 (793 A).
[33] Ibid. 26 (728 C, D).
[34] Ibid. 27–35 (725–40).

After many insistent chapters exhorting avoidance of all contacts with men, and reiterating the argument that even the most fleeting thought of a man constitutes adultery, Basil introduces conversations 'with the servants of the bridegroom'. And in chapter 35 he warns a virgin to be exceedingly cautious while undressing in the presence of 'brothers in Christ'. Other passages mention 'servants of the Lord', and others again speak of 'house-mates', οἰκεῖοι.[35] Who are these men and what is their relationship with virgins?

When listening to the 'servants of the bridegroom' talk about their master the Lord, the virgin must be conscious of the fact that the only way a pure soul can express itself is through the body, in the same way as music is made audible only through instruments. Therefore, when listening to a voice expressing pure thoughts, the virgin must never make the mistake of loving the instrument more than the music. This is a difficult task indeed, since 'vice and virtue, as the Greeks have already said, are close neighbours' (ἀγχιθύρους γάρ φασι καὶ Ἕλληνες τὰς κακίας εἶναι ταῖς ἀρεταῖς). A virgin's greatest mistake is to confuse love for the words with that for the man who utters them; to love the servant as much or, even worse, more than the Lord himself. Unfortunately, several virgins have already succumbed to this error: totally oblivious of their true spouse, they have become the despicable brides of the Lord's servants. Worse, some have degraded themselves still more: they have become the detestable wives of what Basil calls 'strangers' (ἀλλοτρίων: probably non-Christians), a crime that deserves complete expulsion.

In short, seeing that virtue and vice are so close, a virgin must be extremely careful that her love (ἀγαπή) for a 'servant of the Lord', their familiarity and closeness, never turns into carnal lust (σαρκὸς πάθη). If a virgin lives together with a man as if in a pseudo-marriage, she commits a crime worse than a passing act of adultery: since she can never be released from her first marriage, she can never marry the man, to whom she is bound in carnal lust and perpetual sin. On his part, the man who touches the sanctuary of the Lord is worse than any adulterer. He betrays the Lord himself.[36]

---

[35] τοῦ νυμφίου φίλοις, τοῖς τοῦ νυμφίου ... ὑπηρέταις, *De virg.* 36 (740 D, 741 A).
[36] Ibid. 37 (744); and cf. above pp. 47–51.

Yet despite all these dangers a virgin must not hate the Lord's servants, she must not succumb to μισαδελφία.

This is the greatest and most magnificent aspect of virginity, that it constitutes a manifestation already here on earth of the pure seed of the resurrection and the incorruptible life. If at the resurrection no one marries and is married but all are like angels and become children of God (Matt. 22: 30), then all those who lead the virginal life are already angels during their human life, while still ensconced in their corruptible flesh . . . surrounded by constant temptations. . . . Here, the virgins must be most highly admired. They have a female body, but they repress this appearance of their body through *askēsis*, and become, through their virtue, like men, to whom they are already created equal in their soul. And while men through *askēsis* become angels instead of men, so do women, through exercise (διὰ τῆς ἀσκήσεως) of the same virtues, gain the same value as men. So, while in this present life they are equal to men in their soul only, but are hampered in achieving equality because of their female body,[37] they will gain, through virtue, full equality with these men, who have already been made into the angels of the future life. Because if they become angel-like (ἰσαγγέλους), then those who practise asceticism in this life have already succeeded in being just like angels: they have castrated the female and male desires to cohabit through virtue and live amongst men on earth with naked souls.

If the soul is free from desire towards the male or the female, then male or female, passion or desire, no longer exists. All is 'one in Christ' (Gal. 3: 28), because all such male and female aspects of the body are dead, and only the incorrupt soul is alive.[38]

Once a virgin has achieved this state of mind, once she adopts the appearance of a man, has given her voice a masculine firmness, and comports herself like a man (ἀρρενωπὸν τὸ ὄμμα, καὶ στερρὰν ποιεῖν τὴν φωνὴν . . . σώφροσι κινήμασιν ἀνδρείως[39]), then she may live with the brothers in Christ as if in a family, *oikia*, as if both were

---

[37] τῇ δὲ τοῦ θήλεος περιβολῇ πρὸς τὴν ἰσότητα χωλευούσας . . . (772 C: lit. 'they limp towards equality in their female wrapping').

[38] *De virg.* 51 (772); for later implications of these concepts cf. J. Bugge, *Virginitas: An Essay in the History of a Medieval Ideal* (Archives internationales d'histoire des idées, séries mineur 17; The Hague, 1975), 30–47, 58–110, although he over-concentrates on 'gnosis'; Frank, *Angelikos Bios*, 12–35, 98–135, 198–201; U. Ranke-Heinemann, 'Zum Ideal der *vita angelica* im frühen Mönchtum', *Geist und Leben* 29 (1956), 347–57.

[39] *De virg.* 18 (708 B).

'born from one womb'. Then she may extend hospitality towards these brothers and wash their feet. Then she may walk around and perform works of charity like feeding the poor and 'touching the bodies of the dead'.[40]

What arrangements is Basil alluding to, and how does this pertain to Eustathius, Macedonius, and Marathonius, or, indeed, to Basil of Caesarea and his ascetic system? Basil of Ancyra is addressing a fellow bishop with the intention of instructing him in the correct supervision of those within his congregation who have become 'virgins of God'. He develops his norms of correct ascetic behaviour by proceeding in a twofold way: by delineating his understanding of ideal virginity against what he has identified as deviations from that ideal. Therefore his references to the life-style of these ascetics serve primarily to illustrate either the norm or the deviation. Fasting is quintessential for physical control, but detrimental if carried to extremes. The same is true of the rejection of property. An ascetic ought to leave his or her father's house behind, but must not wander around the villages. While marriage is a deplorable state, it must not be condemned on principle. Asceticism represents the highest form of virtue but not a general commandment.

Women became 'virgins', according to Basil, in a public ceremony fashioned after the rite of a secular marriage; they *apparently* departed from their father's house. This may well have been a ritual exodus; virgins may in fact have remained at home, since in descriptions relating to their subsequent life domestics and female servants are mentioned. However, Basil of Ancyra further refers to a 'choir of virgins', as well as to several women living together. Moreover, he warns against women sleeping together in the same bed (and at times, apparently, committing acts of lesbian love[41]), an indication that some virgins at least lived in a community.

Whether in their families or in communities, virgins were not completely secluded; yet Basil makes it clear that they should not leave the house under some frivolous pretence, but may do so to perform works of charity. In general, they are to be a constant example of divine grace for the entire congregation, a living

---

[40] Ibid. 52 (775 A).
[41] In ch. 62 (797 B–C) Basil appears to allude to those kinds of 'dangers'.

testimony to the resurrection, and should occupy a considerable public position regardless of their *de facto* social status. Such freedom of movement is possible because virginity is primarily an internal disposition. Therefore a virgin raped during a persecution or by a demented male does not lose her status, though her body may be defiled. The essential aim of virginity is the pure, virginal soul, in which all external sexual distinction has been obliterated. Women become 'male' through *askēsis*, and express this by wearing a 'pauper's dress'. As a truly 'manly woman', a virgin should be in frequent and close contact with the 'servants of the Lord'.[42] These men may well have been certain members of the clergy who were in some way closely connected with the virgins, possibly responsible for their spiritual guidance.[43]

However, even as members of the clergy, these 'servants of the Lord' deserve a closer investigation. Their relationship to the virgins was very intimate, constituting in some cases a 'spiritual marriage' of the kind already discussed. But whenever Basil talks about these 'brothers in the Lord' he uses the plural—even when addressing one virgin only—and he frequently mentions an οἰκεία or 'family' (as distinct from a natural family). Further, after much prevarication, Basil introduces yet another characteristic of some of these men. A significant number of them misunderstood the demand for chastity, and, in a shocking imitation of a pagan custom popular in the region 'in the old times',[44] they obeyed literally Jesus' saying in Matt. 19: 11–12: 'For there are eunuchs because they were born so from their mother's womb; and there are eunuchs who were made so by men; and there are eunuchs who made themselves so for the sake of the kingdom of Heaven.'

There could be no concept of virginity and chastity more mistaken than to interpret this saying literally, to castrate oneself for the sake of the kingdom of heaven. It is self-evident, accord-

[42] Ordinary men are usually described as ἀνήρ, ἄνθρωπος, ἀρρένος, chs. 2–7, 14–15, 18–19.

[43] Basil felt no need to explain who these servants were. Presumably he could assume his audience's familiarity with their function. The 'fruitful conversations' concerning purity of the soul and the implicit reference to Mark 10: 42–5 point to members of the clergy.

[44] A reference to the cult of Attis-Cybele and the *Galloi*; cf. e.g. H. Graillot, *Le Culte de Cybèle, mère des dieux, à Rome et dans l'Empire romain* (Paris, 1912), 290–7.

ing to Basil, for those familiar with the Old Testament passage referred to by Jesus (Isa. 56: 4–5), that the Lord spoke of a 'mystical castration' (μυστικῆς εὐνουχίας).[45] The goal for all virgins, male and female, is chastity of the soul and this cannot be realized by a violent act of self-mutilation. To remove the offending organs does not remove the underlying desires; castration augments such impulses. Basil has heard of cases in which women had been raped by eunuchs: one of them was 'a canonical virgin of the Church' (παρθένος τις τῆς Ἐκκλησίας κανονική)—a fascinating incident, not least because it may contain the first reference to this official title.[46] A eunuch attacked the 'canonical virgin' and, frenzied by his futile desires, resorted to biting her entire body. To remove the horns does not convert a cow into a horse; likewise, a castrated man remains a man. Therefore the custom of some virgins not only to cohabit, but also to sleep with these

[45] *De virg.* 57–63 (784–97, quotation 797 B). The Hebrew term used in Isa. 56: 4–5, 'God will give the eunuch וְשֵׁם יָד ', 'hand and name', 'power and glory', can also mean 'male organs and posterity' (cf. for שֵׁם Num. 27: 4; Deut. 7: 24, 9: 14, *et al.*; for יָד Isa. 57: 8); the LXX has τόπον ὀνομαστόν as quoted by Basil. Castration for ascetic reasons had long been a controversial topic within the Church; we know of several 3rd-cent. bishops who were highly revered despite the fact that they were 'eunuchs', esp. Melito of Sardis, Eus. *HE* 5. 24. 5; the most celebrated case is Origen, Eus. *HE* 6. 8. Nicaea's can. 1 (AD 325) officially banned the custom for members of the clergy (Hefele–Leclercq i.1, 528, 157 n. 1), but W. M. Calder ('The Epigraphy of the Anatolian Heresies', in *Anatolian Studies presented to Sir William Mitchell Ramsey*, 90) has the following inscription (no. 11), . . . Αὐρ. Ἀππᾷ πρεσβ[υτέρ]ῳ εὐνούκῳ κ[αὶ Ἀντωνείῃ συ[νβίῳ καὶ Ἰουλιανῃ [θ]υγ/ατρὶ . . . , which he dates between 323 and 350; the fact that Aur. Appas had a daughter may indicate an honorific use of 'eunuch', cf. inscription no. 10 (p. 88); Calder also mentions an inscription from Nicomedia (*CIL* iii, Suppl. 2, no. 14188); for an overview cf. H. Chadwick, *The Sentences of Sextus* (Texts and Studies 5; Cambridge, 1959), 109–12; and see K. Hopkins (*Conquerors and Slaves* (Cambridge, 1978), 172–96) on the position of eunuchs at court. A. D. Nock, 'Eunuchs in Ancient Religion', in Z. Stewart (ed.), *Essays on Religion and the Ancient World*, i (Oxford, 1972), 7–15 remains fundamental; also A. Rouselle, *Porneia: De la maîtrise du corps à la privation sensorielle (IIe–IVe siècles de l'ère chrétienne* (Paris, 1983), 158–64.

[46] *De virg.* 61 (196 c); if part of the original text, this would attest to a very early, if not the earliest, use of the title κανονική in the sense of 'religious women'; cf. LSJ s.v. κανονικός; Lampe s.v. κανονικός; cf. also inscription no. 375 (Sengen) bearing two Maltese crosses, Μαρία κανονυκή at *MAMA* i. 195; Calder ('The Epigraphy of the Anatolian Heresies', 81) has an inscription (no. 5) which mentions an ἀσκήτρια τῆς ἁγίας τοῦ Θεοῦ ἐκλησίας.

Christian eunuchs, in the belief that physical integrity alone is the hallmark of true virginity, can only be condemned as utter absurdity.[47]

Clearly, what caused Basil's severe criticism, if not indeed outrage, is an excessively literal interpretation of exactly the way of life he convincingly advocates throughout his entire treatise. The eunuchs castigated here are in fact men who sought to follow the call of abstinence and chastity in the most drastic fashion. Apart from their methods, their aims and intentions were certainly laudable: to lead a virginal life, frequently together with virgins.

This leaves us with two kinds of men striving for ascetic perfection: those who did it the 'right' way, described as 'servants of the Lord' or 'brothers in Christ', and those who did it wrongly and castrated themselves. Both types of ascetics lived together with female virgins and, in fact, it was the principal intent of the treatise, which addresses both male and female ascetics, to regulate the life of 'chaste men and women' who lived together in communities, like brothers and sisters 'from the same womb'. It is precisely this proximity which occasions the ambiguity in Basil's argumentation. The chaste life in common expresses the highest ascetic fulfilment: the obliteration of sexual distinctions, which is the quintessence of an angelic life on earth. Yet this very same closeness may also cause the steepest and most irrevocable fall, since 'virtue and vice' are so closely, if paradoxically, related.

The ascetic landscape prior to and at the time of Basil's arrival on the scene is characterized by an almost bewildering variety of experiments. Yet we also detect the presence of several themes which are replayed again and again, each time with the slightest variation.

The central force, the dynamic figure behind the ascetic development in Asia Minor during the years between *circa* 330 and 360, was beyond doubt Eustathius of Sebaste, the same Eustathius the Philosopher, who so intrigued Basil of Caesarea. This Eustathius and his followers had been condemned at Gangra

---

[47] *De virg.* 61–3 (793–7).

because they rejected all ownership of property, disdained marriage, and crossed the most immutable boundaries between
masters and slaves and between men and women. Under the
'pretext' of asceticism, men and women, slaves and free were
regarded as equal, a fact made apparent through identical attire
for all, the 'philosopher's coat'.

In the eyes of educated Christians, Christianity was the only
true philosophy; to choose an ideal Christian life was tantamount
to choosing a philosophical life. Gregory of Nyssa described his
sister's choice to reject marriage, to perform servile tasks, and to
stay by herself as a philosophical life. Macrina made her decision
when Eustathius was first condemned in Neocaesarea. When
Naucratius adopted the 'philosophical life' he fled to the forests
with a slave, and cared for weak old men. Shortly thereafter Basil
of Caesarea followed suit. All disposed of their property. Macrina
and Emmelia treated their slaves as equals; and Macrina became,
through her *askēsis*, a 'manly woman'.

The name of Eustathius of Sebaste never appears in the *Life of
Macrina*. But, as soon as we are alerted, his presence is felt
throughout the entire work. It was Eustathius who inspired
Marathonius to renounce his career and fortune, and he was the
initiator of Marathonius and Macedonius' establishment of
'hospices' for the poor and the sick, and of communities of
ascetic men and women in Constantinople.

Basil of Ancyra's treatise advocates a middle way, but leaves
no doubt that women, through asceticism, 'become men', and on
that account the properly conducted life of male and female
ascetics in common is the highest form of asceticism. Eustathius
of Sebaste, Marathonius of Nicomedia, Macedonius of Constantinople, Basil of Ancyra and Basil of Caesarea, Peter of
Sebaste, and Gregory of Nazianzus also shared one characteristic:
all were ascetics as well as members of the clergy, 'servants of the
Lord'.

Why was Eustathius excommunicated at Gangra, how does one
account for the silence in Gregory of Nyssa's *Life of Macrina*,
written between 380 and 383? Why do we know so little about
Macedonius and Marathonius? Was it the nature of their ascetic
practices? Or could other factors account for the cloak of silence
which envelops the origins of monasticism in Asia Minor?

HOMOIOUSIAN MONASTICISM

In his *De viris illustribus* 80 Jerome offers this highly intriguing remark:[48] 'Basil, the bishop of Ancyra, . . . was the leader of the Macedonian party together with Eustathius of Sebaste during the reign of Constantius.' This is the same Constantius who had directly intervened against Paul in Macedonius' election as bishop of the imperial see of Constantinople.[49] Constantius II's adherence to the so-called 'Arian' version of Christianity is common knowledge.

Although commonly used in theological and historical accounts, 'Arianism' is a heresiological label, created to describe all those who, like Arius of Alexandria, rejected the same substance of the Father and the Son.[50] The 'Macedonian party', likewise a pejorative name-tag, identified all those who modified the belief that Father and Son were similar into the view that Father and Son were 'similar in being', ὅμοιος κατ' οὐσίαν.[51] Their doctrinal

---

[48] 'Basilius, Ancyranus episcopus, . . . sub rege Constantio Macedonianae partis cum Eustathio Sebastano princeps fuit.'

[49] Paul was elected in 337/8; according to Socrates and Sozomen, a victory of the true Nicene faith over the 'Arian' aberration. Yet neither Socrates and even less Sozomen concealed their sympathies for the alleged villain, Macedonius. Sozomen (*HE* 3. 3 (GCS 50. 104)) mentions that the 'Arians' criticized Paul's election for being based on 'his own motion and against the advice of Eusebius, bishop of Nicomedia, or of Theodore, bishop of Heraclea; upon whom, as being the nearest bishops, the right of conferring ordination devolved.' The 'orthodox' response to this accusation was Alexander's counter-accusation that Macedonius was nothing more than a smooth politician. The supporters of Macedonius reversed the story, saying that 'Paul was more skilled in the transaction of business', whereas Macedonius was austere and pious. Indeed, Sozomen repeatedly emphasizes the ascetic life-style of both Macedonius and Marathonius.

[50] At present, the state of research concerning Arianism is very much in flux; for a general overview and a background to the following section cf. R. Gregg, and D. Groh, *Early Arianism: A View of Salvation* (Philadelphia, 1981), *passim*; R. Gregg, 'The Centrality of Soteriology in Early Arianism', *American Theological Revue* 59 (1977), 260–78; Kopecek, *A History of Neo-Arianism*, i (Patristic Monograph Series 8; Philadelphia, 1979), *passim*; C. Stead, *Substance and Illusion in the Christian Fathers* (London, 1985), *passim*; id. *Divine Substance* (Oxford, 1977), *passim*.

[51] Eventually, one faction within the Homoiousian party rejected the notion that the Holy Spirit, the πνεῦμα, should likewise be seen as ὅμοιος κατ' οὐσίαν with Father and Son which led to their being labelled 'Spiritfighters', *Pneumatomachoi*; H.-Ch. Brennecke, *Studien zur Geschichte der Homöer: Der Osten bis zum Ende der homöischen Reichskirche* (Beiträge zur Historischen Theologie 73; Tübingen

position is, therefore, often described as Homoiousian, and their principal representatives were Macedonius of Constantinople, Basil of Ancyra, and Eustathius of Sebaste. The third major position, held primarily by Athanasius of Alexandria and his followers, argued that Father and Son were of the same substance, ὁμοούσιος. In short, these terms reflect specific positions taken with regard to the doctrine of the Trinity. At this juncture we come to the heart of the matter.

The period spanning the emergence of Arius around 320, the council of Nicaea in 325, and the council of Constantinople in 381 was one of intense debate and conflict between these three major theological positions and their protagonists. These conflicts were aggravated by the fact that the emperors took sides, more often than not different sides in the Eastern and the Western half of the Empire: Constantius favoured the Homoian or 'Arian' position, and Constance in the West upheld the position represented by Athanasius.[52] When Constantius II became the sole ruler in 353, the unity of the divided Church was one of his primary concerns, much as it had been for his father Constantine before him. In his attempts to achieve unity, the doctrinal 'middle ground' represented by the Homoiousian position, firmly anchored within the traditions coined by Origen and propagated by Eusebius of Caesarea,[53] author of the *Historia Ecclesiastica*, was of quintessential importance.[54] In 358 Constantius called for

---

1988), 5–66; P. Meinhold, 'Pneumatomachoi', in *RE* xxi. 1066–1101; M. Tetz, 'Arianismus', in *TR* iii. 692–719.

[52] Much has been written with regard to the situation in the West, cf. especially H.-Ch. Brennecke, *Hilarius von Poitiers und die Bischofsopposition gegen Constantius II* (Patristische Texte und Studien 26; Berlin, 1984), 3–64, 147–95; M. Meslin, *Les Ariens d'occident (335–430)* (Patristica Sorbonensia 8; Paris, 1967), *passim*; Simonetti, *La crisi ariana*, 25–312, esp. 250–312; still very valuable is H. M. Gwatkin, *Studies of Arianism* (Cambridge, 1900²). Concerning the East, by contrast, far less material has appeared; cf. Brennecke, *Studien zur Geschichte*, 1–4.

[53] Ibid. 53 f.; Simonetti, *La crisi ariana*, 3–22.

[54] Soc. *HE* 2. 37, 39–44 (PG 67. 301–24, 332–56); Soz. *HE* 4. 17–19, 22–6, 28–9 (GCS 50. 162–9, 172–82, 184–6); Philost. *Historia Ecclesiastica* 4. 11–12, 5. 1–5 (Philostorgius: Kirchengeschichte, ed. J. Bidez (GCS 21; Berlin, 1972²) 63–9). The entire historiographical tradition concerning the doctrinal developments of the period is Nicaean-orthodox. All other tendencies have been obliterated or suppressed. As a consequence, all who did not originally belong to

an ecumenical synod to reunite the Church of East and West.
For practical reasons this synod actually convened in two cities:
Rimini in Italy and Seleucia in Isauria, in Asia Minor; the official
conclusion took place in Constantinople in 360.[55] The man chosen
by Constantius to prepare a formula which would achieve the
vital compromise between East and West was Basil of Ancyra.[56]
At this point Basil of Ancyra, Macedonius of Constantinople,
and Eustathius of Sebaste were at the height of their influence,
representing in fact a position held by a substantial proportion if
not the majority of bishops in the East. They had little reason
to expect anything less than the success of their compromise
formula which was firmly based on the decisions reached in
Nicaea in 325 and supported by the emperor: Father and Son
were 'similar in everything', ὅμοιος κατὰ πάντα.[57] Yet to their

the Nicaean camp are classified as heretical, and subsumed under the label
'Arian'. Terms such as 'Arian', 'semi-Arian', 'orthodox', and the like are therefore
misleading, and often reflect neither the doctrinal conviction nor the historical
position of the parties thus described. In order to avoid confusion and stereotypes,
I shall use doctrinally descriptive terms—*homoios* ('Arian'), *homoiousios* and
homoousios (Nicaean and then Neo-Nicaean), *anomoios* (Neo-Arian, Eunomian)—
and as often as possible the proper names of the people involved. Especially
helpful were the study by Brennecke, *Studien zur Geschichte* (which gratifyingly
supports many of my findings gathered from the different angle of ascetic institutions), and Dagron, 'Les Moines et la ville', 229–76, esp. 247; id. *Naissance d'une
capitale*, 410–42; see also Kopecek, *Neo-Arianism*, i. 75–172.

[55] Ammianus Marcellinus criticized Constantius' tendency to 'meddle in Church
affairs', 21. 16. 18; for imperial involvement in synodical decisions cf. J.
Gaudemet, *La formation du droit séculier et du droit de l'église aux IVe et V[e]
siècles* (Paris, 1979²), 143–58; K. M. Girardet, *Kaisergericht und Bischofsgericht:
Studien zu den Anfängen des Donatistenstreites (313–315) und zum Prozess des
Athanasius von Alexandrien (328–346)* (Antiquitas 21: 1; Bonn, 1975), 6–51, and
here 106–49; A. Kartaschow and E. Wolf, 'Die Entstehung der kaiserlichen
Synodalgewalt unter Konstantin dem Großen, ihre theologische Begründung und
ihre kirchliche Rezeption', in G. Ruhbach (ed.), *Die Kirche angesichts der konstantinischen Wende* (Darmstadt, 1976), 149–86; for the terminology 'ecumenical'
cf. G. Kretschmar, 'Die Konzile der alten Kirche', in H. J. Maqull (ed.), *Die
Konzile der Christenheit* (Stuttgart, 1961), 13–74.

[56] This formula was also designed to 'contain' the new position represented by
Aetius and his disciple Eunomius, Soz. *HE* 4. 16 (GCS 50. 158), following
Sabinus; Brennecke, *Studien zur Geschichte*, 9 n. 29, 15 f., 40–56.

[57] The formula refers explicitly to the Scriptures (ὅμοιον δὲ λέγομεν τὸν υἱὸν
τῷ πατρὶ κατὰ πάντα ὡς καὶ αἱ ἅγιαι γραφαὶ λέγουσί τε καὶ διδάσκουσι), and
consciously avoids any reference to the *ousia* of the Homoiousian formula
ὅμοιος κατ' οὐσίαν (IV. Sirmian Formula, Ath. *De syn.* 8. 3–7 (*Urkunden zur*

surprise the Fathers at Rimini were highly reluctant and, as a result of events which had at times very little connection with doctrine, the convention at Seleucia sent two opposing delegations to Constantinople in 360.[58] Basil's mission had failed.

Basil of Ancyra and Eustathius of Sebaste were closely allied by their common doctrinal position; this was well known to their contemporaries as well as to those who, like Jerome, wrote a generation later. However, no extant text aligns them explicitly with regard to ascetic practices or concepts, whereas Eustathius and Macedonius clearly shared both ascetic ideas and doctrinal standpoints.[59] Both represented a new type of ascetic life which

Geschichte des arianischen Streites iii, ed. H. G. Opitz (Berlin, 1934), 235. 21–236. 15)). Basil of Ancyra's new formula was sent to Rimini on 27 May 359 with detailed instructions on how to proceed in its discussion. The emperor's surprise must have been considerable when the synod at Rimini declared it to be heretical: Nicaea having already sanctioned the only acceptable formula, a new one was superfluous. Only lengthy and at times rather forceful negotiations led eventually to an acceptance of the imperial position; Brennecke, *Studien zur Geschichte*, 15–40, esp. 19 f.

[58] The developments at Serdica in the autumn of 359 were crucial for the history of the Homoiousian party. One hundred and sixty bishops had gathered under the supervision of two high ranking imperial officials. On the agenda were not only the doctrinal formula, but also some unrelated personnel matters: several bishops were accused of disciplinary failures. These cases, in particular that of Cyril of Jerusalem, became the focus of the entire synod. Doctrinal matters, especially the new, more radical Homoian position, the *anomoios* of Aetius and his supporters, faded into the background. Cyril of Jerusalem's readmission into the *communio*, not theological differences, caused a split: some Homoiousians led by Acacius, bishop of Caesarea in Palestine, disapproved of the general Homoiousian acceptance of Cyril and voted therefore with the Anomoian minority, despite obvious doctrinal differences. Thus, a new faction had emerged, while the Homoiousian majority rejected Basil's formula—Basil and Macedonius were not present—and voted to retain a formula developed at Antioch. Effectively, the synod was deadlocked. After much painful debating, the Homoiousian majority under Basil and Eustathius excommunicated the minority formed by Acacius and the Anomoians. The new party of Acacius and his followers agreed to a new formula defining the relationship between Father and Son as ὅμοιος κατὰ βούλησιν (Soc. *HE* 2. 40. 31 (PG 67. 341 c); Brennecke, *Studien zur Geschichte*, 12, 47 n. 45), and claimed to be fully in accord with Constantius. Soz. *HE* 4. 13–14 (GCS 50. 155–7), cf. 4. 22. 21 (p. 175); Dagron, 'Les Moines et la ville', 247; Kopecek, *Neo-Arianism*, i. 110–32, 158–73; Simonetti, *La crisi ariana*, 239–45, 266; Gwatkin, *Studies of Arianism*, 167 n. 2.

[59] Soc. *HE* 4. 1, 4, 6, 7, 12 (PG 67. 465, 468, 472, 484–96); Soz. *HE* 4. 13–14 (GCS 50. 155–7); Philost. *HE* 4. 12, 5. 1 (GCS 21. 64–6); Dagron, 'Les Moines

involved men and women. Basil of Ancyra wrote a lengthy treatise on ascetic practices (his *De virginitate*), which was distributed to his 'soul-mates' among the bishops and provided them with guidelines for regulating the communal life of male and female ascetics. This represents the sole intellectual testimony of a Homoiousian approach to ascetic practice written by a leader of this doctrinal movement itself, without being filtered through the eyes of its adversaries as was the case at Gangra.

Gangra had condemned Eustathius and his followers. On close inspection, they were accused because they took the Scriptures literally: Eustathius taught nothing that does not have a firm basis in the New Testament. According to Matt. 19: 21, one is perfect only if one goes 'and sell[s] all that [one] possess[es] and give[s] it to the poor'; Matt. 19: 29 requires one to leave 'houses or brothers or sisters or father or mother or children or lands'; according to Mark 12: 25, 'when they rise from the dead, they neither marry nor are given in marriage, but are like angels in heaven'; and Paul in his Letter to the Galatians 3: 28 affirms that 'there is neither Jew nor Greek, there is neither slave nor free, there is neither male nor female; for you are all one in Christ Jesus.'

The Fathers at Gangra were faced with a difficult task. They felt obliged to condemn Christians who did nothing but insist on a literal interpretation of the scriptural teachings—the selfsame teachings, after all, on which they based their own authority, their very *raison d'être*. Yet the Fathers' dilemma is easily intelligible; the socially explosive repercussions of a literal interpretation of at least some of these scriptural teachings hardly needs to be emphasized.

Despite the anathema at Gangra, Eustathius became bishop of Sebaste before 356; Macedonius was already bishop of Constantinople. Sozomen, with sound reason, considered Eustathius to be the founder of monasticism in Armenia, Paphlagonia, and Pontus. Indeed, as Loofs and Gribomont have suggested, it is most likely that it was not Eustathius himself but some of his radical followers who were condemned at Gangra; and that Eustathius personally held more moderate convictions and was therefore able to effect a compromise with the ecclesiastical authorities at the synod.[60]

One of the most striking aspects of Basil of Ancyra's *De virginitate* is its dichotomy, its constant emphasis of the 'middle way' as distinct from rigoristic excesses, while at the same time postulating an ascetic ideal based on rejection of property, separation from the natural family, and the performance of charitable acts. It emphasizes, too, a strict internalization of ascetic ideals, which regards the close proximity of male and female ascetics as the highest achievement, while endowing women with male and men with angelic qualities.

Basil is walking a fine line. There can be little doubt that his treatise propagates essentially the same ascetic ideals as did Eustathius himself, at least as far as the latter's position can be reasonably reconstructed. Indeed, oscillating between requests for moderation and praise of a rigorous ascetic ideal, the treatise virtually reads as if it were a defence of Eustathius against his own radical followers. Ancyra was the home of Theodotus' seven virgins and had, therefore, a long history of ascetic rigorism. When attacking heretics, Basil identifies them once specifically as Marcionists, a well-known rigoristic sect popular in the area,[61] and while it is quite possible that he intended to condemn bona fide Marcionists, it is equally possible that he defined extremist followers of Eustathius as Marcionists. It is unlikely, however, that Basil would describe and attack deviations that may have *resulted* from Eustathius' teachings as being actually *caused* by these very same teachings. This is all the more probable, since the actual differences distinguishing rigorist Eustathians from rigorist Marcionists are, at best, minimal.

*

[60] Ath. *Ep. Aeg. Lib.* 7 (PG 25. 553); Loofs (*Eustathius und die Chronologie*, 83–90) and his followers base this interpretation also on the fact that Eustathius was accused of perjury at Antioch, only three years after Gangra; Dagron, 'Les Moines et la ville', 261 f.; Gribomont, 'Le Monachisme', 403 f.; id. 'Saint Basile et le monachisme', 125–7.

[61] *De virg.* 33 (737 A): οὕτω Μαρκίων καὶ οἱ λοιποὶ τῶν αἱρετικὰ . . . δόγματα . . . ; ibid. 62 (797 B): αἱρετικαῖς ἐννοίαις. Marcionists originated in Sinope (according to Eusebius, in Pontus) and criticized institutions such as the clergy and marriage; Eus. *HE* 4. 11. 9, cf. Just. *I Apol.* 26. 5 (PG 6. 368); A. v. Harnack, *Marcion: Das Evangelium vom fremden Gott* (TU 45; Leipzig, 1921) *passim*; G. Pelland, 'Marcion', in *DSp* x. 311–21.

When Eustathius became bishop of Sebaste around 356/8, he founded a hospice called a πτωχοτροφεῖον or 'feeding-place for the poor'.[62] Between the years 330 and 350, Macedonius and Marathonius had already established a 'feeding-place for the poor' and what our fifth-century sources characterize as 'monasteries' for men and women in Constantinople. Between 336 and 358 Basil of Ancyra sent to his colleague Letoios, bishop of Melitene, his treatise prescribing the norms by which ascetics ought to be integrated into a functioning congregation, and stressing service to the poor and care for the dead (e.g. the washing of corpses). When the other Basil became bishop of Caesarea, he was also the superintendent of a famous hospice and 'feeding-place for the poor'.

In 360 Basil of Ancyra and Eustathius of Sebaste—with the young Basil, future bishop of Caesarea, among their entourage— arrived at Constantinople to represent the majority of the Homoiousian party at the concluding session of the council. In the mean time the balance of power had changed. The minority delegation sent from Seleucia had formed a new alliance with the representatives from Rimini. The Homoiousian *de facto* majority had been outmanœuvred and lost the emperor's support. Their traditional formula, ὅμοιος κατ᾽ οὐσίαν or '*homoiousios*', was rejected and from then on their doctrinal basis was considerably weakened. The Homoians, represented by Acacius (the bishop of Caesarea in Palestine), emerged as the leading faction. An imperial edict declared their formula to be the only valid one, and it was immediately sent to all bishoprics and churches for signature. All Homoiousian bishops, Basil, Eustathius, and Macedonius foremost among them, were excommunicated and expelled from their sees, even though they had signed the new formula. On 27 January 360 Eudoxius took over Macedonius' see at Constantinople. Homoiousians and Homoians, fundamentally of the same doctrinal persuasion until that time, split into two parties, with the Homoiousians losing out.[63]

Basil of Ancyra's *De virginitate* confirms the existence of ascetic

[62] Lampe s.v. πτωχοτροφεῖον; Epiph. *Haer.* 75. 1 (3 GCS 37. 333); Bas. *Epp.* 94 (dating from 372) and 81.

[63] For detailed references cf. Brennecke, *Studien zur Geschichte*, 52–6; Dagron, 'Les Moines et la ville', 246–8; Gwatkin, *Studies of Arianism*, 185 f.; Kopecek, *Neo-Arianism*, i. 299–303.

communities in Ancyra from approximately the 330s onwards. It offers the first insight into what may be called 'Homoiousian' asceticism by a Homoiousian himself. It also confirms that these communities consisted of male and female ascetics, and that they were neither confined to Ancyra nor was their incidence merely sporadic. Perhaps initiated by Eustathius of Sebaste, but certainly inspired by him, such communities were located in major episcopal sees—Constantinople, Ancyra, Sebaste—and they attracted male and female followers in provinces as diverse as Thrace, Bithynia, Galatia, Paphlagonia, Pontus, and Armenia.

It has been the intention of this survey to reconstruct the nature of the phenomenon which prompted the first official, ecclesiastical legislation pertaining to 'virgins of God'. It has become clear that women did not search for ways to dedicate their lives to God in isolation. Their attempts to construct new modes of life were intrinsically linked with those designed by and for men. Yet our initial concentration on women has functioned like a lever: it has opened the door to ascetic practices pursued by male and female ascetics but previously virtually hidden from view, and in any event rarely discussed.

As far as the origin and development of ascetic models for women are concerned, we can distinguish three levels of 'construction': the strictly practical level, where methods to cope with the ordinary implications of daily life as an unmarried woman are devised; the intellectual level, where these new models find their conceptual basis; and, finally, the interaction between these two, the manner in which intellectual concepts are utilized to characterize, justify, and, ultimately, to regulate the process of practical organization.

Initial attempts by individual women to implement their religious aspirations occurred along two diametrically opposite lines: either within society or in complete rejection of society—these two opposites are represented by Juliana and by the unnamed prophetess. The 'daughters' of the homily by the anonymous author, and Macrina the 'virgin widow', in her early years, follow the precedent set by Juliana.

The prophetess, too, found her own followers, if not always quite as radical as herself. Approximately eighty years later, women had again secured an important public role, again within a Montanist congregation, and again based on their religious charisma—the 'seven virgins' under the guidance of Tekousa 'the elder virgin mother'. The earliest canons had already referred to another type of religious woman who likewise lived apart from her natural family, the *syneisaktes*, or virgins who lived in a 'pseudo-marriage' with men, chiefly members of the clergy who were also ascetics.

Virtually all these models chosen by women as diverse as Macrina and the seven virgins have one common thread: they are based on the notion of the family, yet distinct in the degree to which they digress from or transform this basic structure. Indeed, the modification of the family-model is progressive from 'virgin daughters' to 'virgin widows' to 'virgin wives', clearly an increasing contradiction in terms. The last step in this transformation is further characterized by the abandonment of the natural family. It is interesting that this fairly far-reaching transformation is the first model to be officially condemned. If the 'seven virgins' indeed left their natural families, their initiative, the decision to live among similar-minded women under the guidance of the 'elder virgin mother', would signify yet a further move away from the conventional matrix of the family. The combination 'virgin mother' certainly constitutes a paradox.

Progressive detachment from the natural family and the gradual transformation of the family through asceticism is most evident in the last cases discussed, the innovations of Eustathius, Macedonius, and Basil of Ancyra. Here, the process reaches its ultimate expression: by means of asceticism, women understood themselves as having become virgins and men, or 'manly virgins', who could therefore live together with male virgins as complete equals.

We are left with the principal characters of our preceding discussion, Macrina and Basil of Caesarea. Far from being a *creator ex nihilo*, Basil was firmly established in an already existing tradition of organized, communal asceticism. This asceticism, in large part derived from the teachings of Eustathius and the Homoiousian party, had found widespread support and seems to have been among the predominant forms of ascetic life by the time Basil appeared on the scene. Yet our knowledge of Eustathius' profound influence not only on Basil himself, but on his entire family, is largely the result of mere chance. Basil personally acknowledges Eustathius' influence in his early Letter 2; they remained close friends and exchanged several letters; and Eustathius figures prominently in Basil's reminiscence about his earliest ascetic experiences in his Letter 233. Yet the *Life of Macrina* makes no mention of Eustathius' name. The reason for this omission is fairly obvious. At the time of the *Life's* composition disagreements between Basil and Eustathius, primarily concerning the role of the Holy Spirit, had severed all the ties of friendship which had linked them for almost twenty years. Clearly, these later events determined the content of the surviving sources, and make a correct interpretation of earlier events more elusive and complicated.

However, once we identify these elusive elements, the influence of Eustathius' teachings is virtually pervasive in all the written sources dealing with the early ascetic years of Basil and his family.[64] Naucratius furnishes the strongest testimony for such influence, and even Macrina herself, despite Gregory's best efforts, can be seen as responding directly to some of Eustathius' ideas, particularly at the most important stages: for example, the gradual transformation of the household into an ascetic community by legally adopting all former slaves as equals, and the renunciation of all disposable property. At Annesi the women wore a dark cloak, much like the philosopher's gown worn by Eustathius and his followers, a veil, and a pair of simple shoes.[65] However, Macrina and her companions never denied their sex; as commanded in Basil's *RB*, they preserved their feminine appearance and conduct. Macrina is represented as a 'manly virgin', but only internally, with regard to the quality of her character, her soul. If her community had originally included men such as her brother Peter—who was not a brother to the virgins—or indeed male servants, Gregory never makes explicit reference to the fact. Basil's male and female communities were certainly segregated; apart from the hospice in Caesarea, they were primarily located in the countryside, at Annesi. Furthermore, if Macrina held a position of authority equal to that ordinarily held by men, this

[64] Gribomont, 'Basile et le monachisme', 129–43; id. 'Eustathe le Philosophe', 115–24; Maraval, *Macrine*, 51.

[65] It seems that members of Macrina's community wore what was to become the typical monastic habit, Gr. Nyss. *VSM* 29 (Maraval, *Macrine* 236, 238 n. 1).

authority was limited to her community, and never extended to any matter even remotely suggesting a sacramental function— once again as specified in Basil's rules.

Like Basil of Ancyra, Gregory of Nyssa wrote in response, if not in opposition, to particular issues; like Basil of Ancyra he too was walking a fine line. What were these issues he was writing against, what is his subtext? The same concerns that provided the backdrop for at least some of Basil of Caesarea's rules? A convincing case can be made that the models of ascetic life practised with so much variety before and during their own time prompted Basil of Caesarea and Gregory of Nyssa to formulate their concepts in the way they did. Basil of Ancyra, Eustathius, and the Homoiousian ascetic communities certainly figured prominently among those models.

5

Parthenoi, Widows, Deaconesses: Continuing Variety

When Rufinus of Aquileia wrote his continuation of Eusebius' *Historia Ecclesiastica* in *circa* 402, Basil's ascetic innovations had transformed Pontus and Cappadocia. Wandering around cities and the countryside—to paraphrase Rufinus—inducing all to come together, constructing monastic settlements wherever he went, Basil changed the face of the entire province.[1] Sozomen likewise attests to Basil's numerous monastic foundations, and to the fact that 'by teaching the people, he persuaded them to hold like views with himself'.[2] Yet another fifth-century testimony comes from Gaul. John Cassian reports in his *Collationes Patrum*, written in 419 and 426, that a certain Piamun came across Basilian *coenobia* in numerous Pontic villages.[3]

A few decades after his death in 379 Basil had clearly achieved recognition as the dominant figure of ascetic life in Asia Minor. This apparent success prompted his followers as well as contemporary and later historians to take for granted the immediate impact of his ascetic concepts; Basil certainly eclipsed all prior and contemporary ascetic phenomena.[4]

Yet Asia Minor had been alive with a wide range of experiments by the time Basil entered the 'athletic contest'. Far from being confined to what may be called rigoristic extremes, the spectrum of ascetic models then flourishing included a variety of choices available for women—and for men the *Naziraioi* should be kept in mind. Unfortunately, the features of these various models, in particular of the ascetic communities, are still far from

---

[1] Ruf. *HE* 2. 9 (PL 21. 518); F. Thelamon, *Païens et Chrétiens au IVᵉ siècle: L'Apport de l "Histoire ecclésiastique" de Rufin d'Aquilée* (Études Augustiniennes; Paris, 1981), 13.

[2] Soz. *HE* 6. 17 (GCS 50. 258).

[3] John Cass. *Coll.* 17. 7 (PL 49. 1107f.).

[4] Gain, *L'Église*, 154 n. 142.

clearly delineated. Our most important sources, those written by the great Cappadocian Fathers, often function as a dense curtain, allowing us to catch only occasional glimpses: for example, *ex negativo* through canons condemning 'heretical' aberrations, or through writings preserved only by mistaken attribution to an 'orthodox' author. In short, most of our information has survived virtually against the best intentions of our principal authors, namely, the Cappadocian Fathers. However, if indeed such a wide spectrum of ascetic experiments flourished before Basil's time, continued while he was alive, and survived perhaps even after his death, they presumably left their traces. If we can find those traces in the writings of the Cappadocians, then this will lend considerable weight to our hypothesis, since their writings shaped the 'official' concept of how asceticism ought to be practised.

Between 374 and 375 Basil wrote three lengthy letters to a friend and colleague, Bishop Amphilochius of Iconium, dealing with matters related to questions of Church discipline.[5] In the concise form of a commentary on ecclesiastical legislation Basil provides us here with highly interesting insights into both the organizational developments and the day-to-day affairs of a fourth-century Christian community.[6] Three canons (canons 18 and 20 in Letter 199 and canon 60 in Letter 217) are of particular relevance. Here, like the Fathers at Ancyra over sixty years previously, Basil had to judge 'fallen virgins'. However, before elaborating on their fate, Basil provides us with a succinct de-

[5] Bas. *Epp.* 188, 199, 217; Deferrari, *St. Basil: The Letters*, iii. pp. iv–xii, 5 n. 5. In accordance with the canons which form the basis of his discussion, Basil comments primarily on the penalties he considers appropriate for a variety of trespasses in chiefly sexual matters, such as adultery, fornication, putative marriages, incest, homosexuality, and the like. He also discusses intentional and unintentional homicide, abortions, rape, pagan sacrifices, abstention from eating 'swine', and the correct treatment of those who have lapsed into heresy; cf. Grotz, *Die Entwicklung des Bußstufenwesens*, 414–36.

[6] Following the precedent of the ecclesiastical canons, the penalties suggested by Basil vary according to the rank and status of the offender. Cf. Amand (*L' Ascèse monastique*, 145–79) for a more general discussion of Basil's concept of sin and repentance; cf. also E. Baudry, 'À propos du rigorisme de s. Basile: Gravité du péché, libération du pécheur', in J. Gribomont (ed.), *Commandements du Seigneur et libération évangélique: Études monastiques proposées et discutées à S. Anselme* (Studia Anselmiana 70; Rome, 1977), 141–74; S. Giet, 'Le rigorisme de s. Basile', *RSR* 23 (1949), 333–42.

finition of what it is they have strayed from: the status of a *parthenos*.

Canon 18 of Letter 199 begins with a brief summary of the Ancyran Fathers' decision,[7] according to which virgins 'who, after professing to the Lord life in holiness, then, by succumbing to the lust of their flesh, had made their vows void' were considered as guilty as those who had married twice, and were condemned to one year's penance.[8] Basil is no longer content with this state of affairs. He criticizes the Fathers' judgement as being too lenient, 'gently showing indulgence to the weakness of the fallen'. The developments of the past sixty years command a thorough re-examination of the entire subject, 'since the Church, as it advances, is becoming stronger, and the τάγμα τῶν παρθένων (the order of virgins) is now increasing'.

Basil begins his re-examination by clarifying the relative position of virgins and widows, concluding that widowhood is inferior. Consequently, a virgin's fall is far more severe a transgression. Paul in his First Letter to Timothy had already declared that young widows who might wish to remarry would violate their 'first faith' (πρώτην πίστιν) in Jesus Christ.[9] A virgin is 'the spouse of Christ and a sacred vessel dedicated to the Lord'; her trespass equals that of a bride dishonouring her union. Therefore a fallen virgin and the man who keeps her both deserve the same treatment as adulterers: excommunication for fifteen years.[10]

But before deliberating further on punishments, Basil gives his definition of what constitutes a virgin: 'She is named (ὀνομάζεται) a virgin who has willingly consecrated herself to the Lord, and has renounced marriage and preferred the life of holiness.'[11] The foremost prerequisite in 'becoming a *parthenos*' is the woman's

---

[7] Ancyra can. 19 (Mansi, ii. 519 f.).

[8] Legislation concerning *bigamoi* had become more specific by the time Basil wrote Letter 199; Neocaesarea c. 3 (Mansi, ii. 539) mentions no specific punishment but cf. c. 7 (AD 314); later on one year's penance became customary; Hefele–Leclercq, i.1, 328–30; Courtonne, *Un témoin*, 474 f.; Deferrari, *The Letters*, iii. 105–11.

[9] 1 Tim. 5: 11–12.

[10] Ancyra cc. 15 and 19 (Mansi, ii. 525–6); Bas. *Epp.* 188 c. 9, 199 cc. 21, 31, 34, 35, 36, 37, 39, 48 deal with adultery as opposed to fornication; in canon 58 of *Ep.* 217 Basil prescribes fifteen years of excommunication for a married man committing adultery with a married woman.

[11] *Ep.* 199.

personal decision, her free will, unencumbered by external force or persuasion. Therefore a woman's vow cannot be accepted before she has reached an age when 'fullness of reason' (κυρίαν οὖσαν τῶν λογισμῶν) can be assumed. Basil proposes that a girl's vow can only be considered valid if she is at least 16 or 17 years old. The voice of children does not carry the same weight. Yet age alone cannot guarantee the genuine nature of a girl's decision. Basil suggests, therefore, a period of trial, during which the girl has to prove her eagerness and sincerity by persistent petitions to be accepted. At the same time, this period affords those concerned with her enrolment the opportunity to assess the intentions and the suitability of the aspiring *parthenos*. Only after lengthy examination should a young woman be allowed to make her vow, a lifelong commitment, in full consciousness of its consequences. Under these preconditions will any subsequent offence be judged and, justifiably, punished with severity.

Substantial changes in procedure had occurred by the year 375. Sixty years after Ancyra the 'virgins of God' constituted an order, a *tagma tōn parthenōn*. Until then the sole criterion for admission to this order appears to have been a simple vow. Once admitted—the precise term employed by Basil is 'inscribed' (ἐγκαταλέγεσθαι)—members of the order were supported materially, presumably by the entire congregation. This practice led, almost inevitably, to abuse. Many under-age girls were enrolled by their relatives[12] 'not because these girls have an inner urge toward the celibate life (ἀγαμίαν), but in order that their relatives may provide some worldly advantage for themselves'. The *tagma* had, at least in some instances, declined into a charitable institution for girls under 16 without any other means of support—a cheap, convenient, and socially acceptable way to rid oneself of 'superfluous' girls, preferable to marriage since it did not require a dowry.[13] Basil does not reveal much as far as the members' actual living conditions are concerned. His observation regarding the relatives' material advantages may suggest that the *tagma*'s members remained in their family, thus providing income; Basil's use of the term προσάγειν ('to bring forward') in the context of a virgin's profession could, on the other hand, indicate that members lived elsewhere.

[12] More precisely 'parents, brothers, or other relatives', i.e. those who had legal responsibility for and thus authority over these girls.
[13] B. Biondi, *Il diritto romano* (Storia di Roma 20; Rome, 1957), 347–54;

At the time of Basil's letter the *tagma* showed signs of decline and was in dire need of reform. In order to restore the original character of the institution Basil therefore proposes a minimum age, a period of trial comparable to a noviciate, and severe punishment in the case of lapses. In line with the legalistic style of canonical writings, Basil does not comment on the order's position in the congregation (except to say that its members rank higher than widows), and we learn nothing more about a virgin's function.

Canon 20 of the same letter adds a valuable nuance. Apparently, some women had 'professed virginity' while living, according to Basil, 'in heresy'.[14] Should those women break their vows, Basil enjoins leniency; the punishment for lapsed virgins does not apply. Since they made their original profession under conditions the Church considers to be outside its jurisdiction, those women cannot now be held responsible; under 'orthodox' law their original vows are null and void. Once such a woman joins the 'orthodox' fold, her entire previous life is blotted out; her 'new' baptism is a rebirth in the fullest sense of the term.[15]

When discussing the profession made by 'those in heresy', Basil uses exactly the same terms as in the case of 'orthodox' enrolment in the *tagma*. Does this imply that heretics, too, had an 'order of virgins', whose members simply adhered to a different interpretation of the doctrine? At any rate, Basil proposes a general amnesty for lapsed heretical virgins if they return to the orthodox flock. Such an attitude must have gained him new,

---

J. Herrin, 'In Search of Byzantine Women: Three Avenues of Approach', in *Images of Women in Antiquity*, 167–89, here 174–9; E. Patlagean, 'Sur la limitation de la fécondité dans la haute époque byzantine', in *Histoire Biologique et Société* (Annales ESC 24; Paris, 1969), 1353–69. *CTh*. 3. 5. 11 (Mommsen–Meyer, i.2, 137), allows marriage at the age of 10, but 12 seems customary; Leclercq, 'Mariage', 1967; Calder, *MAMA* vii. 56, no. 258, mentions a girl married at 11; E. Patlagean, 'L'Enfant et son avenir dans la famille byzantine (IVᵉ–XIIᵉ)', *Annales de démographie historique* (1973), 85–93.

[14] ἐν αἱρέσι οὖσαν, παρθενίαν ὡμολόγησαν, *Ep*. 199.

[15] Baptism administered by heretical groups and the measures to be taken in case of a 'conversion' to orthodoxy are a notorious problem, reflected in Basil's canonical letters, esp. *Ep*. 188 c. 1. He shares the position taken by Tertullian, Cyprian, and Firmilian of Caesarea; Gain, *L'Église*, 197–200; Gaudemet, *L'Église*, 63–6; J. Hamer, 'Le Baptême et l'Église: À propos des *Vestigia Ecclesiae*', *Irénikon* 25 (1952), 142–64 (160–1 for Basil's position), 263–75.

grateful, and thus especially faithful supporters. Interestingly, the treatment of any heretical virgins who may have 'returned to orthodoxy' without a previous lapse did not seem to have required further specification. Those virgins, if they existed, presumably simply joined the orthodox *tagma*.

Basil's canonical letters present an 'order of virgins' as a fully developed institution. This *tagma* is actually documented for Iconium, Amphilochius' episcopal see, and for Caesarea, but was most probably represented throughout Asia Minor. From the foregoing evidence, however, it is clear that by 375 it had already begun to show signs of internal corruption, caused by both material abuse and doctrinal tensions.

Prior to his correspondence with Amphilochius, Basil had already addressed a letter to a lapsed virgin of precisely the type described above.[16] Perhaps contrary to what one might expect from the stern author of the canonical letters, punishment was not foremost in his mind. Rather—composing indeed a rhetorical as well as a psychological masterpiece which resembles more a homily than a letter—Basil attempts to convince the virgin that true repentance will secure divine grace and thus give her the opportunity of being redeemed.[17] This is not to say that he takes such a transgression lightly. Invoking the testimony of Jeremiah and John the Baptist, who decried the frailty of ordinary mortals, he asks her to imagine their outrage at a bride of the Lord's breach of divine laws.[18] Then he recalls the glory of her former days.

Basil begins by reminding this nameless virgin of her profession (ὁμολογίας) of virginity made before God, the angels, and men (1 Tim. 6: 12), a profession that inaugurated her membership in 'the

[16] *Ep.* 46; S. Y. Rudberg ('Manuscripts and Editions of the Works of Basil of Caesarea', in Fedwick, *Basil of Caesarea*, i. 49–65, here 55) voices doubts concerning the letter's authenticity. However, his statement, which refers primarily to the spurious *Ep.* 45, is somewhat ambiguous, cf. also pp. 46 and 64. J. Bessière (*La tradition manuscrite de la correspondance de Saint Basile* (Oxford, 1923), 346 ff.), P. J. Fedwick ('Chronology', 10 n. 56), M. Forlin Patrucco (*Lettere*, 422 f.), and B. Gain (*L'Église*, 157–9) all accept *Ep.* 46 as authentic, pointing to Rufinus' early translation at PG 31, 1785–90. The precise date of the letter cannot be established; its content could, however, indicate a date after Basil's ordination as bishop in 370.

[17] The 'epistle' is a catch-all literary form, which, indeed, comprises works as diverse as Basil's *Ep.* 22 and Gregory of Nyssa's *Life of Macrina*.

[18] Jer. 8: 23; Matt. 14: 4–8 and parallels; 1 Cor. 7.

solemn company (συνοδία), the sacred chorus of virgins'. He then recalls her grandmother, mother, and sister, who all adopted the ascetic life. Despite their undeniable virtues, the fallen virgin's sister had surpassed her mother and grandmother, since the latter were both widowed, and as such unable to achieve the same ascetic virtue as their physically intact offspring—an interesting and indeed contradictory statement in the light of postulates that 'true virginity' is an internally, not a physically determined 'condition'. All four women shared 'days of calm, heights of enlightenment, spiritual songs, psalms chanted in harmony, holy prayers, a pure and untarnished bed, the procession of virgins, and a frugal table'. Their conduct was reflected in their general appearance, their simple dress, the noble pallor of their faces, attesting to fasts and vigils and coloured only by a blush of modesty, their eyes marked by tears.

Basil portrays his ideal of the perfect virginal life.[19] As before, all practical precepts are mere preparation for the perfection of the virgin's soul, culminating in her marriage to Christ. In the case of the unfortunate addressee, it is precisely this internal quality which will accomplish her redemption: her fall has irreversibly destroyed her physical purity, yet the purity of her soul, the only aspect that matters, may, through true repentance and divine grace, be restored.

Basil, in adherence to the precepts of Paul's Second Letter to the Corinthians 11: 2, considers it his duty to supervise the virgin's spiritual progress, in particular during the difficult period of remorse. He understands himself as the virgin's guardian, 'protecting with thousands of safeguards' (μυρίαις δὲ φυλακαῖς) the 'temple of the Lord', and it will be his task to prepare her for her future marriage to Christ. As a consequence of his function, his charisma, Basil the cleric now occupies the same position as that held by the *paterfamilias* in the anonymous homily *On Virginity*.[20]

[19] *Ep.* 46; cf. also *VSM* 3. 20–6.
[20] Cf. *VSM* 5. 18: φυλακτήριον; for the metaphor of the Lord's 'temple' cf. e.g. Bas. *Ep.* 2. 4; and Amand and Moons, 'Une curieuse homélie', 2. 19–29 (p. 39); Albrecht, *Das Leben der heiligen Makrina*, 87. At *Ep.* 46. 3 Basil juxtaposes an old and a young Paul as a sort of combined νυμφαγωγός, under whose guidance and teachings the virgin left her family home to become Christ's spouse. Various suggestions have been made as to the two Pauls' identity. Most likely, the old and new Paul stand for the Apostle and for Basil himself, as the cleric who received the virgin's vows (cf. Clem. *Ep.* 1. 47: 1 (PG 1. 305)); Patrucco, *Lettere*, 428.

Much like Macrina,[21] the ladies of this family—also belonging to the upper echelons of urban society[22]—had transformed their household into an ascetic community.[23] Basil invites the lapsed virgin explicitly to remember her life among other virgins (*μετὰ παρθένων συμβιώσεις*), excursions (*προόδους*) made in their company, greetings and benedictions (*παρθένων δεξιώσεις*) received from yet other virgins.[24]

In this ascetic household, the role ordinarily occupied by the *paterfamilias* had been transferred to Basil, a member of the clergy, who also acted as spiritual guide. The same transfer had occurred in the case of Basil of Ancyra and Letoios of Melitene. In each instance it was the bishop himself who acted as spiritual guide, though it is not entirely certain that Basil of Caesarea had already been ordained as bishop at the time of Letter 46. Although he eschews in this context the more systematic expression *tagma*, there is little doubt that the lapsed virgin as well as the others were members of this group, and that thus the cleric's function as *paterfamilias* extended to the entire *tagma*.

*

Courtonne (*Lettres*, i. 119 n. 4) suggests Paul the Hermit and Paul the Apostle. For the *paterna potestas* as an aspect of the clerical position cf. B. Biondi, *Il diritto romano cristiano*, iii (Milan, 1954), 1–57; F. J. Felten, 'Herrschaft des Abtes', in F. Prinz and K. Bosl (eds.), *Herrschaft und Kirche: Beiträge zur Entstehung und Wirkungsweise episkopaler und monastischer Organisationsformen* (Monographien zur Geschichte des Mittelalters 33; Stuttgart, 1988), 209–11; Gaudemet, *L'Église*, 558–60; M. Roberti, 'Patria potestas e paterna pietas', in *Studi Albertoni*, i (Milan, 1935), 257–70.

[21] The similarities are indeed startling; one far-fetched possibility is that we are dealing here with one of Basil's relatives, cf. Maraval, 'Encore les frères et les sœurs', 161–6; Gaudentius (*Sermo* 17 (PL 20. 964–5)) mentions two nieces of Basil as superiors of a female convent in Caesarea; they owned relics of the 40 Martyrs.

[22] Work is unusual for the mother, and stands in stark contrast to her former life; the fallen virgin is said to have both written and received many letters and other writings, and Basil's allusion to Plato's *Crito* 50a–54e (Courtonne, *Lettres*, i. 116 n. 2) further attests to their erudition; see also Matt. 5: 28; Deut 5: 21.

[23] An alternative would be to assume that the 'other virgins' were simply members of the same *tagma*, who shared no more than a common aspiration. However, the word *symbiosis* suggests actual life in common.

[24] Lit. 'the extension of the right hand to salute or pray', Lampe s.v.; Rufinus translates 'benedictiones tibi virginum datae' (PG 31. 1787); Gain (*L'Église*, 159 n. 163) quotes Dölger· in interpreting this as a common Cappadocian gesture; Maraval, *Macrine*, 197.

In two other letters Basil introduces a new level of formality by addressing the recipients as κανονικαί.[25] The term is already familiar from Basil of Ancyra's treatise, where it had been used in reference to the mistreated *parthenos tis tēs ekklēsias kanonikē*.[26] Literally, the description means 'subject to a rule', more specifically, an ecclesiastical rule.[27] In Letter 173, addressed to *ΘΕΟΔΩΡΑΝ ΚΑΝΟΝΙΚΗΝ*, Basil identifies both the nature of the rule and that of the 'law-giving' body which issued it. In simple grammatical style, which suggests an addressee of fairly low social origins, Basil lists the regulations that guide Theodora's 'battle' for the perfect ascetic life: '[to carry] out [the] observance [of the Scriptures] even to the smallest details and overlooking none of the written rules'; in such manner are the terms of a virgin's official vow fulfilled.[28] In practice these prescriptions translate into self-control, manual labour, modesty, and frugality (αὔταρκες) in all respects, and caution when conversing with men (συντυχίαις τῶν ἀνδρῶν). Of equal importance is the obliteration of any former distinction of rank, and the avoidance of seeking any exaltation or other advantage. Brotherly love, assiduous prayer, generosity towards those in need, sound faith, moderation in times of irritation, and constant awareness of the Last Judgement are the fundamentals of a life according to the *kanōn*.

The context implies that Theodora was the leader of an ascetic community and the letter, in essence an enumeration of regulations (canons), offers an example of Basil's spiritual guidance: one of the ways in which a bishop and ascetic organized ascetic life in common.[29]

Basil's efforts were not limited to his own diocese. At the beginning of his episcopate he wrote to a group of women in

[25] *Epp.* 52, 173, 188 can. 6.

[26] Bas. Anc. *De virg.* 61 (PG 30. 795); H. Leclercq, 'Chanoinesses', in *DACL* xxiv. 249.

[27] LSJ s.v. κανών; Lampe s.v.

[28] Gribomont ('Les Règles épistolaires', 268 n. 30) wonders whether the subsequent clause, 'this is successfully accomplished by very few of those who have come within our knowledge', is an implicit criticism of Eustathius' followers. Considering the letter's likely date, 374, this is possible, but the context does not seem to imply any criticism, rather the contrary.

[29] Apart from answering a request for guidance on how to lead an ascetic life, the letter, which ends rather abruptly, has on the whole very little personal content.

Colonia, in the diocese of Bishop Bosporius. Bosporius had been one of Basil's opponents in the clashes that had involved the *Naziraioi*, following the death of Dianios. However, in later years, he became a staunch supporter. Whenever he learned of any slanderous allegations against . Basil, he immediately informed him, and on one occasion this prompted Letter 52.[30] The originators of the allegations and thus the recipients of Basil's Letter were several ladies, also addressed as *kanonikai*. These women had been troubled by a matter of paramount doctrinal concern: the word '*homoousios* (consubstantial), which has been ill-received by some'. Appropriately, the title in the manuscript Ambrosianus 604 defines Basil's reply as 'Canon on whether Father and Son are of the same substance'.[31] The ladies had expressed grave doubts as to whether Basil and Bosporius' teaching, namely that Father and Son were consubstantial, was within the boundaries of orthodoxy as defined by the council of Nicaea. Letter 52 thus attests the widespread and dangerous potential of the Trinitarian controversies at the beginning of Basil's episcopate. Indeed, exactly at this time the Cappadocian Fathers were in the process of formulating their terminology and its application to Father, Son, and Holy Ghost. Though eventually of such fundamental and far-reaching consequence, at the time the term *homoousios* itself and especially its meaning were a novelty. In his response to the *kanonikai* Basil has thus to confess that several bishops had dismissed it already as being too obscure (οὐκ εὔσημον)—an indication that Basil and his partisans were constantly faced with potential misinterpretations, controversies, and risks of being accused as innovators.[32]

---

[30] See also *Ep.* 51. For Colonia, modern Aksaray, cf. Hild and Restle, *TIB* ii. 207 f. Bosporius was present at Constantinople in 381; cf. Mansi, iii. 569, xi. 1005. He was accused of heresy but defended by Gregory of Nazianzus and Basil; R. Janin, 'Bosporius', in *DHGE* ix (Paris, 1937), 1330; Hauser–Meury, 'Bosporius', 45–8.

[31] κανὼν περὶ τὸ ὁμοούσιον εἶναι τὸν υἱόν τῷ πατρί, cf. Gain, *L'Église*, 334–43, esp. 336 n. 47.

[32] Bas. *Ep.* 28. Bishop Musonius, for instance, opposed all innovations; for Basil's references to Nicaea cf. Gain, *L'Église*, 332 nn. 33, 34. The amount of literature regarding the formula of Nicaea and Basil's own interpretation is vast; cf. for instance I. Ortiz de Urbina, *Nicée et Constantinople* (Histoire des conciles œcuméniques 1; Paris, 1963), *passim*; or Simonetti, *La crisi ariana, passim*; for Basil cf. e.g. his *De Spiritu Sancto*, 28 (SC 17*bis*, 244 f.).

The *kanonikai* were a case in point. Basil responds to their doubts by asserting both the long tradition of the term 'consubstantial' and its fidelity to the biblical message, and he delivers a very clear definition of the nature of doctrinal authority: 'For, to refuse to follow the Fathers and to refuse to regard their word as of greater authority than [one's] own opinion is an arrogance deserving of reproach'.[33]

Leaving aside the intricacies of the term 'consubstantial', Letter 52 reveals that women entitled *kanonikai* were actively involved in the most pressing doctrinal debates, and that their concerns merited immediate attention, not simply from their local bishop but from a figure of such acclaimed authority as Basil himself—a clear indication of the respect with which these women were regarded. To put it differently, in times of high tension and doctrinal conflict no bishop, especially one like Basil, who attempted to propagate a new doctrinal concept, could afford to lose the support of *kanonikai*.

The foregoing information suggests in fact that *kanonikai* quite possibly occupied a more prominent position within the *tagma* than ordinary virgins. This, albeit in a round-about fashion is supported by a third reference—canon 6 of Letter 188, Basil's first 'canonical' letter to Amphilochius, written in 374: 'The prostitution of *kanonikai* must not be considered a marriage and must be broken at all costs.' In Basil's view, therefore, *kanonikai* were virgins, members of the *tagma*, who must live according to the 'rule'. It is also apparent that, like other members of the *tagma*, *kanonikai* too lived not only with female companions, but also with men in a spiritual marriage, or, indeed, in communities of men and women: Theodora was in fact the leader of such a mixed community.[34] *Kanonikai*, in other words, occupied positions

[33] Was part of the concern that a *kanonikē* interpreted aspects of the doctrine without 'proper', institutionally sanctioned spiritual advice? Bas. *De Spiritu Sancto* 1. 3; 29. 70–5 (SC 17*bis*, 256, 500–14); Matt. 28: 19; 1 Cor. 12: 4–6; E. Amand de Mendieta, 'The "Unwritten" and "Secret" Apostolic Traditions in the Theological Thought of Basil of Caesarea', *Scottish Journal of Theology*: Occasional Papers 13 (1965), 61 f., 64–6; Gain, *L'Église*, 330–43; H. Leclercq, 'Doxologies', in *DACL* iv.2, 1525–36; A. Stuiber, 'Doxologie', in *RAC* iv. 210–26.

[34] Gribomont ('Règles épistolaires', 264–86 (quotation, 265)) proposes a merger of Bas. *Ep.* 173 to Theodora with *Ep.* 22; this suggestion is based on content and formalistic considerations (the abrupt ending of Letter 173 and the absence of an introduction to Letter 22), as well as significant manuscript

of leadership and were influential and outspoken in doctrinal matters; there is thus an indication of a rudimentary hierarchical differentiation within the *tagma* itself.[35] All allusions to the *tagma* thus far have referred to virgins who lived in an urban environment. Yet the *tagma* was not limited to cities. In the year 374 the inhabitants of Venasa, a village near Nazianzus, were greatly perturbed by a series of incidents serious enough to call for the attention of both Basil and Gregory of Nazianzus.[36] Gregory himself had consecrated a certain Glycerius

traditions, and makes 'Théodora . . . soit la secrétaire porte-parole, soit même la principale autorité d'un groupe mixte. . . .' Gribomont (p. 285) also suggests a later date, after 370, but is refuted by Fedwick ('Chronology', 8 n. 29). One would certainly welcome further evidence for Gribomont's suggestion, but can. 6 leaves little doubt that *kanonikai* lived together with men. Around 382/3, John Chrysostom wrote an entire treatise Περὶ τοῦ τὰς κανονικὰς μὴ συνοικεῖν ἀνδράσι, usually known by its Latin title, *Quod regulares feminae viris cohabitare non debeant* (PG 47. 513–32); evidently, the practice remained a common phenomenon; Pall. *Dialogus de Vita S. Johannis Chrysostomi* 5. 15 (*Palladios: Dialogue sur la vie de Jean Chrysostome*, ed. A.-M. Malingrey and P. Leclercq, 2 vols. (SC 341–2; Paris, 1988) 108); C. Baur, *Der heilige Johannes Chrysostomus und seine Zeit*, 2 vols. (Munich, 1930): quoted in the following according to the Eng. trans. by M. Gonzaga, *John Chrysostom and his Time*, 2 vols. (Westminster, Md., 1959–60), here i. 161, 166–70; Clark, *Jerome, Chrysostom, and Friends*, 158–60; L. Meyer, *Jean Chrysostome, maître de perfection chrétienne* (Paris, 1933), p. xviii.

[35] Interestingly, Basil never used the word *kanonikē* in his rules; instead he used *adelphē* or *proestōsa*; Soc. *HE* I. 17 (PG 67. 121), παρθένους τὰς ἀναγεγραμμένας ἐν τῷ ἐκκλησιῶν κανόνι; Gain, *L'Église*, 119f; Deferrari (*The Letters*, ii. 449) mistakenly quotes Soz. *HE* 8. 23; W. Hauschild, *Briefe*, ii. 172; J. B. Valvekens, 'Canonichesse', *DIP* ii. 24–7. The prevailing interpretation of the status of a *kanonikē* is that of a woman leading an ascetic life while being inscribed in the 'order' of the Church, but not living within a monastic community. This residence outside a community is in fact seen as the constitutional aspect distinguishing *kanonikai* from virgins. As the above brief summary has, I hope, demonstrated, such an interpretation is a reflection of later, medieval developments, and over-simplifies the early evidence.

[36] Bas. *Epp.* 169–71 were in fact written by Gregory of Nazianzus (*Epp.* 246–8); cf. A. Cavallin, *Studien zu den Briefen des hl. Basilius* (Lund, 1944), 81–92. Venasa, modern Avanos, is about 12 km. distant from Nazianzus and about 100 km. from Caesarea; it is idyllically described by Gr. Nyss. *Ep.* 20 (*GN* viii.2), 69 f.); see also *TIB* ii. 302; Gain, *L'Église*, 8 n. 19; W. M. Ramsay, *The Historical Geography of Asia Minor* (London, 1890; repr. Amsterdam, 1962), 292; N. Thierry, 'Un problème de continuité ou de rupture: La Cappadoce entre Rome, Byzance, et les Arabes', *Comptes Rendus de l'Académie des Inscriptions et Belles-Lettres* 1977, 98–144, here 129–34.

as deacon, to help the local presbyter with work in the church. Once ordained, Glycerius did anything but attend to his duties. Instead, 'collecting some unfortunate virgins by his own authority and responsibility, some running towards him willingly (and you know how the young are always ready for such adventures), and others against their will, he endeavoured to become the leader of the company' (*Ep.* 169). Not only did Glycerius arrogate to himself the guidance of these virgins, he appropriated all the external signs of a patriarch and caused a state of tumult in the entire congregation. On the occasion of a festival celebrating the local martyrs, he brought off his major coup: he 'captured' as many virgins as he could, and escaped with them into neighbouring Cappadocia, then under Basil's jurisdiction. Basil seems to have managed to contact the group, but by the time he wrote his letter neither Glycerius nor his virgins had returned 'to their mother, the Church'.

That these virgins were part of the *tagma tōn parthenōn* is made evident by the fact that Glycerius regarded his newly usurped position as their leader as a money-making proposition; 'he preferred this source of livelihood, just as another man would choose one or another occupation' (*Ep.* 170)—an interesting insight into the less salubrious aspects of clerical financial administration. When Glycerius took over, the *tagma* appears to have been fairly small, and the revenue correspondingly meagre. He thus set out to increase the income by forcibly enrolling additional members. Yet even that seems to have failed to satisfy his aims: at the festival, which had attracted the usual 'immense crowd', he is said to have displayed his 'chorus of virgins' as a kind of dancing-troupe, presumably in return for some form of payment.[37]

If Glycerius intended to enrich himself by exploiting others under a religious pretext, he was not alone. An edict issued by the emperors Valentinian, Valens, and Gratian on 30 July 370 stipulated that '[ecclesiastics, ex-ecclesiastics, and those men who wish to be called by the name of *continentes*] shall be able to obtain nothing whatever, through any act of liberality or by last will of those women to whom they have attached themselves privately under the pretext of religion'.[38] Though the edict ad-

---

[37] Gallay, *Lettres*, ii. 171 n. 4; Gain, *L'Église*, 256 n. 128.

[38] *CTh.* 16. 2. 20 (Mommsen–Meyer, i.2, 841; Pharr, *Theodosian Code*, 443 f.); cf. also *CTh.* 3. 6. 1 (Mommsen–Meyer, i.2, 140); M. Forlin Patrucco, 'Aspetti di

dresses the Roman congregation, Rome's clerics were not the only ones to abuse their privileges.[39] Still, in Glycerius' case much remains mysterious. But, whatever his motives, the correspondence generated by his misbehaviour proves the existence of a *tagma* of virgins even in small towns such as Venasa.

Stern exhortations, phrased in meticulous style, were one consequence suffered by 'fallen virgins'. More common, and certainly more vicious, was a particular kind of public humiliation: their exalted reputation also made the members of the *tagma* into easy targets for false accusations, if not veritable smear-campaigns. The addressee of Letter 289 was one such 'afflicted woman'.[40] She had 'forgone a husband and the bearing of children and the world' in order to be considered 'worthy of God's approval and of a better name (τοῦ βελτίονος ἀξιοῦσθαι λόγου) among men', but all her efforts were brought to naught by one man who gained access to her house, and, having been denied what he came for, publicly calumniated her by posting placards at the entrances to the church, the market-place, the gymnasiums, and the theatres.[41]

Against such attacks the woman, clearly one of the virgins, found herself defenceless, especially since she had no legal guardian. In her predicament she appealed to the one person she thought responsible for her well-being in the manner of a *paterfamilias* (πατρικός), namely Basil.[42] His response seems to have been not quite as helpful as she expected. He contented himself with 'philosophizing on the suffering of others', which she considered a weak reply: 'For you do not order me to despise the loss of wealth, nor to bear with bodily sufferings, but to be ruined in my very reputation, the damage to which becomes a common damage to the clergy'.

Aside from the personal details, Letter 289 largely confirms

vita familiare nel IV secolo negli scritti dei padri cappadoci', in *Etica sessuale e matrimonio nel cristianesimo delle origini*, 158–79, here 177.

[39] The edict was effective throughout the entire Empire; Jones, *The Later Roman Empire*, i. 171, 470–507; Biondi, *Il diritto romano cristiano*, i. 115–67; ii. 209–40.

[40] Courtonne (*Lettres*, iii. 161 n. 2) considers her to be a widow, but the following quotation supports my interpretation; cf. also Gain, *L'Église*, 119f.

[41] He appears to have been expelled on account of this, but continued 'his vicious campaign'.

[42] The virgin has neither 'brother, friend, relative, servant, freedman' to act on her behalf.

what we have so far learned about the status and circumstances of the virgins,[43] except in one aspect: she felt that the loss of her reputation was a 'common loss to the clergy'. This raises an important issue. What exactly was the virgins' standing in the ecclesiastical hierarchy? So far, all we know is that virgins formed an order and that they were superior to widows. But were they part of the clergy?

*

Basil of Caesarea's letters, certainly the most orthodox of all sources, reveal that institutionalization of this life-style had indeed progressed rapidly. We find an order of virgins with an ever-increasing number of members, both in urban centres and smaller towns. Admission was formalized and guaranteed financial remuneration, distributed by the highest ranking member of the clergy. A rudimentary hierarchy within the *tagma* itself might also have developed. We certainly find an increasing proliferation of titles—instead of simply *parthenoi*, we now find *kanonikai* as well. Yet, despite all these external signs of order and systematization, Basil's letters demonstrate the continuing variety of ways in which the everyday life of a virgin was organized. In practice, there was no fixed manner in which a woman 'dedicated her life to God'. Regardless of their doctrinal affiliation, and seemingly despite episcopal efforts, women continued to follow the now familiar pattern: they pursued their vocation either alone, or in their families, or as members of female communities, or in ascetic communities with men. Gregory of Nazianzus' writings further corroborate these findings.

If Basil's role is that of a leader and an organizer, then his friend and companion Gregory of Nazianzus provides the different voice of the introvert and contemplative poet. To integrate classical erudition with Christianity, and to place the glory of Athens' rhetoric at the feet of Christ, was part of Gregory's mission.[44] In his understanding Christianity was heir to the true values of Greek *paideia*, and he remained convinced that truth could be found only in the fiery power of words, in the rigorous

---

[43] She lived in her own house (ἡμῶν τῷ οἴκῳ), although not necessarily by herself. The context indicates that she was not a member of a community, cf. Gain, *L'Église*, 120.

[44] Gr. Naz. *Carm.* 2. 2. 7. 43 *ad Nemesium* (PG 37. 1554).

battle of thoughts in the arena of learning.[45] This approach to
classical culture, especially to its literary heritage, ensured him a
place among the greatest artists—in the words of Puech 'aucun
époche n'a connu un artiste plus raffiné'.[46]

In 372, in the midst of a period of political upheaval caused
by the emperor Valens' subdivision of Cappadocia into two
provinces, Basil ordained Gregory as bishop of Sasima, an obscure
village where the roads from Cappadocia and Pontus to Cilicia
and Tyana intersected. Gregory, who was at that point managing
the affairs of the diocese of Nazianzus on behalf of his ailing
father, the bishop, never forgave Basil this appointment. He
refused to fight, as he put it, 'about livestock and poultry, as if
the issue were souls and ecclesiastical canons'. To him it was
clear that his election was merely a means to increase Basil's
power-base, or, in Gregory's own words, to satisfy his desire
for 'control . . . of taxes and contributions' that were his due as
metropolitan of Caesarea—a control that was severely threatened

---

[45] Gr. Naz. *Carm.* 2. 2. 4. 58–75 *Nicobuli filii ad patrem* (PG 37. 1510);
B. Wyss, 'Gregor von Nazianz: Ein griechischer-christlicher Dichter des 4.
Jahrhunderts', *Museum Helveticum* 6 (1949), 117–210, here 123 f. (repr. in Libelli
53 (Darmstadt, 1962), here 6 f.). Gregory's attitudes towards erudition gain a
specific significance in the light of Julian's campaign against Christian philosophical
instruction, cf. esp. Gr. Naz. *Or.* 4 and 5 (*Grégoire de Nazianze: Discours*, ed. J.
Bernardi (SC 309; Paris, 1983)); cf. also B. C. Hardy, 'Kaiser Julian und sein
Schulgesetz', in R. Klein (ed.), *Julian Apostata* (Darmstadt, 1978), 387–408; A.
Kurman, *Gregor von Nazianz: Oratio 4 gegen Julian* (Basle, 1988), 6–26; R. C.
Gregg, *Consolation Philosophy: Greek and Christian Paideia in Basil and the Two
Gregories* (Philadelphia, 1974), *passim*; W. Jaeger, *Das frühe Christentum und die
griechische Bildung* (Berlin, 1963), 54 f.

[46] A. Puech, *Histoire de la littérature grecque chrétien*, iii (Paris, 1930), 38;
Gregory's position on classical *paideia* was not solely positive: an example of a
more negative outlook is *Or. Fun.* 43. 11 *In Basilio* (Boulenger, 78); see also
W. Nestle, 'Die Haupteinwände des antiken Denkens gegen das Christentum',
ARW 37 (1941/2), 51–100; especially helpful is the differentiated study by R. R.
Ruether, *Gregory of Nazianzus: Rhetor and Philosopher* (Oxford, 1969), 96,
156–75. His artistic merits add to the historical value of his work; although
'Zunächst verbietet ein klassisches Stilgesetz ihm . . . gegenständliches historisches
oder kultur-historisches Detail zu geben', Hauser-Meury, 15; M. Wittig, *Gregor
von Nazianz: Briefe* (Bibliothek der griechischen Literatur 13; Stuttgart, 1981),
8–13; cf. also F. Lefherz, *Studien zu Gregor von Nazianz: Mythologien,
Überlieferung, Scholiasten* (Bonn, 1958), *passim*; H. M. Werhahn, 'Dubia und
Spuria unter den Gedichten Gregors von Nazianz', *SP* 7 (1966), 337–47.

by the loss of half of his diocese to Anthimus, the newly elected bishop of Tyana.[47]

Shortly before this incident, around Easter 372, Gregory composed a lengthy poem or *protreptikos*, in which he pleaded for the tax exemption of ten needy monks and clerics who lived in the diocese of Nazianzus.[48] It was addressed to Hellenius, the *peraequator* in charge of tax revisions and a friend and former

[47] Gr. Naz. *Carm. de vita sua* 2. 439–62 (*Gregor von Nazianz: De Vita Sua*, ed. Ch. Jungck (Heidelberg, 1974), 74–6); id. *Ep.* 48; for Eng. trans. see Ruether, *Gregory of Nazianzus*, 36 f. Valens' edict has not been preserved; his division was conceived such that Caesarea remained the sole city in Cappadocia Prima, which otherwise consisted virtually exclusively of imperial domains; Cappadocia Secunda on the other hand comprised practically all other remaining cities. The income and political standing of Caesarea, and thus of Basil's episcopal seat, was severely diminished, as was his own episcopal jurisdiction, now contested by Anthimus. Since the ecclesiastical and administrative boundaries no longer overlapped, both bishops claimed supremacy over the other's territory. Gain, *L'Église*, 306–9; S. Giet, *Sasimes: Une méprise de Saint Basile* (Paris, 1941); G. May, 'Basilios der Grosse und der römische Staat', in *Bleibendes im Wandel der Kirchengeschichte*, 47–70; Treucker, *Politische Studien*, 110 n. 427.

[48] PG 37. 1451; the interpretation of any poem by Gregory is hampered by the fact that, as far as I am aware, no comprehensive edition (or translation) of his *circa* 180 poems is yet available, though several individual works have been edited, commented upon, and translated. The largest single selection of his poetical work remains accessible only in the Migne edition, PG 37; see M. Sicherl, 'Berichte über die Arbeit an den Gedichten Gregors von Nazianz seit Koblenz (1976)', in J. Mossay (ed.), *II. Symposium Nazianzenum. Louvain-la-Neuve, 25–28 août 1981* (Studien zur Geschichte und Kultur des Altertums NF 2; Paderborn, 1983), 137–40; *Gregor von Nazianz: Carmina de virtute 1a/1b*, ed. M. Kertsch and R. Palla (Graz, 1985), 7–83; *Gregor von Nazianz: Gegen die Putzsucht der Frauen*, ed. A. Knecht (Heidelberg, 1972), 14. Dating poses similar problems. Most scholars maintain that Gregory began writing poetry only after 382/3; however, some poems clearly stem from an earlier period; cf. E. Dubedout, *De Gregorii Nazianzeni carminibus* (Paris, 1901), 16–23. Equally controversial is whether or not Gregory intended his poems to be circulated. Their predominantly didactic content suggests, however, that he wrote to be read and heard, cf. W. Ackermann, *Die didaktische Poesie des Gregor von Nazianz* (Leipzig, 1903), 8–22, and Wittig, *Briefe*, 62–8; with regard to authenticity cf. Wittig, ibid. 64 n. 164; in general Wyss, 'Gregor von Nazianz', 117–210. As Wittig (op. cit. 65 n. 166) points out, the subjective character of Gregory's poetry has led to comparisons with Augustine's *Confessions*; cf. also Ackermann, op. cit. 8–11; M. Pellegrino, *La poesia di San Gregorio Nazianzeno* (Milan, 1932), *passim*; the same applies *mutatis mutandis* to his letters; cf. especially M. Guignet, *Les Procédés épistolaires de S. Grégoire de Nazianze* (Paris, 1911); Ruether, *Gregory of Nazianzus*, 124–8.

fellow student of Basil and Gregory.[49] Apparently, Hellenius complied.[50] But these monks were not the only ascetics living in Nazianzus. The same poem also refers to παρθενικὰς γυναῖκας, who are eagerly awaiting the coming of their heavenly bridegroom (ll. 225–30). Through their ascetic efforts these women have become like men, not only in wisdom, but even in body (245–6)—and the tax exemption requested by Gregory may even have included them. As he points out, many women have been attracted by the sweet odour of ascetic life: 'Some have joined each other, profiting from their common desire for heavenly life, and following the same rule of life. Others remain with their weak parents or with their brothers and sisters' (255–60). Again, the virgins followed different organizational paths: either in groups, or within their families, or, interestingly, with their brothers—and by using the word κασίγνητος Gregory leaves little doubt that he means 'brothers born from the same mother'.

Another so-called 'moral' poem, the *Praecepta ad virgines*, addresses both female and male ascetics.[51] Without going into the details of Gregory's prescriptions, which largely correspond to those already discussed in the context of similar treatises, two references to organizational features are worth mentioning.[52] In lines 96–124 Gregory exhorts virgins to disdain all men, in particular those called συνείσακτοι ('those introduced into the house'), because the company of these male *syneisaktes* entails a

---

[49] Bas. *Epp.* 71, 98; Hauser–Meury, 'Hellenius', 97; Devos, 'Pièrre Ier de Sébastée', 346–59; the date is derived from Basil's *Ep.* 98 and the fact that 372 was a year for the official census; for the function of a *peraequator* cf. O. Seek, 'Discussor', *RE* v. 1185; for the geographical extent of a *peraequator*'s responsibilities, see *CTh.* 11. 28. 2, 12. 10. 1 (Mommsen–Meyer i.2, 617, 725).

[50] Cf. Bas. *Ep.* 104.

[51] *Carm.* 1. 2. 2 (PG 37. 578); F. E. Zehler, *Kommentar zu den 'Mahnungen an die Jungfrauen' (carmen 1, 2, 2) Gregors von Nazianz*, Diss. (Münster, 1987); the preceding *In laudem virginitatis* (PG 37. 521 f.) is a glorification of virginity employing all the now well-known topoi. Interestingly, Gregory here presents the Trinity as the first and foremost virgin. The *Exhortatio ad virgines*, printed after the *Praecepta* (at PG 37. 632 f.), is not by Gregory, cf. R. Keydell, 'Die Unechtheit der Gregor von Nazianz zugeschriebenen Exhortatio ad Virgines', *ByZ* 43 (1950), 334–7; Bellini, 'La posizione dei monachi e dei vergini', 452–66.

[52] Both the text and the content of the *Praecepta* certainly deserve a closer examination; Zehler, *Kommentar*, provides many interesting references.

twofold risk. Even if the virgins themselves are capable of maintaining their strength and integrity, this does not safeguard the disposition of their companions; and the virgins must not be the unwitting cause of another's harm (σκάνδαλον). Besides, daily contact is a constant distraction and slowly poisons soul and mind with impurity. In the virgins' own minds the heavenly bridegroom will inevitably assume distinctly human, male features with a specific identity. Closeness may easily lead to a 'fall' and, therefore, the concept of uniting similar spirits in chaste love (ἀγάπη), laudable as it may be in and by itself, becomes the vehicle for the devil's fraud and the virgin's ruin.[53] At the same time, there is no harm whatsoever in leading an ascetic life within a community, with one's parents or relatives, or, once again, with one's *natural* brothers (241–55). An interesting line of argument and by now no longer new: while the theory of cohabitation receives approbation, its practical realization is at best reprehended.[54]

Another example of a woman who may have lived with male ascetics is a certain Thecla.[55] This lady—addressed as 'your Piety' (εὐλάβειαν)—shared her 'solitude and philosophical retreat' with her 'beloved children' (*Ep.* 223). Were these her natural or her spiritual children, male or female?[56] Another member of Thecla's family also presided over a monastic community: her brother Sacerdos, Gregory's 'brother' and friend. Sacerdos had begun the ascetic life as an anchorite, and had then become the leader of a 'hospice of the poor' as well as of a monastery. Unfortunately, owing to real or alleged financial irregularities but perhaps for 'Eustathian' connections, he was suspended from all his posts, a blow he did not survive for very long.[57]

[53] Zehler, *Kommentar*, 77–92.

[54] 'If you are linked to elder brothers who come to support the parents of your parents, or who are in need of help themselves, there is no harm in sharing their life with all affection' (l. 245); Zehler, *Kommentar*, 147 f., especially his interesting remarks regarding filial duties.

[55] Gr. Naz. *Ep.* 56, written between 373 and 375; she also received *Epp.* 222–3, concerning the death of Sacerdos; Hauser–Meury, 'Thecla I. 2', 158 f.; Gr. Naz. *Ep.* 57 (= Bas. *Ep.* 321) was addressed to a different Thecla; P. Gallay, *Les Manuscrits des lettres de Saint Grégoire de Nazianze* (Paris, 1952), 126 f.

[56] Gregory always refers to her community in neutral terms. It is equally possible that Thecla and her 'children' are yet another example of an ascetic family centred around one prominent member, here the mother.

[57] Gregory's correspondence regarding Sacerdos' dismissal by bishop Helladius,

In his letters and other writings Gregory further mentions several ladies who, much like Juliana over a century before, lived on their own. The most interesting of these virgins is a certain Russiana, since her case is one of the few instances where we are able to gain a precise insight into the economic foundations of ascetic life, which so often can only be inferred. Russiana was one of Gregory's many relatives, and one of the beneficiaries mentioned in his will.[58] While he was alive Gregory had supported her with an annuity sufficient to ensure an honourable life-style. In his will he stipulates that this annuity should continue until her death, and he further makes arrangements for her to choose a house of her liking, suitable for her life as a virgin; she will enjoy the usufruct of this house, while its expenses will be borne by Gregory's estate. He also designates two servant-girls for her personal use; if she wishes, she may pay them wages or free them. Otherwise, at the time of her death they as well as the house and all her other possessions will become the property of the Church of Nazianzus.[59]

The reception accorded to one of the other two solitary virgins mentioned by Gregory in his letter, a certain Alypiana, confirms that Basil's suggestions regarding enrolment were by 383 widely accepted—at any rate by his supporters. The newly enrolled virgin is entrusted to the care of Eulalios, Gregory's successor in the see of Nazianzus.[60] As already suggested both by Gregory's provision for Russiana and by the slandered virgin's appeal for Basil's protection, spiritual welfare was only one of the responsibilities of a bishop with respect to his virgins. In Letter 159 Gregory asks Theodorus, probably bishop of Tyana, to look after

Basil's successor in Caesarea, is extensive; he clearly considered Sacerdos innocent; Sacerdos' disgrace and death must have taken place in the early 380s; Hauser–Meury, 'Sacerdos', 'Helladius I', 'Castor', 152, 94, 52.

[58] PG 37. 389–96 (p. 392 for Russiana); Hauser–Meury, 'Russiana', 151; F. Martroye ('Le Testament de St. Grégoire de Nazianze', *Mémoires de la Société des Antiquaires de France* 76 (1919–23), 219–63), has a translation: for Russiana see 221 f.; F. Gilliard, 'The Social Origins of Bishops in the Fourth Century', Diss. (Berkeley, 1966), 32.

[59] Biondi, *Il diritto romano cristiano*, ii. 201–29; Gaudemet, *L'Église*, 288, 291–315; Martroye, 'Le Testament', 239–63 for juridical details.

[60] Gr. Naz. *Ep.* 158; Hauser–Meury, 'Alypiana', 'Eulalios', 26, 70; Bas. *Ep.* 199.

Gregory's 'most honourable daughter, the virgin Amazonia', who had fallen seriously ill—an instructive example of the extent of a bishop's responsibility towards these members of his θρέμμα, his flock.[61]

Besides adding detail and thus colour to our concept of a virgin's life, Gregory's writings shed more light on another facet of communal ascetic life, that of natural siblings. Epigram 154 is dedicated to Georgios, a priest, who had 'procured many souls for Christ'.[62] Buried beside him is the 'noble Basilissa, his sister in flesh and spirit' (σὺν δὲ κασιγνήτη σῶμα, φρένας), who 'now shares his grave as she shared his life', most probably as a 'virgin of God'.[63] Theosebia was the name of yet another lady who may have lived with her brother, himself an ascetic and cleric. Her circumstances are, however, slightly more difficult to unravel:[64] she might have been either Gregory of Nyssa's wife who lived with

[61] The date of Letter 159 is uncertain. Hauser–Meury ('Amazonia', 28) assumes a family relationship with Gregory; 'Theodorus VIII', ibid. 165.

[62] Epigr. 154 (*Anth. graeca*, ii. 524) possibly dates from 384; Georgius may be identified with the recipient of Bas. *Ep.* 149, dating from 382/3, cf. Beckby, *Anthologia graeca*, ii. 606 (n. to Epigr. 154); his priesthood is indicated by Gregory's use of the words ἁγνὰς θυσίας; Hauser–Meury, 'Georgius VI', 85 n. 161.

[63] Nothing is known concerning another Basilissa, mentioned in Epigr. 150 (*Anth. graeca*, ii. 522); Hauser–Meury, 'Basilissa II', 38.

[64] Possibly in 385 Gregory wrote to Gregory of Nyssa a letter of condolence occasioned by the death of Θεοσεβίαν, τὴν ὄντως ἱερὰν καὶ ἱερέως σύζυγον καὶ ὁμότιμον καὶ τῶν μεγάλων μυστηρίων ἀξίαν, *Ep.* 197. The epitaph composed on the occasion of Emmelia's death reads: 'she gave life to so many children, sons and daughters, married and unmarried (ὁμόζυγας ἀζυγέας).... Three became glorious priests, one the *syzyge* of a priest', Beckby (*Anth. graeca*, ii. 528). Epigram 164 is dedicated to κλεινῆς τέκος Ἐμμελίοιο, Γρηγορίου μεγάλου σύζυγε, Beckby (*Anth. graeca*, ii. 530). The problem is evidently the term *syzyge*. Originally, *syzyge* denoted objects arranged in pairs, as well as a close relationship between humans, more precisely that of a marriage. If so, Emmelia had a daughter called Theosebia married to a priest called Gregory and a son called Gregory who became a priest and was married to yet another Theosebia, 'des coïncidences bien singulières', but possible. LSJ s.v. συζυγέω III; Aubineau, *Virginité*, 65–76 (quotation, 68). However, *syzyge* may also be translated in the sense of 'associate' or 'collaborator', as used by Paul (Phil. 4: 3); Gr. Nyss. *De virg.* 3. 1. 5–15 (SC 119. 272 f.). J. Daniélou ('Le Mariage de Grégoire de Nysse et la chronologie de sa vie', *Revue des Études Augustiniennes* 2 (1956), 71–8, esp. 73–8) is very much in favour of translating *syzyge* as 'wife'; Gallay (*Lettres*, ii. 164 (n. 3 to *Ep.* 89)), Hauser–Meury ('Theosebia I and II', 171 f.), and Maraval ('Encore les frères et les sœurs', 165) are less certain.

him in a chaste marriage, or his actual sister, one of Emmelia's daughters.[65]

It is a rare coincidence that two authors complement each other as perfectly as Basil of Caesarea and Gregory of Nazianzus. Basil has provided us with structures and regulations, and Gregory has filled the regulations with names, allowing us at least a glimpse of the individuals affected by them. Combined, they portray a picture of ascetic life with more finely delineated contours, and allow us to identify developments of a more general nature.

During the early second half of the fourth century, the years of Basil's and Gregory's respective episcopates, the institutionalization of female asceticism had progressed rapidly. We now find a *tagma tōn parthenōn*, an order of virgins, with well-defined characteristics. Enrolment followed the successful completion of a noviciate and a rigorous examination, and was ratified by a public vow, possibly celebrated with an official procession. The minimum age was set at 16 or 17 years, and members who reneged on their public promises were punished according to a precise code. In return, all the virgin's worldly concerns were taken care of, with her material welfare being ensured by the congregation. Further, the *tagma* welcomed members from all social strata; in fact, the financial support seems to have made it especially attractive for members of the lower classes. However, in part as a result of our sources, most of the women we know personally come from the highest echelons of society, and were connected with each other and with the leaders of the clergy by family relationship.

The sources remain quite ambiguous with regard to the precise function of such a virgin within her congregation, though of course she was the 'temple of the Lord' and the 'spouse of the heavenly bridegroom'. In this capacity, she enjoyed an exalted position, became the 'glory of the clergy' and an adornment for the entire congregation, which was graced by her presence only on the occasion of divine service.

[65] The former solution was suggested by Tillemont (*Mémoires*, ix. 562), 'les lois de l'Église avaient obligé Théosébie d'entrer dans la continence en même temps que son mari avait été élevé à l'épiscopat'; while the laws regarding celibacy of the clergy were at that time by no means as stringent, a *mariage blanc* is a possibility.

According to the exalted descriptions of her position as summarized above, a member of the *tagma* enjoyed a high standing,
simply as a result of her vocation. Yet how does this place her
within the emerging ecclesiastical hierarchy? It is clear that a
virgin's function was purely charismatic; its benefit for the community was entirely intangible, ensured solely through her special
kind of life, her graced or 'chosen' status. The question arises as
to whether and to what degree this charisma differs from that of
the clergy itself.

At this time, the 370s and 380s, the congregation as a whole had
been divided into two principal *tagmata*, the 'chosen', or ordained
(κλῆρος), and the laity (λαός).[66] The newly emerging *tagma* of the
virgins formed one half of an entirely new order, the τάγμα τῶν
μοναζόντων, those who led an ascetic life, either male or female.[67]
How precisely this *tagma* ought to be classified—among the
'chosen', or among the laity—was a perilous decision, fraught
with uncertainties, and its status thus remained long ambiguous.[68]

[66] Originally, the term τάγμα ('what has been ordered or arranged') referred to
military units, such as a brigade or division, but it soon gained the meaning of an
'order', a rank or status within the hierarchy of the early Church; LSJ s.v. τάγμα.
In order to ensure the τάξις or order of the congregation as a whole, these two
basic τάγματα were in turn subdivided into several strictly hierarchical subsections:
the κλῆρος consisted of bishops, χωρεπίσκοποι, presbyters and deacons, and the
minor orders of the subdeacons and the readers. The λαός, apart from comprising
the entire congregation, also consisted of specific orders: those of the deaconesses,
the widows, the catechumens, and the penitents; cf. can. 24 of Laodicea (late 4th
cent.), Hefele–Leclercq, i.2, 1012 f.; Bas. *Ep.* 54: τὸ τάγμα τῶν ἱερατικῶν; *Ep.* 188
c. 3: οἱ ἐν τῷ λαϊκῷ ὄντες τάγματι, a description already employed in can. 5 of
Nicaea (325), Hefele–Leclercq, i.1, 548; A. Faivre, *Naissance d'une hiérarchie:
Les Premières Étapes du cursus clérical* (Théologie historique 40; Paris, 1977),
75–98, 223–8; id. *Les Laïcs aux origines de l'Église* (Paris, 1984), 167–240; Gain,
L'Église, 62 f.

[67] Can. 24 of Laodicea has τοῦ τάγματος τῶν ἀσκητῶν; Faivre, *Naissance*, 229;
Gain, *L'Église*, 118–20; see Gaudemet (*L'Église*, 199–211) for developments
primarily in the Latin West.

[68] Already can. 12 of the *Traditio Apostolica* (TA) (*Hippolyte de Rome: La
Tradition Apostolique d'après les anciennes versions*, ed. B. Botte (SC 11bis;
Paris, 1984²), 68), compiled between 180 and 200, had established the fact that a
virgin cannot be ordained through the imposition of hands. It is her own free will
which makes her into a virgin. This prescription is maintained in the *Testamentum
Domini nostri Jesu Christi*, 1. 46. 1 (TD) (Syriac edition with Latin translation and
commentary by I. E. Rahmani (Mainz, 1899) 106 f.): 'Virgins are not installed or
ordained by men, but have been separated by their own will and take this name.

One development is certain. The relationship between virgins and the bishop or the next highest member of the clergy was close. The bishop was responsible for their spiritual care, as well as their physical and material welfare to the degree of financial trusteeship and possibly legal tutelage.[69] The *patria potestas* of the virgin's natural father seems thus to have shifted largely to a member of the clergy. Bishops requested tax exemptions on their behalf and supervised their financial support (even if this was actually administered by other clerics), and members of the clergy functioned as *oikonomoi*.[70] The *patria potestas* had thus been transferred to a man who was in no way legally related to the woman in his charge; and the woman in turn assumed a social role akin to that of wife, widow, or mother without any legal claim to any of those positions. This shift of *patria potestas* to a non-related male, combined with an increase in the number of women who *de jure* were neither mothers (and could thus not claim *matria potestas*), wives, nor widows, probably caused over time a change in the legal position of women in society, and thus their sphere of action. This remains to be further investigated, however.[71]

One cannot lay hands on to gain virginity since this order (τάγμα) relies on one's own will'; the synod of Antioch (341) is the first in the Orient to specify minor orders; cf. Faivre, *Naissance*, 75–98, 200, 221–3.

[69] In *RF* 27 (PG 31. 988) Basil alludes to the spiritual father as representing the rule (κανών); Gr. Nyss., *De virg.* 23. 6. 8–10 (SC 119. 544), refers to Basil as lawgiver.

[70] For a more general overview and later developments cf. Biondi, *Il diritto romano cristiano*: i. 421–7, legal regulations of monastic orders; i. 435–61 the scope of civil jurisdiction accorded to bishops; iii. 1–57, the *patria potestas*; Cacitti, 'L'etica sessuale', 69–157; H. de Lubac, *Les Églises particulières dans l'Église universelle* (Intelligence et la Foi; Paris, 1971), esp. 175–92; E. Neuhäusler, *Der Bischof als geistlicher Vater nach den frühchristlichen Schriften* (Munich, 1964), *passim*.

[71] Legal studies by both Gaudemet and Biondi suggest a dual development: increasing protection of a woman's material basis combined with a static if not decreasing role in public affairs, both on the grounds of a woman's *infirmitas sexu*; however, women did gain a greater economic role, which had its impact in the long run, heightened no doubt by powerful and influential empresses. The situation is difficult and complex; see Biondi, *Il diritto romano cristiano*, iii. 1–200; J. Gaudemet, 'Le Statut de la femme dans l'Empire romain', 'Aspects sociologiques de la famille romaine', and 'Les Transformations de la vie familiale au Bas-Empire et l'influence du Christianisme', all reprinted in id. *Études de droit*

That the period in question witnessed an increase in institutionalization is demonstrated by the mere notion of a *tagma*. This may, of course, be an impression reflecting precisely the intention of the authors of our sources, who without exception were themselves the organizers and creators of what was, according to them, the norm. Did ascetic life indeed become more streamlined and organized? Given the nature of our sources, the difficulties inherent in answering such a question are evident. What Basil's and Gregory's writings reveal is a *de facto* progress in organization. The practical norms of an ideal ascetic life had become more precise. Yet this precision resulted from a continuing interaction with constantly emerging 'deviations', which had to be addressed and regulated. Thus, even though organizational norms were in the process of crystallizing, this process was in practice much more protracted than a superficial glance at our orthodox sources might lead us to believe.

Judging from the way in which virgins organized their daily lives, the diversity continued. An ascetic woman had to accommodate a variety of practical preconditions—her financial situation, her relationship to her family, the availability of other compatible persons—perhaps simply personal preference. On a different level it appears that asceticism, male and female, was a predominantly urban phenomenon, though again this finding might simply result from our sources: the majority of ascetics addressed by Basil and Gregory lived in urban areas, more precisely, in close proximity to the local bishop.

In fact, the close connection, indeed identity, of ascetics, clerics, and members of the *tagma tōn monazontōn* is a crucial aspect, and perhaps directly responsible for the ambiguity of our sources with regard to the *tagma*'s hierarchical position. A sizeable proportion of the male ascetics were clerics and lived together with

romain, iii (Pubblicazioni della Facoltà di Giurisprudenza della Università di Camerino 4: 3; Camerino, 1979), 225–310; R. Lapart, 'Le Rôle de la materfamilias romaine d'aprés saint Augustin', *Revue du Moyen Age latin* (1945), 129–48; for the economic situation cf. for instance J. Le Gall, 'Un critère de différenciation sociale: La Situation de la femme', in *Recherches sur les structures sociales dans l'Antiquité Classique (Colloque national du centre national de la recherche scientifique, Caen 25–26 avril 1969)* (Paris, 1970), 275–86; E. Volterra, 'Les Femmes dans les "inscriptiones" des rescrits impériaux', in *Xenion: Festschrift für J. Zepos*, i (Athens–Freiburg i.B.–Cologne, 1973), 717–24.

their own sisters or other female relatives, who were themselves ascetics. The sensitive issue of men and women practising ascetic life in common posed a particular problem, and was a clear point of controversy: boundaries between the 'acceptable' and the 'unacceptable' were hard to define and in constant flux. A vast 'grey area' comprised a host of ascetic experiments (not only those involving cohabitation) which surface occasionally in our normative sources, mostly in the context of warnings and condemnations: thus we read of virgins who professed their vows 'in heresy', *kanonikai* who lived with men 'in prostitution', virgins who lived as *subintroductae*. In contrast to such irregularities as these, the notion of the *tagma* as represented by our authors served as a bench-mark, as a blueprint to facilitate the exclusion and marginalization of other forms of ascetic life, which none the less existed.

In the year 314 the Fathers at Ancyra had issued a canon prohibiting 'those, who live together with men as if they were their sisters, from doing so'. Ten years later the third canon of the council of Nicaea condemned all clerics who lived with women other than their direct relatives. More than half a century after these and several other official condemnations, the practice of celibate 'marriage' was alive and flourishing.[72]

At the beginning of his episcopate Basil received a letter (now lost) from a presbyter called Paregorius, a man in his seventies who lived somewhere in the Cappadocian countryside. Paregorius felt imposed upon by his direct superior, the *chorepiskopos*, who had complained about his way of life.[73] This could only have been sheer rancour on the *chorepiskopos*' part, since he, Paregorius, lived according to a well-established custom sanctioned by long

---

[72] Ancyra c. 19 (Mansi, ii. 519); Nicaea c. 3 (Mansi, ii. 670); P. de Labriolle, 'Le "Mariage Spirituel" dans l'Antiquité Chrétienne', *RH* 137 (1921), 204–25, here 210; p. 222 contains a list of councils condemning the practice, which was eventually prohibited by Canon Law (*Decretum Gratiani*); E. A. Clark, 'John Chrysostom and the *Subintroductae*', *CH* 46 (1977), 171–85; repr. in ead. *Ascetic Piety and Women's Faith*, 265–90.

[73] Bas. *Ep.* 55 (AD 370); the name Paregorius is furnished by MSS L and C of the epistolary tradition, and confirmed by the Syriac version of the *Par. syr.* 62: Courtonne retains Gregorius; Achelis, *Virgines Subintroductae*, 46; Gain (*L'Église*, 102) interprets *Ep.* 55 as referring to Paregorius' wife; for a succinct discussion of the *chorepiskopoi* cf. ibid. 94–100; for presbyters ibid. 100–8.

tradition. The truth was that he lived with a 'little woman' (γυναίου) in a spiritual marriage. The woman helped him with his household; he took care of her material needs; and both had evidently grown rather fond of each other. At the same time their union was platonic, an affirmation Basil has no reason to doubt. But Basil replies in no uncertain terms. He is shocked and surprised that Paregorius not only pleads innocence, but dares to feel indignation: Nicaea had 'distinctly forbidden the introduction of women (συνείσακτους) into the household'. In fact he reproaches Paregorius' conduct not only on the grounds that it violates the decisions reached at Nicaea, but also because he wants the best of both worlds: the virtues and future rewards granted to the celibate as well as the earthly advantages of companionship with the other sex. This attitude contradicts the very nature of celibacy: 'to be cut off from the society of women'. Further, Paregorius' example may easily become a stumbling-block for many less virtuous, and thus create a scandal (Rom. 2: 24, 14: 13). Paregorius has to find a male servant. However, he need not abandon the woman to some harsh fate: Basil suggests he 'place her in a monastery' (ἐν μοναστηρίῳ).[74]

Sheer practical advantages kept the institution of the 'spiritual marriage' alive. Paregorius and his 'little woman' lived in the countryside. He was a presbyter and a celibate, the woman an ascetic. Many women like her, wanting to lead a celibate life, had no economic alternative, especially in the countryside where the likelihood of finding similarly minded companions of the same sex may have been quite low. Moreover, since both kept their vow, their union was not only practicable but even admirable, and it did not seem to have diminished either the venerable presbyter's or the virgin's standing in the community. It is only by 370 that, at least for the woman, a practicable alternative emerges: a *monastērion*.[75]

About thirty years earlier, another presbyter, Leontius of Antioch, had become the target of Athanasius of Alexandria for exactly the same reason: he shared his house with a virgin called Eustolion, who, according to Athanasius, was no longer a virgin.

[74] An early usage of the word; the more common word for a female community is *parthenōn*; cf. above, p. 97 n. 70.
[75] Perhaps a Basilian foundation?

Leontius castrated himself to be able to continue living with her—an extreme measure which failed to achieve his purpose: his superiors deprived him of his presbyterial honours.[76] Paregorius and Leontius were members of the clergy. Marriage of clerics was still an accepted practice. Yet, while it was not at all a universally accepted prerequisite for ordination, celibacy was on the rise. All the official regulations that have been mentioned prohibited only the 'spiritual marriage' of members of the clergy, of the ταγμα τῶν ἱερατικῶν.[77] Members of the *tagma tōn monazontōn*, ascetics in other words, were not affected by these regulations, unless they were also members of the clergy. However, before attempting any further clarification of the complexities of the symbiosis between male and female ascetics, the relevance of our observations for the *tagma tōn parthenōn* ought to be summarized.

The institutionalization of female ascetic practice coincided with four interrelated aspects. First, ascetic life continuously rose in esteem. Secondly as a direct result, the numbers of women and men attracted to this life increased. Thirdly, at the same time, asceticism and celibacy gained in significance as prerequisites for clerical office. Lastly, ascetic life made men and women, in theory, into equals. The features that, up to a certain point, distinguish the priest from the lay person are celibacy and ascetic purity. This distinction is emphasized in the liturgical function, where the priest's special charisma, his purity, becomes the prerequisite for his relationship to God.[78] Through the same

---

[76] Rehabilitated, he later became bishop of Antioch; Ath. *Hist. Ar. ad monachos*, 28 (PG 25. 725).

[77] Bas *Ep*. 199 c. 27; for Eustathius' criticism of married clergy cf. Soc. *HE* 2. 43 (PG 67. 135); Soz. *HE* 3. 14. 33 (GCS 50. 123). Ever since Bishop Paphnutius from the Upper Thebais rejected the proposal of Nicaea to oblige all members of the higher clerical ranks to end their marital relationships, the development differed in East and West; Soc. *HE* 1. 11 (PG 67. 101); Soz. *HE* 1. 23 (GCS 50. 44); Faivre, *Naissance*, 219; Gaudemet, *L'Église*, 159–63; R. Gryson, *Les Origines du célibat ecclésiastique* (Recherches et Synthèses, Sect. Hist.; Gembloux, 1970), *passim*; J. E. Lynch, 'Marriage and Celibacy of the Clergy. The Discipline of the Western Church: An historio-canonical Synopsis I,' *Jurist* 32 (1972), 14–38; P. Pampaloni, 'Continenza e celibato del clero: Leggi e motivi nelle fonti canonistiche dei secc. IV e V', *Studia Patavina* 17 (1970), 5–59.

[78] H. Crouzel, 'Le Célibat et la continence ecclésiastique dans l'église primitive: Leurs motivations', in id. *Mariage et divorce: Célibat et caractère sacerdotaux dans l'église ancienne* (Études d'Histoire du Culte et des Institutions Chrétiennes 2; Turin, 1982), 245–371; Gryson, *Les Origines du célibat, passim*.

characteristics, celibacy and asceticism, a woman also enters into a special relationship, a *pactum* or *epangelia*, with the Divine. If continence becomes increasingly a prerequisite for clerical charisma, and if, through an ascetic life, the differences between the sexes are blurred or obliterated, what prevents an ascetic woman from being granted clerical charisma?

It is no coincidence that all precepts addressed to virgins, written with clearly normative intent by such authoritative figures as the Cappadocian Fathers, stress essentially the same points: virgins ought to maintain close connection with a bishop, who acts as spiritual guide, and they should refrain from independent interpretation or teaching of dogmatic issues. These precepts are enhanced by stern exhortations to esteem humility, abstain from talking, and remain inside the house, unseen and unheard. At the same time, we observe an increasing precision in defining the nature of a virgin's charisma and how she ought to live, combined with the use of more differentiated titles such as *parthenos tēs ekklēsias*, or *kanonikē*. It is perhaps equally no coincidence that the duties assigned to a virgin as reflected in these prescriptions appear to be increasingly limited. The sources mention fewer and fewer occasions for actual charitable involvement, or any other occupation beyond 'being a pure vessel', immersed in prayer and meditation, abstaining from any unnecessary mobility. Yet, at the same time, the language used to characterize this increasingly circumscribed ideal endows the virgin with an undiminished, if not augmented, theoretical importance: a reflection of a complex and highly elaborate process. While the theoretical implications of the ascetic charisma suggest an expanding practical role (in other words, could easily call for some concrete recognition of these women's importance within the framework of the ecclesiastical hierarchy), the Fathers seek to prevent this in practice—for social and religious reasons which cannot be discussed here.

Women's demand for ordination has to be denied without at the same time alienating a highly significant sector of the Christian community. The answer, at least in theory, is the notion of an 'internalized' ideal. The true virgin has all the characteristics of the perfect male ascetic combined with her own; she becomes manly in her *virtue*, an exemplar of the 'philosophical life'; her position within the congregation is honoured, and she is granted virtual economic autonomy, but all of this remains internal, and from an administrative point of view, private. She must not translate this status into its exact external representation: she must not alter her appearance into a male one, she must not assume the functions of a cleric (other than prayer), she must not assume a public role which would overstep certain clearly felt limits and thereby contradict that within her which remains female. Thus, female presbyters and female bishops appear only among those condemned as heretics.

This pattern of institutionalization appears to adhere to the classic Weberian model. As soon as female asceticism became too amorphous, too widespread, and in many instances potentially too powerful, efforts at regulation without alienation set in. A new order, the *tagma tōn parthenōn*, with new titles and functions emerges; it is characterized by a clearer definition, allowing for easier supervision. Deviations from the newly created norm are easier to identify and thus to prevent. At the same time, the *de facto* limitations are compensated for by an increase in status—'future bride of the Lord'—which provides satisfaction without threatening the good order (*taxis*) of the existing hierarchy through demands for ordination. The result is the formation of the *tagma tōn parthenōn* as a part of the τάγμα τῶν μοναζόντων, which is clearly separated from the *tagma tōn hieratikōn*.[79] Neither the *tagma tōn parthenōn*, nor the function and significance of its institutional development are without precedent.

When Macrina decided to change her life at the age of 12, she declared herself, without ever having been married, to be a widow. Her choice of 'title' or, better, 'status' was not haphazard. From the earliest period in Jerusalem onwards, widows had held a special position within the Christian congregation, but the first to discuss this special position was Paul in his Letter to Timothy

---

[79] Though the distinction between the male ascetics and the clergy is fluid because of the frequent 'personal union' between cleric and ascetic. At *Ep.* 199 c. 19 Basil distinguishes between two groups of male ascetics: members of the *tagma tōn monazontōn*, who have to proclaim a vow, and others who do not swear a vow and decide to live privately in celibacy. Would one have to assume a similar distinction between members of the *tagma* and others in the case of celibate women? Cf. also Gregory of Nazianzus' reference to the *migadoi* in *Or.* 43. 62 (Boulenger, 186), and to the *Naziraioi*, *Or.* 43. 28 (Boulenger, 120).

(1 Tim. 5: 3–16).[80] Here, he defines three categories of widows: those who have their own means of support and thus no claims against the congregation; those who are entirely on their own and have to be 'honoured', that is, financially supported, by the Church without further conditions ('the real widows'); and, finally, a third group, 'those put on the roll'.[81] This last group, pledged to remain widowed and supported either by their families or by the congregation, had to perform specific duties, consisting of acts of charity, almsgiving, and prayer. To become part of the third group was not a matter of personal choice. A woman had to be 'elected' on the basis of certain prerequisites. She had to be at least sixty years of age, have married only once, reared children, and performed good deeds.[82] Our focus will be on this last category, widows 'placed on the roll'.[83]

By the turn of the first century AD, the term widow or χήρα had already assumed technical meaning. It did not simply de-

[80] The following discussion makes no claim to be exhaustive. For a more detailed treatment of the subject see my forthcoming paper in the *Journal of Early Christian Studies* 'The Order of Widows, the Order of Deaconesses'. Cf. L. Bopp, *Das Witwentum als organische Gliedschaft im Gemeinschaftsleben der alten Kirche* (Mannheim, 1965); still fundamental is J. Daniélou, 'Le Ministère des femmes dans l'Église ancienne', *La Maison-Dieu* 61 (1960), 70–96; Davies, *Revolt of the Widows*, has interesting insights; for a comparison of classical and Old Testament attitudes towards widows cf. Giannarelli, *La tipologia*, 49–66; cf. also B. Grillet (ed.), *Jean Chrysostome: À une Jeune veuve sur le mariage unique* (SC 138; Paris, 1968), esp. 21–83; still fundamental is A. Kalsbach, *Die altkirchliche Einrichtung*, *passim*; LaPorte, *Role of Women in Early Christianity*, 58–70; H. Lesêstre, 'Veuve', in *DB* v. 2411–13; J. Viteau, 'L'Institution des Diacres et des Veuves', *RHE* 22 (1926), 513–37.

[81] J. Chrys. *Vidua eligatur*, 2 (PG 51. 322–3): 'Once poverty is concerned, Paul did not concern himself with age. And what, if at the age of fifty, she is consumed by famine? And, if still young, she has been deprived of the use of parts of her body? Must she sleep until she has reached the age of sixty?'; Daniélou, 'Le Ministère', 78; Grillet, *Le mariage unique*, 37 f.; Gryson, *Le Ministère*, 31–3; Martimort, *Les Diaconesses*, 19–21.

[82] A different view is held by J. G. Davies, 'Deacons, Deaconesses and the Minor Orders in the Patristic Period', *JEH* 14 (1963), 1–15, here 5: 'they were . . . in no sense an active order, rather . . . an organised group of Church pensioners, and to be "on the roll" was to be a recipient of charity.'

[83] Regarding the category of widows who were recipients of alms cf. e.g. Ign. *Ant. Ep. ad Smyr.* 6. 2 (PG 5. 712); Polycarp, *Ep. ad Phil.* 6. 1 (PG 5. 1009); S. Elm, 'Vergini, vedove, diaconisse—alcune osservazioni sullo sviluppo dei cosidetti "ordini femminili" nel quarto secolo in Oriente', *Codex Aquilarensis* 5 (1991), 77–89; Gryson, *Le Ministère*, 34–6.

scribe a woman who had lost her husband; it designated one
having a specific role within the community: a woman who, as an
'altar of God', led an exemplary life of continence, and whose
prayers were therefore of a particular significance for the entire
congregation.[84]
The clearest insight into the role and function of these widows
emerges from certain canonical and liturgical documents originating in the third century. The *Traditio Apostolica*, 'le document le plus ancien et le plus précieux pour l'histoire de la
littérature et des institutions au troisième siècle', lists widows
among a number of congregational office-bearers who rank below
the bishop, the presbyters, and the deacons: they are cited after
the confessor, before the lector, and before virgins.[85] 'When,
however, a widow is instituted (καθιστάναι) she is not ordained
(χειροτονεῖν), but distinguished by [this] name . . . because she does
not offer the oblation or possess liturgical functions (λειτουργία).'[86]
The *Traditio Apostolica* became the model for a variety of later
ecclesiastical constitutions which rephrased and reshaped the
original text to suit the needs of local congregations,[87] the
most important of which are beyond doubt the *Constitutiones*

---

[84] Polycarp, *Ep. ad Phil.* 4. 3 (PG 5. 1009); cf. Tert. *ad uxorem*, 1. 7. 4 (CCSL
1. 381); Ign. Ant. *Ep. ad Smyr.* 13. 1 (PG 5. 717); for interpretations of the
metaphor 'altar of God' cf. Daniélou, 'Le Ministère', 77; Kalsbach, *Die altkirchliche Einrichtung*, 17 f.

[85] B. Botte, 'Le Texte de la Tradition Apostolique', *Recherches de théologie
ancienne et médiévale* 22 (1955), 161–72, here 161; the original Greek text has
been lost and has had to be reconstructed from Syriac, Coptic, and other translations; for the complicated question of authorship cf. B. Botte's introduction to
Hippolyte de Rome: La Tradition Apostolique, 67; Faivre, *Naissance*, 57 f.; the
TA (20, 24, 30 (SC 11bis, 78, 98, 110)) also contains references to indigent
widows.

[86] Botte, *TA* 12 (SC 11bis, 69); for the important distinction between χειροτονία
and simple institution, and its relevance for the increasing division between clerics
and laics cf. Faivre, *Naissance*, 49–67, and the bibliography, ibid.

[87] For the methodological problems involved in the entire genre of canonical
and liturgical writings and their normative aspects cf., to quote but a few, N.
Brox, 'Altkirchliche Formen des Anspruchs auf apostolische Kirchenverfassung',
Kairos 12 (1970), 113; id. *Offenbarung, Gnosis und gnostischer Mythos bei Irenäus
von Lyon* (Salzburger Patristische Studien 1; Salzburg, 1966), 150–8; Cacitti,
'L'etica sessuale', 69–80; D. van den Eynde, *Les normes de l'enseignement chrétien
dans la littérature patristique des trois premiers siècles* (Paris, 1953), 159–87; *La
Didascalie des douze apôtres*, ed. F. Nau (Paris, 1912²), 44.

Apostolorum, whose final redaction can be dated to around 380 in an Antiochene milieu.[88] Here, the arrangement of the 'sacerdotal lists' reveals that a marked change has taken place.[89] By the end of the fourth century widows formed a separate order, but this order, together with that of the virgins, had been relegated to a position inferior to a new female function: the deaconess.[90] Not only does the widow now rank below the virgin and the deaconess; neither widow nor virgin appears in any context relating to official, 'quasi-clerical' functions. This virtual reversal of the widow's role is further reflected in the functions accorded her when compared to those associated with the virgin and the deaconess.

The widows' primary function,[91] according to the *Constitutiones*, is to 'persevere in prayer night and day', and to be calm, meek, and quiet. Widows must never give instruction in the faith, but direct all those who have questions of a doctrinal nature directly to the bishops:

Women are not permitted to teach in the Church, but only to pray and to listen to their teachers. . . . The widow must therefore know that she is the altar of God and that she has to remain at home, not introducing herself under some pretext into the houses of other faithful to become a

[88] The fundamental edition is still that of F. X. Funk (*Didascalia et Constitutiones Apostolorum* (*CA*) (Paderborn, 1905; repr. Turin, 1970)); here the revised edition by M. Metzger (*Les Constitutions Apostoliques*, 3 vols. (SC 320, 329, 336; Paris, 1985–7)) has been used; for the complex textual history of the *CA* as well as its literary genre cf. Metzger's introduction, pp. 13–54, 63–94; for the date and place of origin, pp. 54–62; interestingly, the *CA* was rejected as 'falsified by heretics' in can. 2 of the council of Quinisexe in 681; Faivre, *Naissance*, 77 n. 2.

[89] *CA* 8. 12. 43–4; 13. 14; 28. 7–8; 31. 2; 46. 1 (SC 336. 202, 208, 230, 234, 264); καταλόγου τοῦ ἱερατικοῦ, *CA* 3. 15, 5 (SC 329. 154); *Book VIII*, also known in an abridged form under the title *Epitome of Book VII of the Apostolic Constitutions* or as *The Constitutions of Hippolytus*, is here relevant; cf. Funk, *Didascalia*, ii, pp. xi–xix, 72–96.

[90] In addition to the works already mentioned, cf. also Gain, *L'Église*, 112–15; Gaudemet, *L'Église*, 122 f. (regarding deaconesses), 186 f. (regarding widows); A. Kalsbach, 'Diakonisse', in *RAC* iii. 917–28; C. Vagaggini, 'L'ordinazione delle diaconesse nella tradizione greca e bizantina', *OrChrP* 40 (1974), 145–89.

[91] Widows are not ordained; they are only admitted to their order: *CA* 8. 25. 2 (SC 336. 226), κατατασσέσθω εἰς τὸ χηρικόν; they have to be 60 years of age and must fulfil their vow of continence, which they have made to Christ; Gryson, *Le Ministère*, 96 n. 4.

gadabout; because God's altar doesn't wander around, but is fixed to one place.

Moreover,

as far as women who baptize are concerned, we inform you that those daring to do so place themselves in high danger. This is why we do not condone such a practice, because it is uncertain, or rather, it is illegal and unfaithful. In fact, since the 'head of the woman is the man', it is he who has been chosen for the priesthood.

It is not only pagan atheism, but an aberration against the very laws of nature if women usurp the functions of a priest or baptize.[92]

Some widows regard their status as a profession. They use the support received from the faithful as an investment, lending it out at 'ferocious' interest, being solely concerned with their profits. They do not pray for all, but only for the rich, at the same time constantly comparing and criticizing what has been given to them. Such widows, so the compiler of the *Constitutiones*, are widows in name only, but not in actual fact.

The situation is quite different with regard to the new office-bearers, the deaconesses. In sharp contrast to both the widow and the virgin, the deaconess, at times called ἡ διάκονος, at times ἡ διακόνισσα, is included in the 'sacerdotal lists', albeit always after all other ministries held by men. Furthermore, the deaconess is formally ordained:[93] 'O bishop, you shall lay hands upon her in the presence of the *presbyterium*, the deacons and the deaconesses'. In this context she is mentioned immediately after the deacon, and before the remaining male ministries; the same is true in a passage which compares the deacon to Christ and the deaconess to the Holy Spirit, emphasizing that the Holy Spirit cannot act independently of Christ.

Her functions are well defined. She is to assist the bishop during the baptism of women; but, as the compiler is eager to explain, her sole duty is that of anointing the body of the neophyte whereas the actual rite of initiation is performed by the bishop. Her other functions are to guard the women's entrance to the church; to conduct the examination of strangers; to perform charitable deeds under the surveillance of both bishop and deacons and to act as a liaison between the women and the male

---

[92] *CA* 3. 1–9 (SC 329. 120–44).   [93] Ibid. 8. 19 (SC 336. 220).

members of the clergy.[94] At the end of a lengthy paragraph on the marriage of the clergy (exalting the advantages of celibacy, and failing that, advocating one marriage only, and then not to a widow, courtesan, or slave, who are unsuitable partners for a cleric), it is stipulated, not suprisingly, that: 'as a deaconess, one should select a pure virgin; in absence of that, a widow married only once, faithful and honourable.'[95]

These changes are significant. When the *Constitutiones Apostolorum* were compiled a new function for women had emerged. The precise nature of this function is difficult to assess. On the one hand, the deaconess represents the female aspects of the diaconate with responsibilities unsuitable for men because of matters of decency;[96] yet, within the ranking order of the hierarchy, her position is appreciably inferior to the relatively superior role of the deacon: 'nous devons reconnaître que sa position au sein de la hiérarchie est incertaine et mal fixée'.[97]

Simultaneously, we note a steep decline in the position once accorded to the widow. While still honoured as the 'altar of God', her position now offers no hint of any clerical status and is subordinate to that of the virgin, only marginally above the general laity.

The *Constitutiones Apostolorum* are a fourth-century compilation, drawing in part, as has been pointed out, on the third-century *Traditio Apostolica*. However, they owe at least as much, if not more, to another third-century document, the *Didascalia Apostolorum*.[98] The *Didascalia* were composed around 230 in

---

[94] Ibid. 2. 26. 3 and 6; 57. 10; 58. 6 (SC 320. 236, 238, 314, 322); 3. 8. 1; 16; 19. 1 (SC 329. 140, 154, 160); 8. 10. 9; 11. 11; 12. 43; 13. 4 and 14; 19; 20. 1; 28. 6–7; 31. 2; 46. 13 (SC 336. 168, 176, 202, 206, 210, 220, 222, 230 f., 236, 270).

[95] Ibid. 6. 17. 4 (SC 329. 346).

[96] Davies, 'Deacons, Deaconesses and the Minor Orders', 4.

[97] Faivre, *Naissance*, 94: 'Si nous pouvions dire que théologiquement parlant, la diaconesse était l'aspect féminin du diaconat . . .'; Gryson, *Le Ministère*, 104–9.

[98] The *Didascalia* discusses the role of widows at length; indeed, the compiler of the *Constitutiones Apostolorum* later adapted this section virtually verbatim in his work. In addition to Funk (n. 89 above) standard editions are those by H. R. Conolly (*Didascalia Apostolorum: The Syriac Version Translated and Accompanied by the Verona Latin Fragments* (Oxford, 1929)) and F. Nau (*La Didascalie des douze apôtres*); cf. also *Die syrische Didascalia übersetzt und erklärt*, ed. H. Achelis and J. Fleming (TU 25: 2; Leipzig, 1904); the original Greek is lost with the exception of a few fragments of Book III, and again our text had to be reconstructed from Latin, Syriac, Coptic, Arabic, and Ethiopian fragments.

Syria, more precisely in the Patriarchate of Antioch, and provide exceptional insights into a Christian congregation of the period. A comparison between the *Didascalia* and the later *Constitutiones Apostolorum* reveals the origin of the changes which were to affect and transform the role of both the widow and the virgin. Already during the third century widows were providing occasion for much concern. Not only did many of them abuse their position for the sake of material gain, but their constant 'bargain-hunting' prevented them from executing their designated functions. Allegedly driven by motives of profit, some widows not only neglected their duties, but failed to accept the authority of the bishop and the deacons. Widows taught, baptized, healed and 'wish[ed] to be wiser and to know better, not only than men, but even than the presbyters and the bishops'.[99] It is precisely at this time, in the *Didascalia*, that the new, well-defined office of deaconess appears for the first time.[100]

The appearance of the deaconess and the gradual decline of the order of widows to a position of lesser significance is not a coincidence nor has the fact remained unnoticed. The most common interpretation of this development can be roughly summarized as follows. Both the order of widows and the subsequently developing order of virgins represented essentially an '*état de vie*'.[101] With increasing emphasis on celibacy, the prestige of the status 'widow' diminished steadily in favour of the virgin. The order of widows thus declined from the middle of the third century onwards in tandem with the increasing value placed on morally correct behaviour among members of the clergy. By the end of the fourth century the role of the widow had dwindled into insignificance,[102] its demise being accelerated by the rise of virginity as an ideal and the arrival of the deaconess. While adopting some qualities of the widow's *état de vie*, the deaconess,

[99] *CA* 3. 1–11 (Conolly, 130–45 = Funk, 182–206); Faivre, *Naissance*, 134–6; Gryson, *Le Ministère*, 65–75.
[100] For a detailed analysis of the deaconess's function according to the *Didascalia* cf. Daniélou, 'Le Ministère', 75; Gryson, *Le Ministère*, 75–9; Martimort, *Les Diaconesses*, 31–41.
[101] Faivre, *Naissance*, 111–13; Gryson, *Le Ministère*, 75, 78 f.
[102] Daniélou, 'Le Ministère', 81–4; Faivre, *Naissance*, 82, 112 f., 125 n. 31 for their decline despite J. Chrys. *Hom. Mat.* 66, 125–7; Grillet, *Le mariage unique*, 39 f.; Gryson, *Le Ministère*, 174–5; Metzger, *Les Constitutions Apostoliques*, ii. 60–4.

who exercised a well-defined function, had superseded the widow.[103] The former's sphere of action was from the outset much more limited and easier to control than that accorded to the widow, which could be expanded beyond 'tolerable' limits merely because of the excellence of an individual's conduct.[104] Although clearly restricted in her potential, the deaconess was rewarded for her actual loss in influence by a much higher ranking in the hierarchy: her position of honour, the διηκονίης τιμή, replaced the original independence of the widow.[105] With the rise of the virgin, the widow lost further ground: the virgin possessed the added dimension of physical integrity and thus achieved a more important *état de vie* than the widow; she was therefore also more suitable for the semi-hierarchical function of the deaconesses.

These interpretations appear very convincing. There remains a distinct impression, however, that such interpretations reflect too precisely the sources themselves, namely the canonico-liturgical literature, which is by definition normative, not descriptive. Perhaps also occasioned by today's concerns regarding the ministry of women in the Church, there remain doubts as to whether these hypotheses do in fact attempt to reconstruct the complexity of the historical circumstances.[106] It is not clear that the 'role of widows' had actually declined to the point we are led to believe by the *Constitutiones Apostolorum*; nor is it necessary to dismiss any form of connection between deaconesses and widows as categorically as some scholars have done.[107] The relationship between the order of widows, the order of virgins, and

---

[103] I do not consider justified the strong dismissal of a link between widows and deaconesses that is at times expressed by scholars such as Martimort (*Les Diaconesses*, 41 n. 42: 'Je ne crois pas utile de faire état des Homélies et des Récognitiones pseudo-Clémentines... ; le rapprochement [of widows] que fait Kalsbach, *Altkirchliche Einrichtung*, 21, avec les diaconesses est purement gratuit').

[104] Faivre, *Naissance*, 135; Kalsbach, *Die altkirchliche Einrichtung*, 31.

[105] *MAMA* viii. 59, no. 321; Martimort, *Les Diaconesses*, 124.

[106] The danger of introducing 'Vorstellungen und Motive der Gegenwart' into these texts is particularly acute in areas like this, cf. Faber, *Theorie der Geschichtswissenschaft*, 141; cf. also Gadamer's explicit formulation regarding the 'Willkür und Beliebigkeit aktualisierender Anbiederung mit der Vergangenheit', *Wahrheit und Methode*, 29, 253, 290, 296 (quotation, 284).

[107] Gryson, *Le Ministère*, 174, to quote an explicit example.

the rise of the deaconess was in fact more complex than is generally acknowledged.

The simple fact that the author of the *Constitutiones Apostolorum*, far from merely copying the relevant passages of the *Didascalia*, felt the need to emphasize factors and introduce aspects which further limited the role of both deaconess and widow in favour of that of the virgin could indicate that the order of widows was not yet quite moribund, and that of the deaconess not yet altogether restricted.[108] The actual as opposed to the legally constructed role occupied by the order of widows can only emerge if examined together with that of the virgin and the deaconess, and in the context of the developing ecclesiastical hierarchy in general.

This is not the place to investigate further whether or not the order of widows declined or was suppressed. It ought to have become apparent, however, that the well-established order of widows was the model for the newly developing order of virgins. Both orders earned their legitimization from the way of life adopted by their members; both accepted their members as the result of a free decision, and both were constituted because of their members' capacity to live an extraordinary life. Both afforded women an unusual degree of independence and influence, a position that was soon threatened once it was recognized as a vehicle for abuse and a possible risk for the hierarchy. This was especially the case in the light of the increasing value attributed to the clergy's 'moral' capacity.[109] The creation of a new, well-defined female ministry, the deaconess, served to restrict the potential role of women.

[108] e.g. selection of deaconesses from among the virgins, the subordination of widows to deaconesses, emphasis on the deaconesses' inability to baptize. For a precise and detailed comparison cf. Faivre, *Naissance*, 118–38; Gryson, *Le Ministère*, 95–109; Martimort, *Les Diaconesses*, 55–71; Vagaggini, 'L'ordinazione', 163–73.

[109] Regarding the highly controversial issue of clerical celibacy cf. further Tillemont, *Mémoires*, ix. 562. In all this one must not forget that even bishops could be married until the Justinianic legislation of 527–65 (repeated by the council of Trullo in 691/2, cc. 12, 13, 48 (Mansi, xi. 946))); Soc. *HE* i. 11 (PG 67. 101–4); Nicephorus, *HE* ii. 19 (PG 146. 628); Aubineau, *Virginité*, 73–5; C. Cochini, *Origines apostoliques du célibat sacerdotal* (Paris, 1981), 23–281; Gaudemet, *L'Église*, 159; E. Vacandart, 'Célibat ecclésiastique,' in *Dictionnaire du Théologie Chrétienne*, ii (Paris, 1905), 2068–80.

Further, all these developments have to be seen within the context of the simultaneously raging struggles for doctrinal supremacy. Women formed an important constituent within *all* the rival factions. Simply to exclude them from any office, without some compensation, could have meant the loss of a substantial number of sympathizers to opposing doctrinal or 'heretical' groups.

A closer scrutiny of the epigraphical, literary, and legal evidence regarding the new function of the deaconess in connection with that of the widow and the virgin reveals a high degree of interrelation and complexity.[110] A few examples will illustrate the point: a late fifth-century adaptation of the various constitutional writings, the *Testamentum Domini nostri Jesu Christi* again from Antioch, confers an extraordinary position of influence upon the widow.[111] Widows include women such as Nonna (Gregory of Nazianzus' mother), Emmelia, Lampadion, and Vetiana, and Macrina regarded herself as a widow; Basil discussed the status of widows *vis-à-vis* virgins, and issued canons regarding a widow 'enrolled among the rank of the widows'.[112] A fifth-century inscription found on a richly decorated tombstone in Colonia in Cappadocia reads: 'According to the texts of the Apostle, Maria the deaconess has reared children, engaged in hospitality, washed the feet of the Saints, and distributed bread to the needy'.[113] Maria was a widow according to 1 Tim. 5: 9–10 as well as a

[110] The term διακόνισσα was a neologism soon to become the technical term; Lampe s.v.; Gryson, *Le Ministère*, 86; Kalsbach, *Die altkirchliche Einrichtung*, 46–9; Martimort, *Les Diaconesses*, 99–102; Vagaggini ('L'ordinazione', 155–60) differs.

[111] *TD* 1. 40–3 (Rahmani, 94 f.); for date and origin cf. Botte, *TA* 12, and Faivre, *Naissance*, 98–113; Gryson, *Le Ministère*, 110–19; 118: 'les principales fonctions de la diaconesse . . . étant assumées dans le Testament par les veuves, le ministère des diaconesses . . . se rèduit à presque rien.' Gryson also argues convincingly (ibid. 92–5) that can. 11 of the late 4th-cent. collection of Phrygian rules (known as the canons of the council of Laodicea), which stipulates that those called elder women (πρεσβύτιδας) or leaders (προκαθημένας) must not be installed (καθίστασθαι) in the Church, ought to be interpreted as referring to 'enrolled widows'; an interpretation he bases primarily on parallells with the *TD*.

[112] *Ep.* 199, c. 24; can. 41 discusses ordinary widows; with regard to Nonna cf. Gr. Naz. *Epigr.* 24–74 (*Anth. graeca*, ii. 460–82); Gryson, *Le Ministère*, 91 f.

[113] Modern Aksaray; G. Jacopi, 'Esplorazioni e studi in Paflagonia e Cappadocia', *Bollettino del Reale Istituto di Archeologia e Storia dell'Arte* 8 (Rome, 1937), 3–43, here 34.

deaconess, and a lady of some means.[114] Indeed, a number of fifth- and early sixth-century inscriptions from eastern Phrygia, Galatia, Cilicia, Lycaonia, Caria, and Iconium confirm that a considerable number of deaconesses were also widows.[115] The inscriptions indicate that most of these deaconesses lived within their own families and that in a substantial number of cases these families had clerical connections: Domna was the daughter of a priest; Aurelia Faustina, the mother of a reader; Nonna, the mother of a presbyter; Masa, both the daughter and the wife of a priest; Kyria, the wife, and Messalina, the sister of a priest.[116] One inscription from Nevine in Laodicea refers to 'Elaphia, deaconess of the Enkratites'.[117]

In short, widows were not only not on the decline as a 're-cruiting pool' for deaconesses, but it appears rather that the 'office' of the enrolled widow gradually merged with the function of the deaconess. Perhaps the most instructive evidence for this progressive assimilation is derived from imperial legislation.

On 21 June 390 the emperors Theodosius, Valentinian, and Arcadius stipulated that 'according to the precept of the Apostle,

[114] At the very least, Maria's relatives were able to afford an elaborate tombstone.

[115] *MAMA* i. nos. 323, Νυνης δηακοννυσης, daughter of Kastor, a presbyter (early 4th cent.); 324, Εἰστρατηγὴς διακό (νισσα); 326, τῆ μη (τρί) μου Πρίβι διάκονος; 383, τῆ μητρί μου Ματρώνη διακονίσσης (all from Eastern Phrygia (Axylos)); ibid. nos. 178, Masa, mentioned with presbyters Phrontios and Rhodonos; 194, ἡ μήτηρ αὐτοῦ Αὐρηλ. Φαυστῖνα διάκονος; 226, Paula diakonos (all from Laodicea Combusta); *MAMA* iii, nos. 212, Athanasia; 395, Theodora; 418, Theophila; 744, Timothes; 759, Charitina (all from Kokyros, Cilicia); *MAMA* vii, nos. 120, Celsa, perhaps married to Septemios; 186, διακονίση Σεβ (ήρα) μητ (ρί; 471, Δόμνα διάκονος θυγάτηρ Θεοφίλου πρεσβυτέρου; 539, μητρὶ Νόννη διακονήση; 585, Messalina; *MAMA* viii, nos. 64 and 91; 318, Basilissa; 321. Grégoire, *Recueil des inscriptions grecques-chrétiennes d'Asie Mineure*, i. no. 258 (Arete in Caria).

[116] *MAMA* vii, no. 471; i, nos. 178, 194; vii, no. 539, and cf. n. 115 above; according to Cyril. Scyth. *Vita Euth.* 3 (*Kyrillos von Skythopolis: Das Leben des heiligen Euthymios*, ed. E. Schwartz (TU 49: 2; Leipzig, 1939) 10 f.), the widow Dionysia, mother of St Euthymus, was ordained deaconess in Armenia in 378; Κύρια διάκονος was the wife of the priest Conon, cf. J. R. Stilington Sterret, 'The Wolfe Expedition to Asia Minor', *Papers of the American School at Athens* 3 (1884/5), 198, no. 326. While, as pointed out by Martimort (*Les Diaconesses*, 123–6), much of the epigraphical evidence is subject to 'extraneous' factors, such as where expeditions have been conducted etc., I disagree with Gryson's comment (*Le Ministère*, 149–50, here 150 n. 8) that the inscriptions do not offer insights.

no woman shall be transferred to the society of deaconesses unless she is sixty years of age and has the desired offspring at home. . . .'[118] The edict then lists the conditions under which a deaconess may dispose of her property, which are similar to those already mentioned in the context of the abused virgins of Venasa: no member of the clergy or ascetic may 'visit' a widow to solicit her legacy under the pretext of religion.[119] Only four months later this same law, 'legem quae de diaconissis vel viduis nuper est promulgata', was partially revoked and somewhat mitigated by addressing uniformly: 'vidua, sive diaconissa, sive virgo dicata Deo, vel sanctimonialis mulier'.[120] In this context the terms widow and deaconess have become synonymous and, indeed, many of the widows' shortcomings, deplored so vociferously by the compilers of both the *Didascalia* and the *Constitutiones Apostolorum*, had similarly become faults of the deaconesses. However, from the middle of the fourth century onwards, parallel to the 'rise' of the *tagma tōn parthenōn* and the emergence of the 'widow-deaconess', a different aspect, if not indeed an entirely new type, of deaconess appeared.

Just after Macrina's death Gregory of Nyssa entrusted all funeral arrangements to 'one of those who preside over the chorus, a deaconess called Lampadion'.[121] Lampadion held a special position: she was entitled 'deaconess', was of advanced age, enjoyed Macrina's particular respect, and presided over the chorus of virgins.[122] Chosen either because she was already a

---

[117] Ἐλα(φ)ίη διακονίσση (τῆς τῶν Ἐ) νκρατῶν, *MAMA* i, p. xxv = *MAMA* vii, no. 69, late 4th cent.

[118] 'Nulla nisi emensis sexaginta annis, cui votiva domi proles sit, secundum praeceptum apostoli ad diaconissarum consortium transferatur', issued to Tatianus, *prefectus praetorio per Orientem; CTh.* 16. 2. 27 (Mommsen–Meyer, i.2, 843 f.); for the date cf. Pharr, *Theodosian Code*, 444 f.; the law is difficult to interpret since Tatianus was pagan and Theodosius on campaign in the West; this does not affect the present argument, however.

[119] *CTh.* 16. 2. 20 (Mommsen–Meyer, i.2, 841); Pharr, *Theodosian Code*, 443 f.

[120] *CTh.* 16. 2. 28 (Mommsen–Meyer, i.2, 844); Pharr, *Theodosian Code*, 445; *Novella Marc.* tit. 5 (Mommsen–Meyer, ii. 195).

[121] *VSM* 29. 1–2.

[122] The *choros* is mentioned twice, in *VSM* 16. 5 and 33. 15, in connection with ceremonial functions; J. Quasten (*Musik und Gesang*, 229) therefore suggested that it was a musical body, which is a probable, but too narrow, interpretation; Maraval, *Macrine*, 236 n. 1. Gregory customarily uses the term in a general sense

deaconess, or elevated to the status of a deaconess as result of her position, Lampadion seems to have been Macrina's proxy and successor, thereby ensuring continuity within the tradition of the founder, herself a 'widow';[123] she therefore combined the office of deaconess with that of ἡγουμένη or leader of an ascetic community.

When Gregory of Nazianzus sought a retreat after his unwelcome ordination as bishop of Sasima, he went to the '*parthenōn* at Seleucia', which was guided by 'the holy deaconess Marthana'.[124] Seleucia borders on Cilicia, and is the place where a fourth-century inscription dedicated to 'Timothea, *diakon* of the monastery' was found.[125]

The best-known widow, deaconess, and *hēgoumenē* of an ascetic community was a lady from the highest level of Constantinopolitan society, John Chrysostom's soul-mate and Gregory of Nazianzus' protégé Olympias, 'most venerable and beloved by the Lord'.[126] Born in 361, the daughter of a high-ranking courtier,

(as discussed below p. 96), e.g. *De virg.* 4. 2. 7 (SC 119. 306); in *VSM* 16. 2 and 33. 15 he juxtaposes *choros* with ἡ ἀδελφότης, σύνταγμα τῶν ἀνδρῶν, τάγμα τῶν μοναζόντων.

[123] Lampadion's condition, virgin or widow, is unclear.

[124] 'Sancta diaconissa nomine Marthana, quam ego apud Ierosolimam noveram . . . monasteria aputactitum seu virginum regebat'; *Per. Aeth.* 23. 3 (SC 21. 184); inscriptions referring to the Seleucian monastery are frequent, e.g. *MAMA* iii, nos. 45, 102; other deaconesses as superiors appear in Antioch: Jannia, Valeriana, and possibly Anastasia, cf. *The Sixth Book of the Selected Letters of Severus, Patriarch of Antioch*, ii.2, ed. E. W. Brooks (London, 1904), 364–71; M. Chaine, 'Une lettre de Sévère d'Antioch à la diaconesse Anastasie', *Oriens christianus*, NS 3 (1913), 36; Martimort, *Les Diaconesses*, 134.

[125] Τιμοθέας διακ(όνου) μονῆς, *MAMA* iii, no. 744; an Ephesian inscription refers to another Lampadion *parthenos diakonos*, Grégoire, *Inscriptions grecques*, i. 19, no. 67.

[126] Our primary sources regarding her life and friendships are the original edition of *Vita Sanctae Olympiadis diaconissae*, ed. H. Delehaye, *AnBoll* 15 and 16 (1896/7), 400–23 and 44–51 (Fr. trans. by J. Bousquet in the *Revue de l'Orient chrétien* 11 (1906), 225–50), and in particular A.-M. Malingrey, *Jean Chrysostome: Lettres à Olympias* (SC 13*bis*); an English translation of the *Life* was made by E. A. Clark, *Jerome, Chrysostom, and Friends*, 107–57; cf. also Gr. Naz. *Carmen ad Olympiadem* (PG 37. 1542–9); Libanius, *Epp.* 677–734 (*Libanii Opera*, x, ed. R. Foerster (Leipzig, 1920), 617–60); Palladius, *HL* 56 (Butler, ii. 149 f.); id. *Dial.* 17 (SC 341. 342–8); Soz. *HE* 2. 6, 8. 9 (GCS 50. 193 f., 361). M. T. W. Arnheim, *The Senatorial Aristocracy in the Later Roman Empire* (Oxford, 1972), 70–2; Baur, *Johannes Chrysostomus* = Gonzaga, *John Chrysostom*, ii. 98–100; G. Grego,

Olympias was orphaned at an early age, and became the legal ward of Procopius, prefect of Constantinople. Her education was entrusted to one of the most cultivated ladies of her time, Theodosia, Amphilochius of Iconium's sister and Gregory of Nazianzus' cousin. At the age of 23 Olympias married a man considerably her senior, who died two years later.[127] Theodosius then urged Olympias to marry his relative Helpidius, but she refused.[128] In retaliation, Theodosius sequestered her immense fortune until she reached 30, and restricted her contact with bishops and visits to churches.[129]

In 390, however, as soon as her property had been restored, Olympias, then aged 30 and never having borne children, was ordained as deaconess by Bishop Nectarius. It was no coincidence that her ordination took place shortly after she had made vast donations to the Constantinopolitan church and its bishop. At that time, too, she already presided over a community of fifty women, which she had founded shortly before.[130] In the same year (390) Theodosius issued the edict which prohibited deaconesses from declaring as their heir any church, member of the

'S. Olimpia di Costantinopoli, donna simpatica ed energetica', *Asprenas*, NS 29 (1982), 41–66; E. D. Hunt, 'Palladius of Helenopolis: A Party and its Supporters in the Church of the Late Fourth Century', *JThS*, NS 24 (1973), 456–80, here 476 f.; Matthews, *Western Aristocracies and Imperial Court*, 102–9.

[127] The date of birth is calculated according to Libanius, *Ep.* 672 (Foerster, 613); Pall. *HL* 56 (Butler, ii. 149); Gr. Naz. *Carm. ad Olympiadem*, 97 f. (PG 37. 1549); but the date is controversial: Malingrey (*Lettres à Olympias*, 15 n. 1) places it between 360 and 370; for Olympias' early years cf. ibid., 15–18; Tillemont' (*Mémoires* xi. 416–60), dates her birth to 368: she would then have married at the age of 18; cf. also Baur, *Johannes Chrysostomus* = Gonzaga, *John Chrysostom*, ii. 98 f.; Matthews, *Western Aristocracies*, 102–9; Martimort, *Les Diaconesses*, 135; 'Nebridius 2', 'Olympias 2', 'Seleucius 1', in *PLRE* i.

[128] *Vita*, 3 (SC 17*bis*, 410).

[129] The property was transferred to the new PVC Clementinus (AD 386/7); 'Clementinus 2', in *PLRE* i; Pall. *Dial.* 17 (SC 341. 344); id. *HL* 56 (Butler, ii. 149 f.; *Vita*, 3 and 4 (SC 17*bis*, 410 f., 412–14); for the size of her fortune cf. *Vita*, 5 and 7 (SC 17*bis*, 416, 420); the fortune included property in Thrace, Galatia, Cappadocia, and Bithynia, as well as two palaces in Constantinople; J. Chrys. *Ep.* 8. 10 (SC 17*bis*, 198); Soz. *HE* 8. 9 (GCS 50. 361); Dagron, *Naissance d'une capitale*, 503 f.; Malingrey, *Lettres à Olympias*, 16–20.

[130] *Vita*, 3–8, 14 (SC 17*bis*, 410–16, 418–22, 436) = Pall. *Dial.* 17 (SC 341. 344, 348); Pall. *HL* 56 (Butler, ii. 149–50); Soz. *HE* 8. 9 (GCS 50. 361); Dagron, *Naissance d'une capitale*, 502–4; Malingrey, *Lettres à Olympias*, 15–18, 20 nn. 3, 4; Tillemont, *Mémoires*, xi. 428.

clergy, or 'pauper', and further prohibited any woman under
60 who had not raised children from becoming a widow or
deaconess;[131] this edict he partially revoked only months later.
Olympias' monastery soon increased to two hundred and fifty
members, who included her relative Elisanthia, her sisters
Martyria and Palladia, and her niece, as well as 'many other
members of senatorial families'. Eventually, Nectarius' successor
John Chrysostom ordained Elisanthia, Martyria, and Palladia as
deaconesses, and, after Olympias, Elisanthia in her turn combined
the office with that of *hēgoumenē* of the foundation.[132] In addition to its amalgamation with the role of the widow, therefore,
the role of a deaconess had developed into that of a superior of
a community, clearly demonstrating the underlying honorific
nature of the title. By the fifth century the *hēgoumenē*–deaconess
nexus was common.

Olympias, Macrina, Vetiana, Gregory's companion Theosebia,
almost all the women we know by name, belonged to the Christian
élite, which ruled the newly emerging Christian Roman Empire
both politically and 'spiritually'. Either by birth or by marriage,
most of these women were linked to high-ranking courtiers at
Constantinople, and some of them to the emperor himself. At
the same time, again either by birth, marriage, or personal friendship, these women were closely associated with the most powerful
bishops of the day. Macrina was sister to Basil of Caesarea and
Gregory of Nyssa. Gregory of Nazianzus was their close friend
and a cousin of Amphilochius. Together with Amphilochius' sister,
Gregory had educated Olympias. Olympias supported Gregory
of Nazianzus' successor in the see of Constantinople, Bishop
Nectarius, who was of senatorial rank and ordained without even

---

[131] 'diaconiss[ae] . . . nullam ecclesiam, nullum clericum, nullum pauperem
scriba[n]t heredes', *CTh.* 16. 2. 27, 28 (Mommsen–Meyer, i.2, 843 f.). The edict
was perhaps revoked by Rufinus, Tatianus' opponent and successor, upon realization that the measure had failed to procure the desired results; for another
example of legislation caused by specific incidents cf. Jones, *Later Roman Empire*,
i. 339–41 = *Theod. II Nov.* 7. 2–4, AD 440; *Vita*, 5 (SC 17*bis*. 414); Dagron,
Naissance d'une capitale, 255 f., 496–507.
[132] *Vita*, 6–8 (SC 17*bis*, 418–22); Baur, *Johannes Chrysostomus* = Gonzaga,
John Chrysostom, ii. 99; Malingrey, *Lettres à Olympias*, 421 n. 5; Martimort, *Les
Diaconesses*, 135–7.

having been baptized.[133] He remained bishop until 397, when he was succeeded by John Chrysostom, Olympias' 'soul-mate'. Olympias in particular, but equally so Macrina, Vetiana, and others, had immense wealth at their disposal. All these ladies were widowed.

The prestige of virgins had risen in society and their position was considered honourable in the general climate of esteem for continence. However, large numbers of women who wanted to lead an ascetic life had married and were widowed. Epigraphic evidence assures us that many of these women were wealthy and well connected to clerical families. They constituted an important resource that no bishop, so frequently enmeshed in doctrinal conflicts, could ignore, not least because donations from people like Olympias, Macrina, and many other widows besides transformed the churches, especially those in urban centres and the capital, into powerful economic enterprises.

The picture revealed by our sources is not that of linear development, easily subsumed under one or two theories. The order of deaconesses emerged at a time when the order of widows had grown both powerful and unruly. On the basis of their personal charisma and aided by financial independence, many widows demanded a position similar to that held by members of the clergy. The primary reason for denying widows those functions was the fact that they were women and thus prohibited from 'ruling' over men. Always confronted with 'heretical' challenges, those who attempted to confine the widows within acceptable limits could not simply prevent women from exercising any kind of public authority, especially those who already held a revered position. The answer lay in a new function with clearly defined and easily enforceable boundaries, but with a semi-public, quasi-clerical appeal: the office of deaconess. At the same time, another female role gained increasing significance: that of the virgin. 'Virgins' likewise derived their influence from personal charisma. As in the case of widows, their position was inherently difficult to regulate, but, unlike the case of widows, far fewer women could

[133] Dagron, *Naissance d'une capitale*, 450–65; Forlin Patrucco, 'Aspetti di vita familiare', 171 f.; for Olympias' influence on Nectarius see *Vita*, 14 (SC 17*bis*. 436); Pall. *Dial.* 17 (SC 341. 348).

fulfil its prerequisites. Before long, efforts were made to define this new order. Yet much of the regulatory effort remained theoretical; in practice we find virgin daughters, as well as virgin widows, virgin wives and virgin mothers. Here, the order of deaconesses offered a solution: rather than simply excluding a vast pool of resources a priori, the 'deaconess' served as a new catch-all category that included both widows and virgins.

The status of the deaconess seems to have been actively promoted as a reward and enticement: the 'honour of the deaconess' increasingly acquired the character of a special recognition for services rendered—irrespective of whether or not a woman fulfilled the prerequisites laid down by the bishops themselves (a case in point is Olympias, ordained deaconess in defiance of both ecclesiastical and, indeed, imperial regulation). 'Deaconess' became an honourable title, and the originally quite precise definition of her function diluted. Instead of superseding the role of the widow, the order of the deaconess absorbed the qualities of the widow, and merged them with its own attributes and those of the virgin to form a concept that applied to a vast variety of women: hence the virgin-widow-deaconess as leader of ascetic communities. This shift away from a function towards a title may, however, have initiated the deaconess's demise: as a title, it could easily be replaced by another honorific designation.

The preceding discussion has sought to bring firmer substance to traces of the great diversity of ascetic models chosen by women in orthodox sources. In fact, the work of Basil and Gregory of Nazianzus confirms that women continued to live in a variety of ways: alone, with their natural family, with brothers, in community with other women, and in spiritual marriages with men. It has also become clear that these women came from all walks of life, and that virgins lived both in rural areas and in cities, though those living in an urban environment predominated. This variety continued despite attempts to organize female ascetic life within the parameters of a *tagma* conceived along the lines of the *tagma* of widows, and continued even while the *tagma* of deaconesses was taking shape. In all these endeavours, the main challenge facing the clergy was to gain and preserve the support of female ascetics—often the possessors of vast financial resources and high-ranking connections, as exemplified, again, by Olympias—without granting these women any degree of public influence that could threaten its own prerogatives. Here, the personal relationship between the most powerful ascetic women and the leading bishops of the time becomes important. Such women traditionally held positions of immense influence which were, however, not exercised through an institutional framework. Their *auctoritas* always possessed a different, more individualistic base, which was nevertheless highly effective. Considered as ascetic equals on both an intellectual and a social level, these women—in the normative writings of their relatives—became the aristocratic *exempla* of female ascetic life, powerful without any claims to institutional representation.[134]

In spite of the complex and at times bewildering variety of forms just discussed, all these models are united by a common denominator: they all follow in essence the path initiated by Juliana; they remain within the boundaries of society. Yet the prophetess also found her followers.

[134] P. R. L. Brown, 'The Saint as Exemplar in Late Antiquity', *Representations* 1 (1983), 1–25; for examples from the Latin context cf. Consolino, 'Modelli di santità femminile', 83–113.

6

Symbiosis of Male and Female Ascetics
and the Demise of the Homoiousian Model

One of the central questions driving much of the preceding discussion is encapsulated in two words: orthodox and heretical;
that is, norm and deviation as defined by the party which ultimately succeeded. What constitutes the norm, on what grounds
are certain issues seen as heretical, how are heresies constructed
both at the time of struggle and *ex post facto*, and how does this
process affect the development of institutions? Are institutions
used to exclude deviations? How do they, by definition designed
for continuity, react and adapt themselves to the fluid, rapidly
and constantly changing notions of 'heresy'? Or, to rephrase the
question, given a set number of existing organizational models,
what types of models last and which ones are superseded, and
how and on what grounds is the notion of orthodox and heterodox
utilized to justify this process of selection? One model which
exemplifies the reconstruction of processes obscured after the fact
by a skilful construction and arrangement of events employing
notions of orthodox and heretical, is the communal ascetic life
led by men and women in all its recognizable forms.

In 374, as may be recalled, Basil explicitly condemned the
'prostitution of *kanonikai*'. One year later, in the context of
heretical doctrines spread by the Sabellians and Marcellus of
Ancyra, he wrote:[1]

We are but children, in comparison at least with the perfect [in Mesopotamia and Palestine]. And if women also choose to live according to the
Gospel, and prefer virginity to marriage—they are blessed. . . . But if
these practices cause some irregularities in the lives of these women, I do
not propose to defend them.

---

[1] *EP.* 207; for Sabellianism and the teachings of Marcellus of Ancyra cf. Gain,
L'Église, 362–82; Simonetti, *La crisi ariana*, 66–71, 147–9, 410, 427; id. 'Sabellio
e il Sabellianesimo', *Studi Storici-religiosi* 4 (1980), 7–28; Kopecek, *A History of
Neo-Arianism*, i, *passim*.

Virtually at the same time Basil's younger brother, Gregory of Nyssa, condemns:[2]

others [who] deviate in the diametrically opposed direction. While nominally professing celibacy (ἀγαμίαν), they are in fact in no way distinct from those living in community (τοῦ κοινοῦ βίου): not only do they grant their stomachs all pleasures, they cohabit (συνοικοῦντες) openly with women, declaring this symbiosis (συμβίωσιν) to be a 'brotherhood' (ἀδελφότητα), to hide the perversity of their secret designs under a respectable name: it is mainly because of them that this pure profession is vilified by 'those on the outside' (τῶν ἔξωθεν).

Gregory of Nazianzus joined them. In the late 380s he formulated his thoughts concerning the cohabitation of men and women in ten Epigrams, addressed to *syneisaktes* and *agapētes*.[3] A celibate man should never live with a 'virginal woman', since 'a better hope divided male and female' (Epigr. 12), namely nature itself. In the same way in which black and white, life and death are divided, so should men and women be separated (Epigr. 15). These ἀγαπητοί (literally, the beloved), mix honey with bile (Epigr. 14), oscillating as they do between marriage and prostitution (Epigr. 15). In fact, rather than continue life in this unnatural state, they should marry (Epigr. 15). Certainly, not all of these unions are corrupt; however, there is always the danger of suspicion. And what makes their cohabitation so shocking is the fact that a pure virgin has her eyes fixed on one she calls by the 'sacred name of beloved' (Epigr. 16), a name that is venerable because it belongs to Christ himself (Matt. 3: 17).

The basic argument appears to be the same as the one made by Basil and Gregory of Nyssa. There is, however, at least one profound difference. As shown by Guillaumont, *agapēte* is a term for a male ascetic. Therefore all the just-mentioned passages by Gregory of Nazianzus condemn the communal life not of members of the clergy, but of male and female ascetics.[4] Further-

---

[2] *De virg.* 23. 4. 5–13 (SC 119. 538–40); for the date cf. Aubineau, *Virginité*, 31; τῶν ἔξωθεν ('those on the outside') is an expression originally designating non-Christians; Wittig, *Briefe*, 258 n. 428.

[3] Gr. Naz. Epigr. 10–20 (PG 38. 86–93); Achelis, *Virgines Subintroductae*, 51 f.; A. Guillaumont, 'Le nom des "Agapètes"', *VigChr* 23 (1969), 30–7; M. Santa Maria and J. di Gribomont, 'Agapète (Mulieres et virgines subintroductae)', in *DIP* i. 146–8.

[4] 'Le nom des "Agapètes"', 34–7.

more, Basil mentions *kanonikai*, Gregory of Nazianzus attacks *monachoi* and *agapētes*, and Gregory of Nyssa speaks of an *adelphotēs*, a brotherhood. In each case, all employ the plural of the Greek substantive.

In chapter 49 of his *Historia Lausiaca* Palladius mentions a former slave called Sisinnius, who returned to his native Cappadocia after ten years spent with a hermit in caves near Jericho. Once back in his own country, as a presbyter and thus a member of the clergy, Sisinnius founded a 'brotherhood of men and women', συναγαγὼν ἀδελφότητα ἀνδρῶν τε καὶ γυναικῶν.[5] He guided his community of brothers and sisters with such ascetic firmness that all male and female instincts were eradicated, fulfilling what had been written: 'In Christ Jesus there is neither male nor female' (Gal. 3: 28). Sisinnius' teacher and fellow hermit, Elpidius, was also a Cappadocian and he is said to have come from 'the monastery of Timotheus'. Timotheus for his part can be identified as one of Basil's *chorepiskopoi*, whom he had to reprimand between 368 and 379 because of slackening ascetic zeal.[6] Sisinnius' return must therefore be dated to the late eighties or early nineties, approximately the period in which Gregory of Nazianzus composed his Epigrams.

Some twenty years earlier, Gregory of Nazianzus had written a letter of condolence on the death of a certain Leucadius, who had been the superior of 'a blessed brotherhood of monks and virgins' living in the Cappadocian town Sannabadae.[7] Gregory exhorts both men and women within the community to honour Leucadius' memory by continuing to strive for their common goal: to be true athletes of Christ.

In 375, in the aftermath of the turmoils created by his election to the bishopric of Sasima and the recent death of his father, Gregory 'went as a refugee to Seleucia, to the παρθενών of

[5] *HL* 49 (Butler, ii. 143 f.); this chapter exists only in the B group of MSS; C. Butler (*The Lausiac History of Palladius*, ii, p. liv) confirms its authenticity, also ibid. pp. xlvi–xlviii, l; cf. *Palladio: La Storia Lausiaca*, ed. G. J. M. Bartelink and C. Mohrmann (Vite dei Santi 2; Milan, 1974), p. xii.

[6] Ibid. 385 (n. to ch. 48); Bas. *Epp.* 24 (written AD 368), 291 (written after AD 370).

[7] *Ep.* 238 (after AD 360); Hauser-Meury, 'Leucadius', 112; Sannabadae is modern Halkapınar, *TIB* ii. 271; P. Maas, 'Zu der Beziehungen zwischen Kirchenvätern und Sophisten' (Sitzungsberichte der Preußischen Akademie der Wissenschaften 2; Berlin, 1912), 990 n. 6.

the blessed virgin Thecla', where he remained for four years.[8] The term *parthenōn* has caused considerable perplexity amongst scholars. Literally translated, it means that Gregory retired to the 'female community of the sacred virgin Thecla' at Seleucia, which 'is a somewhat peculiar assumption'. Therefore the phrase ought to be translated as 'the retreat of a female saint', certainly a grammatical possibility.[9] However, we possess quite an accurate description of this community, written a decade later, in the travelogue of the virgin Egeria.[10] Upon visiting Seleucia, she found a spacious precinct enclosed by an 'enormous' wall (doubtless a fortification against the surrounding Isaurians), which contained 'monasteries beyond measure of men and women'.[11]

The picture is a puzzling one. At least three different ways of communal life led by men and women elicited condemnation and attacks on the part of the Fathers. The first was a 'spiritual marriage' between a continent member of the clergy and an ascetic woman. This union, while undoubtedly enriched by mutual friendship, appears to have derived its continuing popularity from a variety of practical advantages for both parties.[12] To the degree in which clerical celibacy increased in popularity, so the practice was repeatedly condemned by official sanctions.

Official sanctions did not affect a similar cohabitation of male and female ascetics. Ascetics as a *tagma* were different from clerics as a *tagma*; though on an individual level the distinction

---

[8] Gr. Naz. *De vita sua*, 545–60, esp. 547 (Jungck, 80, 175 f. = PG 37. 1067); see also *Or. 21 in laud. Ath.* 22 (*Grégoire de Nazianze: Discours 20–3*, ed. J. Mossay (SC 270; Paris, 1980), 154); Gallay, *Lettres* i, p. xiii.

[9] Jungck, *De vita sua*, 175 (n. to ll. 547 ff.): 'eine etwas seltsame Vorstellung'; Jungck has a useful overview of other interpretations of the *parthenōn*, e.g. as a church.

[10] *Per. Aeth.* 23 (SC 21. 182–6), *c.* AD 390; P. Devos, 'La Date du voyage d'Égérie', *AnBoll* 85 (1967) 165–94; J. Wilkinson, *Egeria's Travels* (London, 1971), 228 f.

[11] 'ibi autem ad sanctam ecclesiam nihil est aliud nisi monasteria sine numero virorum ac mulierum . . . etiam sanctis monachis vel aputactitis, tam viris quam feminis, qui ibi erant . . .'; *Per. Aeth.* 23. 2. 13 (SC 21. 184); G. Dagron, *Vie et miracles de S. Thècle* (Brussels, 1978), 57 f., 73–9.

[12] Much of the contemporary literature on *syneisaktes* concentrates on John Chrysostom's and Jerome's writings, cf. E. A. Clark, 'John Chrysostom and the *Subintroductae*', in ead., *Ascetic Piety*, 265–90; R. Rader, *Breaking Boundaries: Male/Female Friendship in Early Christian Communities* (New York, 1983), 62–71; both authors are beyond the scope of this study.

was more often than not blurred. The ascetics' zeal was known
and guaranteed. In theory at least, a union between two ascetics
represented the highest degree of ascetic perfection, of true
Christian *agapē*. The Fathers' position with regard to this second
phenomenon is highly equivocal. The institution as such is rarely
criticized; what causes the harsh judgement are its inherent
dangers. The situation becomes even more nebulous regarding
the third form, communities of ascetic men and women, as represented by the two examples most recently mentioned above:
both Palladius and Gregory of Nazianzus are full of praise for
Sisinnius and Leucadius, both heads of 'communities of men and
women'; moreover, Gregory himself had spent four years in
exactly one of these institutions. On the other hand, Gregory of
Nyssa and perhaps Basil, with his references to the prostitution of
kanonikai, condemn a 'brotherhood of men and women'.[13]

In 374 Glycerius' escapades at Venasa became the subject
of three letters between Gregory of Nazianzus and Basil of
Caesarea.[14] To recapitulate: Glycerius, a deacon, but also a
'difficult' (δύστροπος) though quite able man, had 'on his own
authority and responsibility' collected a group of virgins, invested
himself with the title and apparel of a patriarch, and caused a
state of constant commotion, because 'he proceeded to train the
young men also to engage in the same folly'. After abusing
'his chorus [of virgins] together with the young men' by displaying them at the annual celebration of the local martyrs,[15]

---

[13] Neither Gregory of Nyssa's paragraph in the *De virginitate*, nor Palladius'
chapter on Sisinnius, nor Gregory of Nazianzus' Epigrams refer to *syneisaktes*; for
a different view see Achelis, *Virgines Subintroductae*, 51 f., 66–75; for contemporary developments in the West cf. *inter al.* Giannarelli, *La tipologia femminile*, 88–94.

[14] Gr. Naz. *Epp.* 246–8 (135–8) = Bas. *Epp.* 169–71; *Ep.* 247 (= Bas. 105) is
addressed to Glycerius; for Venasa cf. p. 148 n. 36. Cf. Gallay, *Vie de Saint
Grégoire*, 100–31.

[15] As Basil's reference to the celebration of the martyr Eupsychius (*De Spiritu
Sancto*, 1 (SC 17*bis*, 109)) demonstrates, these celebrations were very popular, cf.
Gr. Naz. *Epp.* 58, 122, 124, 197. They were often continuations of ancient pagan
customs: Venasa, for instance, was the site of a temple of Zeus Ouranios. Gain,
L'Église, 256–62. W. M. Ramsay (*Pauline and Other Studies* (London, 1906),
381) interprets the entire episode concerning Glycerius as a return to pagan
practices, a hypothesis accepted by N. Thierry ('Avanos-Vénasa, Cappadoce', in
Geographica Byzantina (Byzantina Sorbonensia 3; Paris, 1981), 119–29, here
121) and to a lesser degree by W. D. Hauschild (*Basilius von Käsarea: Briefe*

he crowned his outrageous behaviour by leading his band of 'brigands' (ληστρικοῦ συντάγματος) to live dispersed (τὴν διασποράν)[16] in the countryside (actually in Basil's diocese). According to Gregory, Glycerius' act shamed the entire τάγμα τῶν μοναστῶν. However, should he return to Venasa 'with understanding and with becoming steadiness of mind', Gregory promised him and the virgins complete amnesty. To no avail. Several months later the group had still not returned.[17]

At roughly the same time, between 374 and 377, Epiphanius devoted chapter 75 of his *Panarion* to the heresy of a certain Aerius.[18] Under the alleged influence of Arianism, Aerius had attracted a large following of men and women (πολὺν χορὸν ἀνδρῶν τε καὶ γυναικῶν), whom he led 'away from churches, cultivated lands, villages and towns'. Aerius and his male and female followers lived in abject poverty (ἀποταξία) in the wilderness, sleeping, even in the midst of winter, under the open sky with only the occasional shelter of trees or a cave. Aerius had further challenged the bishop's authority, declaring that a bishop is no different from a presbyter or any other cleric. He also rejected any regulation regarding fasts, and the veneration of martyrs.

Aerius was an ascetic, and had been the preferred disciple and long-time confidant of none other than Eustathius of Sebaste. Eustathius himself had ordained him as a presbyter, and had entrusted him with the supervision of 'the *xenodochion*, which in the region of Pontus is called *ptōchotropheion*', the hospice for the poor founded by Eustathius at Sebaste. Soon after Eustathius' election as bishop, between 365 and 370, Aerius resigned from his post in disagreement over Eustathius' advancement in the hierarchy, which left him, in Aerius' eyes, incapable of truly leaving this world.[19]

Roughly a decade later Amphilochius of Iconium, Gregory of Nazianzus' cousin and Basil's friend, presided over a synod at

---

zweiter Teil (Stuttgart, 1973), 171 n. 129) but characterized as 'audacious' by E. Kirsten ('Cappadocia', 884).

[16] Gr. Naz. *Ep.* 246.

[17] Gain, *L'Église*, 256 n. 128.

[18] Epiph. *Haer.* 75. 2. 2–4 (3 GCS 37. 333–6).

[19] Gribomont, 'Le Monachisme', 403 f.; id. 'Le Dossier des origines du Messalianisme', in *Epektasis*, 611–25, here 614.

Side. Twenty-five bishops had gathered to investigate a sect called
'Messalianoi' or 'Euchitai'.[20] They sent a letter with the results of
their deliberations to Flavian, bishop of Antioch, who called for a
synod himself. Here, Flavian used all his diplomatic skills to
expose the leader of the accused, an old man by the name of
Adelphios, and several others along with him, among them a certain Symeon.[21] Flavian then alerted the bishops of neighbouring
Osrhoene.[22] This sect, suddenly under massive attack, first appeared in our
sources about a decade earlier. Epiphanius had mentioned 'the
Messalians, with whom are associated the Martyrians of pagan
origin, the Euphemites, and the Satanians' already before 374 in
his *Ancoratus*.[23] He then devoted the concluding chapter of the
Panarion to 'another heresy, totally ridiculous, of inconsistent

---

[20] Most of the documents relating to the history of Messalianism have been
collected and discussed by M. Kmosko in his introduction to the *Liber Graduum*
(Patrologia Syriaca 1: 3; Paris, 1926), pp. cxvi–ccxcii. This corpus has recently
been assessed and augmented by H. Dörries, 'Urteil und Verurteilung. Kirche
und Messalianer: Zum Umgang der Alten Kirche mit Häretikern', in id. *Wort und
Stunde*, i (Göttingen, 1966), 335–51; also in id. 'Die Messalianer im Zeugnis ihrer
Bestreiter: Zum Problem des Enthusiasmus in der spätantiken Reichskirche',
Saeculum 21 (1970), 213–27; cf. Gribomont, 'Le Dossier', 614 f. The decisions
reached at Side have been preserved by Photius, *Ex Bibliotheca Photii* Cod. LII,
in Kmosko, *Liber Graduum*, cols. cclii–cclx; K. Holl, *Amphilochius von Iconium
in seinem Verhältnis zu den großen Kappadoziern* (Tübingen, 1969²), 31–8;
Tillemont, *Mémoires* viii. 798; for a more general assessment cf. J. Gribomont,
'Le Monachisme au sein de l'église en Syrie et en Cappadoce', *Studia monastica* 7
(1965), 7–24; A. Guillaumont, 'Les Messaliens', *EtCarm* 31 (1952), 131–8; id.
'Un mouvement de "spirituels" dans l'Orient chrétien', *RHR* 189 (1976), 126–9;
id. 'Messaliens', in *DSp* x. (1980), 1074–83; Vööbus, *History of Syrian Asceticism*,
ii. 127–39.
[21] Theod. *HE* 4. 10–11 (GCS 44, esp. 230–1); id. *Haereticum fabularum
compendium* 4. 11; Tim. Const. *De iis qui ad ecclesiam accedunt: De Marcianistis*;
John Damasc. *De Haeresibus compendium* 80, all in Kmosko, *Liber Graduum*,
cols. cxl–cclxi.
[22] Dörries ('Urteil', 335–7, and 'Bestreiter', 218) dates the synod at Side
between 383 and 394; Gribomont ('Le Dossier', 616f.) suggests around 390,
followed here by R. Staats, *Gregor von Nyssa und die Messalianer* (Patristische
Texte und Studien 8; Berlin, 1968), 112 n. 31, and E. Honigmann, *Patristic
Studies* (StT 173; Rome, 1953), 46; Holl (*Amphilochius*, 35–7) discusses the likely
date (after 383) in greater detail.
[23] Paragraph 13 of his *Ancoratus*, which can securely be dated before 374
(*Epiphanius' Werke*, i, ed. K. Holl (GCS 25; Leipzig, 1915), 22).

opinion, leading men and women into error. They are called Messalianoi, which translated means "those who pray" ' (εὐχόμενοι).[24] Messalians originated, according to Epiphanius, in Mesopotamia and had by his time reached Antioch. Indeed, in his *Hymn* 22 *contra haereses* written between 362 and 373 Ephrem of Nisibis composed a verse in praise of those who disdain all heretics, among them 'the Messalians who misbehave themselves'.[25] Apart from their Eastern, perhaps Syrian origin, little is known about this sect prior to Side, when its expansion towards the West and its influence had reached an alarming degree.[26] Who were the Messalians? According to Epiphanius, the Messalians have 'no beginning, no end, neither head nor any roots'. They live without any stability (ἀστήρικτοι), without guidance— Epiphanius says 'without a name' (ὀνόματος)—in total anarchy. Simpletons, poor and homeless, they wander around the country, sleeping in public places, fasting and eating whenever and wherever they please. Instead of working, they beg. In their arrogance, they claim to be prophets, patriarchs, angels, even Christ himself, but the truth is indeed far removed from these lofty claims: women and men 'promiscuously roam around together'.[27]

The testimony of Theodoret of Cyrrhus, Timothy of Constantinople, and Photius, who knew and quoted the original acts of the synods at Side and Antioch, including the statements of the accused, permits us to reconstruct some of the heretics' principal

---

[24] Epiph. *Haer.* 80. 1, 4, 1–2 and 5, 3 (3 GCS 37. 485, 488, 490). The final revision of the *Panarion* took place in 377; as, however, Dörries' excellent analysis ('Bestreiter', 215 f.; refined by Gribomont, 'Le Dossier', 612 f.) demonstrates, Epiphanius knew the sect only from hearsay, aligning it with two other rather obscure groups that were either of pagan origin or bore a slight resemblance to the traits described as Messalian. The main part of the concluding chapter is devoted to orthodox Syrian monasticism in general, which Epiphanius accuses of furthering sectarian tendencies.

[25] Ephrem composed his *Hymns against Heretics* after Jovian had surrendered Nisibis to Shaphur II in 362 and before his death in 373. *Des heiligen Ephraem des Syrers Hymnen contra haereses* (CSCO 169–70, ed. E. Beck (Louvain, 1957), 71 (translation), 79 (text) = Kmosko, *Liber Graduum*, cols. clxxi); Vööbus, *History of Syrian Asceticism*, ii. 87 f.; cf. also Ephrem's *Testament*, ed. J. S. Assermani, *Opera s. Ephraemi*, ii (Rome, 1743), 242, discussed in Gribomont, 'Le Dossier', 612.

[26] Dörries, 'Bestreiter', 220 f.; Holl, *Amphilochius*, 31–7.

[27] ἀναμὶξ ἄνδρες ἅμα γυναιξὶ καὶ γυναῖκες ἅμα ἀνδράσιν ἐπὶ τὸ αὐτὸ καθεύδοντες, ἐν ῥύμαις μὲν πλατείαις, Epiph. *Haer.* 80 (3 GCS 37. 487).

ideas, though once again as seen through the eyes of their adversaries.[28] Timothy has the fullest account of the Messalian
doctrine.[29] According to him, Messalians claimed that by the
force of a spirit they called 'Holy Ghost' (πνεῦμα) and by fervent
prayer, they had attained a state of ἀπάθεια. They were no longer
disturbed by passions and could therefore give themselves up
entirely to meditation upon the divine. *Apatheia* allowed their
souls to be united with the heavenly bridegroom in the same way
that a woman is united with a man, thus rendering all sacraments
superfluous (and also giving a free rein to all forms of behaviour,
because its possessor has transcended every human boundary).
Work was to be shunned at all costs, since it interrupted continuous prayer, which alone could eliminate original sin, and
prevented the faithful from living like the apostles, without
worldly concerns. Messalians, not orphans, widows, or other
indigents, were the only ones who should receive alms, since only
they were truly 'poor in spirit' (πτώχοι τῷ πνευμάτι).

Apatheia, granted by the *pneuma* and achieved through prayer,
lifts the human soul beyond all the confines, rules, and regulations
of society, granting direct access to the divine. One of the most
distinct barriers separating mankind is that of gender. Not surprisingly, 'They elect women as teachers of their dogma and
allow them to be superior not only to ordinary men but even to
priests'.

In the light of the Messalian teachings, the actions of Glycerius
at Venasa now take on a different aspect. This renegade had also
defied the authority of his presbyter, *chorepiskopos*, and bishop;
he had disturbed the annual celebration of martyrs (according to

---

[28] Ibid. (3 GCS 37. 486); Theod. *HE* 4. 10, and id. *adv. Haer.* 4. 11 = Kmosko,
Liber Graduum, cols. cxci–cc.

[29] Tim. Const. *De iis qui ad eccl. acc.* = Kmosko, *Liber Graduum*, cols. ccxxi–
ccxxx; cf. also *Ex Bibliotheca Photii*, ibid. cols. ccliii–cclxi, esp. cclix. Timothy
wrote his legal work regulating acceptance into the Church in the 7th cent.; his
account is primarily based on the decisions reached at Constantinople in 426,
which are harsher than those reached at Side. This is a result of the definitive
character of the decisions of Ephesus (see below) as well as of the fact that he
had easy access to the acts of Constantinople, cf. H. Dörries, *Symeon von
Mesopotamien: Die Überlieferung der messalianischen "Makarios"-Schriften* (TU
55: 1; Leipzig, 1941), 425–9; id. 'Urteil', 335–44; id. 'Bestreiter', 218–25; for an
excellent discussion of the circumstances leading to the harsher judgement at
Constantinople cf. Gribomont, 'Le Dossier', 614–19.

Epiphanius, the Messalians did not venerate martyrs); and he had rallied a group of ascetic men and women, with whom he finally disappeared into the Cappadocian countryside. The parallels to Aerius' case are even more evident. An ascetic of long standing, he became suddenly dissatisfied with the stable life and ecclesiastical career of his mentor and friend, Eustathius. In an act of 'revolt' he rekindled the original intentions of his master, and in this he was supported by a substantial portion of the ascetics in Sebaste. Men and women left together to adopt a life of absolute poverty disregarding all the conventions of society.

What distinguishes Eustathius' followers condemned at Gangra from the Messalians condemned around 390 at Side appears to be little else than the interim of sixty years.[30] Aerius was a radical disciple of Eustathius, and Eustathius' radical faction had been condemned at Gangra for exactly those errors (all based on ascetic principles) that Aerius tried to revive: disregard of the clergy, condemnation of the celebration of martyrs, absolute poverty leading to an unsettled life, disruption of families, equality—and thus indiscriminate community—of men and women. Glycerius' followers were already virgins, yet most of them had remained part of their families. Aerius on the other hand presided over an organized ascetic community at the time of his 'revolt'; most of his followers, men and women, were equally members of this community. According to Theodoret, Letoios of Melitene wrote to Flavian around the time the synod at Antioch had condemned the Messalians, and asked for support since 'this pestilence had already affected many monasteries, or rather the hovels of brigands'.[31] All these cases involved considerable numbers of men and women who were ascetics, but were living a settled life in communities.[32]

According to their adversaries' description, these heretics were

---

[30] Gr. Naz. *Epp.* 246–8 = Bas. *Epp.* 169–71; Epiph. *Haer.* 75 (3 GCS 37. 333 f.); Gangra cc. 3, 4, 6, 11, 19, 20 (Hefele–Leclercq, i.2, 1034, 1035, 1037, 1041 n. 36, 1041); cf. especially Gribomont, 'Le Monachisme', 402–10, 414 f.; id. 'Monachisme enthousiaste', 130–5; Hauschild, 'Eustathius', 547 f. E. Peterson ('Die Häretiker der Philippus-Akten', *ZNW* 21 (1932), 97–111, and 'Zum Messalianismus der Philippus-Akten', *Oriens Christianus* 29 (1932), 172–9) is the first to have connected the Messalians with those condemned at Gangra.

[31] Not the addressee of Basil of Ancyra's treatise; Theod. *HE* 4. 11 (GCS 44. 230), σπήλαια λῃστρικά; Glycerius' group was also called a band of brigands.

[32] χορός and πολὺς χορός; Gr. Naz. *Ep.* 246; Epiph. *Haer.* 75 (3 GCS 37. 334).

in essence anarchists (in the case of the Messalians this is derided as resulting from the adherents' lowly origin); as such, they were without rules, regulations, or other recognizable signs of order, and thus totally bereft of any civilization. However, our adversarial sources are inconsistent. They also confirm that, paradoxically, the disdain for ecclesiastical institutions resulted in anything but anarchy: far from being simply disorganized mobs, these groups were in fact structured according to the same hierarchical principles as those they despised and attacked.[33] However, in the heretics' case the legitimization, the prerequisites for leadership, were different. At least according to a council convened at Constantinople in 426, the Messalians elected women not only as teachers of dogma but also as leading members of their clergy; 'in thus making women into their heads, they bring shame to the head of Christ our Lord' (canon 18).

The female followers of Eustathius were condemned at Gangra because they cut their hair, denied male 'power over their heads', and 'became men'.[34] Montanists, the sectarian milieu in which the *Life of Theodotus and the Seven Virgins* originated, described themselves as martyrs, apostles, and catechists, and wrote 'catholic letters'. 'In their community they also have female bishops, female presbyters and others.' This is the very same milieu in which women as prophetesses played a pivotal role in the liturgy, the milieu of our prophetess on her way to the 'New Jerusalem'.[35] This prophetess travelled with a deacon and a *presbyter rusticus*, and among her many offences was the administering of baptism. Again and again the 'canonic-liturgical' literature quoted in the context of widows prohibited women from administering sacraments, particularly baptism.

A clear thread links the third-century prophetess condemned by Firmilian in Cappadocia with all those unnamed women condemned by the Fathers at Gangra, Side, Antioch, and Constantinople. Time and again, enthusiastic groups returned to specific aspects of the Gospels, aspects with a distinctly apocalyptic character. Guided by sayings which demanded absolute renunciation

---

[33] Aerius and Glycerius adopted the insignia of a cleric and Aerius further claimed that presbyters and bishops should have the same rank, Epiph. *Haer.* 75 (3 GCS 37. 334).

[34] Can. 17 (Hefele–Leclercq, i.2, 1040), referring to 1 Cor. 11: 10.

[35] Epiph. *Haer.* 49 (2 GCS 31. 243); Eus. *HE* 5. 14–18.

of all worldly considerations, these men and women rejected all structures of society. Through the power of uninterrupted prayer or through prophetic faculties, they professed to have achieved communication, even union, with the divine, above and beyond all social conventions and ecclesiastical requirements and benefits.

For these men and women the demands of asceticism superseded all those constraints and commandments which constitute the order of society. They did not obey, they did not work, they did not procreate, they did not distinguish between slave and free, male and female. However, the whole picture is not quite as simple as that. Our information is so scanty that it is extremely difficult to chart developments, but it appears as if the most radically enthusiastic movements—whether called Montanists, Encratites, Apotactics, Eustathians, Messalians, or Euchitai— were truly, if ever, 'anarchic' only at the outset. Processes of hierarchization, organization, and settlement began virtually immediately. All these groups had leaders, even though their capacity was based on their *pneuma*, in this context their ascetic excellence. Thus, women could and did exercise the same prominent role, and fulfil the same public functions, as men.

Even if based on different principles, and thus offering otherwise unattainable opportunities to certain kinds of people, in particular women, these groups were organized in a hierarchical structure. The existence of a clerical hierarchy is not the only characteristic that these fringe groups shared with 'the Church', or indeed with society as such. It appears in fact that at almost all times two kinds of radical, enthusiastic groups existed side by side. To begin with, there were the initiators, instigating the first breakaways, and usually characterized by a severely rigoristic message. These were people like Montanus and his prophetesses, Glycerius, perhaps the young Eustathius, and the earliest Messalians. As soon as the first phases of radical rupture had passed, the breakaway groups were forced to adapt themselves to the constraints of nature and society. The extremes of the climate forced them to settle; settlement required rudimentary organization, and a process of institutionalization set in, mirroring more or less precisely that of the 'great Church'—which had after all undergone a similar transformation. As soon as this process of stabilization and organization had brought the breakaway groups closer to established ones, and their everyday life was no longer all that radically distinct, dissatisfied members broke away, and the cycle renewed itself.

In other words, at any given time the spectrum within the so-called heretical movements ranged from the radically extreme to the virtually 'orthodox', the latter being distinguished in their organizational as well as doctrinal outlook only marginally, if at all, from the Great Church. In this grey area of moderate forms, factors other than ascetic practice and doctrinal adherence decided survival or condemnation. Those who pronounced the decision, mainly the leaders of the clergy, the social élite, were confronted with a complex and intricate problem, which demanded complex and intricate solutions.[36]

The third ecumenical council gathered at Ephesus in 431 to reach, among other issues, the final verdict on the subject of the Messalians. It reaffirmed the decisions of Constantinople and made them into the touchstone of orthodoxy; in this matter the council had the help of additional evidence: a book entitled *Asketikon*, written by one of the Messalian leaders called Symeon.[37] Excerpts of this book have been preserved, and led to a trail-blazing discovery. In 1920 the Belgian Benedictine Dom L. Villecourt identified the excerpts as part of a corpus that had been commonly attributed to the famous Egyptian Desert Father Macarius. Moreover, later research not only corroborated Villecourt's findings, but established that the entire Macarian corpus was, in fact, the work of Symeon the Messalian.[38] The significance of this finding can hardly be overestimated; 'the identification of Macarius with a "Messalian" author does imply a basic judgement upon the entire tradition of Eastern Christian spirituality. For indeed, if "Macarius" is Messalian, this entire tradition is Messalian as well.'[39]

---

[36] Patlagean, *Pauvreté économique*, 128–55.

[37] Gribomont ('Le Dossier', 616–19) assumes that the synod of Constantinople had already had access to the *Asketikon*.

[38] L. Villecourt, 'La Date et l'origine des "Homélies spirituelles" attribuées à Macaire', *Comptes Rendus des séances de l'Académie des Inscriptions et Belles-Lettres* (1920), 250–8; id. 'La Grande Lettre grecque de Macaire, ses formes textuelles et son millieu littéraire', *Revue de l'Orient Chrétien* 22 (1920/1), 29–56; his work has been substantially advanced by Dörries, *Symeon von Mesopotamien*, passim.

[39] The heated debate surrounding the Macarian corpus has been summarized and advanced by J. Meyendorff, 'Messalianism or Anti-Messalianism: A Fresh

W. Jaeger's edition of Gregory of Nyssa's ascetic works begins with a treatise entitled *Hypotyposis* or *De instituto Christiano*, a 'guidebook' for the practical path towards ascetic perfection. On close inspection, this treatise parallels in large parts Symeon-Macarius' *Great Letter*.[40] In a second text, entitled *In suam ordinationem*, Gregory of Nyssa praised certain pneumatic ascetics from Mesopotamia, 'who rejuvenate amongst us the charismata of the primitive Church'. He further expressed his hopes that these ascetics would help to bring the dissident 'Macedonianoi' or 'Pneumatomachoi' back into the Church. Quite probably, this text was written on the occasion of the Constantinopolitan council of 381.[41]

In 371 Basil asked his younger brother Gregory of Nyssa to write a treatise extolling the virtues of virginity.[42] Chapters 7, 15–18, and 21–22 of Gregory's *De virginitate* are devoted to concrete aspects of ascetic life, drawing directly from the experiences of his elder brother. Indeed, throughout his work Gregory has 'taken it to heart to treat . . . [the beauties of virginity],

Look at the "Macarian" Problem', in Granfield and Jungmann, *Kyriakon*, ii. 585–94 (quotation, 586); cf. also I. Hausherr, 'L'Erreur fondamental et la logique du messalianisme', *OrChrP* 1 (1935), 328–60.

[40] *GN* viii. 1, 1–89; both treatises follow the same organizational structure, and use the same biblical citations. However, they differ greatly with regard to vocabulary and literary style. By now, the consensus tends to view Gregory's work as a revision and modification of the *Great Letter*; cf. especially Staats, *Gregor von Nyssa*, 1–15 and *passim*. This has led some to doubt Gregory's authorship of *De inst.*, cf. M. Canévet, 'Le "De instituto christiano" est-il de Grégoire de Nysse?', *REG* 82 (1969), 404–23, following J. Daniélou, 'Grégoire de Nysse et le messalianisme', *RSR* 48 (1960), 119–34; J. Gribomont, 'Le De Instituto Christiano et le Messalianisme de Grégoire de Nysse', *SP* 5 (1962), 312–22; id. 'Le Dossier', 623 f.

[41] E. Gebhardt, *GN* ix. 336–8, and id. 'Titel und Zeit der Rede Gregors von Nyssa "In suam ordinationem"', *Hermes* 89 (1961), 503–7 (esp. 506); the title remains debated: Gribomont, 'Le Dossier', 621–5; R. Staats, 'Die Asketen aus Mesopotamien in der Rede des Gregor von Nyssa', *VigChr* 21 (1967), 167–79; id. 'Die Datierung von "In suam ordinationem" des Gregor von Nyssa', *VigChr* 23 (1969), 58–9; G. May, 'Die Datierung der Rede "In suam ordinationem" des Gregor von Nyssa und die Verhandlungen mit den Pneumatomachen auf dem Konzil von Konstantinopel 381', *VigChr* 23 (1969), 38–57.

[42] For the date of *De virg.* cf. Aubineau, *Virginité*, 29–33, 81 f., and for Basil's request Gr. Nyss. *De virg.* pr. 2. 2–21; 23. 2. 5, 6 (SC 119. 250, 525); J. Gribomont ('Le Panégyrique de la virginité', 250) proposes a date closer to 378; id. 'Le Dossier', 621.

obeying in every respect the authority of the one who asked us to do so'.[43] Gregory thus stresses unequivocally that the only path towards ascetic perfection lies in the observance of a rigorous regimen under the guidance of a master such as Basil.[44] Without such guidance, dangers would lurk everywhere. Thus, extreme mortification of the body could be counterproductive to the ascetic perfection of the soul, an argument already familiar from Basil of Ancyra's treatise.[45] Then there are some individuals who, in the enthusiasm of their youth, might think that they do not need to follow a slow, laborious regime as prescribed by written instructions. Under the illusion of having found a more direct way to achieve perfection—without a master, and disregarding the precepts of the Book of Proverbs and the apostle Paul—such Christians could refuse to work for their food and eat that of others, masters in the art of laziness. They could become dreamers, attributing greater authority to their delusions than to the Scriptures, confusing their imagination with divine revelation.

Gregory clearly had more than a passing acquaintance with such forms of behaviour, for he goes on to describe a variety of errant ascetics: those who 'are the sort that insinuate themselves into private houses',[46] and others who consider their antisocial (ἄμικτόν), savage life to be a virtue. Some fast to the point of starvation, others follow the diametrically opposite path, for 'not only do they grant their stomachs all pleasures, they co-habit (συνοικοῦντες) openly with women, declaring this symbiosis (συμβίωσιν) to be a "brotherhood"'.

Rather than listing wholesale accusations, Gregory distinguishes between different practices. But, according to him, not all these ascetics are damnable heretics, a number are simply examples of good intentions gone awry.[47] Thus he still considers them part of

[43] *De virg.* 2. 15 (SC 119. 271).
[44] Ibid. 23. 1. 12–15 (SC 119. 522); the discipline is outlined in ch. 7, and is based on Basil's precepts.
[45] *De virg.* 22 (SC 119. 511–21), cf. notes for cross-references to Bas. Anc. *De virg.*
[46] 'And they get miserable women into their clutches, women burdened with a sinful past, and led on by all kinds of desires', 2 Tim. 3: 6; Gregory omits the second part, cf. Aubineau, *Virginité*, 537 n. 3.
[47] *De virg.* 23 (SC 119. 521–53), quotation, 23. 4. 9 (SC 119. 539f.); Dörries, 'Bestreiter', 217–18; Gribomont, 'Le Dossier', 621f., 624; id. 'Le Monachisme', 414f.

the *tagma tōn monazontōn*; like Glycerius they are temporarily lost sheep which can easily be brought back to the flock with some good will on both sides. He also differentiates clearly between these wayward ascetics and the strictly dualistic groups, who condemn the body and marriage outright and on principle.[48] 'Chez Grégoire, . . . nous avons trouvé une sympathie à l'égard des idées macariennes [i.e. Messalian], fort différente de l'attitude sévère d'un Amphiloque d'Iconium.'[49] Or to put it differently, there were Messalian circles whose intellectual calibre and ascetic teachings, even if not all their doctrines, strikingly resembled those of a Gregory of Nyssa himself.

Gregory of Nyssa's sympathies for certain Messalian circles, such as the one around Symeon-Macarius, almost precisely mirror Basil's own sympathy for Eustathian teachings and his downright dependence on them. Basil admired and emulated Eustathius' ascetic doctrines, even though some critics found them too radical, and others not radical enough. Basil and Gregory, Eustathius and Symeon-Macarius are thus perfect examples for marking the boundaries of the grey area where neither ascetic teachings and practice, nor doctrinal provenance alone account for the dividing line between what was to become orthodox and what heretical. There is, however, one decisive issue, one aspect which may be seen as a touchstone: their attitude towards (and treatment of) the communal life of ascetic men and women, and as a consequence their conceptualization of the public role attributed to and resulting from the ascetic qualities of women.

The development, distribution, and final establishment of asceticism according to the Basilian model had to overcome countermodels far more complex and difficult to cope with than simply resurgent radical fringe groups. The history of Eustathius and his followers, that of Homoiousian asceticism and the Homoiousian party, constitutes a test-case for demonstrating some aspects of the processes and developments leading to an eventual establishment of orthodox asceticism according to the Basilian model.

In 360 the synod of Constantinople, sanctioned by the emperor

---

[48] As those mentioned at *De virg.* 7. 1. 10 (SC 119. 350); to quote Gribomont ('Le Dossier', 622), 'les lecteurs de Grégoire, jeunes gens attirés par la virginité, se trouvent seulement mis en face de l'alternative de se soumettre à un père spirituel ou de risquer une telle déviation.'

[49] Gribomont, 'Le Dossier', 624.

Constantius, had excommunicated the leading Homoiousian bishops. This event marks the party's first major defeat, and resulted from a personal vendetta rather than doctrinal disagreements.[50] However, the Homoiousians were far from being conquered. The ban of 360 affected less than twenty bishops, most of them from Asia Minor. Although the formula defining the nature of the Trinity finally accepted by the Synod of Constantinople was to be signed by all Eastern bishops, and those who refused were to be exiled, this sanction seems never to have actually been implemented.[51] Among those who signed the formula of Constantinople were Dianios of Caesarea and Gregory the Elder of Nazianzus. In both cases their signatures caused widespread resentment amongst a particular group of their congregation: those 'who had left the world', the *Naziraioi*. In Caesarea the death of Dianios in 362 brought the divisons into the open. The ascetics favoured Basil, who, it will be recalled, was the disciple of Eustathius, and had accompanied Eustathius, Basil of Ancyra, and Macedonius to the fateful synod at Constantinople. At Nazianzus the ascetics refused to obey their bishop, Gregory the Elder, and pledged their loyalty to Eustathius and Macedonius. In 360 Gregory the Younger, later of Nazianzus, supported his father's decision to sign the Homoian, that is, 'Arian', formula of Constantinople, a move which he characterized ten years later, and under very different circumstances, as the result of fraud.[52] In Constantinople Macedonius' successor Eudoxius faced wide-

[50] Cf. the discussion above, pp. 127–9; also Brennecke, *Studien zur Geschichte*, 5–56; Dagron, 'Le Monachisme', 247; Kopecek, *Neo-Arianism*, ii. 299–303; W. Löhr, *Die Entstehung der homöischen und homöusianischen Kirchenparteien—Studien zur Synodalgeschichte des 4. Jahrhunderts*, Diss. (Bonn, 1986).

[51] Brennecke, *Studien zur Geschichte*, 56–66, esp. 58 n. 14; Gwatkin, *Studies of Arianism*, 185 f.; Simonetti, *La crisi ariana*, 338–43; for the fate of the Neo-Arians cf. Kopecek, *Neo-Arianism*, *passim*; and *Eunomius: The Extant Works*, ed. R. P. Vaggione (Oxford, 1987), *passim*.

[52] Gr. Naz. *Or.* 4. 10 (*Grégoire de Nazianze: Discours 3–5*, ed. J. Bernardi, (SC 309; Paris, 1983), 100). The conflict revolving around the opposition to Gregory the Elder's signature is also referred to in Gr. Naz. *Or.* 6. 12 (PG 35. 737) and *Or.* 18. 18 (ibid. 1005); cf. the discussion in Bernardi's Introduction, SC 309, pp. 25–7. The conflict lasted probably from 360 to 364, though Wittig (*Briefe*, 17–19) has it end in 361, and the older literature has it begin around 362; cf. Brennecke, *Studien zur Geschichte*, 60–2, 150–2; cf. also his observations concerning the martyrdom of Eupsychius of Caesarea and Basil's role in the conflict surrounding Dianios' signing.

spread resistance among Macedonius' ascetic followers.[53] Not only did the ascetics continue their support of the Homoiousian cause, but it soon became clear that only the more conspicuous leaders of the Homoiousian party had been directly affected by the defeat of 360. Many retained their sees simply because they had not exposed themselves at the council of Serdica. In fact, the leading Homoian (or 'Arian') bishops were generally very conciliatory, evidently in an effort to avoid open hostility.

Constantius died on 3 November 361, and on 11 December his nephew Julian, later known as the Apostate, arrived in the capital as the new emperor. Almost immediately, little more than a year after their deposition, prominent Homoiousian bishops rallied again around Macedonius.[54] For his part, Julian intended not only to restore paganism, but also to undermine his uncle's Christian policies, and he knew exactly how to exploit intra-Christian controversies to further these aims: he declared a general amnesty for all bishops deposed under Constantius, principally the Homoiousians and the Anomoians following Aetius and Eunomius. Even if not all exiled Homoiousians were able to regain their sees, which had been taken by others in the mean time, they certainly convened a number of synods, at which they immediately distanced themselves from the formula of Constantinople that they had signed barely two years earlier. From this time on, Sozomen talks about the 'Macedonians', including Eustathius, as a separate group within the doctrinal spectrum. Macedonius presumably died shortly thereafter; his place in the movement, especially in the region of Constantinople and its neighbouring provinces, was taken by Marathonius, now bishop of Nicomedia, and Eleusius, bishop of Cyzicos.[55]

The Homoiousians had retained their strength, even under adverse conditions. In 363 a Homoiousian delegation headed by Basil of Ancyra intercepted Julian's successor Jovian on his

---

[53] Soc. *HE* 2. 38 (PG 67. 324); Soz. *HE* 4. 20 (GCS 50. 170); P. Franchi de' Cavalieri, 'Una pagina di storia bizantina del secolo IV: Il martirio dei santi notari', *AnBoll* 69 (1946), 132–75, here 170, ll. 21–4, and see Brennecke, *Studien zur Geschichte*, 187 n. 41 for problems involving the passage in Franchi, p. 171, ll. 1–10.

[54] Soc. *HE* 2. 45. 2 (PG 67. 357); Soz. *HE* 4. 27. 2 (GCS 50. 184); Philost. *HE* 5. 1 (GCS 21. 66); Brennecke, *Studien zur Geschichte*, 81–6, 100–9; Meinhold, 'Pneumatomachoi', 1074 f.

[55] Soz. *HE* 5. 14. 1 (GCS 50. 213).

return from the ill-fated Persian campaign, and petitioned for rehabilitation and reinstallation in their sees.[56] At that time the diocese of Asiana was still governed by a majority of Homoiousian bishops.[57] Their strongholds were in the west and south-east: the province of Asia, the Hellespont (which was under the guidance of Eleusius), and Caria. Thrace and Phrygia were chiefly Homoian, and the positions in the diocese of Pontica were *de facto* divided between Homoians in Bithynia and Galatia, and Basil of Caesarea's just-emerging Neo-Nicaean movement. However, strong Homoiousian tendencies prevailed in Paphlagonia, Honorias, Hellenopontus, Pontus Ptolemoniacus, and the two Armeniae. Even Cappadocia, the Neo-Nicaean stronghold, had Homoian bishops and a sprinkling of Homoiousian ones.[58]

Despite the events of 360, and regardless of growing internal divisions, the Homoiousians were as numerous as ever, and continued to insist on regaining their pre-360 standing. Homoiousian synods assembled with full imperial sanction in 364 and 365/6,[59] and even the Western Church and Valens' Western co-regent Valentinian became involved in the struggle.[60] A delegation

---

[56] Soc. *HE* 3. 24. 1, 25. 2 (PG 67. 449, 452); Soz. *HE* 6. 4. 3 (GCS 50. 240).

[57] The primary sources for the following years under Valens are Amm. Marc. Books 26–31; and Zosimus, *Historia Nova*, 4. 1–24 (*Zosime: Histoire Nouvelle*, ed. F. Paschoud, 3 vols. (Paris, 1978–89) ii.2, 262–86).

[58] It is, despite inevitable shortcomings, possible to paint an at least approximately correct picture of the doctrinal constellation in the East at the time of Valens' accession. Cf. M. Le Quien, *Oriens Christianus*, 3 vols. (Paris, 1740; repr. Graz, 1958), esp. vol. 1; Brennecke, *Studien zur Geschichte*, 186–206; Hauschild, *Die Pneumatomachen*, 211–16; Ritter, *Das Konzil*, 73.

[59] In 364 the synod at Lampsacus under Eleusius demanded again the reversal of 360, without direct result. However, Lampsacus forced the leaders of the Homoian Church to recognize the continuing strength of the opposition and to organize a synod at Nicomedia in 365/6; here Eleusius had to defend his position, and was forced to sign the formula of Constantinople—but he revoked his signature as soon as he had returned to Cyzicos. In 365 Valens issued an edict upholding the decisions of Constantinople and deposed once more all those bishops removed under Constantius II and recalled under Julian. However, the edict had little effect. Eustathius remained in Sebaste, and in the Hellespont Homoiousians retained their majority; Soz. *HE* 6.12.5 (GCS 50. 252); Brennecke, *Studien zur Geschichte*, 208–16f.; Hauschild, *Die Pneumatomachen*, 195 n. 1.

[60] Soc. *HE* 4. 12. 2–12 (PG 67. 484); Soz. *HE* 6.10.3 (GCS 50. 249). Technically Valentinian held the higher rank and Valens would have had to follow his lead in religious questions as well. To achieve their aims the Homoiousians needed the support of the Western churches, adherents of the Nicaean formula.

headed by Eustathius of Sebaste and others visited Western congregations, and succeeded in reaching the first agreement since 342 between Western doctrinal factions and a segment of the Eastern Origenistic-Eusebian coalition.[61] However, these successes proved to be only temporary.

The erosion of the Homoiousian party's inner unity was irreversible. After 367 one Homoiousian section drifted increasingly towards the new Nicaean party represented by Basil of Caesarea, whereas others rallied around a newly emerging doctrinal movement led by Eustathius of Sebaste, and soon known as the 'Pneumatomachoi', those who fight the ἁγιὸν πνεῦμα. According to this doctrinal persuasion, the concept of the ὅμοιος κατ' οὐσίαν applied solely to Father and Son, and did not include the Spirit.[62] The eroding unity of the Homoiousians, the rising impact of the

Numerous Homoiousian synods appear to have debated this strategy in 365/6, all stressing once more the Nicaean basis of the *homoousios* in the Homoiousian interpretation of ὅμοιος κατ' οὐσίαν. This was the theological basis for their mission to Rome; cf. especially Brennecke (*Studien zur Geschichte*, 219 n. 257) for a discussion of the doctrinal implications of the identification of *homoousios* with the classical formula ὅμοιος κατὰ πάντα.

[61] Unfortunately, the delegation did not meet Valentinian, who was campaigning in Gaul and Belgium. After initial difficulties, negotiations with Bishop Liberius of Rome resulted in the latter's acceptance of the Homoiousian position, which was also supported by a Sicilian synod; cf. Simonetti, *La crisi ariana*, 395–9. This *rapprochement* with the West (short-lived since Liberius died on 24 Sept. 366) forced the Homoiousians, once back in Asia Minor, to renegotiate their stance *vis-à-vis* another group who adhered to a new interpretation of the Nicaean *homoousios* and were also in the Origenistic-Eusebian tradition: the so-called Melitians. The leader of this group, Melitius, had changed his initially anti-Homoiousian stance after he was deposed as bishop of Syrian Antioch in 360, thus becoming a potential Homoiousian partner. Eusebius of Caesarea, with substantial support from his presbyter Basil, later bishop of Caesarea, and then still his close friend, assembled a synod in Tyana, where all Melitians accepted the newly reformed Homoiousian creed; and another synod was planned for 367, when all newly allied parties would re-emphasize their adherence to the stipulations of Nicaea. However, Valens simply prohibited this assembly; Brennecke, *Studien zur Geschichte*, 66–81, 219–21; Kopecek, *Neo-Arianism*, ii. 392–430; Simonetti, *La crisi ariana*, 360–99.

[62] i.e. the Holy Spirit was not of divine substance, but a 'servant', comparable to the angels; Soc. *HE* 2. 45 (PG 67. 360). The differences between *Pneumatomachoi* and *Macedonianoi* and the eventual amalgamation of these terms in heresiological literature have been fully discussed by Meinhold, 'Pneumatomachoi', *RE* xxi. 1066–78, cf. also 1078–85 for the events of 367; Hauschild, *Die*

Cappadocian Fathers' interpretation of the Nicaean *homoousios*, and the conflicting opinions regarding the nature of the Holy Spirit also caused an increasing division between Basil, newly elected bishop of Caesarea, and his friend and ally Eustathius of Sebaste. Their growing disagreements culminated in the final rupture of their twenty-year friendship in 373.[63]

In the following years Basil's former friend and ascetic mentor became his sworn enemy as the leader of the Πνευματομάχων αἵρεσις. Indeed,

now the reckless and impudent heresy of the Arians, being plainly cut off from the body of the Church, remains in its own errors, and harms us but little because their impiety is evident to all. But those who have clothed themselves in the skin of a sheep, and present a gentle and mild appearance . . . and because they have come from amongst ourselves, easily inflict injury on the simpler folks, these are they who are harmful and difficult to guard against. . . . And we must mention [him] by name . . . Eustathius of Sebaste in Armenia Minor.

For Basil, the true threat was neither the Homoians who controlled the Church with the help of the emperor, nor those whose heretical error was plainly in evidence, but the Homoiousians who had indeed 'come from amongst ourselves'.[64]

Pneumatomachen, 176–90, 192–201, 236–9; F. Loofs, 'Macedonius', in *Realenzyklopädie für protestantische Theologie und Kirche*, xii (Leipzig, 1903), 41–8, here 47; Ritter, *Das Konzil*, 68–77 has a different chronology; for 367 and its consequences cf. Brennecke, *Studien zur Geschichte*, 220–4; Pruche, *Basile de Césarée: Sur le Saint-Esprit*, 41–110, 154–225.

[63] Brennecke (*Studien zur Geschichte*, 226–31 with n. 13) claims that Basil's election was pushed through by other bishops against the resistance of the local upper classes; Hauschild, *Die Pneumatomachen*, 191–210; May, 'Basilios der Große', 47–70; id. 'Die großen Kappadokier und die staatliche Kirchenpolitik von Valens bis Theodosius', in G. Ruhbach (ed.), *Die Kirche angesichts der konstantinischen Wende* (Darmstadt, 1976), 322–37; E. Schwartz, 'Zur Kirchengeschichte des vierten Jahrhunderts', in id. *Gesammelte Schriften*, iv (Berlin, 1960), 1–110.

[64] *Ep.* 263; cf. also *Epp.* 125, 126, 130, 244; J. Bernardi, *La Prédication des Pères Cappadociens* (Paris, 1968), 85–8; Brennecke, *Studien zur Geschichte*, 226–42, esp. 230 n. 45; H. Dörries, *De Spiritu Sancto: Ein Beitrag des Basilius zum Abschluß des trinitarischen Dogmas* (Abhandlungen der Akademie der Wissenschaften in Göttingen, phil.-hist. Kl. 3: 39; Göttingen, 1965), 28–42, 94–120; Gain, *L' Église*, 324–84; cf. Loofs (*Eustathius und die Chronologie*, 6–34) for the fundamental chronological reconstruction; May, 'Basilios der Große', 64; Schwartz, 'Zur Kirchengeschichte', 54–64.

Homoiousians, as this excursus shows, had not only been the major doctrinal force in the East before 360; they retained influence and positions well into the 370s and, indeed, until the second ecumenical council held at Constantinople in 381. However, what significance do these doctrinal disputes have for the development of the ascetic organization of men and women?

Some twenty years before Basil of Caesarea emerged as the 'founder' of asceticism and monasticism, the leaders of the Homoiousian party, Eustathius, Macedonius, and Basil of Ancyra, had introduced an organized monastic movement to Asia Minor. In various characteristics this movement adopted the principles and guide-lines contained in Basil of Ancyra's *De virginitate*. It was marked by a strong social commitment made manifest in its close association, if not actual identity, with 'hospices for the poor', and was primarily an urban movement, centred in cities where its leaders were bishops as well as ascetics. Its following was considerable, and included members from the highest echelons of society. Not surprisingly, the ascetics seem to have had a decisive voice in episcopal decisions; moreover, the movement was based on ascetic—the fifth-century sources say 'monastic'—communities of men and women. These men and women lived together. They could do so because it is 'the greatest and most magnificent aspect of virginity, that . . . all those who lead the virginal life are angels during their human life already'.[65]

Gregory of Nazianzus wrote to a community of men and women in Sannabadae in Cappadocia, and he addressed several Epigrams to male and female *agapētes* who practised an ascetic life in common.[66] Sisinnius was the leader of a community of men and women, equal in Christ, also located in Cappadocia. Gregory of Nyssa mentions *adelphotēs*, brotherhoods of men and women. The *kanonikē* Theodora was the leader of a community of men and women. Marthana guided a monastery of men and women. Even Macrina's early ascetic community included at least her brother Peter, if not other men as well.

---

[65] Bas. Anc. *De virg.* 37 (PG 30. 744); Soc. *HE* 2. 38. 2 (PG 67. 324); Soz. *HE* 4. 20. 2 (GCS 50. 170); Dagron, 'Le Monachisme', 252 f.; id. *Naissance d'une capitale*, 514 n. 2; Patlagean, *Pauvrété économique*, 133–45.
[66] Guillaumont, 'Le nom des "Agapètes" ', 30–7.

In addition, numerous virgins lived together with ascetic men in what was described as a 'spiritual marriage'. Others lived with their natural brothers who were often members of the clergy as well as ascetics. Widows and deaconesses, also bound by a vow of chastity, lived with their male relatives or with members of the clergy in a *mariage blanc*. Yet again, other groups of men and women followed a peripatetic life of absolute poverty together. All the sources that provide these instances date from the period between the 360s and the 390s.

Three major trends of ascetic practice emerge: the peripatetic life of rigorously ascetic men and women who completely rejected society; men and women who together practised an ascetic life in the context of their homes and families; and lastly, settled, organized ascetic communities of men and women. These communities again fall into two groups: the Homoiousian foundations, and those which followed the model of Basil of Caesarea.

In all but Basil's model, men and women practised the ascetic life together, in community. All but Basil's model had a long tradition. The communities of men and women together date back to the 330s, and they constituted the majority of ascetic organizations. In short, communal asceticism in Asia Minor originated and developed along Homoiousian lines. From the beginning, and well into the middle of the fourth century, ascetic communities of men and women were the rule, not the exception.[67] These communities were mostly situated in the major urban centres. Their inhabitants, despite the fact that they were 'those who had withdrawn from the world', played an active and vociferous role in all ecclesiastical decisions. They were present during the fierce controversies surrounding both the election and the dismissal of Macedonius in Constantinople; some of his ascetic supporters, called 'the poor' (πτωχοί or φιλόπτωχοι), followed him into exile. Eustathius' varied career involved his ascetic followers; urban ascetics opposed the acceptance of the Constantinopolitan formula by Gregory the Elder of Nazianzus and Dianios of Caesarea; and ascetics favoured their fellow ascetic Basil as suc-

---

[67] Gain, *L'Église*, 155 n. 145, referring to Justinianic Laws and those of the second council of Nicaea; cf. Gribomont, *Histoire du Texte des Ascétiques*, 54, 60, 222, 294, and index, p. 343, s.v. 'monastères doubles'; id. 'Eustathe', *DSp* iv. 1711–12.

cessor of Dianios.[68] In the intense struggle for doctrinal supremacy the support of the ascetics often played a decisive role; and the bishops in question addressed themselves to ascetics not only to regulate their behaviour, but also to gain their support.

Both tasks were difficult. The first question is whether there were any real differences, or actual practical advantages that would attract an ascetic to one particular model, in our case Basil of Caesarea's, in preference to another one, that of the Homoiousians.[69] If so, what were they? Or, was the distinction grounded not in practical concerns at all, but rather tied to the leaders, their charisma, and their particular doctrinal position?[70] Or do we find a combination of all these elements?

Basil of Caesarea was not the inventor of communal ascetic life in Asia Minor. The question is, was he its reformer? And if so, how, as a representative for so long a time of a doctrinal minority, did he manage to propagate his ascetic concepts?

In Chapter 62 of his funeral oration *In laudem Basilii*, Gregory of Nazianzus offers the following appraisal of his friend's monastic achievements:[71]

He reconciled most excellently and united solitary (ἐρημικοῦ βίου) and community life (μιγαδός). These had been in many respects at variance with each other and rife with dissension (μαχομένων), while neither of them was in absolute and unalloyed possession of good and evil: the one being rather more calm (ἡσυχίου) and settled, tending to union with God, yet not free from pride, inasmuch as its virtue lies beyond testing or comparison; *the other, which is more oriented towards practical service* (πρακτικωτέρου), *being not free from the tendency to turbulence* (θορυβῶδες). [Basil] founded cells for ascetics (ἀσκητήρια) and hermits (μοναστήρια), but at no great distance from his cenobitic communities (κοινωνικῶν καὶ

---

[68] Brennecke, *Studien zur Geschichte*, 59–62; Dagron, 'Le Monachisme', 253–76; Gain, *L'Église*, 383.

[69] Gribomont, 'Monachisme enthousiaste', 123–43; M. Forlin Patrucco, 'Vocazione ascetica e Paideia greca', *Rivista di Storia e Letteratura religiosa* 15 (1979), 54–62.

[70] For the problem of a link between dogma and ascetic practice cf. e.g. W. Hauschild, *Gottes Geist und der Mensch* (Munich, 1972), 290; A. Le Boulluec, *La notion d'hérésie dans la littérature grecque (II*e*–III*e *siècles)*, 2 vols. (Études Augustiniennes; Paris, 1985), i. 1–20, and *passim*.

[71] Rendered here in the translation given by C. G. Browne and J. E. Swallow in the Nicene and Post-Nicene Fathers series 7 (Ann Arbor, 1955) 415 f.; Gr. Naz. *Or*. 43. 62 (Boulenger, 186 f.; commentary, ibid. pp. civ–cvii).

μιγάδων), and instead of distinguishing and separating the one from the other, as if by some intervening wall, he brought them together and united them, in order that the contemplative spirit might not be cut off from society (μήτε τὸ φιλόσοφον ἀκοινώνητον), nor should the active life be unaffected by the contemplative (τὸ πρακτικὸν ἀφιλόσοφον).

Here we have the key to an accurate understanding of Basil's ascetic achievement—and a passage which has also been the cause of some consternation among its translators and commentators. For example, according to W. K. L. Clarke, 'this version is open to grave objection. To begin with, . . . Basil's great contribution to monasticism was the establishment of community life. Could his bosom friend . . . have dismissed one of the great works of his life with a few deprecatory remarks . . . ?' 'Basil is represented as instituting a *tertium quid* by the side of two existing forms of asceticism. The first is clearly the solitary life; what is the second?'[72]

The issue at hand is evident. What precisely did Gregory have in mind when talking about the *migados bios*? He contrasts two notions: the *erēmikos bios* and the *migados*. The *erēmikos bios* excels in its contemplative merits, *philosophia* and ἡσυχία. The *migados bios* on the other hand is more 'practical and more useful', yet prone to disruptions and agitation. In his autobiographical poem *De vita sua* Gregory repeats this exact description when discussing his own choice of life after his return from Athens. Those who devote their life to the *praktikē* are more useful to others, yet gain nothing for themselves, and often descend into 'turbulences'; those who remain 'outside' are more concentrated in their devotion to God, but serve only themselves. Therefore Gregory tried to find a middle way between the *erēmikos* and the *migados*, intending to preserve the contemplation of the one and the usefulness of the other.[73]

---

[72] Clarke, *St. Basil the Great*, 109–13 (quotation, 112); I am surprised by the lack of discussion of the *migadoi* among contemporary scholars; Gain (*L'Église*, 131) devotes a few paragraphs to the question, quoting P. Deseille (*L'Évangile au désert des premiers moines à s. Bernard* (Chrétiens de tous les temps 10; Paris, 1965), 36), who interprets the cenobites and *migadoi* as 'une ébauche de l'institution des hésychiastes, telle que la législation byzantine postérieure la sanctionnera'.

[73] *De vita sua* 291–311 (Jungck, 68; commentary, 165 f.); for the same topic cf. *Gregorii Nazianzeni Σύγκρισις βίων*, ed. H. M. Werhahn (Klassisch-philologische

The term 'practical life' evidently has a specific meaning. Both Gregory of Nazianzus and Gregory of Nyssa use it essentially in the Aristotelian sense of φιλοσοφία πρακτική as opposed to φιλοσοφία θεωρητική, yet they invest these expressions with a new, more precise meaning: both terms now refer to different forms of monastic life. Thus, Gregory describes Basil as the epitome of philosophical life, both in its practical and its theoretical form; hence his definition of the 'practical life' is made quite clear: it is the kind of life led by those ascetics who, having abandoned the world, continue to serve others and to perform their civic duties, for example as a bishop—these are the *migadoi*.[74] According to Gregory, Basil's innovation was to build *askētēria* and *monastēria* not far from the cenobitic communities described as *koinōnikōn* and *migadōn*. In the same eulogy Gregory rhetorically asks what joys remain for the μοναστῶν ἢ μιγάδων (the monks or *migadoi*) now that Basil is gone. In his second discourse in defence of his flight to Pontus, Gregory distinguishes two groups of celibates: the hermits, and those who live in community (κοινωνικῶν καὶ μιγάδων). Lastly, praising Athanasius the Great, Gregory underlines that Athanasius, like Basil, reconciled two forms of life: the 'utterly monastic (μοναδικόν) and solitary (ἄμικτον) life', and the life of those who cherish 'love in community (νόμον ἀγάπηες τῃ κοινωνίᾳ), at once solitaries (ἐρημικοί) and cenobites (μιγάδες)'.[75]

Gregory's description of Basil's ascetic achievements could hardly be more accurate. From two existing forms he created a new one which combined the advantages of both. One was the solitary life of the hermit, the life led by Naucratius, the young Basil, and Eustathius' more radical followers. The other was the one led by Homoiousian ascetics, who lived in communities, were actively involved in charitable works, often as members of the urban clergy, vocal in doctrinal questions, and thus prone to

Studien 15; Wiesbaden, 1953) = *Comparatio vitarum*, PG 37. 649–67; Gr. Naz. *Or. 12 ad Patrem*, 4, 5 (PG 35, 848–9); and *Or. 25 in laud. Heronis Philosophi*, 4, 5 (PG 35, 1201, 1204).

[74] Gr. Naz. *Or. 43. 23* (Boulenger, 108–9); *Évagre le Pontique: Traité Pratique ou Le Moine*, i, ed. A. and C. Guillaumont (SC 170; Paris, 1970), 38–52, esp. 45–48; Malingrey, *Philosophia*, 207–61, esp. 253–7.

[75] Cf. below, p. 354. Gr. Naz. *Or. 43. 66* (Boulenger, 198); id. *Or. 2 de fuga sua*, 29 (PG 35. 437); *Or. 21 in laud. Ath.* 19 (PG 35. 1104).

'turbulences'. In short, the life led by those who supported the young Basil against bishop Eusebius, the *Naziraioi*.[76]

Migas, the crucial expression, literally translated means 'mixed in confusion' or 'pell-mell' and is usually interpreted as meaning 'the mingling of two opposites, for example the ascetic life and the world'.[77] As we have already seen, Gregory uses it in the sense of 'ascetics living in common', as opposed to the solitary ascetic, ἄμικτος. Without stretching the meaning too far, what prevents us from interpreting *migas* as describing Homoiousian ascetic communities, where *men* and *women* lived 'mixed together'?

Basil created a model that differed from both the *erēmikos bios* and the *migados bios* as practised by Homoiousian ascetics, while drawing upon the concepts developed by both. Of course, as I have repeatedly pointed out, all attempts at reconstructing this kind of life are severely hampered by the lack of information. If the features of Homoiousian asceticism *are* those developed in the preceding discussions, then the organization of Basil's *tertium quid* differed in three significant ways.

Annesi itself, and some other communities founded by Basil, were situated in the countryside. Separation from the world was enhanced by the retreat into the ἔρημος, the wilderness, which favoured 'contemplation'.[78] Secondly, as a direct result, ascetics following the Basilian model were less likely to engage in doctrinal disputes or vociferous 'turbulences' with regard to clerical appointments. Finally, in Basil's ascetic communities men and women were separated. His communities included women of course, but were structured as double monasteries, where men and women lived together, like angels, but were separated by

---

[76] Gr. Naz. *Or.* 43. 28 (Boulenger, 120); trans. (see n. 71 above), 405; Gain, *L'Église*, 383 n. 122; the usual interpretation of *migas* is that of 'the ascetic life lived in the world'. This widely accepted (and repeated) interpretation (cf. e.g. Fedwick, *Church and Charisma*, 163 f; Gain, op. cit. 122–60) is somewhat vague. What does 'the ascetic life lived in the world' mean in practical terms? In W. K. L. Clarke's almost vehement defence of this meaning of *migas* (*St. Basil the Great*, 109–13), the intention to salvage the exclusivity of Basil's foundation is evident, but this should not lead to an unquestioned adoption of the definition.

[77] LSJ s.v. μιγάς; Lampe s.v.; Clarke, *St. Basil the Great*, 112.

[78] Amand, *L'Ascèse monastique de saint Basile*, 118–28; Clarke, *St. Basil the Great*, 86 n. 2; Fedwick, *Church and Charisma*, 15–23; J. Gribomont, 'Le Renoncement au monde', 282–307, 460–75 (esp. 295–301).

'intervening walls', like humans. Apart from these purely organizational differences, Basil also followed a doctrinal course that gradually separated him from the Homoiousian party, especially from those who challenged the divinity of the Holy Spirit.

Despite these differences, Homoiousian and Basilian asceticism had much in common, in their organizational framework as well as in their doctrinal concepts. To a certain degree, both models had been developed in response to enthusiastic movements.[79] Both offered, in other words, a middle way between radical withdrawal—denying all that is of this world—and the established hierarchical structure of everyday life. Both represented a step beyond the individual ascetic life practised by many within their family. Both offered women in particular a different approach to ascetic life: no longer within the bosom of their own family, but within the community of ascetic 'brothers and sisters'. But in Basil's model two major issues which could and did give rise to controversies and complications had been modified: the degree of involvement in the world and the accompanying byproduct of ascetics as an intra-urban doctrinal lobby had been counteracted by a move to the country; and potential conflicts arising from the 'cohabitation' of men and women had been counteracted by physical separation. Basil was, in other words, the first great reformer of communal ascetic life.

Several examples illustrate this point. In the 360s, while still a presbyter, Basil founded a hospice at Caesarea, giving it the name that had become synonymous with Eustathius' foundation in Sebaste and those of Macedonius in Constantinople: a πτωχο-τροφεῖον. By 372 this hospice had developed into a 'new city', containing quarters for bishop and clergy and housing for the poor and sick.[80] Sacerdos, brother of Thecla, associate of Gregory

---

[79] Basil never required absolute poverty, no relative was to be deprived by someone's decision to become an ascetic; he accepted slavery; his communities developed under the protection of the local clergy; and he placed great importance on work and obedience (cf. above, pp. 70–2). While the latter aspects distinguish Basil's model from radical groups, these aspects appear not to have differed significantly from what we know about Homoiousian organizations, Dagron, 'Les Moines et la ville', 251–3; id. *Naissance d'une capitale*, 510 f.

[80] Lampe s.v. πτωχοτροφεῖον; Epiph. *Haer.* 75 (3 GCS 37. 333); Gr. Naz. *Or.* 43. 63 (Boulenger, 188 = PG 36. 577 c); Bas. *Epp.* 150, 94 (dating from 372), 81; Soz. *HE* 6. 34 (GCS 50. 291); Clarke, *St. Basil the Great*, 59–61; Patrucco, *Lettere*, 367 f.

and an ascetic member of the clergy, was in charge of a 'hospice of the poor'. In two undated letters addressed to Numerius, a prefect, Basil mentions a *chorepiskopos* in charge of a 'hospice of the poor', and indicates that these institutions were tax-exempt. The second of these letters further informs us that the addressee had supported yet another 'hospice of the poor' in Amasia.[81] In 372 Basil invited two ascetics to visit him, to resolve some dissension, but he realized that 'men who have chosen the life of the poor and must always provide for the most necessary items with their own hands cannot be absent for a long time'.[82] Could this suggest another hospice?[83] Whatever the answer in this case, the other examples above clearly illustrate that Basil perpetuated the Homoiousian practice of combining ascetic life with service to the poor—in particular, with the establishment of *ptōchotropheia* situated just outside the cities.[84]

Further, as emphasized by Gribomont and others, Basilian asceticism grew out of Eustathius' ascetic concepts with which it retained close links. Similar links can be seen between Basil's ascetic principles and those represented by the 'moderate Messalian' group around Symeon-Macarius, who himself was apparently well known and liked by Basil's brother Gregory of Nyssa. On the other hand, radical Eustathians were likewise connected to the radical Messalians.[85] There can be little doubt that the relationship between Homoiousian and Basilian ascetic

[81] *Epp.* 142, 143.

[82] Bas. *Ep.* 259.

[83] Another letter, of 372/3, purports to have been written by a certain Heraclides to Amphilochius, after Hercalides' visit to Caesarea, when he refrained, 'however, from visiting the city itself, [and] took refuge in the neighbouring poor-house'; Bas. *Ep.* 150; Fedwick ('Chronology', 13) does not indicate authorship; Hauschild (*Briefe*, 166 n. 147), mentions Basil as author; see also Clarke, *St. Basil the Great*, 61; Holl, *Amphilochius*, 12. A very interesting remark concerns the administration of property: the ascetics are supposed to hand their property over in trust to the superintendent of the *ptōchotropheion*.

[84] Gain, *L'Église*, 271 f., 277–87; M. Forlin Patrucco, 'Social Patronage and Political Mediation in the Activity of Basil of Caesarea', *SP* 17: 3 (1982), 1102–7.

[85] V. Desprez, 'Les Relations entre le Pseudo-Macaire et S. Basile', in *Commandements du Seigneur et libération évangélique: Études monastiques proposées et discutées à S. Anselme, 15–17. 2. 1976*, ed. J. Gribomont (Studia Anselmiana 70; Rome, 1977), 208–21; Dörries, *Symeon von Mesopotamien, passim*; Gribomont ('Monachisme enthousiaste', 143 f.) discusses the relationship between Basil and Symeon-Macarius.

concepts is close and complex, and that both had to confront similar enemies.

Thus, there arises the question of how Basil sought to convince his contemporaries that his ascetic ideal was indeed distinct from the Homoiousian one, and that his articulation of this ideal was superior to the established Homoiousian tradition, a particularly daunting task at a time when the Homoiousians still represented a much more powerful doctrinal position. Basil's principal strategy was to ensure that as many of his relatives and close friends as possible became high-ranking members of the clergy.[86] Along with considerable political influence, he used his own office and theirs to impose his new ideas on his subordinates, to a degree which caused open resentment in some quarters.[87] 'Basil seems always to have thought that his friends and his relatives were there to support and enhance his own ambitions and ideas.'[88] These 'ideas' of course included his ascetic concepts, and their propagation and implementation were among his chief interests.

Together with his influential friends and relatives Basil began to publish numerous writings, containing the norms and guidelines for the implementation of his concepts. As the previous analysis has demonstrated, these works not only impressed upon their recipients the correct doctrine, but also the proper ascetic practice associated with it: that devised or at least sanctioned by Basil himself.

[86] Gregory became bishop of Nyssa in 372, Aubineau, *Virginité*, 29 n. 3, 81 f.; in the same year Gregory of Nazianzus was appointed bishop of Sasima, Patrucco, *Lettere*, 255; Gallay, *Lettres*, i, pp. xi–xiv; Giet, *Sasimes*, *passim*; Hauser-Meury, 41 f.; Loofs, *Eustathius und die Chronologie*, 76–8. Peter was ordained bishop of Sebaste; two other relatives, an uncle Gregory and a certain Poimenius were both bishops; Amphilochius was ordained bishop of Iconium in 373. Holl (*Amphilochius*, 14–26) provides interesting insights into Basil's strategic thinking; Melitius' case has been discussed briefly, cf. Brennecke, *Studien zur Geschichte*, 218–22, 226, and R. E. Snee, 'Gregory of Nazianzen's Constantinopolitan Career, A. D. 379–381', Diss. (Washington, DC, 1981), 120–36. Among the *chorepiskopoi* are Timotheus (Bas. *Epp*. 24, 291) and the father of Evagrius Ponticus (Pall. *HL* 38 (Butler, ii. 16–23))); Guillaumont, *Traité Pratique*, i. 21 f. Also very illuminating are e.g. Basil's Letters 81, 200, and 205. For Basil's use of familial connections see also Forlin Patrucco, 'Aspetti di vita familiare', 171–3; R. Van Dam, 'Emperor, Bishops, and Friends in Late Antique Cappadocia', *JThS* NS 37 (1986), 53–76.

[87] Bas. *Epp*. 56, 94.

[88] Van Dam, 'Emperor, Bishops, and Friends', 69.

Three works, beyond those already discussed, are particularly representative of this strategy. About 372/3 Basil asked his younger brother Gregory of Nyssa to write the treatise *De virginitate*. This was specifically designed to encourage obedience to 'the authority of the one who authorized us'—that is, to emphasize in all aspects the superiority of Basil's ascetic concept.[89] Indeed, when criticizing 'enthusiasts', Gregory's main point of contention is not primarily their ascetic practice, but their failure to adopt Basil's model.[90]

A letter by a certain Heraclides (numbered as Letter 150 of Basil), and addressed to Amphilochius, is a second example of the prescriptive writings. The author follows almost exactly Gregory's line of argument. His youth and as yet unbridled ascetic zeal reinforce his tendency to overestimate his own potential; therefore, he concedes, he needs 'a great and experienced teacher' to guide him safely towards perfection. This insight has led Heraclides to abandon the more radical ascetic course that he and Amphilochius had chosen, which prompts Amphilochius to accuse him of desertion. However, Heraclides, acquainted with Basil's ascetic teachings because of his sojourn in the hospice at Caesarea, remains steadfast and attempts to persuade Amphilochius to follow suit: 'you [would not] have counselled me to leave this person and go wandering in the desert. For while the caves and the rocks will wait for us, yet the aid which true men can give will not always abide with us.'[91]

Letter 295 is a particularly illustrative example of Basil's at-

[89] Cf. n. 43 above.
[90] *De virg.* 7. 2. 6–23 (SC 119. 354–6); Daniélou, 'Gregoire de Nysse', 119–34; Dörries, 'Bestreiter', 217 f.; id. 'Urteil', 346–51; Gribomont, 'Le Dossier', 21–5; for the importance of the leader and spiritual father cf. I. Hausherr, 'Direction spirituelle, ii, Chez les chrétiens orientaux', in *DSp* iii. 1008–60, here 1008–21; A. de Vogüé, *L'Expérience de Dieu dans la vie monastique* (Abbaye de la Pierre-qui-Vive, 1973), 51–64.
[91] Bas. *Ep.* 150; Holl, *Amphilochius*, 11–13; in fact, both Letter 150 and Gregory of Nazianzus' correspondence regarding Glycerius (esp. *Ep.* 247 = Bas. *Ep.* 170) imply the same strategy: to induce as many 'radicals' as possible to 'return' to moderate 'Basilian' practices. Gregory never threatened Glycerius seriously; instead he offered pardon in case of his return. Basil, to whose sphere of jurisdiction Glycerius had obviously fled, also acted with great leniency; Gribomont, 'Le Dossier', 624 n. 76; Meyendorff, 'Messalianism or Anti-Messalianism', 589.

tempts at persuading others to follow his path.[92] Basil had previously visited the community of monks which he now addresses in writing. On his visit he had already impressed upon them the necessity of living according to his principles of life in common, 'after the fashion of the Apostles'. These words had not been idle talk, but teachings that Basil wished to be observed. Therefore he has dispatched a brother who will oversee their zeal and 'arouse them from [their] lethargy, and make clear to us what stands in the way'. Somehow, despite their good intentions to exchange their isolated lives for a communal one, this has not yet been properly effected. Such reluctance is in no small part caused by those who have unsettled the monks' right faith in the Fathers (of Nicaea). These people who seek to disturb their faith fail to realize that rigoristic ascetic practice alone will not grant salvation. Nor, for that matter, will correct faith without good deeds. Both practised together are the sole guarantee.[93]

This letter gives a clear account of the crucial steps: a visit from Basil himself, followed by writings containing the rules and regulations conducive to correct ascetic life in common, to be supervised by one of Basil's trusted confidants, who furthermore ensures the correct doctrinal convictions.[94] Yet this comprehensive strategy alone seems to have proved insufficient. At least for Basil's own time the results are difficult to ascertain. We possess comparatively few references to actual Basilian foundations, and it is virtually impossible to distinguish between an original Basilian foundation and a reorganized Homoiousian community.[95]

---

[92] Cf. also *RF* 7 (PG 31. 928).

[93] For similar sentiments see *Ep.* 262, addressed to Urbicius, where Basil demands news regarding the 'behaviour' of Urbicius' monks; Gain, *L'Église*, 135–7. *Letters* 173 and 22 combined, if accepted as a single communication, could attest to an attempt to reorganize Theodora's community; Gribomont, 'Règles épistolaires', 264–87.

[94] Basil did not fail to promote his proposals by personal appearances. His letters give abundant evidence of his own travels and those of his envoys like Meletius, Gregory of Nyssa, or Amphilochius; *Epp.* 200, 259; Aubineau, *Virginité*, pr. 2. 2–21 (SC 119. 250, 31 n. 2); Fedwick, *Church and Charisma*, 142–53; Holl, *Amphilochius*, 20–7.

[95] However, a number of Basilian ascetic communities proper are referred to, one of them being, of course, Annesi. At the end of 375, Basil would have liked to visit ΤΟΙΣ ῾ΥΦ᾿ ῾ΕΑΥΤΟΝ ΑΣΚΗΤΑΙΣ, but he has instead to send his confidant Meletius (*Ep.* 226). Interestingly, the letter contains a doctrinal discussion and

It is easier to reconstruct the manner in which outright rigoristic movements, which intended to remain so, were dealt with. The most obvious way to channel rigorist zeal was by oppression, first by the clergy and secondly, with the support of the empire, by the civil authorities. The clergy's most efficient instrument for influencing ascetic behaviour was excommunication by a synod. The synod at Gangra that condemned radical Eustathians was followed by a succession of others, at Antioch, Constantinople, Sirmium, and Side, to name but a few.[96] However, enthusiastic (i.e. radical) movements continued, attesting to the fact that this form of punishment remained ineffective. The enthusiasts' continued vigour suggests that their way of life met existing needs, and responded to ongoing demands.

Furthermore, such radical movements were constituted on strict and scrupulous observance of the most fundamental authority, the Scriptures—or at least selected passages of the Scriptures—and the radicals thereby denied outright the legitimacy of those who, in their view, misinterpreted the same: the clergy. Decisions made by such clergy could therefore be simply ignored with impunity. Not surprisingly, the ecclesiastical authorities resorted to more effective measures: imperial legislation.[97]

warnings against heretics, suggesting that even his own monks could be led astray; similar circumstances are possible in the case of *Ep.* 259. Basil's *Ascetica* also contain references to other communities; see e.g. *RF* 35 (PG 31. 1004), where brothers ask whether it would be advisable to have more than one *adelphotē* in the same village. Basil deems this unwise since rivalries are likely to ensue; it seems a little far-fetched to assume on the basis of this passage that each town had its own community, as is the view of K. S. Frank (*Basilius von Caesarea: Die Mönchsregeln* (St Ottilien, 1981), 61, 63 f.); but cf. Bas. *RF* 30, 43, 54 (PG 31. 991, 1029, 1044). In *Ep.* 313 Basil asks for tax exemption for a home owned by him in Galatia. Does this refer to one of his communities, since monastic communities were tax-exempt (and enjoyed a number of other legal privileges)? Cf. *Epp.* 154, 256, 262, 284; Clarke, *St. Basil the Great*, 59; H. R. Hagemann, 'Die rechtliche Stellung der christlichen Wohltätigkeitsanstalten der östlichen Reichshälfte', *Revue internationale des droits de l'Antiquité* 3 (1956), 265–83.

[96] Dörries, 'Bestreiter', 218–27; id. 'Urteil', 334–40, 347 f.; Gribomont, 'Le Dossier', 614 f.; id. 'Monachisme enthousiaste', 130–5; E. Honigmann, 'Samus of Seleucia in Isauria', in id. *Patristic Studies*, 43–6.

[97] For a discussion of the fundamental problems facing ecclesiastical authorities when resorting to coercive measures executed by state organs, cf. P. R. L. Brown, 'Saint Augustine's Attitude to Religious Coercion', *JRS* 54 (1964), 107–16; id. 'Religious Coercion in the Later Roman Empire: The Case of North

Theodosius' accession to the throne of the Eastern Empire initiated another period during which a ruler actively sought to establish unity in the Church, this time under the banner of the Western interpretation of Nicaea, which was shared by the three Cappadocian Fathers. The famous edict promulgated on 28 February, 380 in Thessaloniki and addressed to the citizens of Constantinople heralded a new dawn for the Neo-Nicaean faction within the Eastern Empire.[98] It stipulated:

> that all the peoples who are ruled by the administration of our Clemency shall practise that religion which the divine Peter the Apostle transmitted to the Romans . . . the religion followed by the Pontiff Damasus and by Peter, bishop of Alexandria. . . . Those persons who follow this rule shall embrace the name of Catholic Christians. The rest, however, whom We adjudge demented and insane, shall sustain the infamy of heretical dogmas, their meeting places shall not receive the name of churches, and they shall be smitten . . . by the retribution of Our own initiative.

On the same day and in the same context the emperor decreed further, that 'those persons who through ignorance confuse or through negligence violate and offend the sanctity of the divine law commit sacrilege'.[99] Thus, bishops representing the 'Catholic

---

Africa', *History* 48 (1963), 283–305; R. A. Markus, '*Coge intrare*: The Church and Political Power', in id. *Saeculum: History and Society in the Theology of Saint Augustine* (Cambridge, 1970), 133–53; unfortunately for us, all three articles are based on Augustine.

[98] *CTh.* 16. 1. 2 (Mommsen–Meyer, i.2, 833); Pharr, *Theodosian Code*, 440; born in Cauca in Spain, Theodosius came from a region of the Empire long under the influence of the Athanasian interpretation of Nicaea. Although he was not baptized when Gratian elected him co-regent on 19 Jan. 379 in Sirmium, Theodosius soon made it his primary internal political aim to restore order within the Church on the basis of this same interpretation of Nicaea; W. Ensslin, *Die Religionspolitik des Kaisers Theodosius des Großen* (Sitzungsberichte der Bayrischen Akademie der Wissenschaften, phil.-hist. Kl. 1953, 2; Munich, 1953), 5–28; id. 'Staat und Kirche von Konstantin dem Großen bis Theodosius dem Großen', in *Die Kirche angesichts der konstantinischen Wende*, 74–86; Gaudemet, *L'Église*, 598–620; P. Joannou, *La Législation impériale et la christianisation de l'Empire romain* (OrChrA 192; Rome, 1972) 43–52, 78–106; N. O. King, *The Emperor Theodosius and the Establishment of Christianity* (London, 1961), 50–69; J. Rougé, 'La Législation de Théodose contre les hérétiques', in *Epektasis*, 635–49.

[99] 'Qui divinae legis sanctitatem aut nesciendo confundunt aut neglegendo violant et offendunt, sacrilegium committunt' *CTh.* 16. 2. 25 (Mommsen–Meyer, i.2, 843); Pharr, *Theodosian Code*, 444; Ensslin, *Die Religionspolitik*, 98 f.

Church' had been given full rein to invoke the punitive power of the state against those who strayed from the flock.[100]

In 369 Valentinian I had already issued an edict which punished those who had 'usurped' the garb of a philosopher. Only those approved by an exacting panel, and thus officially separated 'from this filthy crowd', were allowed to wear these coats.[101] In 372 the same Valentinian had prohibited all Manichaean assemblies. In 381 Theodosius not only denied Manichaeans the right to assemble, but he also revoked, retroactively, their rights to bequeath or inherit property, thus severely infringing their rights as Roman citizens. He included in the edict 'those who defend themselves with dishonest fraud under the pretence of those deceptive names . . . the Encratites, Apotactites, the Hydroparastatae, or the Saccophori'[102]—all of them enthusiasts.[103] In 382 Theodosius forbade so-called Manichaeans to 'flee the company of the good under false pretence of the solitary life and . . . choose the secret gatherings of persons of the lowest classes'—that is, the company of the 'poor'. In the same edict, any of the previously listed enthusiasts are, if apprehended, to be punished with the 'supreme penalty'.[104] In short, between 381 and 383 no less than four edicts severely restricted enthusiastic activities. In 390 Valentinian and Theodosius issued the edict regulating the enrolment of deaconesses, as discussed in the context of Olympias. In its second half they decreed that:

Women who cut off their hair, contrary to divine and human laws, at the instigation and persuasion of some professed belief, shall be kept away from the doors of the churches. It shall be unlawful for them to approach the consecrated mysteries, nor shall they be granted . . . the privilege of frequenting the altars which must be venerated by all.

Bishops who allowed a woman with a shaved head to enter their church—who even knew of such an occurrence—were expelled

---

[100] W. K. Boyd, *The Ecclesiastical Edicts of the Theodosian Code* (Studies in History, Economics and Public Law 24: 2; New York, 1905), 33–70; King, *The Emperor Theodosius*, 50–9.

[101] *CTh*. 13. 3. 7 (Mommsen–Meyer, i.2, 742); Pharr, *Theodosian Code*, 388; issued in Sirmium and addressed to Probus, the praetorian prefect of Rome.

[102] *CTh*. 16. 5. 3, 7 (Mommsen–Meyer, i.2, 855, 857); Pharr, *Theodosian Code*, 450–2; for a description of these heresies cf. Gain, *L'Église*, 366–70.

[103] G. Blond, 'Encratisme', in *DSp* iv. 628–42.

[104] *CTh*. 16. 5. 9 (Mommsen–Meyer, i.2, 858); Pharr, *Theodosian Code*, 452.

from their office.[105] In 398 and 410 two further edicts banned 'Montanists' and 'Priscillians', and in 428 another edict added explicitly the Messalians, the Euchitai, and the so-called Enthusiasts to those already condemned.[106]

Nevertheless, the early fifth-century lives of Alexander Akoimetos and of the monk Hypatius, as well as Nilus of Ancyra's treatise *On Voluntary Poverty* of *c*.430, tell of monks wandering around the countryside in extreme poverty, 'lacking all earthly possessions'.[107] An entire literary tradition revolves around the theme of women disguised as male ascetics, the most famous exemplar being the sixth-century *Life of Matrona*.[108] Women and men continued to live as wandering ascetics; women continued to shave their heads and 'become male'. In other words, even though radical movements were easier to identify and thus easier to suppress, both the ecclesiastical and imperial legislation failed to eradicate them entirely. Not surprisingly. As Sozomen reports of Theodosius:[109] 'great as were the penalties adjudged by the laws against heretics, they were not always carried into execution, for the emperor had no desire to persecute his subjects, he desired only to enforce the uniformity of belief about God through the medium of intimidation.' Thus the 'war on heretics' had to be

[105] 'Feminae, quae crinem suum contra divinas humanasque leges instinctu persuasae professionis abscinderint, ab ecclesiae foribus arceantur. . . . Hoc absque dubio emendandis pro lege erit, emendatis pro consuetudine, ut illi habeant testimonium, isti incipiant timere iudicium', *CTh*. 16. 2. 27 (Mommsen–Meyer, i.2), 844; Pharr, *Theodosian Code*, 444 f.; given the recipient, the *Praefectus Praetorio Orientis* Tatianus, this edict affects the entire East. The parallels with Gangra's c. 17 are evident, Hefele–Leclercq, i.2, 1040.
[106] *CTh*. 16. 5. 34 (AD 398), 48 (AD 410) (Mommsen–Meyer, i.2, 866, 871); Pharr, *Theodosian Code*, 455, 458; *CTh*. 16. 5. 65 (AD 428) (op. cit. 878); Pharr, op. cit. 462 f.; Holl, *Amphilochius*, 36–8.
[107] *Vie d'Alexandre l'Acémète*, ed. E. De Stoop (Patrologia Orientalis 6: 5; Paris, 1911); Vööbus, *History of Asceticism* ii. 185–96; *Callinicus: De vita S. Hypatii*, ed. H. Usener (Leipzig, 1895); Nilus, *De voluntaria paupertate* (PG 79. 725–997).
[108] Patlagean, 'L'Histoire de la femme déguisée', 597–623; ead. *Pauvrété économique*, 135–7; Dagron, *Naissance d'une capitale*, 513 f.; Gribomont's query ('Monachisme enthousiaste', 133), 'Ces cas de féminisme militant furent-ils rares, limités aux années 340, ou à la ville de Constantinople? Le phénomène semble avoir disparu sans laisser des traces, sinon peut-être parmi les disciples d'Aère', seems thus answered and corrected.
[109] *HE* 7. 12. 11 (GCS 50. 316).

won by other means;[110] for example, by offering models of ascetic
life which would remain within the frameworks of society yet
allow for ascetic fulfilment[111]—models such as Basil's, which
could reform and 'domesticate' former enthusiasts of the type
that Basil, Gregory of Nazianzus, Gregory of Nyssa, Amphilochius of Iconium, and his friend Heraclides had once been
themselves.[112]

If imperial legislation had to be invoked—albeit with mixed
results—in the 'war on heretics', it was the same imperial influence which greatly enhanced the ultimate success of Basil's
ascetic concepts. The Homoiousian party led by Eustathius'
followers, the 'Pneumatomachoi', continued to exercise considerable influence until 379 (the year of Basil's death), when a synod
at Antioch condemned their teachings by a narrow majority as
heretical.[113] Notwithstanding Antioch, the sheer number and ecclesiastical standing of the Homoiousians and 'Pneumatomachoi'
prompted the emperor Theodosius himself to initiate conciliatory
negotiations with them on the eve of the second ecumenical
council assembled in Constantinople in 381.[114] His initiative, by
no means the rash action of an uninformed outsider, followed a

---

[110] Bas. *Ep.* 242. 2: ὁ αἱρετικὸς . . . πόλεμος.

[111] Families especially were strongly opposed to radical teachings; cf. on
this topic the fundamental article by L. Cracco Ruggini, 'Simboli di battaglia
ideologica nel Tardo Ellenismo', in O. Banti *et al.* (eds.), *Studi Storici in onore di
O. Bertolini*, i (Pisa, 1972), 176–300, esp. 288–300; again Gregory's letter concerning Glycerius is instructive (Gallay, *Lettres*, ii. 136). A sentence in Basil's
Letter 119 to Eustathius, written a year before the events at Venasa, describes the
feelings of the general public very aptly: 'no profession is at this moment more
suspect to the people here than that of the ascetic life' (Courtonne, *Lettres*, ii.
25).

[112] Gr. Naz. *Epp.* 4–6; Bas. *Epp.* 2, 14; Gr. Nyss. *De virg.* 23. 6 (SC 119. 544);
Gr. Naz. *Carm. ad Olympiadem*, l. 102 (PG 37. 1550); Patrucco, *Lettere*, 31 f.;
Holl, *Amphilochius*, 10–13, 31–5.

[113] Bas. *Ep.* 244 on the occasion of the synod at Cyzicos; May, 'Die Datierung',
47–53; Meinhold, 'Pneumatomachoi', *RE* xxi. 1085; Ritter, *Das Konzil*, 68–78.

[114] Interestingly, none of the bishops of the classically Homoiousian areas had
been formally invited; cf. E. Schwartz, 'Über die Bischofslisten der Synoden von
Chalcedon, Nicaea und Konstantinopel' (Abhandlungen der Akademie der
Wiss. Mainz, NF 13; Mainz, 1937), 83; Ritter, *Das Konzil*, 39. For the Pneumatomachian negotiations see Soc. *HE* 5. 8 (PG 67. 576–77); Soz. *HE* 7. 7. 2–5 (GCS
50. 308); Gr. Naz. *De vita sua* 1703–96 (Jungck, 136–41); May, 'Die Datierung',
48–57; Ritter, op. cit. 68 n. 5, 78, 253–70.

conscious policy to incorporate this substantial minority into the new Nicaean coalition.[115]

For reasons difficult to assess, the negotiations failed.[116] An edict issued on 25 July, 383 in Constantinople included the Macedonians and 'Pneumatomachoi' among the banned heresies, together with the Arians, the Manichaeans, and other enthusiastic groups. The same ban is twice reiterated during the following year.[117] The fate of the Pneumatomachian–Homoiousian party was thus sealed and that of their ascetic organizations with them. Although the institutions had been well organized and popular, they could no longer be mentioned, let alone praised.[118] The history of the Homoiousians, now called Macedonians or Pneumatomachoi, had to be rewritten.[119] Whatever was known of the positive aspects of Homoiousian asceticism had to be ignored, and Basil of Caesarea was henceforth acknowledged as the one and only true founder of ascetic communities in Asia Minor.

However, the empress Flacilla, Theodosius' wife, visited hospices and *ptōchotropheia* modelled on those founded by Macedo-

---

[115] In fact, given the Pneumatomachian–Homoiousian adherence to the formula of Nicaea, sanctioned by Pope Liberius of Rome, Theodosius' attempt was not as improbable as later made out. Indeed, Gregory of Nyssa's (mistitled) discourse *In suam ordinationem* (PG 46. 543–54, esp. 549 B–D, 553) sheds light on the sympathies the Pneumatomachoi could still command; they are described as brothers standing in the middle between the true faith and heresy, and are praised for their ascetic impetus; cf. J. Daniélou, 'La Chronologie des sermons de Grégoire de Nysse', 357 f.; Gribomont, 'Le Dossier', 622; May, cf. n. 114 above. Meinhold, 'Pneumatomachoi', *RE* xxi. 1087.

[116] Of course, one of our main sources for the history of the council is Gregory of Nazianzus, who was its leader for the initial three months (i.e. the period of his troubled tenure as bishop of Constantinople). It is well known that his attitude towards the Pneumatomachian position was even more intransigent than Basil's, and was shared by Amphilochius, who had already condemned the sect in 376; cf. May, 'Die Datierung', 49 f.

[117] Soc. *HE* 5. 8. 4 (PG 67. 577); Soz. *HE* 7. 7. 3 (GCS 50. 308); *CTh.* 16. 5. 11, 12, 13 (Mommsen–Meyer, i.2, 859 f.); Pharr, *Theodosian Code*, 452 f.; Meinhold, 'Pneumatomachoi', *RE* xxi. 1086.

[118] Dagron, *Naissance d'une capitale*, 439–42, 511.

[119] In 380 Jerome, *Chronicon* 235 (*Die Chronik des Hieronymus*, ed. R. Helm (GCS 47; Berlin, 1956²), 342), comments on the 'heresiarch Macedonius'; a 5th-cent. Constantinopolitan bishops' list (Theod. *HE* 5. 40. 8 (GCS 44. 349)) mentions Macedonius as 'the Pneumatomachian heresiarch'; Eustathius' fate was similar, see Meinhold, 'Pneumatomachoi', *RE* xxi. 1072, 1075; for a more general overview cf. Le Boulluec, *La Notion d'hérésie, passim*.

nius and Marathonius; Sozomen knew of flourishing Macedonian monasteries in his day; and the empress Pulcheria discovered the remains of the *Forty Martyrs of Sebaste* in a Macedonian monastery.[120] Moreover the ascetic cohabitation of men and women continued to enjoy popularity, not only among rich young ladies and their subservient monks.[121] Justinian passed a *novella* banning *monastēria dipla*, dual monasteries, a ban repeated by canon 20 of the second council at Nicaea in 787.[122] The notion of an automatic, swift conversion of the entire Cappadocian and Pontic ascetic movement into a homogeneous Basilian community is false. Organizational differences, and female religious practices in particular, indicate a long period of adaptation before Basil's model was widely accepted, if that was ever truly the case.

Basil of Caesarea—in his doctrine as well as his ascetic concepts—was an outstanding reformer, and in that sense he was an innovator. Like most reformers, he derived his new concepts—such as his reinterpretation of the Trinity—from existing structures and models, but he invested these with new meaning and thereby subjected them to change.

In the case of his doctrine, Basil's new concepts altered and reinterpreted Scriptural precepts—and it is here that he no doubt encountered the strongest resistance. As for his ascetic concepts, the *pièce de résistance*, the aspect where novelty caused the greatest dilemma, was the life of male and female ascetics in common. The Scriptures are quite clear: if ascetic life makes humans resemble angels while still on earth, and if angels neither marry nor are given in marriage, and are thus asexual, then ascetics are above and beyond sexual distinction—'there is neither male nor female in Jesus Christ' (Gal. 3: 28). Thus the highest form of ascetic life is that of men and women together. The dangers inherent in this concept, especially once the movement loses its first rigour, are self-evident. The problems arise, how-

---

[120] Soz. *HE* 4. 27. 4, 9. 2. 1–3 (GCS 50. 184, 392); Theod. *HE* 5. 19. 2–3 (GCS 44. 314).

[121] Dagron, *Naissance d'une capitale*, 512 f. with references to John Chrysostom.

[122] Just. *Nov.* 123. 36, μοναστηριῶν διπλῶν; Boulenger, *Discours funèbres*, p. cv; Gain, *L'Eglise*, 155 n. 145; this led to the 'anti-feminist' revision of some of the MSS of Basil's *Ascetica*; Gribomont, *Histoire du texte des Ascétiques*, 222, and index, p. 343 s.v. 'monastères doubles'.

ever, in the process of reform and change itself, since the element to be reinterpreted and superseded is the normative basis not only for asceticism but for Christianity itself: the Scriptures.

Not surprisingly, the Fathers' attitude to communal ascetic life for men and women was highly ambiguous, and the process of drawing the boundaries became an intricate and prolonged affair. Life in common could not be condemned outright, nor could it be allowed to continue in its original, albeit more Scriptural fashion: thus Basil's reformed communities offered a compromise, an alternative. Men and women lived together, but they were separated. *Mutatis mutandis*, the same is true for the other essential aspects of ascetic life, poverty and renunciation. These practical developments find, of course, their complement in the theoretical justification, as exemplified by Macrina. She became a 'manly virgin' in her virtue alone, not in her external appearance; she gave away her property, but did not impoverish her community; she was a figure of authority, but not a part of the hierarchy.

Indeed, though never mentioned explicitly, one subject of the reforms and of the doctrinal and legal struggles leading to their success was that of women. The decision between Eustathius and his Homoiousian model of ascetic life and that proposed by Basil directly affected the ways in which women could henceforth realize their ascetic ideals: they would act no longer in concert with their 'brothers in Christ', and would be less and less involved in charitable works and direct doctrinal conflicts—or so it appears. As has already become evident, the decision took a long time to make, and it is doubtful that all forms of communal ascetic life, despite the impression generated by our 'orthodox' sources, disappeared entirely. But, are Basil and thus Asia Minor an anomaly, or are they together representative of a pattern in the making of monasticism in Late Antiquity?

II Egypt

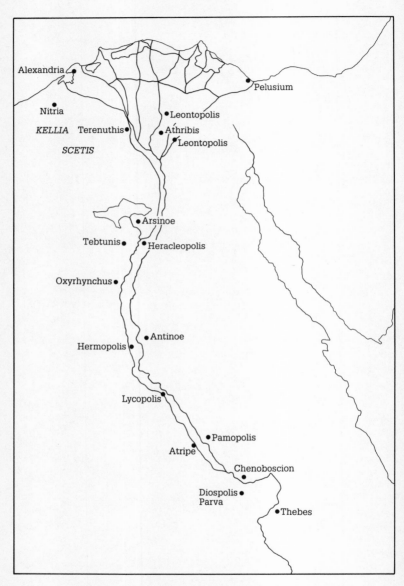

MAP 3. Locations of female ascetics in Egypt

7

Canons and Papyri

THE CANONS

One day in the year 270 a young Egyptian, then 'eighteen or even twenty years old', 'considered, while he walked home, how the apostles, forsaking everything, followed the Saviour'. This day not only changed the young man's life, but it made him, through the work of Athanasius, into the *pater eremitorum*, the archetypal Desert Father, whose sufferings and labours kindled the imagination for generations to come.[1] However, at this fateful moment Antony was not yet the solitary hermit. Though recently orphaned, he had 'one quite young sister'. Faced with the dilemma of having to abandon either his sister or his desire to 'forsake everything', Antony found an interesting solution. According to Athanasius' *Vita Antonii*, he placed his younger sister 'in the charge of respected and trusted virgins' to be raised εἰς παρθενίαν, 'in virginity'.[2]

[1] Ath. *V. Ant.* (PG 26. 835–976); here c. 2 (841); and *Athanasio: Vita di San Antonio*, ed. G. J. M. Bartelink and C. Mohrmann (Vite dei Santi 1; Milan, 1974), based on the oldest Latin translation edited by H. Hoppenbrouwers, *La plus ancienne version latine de la Vie de s. Antoine de s. Athanase: Étude de Critique textuelle* (Nijmegen, 1960), for a discussion of the manuscript tradition cf. pp. xxviii f. and lxxi–lxxiv. The English translation used mainly in the following is by R. C. Gregg, *Athanasius: The Life of Saint Antony and the Letter to Marcellinus* (New York, 1980). See also B. R. Brennan, 'Dating the Vita Antonii', *VigChr* 30 (1976), 52–4; G. Garitte, *Un témoin important de la Vie de s. Antoine de s. Athanase: La Version inédite des Archives de saint Pierre à Rome* (Brussels, 1939), *passim*; id. 'Le Texte grec et les versions anciennes de la Vie de s. Antoine', *Studia Anselmiana* 38 (1956), 1; M. Tetz, 'Athanasius', in *TRE* iv. 333–49.

[2] εἰς παρθενῶνα, Ath. *V. Ant.* 3 (PG 26. 844 A) and c. 54 (921 B); 'sororem quoque suam commendavit notis et fidelibus virginibus ut nutrientur ad virginitatem' (Bartelink, pp. 10, 191). A *parthenōn* denoted at that time the female part of a house, but in connection with pious virgins it must indicate something else; Lampe s.v. παρθενών; *Lexicon Athanasianum*, ed. G. Müller (Berlin, 1944–52), s.v. What exactly Athanasius had in mind—especially considering the early date of the episode (c.270)—created enormous speculation, until G. Garitte ('Un

Athanasius composed his life of Antony much later, shortly after the saint's death in 356. Nevertheless, this incident suggests that long before Antony departed to the desert, Christian women were already known as 'virgins' or *parthenoi*, not because of their physical condition but because of their way of life.[3] Indeed, traces of these women and, more importantly, of their particular life appear in other sources, dating back as early as the third century AD. Taking as a beginning once again those sources that are specifically intended to regulate the daily life of a Christian congregation, the so-called canonical collections, only three collections are relevant here: the *Canons of Hippolytus*, the *Pseudo-Basilian*, and the *Pseudo-Athanasian Canons*.[4]

couvent de femmes au IIIe siècle?', 150–9, esp. 151–3 for discussion of secondary literature, and 157 f. for textual revision) identified the problem as textual rather than historical; thus Athanasius' passage does not indicate the existence of a female religious community called *parthenōn*.

[3] For the historicity of the *Vita Antonii* cf. Bartelink and Mohrmann, *Vita di Antonio*, pp. xxviii, lxxv–lxxxiii; L. Bouyer, *La Vie de s. Antoine* (repr. Spiritualité Orientale 22; Bellefontaine, 1977), esp. 119, 122; H. Dörries, *Die Vita Antonii als Geschichtsquelle* (Nachrichten der Akademie der Wissenschaften Göttingen, phil.-hist. Kl. 14; Göttingen, 1949; repr. in id. *Wort und Stunde*, i. 145–224).

[4] For the methodological complexities involved in using the so-called canonical literature cf. N. Brox, 'Altchristliche Formen des Anspruchs auf apostolische Kirchenverfassung', *Kairos* 12 (1970), 113–17, 135; Cacitti, 'L'etica sessuale', 74–85; Faivre, *Naissance*, 37–45; Gaudemet, *L'Église*, 45–7; O. Meinardus, 'A Study on the Canon Law of the Coptic Church' *Bulletin de la Société de l'Archéologie copte* 16 (1961–2), 231–42, here 232 f., 238. These three collections, although they incorporate earlier material originating from other parts of the Roman Empire, were compiled in Egypt and intended exclusively for their immediate vicinity; E. Wipszycka, *Les Ressources et les activités économiques des églises en Egypte du IVe au VIIIe siècle* (Papyrologia Bruxellensia 10; Brussels, 1972), 14–20. The *Apostolic Church Order* (*Die allgemeine Kirchenordnung, frühchristliche Liturgien und kirchliche Überlieferung*, i, *Die allgemeine Kirchenordnung des zweiten Jahrhunderts*, ed. T. Shermann (Paderborn, 1914)), dating from the beginning of the 4th cent., has only two references to women of which one is to widows: 'Cephas said: three of them ought to be installed (καθιστανέσθωσαν), two who persevere in prayer ... and one to assist women in want' (can. 21, Shermann, pp. 29–30). The other reference discusses the possibility of creating offices for women, only to conclude that they are not called for (Shermann, 31–3). Though providing useful insights into the function of the 'widow', the *Apostolic Church Order* is only of tangential relevance to the topic at hand; see also J. P. Arendzen, 'An Entire Text of the "Apostolic Church Order"',

The *Canons of Hippolytus*, revised between 336 and 340 on the basis of the Roman *Apostolic Tradition*, are the oldest collection compiled with a rural Egyptian audience in mind.[5] They do indeed confirm the existence of women and men characterized as virgins. Thus, canon 7 stipulates that virgins (*parthenoi*) need not be consecrated by the 'laying on of hands'; a simple proclamation sufficed. However, the virgins here addressed are celibate sub-deacons and lecturers and not female virgins.[6] Canon 18 exhorts virgins to wear a thick veil to church (a *pallium*), but here the addressees are young, unmarried women.[7] Canon 32, finally, stipulates that 'The virgins and widows fast frequently and pray for the Church'.[8] Virgins and widows are two distinct groups, set apart from the lay community, and play a role very much like that already known from Asia Minor. The congregation knew 'enrolled widows', who were selected in accordance with Paul's prescription from Timothy 5: 9,[9] but they were 'not ordained, . . . prayers are said over them; since ordination is only for men.' However, they were held 'in the highest esteem because of their great achievements in praying, caring for the sick and much fasting', and were remunerated by the congregation. Canon 32

JThS 3 (1901/2); 59–80; B. Botte, 'Les Plus Anciennes Collections Canoniques', *L'Orient syrien* 5 (1960), 331–50, esp. 335; for the date cf. A. v. Harnack, *Die Quellen der sogenannten apostolischen Kirchenordnung*, ii (TU 2: 5; Leipzig, 1886), 55; *Didascaliae Apostolorum canonum ecclesiasticorum traditionis apostolicae versiones latinae*, ed. E. Tidner (TU 75; Berlin, 1963), 105–13.

[5] The Greek original is lost; only an arabic translation of a Coptic version has been preserved and edited by R. G. Coquin, *Les Canons d'Hippolyte* (Patrologie Orientale 31:2; Paris, 1966), 318–31; Botte, *La Tradition apostolique*, 14–17; for the dating cf. id. 'L'Origine des canons d'Hippolyte', in *Mélanges M. Andrieu* (Strasburg, 1956), 53–63. See also H. Brakmann, 'Alexandria und die Kanones des Hippolytus', *JAC* 22 (1979), 139–49; Faivre, *Naissance*, 69–75; J. M. Hanssens, 'L'Édition critique des canons d'Hippolyte', *OrChrP* 32 (1966), 540f.; *Die Kirchenrechtsquellen des Patriarchats Alexandrien*, ed. W. Riedel (Leipzig, 1900), 193–230; Wipszycka, *Les Ressources*, 19.

[6] As affirmed by both Coquin (*Les Canons*, 323) and Botte (*La Tradition apostolique*, 33), on the basis of canon 12 of the *Apostolic Tradition*; cf. also Botte, 'L'Origine des canons', 61; Riedel, *Die Kirchenrechtsquellen*, 205.

[7] Coquin, *Les Canons*, 373–5.

[8] Ibid. 403.

[9] Can. 9; Coquin, *Les Canons*, 361; Gryson, *Le Ministère*, 31–3; Martimort, *Les Diaconesses*, 19–21.

suggests a similar arrangement for women entitled 'virgins'. Both
categories were required to fast and pray, and both were required
to lead a chaste life.[10] In other words, the *Canons of Hippolytus*
confirm that women of a variety of ages were leading a life *eis
parthenian*, in virginity—just like the ones who were entrusted
with the education of Antony's sister—and formed part of a long-
standing tradition. These women lived as part of their village,
distinguished solely by a stricter religious life, and not in some
special community.

The *Pseudo-Basilian Canons*, which—as their title suggests—
have very little to do with the Cappadocian bishop under whose
name they were transmitted, add further insights.[11] Here, Canon
5 (Riedel, p. 239) mentions a certain degree of censure—punishment would be too strong an expression—as appropriate for a
virgin who breaks her promise: her marriage is shameful. Canon
32 (Riedel, p. 249) deals with another, now well-known, phenomenon: it condemns ascetic men who lived together with celibate
women.

Finally, Canon 36 (Riedel, p. 254) echoes the *Canons of
Hippolytus* by declaring that widows and virgins are under the
same rule (νόμος) and in the same position (τόπος), but not in the
same order (τάγμα): virgins occupy a higher order. They are in
the first *tagma*, while widows are in the second. In contrast to the
widows, virgins are not officially elected and must not be dressed
by their parents 'in the garment of a virgin'. On the contrary,
their decision has to be made of their own accord, after careful
self-examination, and in case of failure the blame will be exclusively theirs.

[10] See Faivre, *Naissance*, 106–9, 131–5, for comparable prescriptions in the
major non-Egyptian canonical collections. The best known of these collections,
mostly compilations drawing from the Roman *Apostolic Tradition*, had a profound influence on the entire Orient, including Egypt.

[11] They represent an originally Greek collection compiled during the 4th and
5th cent., which contains elements from significantly earlier periods. To com-
plicate matters, the sole version now known is in Arabic and underwent further
noticeable changes; here I use the German translation by Riedel, *Die Kirchenrechtsquellen*, 213–83; some Coptic fragments have been published by W. Crum,
The Coptic Version of the Canons of St. Basil (Proceedings of the Society of
Biblical Archaeology 26; London, 1904), 57–62; G. Graf, *Geschichte der christlichen arabischen Literatur*, i (Rome, 1944), 606–7; Wipszycka, *Les Ressources*,
17–18.

Widows and virgins together are 'to be a light for the congregation' through fasting, praying, and continence. Virgins in particular have to be strict with themselves: they must not leave their house during the day, and certainly never by night, should not drink wine, except when ill, and ought to refrain from using too much perfume. Neither widow nor virgin must ever lie or argue. Virgins are not allowed to become servants, since she who serves the Lord cannot serve in the world. Again, most virgins appear to have lived alone, in their own house, their manual labour supplementing their means, which at times were meagre.

The *Pseudo-Athanasian Canons*, compiled between 350 and 450 by an unknown Egyptian author, add some colour to this information.[12] Ten of its 107 canons deal with virgins, and by then their number had increased. In fact, the canons reflect the existence of two distinct groups: virgins who lived within a family and those who formed their own community.

'In every house of Christians it is needful that there be a virgin, for the salvation of this whole house is this one virgin.' At times a mother may vow to 'give her daughter unto the Lord', but in general it was the duty of both parents to educate all their children in 'virginity', whilst paying constant attention to discover 'which among [the] daughters is worthy of holiness'.[13] Thus, here it was the parents who decided their child's fate, and, in contrast to the *Pseudo-Basilian Canons*, a woman's own decision is nowhere mentioned. Parents had to observe a daughter's every movement, her preferences, and her general behaviour. If her eyes

---

[12] Internal dating of individual canons is therefore difficult, and the information offered may reflect late 4th- and early 5th-cent. developments. The question of authorship remains disputed. The Greek original is lost, and only a few Coptic and Sahidic fragments dating from the 6th or 7th cent. as well as a complete Arabic version (*The Canons of Athanasius*, ed. and trans. W. Riedel and W. Crum (Amsterdam, 1973²)), have been handed down, cf. Riedel and Crum's introd. pp. vii–xxv. Riedel proposes a metropolitan or archbishop as actual author and argues for Athanasius as a sponsor if not indeed author; Coquin, *Les Canons*, 328; Graf, *Geschichte*, 605, proposes the first half of the 4th cent. as the most likely date; A. Martin, 'Aux origines de l'Église copte: L'Implantation et le developpement du Christianisme en Égypte (Ier–IVe siècle)', *REA* 83 (1981), 35–56 leaves the authorship undecided; Wipszycka, *Les Ressources*, 14–16. Neither the *Pseudo-Athanasian* nor the *Pseudo-Basilian* collection have found much attention in scholarly works discussing the history of Christian Egypt or that of canonical literature.

[13] cc. 98 and 97 (Riedel and Crum, *The Canons*, 62).

were steadfast, if she was obedient even when faced with drudgery and reprimands, if she chose fasting over eating and drinking, then she was suited for 'the vow' and 'shall be appointed to the habit' or σχῆμα. If a girl thus singled out had not mastered all these demands by the time she reached the age of 30, she had to be given in marriage. Nothing is said concerning the precise manner of the appointment, nor the content of the vow, other than that the virgin remains pure 'unto Christ, her living bridegroom, who dieth not'.

Once appointed to the habit, a virgin led a life quite distinct from that of her family members: she fasted until evening and then had to prepare her own food (did some rely on the help of servants?) consisting of 'cakes of bread and fried cakes and fine flour mixed with fat and honey'. Virgins were not supposed to visit the church alone, but only with their mothers or sisters. On the eve of special holidays virgins had to attend service in a community of virgins or in a *monē*, not in the main church.[14]

If a rich lady did not have a daughter, she should elect a suitable maid as 'virgin'. This maid had then to be treated like a daughter, kept secluded, and placed in charge 'of the ordering (lit. "canons") of the household'. But interesting restrictions applied: 'Rich women shall not keep by them virgin nuns in the part of servants, as (do those) that send them unto the places of gold workers or of dyers, so that their habit, *schēma*, is despised.'[15] Once a virgin, a woman could no longer be treated in any way reminiscent of slavery, regardless of her former status.

As already mentioned, other virgins had left their parental home to live a secluded life in an organization described as a convent of virgins, community of virgins, or even a monastery, under the guidance of a mother.[16] Canon 48 prohibits a priest

---

[14] c. 98 (Riedel and Crum, *The Canons*, 62–4).

[15] cc. 103, 104 (Riedel and Crum, *The Canons*, 66–7). For the role and importance of the purple trade cf. Pliny, *Hist. Nat.* 21. 45–6, also ibid. 9. 124–42. Eus. *HE* 7. 32. 2–3 suggests that already by the 1st cent. AD purple and its manufacturing had become an imperial monopoly, many of those employed being former slaves; M. Reinhold, *History of Purple as a Status Symbol* (Coll. Latomus 116; Brussels, 1970); R. J. Forbes, *Studies in Ancient Technology*, iv (Leiden, 1964²), 99–150 for technical aspects; H.-J. Horn, 'Gold', in *RAC* xi. 895–930; Jones, *The Later Roman Empire*, ii. 836–7, 862–3.

[16] cc. 48, 92, 99; the absence of the original Greek text defies further specification.

from visiting such a community unless he is old, married, or re-nowned for extreme abstinence.[17] To receive additional spiritual advice, the entire community visited the church 'before the reading of the Psalms, and when they come forth they shall walk by twos and their mother before them, and they shall not talk evil talk.' Like their counterparts in households, virgins in convents could not attend church on special holidays, such as those of local martyrs and particularly not at night. Both male and female virgins fasted until sunset, including the Sabbath and Sunday, and wine was only for the sick. Virgins were not to talk to married women and might visit their relatives only in the company of another virgin.[18] All virgins could inherit and bequeath property. In the absence of natural heirs, the property would be distributed among the poor, but even close friends might count as heirs. Convents had an additional source of income: rich women were exhorted to spend entire nights praying in these convents 'because of a day of judgement upon [their] son or husband', and the virgins, too, would pray with them. All expenses were then paid for by the visitors.[19]

Much as in Asia Minor, in Egypt, too, and more precisely in the so-called *koinē*, women were known, at the very latest from the end of the third century onwards, to lead a life dedicated to God. These women held the title of widow or virgin, achieved their status through a vow, and expressed it by wearing a specific habit. To be a virgin did not confer a particular function within the congregation but granted a revered position based on the special nature of a woman's prayers. A virgin's property-rights were in no way altered by her status. *Parthenoi* most commonly lived within their families; of the three canonical collections named above, only the *Pseudo-Athanasian Canons* refer to or-ganized communities.

Canonical collections are by definition the reflection of an ideal, circumscribed by restrictions and exhortations; they are unlikely to reflect what may be called historical reality. However,

[17] Based here on the text of the Coptic fragment, Riedel and Crum, *The Canons*, 121–2; cf. 35–6.

[18] c. 92 (Riedel and Crum, *The Canons*, 61–2); the fact that relatives can be visited, with permission from the mother, contradicts the strict seclusion recommended in cc. 99 and 101.

[19] cc. 99, 102 (Riedel and Crum, *The Canons*, 64, 66).

despite their prescriptive nature, the three collections discussed seem to have responded to some, at times contradictory, developments. In the following pages the bare bones will be filled with more life in an attempt to reconstruct some of the processes that may have led to those developments.

THE PAPYRI

In Egypt fourth century canonical and literary sources find a unique complement in the papyri. In particular when compared to the canons, papyri are a genre of sources virtually on the opposite end of the spectrum. Where canons seek to convey a normative concept and are thus deliberate and stylized, the papyri contain largely accidental information, generally as a by-product of other everyday activities. An investigation of this type of source-material (consisting mainly of personal and business letters, tax receipts, and rent contracts) for traces of 'virgins' reveals indeed few, but invaluable insights.[20]

The left margin and the opening line of papyrus *PSI* vi. 698 are severely damaged, making a precise dating difficult: it could have been written on 24 January 391 or 392, 'during the year of the consulship of Fl. Tatianus and Symmachus' or in the subsequent year. The document comes from Oxyrhynchus and deals with a

[20] A careful survey of all 3rd- and 4th-cent. papyri identified as Christian results in a small yet by no means insignificant dossier of papyrological evidence, in which documents relating in some fashion to ascetic women form only one-sixth of the papyri relating to asceticism. E. G. Turner (*Greek Papyri: An Introduction* (London, 1980²)), has a list of abbreviations of the major collections used below. The principal collections of Christian letters are by G. Ghedini, *Lettere cristiane dai papiri greci del III e IV secolo* (Milan, 1923); M. Naldini, *Il cristianesimo in Egitto* (Florence, 1968) (reviewed by E. Wipszycka, 'Remarques sur les lettres privées chrétiennes des IIᵉ–IVᵉ siècles (à propos d'un livre de M. Naldini)', *Journal of Juristic Papyrology* 18 (1974), 203–21); and by G. Tibiletti, *Le lettere private nei papiri greci del III e IV secolo d. C. Tra paganesimo e cristianesimo* (Vita e Pensiero 15; Milan, 1979), which has been used in the following for dating. J. Van Haelst ('Les Sources papyrologiques concernant l'Église en Égypte à l'époque de Constantin', in *Proceedings of the 12th International Congress of Papyrology, 13–17 August 1969* (American Studies in Papyrology 7; Ann Arbor, 1970), 497–503), mentions 66 documents.

fairly rare legal procedure, the division of an inheritance.[21] Lines
6–7 describe the lion's share of the inheritance, a plot of land, by
denoting its boundaries with neighbouring plots: '. . . in the south
[the plot] is limited by the public lane, in the east by [the pro-
perty] of *Ανν . . . μοναχή*, and in the west by the inheritance of
Aprion.' Who was Ann . . . *monache*? According to the editors,
'Annitos' is the genitive of a female name otherwise unknown,
and *μοναχός*, originally the top-copy of a document or a piece of
clothing, means 'single' or 'alone'.[22]

Eight or nine years later, in June or July 400, another document was written, also in Oxyrhynchus: *P. Oxy.* xliv. 3202.[23] This
document contains a lease following the conventions common to
this kind of transaction. An *exēdra*, or 'one ground-floor room,
namely a hall, together with the one cellar in the basement, with
all appurtenances' is leased to 'Aurelius Jose, son of Judas, Jew'
from the first of the month Mesore, by 'Aurelia Theodora and
Aurelia Tauris, daughters of Silvanus . . . *μοναχαῖς ἀποτακτικαῖς*'
Two sisters owning a fairly large house in the Cavalry Camp
quarter were letting part of the building to a man clearly identified
as adhering to a religion other than their own.

P. Lips. 43 was probably written before 371 in the town of
Hermopolis. The document again deals with the division of an
inheritance but is of a slightly different nature. The heirs of
Bessarion accuse a certain Thaesis, herself also an heir, of having
illegally appropriated Christian books from the inheritance before
its official division. The case is to be tried in the court of the
'catholic church' (*κ(αθ)ολικῆς ἐκκλησίας*) by bishop Plusianos in
the presence of magistrates acting as witnesses.[24] The defendant,
who ultimately inherits the larger portion of the inheritance, is

---

[21] Cf. *P. Oxy.* iii. 503; *P. Ryl.* ii. 156; *BGU* i. 194; *P. Tebt.* 382; Johnson and
West, *Byzantine Egypt*, 39–66, esp. 64; R. Taubenschlag, *The Law of Greco-
Roman Egypt in the Light of the Papyri, 332 BC–640 AD* (New York, 1944–8;
repr. Warsaw 1955), 317.

[22] *PSI* vi. 698 with n. 7 ad loc.; LSJ s.v. *μοναχός*.

[23] Re-edited in G. H. Horsley (ed.), *New Documents Illustrating Early
Christianity* (Macquarie University, 1981), 126–30 no. 82.

[24] It is unlikely that this Plusianos is identical with the bishop from Lycopolis
known in the context of Athanasius' dealings with Meletians; W. Ensslin,
'Plusianos', in *RE* xxi. 1, 616; R. A. Riall, 'Athanasius Bishop of Alexandria: The
Politics of Spirituality', Diss. (Cincinnati, 1987), 41–3, nn. 60, 62.

mentioned without patronymic, legal adviser, or relatives; she is called Thaesis *aeiparthenos* (Θαῆσιος ἀειπαρθ(ένο)υ).

In 371 two citizens of Panopolis confirmed that they had obtained a receipt for clothes that their father procured for the army as part of his taxes (*P. Lips.* 60).[25] These two citizens were Αὐρήλιο[ς . . . ἀδελφὴ Διδύμη ἀειπάρθενος (Didyme *aeiparthenos*). *P. Mich. inv.* 431 is a fourth-century letter transmitting greetings to Νόναν μετὰ τῆς ἀειπαρθένου θυγατρός (Nona with her *aeiparthenos* daughter).[26]

P. Laur. ii. 42 is another letter from the region of Oxyrhynchus, written at the end of the fourth century.[27] On the verso someone expresses his concern at the behaviour of a sailor, a drunkard; and on the recto the writer criticizes actions towards a certain 'Aetheas, who is a Christian, and because of that, although she is a laywoman, she never mingles in the affairs of the world'. To summarize briefly: thus far three women called *monache* have been mentioned; two are sisters, also characterized as *apotaktikai*; three women are described as *aeiparthenoi*; and one woman is a Christian and a laywoman but behaves uncharacteristically.

In the early part of the fourth century a certain 'Didyme and the sisters' wrote to a 'Kyria and her *adelphē* Atienatia' and to a 'kyria and *adelphē* Sophias'.[28] Both letters, *P. Oxy.* xiv. 1774 and

[25] Apparently a frequent practice to compensate for shortages in the government-owned *fabricae*, or *gynaecia*, Jones, *The Later Roman Empire*, 837; cf. also Girardet, *Kaisergericht und Bischofsgericht* 57; Riall, 'Athanasius of Alexandria', 46.

[26] Edited by H. C. Youtie, 'Short Texts on Papyri', *ZPE* 37 (1980), 211–19, here 216–17.

[27] Re-edited by Tibiletti, *Lettere private*, 196 f., no. 34, and Horsley, *New Documents* (1982), 172–4, no. 102; Tibiletti proposes to read line 2 as χρηστιανὴ οὖσα; Horsley translates: '. . . to do such a thing to Atheas, since you are a Christian, because she also is a laywoman . . .' While grammatically feasible this solution is less probable since *a*) it supposes a different relation and meaning of two consecutive forms of οὖσα, whereby both the addressee and Atheas have to be women quarrelling with each other; *b*) if it was a parenthesis, χρηστιανὴ οὖσα would have to appear earlier, after ποιῆση(ς) for instance; cf. S. Kapsomenakis, *Voruntersuchungen zu einer Grammatik der Papyri der nachchristlichen Zeit* (Munich, 1938); M. Mondini, 'Lettere femminili nei papiri greco-egizi', *Studi della Scuola Papirologica* 2 (1917), 29–50.

[28] Re-edited by Naldini, *Il cristianesimo*, 173–80, nos. 36, 37; and by A. Emmet, 'A Female Monastic Community in Egypt?' in A. Moffat (ed.), *Maistor: Classical, Byzantine and Renaissance Studies for Robert Browning* (Byzantina Australiensia 5; Canberra, 1984), 77–83; text on pp. 79 f.

SB iii. 9746, deal with business matters conducted by Didyme on behalf of the sisters. The recipients are likewise sisters who live with other sisters, though brothers are mentioned as well. Both letters end with greetings in the Lord.

P. Iand. 100 dates from the second half of the fourth century. A certain Bessemios had business dealings with the Fathers Doilos and Valerios and greets a number of brothers, amongst them 'Aron and Maria and Tamunis together with all the brothers of the monastery'.[29] In *P. Lond.* vi. 1926 a lady named Valeria wrote to a well-known ascetic who lived in the Heracleopolite *circa* 340.[30] Valeria suffered from a respiratory disease and trusts that the revered Apa Paphnutius, being an ascetic and very devout, will be able to help her. At the same time she asks him to greet her daughters, Bassiane and Theoklia. Finally, a third century papyros, *SB* viii. 9882, transmits the greetings of 'Amma Thaubarin and Appa Dios and the brothers . . .'

The first three women mentioned are called *monachē* and *monachē apotaktikē*. *Monachos* in a metaphorical sense appears for the first time in literature around 330, in Eusebius' *Commentarium in Psalmos*, where he defines *monachoi* as those who advance Christianity by being in the forefront of the battle.[31] *P. Co.*vii.171, a petition dating from 7 June 324, refers to an 'Isidor monachos' and thus antedates Eusebius' usage. *Monachos*, with its connotations of 'alone, single' and even 'single-minded', was indeed an apt description of a social phenomenon by then well established and ubiquitously recognized, that of a male ascetic. However, the term *monachos* remains rare in

---

[29] ἀσπάζομαι Ἄ(ρων) καὶ Μαριὰμ καὶ Ταμοῦνι καὶ τοὺς ἀδελφοὺς πά(ντα)ς τοὺς ἐν τῷ μοναστηρίῳ; re-edited by Naldini, *Il cristianesimo*, 339, no. 87; Van Haelst ('Les Sources papyrologiques', 498 f.) dates it to the early 4th cent.

[30] H. J. Bell, *Jews and Christians in Egypt: The Jewish Troubles in Alexandria and the Athanasian Controversy* (London, 1924; repr. New Haven, 1972), 108–10; re-edited by Tibiletti, *Lettere private*, 185 f. with n. 28; date: Bell, op. cit. 101 f.; E. A. Judge, 'The Earliest Use of Monachos for "monk" (P. Coll. Youtie 77) and the Origins of Monasticism', *JAC* 20 (1977), 72–89, here 83.

[31] Eus. *Comm. in Ps.* 67. 7 (PG 23. 689 B); for the date cf. J. Moreau, 'Eusebius von Cäsarea', in *RAC* vi. 1064; A. Adam, 'Grundbegriffe des Mönchtums in sprachlicher Sicht', *ZKG* 65 (1953), 209–39; Judge, 'The Earliest Use', 74 f., 86; F. E. Morrad, 'Monachos, moine: Histoire du terme grec jusqu'au 4ᵉ siècle', *Freiburger Zeitschrift für Philosophie und Theologie* 20 (1973), 332–411, esp. 336–40.

papyri. The only other occurrence is in a damaged address in *P. Lond.* vi. 1925.[32] It is thus all the more significant that three women with this title appear in papyri, 'Ann ... *monachē*' and the two sisters, and most significant of all 'Ann ... *monachē*' is the earliest occurrence.[33] None of the *monachē* seems to have had close relatives; all of them lived in a village and owned property.

'Ἀποτάσσειν, originally 'to detach' (for instance, soldiers), gained a new significance in the wake of Luke 14: 33: 'whoever of you does not renounce all that he has cannot be my disciple.'[34] *Apotaktikos* soon became a title indicating a religious person who no longer owned worldly goods; in fact 'the form *apotaktikos* was an accepted professional identification'.[35] But six of the eight *apotaktikoi* mentioned in papyri—people defined as 'having renounced the world'—are known to have owned property and lived in villages. Now, the same word appears in a slightly differ-

[32] E. A. Judge, 'Fourth-Century Monasticism in the Papyri', in *Proceedings of the 16th International Congress of Papyrology, New York 24–31 July 1980* (American Studies in Papyrology 23; Ann Arbor, 1981), 613–20, esp. 613–15; id. 'The Earliest Use', 72–9.

[33] An unknown taxpayer from Skar in a 4th-cent. tax-list from the Hermopolite in *CPR* v. 26 is the only other example known to me.

[34] LSJ s.vv. ἀποτάσσω and ἀποτακτικός; Lampe s.vv.; A. Emmett, 'Female Ascetics in the Greek Papyri', *JÖB* 32 (1982), 507–13, esp. 510 f.; Horsley, *New Documents*, 128; Judge, 'Fourth-Century Monasticism', 616–20; E. Wipszycka, 'P. Berl. inv. 11860 A–B: Les Terres de la congrégation pachômienne dans une liste de payements pour les *apora*', in J. Bingen, G. Cambier, and G. Nachtergall (eds.), *Le Monde grec: Pensée, littérature, histoire, documents. Hommage à C. Preaux* (Brussels, 1975), 625–36, here 632–4.

[35] Theodore, Pachomius' successor (below, p. 363), addresses the superiors of Pachomian communities as *apotaktikoi* in *Praeceptum* 49 (A. Veilleux and A. de Vogüé (eds.), *Pachomian Koinonia*, ii (Cistercian Studies Series 46; Kalamazoo, 1981), 152); cf. also the *First Greek Life of Pachomius* (= *G*[1]), 24, 39 (*Sancti Pachomii vitae graecae*, ed. F. Halkin (Subsidia Hagiographica 19; Brussels, 1932) 15, 24), *The Bohairic Life of Pachomius* (= *SBo*) 185 (A. Veilleux and A. de Vogüé, (eds.), *Pachomian Koinonia*, i (Cistercian Studies Series 45; Kalamazoo, 1980) 220), and *Pach. catech.* (*Œuvres de S. Pachôme et de ses disciples*, ed. T. Lefort (CSCO 160; Louvain, 1956), 17). An Athanasian letter uses the term in connection with anchorites, A. Van Lantschoot, 'Lettre de s. Athanase au sujet de l'amour', *Le Muséon* 40 (1927), 287; and several papyri employ it; Judge, 'Fourth-Century Monasticism', 613 (quotation, 616); H. Maehler, 'Häuser und ihre Bewohner im Fayum der Kaiserzeit', in G. Grimm, H. Heinen, and E. Winter (eds.), *Das römisch-byzantinische Ägypten: Akten des intern. Symposions, 27–30 Sept. 1978 in Trier* (Aegyptiaca Treverensia 2; Mainz, 1983), 119–37, here 119–32.

ent context in Luke 14: 26: 'If anyone comes to me and does not hate his own father and mother, and wife and children and brothers and sisters, yes, and even his own life, he cannot be my disciple.' In fact, none of the *apotaktikoi* mentioned in papyri had a spouse or close relative, except the two sisters who leased their *exēdra* and one man who adopted his brother's son.[36]

The same is true for the three women called *aeiparthenoi*. Again, they all lived within villages, and neither patronymics nor husbands are mentioned. One of the women lived with her brother, the other with her mother, whether spiritual or otherwise is impossible to say. However, before jumping to conclusions, one has to consider that the term *aeiparthenos* ('forever-virgin') 'could . . . be simply a legal way of indicating that [these] were unmarried women'.[37] In such a case would not *parthenos* be sufficient? If a woman was not married, this status was relatively easy to alter and there is no need to add 'forever'. Moreover, the *aeiparthenos* Thaesis was tried by a bishop in the court of a catholic church for the theft of Christian books.[38] Nonna, the name of the mother of the *thygatēr aeiparthenos*, is predominantly Christian and the ascetic mother–daughter combination one of the most common organizational forms.[39] That both Didyme and her brother had to pay their father's tax does not preclude Didyme's religious involvement.[40] All three women, rather than

[36] *P. Lips.* 28, dating from 381.

[37] Emmett, 'Female ascetics', 507–10; Judge, 'Fourth-Century Monasticism', 616, cautions against over-optimistic ascetic usage.

[38] For *P. Lips.* 43 cf. S. Elm, 'An Alleged Book-theft in Fourth Century Egypt: P. Lips. 43', *SP* 18 (1989), 209–15; in the early 5th cent. *aeiparthenos* becomes the epithet of the Virgin Mary together with *theotokos*; G. Giamberardini, *Il culto mariano in Egitto*, i (Jerusalem, 1975), 122–6.

[39] For Nona or Nonna cf. *P. Mich. inv.* 1373 = *ZPE* 21 (1976), 26–8; SB vi. 9622; J. Barns, 'A Fourth-Century Deacon's Petition from Theadelphia', *SP* 1 (= TU 63; Berlin, 1957), 3–9; F. J. Dölger, 'Nonna: Ein Kapitel über christliche Volksfrömmigkeit des 4. Jh.', *Antike und Christentum* 5 (1936), 44–75; J. M. Hanssens, 'Nonnos, nonna et Nonnus, nonna', *OrChrP* 26 (1960), 29–41; L. C. Youtie ('P. Corn. 29: Nonna's Order', *ZPE* 27 (1977), 138) points to the fact that the name Nona or Nonna never appears before the 4th cent.; for other examples of a mother–daughter relationship cf. Pall. *HL* 31, 60 (Butler, ii. 86, 154); Ps.-*Ath.* c. 97 (Riedel and Crum, 62).

[40] For the taxation cf. e.g. *CTh.* 11. 9. 1, 2 (AD 323), 7. 6. 3 (Mommsen–Meyer, i. 2, 592, 325); *P. Isid.* 54; *P. Oxy.* xii. 1424, 1448; J. Lallemand, *L'Administration civile de l'Égypte de l'avènement de Dioclétien à la création du*

simply being unmarried, must, therefore, have made a definite decision to remain unmarried, and that decision was known to a larger public.

All the women discussed so far led an unconventional life and were easily identifiable—for instance through a distinct way to dress. More importantly, the phenomenon of such women had existed long enough to give rise to specific titles that were unanimously recognized and accepted in legal documents.[41] All the titles presupposed celibacy and one of them indicated withdrawal from the world, but none specifically required renunciation of possessions. Indeed, virtually all the documents deal with property issues.

The only papyrus that alludes to the more scriptural meaning of *apotaktikos* never actually mentions the word. It is the letter referring to some unspecified 'deed' done to 'Atheas, who is a Christian, and because of that, although she is a λαε(ι)κή, she never mingles in the affairs of the world' (*P. Laur.* ii. 42). An intriguing sentence. The epithet χριστιανός, given to the adherents of the religion by hostile outsiders, soon became synonymous with persecution and martyrdom, the *nomen ipsum* being often sufficient for condemnation. Consequently, the term was rarely used by 'Christians' themselves until the late third century, when it was precisely its connection with martyrdom that gave it a new, glorifying significance. During the fourth century the term began to be more widely accepted, especially because it emphasized the close connection between the *christianoi* and Christ.[42] In our context, however, *christianos* had a more specific meaning because of its juxtaposition to the term *laikos*.[43] *Laikos*, which—as

diocèse (*284–382*): *Contribution à l'étude des rapports entre l'Égypte et l'Empire à la fin du IIIe et au IVe siècle* (Académie royale de Belgique. Cl. des lettres, Mémoires 57: 2; Brussels, 1964), 191–3.

[41] *P. Amh.* 142; *SB* iv. 7449; Judge, 'The Earliest Use', 86 n. 39.

[42] H. Karpp, 'Christennamen', in *RAC* ii. 1114–38, here 1131; the only other evidence for *christianos* is *P. Oxy.* xliii. 3149 (5th cent.); E. A. Judge and S. R. Pickering, 'Papyrus Documentation of Church and Community in Egypt to the Mid-Fourth Century', *JAC* 20 (1977), 47–71, esp. 66–69; cf. 67 n. 78 for possible Montanist connections.

[43] Tibiletti (*Lettere private*, 48 f., 197 n. 3) rightly remarks that to refrain from mingling with the deeds of the world '. . . non necessariamente vi si deve vedere un'accezione morale negativa', contrary to the editor of the papyrus, Pintaudi (p. 50 f.), who translates 'non si é mai macchiata delle colpe del mondo'.

we have discussed—by the fourth century generally indicated the congregation as distinct from the clergy, is here set in opposition to something else.[44] Atheas refrained from dealing with the πράγματα τοῦ κόσμου because she was a Christian, and *although* she was a laywoman. In other words, her behaviour appears to have been characteristic of someone who was not simply *laikos*, but of someone who could easily be taken for being superior to a lay-person, if not for a member of the clergy itself. Was Atheas an *apotaktikos* or a *monachē*?[45] Why then was she not described as such? Or was she an intensely religious woman who, because she was married or widowed, failed to fulfil the one vital prerequisite of a *monachē*?[46]

The seven papyri discussed so far corroborate the information gained from the canonical collections. All these sources mention celibate women living within their village community together with mothers, sisters, or brothers, and often owning the property they inhabited.[47] The *Pseudo-Athanasian Canons* also mention communities of women, likewise within villages. It is therefore not inconceivable that traces of similar organizational forms exist in the papyri. The two letters written in the early fourth century by 'Didyme and the sisters' to Atienatia and Sophias could indeed reflect aspects of life within just such a community.

Both letters deal with business transactions. In her letter to

[44] LSJ s.v. λαικός, originally 'common, belonging to the people'; cf. *SB* v. 8008 (216 BC). It is never used as opposed to baptized, the technical term for which is 'catechumenes'. In opposition to clergy it appears as early as Clem. Alex. *Strom.* 3. 12. 90 (GCS 52 (15), 237); Faivre, *Naissance*, 75–96, 223–8; id. *Les Laïcs aux origines*, 167–240; L. de la Potterie, 'L'Origine et le sens primitif du mot laïc', *Nouvelle Revue Théologique* 80 (1958), 840–53; and the discussion above, p. 159; *P. Laur.* ii. 42 is perhaps the earliest usage in papyri.

[45] As discussed above (p. 164), the τάγμα τῶν μοναζόντων did not form part of the clergy; Wipszycka, 'Remarques sur les lettres', 209.

[46] One other factor is interesting: the only other contemporary papyrus using *christianos* in the sense of 'specific' behaviour is Melitian, *P. Lond.* vi. 1919, where a brother is supposed to pray as 'Christian in Christ'; the Melitians will be discussed below, Ch. 11.

[47] Another 3rd/4th-cent. papyrus, *P. Oxy.* xii. 1592, contains the fragment of a letter in which a woman fervently expresses gratitude for a letter received from κ[υρι]ή μου π[άτε]ρ—a letter which might refer to the special relationship between virgins and their priest as is implied by the *Ps.-Ath.* c. 48 (Riedel and Crum, *The Canons*, 35 f.); see also c. 6 (ibid. 13); Naldini, *Il cristianesimo*, 159, no. 31; Wipszycka, 'Remarques sur les lettres', 213.

Sophias, Didyme acknowledges the receipt of travelling provisions from 'brother Piperas', and of seven double containers of wine and a leather bag of unripe grapes she has received on behalf of an absent 'sister'. Other items have not yet arrived, though Didyme *has* received a piece of linen for one Loukilos, and has sent off two sandals paid for out of Loukilos' account, for which she has not yet had a receipt. She is also awaiting a reply regarding an ostrich egg and a small basket in purple wrappings for Pansophios' wife, as well as a head-band and two cakes dispatched for the 'good Biceutia'. She further reports that 'sweetest Didyme's' implements were found in Severos' wool-bag, and as soon as she can find a suitable courier, she will return the grape-bag and other containers. In the other letter, Didyme informs Atienatia that she has credit for 1,300 *denarii*, and invites her to place more orders, if necessary. At the same time, Didyme has received two cakes for Atienatia, and their amount will be deducted from the total.[48]

We could here be faced with a group of natural sisters running a small business, which specialized in the distribution of goods.[49] Most of the people mentioned are women referred to as 'sisters', a fairly common form of address, and there can be little doubt that both author and recipients were Christian.[50] However, several observations speak against a natural family and in favour of a different kind of organization.

Didyme clearly operates on behalf of her sisters, who include a 'Kyria and a *kyria* Valeriana' (or two Valerianae). Lady, or *kyria*, is a much rarer form of address and not likely to describe a natural sister.[51] Associated with Didyme are a Loukilos, a Severos, an Aionios, the 'brother Piperas', and Nautesiphares, both the latter acting as couriers. Sophias' group includes several

---

[48] The meaning is slightly doubtful: αὐτῶν, 'with these, out of these', i.e. these 1,300 *denarii*.

[49] Emmett, 'Female Monastic Community', 79–83; Wipszycka, 'Remarques sur les lettres', 208 f.

[50] L. Dinneen, *Titles of Address in Christian Greek Epistolography to 527 A. D.* (Washington, DC, 1929), 12–17; Tibiletti, *Lettere private*, 93 f., 102; Naldini, *Il cristianesimo*, 15.

[51] Tibiletti, *Lettere private*, 32–4; K. Mentzu-Meimare (῾Η παρουσία τῆς γυναίκας στίς ἡλλενικές ἐπιγραφές ἀπό τόν Δ μεχρί τόν Ι μ.Χ. αἰῶνα (*JÖB* 32: 2; Vienna, 1984), 433–43), mentions only three inscriptions: nos. 144–6, (p. 442), cf. also nos. 31–2 (p. 434); S. Davis (ed.), *Spoglio Lessicale Papirologico* (Milan, 1968), s.v. κυρία.

sisters, another Didyme described as γλυκυτάτη, Italia, Theodora, the καλή Biceutia, and an unidentified lady, who seems to belong to Didyme's group, but is temporarily staying elsewhere, perhaps with Sophias. Sophias' 'circle' further includes a certain φίλτατος Favorinos, Pansophios and his wife, Loukilas, and Philosophios.[52] The letter addressed to the '*kyria* and sister Atienatia' mentions the 'blessed (μακαρεία) sister Asous', her mother, and others.[53]

Didyme received orders for unspecified goods, which she then forwarded, expecting acknowledgements of receipt. She also received advance payments and was able to make disbursements out of other people's accounts, while she kept the books. The goods traded consist mainly of agricultural produce and items for day-to-day use, such as grapes, wine, cakes, a head-band, cloth, and sandals. The most unusual item is the ostrich egg. While a rare delicacy, ostrich eggs were also used in churches as symbols of light.[54] None of the items mentioned, with the possible exception of the wine, would have been unacceptable in ascetic circles; in fact, given the information of the *Pseudo-Athanasian Canons*, the relative frequency of 'cakes' is interesting.[55]

The potentially hierarchical structure implied by the use of *kyria*, epithets such as *makarios*, a prayer, the use of *nomina sacra*, and the close relationship of the sisters have all led to the assumption that Didyme, Sophias, and her sisters formed a monastic group.[56] While caution is advisable, the evidence

---

[52] While often used for children, γλυκυτάτος is by no means restricted to them; Dinneen, *Titles of Address*, 43; D. Koskenniemi, *Studien zur Idee und Phraseologie des griechischen Briefes bis 400 A. D.* (Helsinki, 1956), 103 f.; φίλτατος, Favorinos' epithet, is, according to Tibiletti, *Lettere private*, 43 f., at times used for members of the clergy; Dinneen, op. cit. 17.

[53] Lampe s.v.; Dinneen, *Titles of Address*, 81, 83 f.; Tibiletti, *Lettere private*, 39 f.

[54] Emmett, 'A Female Monastic Community', 83, no. 28, referring to L. Durrell, *Mountolive* (London, 1958), ch. 5: 'the long hanging lamps had ostrich eggs suspended under them'; G. Galavaris, 'Some Aspects of Symbolic Use of Lights in the Eastern Church: Candles, Lamps and Ostrich-eggs', *Byzantine and Modern Greek Studies* 4 (1978), 69–78.

[55] For the cakes and the dress cf. *Ps.-Ath.* c. 98 (Riedel and Crum, 62); c. 92 forbids wine except for the sick (ibid. 59); Pall. *HL* 59 (Butler, ii. 153; Judge, 'The Earliest Use', 86 nn. 39, 40).

[56] The editor, G. Manteuffel ('Epistulae privatae ineditae', *Eos* 30 (1927), 211–14), suggests that both letters are from the same author; P. Barison ('Ricerche sui

favours a community of women and men who are not relatives and are united by other than business interests alone: at the very least by their shared Christianity, but perhaps by ascetic principles as well. In fact, we could here be presented with 'groupes de gens qui s'unissaient et acceptaient une certaine forme d'organisation afin de mener une vie religieuse commune, mais qui ne brisaient pas leurs liens avec le "monde".'[57] For the present this somewhat vague conclusion has to suffice, but the two papyri have presented us with a potential model of ascetic life for women, aspects of which might reappear in literary sources.

Another letter dealing with business matters is that sent by Bessemios to two superiors and the brothers of a community. These matters include the sale of a small number of unspecified goods, several cheeses, and a *kolobion*, or tunic. Here, as in Didyme's letters, the actual volume of business is small, although one or even two monastic communities are involved.[58] After several greetings to brothers mentioned by name, Bessemios continues by greeting 'Aron, Maria and Tamunis, and all other brothers in the monastery'. Maria and Tamunis are female names.[59] Two

monasteri dell'Egitto bizantino ed arabo secondo i documenti dei papiri greci', *Aegyptus* 18 (1938), 138) as well as Ghedini (*Lettere private*, 141) and Naldini (*Il cristianesimo*, 173) consider these to be monastic communities.

[57] *Ps.-Ath.* cc. 103 and 104 (Riedel and Crum, 66 f.) clearly indicate what kinds of business were unsuitable for ascetics, which implies that they were allowed and accustomed to make a living by means of other business transactions; *P. Oxy.* xvi. 1682, 1773; *P. Ryl.* ii. 165; for the notion of business-guilds cf. E. Wipszycka, 'Les Confréries dans la vie religieuse de l'Égypte chrétienne', in *Proceedings of the 12th International Congress of Papyrology* (American Studies in Papyrology 7; Toronto, 1970), 511–25 (quotation, 511), cf. esp. the *philoponoi* 512–20. E. Lüddeckens, 'Gottesdienstliche Gemeinschaften im pharaonischen, hellenistischen und christlichen Ägypten', *Zeitschrift für Religions-und Geistesgeschichte* 20 (1968), 193–211; M. Muszynski, 'Les "associations religieuses" en Égypte d'après les sources hiéroglyphiques, démotiques et grecques', *Orientalia Lovaniensia Periodica* 8 (1977), 146–74.

[58] For the *kolobion-lebiton* cf. Judge, 'Earliest Use', 86 nn. 40–2. The sale of some of these goods proved difficult because only one offer of 4,000 talents had been made, which might appear to be high, but is actually a moderate sum given the inflation rate towards the end of the 4th cent.; R. Bagnall and P. Sijpesteijn, 'Currency in the Fourth Century and the Date of CPR V 26', *ZPE* 24 (1977), 111–24; R. Bagnall, 'P. Oxy XVI 1905, SB V 7756 and Fourth Century Taxation', *ZPE* 37 (1980), 185–95; Bowman, 'Economy of Egypt', 23–40.

[59] D. Foraboschi, *Onomasticon Alterum Papyrologicum*: *Supplemento al Namenbuch di F. Preisigke*, (Milan, 1967–71), s.v. 'Tamunis'; cf. above n. 29.

interpretations are possible: either Aron, Maria, and Tamunis are for some reason included in the greetings to all brothers without actually being a part of the monastery, or the two women are also members of the monastic community.

The notion of male and female ascetics living in close proximity is further emphasised by *P. Lond.* vi. 1926, written by a certain Valeria. As has been mentioned, she asks a famous ascetic for his help in healing her illness and praying for her well-being. She also asks the ascetic to include her daughters—one must presume her natural daughters—in his prayers. This request (line 20) prompted Tibiletti to remark: 'l'integrazione dà adito a perplessità, essendo più verosimile che le figlie siano con la madre.' However, Valeria wrote quite clearly, 'I greet my daughters . . .'— a remark that can only be explained if Valeria's daughters did not live with their mother but with the ascetic Apa Paphnutius.[60] Valeria's daughters were closer to the ascetic than to their mother. Apa Paphnutius was an anchorite who had withdrawn into the desert.[61] Is it possible that women lived in his vicinity?

The etymology of the term ἀμμά or ἀμμάς is another interesting facet of early female asceticism. Originally *amma* meant mother, more specifically 'foster-mother' or 'nurse'. In this sense it appears in a small number of papyri, mainly from the second or third century, usually without proper name or patronymic, and thus perhaps emphasizing the professional nature of the term.[62] Then there is a gap in the papyrological evidence until the fourth century, when one papyrus mentions '*ammas* Eva and Maria'.[63]

[60] Προσαγ[ορε]ύω τὰ[ς θυγατ] έρα[ς] μου, καὶ μνήσθητι αὐτῶν ἐν τῇ ἀγίᾳ σου προσευχῇ, Βασσιανῆς καὶ Θεοκλίας, Tibiletti, *Lettere private*, 186, no. 28, ll. 19–20.

[61] At least two anchorites called Paphnutius are known; the most likely here is the one mentioned in the *Historia Monachorum in Aegypto*, 14 (ed. A. J. Festugière (Subsidia Hagiographica 34; Brussels, 1961), 102, with a translation by id., *Enquête sur les Moines d'Égypte; Les Moines d'Orient*, iv. 1 (Paris, 1964); both text and trans. repr. in Subsidia Hagiographica 53 (Brussels, 1971²); both lived in the Heracleopolite during the early part of the 4th cent., and may be identical with the Melitian *anachoretes* mentioned at Epiph. *Haer.* 68. 5 (3 GCS 37. 145); Bell, *Jews and Christians*, 101 f.; Brown, 'Rise and Function of the Holy Man', 80–101; Judge, 'The Early Use' 83 n. 33.

[62] LSJ s.v. ἀμμά; Lampe s.v.; *SIG* 2868; *SB* v. 8212 (AD 130); *P. Mich.* viii. 488; *P. Mich.* iii. 209; *P. Oslo* iii. 153; *BGU* ii. 449; *P. Tebt.* 23; the exception is *P. Oslo* iii. 153.

[63] *P. Oxy.* iv. 1874; only one of the pre-4th-cent. papyri mentions an *amma* by name.

By this time the term begins to acquire a new technical meaning: 'spiritual mother' or *pneumatika*, eventually 'leader of a community', a shift mirrored in late fourth- and early fifth-century papyri speaking of *'hagia ammas* Christina' or *'hagia* Thekla and *amma* Iouliana'.[64] Thus, *SB* viii. 9882, dating from the third century, could shed some light on a development that is interesting not only from the semantic point of view. It transmits greetings from an 'Ammas Thaubarin and Appas Dios together with the brother . . .' Like *ammas, appas* is rare in papyri before the fourth century, when, parallel to *amma* or *ammas, apa* or *appas* assumes the meaning 'ascetic' or 'clerical personality'.[65] *SB* viii. 9882 could suggest a natural father and mother but addressed in an unusual way; or else it could represent a step in the transition to a more honorific title which precedes the Christian usage of *amma* and *appa* as titles for *pneumatikoi*.

The very fragmentary *P. Strass.* 1900, dating most likely from the second half of the fourth century, is perhaps the most intriguing of all the papyri discussed so far.[66] It involves three men and three women. The men are a certain *kyrios* and brother Ioulianos in Alexandria, *kyrios* Phoibammon, and a *kyrios* Philoxenos, who is a *didaskalos* and also the recipient of the letter. The women, mentioned without patronymic or relatives, are *kyria* Xenike, *kyria* Arsione, and Κυρ] ίαν τὴν διδάσκ [αλον.[67] Phoibam-

---

[64] *SB* v. 8714; *P. Oxy.* xxvi. 2414; *PSI* viii. 953; and many more; *SB* vi. 9158 is perhaps an exception. For literary evidence cf. e.g. Pall. *HL* 34, 59 (Butler, ii. 99, 153).

[65] One 2nd-cent. papyrus has *apa* as a religious title and it appears twice in the sense of 'father', once in an ambiguous context, cf. *P. Mert.* i. 28, and the comment by the editors H. Bell and F. Roberts, 104 (n. to l. 16); *BGU* iii. 714; for ἀπα cf. Lampe s.v., and *P. Lond.* vi. 1913–20; *P. Herm. Rees* 8–10 and 43. According to H. Leclercq ('Ama', in *DACL* i. 1306–23, here) 'apa et ama correspondent aux doublons honorifiques égyptiens . . . ces titres ont été parfois conservés à ceux qui étaient morts.' Here, both Thaubarin, a name rare after the 2nd cent., and Dios are alive.

[66] Re-edited by M. Nagel, 'Lettre chrétienne sur papyrus (provenant de milieux sectaires du IVᵉ siècle?)', *ZPE* 18 (1975), 317–23.

[67] There might have been a fourth woman called Aletheia, ll. 7/8; Nagel (op. cit. n. to l. 7) points out that the name Xenike is not attested elsewhere; he further mentions (n. to l. 5, and 319 n. 2) that Kyria when written out fully indicates the proper name, otherwise it is usually abbreviated; cf. also the Kyria in Didyme's letter, against Emmett, 'A Female Monastic Community', who translates 'lady Valeriana and the other lady Valeriana' (p. 80).

mon is the only man who lives in a household (*oikia*) near the three women.[68]

Διδάσκαλος as a title for men is rare in papyri, and used mostly in the context of contracts regulating apprenticeship.[69] As far as the use of the term in a broader Christian context is concerned, we are confronted with a complex picture. Certainly from the second century onwards Alexandria had its own school or *didaskaleion*. Originally guided by laics, among them Clement and Origen, it was increasingly placed under the direct supervision, if not control, of the bishop, so that by the fourth century lay leaders such as Didymus the Blind were the exception, not the rule.[70] During Origen's time it was, according to Socrates, an old Alexandrian custom for *didaskaloi* to conduct regular prayer sessions, where they taught and interpreted the Scriptures, independent of clerical participation. Other second- and early third-century sources confirm the existence of teachers, both laics and members of the clergy, in charge of instructing catechumens.[71]

However, as early as the middle of the third century, Cyprian mentions *presbyteri doctores*, teachers who were priests, an institution which is perhaps reflected in the *presbyteroi katēchētēs* of the third *Pseudo-Clementine Homily*.[72] Like Cyprian, Basil of

[68] For *oikia* cf. also M. T. Cavassini, 'Lettere cristiane nei papiri greci d'Egitto', *Aegyptus* 34 (1954), 274; B. Grimm, *Untersuchungen zur sozialen Stellung der frühen Christen*, Diss. (Munich, 1975), 198–201; for Phoibammon's epithet καλός cf. Nagel, 'Lettre chrétienne', n. to l. 10; Tibiletti, *Lettere private*, 37; Dinneen, *Titles of Address*, 38, 93 f.

[69] I am aware of 32 occurrences only; Davis, *Spoglio Lessicale*, s.v. διδάσκαλος; Nagel, 'Lettre chrétienne', 321 n. 8.

[70] Soc. *HE* 5. 22 (PG 67. 637); Pall. *HL* 4 (Butler, ii. 19, 187 n. 12); Eus. *HE* 5. 10. 1–4, discussing the διδασκαλεῖον; R. M. Grant, 'Theological Education at Alexandria', in B. A. Pearson and J. E. Goehring (eds.), *The Roots of Egyptian Christianity* (Studies in Antiquity and Christianity; Philadelphia, 1986), 178–89; M. Hornschuh, 'Das Leben des Origines und die Entstehung der alexandrinischen Schule', *ZKG* 71 (1960), 1–25, 193–214, for *didaskaloi*, esp. 200–9; B. Kramer, 'Didymus v. Alexandria', in *TRE* viii. 741–6.

[71] Soc. *HE* 5. 22 (PG 67, 637); R. Gryson, 'L'Autorité des docteurs dans l'Église ancienne et médiévale', *Revue Théologique de Louvain* 13 (1982), 63–73, esp. 65.

[72] Cyprian *Ep.* 29 (ed. Bayard, i. 70 f.): [*doctores audientium*] *lector doctorum audientium*; cf. V. Saxer, *Vie liturgique et quotidienne à Carthage vers le milieu du IIIᵉ siècle* (Rome, 1969), 78. The term used in *Ps.-Clem. Hom.* 3. 71 (*Die Pseudoklementinen*, i, *Homelien*, ed. B. Rehm (GCS 42; Berlin, 1953), 82 f.), written between 325 and 381 in a Syro-Palestinian milieu, is πρεσβυτέρους [,] κατηκητάς; Faivre, *Naissance*, 153–61.

Caesarea also speaks once of 'presbyters and *didaskaloi*', men important enough to be subjected to 'Arian' attacks. Basil himself expressed the wish to be a *didaskalos* for his monks, and he is indeed called a *didaskalos* by his brother.[73] It appears as if, during the third and by the fourth century, the role and function of the *didaskaloi* had become increasingly absorbed and subsumed by members of the clergy, reducing the title itself to a mere honorific without any clerical, that is to say institutional, value.[74]

The situation becomes even more complex with regard to women. At first glance, the Christian position regarding women who act as *didaskaloi* or teachers is without ambiguity: 'I permit no woman to teach or to have authority over men; she is to keep silent' (1 Tim. 2: 11–14). Numerous treatises and canons reiterate this interdiction.[75] However, as our sources from Asia Minor have amply demonstrated, the situation was far from being resolved. Macrina was called a *didaskalos* and *paidagogos*. Theodoret of Cyrrhus mentions two women called *didaskalos*—one the leader of a chorus, the other a deaconess—who lived in Antioch at the time of Julian the Apostate.[76] The *Acts of Thecla* exhort the heroine to 'teach the word' in the world; Tekousa in the *Life of Theodotus* and the virgins in Basil of Ancyra's *De virginitate* all had an educational function, both directly and more indirectly as exemplars.[77]

---

[73] Bas. *Ep*. 248 speaks of πρεσβυτέρων καὶ διδασκάλων; Gain (*L'Église*, 111 n. 207) points to their importance; cf. Bas. *Ep*. 207 c. 2, dating from 375, where Basil wishes to be the monks' διδάσκαλος, a title indeed given to him by Gr. Nyss. in the prologue to his *De hom. opificio* (PG 44. 125).

[74] *Didaskaloi* do not appear in any of the 4th-cent. lists classifying clerical offices; G. Bardy, 'L'Église et l'enseignement', 525–47; Gryson ('L'Autorité des docteurs', 65–8) argues that the minor order of the 'lecturer' may be the stunted remnant of the former *didaskaloi*.

[75] *DA* 3. 5. 3–6 (Funk, 188–90); *CA* 3. 6. 1–2 (SC 329. 132); Epiph. *Haer*. 78; 79 (3 GCS 37. 473, 476); Did. Alex., *Trin*. 3. 41. 3 (PG 39. 988c–989a (the attribution of the *Trin*. to Didymus has become increasingly doubtful, cf. Kramer, 'Didymus', 743)).

[76] Gr. Nyss. *VSM* 12. 13; 19. 7; 26. 9; Gr. Nyss. *Ep*. 19. 4 (*GN* viii.2, 64); Theod. *HE* 3. 14. 1; 19. 4 (GCS 44. 190, 192, 198).

[77] Orig. *Comm. S. Joh*. 32. 12 (GCS 10. 444); *Const. Eccl. Apost*. 24–8 (ed. Schermann, 31–3); *Ac. Paul. et Thecl*. 39–41 (ed. Lipsius and Bonnet 1, 265–7); *Vita Thecl*. (ed. Dagron, 274); Bas. *Ep*. 223; Albrecht, *Das Leben der heiligen Makrina*, 221–33.

Eusebius in his *Life of Constantine* reports that in 324 Licinius

> passed a second law, which enjoined that men should not appear in company with women in the houses of prayer, and forbade women to attend the sacred schools of virtue, or to receive instruction from the bishops, directing the appointment of women to be teachers of their own sex. These regulations being received with general ridicule, he devised other means for effecting the ruin of the Churches.

The edict has not been attested elsewhere.[78] However, Eusebius notwithstanding, Christian women were being instructed by other women and the notion of a woman acting as an instructor was not at all alien. In other words, women were allowed to receive education, mainly through women teachers, and they were praised as educational models but were not allowed to teach. This apparent paradox can be solved when considering the degree of officiality involved.

Women were allowed to teach in private, but not in public, hence not if men were involved.[79] Evidently, the distinction between private and public was marginal and often unclear, as demonstrated by the frequent canonical condemnations. The dividing line became even more attenuated in the context of asceticism, where the distinction between the sexes disappeared. It comes as no surprise that radical ascetic groups like the Montanists or the Messalians knew *gynaiakai didaskaloi*.[80] Furthermore, that pagan women achieved fame as eminent teachers of philosophy, especially in Alexandria, is well known. Thus Hypatia, perhaps the best-known of such philosophers, not least because of her brutal murder in 415, counted Christians among her pupils. *Kyria hē didaskalos* is thus not an anomaly, nor does the papyrus perforce have to belong to a 'heretical' milieu.[81]

---

[78] Eus. *V. Const.* 1. 53. 1 (GCS 7. 32); trans. E. C. Richardson, *The Life of the Blessed Emperor Constantine* (Nicene and Post-Nicene Fathers of the Christian Church, 2nd ser., 1; Grand Rapids, 1961²), 481–559, here 497; though the legislation is not confirmed elsewhere, there is no palaeographical doubt concerning this passage; cf. Orig. *Hom. Is.* 6. 3 (GCS 33. 273). *P. Oxy.* xxxvi. 2785 (Tibiletti, 191, no. 31) is a corroboration: it mentions a 'sister' and several catechumens recommended to 'papas Sotas'.

[79] Gryson, *Le Ministère*, 58, 173–9.

[80] Epiph. *Haer.* 49 (2 GCS 31. 241); Tim. *De rec. haer.* (PG 86. 52 B).

[81] Soc. *HE* 7. 14–15 (PG 67. 768); for Sosipatras cf. *Eunapius: The Lives of the Sophists*, 400–2; Griggs, *Early Egyptian Christianity*, 191; S. Wolf, *Hypatia*,

Although few in number, the papyri mentioning Christian women who led lives that gained them special recognition as *monachē, aeiparthenoi, apotaktikai, Christianē, didaskaloi*, or simply as religious women, confirm the evidence of the canons. At the same time, they raise numerous new questions. None of the women bearing a distinct title is associated with either a patronymic, a male relative, or a *kyrios* (a legal tutor), despite the fact that most documents pertain to legal transactions: divisions of inheritance, rent-contracts, receipts for tax payments. In theory, a woman could not perform these kinds of legal acts without a male representative or *kyrios*.[82] In practice, of course, there were exceptions. It is certainly worth noting that, on our evidence, all these exceptions are women bearing a religious title, and that they are mentioned without a *kyrios* in exactly those cases where as a rule women were required to have one.[83] As already observed in Asia Minor, a comprehensive study of a woman's position in Roman and Byzantine law is lacking, and it is thus impossible to assess the precise significance of this observation.[84] However, as in Asia Minor, the possibility that a reli-

---

die Philosophin von Alexandrien: Ihr Leben, Wirken und Lebensende nach den Quellenschriften dargestellt (Vienna, 1879), for further evidence of female philosophers. Nagel ('Lettre chrétienne', esp. 321 nn. 8, 10, 322 n. 14), reaches a similar conclusion though his argumentation is somewhat biased. He does not mention the 'orthodox' sources and, once in favour of a heretical origin, he discards other evidence as irrelevant; Orig. *Frag. I Cor.* 74, ed. S. Gaselee, *JThS* 10 (1909), 41 f.; G. Ficker, 'Widerlegung eines Montanisten', *ZKG* 26 (1905), 447–63; Labriolle, *La Crise montaniste* 493 f., 554; Gryson, *Le Ministère*, 39 f., 106, 128–35.

[82] The legal position of women in Egypt is determined in general by the relationship between Graeco-Egyptian and Roman law, combined with the effects of Christianity. Accurate statements are therefore difficult to make; *CTh.* 2. 17. 1, 1 (AD 324, Mommsen–Meyer, ii.2, 102); M. Kaser, *Das römische Privatrecht*, ii, *Die nachkonstantinische Entwicklung* (*Handbuch der Altertumswissenschaften* 3, *Rechtsgeschichte des Altertums* 3. 2; Munich, 1975²), 140; B. Kübler, 'Über das "Ius liberorum" der Frau und die Vormundschaft der Mutter', *Zeitschrift der Savigny-Stiftung für Rechtsgeschichte, Röm. Abt.* 30 (1909), 154–83; ibid. 31 (1910), 176–95, esp. 174 f.; E. Seidl, *Rechtsgeschichte Ägyptens als römischer Provinz* (St Augustin, 1973), 140; P. J. Sijpesteijn, 'Die "χωρὶς κυρίου χρηματίζουσα δικαίῳ τέκνων" in den Papyri', *Aegyptus* 45 (1965), 177–89.

[83] Kübler, 'Über das "Ius liberorum"', 174, 180; Seidl, *Rechtsgeschichte Ägyptens*, 140; Sijpesteijn, Die "χωρὶς κυρίου χρηματίζουσα δικαίῳ τέκνων"', 173–7, 188 n. 3; R. Taubenschlag, 'La Compétence du kyrios dans le droit gréco-égyptien', in *Opera Minora*, ii (Warsaw, 1959), 353–77, esp. 353, 369–77.

[84] Taubenschlag, 'La Compétence', 353.

gious title endowed a woman with a different legal status comes to mind and must remain an important concern.

Further, none of the papyri mentions the title used almost exclusively in the literature discussed in Asia Minor: *parthenos*. Instead, we find a great variety of titles in a variety of geographical locations reflecting the great variety of circumstances in which these women lived.[85] Whilst the absence of *parthenos* may be due to the small number of extant papyri, the discrepancy between the consistent use of *parthenos* in the literature and the far greater variety of titles in the papyri could indicate a unifying intent on the part of the authors of the literature, usually bishops.

The Canonical collections on the one hand, and papyri on the other, have given us two almost diametrically opposite pathways into the life of 'virgins of God' in Egypt. Both kinds of sources span several centuries, beginning as early as the third and carrying us well into the fifth. Their information parallels and corroborates much of what we know from Asia Minor: women practised their lives as virgins in a great variety of ways, but primarily as independent individuals within their village—or city—community, in full possession of their property, and with a remarkably wide radius of legal action. However, once again, 'grey areas' have emerged as well: women may have lived with anchorites in the desert, in communities with brothers, with members of the clergy. Moreover, it is clear that a virgin is as often a man as a woman. These aspects will guide our investigation of the Egyptian literary sources, which are not only much better known, but are also more homogeneous, and almost entirely 'orthodox', i.e. of accepted and widely recognized normative value. Thus, if these sources describe aspects of religious practice as marginal or unusual, such judgements and representations carry a different significance from a similar statement made in 'marginal' sources such as the anonymous *Homily on Virginity* or Basil of Ancyra's *De Virginitate*. In the sources dealing with Egypt—often written by outsiders for outsiders—most aspects of ascetic life have a consciously crafted normative value, which has to be seen as 'ortho-

---

[85] The *monachē* are mentioned in papyri from Oxyrhynchus and the Hermopolite; the *apotaktikai* also lived in Oxyrhynchus; and the *aeiparthenoi* in Panopolis, the Hermopolite, and an unknown location.

dox' and therefore generally accepted. What may appear to us as marginal in these sources was the norm for their authors, unless specifically characterized as deviation. This is most clearly evident in a specific Egyptian genre, that of the *Apophthegmata Patrum*.

8

Desert Mothers and Wandering Virgins: The *Apophthegmata Patrum*

Sometime between AD 297 and 300 a young man was forced into marriage by his relatives. Unable to resist their pressures, he nevertheless devised a compromise solution: as soon as the official ceremony was over, he announced to his new wife that he did not intend to consummate the marriage. Instead, he proposed that both retain their virginity. Some time afterwards he decided to take his proposition a step further and departed into the desert. The place he chose as his future residence was a mountain range called Nitria in the desert of Scetis, south of Lake Mareotis. The story of the chaste wedding-night and its consequences is quite possibly a legend; it is not a legend that between 315 (or 325) and 337 the young man, called Amoun, became the founder of a new type of ascetic life specific to the area: the semi-hermitic or semi-anchorite life of the Scetis.[1]

Amoun's model of ascetic life in the desert was based on loosely connected groups, close enough to allow regular contacts

[1] For Amoun cf. Ath. *V. Ant.* 60 (PG 26. 930); Pall. *HL* 8 (Butler, ii. 26); *HM* 22 (Festugière, 128); Soc. *HE* 4. 23. 3–11, (PG 67. 509–12); Soz. *HE* 1. 14. 1–8 (GCS 50. 30); *Apoph.* Amoun 1–3 (Guy (= J.-C. Guy, *Les Apophtegmes des Pères du Désert* (Textes de Spiritualité Orientale 1; Begrolles, 1968)), 59–60); for dates and the locality cf. G. J. Bartelink (ed.), *Palladio: La Storia Lausiaca* (Scritti Greci e Latini, Vite dei Santi 2; Milan, 1974), 320 (n. 1 to c. 8); W. Bousset, *Apophthegmata: Studien zur Geschichte des ältesten Mönchtums* (Tübingen, 1923), 60 f.; Butler, *The Lausiac History of Palladius*, i. 297; D. J. Chitty, *The Desert a City: An Introduction to the Study of Egyptian and Palestinian Monasticism under the Christian Empire* (Oxford, 1966), 11; J.-C. Guy, *Paroles des Anciens: Apophtegmes des Pères du Désert* (Collection des Points, Séries Sagesse 1; Paris, 1976), 6 f.; id. 'Les Apophthegmata Patrum', in *Théologie de la vie monastique* (Théologie 49; Paris, 1964), 73–88, here 74; id. 'Le Centre monastique de Scété dans la littérature du Vᵉ siècle', *OrChrP* 30 (1964), 129–47; and in particular A. Guillaumont, 'Histoire des moines aux Kellia', *Orientalia Lovaniensia Periodica* 8 (1977), 187–203; Heussi, *Ursprung*, 75–8.

between the ascetics but far enough apart to ensure the advantages of solitary meditation. He soon attracted followers, and the movement did not remain confined to the mountains of Nitria. As ascetics moved further into the outer desert, the *panerēmos*, new communities emerged: the Cells or Kellia, Scetis (the present Wadi Natrun, an extensive depression of salty marshlands), and settlements in the mountains of Pherme and Petra.[2]

Before long Amoun and his followers had 'made the desert a city' (ἡ ἔρημος ἐπολίσθη[ν]), populated by 'heroic' Fathers such as Abba Macarius the Egyptian (not to be confused with his equally important namesake Macarius the Alexandrian or the Citizen), Abba Pambo, Bessarion, Esaias, Paesios, Paul the Simple, Pior, Athre, Or, and Sisoes.[3] The generation of pioneers lasted until the end of the fourth century; both Macarii died in their nineties. The suceeding generation, dominated by such figures as bishop Theophilus of Alexandria, Evagrius Ponticus, the presbyter Isidor, and the Roman senator Arsenius, reached well into the fifth century.[4]

[2] The site of Nitria has been identified as modern El-Barnugi; about 15 kilometres south-west of Hermopolis Parva, modern Damanhur; the Kellia were about a day's walk (between 15 and 20 kilometres) further south, and the desert of Scetis is about another 64 kilometres further south of Nitria; the exact location of Pherme, the mountain north of Scetis, remains unknown; Cass. *Coll.* 6. 1. 3 (PL 49. 647); Bousset, *Apophthegmata*, 60 n. 2; id. 'Das Mönchtum der sketischen Wüste', *ZKG* 42 (1923) 1–41; Chitty, *The Desert*, 11, 29; H. G. Evelyn-White, *The Monasteries of the Wadi n' Natrun*, ii, *The History of Nitria and Scetis* (New York, 1932–7); A. Guillaumont, 'Les Fouilles françaises des Kellia, 1964–69', in R. Wilson (ed.), *The Future of Coptic Studies* (Louvain, 1978), 203–8; Guy, 'Le Centre monastique de Scété', *passim*; Heussi, *Ursprung*, 157 n. 1; R. Kasser, *Kellia 1965: Topographie génerale, mensurations et fouilles aux Qouçour' Isa et aux Qouçour el-'Abid, mensurations aux Qouçour el-'Izeila*, (Recherches suisses d'archéologie copte 1; Geneva, 1967), esp. 7–11; C. Lialine, 'Erémitisme en Orient', in *DSp* iv. 936–53.
[3] Well-known quote from Ath. *V. Ant.* 14 (PG 26. 865); Zachar. 1, Poemen 61, Poemen 174 (Guy, 98, 229, 250); Cass. *Coll.* 2. 13 (PL 49. 543 A); for the use of 'abba' or 'abbas', cf. J. Dupont, 'Le Nom d'abbé chez les solitaires d'Égypte', *Vie Spirituelle* 77 (1974), 216–30; H. Emonds, 'Abt', in *RAC* i. 45–55; J. Gribomont, 'Abbas', in *DIP* i. 23–6; Heussi, *Ursprung*, 166 n. 1; J. de Punet, 'Abbé', in *DSp* i. 49–57; B. Steidle, 'Abba-Vater', *Benediktinische Monatsschrift* 16 (1934), 89–94.
[4] Fathers such as Theodore of Pherme and Cronios belong to an 'interim' period; Pambo 11 in Berlin MS cod. p. 72 d; Soc. *HE* 4. 23 (PG 67. 513); Ruf. *HE* 2. 4. 8 (PL 21. 511 f.); Bousset, *Apophthegmata*, 61–6; Guillaumont, 'Histoire

The men who dwelt in the desert lived extraordinary lives shaped by their extraordinary surroundings. It is therefore not surprising that they found new modes of expression that resulted in the literary genre of the so-called *Apophthegmata Patrum*.[5] As indicated by their name, these *Sayings or Apophthegmata* originated as an oral tradition. Experienced Fathers acting as spiritual guides gave practical instructions and words of charismatic wisdom for the benefit of younger ones. Often introduced by the plea, 'Father, give me a word', most *Sayings* are rather laconic, especially the earlier ones, since silence was one of the strictest rules of the desert, and loquacity therefore shunned.[6] These charismatic *Sayings* were of fundamental importance and are the expression of one of the most vital aspects of desert

des moines', 187–91; Heussi, *Ursprung*, 135–43. Subsequent periods of Scetis' history go beyond the scope of this discussion.

[5] From the very beginning compilers, especially Pelagius, created three (at times overlapping) collections of *Sayings*, the so-called 'alphabetic', 'systematic', and 'anonymous' *Sayings*. The Greek original of the 'alphabetic' collection is published in PG 65, 71–440; but because of the defects of the PG edition, the following is based on its French trans. by J.-C. Guy, *Les Apophtegmes des Pères du Désert* (see n. 1 above). The English quotations follow the translation by B. Ward, *The Sayings of the Desert Fathers* (Oxford, 1975), except where I thought changes to be necessary. An 'anonymous' collection (the first 400 *Sayings* only) was edited by F. Nau in vol. 12–14 and 17–18 of the *Revue de l'Orient chrétien* (1907–13) (= N); and a 'systematic' collection in Latin by H. Rosweyde, *Vitae Patrum*, v–vi (Antwerp, 1615), re-edited in PL 73, 851–1022. The latter was translated by L. Regnault, *Les Sentences des Pères du Désert: Les Apophtegmes des Pères* (Solesmes, 1966), cf. also intr. 1–21; for the highly complex manuscript traditions cf. J.-C. Guy, *Recherches sur la tradition grecque des Apophthegmata Patrum* (Subsidia Hagiographica 36; Brussels 1962), esp. 1–11; additions of lesser-known *Apophthegmata* are in L. Regnault, *Les Sentences des Pères du Désert: Nouveau Recueil* (Solesmes, 1977), and id. *Les Sentences des Pères du Désert: Troisième recueil et tables* (Solesmes, 1976); Bousset, *Apophthegmata*, 1–60, 76–93; Guy, 'Apophthegmata', 73 f.; Heussi, *Ursprung*, 133–5, 141.

[6] εἰπέ μοι ῥῆμα; εἰπέ μοι λόγον; for instructions cf. e.g. Ant. 26, 27, 38, Ammoun 2, Zachar. 3, Poemen 174, Felix 1 (Guy, 26, 27, 29, 58, 99, 250, 312); commandments to preserve silence are truly ubiquitous, cf. for example Andreas 1 (Guy, 65), Theophil. 2 (Guy, 114), and the index to Regnault, *Les Sentences* (1976), s.v. 'silence'; Bousset, *Apophthegmata*, 77–9; Guy, 'Apophthegmata', 75–7; id. *Paroles des Anciens*, 13; I. Hausherr, *Direction spirituelle en Orient autrefois* (OrChrA 144; Rome, 1955), 56–105; Heussi, *Ursprung*, 146–53, 164–86; P. Rousseau, *Ascetics, Authority, and the Church in the Age of Jerome and Cassian* (Oxford, 1978), 9–32, for a summary of Heussi's and Bousset's points; Ward, *The Sayings*, 19–21.

asceticism. In the words of Abba Moses: 'The monk who is under the guidance of a spiritual Father and who does not practise obedience and humility, even if, on his own, he fasts or does everything else he considers good, will not attain a single virtue and will not understand what it means to be a monk.'[7] Considering the impact of the elders' *Sayings*—many travelled great distances to hear a 'word'—it is not surprising that written versions were soon in circulation.[8] Exactly when the written tradition began is not certain, but a rudimentary corpus existed before 399.[9] Naturally, this corpus became enlarged and altered in the process of accumulation, presenting the scholar with 'le problème philologique . . . des plus complexes que pose l'édition des textes patristiques.'[10]

The world inhabited by the Desert Fathers is unique in its starkness. It was a world of constant, relentless battle, of ceaseless resistance against the sheer overwhelming force of the environment, as well as the equally ceaseless resistance against the demons that assailed the 'inner man'. The desert was the ultimate arena, where the true athletes fought to achieve the 'imitatio Christi'. It was a world characterized by constant attempts to control the stirrings of mind and body, thus granting a constant state of readiness, free from all ties which hold the ascetic attached to this world, the *kosmos*. In Theodore of Pherme's words, for the Desert Father 'three things [are] fundamental . . . poverty,

[7] PE I 20, 9 (Regnault (1977), 163) (PE = Paulos Euergetinos, Συναγωγὴ τῶν θεοφθόγγων ῥημάτων καὶ διδασκαλίων τῶν θεοσόφων καὶ ἁγίων πατέρων (Venice, 1783), repr. as *Receuil des paroles et d'enseignements des Pères* (Athens, 1957–66)).

[8] Despite a general aversion to the intellectualism represented by written traditions (Arsenius 5, 6, Evagrius 7 (Guy, 31, 94)), Greek-speaking, i.e. perhaps more educated, monks received special mention, Cass. *Coll.* 16. 1 (PL 49. 1011); Heussi, *Ursprung*, 152, 158 f.

[9] Evagrius Ponticus uses a small collection of *Sayings* in his *Praktikos* 91–100 (*Évagre le Pontique: Traité Pratique ou Le Moine*, ii, ed. A. and C. Guillaumont (SC 171; Paris, 1971), 692–710), that is before 399; they appear also in Cass. *De Coen. Inst.* (*Jean Cassien: Institutions Cénobitiques*, ed. J.-C. Guy (SC 109; Paris, 1965), *passim*); Bousset, *Apophthegmata*, 66–8; Guy, *Paroles des Anciens*, 11–13; id. 'Apophthegmata', 77; id. 'Note sur l'évolution du genre apophtegmatique', *RAM* 32 (1956), 63–8; Heussi, *Ursprung*, 135–44.

[10] Guy, *Recherches*, 1; id. 'Note sur l'évolution' (see n. 9 above), 68; id. 'Remarques sur le texte des Apophthegmata Patrum', *RSR* 43 (1955), 252–8.

asceticism, flight from men.'[11] The only attachment a Desert Father was not only permitted but exhorted to cherish was that to his fellow athlete: 'The old men say: "Everyone must take upon himself all that afflicts his neighbour, suffer with him in all circumstances and cry with him . . ."'[12]

It was a world of men. Women had no place in such an environment. Not only that: the desert world, in its complete isolation, had been created in part for the exact purpose of escaping from women and all they represented.[13]

At Scetis lived a brother who was an experienced fighter. The enemy evoked in him the memory of a beautiful woman and tormented him severely. One day, through Providence, another brother came down from Egypt to Scetis, and, in the course of the conversation, told him that the wife of so-and-so had died. This was precisely the woman who so troubled him. At this news, he took his coat and departed by night to the place where she had been buried. He opened the tomb, gathered the liquid flowing from the cadaver with his coat, and brought it back into his cell. The stench was intolerable, but he stared at this infection in front of his eyes, fighting his thoughts by saying: 'See here what you desired; well, now you have it, sit down again.' And he subjected himself to this stench until the battle in him had ceased.

One needs hardly to be more explicit.[14] Many other *Sayings* emphasize similar sentiments, such as Abba Theodore of Pherme's warning, 'do not sleep in a place where there is a woman', or Daniel's *Saying*: 'never put your hand in the dish with a woman, and never eat with her; thus you will escape a little the demon of fornication.'[15] It was fear of the 'demon of fornication' and the almost inescapable power of his temptation that led many into the desert, away from all women, who were nothing but

[11] To give but a few examples: Ant. 33, Theod. Pherme 5, Zachar. 1, 3 (Guy, 28, 106, 98 f.); Guy, 'Apophthegmata', 76–83; Heussi, *Ursprung*, 160–4, 186–205, 213–29, 244–9; Regnault, *Les Sentences* (1966), intr. 1–21; Ward, *The Sayings*, 19–25.

[12] Quotation, N 389 (Regnault (1977), 48); there are numerous *Sayings* exhorting hospitality, e.g. Cass. 1, Macar. Aeg. 4, Matoes 6, Sisoes 28 (Guy, 154, 169, 190, 283); systematic collection under 'hospitality' (Regnault (1966), 189–95).

[13] Other *Sayings* rebuking women include Abraham 1, Theodore 4, 5, Cyros 1, Lot 2, Olympios 1, Poemen 11, 13, 14, 59, 115, 154, Paphnut. 5 (Guy, 61, 106, 161, 163, 210, 219, 228, 240, 247, 265).

[14] Anonymous N 172 (Regnault (1966), 73).

[15] Theod. Pherme 17, Daniel 2 (Guy, 108, 79); N 593 (Regnault (1977), 130).

temptation personified, for 'it is through women that the enemy wars against saints'. However, even the desert was not safe. Despite all efforts, as reflected in Arsenius' reply to a woman who came to see him, 'how dare you make such a journey? Do you not realize you are a woman and cannot go just anywhere?', women did just that.[16] They went everywhere, even into the desert.

The *Apophthegmata* in fact contain numerous *Sayings* typifying different categories of women, which are employed to serve various purposes in the process of edification.[17] Very often, undoubtedly as a result of their real presence in the desert, the women mentioned in the *Apophthegmata* are demons incarnate, sent by Satan himself. Thus, the *Sayings* illustrate heroic struggles as well as shameful falls, and at the same time emphasize the power of divine redemption. An anonymous *Saying* provides a succinct example: 'A brother was tempted violently by the demons: they changed themselves into beautiful women and tempted him for forty days without interruption, to make him yield to sin. But, seeing that he resisted with manly courage and could not be overcome, God, who saw his beautiful combat, granted him never to be tempted again.'[18]

Other women, more specifically former courtesans and prostitutes, exemplified the reforming powers of the Desert Fathers. Typically, these fallen women were either moved to repentance, or rose to saintliness: the newly converted joined a 'monastery of virgins'—a *topos* corresponding to the salvation of former robbers.[19] One *Saying* belonging to this category of the reformed

---

[16] Arsenius 28 (Guy, 36).

[17] Regnault, *Les Sentences* (1976), index s.v. 'femme'.

[18] Ant. 29, Anonymous 57 (Guy, 27, 342); Anonymous N 188 (Regnault (1966), 80).

[19] The example of Pelagia is just one illustration of the enormous popularity enjoyed by the theme of 'saved prostitute'; H. Delehaye, *Les Légendes hagiographiques* (Subsidia Hagiographica 18; Brussels, 1927³), 186–8; P. Petitmengin, *Pélagie la Pénitente: Métamorphoses d'une légende*, 2 vols. (Études Augustiniennes; Paris, 1981), esp. i. 13–37; the Egyptian counterpart is the *Vita Mariae Aegypticae* (PG 87: 3. 3697–726); for other examples in the *Apoph.* cf. Ephrem 3, John Colobos 16 (Guy, 89, 124); John of the Cells 1 (Mark 2: 15; Matt. 21: 31; Guy, 145); Serapion 1, Timotheus 1 (Guy, 294, 308); Heussi, *Ursprung*, 159 n. 2; for further examples of courtesans cf. Regnault, *Les Sentences* (1976), index s.v. 'prostitute'; Ward, *The Sayings*, 23 f.

prostitute differs from the usual accounts. It is the story of Paesia, related in *Saying* 47 by John the Dwarf or John Colobos, a Father of the second generation.[20]

As a young girl, Paesia was left an orphan. Prompted by the Fathers in Scetis, she decided to turn her father's house into a hospice (ξενοδοχεῖον) for the Fathers, and served them with great hospitality for many years.[21] At a certain point, however, her resources were exhausted and she was left destitute. Her only choice was to become a prostitute. Learning of this tragic fate, the Fathers in their chagrin appealed to John, saying: 'we have learnt that this sister is living an evil life. While she could, she gave us charity, so now it is our turn . . . to go to her assistance. . . .' John went to see her, only to be rebuffed by the concierge, who accused the Fathers of having eaten all her mistress's bread already and mocked his insistence that he had something very useful to offer her. Finally, he was admitted. Looking at Paesia, John was moved to tears, since he saw 'Satan playing in [her] face'. Upon this, Paesia asked him whether it was possible to repent, and he assured her that it was.

She said, 'Take me wherever you wish.' 'Let us go,' he said, and she got up [from the bed] to go with him. . . . When they reached the desert, the evening drew on. He, making a little pillow with the sand, and marking it with the sign of the cross, said to her: 'Sleep here.' Then, a little further on, he did the same for himself. . . .

During the night the Father awoke to see a shining path leading a woman to heaven. Paesia had died.

Two aspects distinguish Paesia's story from other accounts of converted courtesans. Already as a young girl, she had enjoyed close contact with the Desert Fathers, and under their influence she turned her father's house into an unique institution: a hospice for the desert monks, owned and supervised by a woman.[22] The character of Paesia's salvation is equally unique. Irrespective of

---

[20] *Saying* 40 at PG 65, 218, and Ward's translation; Guy, 132.

[21] εἰς λόγον τῶν πατέρων; Migne translates 'ad usum', followed by Ward; Guy has 'à l'intention'.

[22] The hospice would have been in or near Terenuthis or perhaps in the village of Nitria (el Barnugi); N. Russel, notes to *HM* 22 (*The Lives*, 137 n. 3); Jos. Panepho 1 (Guy, 140) mentions lodgings for visiting brothers; N 153 (Guy, 375) involves a *hospitalier* in Syria; Heussi, *Ursprung*, 163, 254–6; Ward, *The Sayings*, 22 f.

all hostility towards women and all fears regarding their presence in the desert, the desert was precisely where John took Paesia to save her. Paesia's exodus was sudden, unprepared, and based on her own very explicit decision.[23] Her separation from this world, in which she had fallen, was the beginning of Paesia's redemption; it was completed in the 'other' world, the desert.

Indeed, on an abstract level, Paesia's story comprises all the important features associated with the desert. The conception of the desert, as reflected in the *Apophthegmata*, is primarily that of a place of sterility and death, the dwelling-place of savage animals and equally savage demons.[24] It is, however, also a place of supreme purity, where 'the air is more pure, the sky more open, and God more familiar'.[25] It is the place where Jesus fought temptations, and where his follower, the ascetic, battles against his internal demons, his temptations, and afflictions. If successful, it is here that he might also find God, that is to say redemption, through *hēsychia*, tranquillity, and solitude.[26] In the desert both the battle and the subsequent state of purity and redemption reach their highest intensity. John is thus justified in saying: 'One single hour of repentance has brought [Paesia] more than the penitence of many who persevere without showing such fervour in repentance.'

Leaving her village so abruptly, Paesia left behind her entire past to enter a realm where she could overcome her sins in a concentrated struggle. This intense act of purification meant, in her case, the end of her life on earth as well. Beyond doubt,

---

[23] 'Abba John noticed that she did not make any arrangements with regard to her house; he said nothing, but he was surprised' (Ward, *The Sayings*, 94).

[24] I. Keimer, 'L'Horreur des Égyptiens pour les démons du désert', *Bullet. de l'Institut d'Égypte* 26 (1944), 135–47; *Philo: De vita contemplativa*, ed. F. Daumas and P. Miquel (= vol. xxix of *Les Œuvres de Philon d'Alexandrie*, ed. R. Arnaldez (Paris, 1963)), introd., esp. 60–6.

[25] 'Ubi purior aer est et caelum apertius et familior Deus', Orig. *Hom. in Luc.* 11 (*Homélies sur S. Luc*, ed. H. Crouzel *et al.* (SC 87; Paris, 1962), 192 f).

[26] Matt. 4: 1; cf. in particular the excellent article by A. Guillaumont, 'La Conception du désert chez les moines d'Égypte', *RHR* 188 (1975), 3–21, esp. 3–16. Hos. 2: 16; Jer. 2: 2–3; Isa. 40: 3; 2 Macc. 5: 27; Philo, *De vita contemplativa*, 22–3 (Daumas and Miquel, 92 f.); Ath. *V. Ant.* 9–13, 50–2 (PG 26. 856–64 B, 916–20 A); Cass. *Coll.* 24. 2–3 (PL 49. 1286–8); Arsenius 13, Ant. 11 (Guy, 32, 22); J. Gribomont, 'Eremo', in *DIP* iii. 1260–4; Heussi, *Ursprung*, 108–15, 193; U. W. Mauser, *Christ in the Wilderness: The Wilderness Theme in the Second Gospel and its Basis in the Biblical Tradition* (London, 1963), *passim*.

however, John the Dwarf affirms that the desert as the place of intensified religious struggle and experience is meant for women as well as for men—in clear contradiction of Paphnutius' saying: 'I do not allow the face of a woman to dwell in the desert, because of the battle with the enemy.'[27]

Paesia was not alone. Many other women came to the desert, driven by religious reasons. *Parthenoi* came to seek spiritual advice from the famous Fathers, some of them from remote places, attracted like their male counterparts by the hope of 'receiving a word'. In a number of cases these visits occurred on a regular basis: after all, the 'desert' Fathers, so remote in theory, were in practice often only a few miles distant from the villages of the Nile valley.[28] In other cases matters did not rest at occasional visits.

Several *Sayings*, characteristically from the second or later generations, mention 'virgins' who lived with Fathers as their servants. In one case the chaste nature of this union was called into question and had to be certified by a miracle. As death approached, the suspected man asked the Fathers to plant his stick on his grave: 'if it grows and bears fruit, know that I am pure from all contact with her.' Indeed, the stick budded and produced fruit after three days—the chaste union was sanctified by a divine miracle. Another very old Father from Scetis returned to Egypt because of a grave illness. A pious virgin joined him as his servant. This union evidently did not remain pure: before long, the Father recovered and the virgin became pregnant.[29]

These examples of cohabitation occurred most probably in villages, certainly so in the second, 'unholy', case. However, men and women lived together in the desert as well. A young man wanting to become a Desert Father saw a cell shaped like a tower and vowed to serve until death whomever he found living in this cell. He knocked, an old Father opened, and, being told of the

[27] Eudemon 1, cf. Sopatros 1 (Guy, 95, 292).

[28] Arsenius 28 (Guy, 36); N 13, N 518 (Regnault (1977), 16, 88).

[29] Cassian 2 (AD 360–435) (Guy, 154); it is not entirely certain whether this union took place in the desert itself or in a village close by; another Father, Spyridon, who lived in Cyprus as a shepherd and was eventually chosen as bishop of his village, lived with his daughter, 'who participated in her father's piety'; Spyridon 2, Anonymous 55 (Guy, 297, 342); N 32 (Regnault (1977), 22) has a variation of the sick brother served by a sister and then falling into temptation; here it is a bishop, who then becomes a monk as a penance.

young man's desire, said, 'if you want to make progress, go to a monastery, because I have a woman living with me.' The young man declared that he did not care whether the woman in question was a wife or a sister, his decision was made. Moved by this perseverance, the woman departed and joined a monastery. In another case a brother about to be found out, hides the woman he is living with, in a large trunk.[30]

The examples of Fathers living more or less permanently with virgins or women all belong to the later generations. However, though never condoned, the mere fact of cohabitation is not condemned outright either; what is criticized sharply are the sins committed as a consequence. Moreover, the practice of cohabitation led all too easily to suspicions, often groundless but at times based on sound reason—in short, we find a line of argument almost identical to that found in the authors from Asia Minor.

In 391, at the time the temples of Alexandria were overthrown, Abba Bessarion and his disciple Doulas went to visit John of Lycopolis.[31] On their way they entered a cave inhabited by an old Father who was completely immersed in his work. He was plaiting palm-leaves into ropes. As he neither raised his eyes nor acknowledged their presence in any other way, Bessarion and Doulas decided to leave him undisturbed. On their return journey they passed again by the old Father's cave and again they entered. What they found was only the Father's corpse. Doulas continues:

The old man said to me, 'Come, brother, let us take the body; it is for this reason God has sent us here.' When we took the body to bury it we perceived that it was a woman. Filled with astonishment, the old man said: 'See how the women triumph over Satan, while we still behave badly in the towns.'

Women's quest for ascetic perfection did not end at the boundaries of the villages and the fertile land. Like men, they ventured into the desert and here became true desert 'Fathers'; they 'became men.' As solitary desert-dwellers, all their female characteristics disappeared, not least because of their extreme living conditions.

---

[30] PE I 27, 3 (Regnault (1977), 169); Ammonas 10 (Guy, 54).
[31] Bessarion 4 (Guy, 68); N 162 (Nau, 63); Soz. *HE* 7 15. 10 (GCS 50. 321); K. G. Müller, 'Alexandria I', in *TRE* ii. 248–61; esp. 256 f.

A certain Theodora, the wife of a tribune, 'reached such a depth of poverty that she became a recipient of alms and finally died in the monastery of Hesychas near the sea.' These are Palladius' words in a chapter of his *Lausiac History* devoted to 'manly women' (γυναικῶν ἀνδρείων), women 'who through God's grace have fought battles equal to men'.[32] Precisely those characteristics also ennobled another Theodora, known as *amma* Theodora.[33] Amma Theodora lived towards the end of the third century in the desert of Nitria or Scetis, a contemporary of bishop Theophilus of Alexandria, with whom she kept regular contact.[34] She was a true desert 'mother', a formidable figure, whose *Sayings* were sought after by many Fathers. At approximately the same time an acquaintance of Apa Paphnutius lived in a cell with a terraced roof 'beside the river' in the desert belonging to the 'district of Pelusium'.[35] Her name was Amma Sarah. Last in the line, and perhaps best known through her fifth-century *Life* (wrongly attributed to Athanasius), is Amma Syncletica.[36]

The central theme of Theodora's *Sayings*, only once addressed to 'virgins and monks', is self-discipline, or 'knowing how to profit in times of conflict' (Col. 4: 5), when circumstances are extreme and seemingly unbearable.[37] Thus, in addressing both

---

[32] Pall. *HL* 41 (Butler, ii. 128, 219 n. 78); Bartelink, *La Storia Lausiaca*, 377 (nn. 15 and 16 to ch. 41); Hunt, 'Palladius of Helenopolis', 477.

[33] The honorific *amma* is already familiar from the papyri; Hausherr, 'Direction spirituelle', 261–75.

[34] Theodora (Guy, 116–19); Theophilus lived between *c*.345 and 412; the most comprehensive reconstruction of his history to date is by A. Favale, 'Teofilo di Alessandria (352c.–412)', *Salesianum* 18 (1956), 215–46, 498–535, and no. 19 (1957), 34–83, 215–72, here no. 18, 507–16; the location of Theodora's dwelling is not known; her acquaintance with Theophilus may indicate that she lived in Nitria, Kellia, or even Scetis, comparatively close to Alexandria.

[35] Sarah (Guy, 298 f.).

[36] Ps.-Ath. *Vita Sanctae Syncleticae* (PG 28. 1485–1558); *Vie de Sainte Synclétique*, ed. O. Bernard (Spiritualité Orientale 9; Solesmes, 1972); for the date and authorship see Bernard's introd. 3 f.

[37] An example for Heussi's important observation that 'eine bestimmte mönchische Tugend . . . des öfteren an einem bestimmten einzelnen Mönche verdeutlicht [wird], der Betreffende ist dann das sprichwörtliche Muster für eine bestimmte Sache . . . das *leitende* Interesse, das bei der Bildung der Traditionen wirksam war, [haftete] am *Sachlichen*, an der vorbildlichen Askese, und . . . die *Personen* [dienten] zunächst lediglich zur Verdeutlichung der *Sache*' (emphasis is Heussi's), *Ursprung*, 142.

monks and virgins, she praises the virtue of living in 'peace with oneself' (ἡσυχάζειν). However, as soon as this blessed state has been reached, the ascetic is immediately attacked by the evil of ἀκηδία (depression, self-loathing, listlessness), a vice specific to the desert and difficult to capture in translation. Amma Theodora is in fact one of the earliest desert-dwellers (and the only one in the *Apophthegmata*) to give us a definition of this condition, which causes faintheartedness, evil thoughts or λογισμοί, and unreasonable 'wanderlust': 'It also attacks your body through sickness, debility, weakening of the knees, and all the members. It dissipates strength of soul and body, so that one believes one is ill and no longer able to pray.'

Significantly, Theodora's description of *akēdia* echoes that given by her contemporary Evagrius Ponticus, arguably the most outstanding intellect of the desert, in his theoretical treatise on the ascetic's progress towards perfection, the so-called *Praktikos*.[38] In the *Saying* in which she defines *akēdia* Theodora talks in fact about a monk sucessfully overcoming his fever; in another she praises a formerly rich monk's victory over his body, which is now 'infested with vermin'. Considering this preoccupation with the body and its afflictions, it is perhaps not coincidental that Theodora also mentions 'a Christian discussing the body with a Manichaean'. The Christian's attitude here represented ('give the body discipline and you will see that the body is for him who made it') corresponds exactly with that expounded half a century earlier by Serapion of Thmuis in his refutation *Against the Manichees*—a testimony to the unabated Manichaean challenge to Egyptian asceticism.[39]

[38] Theodora 4 and 8 (Guy, 117 f.); Evagr. Pont. *Pract*. 9 (SC 171. 512) stresses internalized anger and frustration with the monk's state as one of the major sources for *akēdia*; Evagrius (345–99/400), a native of Ibora in Pontus, spent the latter half of his life in the Egyptian desert; cf. Elm, 'Evagrius Ponticus' *Sententiae ad Virginem*', 105–11; Guillaumont, 'La Conception du désert', 19–21; on the psychological astuteness of the *Apophthegmata*'s observations cf. also Heussi, *Ursprung*, 203–5; S. Wenzel, 'Ἀκηδία: Additions to Lampe's Patristic Greek Lexikon', *VigChr* 17 (1963), 173–6.

[39] Theodora 5 (Guy, 117); Serapion of Thmuis, *Adversos Manichaeos*, esp. ch. 5, (*Serapion of Thmuis: 'Against the Manichees*,' ed. R. P. Casey (Harvard Theological Studies 15; Cambridge, 1931), 31); Serapion was a contemporary of Antony and Athanasius of Alexandria; he died in 359, see Casey, p. 5. Alexander of Lycopolis' *Contra Manichaeos* (*Alexandre de Lycopolis: Contre la doctrine de*

Two other *Sayings* are worth mentioning. Theodora exalts those who suffer insults with great patience; and she discusses at length the ideal characteristics of a *teacher*: 'let him be a stranger to the desire for domination, vainglory, and pride; one should not be able to fool him by flattery, nor blind him by gifts, nor conquer him by the stomach, nor dominate him by anger; but he should be patient, gentle, and humble as far as possible; he must be tested and without partisanship, full of concern, and a lover of souls.'

Those who compiled the *Apophthegmata* regarded Theodora as the perfect representative of the qualities an ideal teacher ought to possess.[40] Neither they nor the many Fathers who came to seek out her words of wisdom considered her sex to be either a hindrance to her teaching abilities or a detriment to her standing as a desert ascetic. She, like all the other Desert Fathers, was a charismatic, a *pneumatophoros*, and therefore a model to emulate, as she herself emulated her own *exemplum*: 'as pledge, example, and as prototype we have him who died for us and is risen, Christ our God.'[41]

The region of Amma Sarah's dwelling, unlike Theodora's, is well known: the desert of Pelusium was a popular retreat with a

Mani, ed. A. Villey (Paris, 1985)) is particularly informative regarding the early 4th cent. Manichaean presence in Lycopolis; see in general S. Lieu, *Manichaeism in the Later Roman Empire and Medieval China* (Manchester, 1985); the relationship of Manichaeans (and of Gnostics in general) with asceticism is much debated in scholarship; cf. for example L. Koenen, 'Manichäische Mission und Klöster in Ägypten', in *Das römisch-byzantinische Ägypten*, 93–108; A. Guillaumont, 'Gnose et Monachisme: Exposé introductif', in J. Ries (ed.), *Gnosticisme et monde hellénistique: Actes du Colloque de Louvain-la-Neuve (11–14 mars 1980)*, (Publ. de l'institut orientaliste de Louvain 27; Louvain-la-Neuve, 1982), 301–10; L. Leloir, 'Infiltrations dualistes chez les Pères du Désert', ibid. 327–36; G. S. Stroumsa, 'The Manichaean Challenge to Egyptian Christianity', in Pearson and Goehring, *The Roots of Egyptian Christianity*, 307–19; in our present context of organizational aspects, the distinction between a 'gnostic' and a 'non-dualistic' basis for ascetic practices is not of primary importance.

[40] Hausherr, 'Direction spirituelle', 56–105; Heussi, *Ursprung*, 141–4, 164–86, 198–205.

[41] Theodora 10 (Guy, 119); Guy, *Paroles des Anciens*, 8–12; Heussi, *Ursprung*, 164–7, 266–71; F. Normann, *Christos Didaskalos: Die Vorstellung von Christus als Lehrer in der christlichen Literatur des ersten und zweiten Jahrhunderts* (Münsterische Beiträge zur Theologie 32; Münster, 1967), *passim*.

substantial number of desert-dwellers.[42] Sarah certainly lived in the midst of Desert Fathers, and it may be a result of the comparatively close quarters that—unlike Amma Theodora, who never mentions the topic—she speaks quite forcefully on the subject of fornication. Sarah's *Sayings* begin by emphasizing her thirteen years of warfare against the demon of fornication, overcoming it only with the help of her master, Christ.[43] Her *Sayings* also reflect far more strongly the fact that she was a woman, and, in contrast to Theodora, it is here that we find open signs of opposition to her presence in the desert. Thus she says: 'if I prayed to God that all men should approve of my conduct, I should find myself a penitent at the door of each one, but I shall rather pray that my heart may be pure towards all.' Clearly, Sarah encountered doubts regarding her legitimacy as a desert-dweller.

Another time, two old men, great anchorites, came to the district of Pelusia to visit her. When they arrived one said to the other, 'Let us humiliate this old woman.' So they said to her, 'Be careful not to become conceited thinking to yourself: "Look how anchorites are coming to see me, a mere woman."' But Amma Sarah said to them: 'According to nature I am a woman, but not according to my thoughts.'

This conviction Sarah emphasizes even more clearly in *Saying* 9, addressing the brothers: 'It is I who am a man, you who are women.'

Sarah's position and ascetic legitimacy did not remain unchallenged. While criticism of aberrations is a staple of the *Apophthegmata*, the validity of a Desert Father's quest, and thus the validity of his ascetic practices, is hardly ever questioned. In fact, the Fathers in the *Apophthegmata* are very careful to avoid fundamental debates and instead represent their ascetic practices as something universally accepted, quite beyond the need for legiti-

---

[42] Ammonathas 1 (Guy, 66), an interesting *Saying* dealing with the *capitatio* form of taxation of monks, and as such, supporting evidence for the *P. Lips.* 60; Isaia 4 (Guy, 100); the Pelusium here is most likely the one in the Fajum (Arsinoite) near Theadelphia, close to an eastern arm of the Nile, not the metropolis of Augustamnica, cf. Amm. Marc. 22. 16. 3; H. Kees, 'Pelusion', in *RE* xix., 407–15; R. Pietschmann, 'Augustamnica', ibid. ii. 2362.

[43] Sarah 1 and 2 (Guy, 298).

mation; elements of conflict or controversy are unusual.[44] The open criticism of Amma Sarah is thus exceptional and a clear indication that she was confronted by a particular need to justify her ascetic existence, not as a desert-dweller, but as a woman.

Sarah's basic argument is by now a familiar one: it is one that the Eustathian women could very well have used, the same as that brought forward in Basil of Ancyra's *De virginitate*, or, indeed, in Gregory of Nyssa's eulogy on Macrina, albeit in a more subtle form; it is the same as that expressed by the leader of a group of virgins in an anonymous *Saying* to a passing monk who made a detour to avoid the women: 'If you were a perfect monk, you would not have seen us as women.'[45] For the perfect ascetic the question of male or female no longer exists, because he or she has risen above the limits determined by the body; asceticism means annihilation of sexual distinction. The desert 'mothers' present the opportunity to introduce yet another nuance into the development of this concept.

One of the most fundamental driving forces motivating the desert ascetic was the desire to become a true 'athlete', a 'fighter for Christ', 'not contending against flesh and blood, but against the principalities, against the powers, against the world rulers of this present darkness' (Eph. 6: 12), 'stripped of all earthly fabric and crucified . . . instructed by an elder in the art of combat. This is what God does to grant us victory.'[46] The image of the athlete

[44] Even the most fundamental conflict—that between the developing ecclesiastical hierarchy and charismatic ascetics (as proposed by Heussi and Reitzenstein: for refs. see this note *ad fin*.)—finds expression only in the occasional refusal of a clerical post offered to an ascetic or in random remarks remotely critical of the clergy, such as e.g. Arsenius 7, 8, Apphy, Theophilus 2, Netras (Guy, 31 f., 64, 114, 206); Cass. *De coen. inst.* 11. 18 (SC 109. 445). The same is true for the clashes between desert ascetics and cenobites, cf. Macarius the Citizen 2 (Guy, 200); PE I 25, 2 (Regnault (1977), 169); N 171 (Nau, 63). On the whole, references to conflicts caused by the Fathers' ascetic practices and their legitimacy are, for obvious reasons, extremely rare; Griggs, *Early Egyptian Christianity*, 101–3; Heussi, *Ursprung*, 182–6; R. Reitzenstein, *Historia Monachorum und Historia Lausiaca: Eine Studie zur Geschichte des Mönchtums und der frühchristlichen Begriffe Gnostiker und Pneumatiker* (Göttingen, 1916), 185–210.

[45] N 23 (Guy, 326); the same sentiment is also vividly expressed by Abraham 1 (Guy, 61).

[46] N 143 (Nau, 59); '[like] the athlete who strips off his clothes to fight in the arena'; R. Draguet (ed.), *Les Pères du Désert: Textes choisis* (Paris, 1949), 54–7;

locked in fierce combat is, of course, thoroughly male, and thus, at least in theory, thoroughly unsuitable for women. However, there was one area where women had long since joined the battle and had proved that their fierceness and determination equalled, or even surpassed, that of men: martyrdom.

Already in the Book of Maccabees women had demonstrated that, although 'softer of soul than men', they nevertheless 'despised the most dreadful tortures' and were able to fight a holy war in utter calmness and composure. Indeed, the heroine, like Macrina so many centuries later, 'took her womanly thoughts and fired them with a manly spirit', thus following the example of the Stoic sage, the quintessential ideal of manly virtue.[47] Not surprisingly, such an internal attitude found its external manifestation. A passage in the *Passio Perpetuae* vividly expresses one step in the process of transformation that led to an external manifestation of inward 'manliness'. Here, shortly before her extreme trials, the heroine sees herself in a vision 'expoliata sum et facta sum masculus; et coeperunt me fauisores mei oleo defricare, quomodo solent in agone'; '. . . stripped of [my clothes], I became a man; and my seconds began to rub me down with oil (as they are wont to do before a contest).'[48]

The end of the persecutions ended the glories of martyrdom.

the image of the athlete soon became the image of the male saint *per se*, thus combining and unifying in it, almost as the generic concept, the three highest forms of perfection open to men: bishop, martyr, and ascetic; cf. Giannarelli, *La tipologia femminile*, 25; Guillaumont, 'La Conception du désert', 12–16.

[47] 4 Macc. 15: 5; 16: 2; 17: 11–16 (*The Apocrypha and Pseudepigrapha of the Old Testament in English*. ii, ed. R. H. Charles (Oxford, 1913), 680–2); 2 Macc. 7: 21 (*II Maccabees: A New Translation with Introduction and Commentary*, ed. J. Goldstein (New York, 1983), 290); Th. Baumeister, *Die Anfänge der Theologie des Martyriums* (Münsterische Beiträge zur Theologie 45; Münster, 1980), 38–51; 245 f.; O. Perler, 'Das vierte Makkabäerbuch, Ignatius von Antiochien und die ältesten Märtyrerberichte', *Rivista di Archeologia Christiana* 25 (1949), 47–72.

[48] *Passio SS. Perpetuae et Felicitatis*, 10. 7 (*The Acts of the Christian Martyrs*, ed. H. Musurillo (Oxford, 1972), 118 f.); a similar imagery is used to characterize e.g. Blandina in *The Martyrs of Lyons*, 1. 17. 41–2, 55–6 (Musurillo 66, 74, 78–80); Eus. *HE* 5. 1. 18–19, the battle of Potamiena is described at 6. 5. 1–5; H. v. Campenhausen, *Die Idee des Martyriums in der frühen Kirche* (Göttingen, 1936), *passim*; for the psychological significance of religious transvestism cf. still M. Delcourt, 'Le Complexe de Diane dans l'hagiographie chrétienne', *RHR* 153 (1958), 1–33; F.-J. Dölger, 'Der Kampf mit dem Ägypter in der Perpetua-Vision: Das Martyrium als Kampf mit dem Teufel', *Antike und Christentum* 3 (1932), 177–88.

But in the same way in which Antony, the *primus eremita*, transformed the once-only death of the martyr into the daily martyrdom of the ascetic, women also transformed their once-only battleground and joined the long drawn out fight against the demons of their own desires.[49] In the process, the transformation of women into athletes and thus into men no longer remained solely a metaphorical concept or the momentary transfiguration of a vision. The transformation became real and permanent, in part quite simply as a result of the harsh life in the desert. After long periods of fasting, all external remnants of feminine features disappeared: the women of the desert had truly become 'fathers' and 'athletes', fighting against the same demons, suffering the same extremities. In so doing, women and men not only became equals, as 'men of God', but women even achieved a form of superiority. Since their nature was by definition seen as 'weaker' and softer, their ascetic achievements in comparison to those of men were in effect greater; as Bessarion put it: 'see how the women triumph over Satan, while we still behave badly in the towns.' Or in Syncletica's words: 'those who are great athletes must contend against stronger enemies.'[50] Not surprisingly, the motif of the religious transvestite, exemplified by Bessarion's mother, enjoyed continuous popularity. Numerous stories circulated, centred around women hiding in, living in, and even guiding male monasteries; and such stories were often embellished by dramatic accusations of 'fornication' suffered patiently by the heroine until she is finally vindicated by the discovery of her true sex after her death.[51]

[49] καθ᾽ ἡμέραν μαρτυρῶν, Ath. *V. Ant.* 47 (PG 26. 912); Guillaumont, 'La Conception du désert', 15–18; id. 'Gnose et monachisme', 307f.; Heussi, *Ursprung*, 108–15; E. E. Malone, *The Monk and the Martyr: The Monk as the Successor of the Martyr* (Studies in Christian Antiquity 12; Washington, DC, 1950), *passim*; id. 'The Monk and the Martyr', *Studia Anselmiana* 38 (1956), 201–28.

[50] Cf. Syncletica 14 = 905 = *Vita Syncl.* 26 (Regnault (1976), 17); Pall. *HL* 41 (Butler, ii. 128); Bessarion 4 (Guy, 68); Hausherr, 'Direction spirituelle', 254–7.

[51] F. A. Angarano, 'Teodora, penitente di Alessandria', in *Bibliotheca Sanctorum*, xii. (Rome, 1969), 220f.; legends of monks later discovered to be 'nuns' soon became a staple, cf. e.g. that regarding emperor Zeno's daughter, N. Giron, *Légendes coptes* (Paris, 1907), 59; and the discussion of the genre by Delehaye, *Les Légendes hagiographiques*, 59f., 188–192; Tillemont, *Mémoires*, xvi. 165–7; Anson, 'The Female Transvestite', 1–32; Cameron, 'Neither Male nor Female', 60–7; Giannarelli, *La tipologia femminile*, 25–8, 86–8; Patlagean, 'L'Histoire de la femme déguisée', 597–623.

Bessarion's female 'father' remained anonymous. The account of his encounter with the transvestite desert mother, buried within a *Saying* praising a fourteen-day fast, is in fact the *Apophthegmata*'s only explicit mention of a female desert-dweller whose appearance had become that of a man. Neither Theodora, Sarah, or Syncletica is depicted as having male features. To be precise, no mention at all is made regarding their external appearance, except for the fact that all three are clearly identified as women, 'mothers'. Quite evidently, actual change of appearance was not a unanimously accepted practice. Even Sarah's theoretical maxim, 'according to nature I am a woman, but not according to my thoughts', met with criticism.

Despite the theoretical concept that ascetic perfection surpasses sexual distinction, the actual presence of female ascetics in the desert presented a highly complex issue. The only women featured in a prominent fashion are those who achieved the highest levels of ascetic perfection without transforming their external appearance into that of a man: Theodora, Sarah, Syncletica. Only Sarah's position—and here she might be the representative of a 'theme', namely that of gender—is called in question.[52] At the same time, a female 'Father' appears only once, in passing, but is presented with undiluted admiration. The question arises of whether the notion of the female 'Father', the most radical form of ascetic transformation a woman could achieve, had perhaps undergone a process of 'domestication' by the time Theodora, Sarah, and finally Syncletica entered the *Apophthegmata* as mothers or 'ammai'.[53]

Women left their families, villages, and communities in search

[52] Heussi, *Ursprung*, 142 f.

[53] Sources concerning these developments are not only scarce but also difficult to assess because of the continuous 'layering' of *Sayings* and legends around specific figures over a period of 200 years. Nevertheless, the specific choice of a role, the specific emphasis of aspects attributed to great female figures, speaks for itself. Thus, in a later Armenian version Sarah is depicted as living in fact with other sisters, Arm. 2 19 (35) A (Regnault (1977), 259); the same is true for Syncletica, who, strictly speaking, is said to have lived in a tomb near Alexandria rather than in the desert (*Vita Syncl.* 11 (Bernard, 9, 4–8)), and soon found a large circle of female followers to whom her *Sayings* are addressed. In this context Theodora's role as a teacher gains further in importance: clearly, in later sources the emphasis was placed on the teaching of women. On the other hand, legends concerning transvestites also increased, cf. for instance Anson, 'The Female Transvestite', 12. *The Life of Syncletica*, one of the oldest hagiographic writings

of religious fulfilment in the desert. They did so on their own, undaunted by extremes of nature or fierceness of attacks by humans or demons. In the process these women 'became men' in the strength of their soul and the success of their ascetic achievements, and at times also in their outer appearance. However, life as a desert ascetic was not the only form of extreme asceticism pursued by women. It appears that some chose an ascetic life at least as marginal and perhaps more alien than that of a desert-dweller, who at least belonged to a revered and elect group living in specific locations. In *Saying* 6 Amma Syncletica remarks: 'Just as the bird who abandons the eggs she was sitting on prevents them from hatching, so the monk or the virgin grows cold and their faith dies, when they go from one place to another.'[54] What does she have in mind?

The disciple of Apa Sisoes said to him, 'Father, you have grown old. Let us move a little closer to the settled land.' The Old Man said, 'Where there is no woman, that is where we should go.' The disciple said to him, 'What other place is there that has no woman, if not the desert?' The Old Man said to him, 'Take me to the desert.'[55]

As has become amply apparent, Abba Sisoes' *Saying* represents more an ideal than an accurate description of reality. Women were in the desert, not only as apparitions in the minds of tormented Fathers, but as real human beings. Like men, women ventured into the desert for specific reasons, frequently other than religious ones. Many women were forced into the desert by circumstances as diverse as the 'professional journey' of a group of actresses or the threats of tax-collectors.[56] Many others were drawn by the most obvious and natural reason: to visit their

depicting a woman, has, despite its highly interesting parallels to Ath. *V. Ant.*, the *VSM*, and Evagrius' *Sententiae ad Virginem*, found surprisingly little attention, cf. Albrecht, *Das Leben der heiligen Macrina*, 303 f.; Elm, 'Evagrius Ponticus' *Sententiae ad Virginem*', 102–7.

[54] Syncletica 7 (Guy, 301).

[55] Sisoes 3 (Guy, 276), trans. Brown, *The Body and Society*, 242; cf. S. Elm, 'Formen des Zusammenlebens männlicher und weiblicher Asketen im östlichen Mittelmeerraum während des vierten Jahrhunderts nach Christus,' in M. Parisse and K. Elm (eds.), *Doppelklöster und andere Formen der Symbiose männlicher und weiblicher Religiosen im Mittelalter* (Berliner Historische Studien 18; Ordensstudien 8; Berlin, 1992), 13–24, here 13.

[56] *HM* 14. 5–6 (Festugière, 103 f.); Festugière, *Enquête*, 91 f.; for examples of those ruined and 'persecuted' by tax-collectors cf. e.g. N 66, N 566 (Regnault

fathers, sons, husbands, and other relatives.[57] Illness also brought women into the desert. One of the most pronounced charismatic faculties of the Fathers was their power to heal, and many came to seek their assistance. Stories of miraculous healings abound, ranging from exorcisms to cures of breast cancer and other disfiguring growths.[58] Women seeking cures were clearly driven by their faith in the Fathers' supernatural faculties; in other words, by a motive that can be described as religious. It is this religious aspect of their journey into the desert which also motivated an entirely different group of women who travelled to Egypt: women on pilgrimage.

Pilgrimages to Jerusalem and the Holy Land begin in the middle of the second century with Melito of Sardis' excursion to 'the place where these things were preached and done'.[59] However, they truly gain popularity almost one hundred years later, during the late third and early fourth century. The pilgrimage of the Montanist prophetess of Caesarea may well have been purely spiritual, yet it could have been inspired by the actual pilgrimage of her contemporary and countryman, bishop Alexander of Cappadocia.[60] Alexander went to 'Jerusalem to pray and investigate the holy places', and remained there as a bishop.[61] Others soon

(1977), 36, 105); 1709 (Regnault (1976), 37); for a mime wandering around cf. Arm. 2 373 (57) B (Regnault (1977), 270); cf. also *SBo* 14, and *G*¹ 8 (*Koinonia*, i. 36, 303).

    [57] Mark 3, 4, Timoth. 1, Carion 2, Poemen 5 (Guy, 193, 308, 159, 215); A. Borias, 'Le Moine et sa famille (chez les Pères, Pachôme et Basile)', *Collectanea Cisterciensia* 40 (1978), 82–7; Heussi, *Ursprung*, 196–8.

    [58] Macarius the Egyptian 6 (Guy, 170) cured a woman's possessed child; Daniel 3 (Guy, 79) cured a possessed woman; Longinus 3 (Guy, 164) healed a woman of her breast cancer; Arm. 2 447 (115) B (Regnault (1977), 272) also refers to Longinus' healing of a woman; B. Kötting, *Peregrinatio Religiosa* (Münster, 1950), 168–70, 300–2, 394 f.; J. Wilkinson (*Jerusalem Pilgrims before the Crusades* (Warminster, 1977), 34) mentions e.g. St Menas, which was already a pagan sanctuary of healing, cf. ibid. 88 n. 53.

    [59] Eus. *HE* 4. 26. 14; E. D. Hunt, *Holy Land Pilgrimage in the Later Roman Empire AD 312–460* (Oxford, 1982), 3–5.

    [60] Elm, 'Perceptions of Jerusalem Pilgrimage', 219–23.

    [61] Eus. *HE* 6. 11. 1–2, *c.* AD 212; H. Donner, *Pilgerfahrt ins Heilige Land: Die ältesten Berichte christlicher Palästinapilger (4.–7. Jahrhundert)*, (Stuttgart, 1979), 20 f.; Kötting, *Peregrinatio Religiosa*, 88 n. 24, 322; Egeria, *Per. Aeth.* = Pétré, *Éthérie: Journal de voyage* (SC 21. 18–21).

followed his example. Many of these pilgrims were women, often, but not exclusively, from the highest echelons of society, most notable among them being the empress Helena, who visited the Holy Land in 326.[62] The reasons for such a noticeable presence of female pilgrims can only be surmised, but Basil of Caesarea might provide us with a possible clue: 'whoever is anxious to make himself perfect in all the kinds of virtue must gaze upon the lives of the saints (and the Scriptures) as upon statues, so to speak, that move and act, and must make their excellence his own διὰ μιμήσεως (by imitation).'[63]

Which saints or scriptural passages were women supposed to follow? While in theory there may not have been 'grande différence à faire entre ascètes des deux sexes',[64] women may in practice have wanted to follow their own 'female models'. The few passages of the New Testament in which women play a truly significant role take place in Jerusalem. It is to Jerusalem that Mary accompanies Joseph and Jesus; it is to Jerusalem that the women in Jesus' company follow their master; and it is in Jerusalem that women become instrumental in Christ's burial and resurrection.[65] Desire to emulate the women present at the Holy Sepulchre might thus have been a strong attraction inducing many a woman to go to 'Jerusalem to pray'.[66]

The Holy Land was, however, not the only destination which attracted pilgrims. The spreading fame of the new ascetics resulted in an expanded itinerary, facilitated by the fact that Alexandria was the port of entry for many on the way to Jerusalem; pilgrims began to visit the Egyptian Desert Fathers as well.[67] Eustathius

---

[62] Eus. *V. Const.* 3. 42 (GCS 7. 95); Hunt, *Holy Land Pilgrimage*, 28–49; Kötting, *Peregrinatio Religiosa*, 90–3.

[63] Bas. *Ep.* 2, addressed to Gregory of Nazianzus; Paul. Nol. *Ep.* 49 (ed. W. v. Hartel, CSEL 29. 402).

[64] Hausherr, 'Direction Spirituelle', 267.

[65] Mark 10: 32; 14: 3–9; 15: 40–2; 16: 1–13; Matt. 27–8; Luke 2: 22–4, 41–2; compare also the account of Mary's visit to Elisabeth, Luke 1: 39–42.

[66] Hunt, *Holy Land Pilgrimage*, 83–91; G. Vikan's discussion of 6th-cent. votive gifts depicting incense-bearing women ('Pilgrims in Magi's Clothing: The Impact of *Mimesis* on Early Byzantine Pilgrimage Art' (unpubl. paper, *11th Annual Byzantine Studies Conference, Oct. 25–27*; Toronto, 1985) 29 f.) supports this suggestion.

[67] *Expositio totius mundi et gentium*, ed. J. Rougé (SC 124; Paris, 1966) 29; J. Rougé, *Recherches sur l'organisation du commerce maritime en Méditeranée sous l'Empire Romain* (Paris, 1966), 126–8; Kötting, *Peregrinatio Religiosa*, 188–210.

of Sebaste is said to have visited the early Desert Fathers in the 320s; Basil of Caesarea followed suit in 356, and the 'servant of God Poimenia' visited John of Lycopolis in the middle of the fourth century.[68] The Roman 'virgin of senatorial rank' who came to visit Arsenius, also Egeria, Paula, and her daughter Eustochium, and Melania the Elder and the Younger all came during the 390s and later.[69] For reasons of safety—the long routes were fraught with dangers—almost all the pilgrims mentioned travelled in groups; and quite often in style.[70] Although the entourage was not always as splendid as in the case of Poimenia (who was accompanied by several ships carrying, among others, her eunuchs, Moorish slaves, and the bishop Diogenes), female pilgrims travelled as a rule with members of the clergy or trusted ascetics. Egeria was accompanied by monks, clerics, and sometimes bishops; Paula and Eustochium's entourage included Jerome; and the Roman noblewoman visiting Arsenius was at least introduced to the Father by the famous bishop Theophilus.[71]

More important than their number, however, is one other characteristic shared by all pilgrims: they went to Jerusalem to pray, and they all intended, at least at the outset of their journey,

---

[68] Pall. *HL* 35 (Butler, ii. 106; P. Devos, '"La Servante de Dieu" Poemenia d'après Pallade', *AnBoll* 87 (1969), 189–212; A. Guillaumont, 'Le Dépaysement comme forme d'ascèse, dans le monachisme ancien', *Annuaire École Pratique des Hautes Études, Sciences Religieuse* 76 (1968/9), 31–58, here 37–9.

[69] *Per. Aeth.* 49. 1–2 (SC 21. 264); Arsenius 28 (Guy, 36); Jer. *Ep.* 108 *ad Eustochium* (*Sancti Eusebii Hieronymi Epistulae*, ii, ed. I. Hilberg (CSEL 55; Vienna, 1910), 306–51); id. *Epitaphium S. Paulae = Ep.* 108. 6–14; Pall. *HL* 46 (Butler, ii. 134); *Gerontius: Vie de Sainte Mélanie*, ed. D. Gorce, (SC 90; Paris, 1962).

[70] Hunt, *Holy Land Pilgrimage*, 50–82; Kötting, *Peregrinatio Religiosa*, 363–81, 387 f.; Pétré, *Éthérie* (SC 21. 24–6); Wilkinson, *Jerusalem Pilgrims*, 16–32.

[71] Pall. *HL* 35 (Butler, ii. 106); *Per. Aeth.* 1. 2; 10. 3; 13. 2; bishops, 3. 7; 10. 8; 15. 3; 19. 5 (SC 21. 96, 106, 132, 136, 138, 146, 152, 164); Jer. *Ep.* 108 (CSEL 55. 306–51); *Ep.* 3 *ad Ruf.* (CSEL 54. 12–18); in *Ep.* 54. 13. 3 (CSEL 54. 479 f.) Jerome criticizes a woman flitting about the East in a style fit for Nero or Sardanapallus, perhaps an allusion to Melania the Elder, cf. Elm, 'Evagrius Ponticus' *Sententiae ad Virginem*', 117 f.; Donner, *Pilgerfahrt* 139; Hunt, *Holy Land Pilgrimage*, 76–82; Wilkinson, *Jerusalem Pilgrims* 20 n. 52, 81, 126, 133; apart from the safety advantages, μίμησις or re-enactment of scriptural events was also more suited to pilgrimage in groups, in imitation of the archetypal pilgrims, the three Magi, Matt. 2: 1–15; Kötting, *Peregrinatio Religiosa*, 297–300, 394; Vikan, 'Pilgrims in Magi's Clothing', 29, and *passim*.

to return to a settled life.[72] Now Amma Syncletica expressed her warning as follows: 'If you find yourself in a monastery, do not go to another place, for that will harm you a great deal . . . the monk or the virgin grows cold and their faith dies, when they go from one place to another.' Does she have pilgrims in mind, temporarily 'going from one place to another', or does she refer to a fundamentally different phenomenon: perpetual wandering as a way of ascetic life?[73]

Inspired by scriptural passages such as 'they were afflicted, ill-treated; wandering over deserts and mountains, and in dens and caves of the earth',[74] wandering became for many *the* choice of an ascetic life, representing in fact 'une institution parfaitement naturelle, puisque ces chrétiens suivaient l'exemple de Jésus, qui, lui-même, avait été un xenos'.[75] Accordingly, the practice, though particularly pronounced in Syria, was, as we have seen, known and widespread in Asia Minor. The same seems to have been the case in Egypt.[76] The *Apophthegmata* themselves bear witness to those wanderers, most notably in the *Sayings* of Bessarion.

[72] Eus. *HE* 6. 11. 1–2; Kötting, *Peregrinatio Religiosa*, 302, 304; Turner, *Image and Pilgrimage in Christian Culture*, 1–20, 34–9.

[73] W. Bousset, 'Das Mönchtum der sketischen Wüste', 27–41; H. v. Campenhausen, 'Die asketische Heimatlosigkeit im altkirchlichen und frühmittelalterlichen Mönchtum', in *Tradition und Leben: Kräfte der Kirchengeschichte* (Tübingen, 1960[2]; repr. from *Sammlung gemeinverständlicher Vorträge* 149; Tübingen, 1930) 290–317; Heussi, *Ursprung*, 30, 166, 206–10; Reitzenstein, *Historia Monachorum*, 49–77.

[74] Heb. 11: 37–8; cf. also Gen. 12: 1; Ps. 28: 13; Heb. 11: 8–13; 1 Pet. 2: 11; 2 Cor. 5: 6.

[75] G. Quispel, 'L'Évangile selon Thomas et les origines de l'ascèse chrétienne', in *Aspects du judéo-christianisme* (Travaux du Centre d'études supérieures spécialisé d'histoire des religions; Strasburg, 1965), 44, cf. 50; G. Florovsky, 'Theophilus of Alexandria and Apa Aphou of Pemdje', in S. Lieberman *et al.* (eds.), *H. A. Wolfson Jubilee Volume I* (American Academy for Jewish Research; Jerusalem, 1965), 275–310, esp. 291 f.; Guillaumont, 'Le Dépaysement', 32 f.; G. Kretschmar, 'Ein Beitrag zur Frage nach dem Ursprung frühchristlicher Askese', *Zeitschrift für Theologie und Kirche* 61 (1964), 27–67; G. Ladner, 'Homo Viator: Medieval Ideas on Alienation and Order', *Speculum* 42 (1967), 233–59; Rousseau, *Ascetics*, 43–9.

[76] A. Veilleux, 'Monasticism and Gnosis in Egypt', in Pearson and Goehring, *The Roots of Egyptian Christianity*, 271–306, esp. 302–4; Vööbus, *History of Asceticism*, i. 152–8; as evidence for possible Manichaean influence in the practice of wandering in Egypt cf. P. Nagel, 'Die Psalmoi Sarakoton des manichäischen Psalmenbuches', *Orientalistische Literaturzeitung* 62 (1967), 123–30.

His life had been like that of a bird of the air, or a fish, or an animal living on earth, . . . the care of a dwelling did not trouble him, and the desire for a particular place never seemed to dominate his soul; . . . He always lived in the open air, afflicting himself on the edge of the desert like a vagabond.

Macarius the Egyptian attests to similarly extreme practices when he relates how, in the midst of animals drinking from a well in the desert, he saw two naked men,

and my body trembled, for I believed they were spirits. Seeing me shaking they said to me, 'Do not be afraid, for we are men.' Then I said to them, 'Where do you come from, and how did you come to this desert?' They said, 'We come from a monastery and having agreed together, we came here forty years ago.'

Macarius is full of admiration for these extraordinary champions of endurance. Finding himself unable to rival their practices, he claims that he himself is not yet a monk, but has at least seen true monks—both Bessarion and Macarius the Egyptian, it is worth noting, belonged, to the earliest generation of desert ascetics.[77]

Ξενιτεία, the notion that the one who wants to imitate Christ has to be a stranger on this earth, found its expression in Egypt not only in an exodus into the alien world of the desert, but also in its most literal sense: asceticism as a continuous exile, a perpetual pilgrimage, a life of wandering.[78] However, all of the few

---

[77] Bessarion 12 (Guy, 70); Macarius 2 (Guy, 167), a story reminiscent of John of Ephesus' *Commentarii de beatis Orientalibus*, 53 (ed. and trans. E. W. Brooks (Patrologia Orientalis 19; Paris, 1926), 179); cf. also ibid. chs. 12, 17, 22, 39, 51, 52 (Patr. Or. vols. 17–19). Palladius (*HL* 37 (Butler, ii. 109–16)) relates the story of the migrant Serapion, called the Sidonite because his clothing was made of a thin material of that name; Bousset, 'Das Mönchtum', 27–41, esp. 35–7; J. Hechenbach, *De nuditate sacra sacrisque vinculis* (Giessen, 1911); Heussi, *Ursprung*, 207 f.; M. Lurker, 'Nacktheit', in: *Wörterbuch biblischer Bilder und Symbole* (Munich, 1973), 218–20. Interesting from a different angle is P. F. Beatrice, 'Le tuniche di pelle: Antiche letture di Gen. 3, 21', in U. Bianchi (ed.), *La tradizione dell'enkrateia: Motivazioni ontologiche e protologiche. Atti del colloquio internazionale, Milano, 20–23 aprile 1982* (Rome, 1985), 433–84. Numerous more or less legendary stories circulated concerning male and female ascetics living completely in the wilderness; many of them involved the so-called 'Boskoi': Soz. *HE* 6. 33 (GCS 50. 289); Theod. *HR* 1 (Jacobus), 27 (Baradatus) (SC 234. 160; SC 257. 216); Evagrius Scholasticus, *HE* 1. 21 (*Kirchengeschichte*, ed. J. Bidez and L. Parmentier (London, 1898), 30); Campenhausen, 'Die asketische Heimatlosigkeit', 294 n. 13; T. Špidlík, 'Boskoi', in *DIP* i. 1538.

[78] Guillaumont, 'Le Dépaysement', 32–41, 46–50.

examples relating to this particular form of ascetic life in the *Apophthegmata* concern men. Could Amma Syncletica's *Saying* imply that women also chose perpetual *xeniteia* as the manifestation of their ascetic intentions? Could they too have taken Abraham as a model, literally following God's commandment to 'go from your country and your kindred and your father's house to the land that I will show you'; imitating those women, 'who, when he was in Galilee, followed him and ministered to him; and there were also many other women who came up with him to Jerusalem?'[79]

More conclusions may be drawn from two fragmentary letters addressed to Rufinus of Aquileia and Melania the Elder, written by Evagrius Ponticus, the desert ascetic already mentioned in the context of Amma Theodora.[80] Here Evagrius, already a famous desert ascetic who, typically, considers himself unworthy even to pray to God since he is still subject to worldly thoughts and influences, gives the following advice:

As regards the chaste deaconess Severa, I praise her intentions but I do not approve of her undertaking. I do not see what she will gain from such a long walk over such a laborious route; whereas, with the help of the Lord, I could easily demonstrate the damage she and those with her will suffer. Thus, I beseech your holiness to prevent those [women] who have renounced the world from needlessly walking around over such roads; because I wonder how, travelling over those distances, they can avoid drinking the waters of Gihon (*Γηών*), either in their thoughts or in their deeds. Such behaviour is misguided (*ἀπαλλοτρία*) for those who live in chastity (*τῶν σωφρονῶν*).[81]

---

[79] Gen. 12: 1; Mark 15: 40–1.

[80] W. Frankenberg (ed.), *Euagrius Ponticus, Epp.* 7 and 8 (Abhandlungen der königlichen Akademie der Wissenschaft zu Göttingen, phil.-hist. Kl., NF 13: 2 (Berlin, 1912; repr. Nendeln, 1970), 571 and 73); Ger. trans. by G. Bunge, *Briefe aus der Wüste* (Sophia 24; Trier, 1986), 220 f.; A. Guillaumont, 'Evagrius Ponticus', in *TRE* x. 565–70; the manuscripts do not bear the original address (cf. Bunge, *Briefe*, 173 f., 179–81); the addressee has therefore to be determined by internal factors; the recipient of Letter 7 for instance is addressed as *ὁσιότητος*, a title as a rule reserved for bishops (Bunge, *Briefe*, 180, 336); e.g. Eus. *V. Const.* 2. 46 (GCS 7. 61); Ath. *Ep.* 1 *ad Serap.* 1 (PG 26. 552).

[81] My own translation; to describe oneself as unworthy is a common topos; cf. for instance Bessarion 4, Macarius 2, Moses 2, Matoes 11 (Guy, 68, 168, 183, 191); Guillaumont, 'Evagrius Ponticus', 565–9; id. *Les 'Képhalaia Gnostica' d'Evagre le Pontique et l'histoire de l'origénisme chez les Grecs et chez les Syriens* (Patristica Sorbonensia 5; Paris, 1966); Heussi, *Ursprung*, 190 f.

In his Letter 8 Evagrius exhorts (presumably) Melania the Elder again to

> teach your sisters and your sons not to take a long journey or to travel through deserted lands without examining the matter seriously. For this is misguided (ἀπηλλοτριωμένον) and unbecoming to every soul that has retreated from the world; . . . And I wonder whether a woman roaming about and meeting myriads of people can achieve such a goal.

Apparently, the chaste deaconess Severa had some close connection with Melania the Elder; in fact, Evagrius' Letters 19 and 20 suggest that she was a member of the ascetic community founded by Melania the Elder in Jerusalem—an interpretation that gains additional support from the fact that, so far, 'nous n'avons pas trouvé trace de diaconesses dans les documents et monuments de l'Église d'Égypte'.[82] It is clear that Severa and the women with her proposed to attempt 'a long walk over a laborious route' which would cover a great distance and expose them to all kinds of dangers, both physical and spiritual. As suggested by the context of all four letters, Severa and her companions intended to visit the famous Fathers of the desert, Evagrius in particular.

While praising Severa's intentions, namely to gain greater insight into the ascetic practices of the Fathers, Evagrius clearly disapproves of the method by which she and her companions wish to achieve this aim: 'reliving' the desert-life in person, via *mimēsis*, albeit for a limited period of time. In trying to dissuade Severa, more precisely by instructing Rufinus and Melania to prevent any such journeys, Evagrius argues a fine line. On the one hand, the motive, in effect a pilgrimage to the desert, is laudable and pious; on the other hand, practical considerations speak against such a journey. The route is long and fraught with

---

[82] Bunge, *Briefe*, 179 f., 232; Guillaumont, 'Evagrius Ponticus', 565; Martimort, *Les Diaconesses*, 73–93 (quotation, 73); for allusions to an office like that of the deaconess in Egypt cf. Clem. Alex, *Paed.* 3. 12. 97. 2 (GCS 12. 289); id. *Strom.* 3. 6. 53. 3–4 (GCS 52 (15, 220); Orig. *De Orat. 28. 4* (ed. P. Koetschau (GCS 3; Berlin, 1899) 377); id. *Hom. in Luc.* 17. 10 (ed. M. Rauer (GCS 49; Berlin, 1959²) 110); *Can. Hipp.* 9 and 19 (Coquin, *Les Canons*, 363, 379). The question of the existence of deaconesses in Egypt remains worth investigating; a late 4th-cent. Cilician inscription (*MAMA* vii. no. 186, near Hadrianopolis), commemorating a 'deaconess Severa' has some curiosity value; Mentzu-Meimare, 'Η Παρουσία, 433–43.

dangers, most notably the danger of 'drinking from the waters of Gihon',[83] that is of defiling oneself with all the evils of this world.

However, beyond simply pointing to the unavoidable hazards of travel, Evagrius seems to have something else in mind. In Letter 8 in particular, he exhorts the addressee to prevent her 'sisters and sons' who have 'renounced the world'—clearly they are virgins and monks—from περιαγομένη, 'roaming about' and 'travelling through deserted lands'. Female ascetics especially are exposed to extreme dangers if they 'roam about and meet myriads of people'. Evagrius' language need not only suggest a pilgrimage (i.e. an extended visit to either the desert or Jerusalem); his use of terms such as 'roaming about' implies a different practice, to be condemned even more forcefully.[84]

In two other works Evagrius (not an author known for the simplicity and clarity of his writings) refers more explicitly to the phenomenon he has in mind. In a small collection of precepts for the correct ascetic life—intended likewise for Melania's ascetic community and copied once more for the same deaconess Severa—he warns virgins against the words of 'wandering old women', (γραῶν φεῦγε κυκλευουσῶν). In a parallel text intended for monks, he counsels the recipients to flee wandering monks (κυκλευταὶ μοναχοί), a warning reiterated in various versions

---

[83] The 'Gihon', one of the rivers of paradise (see Gen 2: 13), 'flows through Egypt, and means "that which wells up from the opposite world", and by Greeks is called Nile' Jos. *Antiqu.* I. 39; A. v. d. Born, 'Gehon' and 'Gihon', in *Dictionnaire Étymologique de la Bible* (Tournhout–Paris, 1960), 726, 740; here not the 'Gihon' which is one of Jerusalem's water-sources; cf. also Epiphanius' commentary on Genesis 2, the story of Eden, intended as a rebuttal of Origen's allegorical method of biblical exegesis: 'I have seen the waters of Γηών with my own eyes and have drunk real water from the Euphrates'; Epiph. *Ep. ad Johannem Episcopum* = Jer. *Ep.* 51. 5 (CSEL 54. 404); W. Schneemelcher, 'Epiphanius v. Salamis', in *RAC* v. 909–27, esp. 924f. Egypt in its turn represents slavery, oppression, wealth, corruption, and false idols—in short, all the sins of the world; accordingly, its waters must never be drunk by the faithful. Cf. e.g. Isaiah's prophecy at 19: 1–15; also Exod. 1–2; Jer. 2: 18; 24: 8; Josh. 30; 36: 6; Hos. 2: 16; 7: 12; Zech. 14: 18–19; Acts 7; Heb. 11: 23–7.

[84] Pilgrimage is usually expressed by words like ἀποδεμεῖν together with a specific destination or purpose, e.g. 'to Jerusalem', or 'in order to see, to gaze at'; Eus. *HE* 6. 11. 1–2; Gr. Nyss. *Ep.* 2 (*GN* viii.2, 11); J. Chrys. *Hom.* 8. 2 *in Ep. ad Eph.* (PG 62. 57); Kötting, *Peregrinatio Religiosa*, 7–11; Wilkinson, *Jerusalem Pilgrims*, 40 f.

throughout the *Apophthegmata*.[85] Some women as well as some men interpreted ascetic life as a permanent *xeniteia*, as a life of constant wandering. Evagrius thus seems to support Syncletica's warnings, which were also meant to dissuade virgins and monks from such practices.

As Evagrius' letters have already highlighted, the difference between an extended pilgrimage, ascetic life as a perpetual migration, and the spiritual concept of asceticism as internal exile from the values of this world is a fine one—a potential dilemma expressed again most succinctly by a Desert Father: 'should I wander in the deserts, or should I go to a foreign land where no one knows me, or should I shut myself up in a cell without opening the door to anyone, eating only every second day?'[86] Actual pilgrimage resulted in long periods of instability, and while there may have been an intention to return to settled life, this might often have been lost *en route*.

Further, all types of wandering, actual and spiritual, arose from the same theoretical concept: perfection as a long journey towards the divine, towards the heavenly Jerusalem. The challenge lay thus in the encouragement of the internal journey performed by the ascetic who led a stable life within the confines of his or her cell, while a literal interpretation of the pilgrimage had to be discouraged: strongly so in its perpetual form, less so in its temporary variation. To quote Gregory of Nyssa: 'Beloved, tell the brothers the following: they should leave their body behind and go to the Lord, not from Cappadocia to Palestine.'[87] However, as the preceding discussion has shown, despite all adversities women sought to achieve ascetic perfection in the

---

[85] Evagr. Pont. *Sententiae ad Virginem*, 13; *Sententiae ad Monachos*, 81 (*Euagrius Ponticus: Nonnenspiegel und Mönchsspiegel*, ed. H. Gressmann (TU 39; Leipzig, 1913), 147, 160); cf. e.g. Ammonas 4, Isaiah 3, John Colobos 2 (Guy, 52, 100, 120); Bousset, 'Das Mönchtum', 31–9; G. Constable, 'Monachisme et pélerinage au Moyen Âge', *RH* 258 (1977), 3–27; Guillaumont, 'Le Dépaysement', 51 f.; Reitzenstein, *Historia Monachorum*, 49–52.

[86] Ammonas 4 (Guy, 52).

[87] Gr. Nyss. *Ep.* 2. 18 (*GN* viii.2, 16, ll. 18–20); B. Kötting, 'Gregor von Nyssa's Wallfahrtskritik', *SP* 8 (1962), 360–7; in Jerome's words, 'non Hierosolymis fuisse, sed Hierosolymis bene uixisse laudandum est' (*Ep.* 58 *ad Paul. Presb.* 2–4 (CSEL 54. 529–33)); Constable, 'Monachisme', 6, 15 f.; Elm, 'Perceptions of Jerusalem Pilgrimage', 220 f.; Guillaumont, 'Le Dépaysement', 34; Wilkinson, *Jerusalem Pilgrims*, 43.

xeniteia, in exile: by abandoning home and familiar surroundings to 'go and visit the holy places'; by leaving their female body behind and embarking on an internal exile in the confinement of their cell in the desert; or by wandering permanently over 'laborious routes and through deserted lands', all in search of perfection.

All three kinds of sources discussed so far, the canons, the papyri and the *Apophthegmata Patrum*, are unique to Egypt; in particular the latter two, the papyri and the *Apophthegmata*. All three represent furthermore three entirely different genres. The canons contain concepts considered normative by Church authorities; the papyri represent the opposite end of the spectrum as an entirely secular type of source without any special attempt at normativity; and the *Apophthegmata* stand somewhere in between. They are a compilation of undoubtedly normative character, yet produced by a group of people who by no means considered themselves part of the ecclesiastical hierarchy, who were in fact more often than not opposed to members of this hierarchy: the ascetics populating the 'other world' of the Egyptian desert. None of these three kinds of sources sought to address ascetic women in particular; on the contrary, at least as far as the *Apophthegmata* were concerned, women were to all intents and purposes banned from the world of their heroes, that of the Desert Fathers.

Yet, women who pursued an ascetic life are represented in all these sources, and what is more, all three sources provide us with mutually corroborating evidence. As in Asia Minor, women in Egypt pursued their ascetic life within the confines of their own home and their own family—living alone, with their natural brothers and sisters, and in pseudo-marriages—or else in community with others, whether men or women. Again, as in Asia Minor (and seemingly more frequently) women broke these confines: they, as well as men, withdrew into the desert. It was here that they became most truly 'men', but it was also here, in the most radical ways of withdrawal, that we find the greatest degree of variation and ambiguity. Ascetic women were mothers, teachers, pilgrims, transvestites, and wanderers: models of life which were certainly uncommon, and representative in fact of a progression; an increasing alienation from well-known patterns and surroundings to completely foreign ones, sought out for purely ascetic reasons. This gradual process of alienation can also be understood as spiritual progress, a spiritual progress which was, however, subject to subtle differentiations. A woman as an ascetic mother, settled within her cell, was acceptable; a woman who did the same but changed her external appearance was cause for concern; women who embarked on a pilgrimage were tolerated, women who chose perpetual *xeniteia* were clearly condemned. These differentiations in our sources can be seen as attempts to control and steer. Clearly, women (and men) on the road were even less 'controllable' by ecclesiastical authorities than those in the desert, and, living in perpetual motion, the creation of ascetic practices was solely at their own discretion, unencumbered by the demands for obedience and regularity which were the staple of 'orthodox' ascetic life.

9
Pachomius and Shenoute: The Other Classic Model

Tensions between male and female, between settled and wandering life, between members of the clergy and desert-dwellers, were not the only ones the Desert Fathers had to come to terms with. In time tensions also arose between the anchorite or semi-anchorite life *per se* and yet another organizational model, which emerged at the same time as the deserts of Lower Egypt began to be populated. This model originated in Upper Egypt, in the Thebaid, and was in principle based on the same premises as the ascetic life represented by Antony and Amoun, but it carried the aspects of hospitality, charity, and mutual dependence to their logical conclusion: Pachomian cenobitism.[1]

---

[1] Pachomian cenobitism is evidently not the focus of this discussion, and only its basic outlines will be dealt with in the following pages. Any reconstruction of the development of Pachomius' cenobitic model is complicated by the difficulties of the manuscript-tradition despite recent advances, cf. J. Goehring, 'New Frontiers in Pachomian Studies', in Pearson and Goehring, *The Roots of Egyptian Christianity*, 236–57. Most of our sources date from the middle to late 4th cent., the period of Pachomius' successors Theodore and Horsiesios. These are primarily the *Letter to Ammon* and the *Lives: Sancti Pachomii Vitae Graecae*, ed. F. Halkin (Subsidia Hagiographica 19; Brussels 1932($= G^1$); *S. Pachomii Vita Bohairice Scripta*, ed. L. T. Lefort (CSCO 89; Louvain, 1953²) ($= SBo$); *S. Pachomii Vitae Sahidice Scriptae*, ed. id. (CSCO 99–100; Louvain, 1952²), ($= S^{1-3}$); all translated into English by A. Veilleux, *Pachomian Koinonia*, i, *The Lives of Saint Pachomius and his Disciples*; for a detailed review of research concerning the priority of the various *vitae* cf. J. E. Goehring, *The Letter of Ammon and Pachomian Monasticism* (Patristische Texte und Studien 27; Berlin, 1988), 5–23. Goehring follows in essence H. Achelis' earlier assessment ('Revue: Grützmacher, *Pachomius und das älteste Klosterleben*', *Theologische Literaturzeitung* 9 (1896), 240–4 (quotation, 241)), namely that in each *Life*-tradition 'findet sich soviel Gutes und soviel Sekundäres, daß man bald der einen, bald der andern Recht geben muß'; all extant *Lives* are compilations derived from earlier, unknown versions. As a consequence, every episode needs to be examined individually. Writings deriving from Pachomius' lifetime are limited to two letters and two

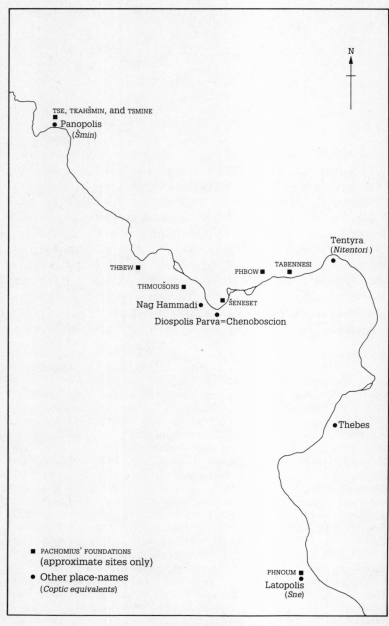

MAP 4. The Pachomian Nile

In 292 a pagan couple living in or near the town of Latopolis, in the diocese of Sne (see Map 4), celebrated the birth of a son whom they called 'Great Eagle' or Pachomius. Little is known of his childhood and adolescence before the year 312. In that year the 20-year-old Pachomius was drafted into Maximius Daia's army and sent down the Nile.[2] Though the period of service was short in this case, life was difficult for young conscripts. While stationed in Thebes they were quartered in a prison, in such squalor that they aroused the pity of some local Christians. Their rather unexpected gesture of charity and kindness made a deep impression on the young Pachomius. Discharged in 313, he made his way back up the Nile to the south until he came to 'a deserted village called Šeneset, scorched by the intensity of the heat. And he began to think about the place, in which there were not many but few inhabitants. He went down to the river, into a small temple called "the place of baking the bricks" (Pmampesterposen)', and settled there to grow vegetables and palm-trees. Before long, he was baptized.[3]

Remembering his own experience in Thebes, Pachomius began to share his food with the village's destitute and with passing strangers. Soon his kindness attracted more and more people to the point where he felt overwhelmed: 'This service of the sick in

Instructions, translated by A. Veilleux (*Pachomian Koinonia*, iii (Cistercian Studies Series 47; Kalamazoo, 1982)), though the Pachomian authorship of the *Instructions* remains debated; cf. T. Orlandi, 'Coptic Literature', in Pearson and Goehring, *The Roots of Egyptian Christianity*, 51–81, here 60f.

[2] *SBo* 3–7 / *G*[1] 2–5; Latopolis (in Coptic Sne) is the modern Isna, D. J. Chitty, 'A Note on the Chronology of Pachomian Foundations', *SP*2 (TU 64; Berlin, 1957), 379–85; H. Bacht, 'Pakhome—der grosse "Adler"', *Geist und Leben* 22 (1949), 367–82; L. T. Lefort, 'Les Premiers Monastères pachômiens: Exploration topographique', *Le Muséon* 52 (1939), 379–408; *SBo* 7 / *G*[1] 4, 5a mention erroneously Constantine and the Persians. P. Ladeuze (*Étude sur le cénobitisme Pakhômien pendant le IVe siècle* (Louvain, 1898; repr. Frankfurt, 1961)), identified the campaign as that of Maximius Daia against Licinius; cf. for the following P. Rousseau, *Pachomius: The Making of a Community in Fourth-Century Egypt* (Berkeley, 1985) 57–76.

[3] *SBo* 8 / *G*[1] 5b; the Greek name is Chenoboscion (modern Kasr-es-Sayad) in the diocese of Diospolis Parva, Coptic Hew; *SBo* 8 calls the temple Pmampiserapis, but Pmampesterposen in 51; the latter is the correct version; Pachomius was probably baptized around Easter; Veilleux, *Pachomian Koinonia*, i. 266 (n. 2 to *SBo* 3); 267 nn. 1, 2 to *SBo* 8; Lefort, 'Les Premiers Monastères', 379, 390, 397–9.

the village is no work for a monk. It is only for the clergy and the faithful old men. From this day on, I will no longer undertake it'—though in fact Pachomius remained three more years in the village, engaged in charitable work. Only then he 'sought to become a monk and to give himself up to the anchoritic life' practised already by 'all the neighbouring brothers, and . . . those on all that mountain'. Thus, in *c*.316 Pachomius became the disciple of the famous anchorite Apa Palamon, 'a great monk who had settled a little way from the village and had become a model and a father for many in his vicinity'. This entire interim stage, when Pachomius lived in the community performing the work of 'faithful old men' is omitted in the *Greek Life* (*G*¹), which only rejoins the *Bohairic Life* (*SBo*) at Palamon's initiation of the young Pachomius into the rigours of desert asceticism:[4] severe fasting on a diet of rock-hard bread, salt mixed with ashes, very little water and oil; constant and uninterrupted prayer, made possible through strenuous work and frequent vigils; strict silence; and absolute obedience to the spiritual Father.[5]

After seven years of 'apprenticeship' with Palamon, Pachomius wandered one day, as was his custom, upstream through the acacia forest from which Šeneset derives its name. After fifteen kilometres he happened upon another completely deserted village called Tabennesi. Upon entering this village, a divine apparition ordered him to found an ascetic community in this very place.[6] He obeyed and was soon joined by his elder brother John. Both lived harmoniously, if extremely rigorously, as anchorites

<hr/>

[4] *SBo* 8b, 9 / *G*¹ 6; *SBo* 10, 14; cf. Veilleux, *Pachomian Koinonia*, i. 16, 18.

[5] Cf. *SBo* 77; Veilleux, *Pachomian Koinonia*, i. 268 (n. 5 to *SBo* 10), 277 (n. 1 to *SBo* 59); H. Bacht, 'Agrypnia: Die Motive des Schlafentzugs im frühen Mönchtum', in G. Pflug, B. Eckart, and H. Friesenhahn (eds.), *Bibliothek-Buch-Geschichte: K. Köster zum 65. Geburtstag* (Frankfurt, 1977), 353–69; Heussi, *Ursprung*, 218–66; A. v. d. Mensbrugge, 'Prayer-time in Egyptian Monasticism (320–450)', *SP* 2 (TU 64; Berlin, 1957), 435–54, esp. 435–8; W. Nauck, *Salt as a Metaphor in Introductions for Discipleship* (Studia Theologica cura Ordinum Theologorum Scandinavicorum edita 6; Lund, 1953), 165–78; F. Ruppert, *Das pachomianische Mönchtum und die Anfänge klösterlichen Gehorsams* (Münsterschwarzacher Studien 20; Münsterschwarzach, 1971), 11–18.

[6] *SBo* 17 / *G*¹ 12; modern Nag'-el-Sabrīyāt; Veilleux, *Pachomian Koinonia*, i. 269 (n. 2 to *SBo* 17); Pachomius informed Palamon of his vision as soon as he had returned and both went upstream to construct a new abode. Palamon did not survive the move for long, he died the same year (*SBo* 18 / *G*¹ 3b); Lefort, 'Les Premiers Monastères', 393–7; Ruppert, *Das pachomianische Mönchtum*, 31–41.

or semi-anchorites, until, prompted by yet another vision, Pachomius enlarged the wall surrounding his own dwelling to house others.[7]

'The greatness and fame that [Pachomius] attained in later years, together with the usual *post-mortem* enhancement, are presupposed throughout the accounts' of all of Pachomius' *Vitae*.[8] Nevertheless, both *SBo* and G^1 agree in some essential aspects. Corroborating the *Life of St Antony*, the *Lives* of Pachomius attest to a widespread tradition of anchorite life, long before either Antony or Amoun took to the desert. Men had lived as ascetics in caves just on the edge of villages since the middle of the third century, and when Pachomius joined Palamon, he not only joined an established Father and teacher, but an entire and close-knit community of ascetics that had already developed a host of ascetic customs.[9] Thus Pachomius' new approach to ascetic life was again firmly rooted in tradition, and 'development beyond this stage in either a coenobitic or a semi-eremitic direction, was neither predictable nor inevitable'.[10]

According to the *Lives*, Pachomius' quest for ascetic life in common was prompted by his realization that the solitary way neglected the commandment to active charity, impressed upon him as fundamental by his own first encounter with Christianity.[11] However, the very corner-stone of desert asceticism, namely the charismatic power of its pioneers, attracted followers, who inevitably formed themselves into groups. These groups had eventually,

---

[7] *SBo* 19, 22 / G^1 14, 15, 23 / S^1 fr. iii.

[8] Goehring, *The Letter of Ammon*, 23.

[9] H. Bacht, 'Antonius und Pachomius: Von der Anachorese zum Cönobitentum', in *Antonius Magnus Eremita* (Studia Anselmiana 38; Rome, 1956), 66–107; id. 'La Loi du "retour aux sources": De quelques aspects de l'idéal monastique pachômien', *Revue Mabillon* 51 (1961), 6–27; G. M. Colombas, *El Monacato primitivo*, 2 vols. (Madrid, 1974–5), here i. 90–3; Ruppert, *Das pachomianische Mönchtum*, 84–90; Veilleux and de Vogüé, *Pachomian Koinonia*, i, pp. xv–xviii.

[10] Rousseau, *Ascetics*, 36.

[11] Ruppert, *Das pachomianische Mönchtum*, 11–18, 93–9; D. Amand de Mendieta ('Le Système cénobitique basilien comparé au système cénobitique pachômien', *RHR* 152 (1957), 31–80, here 39f.) suggests a military basis for Pachomius' organization. This has been refuted e.g. by Colombas (*El monacato primitivo*, i. 90–4) and Ruppert (op. cit. 184–8, 264–71); but cf. the study by P. Nagel, 'Diktion der römischen Kommandosprache in den Praecepta des Pachomius', *Zeitschrift für ägyptische Sprache und Altertumskunde* 101 (1974), 164–71.

despite their avowed break with society, to be organized somehow; and this raised immediately the question of the correct
organization. Should asceticism focus on the 'nourishment of
souls' in community or on the perfection of each soul 'in isolation', while in constant contact with a master? The distinction is
a fine one, and the organization of various forms of community
developed slowly in years of trial and error.[12]

Pachomius' brother John was the first to challenge his concept,
and their dispute ended in appeasement rather than a convincing
victory for Pachomius.[13] Nevertheless, Pachomius soon attracted
followers. About 324 three Fathers called Apa Psentaesi, Sourous,
and Psoi joined him, and before long the community had expanded to 100 monks. All lived in separate dwellings surrounding
that of Pachomius but shared their material needs under his
guidance. 'He gave them a rule: each man was to fend for
himself, and manage matters on his own.' This experiment, still a
far cry from Pachomius' ideal of the *koinōnia* as described in
Acts 4: 32, almost ended in failure. After five years he was
forced to expel some of the brothers.[14] Even so, the community
continued to grow, thus requiring an increasingly stringent organization, strictly based on scriptural prescriptions. Monks lived
together in several houses, each with stewards, assistants, and
specialized tasks. Officers rotated every three weeks; and set
times for prayers, meals, and work were established.[15]

---

[12] G^1 120; Rousseau (*Ascetics*, 33–55) sees a shift from the charisma of the
word to that of the example as essential for the changing nature of ascetic
practice; Ruppert, *Das pachomianische Mönchtum*, 46–51, 464–6.

[13] *SBo* 19 / G^1 14, 15 / $S^1$7; A. Levis, 'Koinonia e communidad en el monacato
pacomiano', *Claretianum* 15 (1975), 269–327, esp. 299 n. 71.

[14] S^1 1, translation by P. Rousseau, *Ascetics*, 34; *SBo* 23 / G^1 25a, 24, 25b /
S^1 10; H. Bacht, 'Vom Umgang mit der Bibel im ältesten Mönchtum', *Theologie
und Philosophie* 41 (1966), 557–66; Ruppert, *Das pachomianische Mönchtum*,
57–9, 128–58, and in general, 104–356; S. Schiwietz, 'Geschichte und Organisation der pachomianischen Klöster im vierten Jahrhundert', *Archiv für katholisches Kirchenrecht* 81 (1901), 461–90, 630–49.

[15] *SBo* 25 / G^1 29, 26b, 27; *HM* 3 (Festugière, 39 f.); Pall. *HL* 7. 18. 32 (Butler,
ii. 26, 52, 87); *Pachomiana Latina: Règle et épitres de s. Pachôme, épitre de s.
Théodore et 'Liber' de s. Orsiesius, Texte latin de s. Jérôme*, ed. A. Boon and L.
T. Lefort (Bibliothèque de la *Revue d'Histoire Ecclésiastique* 7; Louvain, 1932),
3–74; *Œuvres de S. Pachôme et de ses disciples* (Coptic edn.), ed. L. T. Lefort
(CSCO 159; Louvain, 1956), 30–6, 80; Eng. trans. by A. Veilleux, *Pachomian
Koinonia*, ii. 7–13; 141–223.

Pachomius soon founded other monasteries. First was Phbow, about five kilometres downstream (this was the headquarters from 337 onwards), and before 345 an entire second generation of foundations emerged in the region of Panopolis, near Lato-polis, and again near Diospolis Parva.[16] Before his death in 346 Pachomius had founded nine monasteries with reportedly over 3,000 inhabitants. Most Pachomian monks were Coptic speaking peasants, but several brothers clearly belonged to the Graeco-Roman élite. His new ascetic model, the *koinōnion*, had cata-pulted Pachomius to the summit of ecclesiastical fame. Many came from far away to seek his advice. One of the first was Athanasius, bishop of Alexandria, who made the journey up the river in 329.[17] In time, Pachomius' ascetic concepts transformed the shape not only of monasticism in Thebes, but—through Jerome's translations–of the entire ascetic world. Pachomius 'in-troduced a society into the Church; [while] Constantine intro-duced the Church into society.'[18]

PACHOMIAN FOUNDATIONS FOR WOMEN

In 329, around the time of Athanasius' visit, Tabennesi received another guest who arrived from the opposite direction, coming downstream from further south.[19] This visitor, 'a virgin from birth' called perhaps Maria,[20] was Pachomius' sister. It had been

[16] *SBo* 49 / *G*[1] 54a; *SBo* 54, 56, 57 / *G*[1] 80, 83; the account of the *Bohairic Life* is much more detailed; Chitty, 'Chronology', 380–5; Lefort, 'Les Premiers Monastères', 380–5.

[17] For references to non-Coptic brothers cf. *SBo* 89a and b, 90, 91 / *G*[1] 94, 95, but also the history of Pachomius' successor Theodore; B. Büchler, *Die Armut der Armen: Über den ursprünglichen Sinn der mönchischen Armut* (Munich, 1980), 9–36; for Athanasius' visit, *SBo* 28 / *G*[1] 30, and below pp. 362–63.

[18] De Vogüé in Veilleux and de Vogüé, *Pachomian Koinonia*, i, p. xxi; Pall. *HL* 7 (Butler, ii. 26); Cass. *De coen. inst.* 4. 1 (SC 109. 123); Soz. *HE* 3. 14 (GCS 50. 119–21); H. Bacht, 'L'Importance de l'idéal monastique de s. Pacôme pour l'histoire du monachisme chrétien', *RAM* 26 (1950), 308–26; Colombas, *El monacato primitivo*, i. 97; H. v. Cranenburgh, 'Confrontation entre les règles et la littérature pachômienne posterieure', *Vie Spirituelle*, Suppl. 86 (1968), 394–424; C. de Clerq, 'L'Influence de la Règle de saint Pacôme en Occident', in *Mélanges d'Histoire du Moyen Âge dediés à la mémoire de L. Halphen* (Paris, 1951), 169–76.

[19] According to *SBo* 27 this took place shortly before Athanasius' visit, and according to *G*[1] 32 shortly afterwards.

[20] According to *SBo* 27; not in *G*[1] 32.

more than fifteen years since Pachomius had last seen any of his relatives or his home. But, when he learnt of his sister's arrival and her wish to see him, he did not go to the door himself. Instead, he sent the doorkeeper to tell her: 'Do not be distressed . . . because you have not seen me. But if you wish to share in this holy life so that you may find mercy before God, examine yourself on every point. The brothers will build a place for you to retire to. And doubtless, for your sake the Lord will call others to you. . . .' Maria's self-examination proved successful. Brothers were sent 'to build a monastery for her in that village, a short distance from his own monastery. . . .'

After she had passed a brief period of solitary life, other women joined Maria. As soon as Pachomius learned that 'they grew in number little by little', 'he appointed an old man called Apa Peter, whose "speech was seasoned with salt", to be their father and to preach frequently to them on the Scriptures for their souls' salvation. [Pachomius] also wrote down in a book the rules of the brothers and sent them to them through [Peter], so that they might learn them.'[21] Eventually, other selected brothers were dispatched to the women's community to perform necessary labours. Maria became the monastery's mother and elder.

Nothing could be more natural and straightforward than the foundation of this female branch, at least according to the rendering given by the two *Lives*. Pachomius has a sister, who comes to visit her long-lost brother. This sister fulfils all preconditions for ascetic life, in particular that of virginity. Pachomius therefore suggests that she follow in his footsteps and she concurs. A monastery is built for her, guided by the brother's confidant and governed according to the same regulations as his own community. Indeed, we are given the impression that Pachomius was prompted to write down the regulations governing his own community precisely because of the need to transfer them to the new female foundation. This 'book [of] the rules of the brothers' intended for the women may well have been the nucleus of the ever expanding and developing corpus of regulations now known as the *Praecepta*: the *Praecepta ac Instituta*, the *Praecepta at Leges*, and the *Praecepta atque Judicia*.[22]

---

[21] *SBo* 27 / *G*[1] 32.

[22] *SBo* 23 / *G*[1] 25 / *S*[1] 17 refer to rules based on the Scriptures, which Pachomius gave to his first followers. This does not conflict with the impression

However the original female community may have been founded, there can be little doubt that it represented a perfect solution to several common problems. First, it offered the benefits of the Pachomian system to a sizeable proportion of the population, namely women. Further, it addressed a dilemma faced by virtually every ascetic: like Antony before him and Basil several decades later, Pachomius and most of his followers had a family. But unlike Antony, who gave his sisters to 'pious virgins' and thus freed himself of all responsibility, Pachomius expanded his original concept to include his sister. In so doing, he created an ideal way in which two seemingly contradictory demands of an ascetic's life could be combined: the ascetic, like Pachomius himself, could completely sever all ties with his family without having to relinquish all responsibilities towards it—and the weight and the extent of those responsibilities upon the individual cannot be overestimated.[23]

The foundation of a female monastery was again in essence the organizational transformation of a natural condition. Pachomius' foundation, like Basil's, was a family affair. Very often, conversion of one family member to the ascetic life initiated a chain reaction: other relatives eventually followed suit—Pachomius' first, albeit reluctant, follower was his brother John.[24] Like Basil,

that the women's arrival on the scene necessitated the fixing of these regulations in writing; Veilleux and de Vogüé, *Pachomian Koinonia*, ii. 7. These writings were probably from the outset devised in four different versions: one for the superior of the entire complex, one for the house-masters and stewards, one covering communal activities such as the *synaxis*, and one regulating punishments. The first versions of these regulations—as mentioned at n. 1 above, probably only two *Instructions* are of Pachomian origin—were altered and expanded over the years, and thus reflect later developments. However, it was the later rules which truly influenced the future of monasticism; Büchler, *Die Armut*, 14; Chitty, 'Chronology', 380; Lefort, 'Les Premiers Monastères', 387–93; and in particular Orlandi, 'Coptic Literature', 60–4; I have not been able to consult Orlandi's *Pachomiana Coptica* (in press).

[23] Cf. the excellent chapter on 'The Body and the City' in P. R. L. Brown's *The Body and Society*, 5–32.

[24] Drastic attempts to sever all family ties, demonstrated in Pachomius' reaction to Maria's visit and repeated by his disciple Theodore's reaction to a visit by his mother and younger brother (*SBo* 37), resulted frequently in a conversion of family members to monastic life; Borias, 'Le Moine et sa famille', 85–7, 94–9, 216 f.; I. Hausherr, *Études de spiritualité orientale* (Rome, 1969), 334–41; P. Rousseau, 'Blood-relationships among Early Eastern Ascetics', *JThS* NS 23 (1972), 135–44; 25 (1974), 113–17.

Naucratius, Emmelia, and Macrina, who all experimented with different organizational solutions, Pachomius also went through several experimental phases in the creation of his institutional structure. This structure was a transformed version of his own natural family and offered an immediate solution to all his followers who found themselves in a similar position.[25] Here, as in the original family, the ascetics' sisters, mothers, wives, and daughters were provided and cared for, and supervised by brothers who replaced the original *paterfamilias*, while at the same time all natural family ties were effectively severed. The rules and regulations are a precise reflection of this process. As in the later case of Basil's *Ascetica*, Pachomius' regulations evolved out of and were intended for the male community and its branches. They were then simply handed on to the sisters, implying that the female community differed little from other male branches. The sole exceptions are the few passages which address specific concerns arising out of the contact between both communities.

For a brief period Pachomius' sister and her emerging community lived the ascetic life without the benefit of her brother's teachings. But as soon as the community increased, Pachomius ensured the correct implementation of his rule through Apa Peter. Peter's function did not remain limited to Maria's community. He also supervised Pachomius' second foundation for women near Tsmine. Whether or not this foundation had a female superior as well remains, interestingly, unknown. Upon Peter's death, his office was divided: Apa Titoue succeeded him at Tabennesi and Apa Eponyches took over responsibility at Tsmine.[26]

What precisely was the function of Peter and his successors, in

---

[25] The parallels between Pachomius and Basil do not end there; both had less successful brothers, John and Naucratius, who are portrayed as embodying the ideal of *anachōrēsis*, while Pachomius and Basil themselves promoted the community ideal; and both had sisters, Maria and Macrina, who guided female communities closely linked to their brothers' foundations.

[26] G^1 79, 123; G^1 134 mentions the second foundation in passing, but it does not appear in *SBo*, and its location is disputed; cf. Bartelink, n. 1 to *HL* 33 (p. 362); Chitty, 'Chronology', 383; Colombas, *El monacato primitivo*, i. 104; Lefort, 'Les Premiers Monastères', 403 f. Titoue is listed as a prominent father in G^1 79 and *SBo* 94 and as a great brother in G^1 123; he was still alive under Horsiesius; the fact that he is in charge of the first female foundation suggests its size and importance. Eponychos does not reappear as far as I noticed; Veilleux, *Pachomian Koinonia*, i. 272 (no. 6 to *SBo* 27).

particular in relation to both Pachomius and his sister Maria, the 'mother and worthy elder' of the female community? The title 'elder' is clearly honorific, reflecting the position and spiritual advancement of its bearer. In its Coptic form, 'chello', the title is even more significant. Even if applied to a woman, it is primarily male in its connotations, thus suggesting an 'elder brother' rather than a sister: a fact reminiscent of Amma Sarah, Theodora, and the 'Father' of Bessarion.[27] Yet, despite Maria's own spiritual potential and the presence of written rules, her community was controlled by a father as adviser and supervisor.

Prima facie the reasons for Peter's presence were largely practical. Both the male and the female communities followed the same organizational principles.[28] Therefore the sections within the *Praecepta* that deal explicitly with sisters respond only to very specific points: for example, could relatives living as members of the respective communities visit each other?[29] Seeing that *de facto* the severance of family ties prescribed in Luke 14: 26–7 could only be observed up to a point, one of Apa Peter's and his successors' obligations was to co-ordinate visits between brothers and 'a mother, sister, or daughter, some relatives or cousins, or the mother of [their] own children'. These visits were permitted for 'any clear reason, and if some paternal inheritance is due to them from the time before the renunciation of the world and their entry into the monastery'. Given these preconditions, it was Apa Peter's task to make known the request to the respective superior, whose prerogative it then was to grant permission. Only after everything had been approved on the male side, did Peter send word to the mother who then 'released' the 'requested'

---

[27] Above, pp. 262–7. 'Elder' is an addition of *SBo* 27; 'chello' or 'hello' is usually translated as 'old man' (sometimes 'woman' according to prefix and dialect), developed perhaps parallel to the topos *puer senex*; Gr. Naz. *Or.* 43 (PG 36; 526); Cyr. Scyth. *V. Sabae* 11 (ed. E. Schwartz (TU 49; Leipzig, 1939) 94); Bartelink, *La Storia Lausiaca*, 332 (n. 12 to *HL* 17); W. C. Crum, *A Coptic Dictionary* (Oxford, 1939), s.v. 'chello'; E. R. Curtius, *Europäische Literatur und lateinisches Mittelalter* (Bern–Munich, 1961³), 108–11; Festugière, 'Lieux communs', 137–9; Lefort, *Vita Bohairice* (CSCO 89), 27 l. 10; Veilleux, *Pachomian Koinonia*, i. 272 (n. 3 to *SBo* 27); W. Westendorf, *Koptisches Handwörterbuch* 5 (Heidelberg, 1974), 366.

[28] Colombas, *El monacato primitivo*, i. 99–115; Ruppert, *Das pachomianische Mönchtum*, 104–356; Schiwietz, 'Geschichte und Organisation', 226–33, 454–75.

[29] *Pr.* 143 (Veilleux, *Pachomian Koinonia*, ii. 166–7).

sister. Both Peter and the 'mother' were present throughout the entire visit to prevent the discussion of worldly matters.[30]

Another prescription concerned the burial of a sister—another occasion for brothers and sisters to come into close contact. When a sister died she was laid out in the oratory, presumably that of the female community, and the mother covered her with a shroud. Then Peter sent word to Pachomius, who selected chosen brothers to carry the bier to the mountain. 'The virgin sisters followed behind the bier while their father walked after them and their mother before them.'[31]

Although Peter acted as go-between for Pachomius and the head of the female community, nevertheless his functions extended somewhat further, as indicated by the fact that he supervised the implementation of the rules and was actively involved in arranging all contacts between male and female members. The most important and frequent occasion for those contacts, however, was the economic relation between the communities, which also mirrored that of a natural family. The sisters were responsible for the production of textiles and garments for all Pachomian communities, male as well as female.[32] The raw materials, such as flax, were provided by the male communities, and Apa Eponyches (and presumably Apa Peter before him) organized the transfer of these goods between the male and female communities. By the time Pachomius' successor Theodore had founded a third female community, the sisters seem to have produced a surplus. It is possible that they may have attempted to sell that surplus themselves, since *Praeceptum* 119 prohibits the presence of 'weaker vessels' on board ships owned by the

---

[30] Borias, 'Le Moine et sa famille', 97–9.

[31] *SBo* 27 / G^1 32; *Pr.* 127–8 (Veilleux, *Pachomian Koinonia*, ii. 164); E. Revillout, *Funérailles des moines égyptiens au temps de saint Antoine et de saint Pacôme*, *Bulletin Académie Delphinale*, 2nd ser. (1856–60), 374–86; Rush, *Death and Burial*, 91–133, 196–208.

[32] G^1 134; the mention of wool is a later addition, Veilleux, *Pachomian Koinonia*, i. 421 (n. 2 to G^1 134). The account of the sisters' economic activities is nicely corroborated by G^3 44: a sister went outside the monastery to relieve herself and was asked by a passing tailor whether the sisters needed his help; she said: 'we have our own tailors.' The encounter is quite likely as, according to Lefort ('Les Premiers Monastères', 395 f.), the Roman road passed close by the monastery.

community.[33] In return for the sisters' work, the brothers supplied all other material needs and the sisters depended on them for everything from assistance in manual work to the provision of food. Several select brothers known for their intergrity were entrusted with these responsibilities within the female communities. They had to return daily to their own community before the evening meal; in other words they did not live permanently with the sisters. Nothing, however, is said concerning the living arrangements for Apa Peter and his successors; they most probably lived in the female community.[34]

The account of the foundation of the women's community given by the *Lives* as well as the information gathered from the *Praecepta* offer very few insights into the actual relationship between Pachomius, the 'mother' of the female community, and the supervising father. Peter and his successors were responsible for various practical concerns. Beyond that, however, it appears that they held a position similar to those who had been chosen by Pachomius as 'his assistants to take care of the brothers' souls', the role of a spiritual adviser in other words. If so, then this function—most often held by a member of the clergy—was entrusted to a member of the Pachomian community, without clerical affiliation.[35]

The picture as presented reveals an organizational model based on clear-cut principles: Pachomius and his main monastery were at the centre of the entire system, much as the *paterfamilias* was at the centre of his household. It was here that the decisions were ultimately made. Like the subsequent male foundations, the women enjoyed only a relative independence; indeed, their link to the male community was even closer than that between subsequent male foundations and the 'Great Monastery'. While probably in charge of the day-to-day affairs within her com-

---

[33] The context of *Pr.* 119 suggests that monks were forbidden to take ordinary women on board their ships. For the expansion of the communities' wealth and business activities cf. in particular Büchler, *Die Armut*, 23–6. This third community was located in the village of Bechne near Hermonthis, Veilleux, *Pachomian Koinonia*, i. 421 (n. 1 to G^1 134); Colombas, *El monacato primitivo*, i. 109 f.; Heussi, *Ursprung*, 126 f.

[34] G^1 32.

[35] G^1 27.

munity, the mother was subjected to the supervisor's control in all dealings between brothers and sisters, as well as in all spiritual matters. Most importantly, the subdivision of labour led to a virtually complete economic dependence of the sisters upon the brothers, with the sole exception of textile products. Interestingly, 'mothers' of the two subsequent female foundations are nowhere mentioned.[36]

Seen in this light, the story of the foundation of Maria's community takes on a very definite symbolic character: it anticipates precisely the future developments. Consequently, our distinctly hagiographic sources contain no indication of potential tensions between the mother and the supervising father.[37] We do not possess a separate account, no *Life of St Maria*, to offer a different perspective on the female branches of the Pachomian *koinōnia*.[38] The situation is quite different, however, in the case of yet another monastic system that emerged only shortly after that of Pachomius.

SHENOUTE OF ATRIPE

Pachomius' immense impact on later generations was not quite matched by his influence on his contemporaries, especially since

[36] It is worth noting that the female foundations appear to have been located further inside the actual villages than their male counterparts.

[37] Goehring, 'New Frontiers in Pachomian Studies', 244–6; within this context it is worth pointing out that 'Maria' and 'John', like Pachomius himself children of pagan parents, have Jewish-Christian names, whereas Pachomius' own name is pagan. In general, the change to genuinely Christian names took time; they were certainly not widely used before the middle of the 4th cent.; Bagnall and Sijpesteijn, 'Currency in the Fourth Century', 121; R. S. Bagnall, 'Religious Conversion and Onomastic Change in Early Byzantine Egypt', *Bulletin of the American Society of Papyrologists* 18 (1982), 105–24, here 107–12.

[38] The only possible discrepancy could be provided by S^1 24's mention of Pachomius' nephew, who had to be expelled from the monastery because of misconduct. Of course, Pachomius might well have had more than one sister, but this nephew could have been Maria's son, in which case she was not a 'virgin from birth', a characterization significantly omitted by G^1 32; according to Lefort, S^1 is the most primitive of the Sahidic fragments and indeed one of the earliest extant *Lives*; cf. Goehring, *The Letter of Ammon*, 13–22; Rousseau, *Pachomius*, 37–55; Veilleux, *Pachomian Koinonia*, i. 1–6, 8–12, 18; id. *La Liturgie dans le cénobitisme pachômien au quatrième siècle*' (Studia Anselmiana 57; Rome, 1968), 1–159.

the charisma of the founder lost much of its lustre under his successors.[39] Neither was Pachomius' system of *koinōnia* immediately accepted by everyone. Around the middle of the fourth century two anchorites, Apa Pgol and Apa Pschai, were living in the desert near Smin.[40] Pgol and Pschai soon transformed their cells into monastic communities. Pschai founded his community, called the Red Monastery, on the mountain Psou near modern Sohāg, and Pgol's foundation was located about an hour further south in the Theban desert, just outside the ruined village of Atripe. Because of the colour of its walls it became known as the White Monastery. Both monasteries grew in an area which already housed four Pachomian *koinōnia*, three for men and one for women. Although we know very little of Pschai's foundation, we have a somewhat clearer picture of Pgol's, thanks to the fact that he also furnished his community with rules, which were decidedly non-Pachomian and had their own marked characteristics.[41]

One of these characteristics was a heightened austerity. Pgol's and Pschai's communities were situated in the desert itself, not in a deserted village like Tabennesi. Pgol never abandoned his

---

[39] Büchler, *Die Armut*, 9–110.

[40] *SBo* 52, 54 / *G*[1] 83, 81a; *Œuvres de Shenoudi*, ed. E. C. Amélineau (Paris, 1907–14); *Sinuthii Archimandritae Vita et Opera Omnia*, ed. J. Leipoldt and W. C. Crum (CSCO 41, 42, 73 (Script. Coptici 1, 2, 5); Paris, 1908, 1913); Lat. trans. H. Wiesmann (CSCO 96, 108, 129 (Script. Coptici 8, 12, 16); Paris, 1931, 1936; Louvain, 1951), here CSCO 96. 55, 145; *Besa: The Life of Shenoute* (= *VShen*), trans. D. Bell (Cistercian Studies Series 73; Kalamazoo, 1983); *Letters and Sermons of Besa*, ed. K. H. Kuhn (CSCO 157, 158; Louvain, 1956); J. Barns, 'Shenoute as an Historical Source', in *Actes du Xème Congrès International des Papyrologes* (Warsaw, 1964), 151–9; Chitty, 'Chronology', 383 f.; J. Leipoldt, *Schenute von Atripe und die Entstehung des national ägyptischen Christentums* (TU 25, NF 10; Leipzig, 1903), 36–8; Orlandi, 'Coptic Literature', 64–70; J. Timbie, 'The State of Research on the Career of Shenoute of Atripe', in Pearson and Goehring, *The Roots of Egyptian Christianity*, 258–70. As pointed out by most modern scholars, in particular in Timbie's article, any study of Shenoute's historical standing and circumstances is hampered by the absence of a comprehensive critical edition of his works. Therefore, despite their evident flaws, Leipoldt's and Amélineau's works remain fundamental for the following.

[41] Today the monasteries are called Dēr el-ahmar and Dēr el-abiad. Leipoldt (*Schenute*, 36–9 n. 3, 194 f.) assumed that Pschai's monastery isolated itself by its adherence to the language of its surroundings, Ahmimic, while the language of the developing monastic culture was Sahidic; Bell, *The Life of Shenoute*, 2; Colombas, *El monacato primitivo*, i. 115–18.

anchorite roots, and this fact in turn influenced his ascetic regulations. Even as superior of his community, he continued to retreat into the desert for long periods at a time; indeed, his 'rule' consisted mainly of letters written to his monks during those retreats. Not surprisingly, the ascetic routine in Pgol's community was much harsher than in the Pachomian *koinōnia*, which was perhaps the reason why he (and Pschai) did not attract many followers; Pgol's foundation amounted to around thirty monks just before his death. However, those who came included women. Already during Pgol's lifetime a female community had grown up next to his own at Atripe.[42]

Neither Pgol nor Pschai would ever have entered 'history', that is, our sources, had they not shared the fortune of Pachomius' mentor, Apa Palamon. They found a disciple who was not only to succeed but to far surpass them: Pgol's nephew Shenoute or 'Son of God'. Born in the nearby town of Shandawīl (the date of his birth is unknown), Shenoute had entered Pgol's monastery as a young boy. About 383/5, at roughly the age of 30, he suceeded Pgol as the superior of the White Monastery, and during the next eighty years or so, until his death in 466, he transformed Pgol's foundation into one of the largest and most influential monasteries in Egypt.[43]

Yet Shenoute's name never once appears in any Greek source, despite the fact that, in apparent contrast to Pachomius, he sought to incorporate all the 'international' Greek Christian literary genres into his own Coptic *opus*—an *opus* which reveals careful study of the stylistic elements of the 'second sophistic'. Indeed, Shenoute's impact on the creation of a Coptic literature is rivalled only by his importance for the development of Coptic monasticism: whether he was aware of it or not, Shenoute was one of the founders of monophysite monasticism and the fore-

---

[42] Besa, *Sinuthii Vita Bohairice*, 3–9 (CSCO 129. 2–4). Several of Pgol's followers continued the anchorite life and only visited the monastery four times a year. Apparently, Pgol's contemporaries and immediate followers were quite aware of the differences between his and Pachomius' rules and found it necessary to defend Pgol's 'deviations'; Leipoldt, *Schenute*, 38 nn. 2, 3, 100f.

[43] Besa, *VShen* 3–10 (CSCO 129. 1–4); Leipoldt, *Schenute*, 39–45; 188–91. Most modern scholars follow J. Bethune-Baker ('The Date of the Death of Nestorius: Schenute, Zacharias, Evagrius', *JThS* 9 (1908), 601–5) in dating Shenoute's death to 466.

most representative of Coptic Christianity during its 'struggle against the Hellenized, pagan element in the area'. At least as far as Coptic Christianity is concerned, there can be little doubt that Shenoute's importance, in clear contrast to his 'international' fate, far surpassed that of Pachomius.[44]

Under Shenoute's leadership the White Monastery became the monastic centre of the region with thousands of inhabitants. Though numbers given by ancient authors always have to be taken with a grain of salt, the figures of 2,200 monks and 1,800 nuns seem to be quite plausible.[45] Indeed, the term 'monastery' is somewhat misleading. We are actually confronted with a monastic compound, which extended from 'the brook north of Atripe north up to the brook south of Pschai's house . . . in the desert, in which he initially lived', an area covering at least ten square kilometres. The landholdings of the White Monastery were sufficient to permit not only intensive farming, but also to house several smaller daughter communities described by Shenoute as συναγωγαί. The larger of these συναγωγαί were situated in 'the village' south of the main monastery; other, smaller communities were located further north.[46]

The precise arrangement of the ascetics' living accommodation in these *synagōgai* gives rise to some uncertainties. What does Shenoute imply by 'village'? According to Leipoldt, he means just that: an ordinary village within the monastic compound, inhabited by lay-persons. Beyond doubt, the 'village' to the south housed the main community of the women. Several male ascetics are also mentioned as having lived there, but it is unclear whether, on a smaller scale, the same arrangement was true for the so-called 'community in the north'. Two aspects concerning the female monasteries are immediately worth noting: they were

[44] In particular since the latter's foundations began to suffer under incompetent leadership after Horsiesius' death; most later superiors remain anonymous. However, Leipoldt's assessment ('Schenute hat ferner als der Erste eine national ägyptische Auffassung des Christentums geprägt', *Schenute*, 188) requires modification in the light of recent studies which have revealed the plurality of Egyptian currents and attitudes; Barns, 'Shenoute as a Historical Source', 151–9; Orlandi, 'Coptic Literature', 64, 69; Timbie, 'Dualism and the Concept of Orthodoxy', 42–5; ead. 'The State of Research', 258–70.

[45] Arabic version of Besa's *VShen*; Leipoldt, *Schenute*, 93 f.

[46] Shen. 74 *De vita mon.* 21 (CSCO 108. 72); approx. 50 square km. if it extended east towards the Nile; Leipoldt, *Schenute*, 95–7.

located within 'villages' and a certain number of 'elder brothers' lived permanently with the nuns.[47]

Whatever their precise arrangement, all daughter communities or *synagōgai* were entirely dependent upon the White Monastery. They all followed the same rule and were subject to Shenoute's authority to an even greater degree than the Pachomian foundations were to that of Pachomius. One reason behind this strict centralization was the desire to ensure equal treatment of all ascetics, whether in the main monastery or in a smaller one, whether male or female. This concept was reinforced by the economic structure of the *synagōgai*: the food for all inmates was prepared in the main monastery, all received the same garments, and all other necessities were also provided centrally. To strengthen and enhance their sense of community, all inhabitants of the monastic complex came together at a quarterly meeting.[48]

The relationship between the male and female communities within Shenoute's foundation differed quite markedly from that within the Pachomian community: at the time Shenoute took over, a female community was already in existence, and although we have no precise information, it appears likely that women had joined Pgol at a very early stage of his own communal endeavours.[49] Hence, Shenoute's rules and 'canons' were not originally conceived for a male community only and then simply passed on to a later female addition. They were from the beginning conceived for and addressed to *men and women* alike, 'sive mas sive femina'. We further possess a fairly large corpus of letters addressed to nuns, written not only by Shenoute but also

[47] Shenoute's language is not always as precise as we would like. The location of the female community in the village was partially decided by security concerns: around 400 the banks of the Nile were subjected to recurrent attacks of Bedouins (Blemys) or Ethiopians. In case of danger a monastery within a village also inhabited by others was far safer than one at the edge of it or actually in the desert; Shen. *Ep.* 7 *ad Tachom* (CSCO 96. 7); Besa, *VShen* 89, 107–8 (CSCO 129. 24, 29f.); Shen. *Epp.* 20, 21 *de Aethiop. invas.* (CSCO 96. 37–41); G. Fiaccadori, 'Teofilo Indiano', *Studi Classici e Orientali* 33 (1983), 295–331, no. 34 (1984), 271–308, here no. 34, 289–92; Ladeuze, 'Étude sur le cénobitisme', 211; Leipoldt, *Schenute*, 92, 97; H. Sethe, 'Blemyes', in *RE* iii. 566–8.

[48] Shen. 74 *De vita mon.* 21 (CSCO 108. 72); according to Leipoldt (Schenute, 37 n. 8, 97 n. 2, 116f.) these meetings did not include the sisters.

[49] Thus, we know for example of an entire family which joined Pgol's foundation, Leipoldt, *Schenute*, 37 n. 8.

by his successor Besa. Thus our insights into the relationship between the male and female communities are much more comprehensive than in the case of Pachomius.[50]

No one—men, women, and possibly even children—was admitted to the community without having passed a period of probation, which lasted for two to three months. During this period the novices had to stay at the 'gate-houses of the community of the Lord', and it was here that their true intentions and capacities were tested. Having successfully completed this period of trial, the novices had to fulfil two further requirements to be formally admitted: to renounce all possessions and to swear a solemn oath, the διαθήκη, in front of the altar, declaring their willingness to abide completely by the rules of the monastery, to keep their bodies pure, and to refrain from stealing, lying, and committing perjury.[51]

Renunciation of all property seems to have developed into a point of contention. Shenoute demanded a written, legally binding document, which could be used in all potential cases of dispute, but the recipient of the renounced property was never specified. The monastery demanded nothing but accepted donations that were irrecoverable. Those who left the monastery did so in disgrace and could not reclaim their former possessions. Once inside, all property was strictly owned in common: one of Besa's sharpest letters, to the nun Aphthonia, was prompted by her acceptance of a gift from her parents.[52]

Life within Shenoute's communities followed an order which

[50] For Besa cf. also K. H. Kuhn, 'A Fifth-century Abbot', *JThS* 5 (1954), 36–48 (1: 'Besa and His Background'), 174–87 (2: 'Monastic Life in Besa's Day'), no. 6 (1955), 35–48 (3: 'Besa's Christianity').

[51] For the noviciate cf. Leipoldt, *Schenute*, 112 f.; Kuhn, 'A Fifth-century Abbot, 2', 180; the text of the διαθήκη or covenant is translated by Leipoldt, *Schenute*, 109 and 195 f.; cf. Lampe s.v. διαθήκη. Leipoldt (op. cit. 106–13) assumes that both vow and noviciate were Shenoute's innovations. Interestingly, in the text of the vow there is little direct emphasis on continence; indeed, Shenoute mentions the term *parthenia* (virginity) only twice in his entire writings, cf. also T. Orlandi, 'Giustificazioni del'encratismo nei testi monastici copti del IV–V secolo', in Bianchi, *La tradizione dell'enkrateia*, 341–68.

[52] Under Besa the monastery became the sole recipient of all renounced property and in turn allocated some of the funds to charity; Besa, fr. 31 *On those who have renounced their constancy* (CSCO 158. 101); id. fr. 13 *To Aphthonia* (ibid. 36–8).

was often more rigorous even than that in Pachomius' *koinōnia*. All monks and nuns shared a cell with another, so that no-one was ever unobserved—the Pachomian arrangement, by contrast, provided each brother and sister with their own cell. However, Shenoute's brothers were allowed to sleep on a bed, while Pachomius' monks had to sleep on chairs; and Shenoute did not require nightly vigils. There was only one meal a day, consisting of bread, water, and occasionally vegetables— apparently this meagre fare was still too much for some women in the female communities, whom Shenoute exhorts to eat regularly. Seclusion was severe; even though we know that many who joined the monastery had relatives, no visits by members of the opposite sex were permitted.[53] Similar severity can be detected in prescriptions dealing with conduct among the sisters and brothers themselves. Everything that involved bodily contact, even oiling and bathing the sick, had to be performed under the suspicious eyes of the superior and between ten and thirty elders.[54] Any transgression was punished severely: by beatings, by downgrading the sinner to the level of a novice, and ultimately by expulsion, a threat which seemed to have been particularly effective.[55]

The female community followed the same organizational principles as the male ones. It was guided by a 'mater et anus' or 'mother and elder (chello)', who was, in turn, assisted by a 'second' and a committee of elder sisters. The leader of the smaller community to the north seems to have been subordinate to the mother of the main community, whose responsibility it was to supervise the smaller one through regular visits.[56] Like those in Pachomius' *koinōnia*, the sisters' principal duty was the manufacture of textiles. As already mentioned, several brothers lived permanently within the female community and assisted them in

[53] Shen. 60, 71, 74 *De vita mon.* 7, 18, 21 (CSCO 108. 36–8, 63–4, 71); for the sleeping arrangements see Leipoldt, *Schenute*, 98 n. 1; for nightly vigils etc. see ibid. 128, 131, 145 f.; special burial arrangements are again made for sisters (CSCO 108. 37), conforming largely to those of Pachomius (Leipoldt, op. cit. 133 f.).
[54] Although the sick were in general treated extremely well; Shen. 79 *De vita mon.* 26 (CSCO 108. 101 f.).; Leipoldt, *Schenute*, 120–3.
[55] Kuhn, 'A Fifth-century Abbot, 2', 180; Leipoldt, *Schenute*, 129.
[56] A difficult situation to clarify. In 71 *De vita mon.* 18 (CSCO 108. 64) Shenoute addresses the 'mater sive matres vicinarum omnes' ('the mother as well as the mothers of those women in the village'); Leipoldt, *Schenute*, 96 f., 138 f.

all other labours. Like all the other *synagōgai*, those of the sisters received their food from the White Monastery.[57]

Equality, to have 'all together the same in all things', was one of Schenoute's leitmotifs.[58] This equality existed not only among all brothers and all sisters respectively, but extended also to the relationship between the sexes, 'sive mas sive femina'. Shenoute expressed this notion of equal standing quite explicitly in canon 52 of his rule *De pietate feminarum*:

Or has the kingdom of heaven solely been prepared for men? So that it has not been prepared for women to enter as well? . . . Indeed, just as there are many men who are at times strong and many women who are weak, there are on the other hand many women who are at times strong and victorious, and many men, too, who are inferior to them and weaker [than they are]. The same battle has been assigned to men and women, and the same crown stands before those men and women who together will have persevered.[59]

Several practical arrangements correspond to this theoretical concept. First, the mother of the main monastery, like Shenoute himself, supervised her respective daughter house. Secondly, *female* as well as male ascetics were permitted to withdraw into the desert. Following Pgol's footsteps, Shenoute regularly sought refuge from his duties by retreating into a cave in the desert. This was not solely the privilege of the superior: some brothers as well as some sisters lived permanently in the desert. A father called Psoti brought them food from the monastery, and they were expected to attend the quarterly meetings to reinforce their ties to the monastery and demonstrate their loyalty. Of course, their ascetic practices were subject to close scrutiny, and any transgression was punished with extreme severity: one offending

---

[57] Shen. 67, 76 *De vita mon.* 14, 23 (*praecepta pistrinae*) (CSCO 108. 53, 88–9); Shen. 60 *De vita mon.* 7 (CSCO 108. 36f.); Leipoldt, *Schenute*, 61, 96 n. 5, 99–103, 113–17, 134–9, esp. n. 6; the mother's title is the same as Maria's (above, p. 293); Ladeuze, 'Étude sur le cénobitisme', 303 n. 6. Besa explicitly mentions the brothers who lived in the female community; however, Ladeuze's conclusion that the Pachomian *koinōnia* observed the same practice is not quite as certain.

[58] Shen. 71, 77 *De vita mon.* 18, 24 (CSCO 108. 62f., 99f., and *passim*).

[59] CSCO 108. 23, 5–21.

anchorite was expelled and his cave completely destroyed to annihilate his memory.[60]

This raises the question of whether women participated in the general meetings. Theoretically, Shenoute addressed the prescription requiring those meetings to women as well as men. However, in the light of the strict requirements separating the sexes it seems unlikely that women actually participated in a meeting where the potential for unsupervised contacts with the opposite sex was unlimited. This does not at all preclude the possibility that the women had their own meeting under the supervision of the mother. In fact, despite the frequent emphasis on the equality of men and women, the question arises as to what degree the theory actually did correspond to the practice: a question without easy answers as Shenoute himself realized only too well.

Controversies, strife, at times open rebellion, were part of life in the White Monastery. Maintaining control over his numerous followers was one of Shenoute's main concerns. Often physical punishment was his last resort, and in many ways his rules resemble an elaborate penal code. It is certainly possible that the often maligned violence of Shenoute's character—yet another aspect in need of revision—caused much resentment, but to focus on the potential psychological make-up of the leader is a questionable methodological approach, offering few valuable explanations. Shenoute was not merely a violent authoritarian—controversies did not cease after his death—and his punishments were often well deserved: monks and nuns stole everything they could lay their hands on, called each other 'nasty' names such as 'crooked nose', and caused trouble in a multitude of ways. But more importantly, disagreements were caused simply because of circumstances, and this is particularly true of the women and their leader.[61]

[60] Shen. 74 *De vita mon.* 21, 'omnes qui in locis territorii nostri desertis versantur . . . sive mas erit sive femina' (CSCO 108. 72–3); Besa, *VShen* 103, 115, 122–4, 144, 'fratribus montanis' (CSCO 129. 28, 31 f., 37); Leipoldt, *Schenute*, 104–6.

[61] Kuhn, 'A Fifth-century Abbot, 2', 178–84; Leipoldt, *Schenute*, 147–53; Orlandi, 'Coptic Literature', 65; Timbie, 'The State of Research', 264 f.; Veilleux, introd. to Bell, *The Life of Shenoute*, 5.

In clear contradiction of all theoretical pronouncements, Shenoute demanded supreme authority over the female community and its leader. On a practical level he ensured this—as in the case of Pachomius—through an elder brother. This brother was specially chosen to supervise the female monastery and was again more than a spiritual adviser. His principal duty was to keep Shenoute abreast of all developments in the female community. The mother on her own could decide nothing of any significance. Everything important required Shenoute's prior consent negotiated through the elder brother. This was especially true with regard to disciplinary matters, where Shenoute reserved absolute authority for himself. He was the only one who could judge trespasses and administer the appropriate penalties, rarely in person, but through his representative, the elder brother. One letter addressed to a mother contains remarkable evidence for the practical execution of this prerogative.[62]

This letter lists ten offenders, their crimes, and punishment: in most cases beating of the feet. An interesting hierarchy of crimes emerges: 'Taese, the sister of the little Pschai, of whom you notified us that she ran to Sansno in carnal desires: fifteen strokes.' The same amount was given to 'Dschenbiktor, the sister of the little John, of whom you notified us that her understanding and judgement were not completed'. Stealing merited twenty to thirty strokes, as did the action of 'Sophia, sister of the little old man': she had hit the elder brother in the face. The crimes of lying, disobedience, and attempts to teach others were the worst: 'Sansno, the sister of Apa Hello, she who says: I teach others: forty strokes.' Some receive beatings for crimes known only to Shenoute, and one escapes altogether: 'And her sister Apolle would also have merited beatings. But this time we will forgive her the forbidden familiarities and the dress which she donned with vain desires. . . . Because I know that she is very fat and round and therefore could not tolerate [the beatings] well.' Clearly, lying, the failure to make appropriate disclosures, attempts to teach others, and general disobedience were the most threatening offences and thus punished hardest, the penalties

---

[62] Since I am not aware of any English translation of this remarkable document I will quote extensively in what follows; Leipoldt, *Schenute*, 142 f.

surpassing even those for stealing and sexual desire for other sisters.[63]

The exact fashion in which the beatings were administered is also prescribed. The offender sits on the ground and the elder brother beats her feet, which are held up to him by the mother and her second, a certain Tachom, while other elder sisters restrain the recipient. The elder father alone, and not the mother, could adjust the punishment if the situation should require modifications or indeed leniency.

Shenoute, as demonstrated by the letter, was well informed. Most of the punished sisters had relatives among his monks, so that he may well have known things that not even the mother was aware of. However, precisely these two issues—Shenoute's insistence on being always informed, as well as the fact that he alone, and in his absence, the elder father, had ultimate control over disciplinary matters—caused the gravest rifts. How can someone who is subjected to the supervision of a mere father be an effective leader herself?

The easiest way to challenge Shenoute's demand for absolute control was to withhold information. Indeed, the flow of information between the male and female superiors was neither as voluminous nor as uninterrupted as was evidently expected: 'we have already said and written time and again, that the mother as well as the mothers of those in the village write to us here in detail about all things they might require.' Shenoute even promised to do the same in return, but in vain. Besa likewise had to admonish a nun in charge of a community to 'speak the truth . . . and send to us a sound report and not to dissemble'.[64] The mothers did not seem to be too interested in readily revealing everything that happened within their communities, and they had good reason to disobey.

Shenoute's Letter 7 is addressed to a lady whose name is

---

[63] Cf. also Shen. 54 *De vita mon.* 1, 'conspirantes sciscitabitur, sic etiam matrem communitatis et, quae ab ea proxima est, vicariam . . . conspirantes universas' (CSCO 108. 26); and 79 *De vita mon.* 26 (CSCO 108. 101 f.) as an example of the many warnings against undue sexual contacts.

[64] 'Ac nos quidem omnes, quibus hic indigebimus, res vobis scribemus', Shen. 71 *De vita mon.* 18 (CSCO 108. 64 ll. 24–6); Besa, fr. 39 *To a nun in charge in a convent* (CSCO 158. 122); Leipoldt, *Schenute*, 139, 153–5.

already familiar, 'ad Tachom Matrem'.[65] At the time of the beatings Tachom was the 'second' who helped the mother, now she has become her successor. Her former position allowed Tachom to witness the damaging effect of Shenoute's demand for authority—rendered more painful by its execution through the elder—on the mother's capacity to govern in her own community: Tachom refused to make similar concessions, and she appears to have rejected the elder brother's competence point-blank. To question the elder's legitimacy was to question Shenoute himself; Letter 7 is his response to the challenge, a clear demonstration of his capacity to rule.

Responding to her claims 'like a barbarian to a barbarian, and not like a father to a mother or a brother to a sister', he follows the only possible strategy: to reverse her line of argument. 'And if he, whom we sent to you, is not your father—and according to the order and the laws of God he is—then you are also for your part not mother.' Does she not realize that her questioning of the father's authority attacks the very foundation of the entire organizational structure of which she herself is a part? Thus, her negation of the father's authority is no mere act of disobedience, it is a *discidium*, a 'tearing assunder', of all order. Such a monstrous crime could only be conceived by a fool suffering from hubris, as were those who built the Tower of Babel. Tachom's behaviour will have the same result: confusion and stupidity; neither, of course, being characteristics befitting a leader.[66] Theory alone seldom suffices. Thus Shenoute opens his letter with a reminder of an occasion when he came to punish the nuns in person, 'so that the entire village in which you live was filled with your imbecile voice'.[67]

Letter 7 is a fragment; Tachom's original letter is lost. But as Besa's later letters attest, we are here not simply confronted

---

[65] Shen. *Ep.* 7 (CSCO 96. 7 f.); Leipoldt, *Schenute*, 153–5, 213; Tachom is the feminine of Pachom.

[66] 'Si negas, quem nos ad te misimus, . . . tu quoque discidium inter nos et te effecisti' . . . 'Miror autem, quod saepissime Deus linguam vestram apud vos . . . confuderit. [Gen. 11: 7 f.] . . . Sed si mater sapiens non es, profecto quid faciant omnes illae, quae matrem te apellant, ut sine te sapientes fiant?' (CSCO 96. 7–8).

[67] 'Ubi sunt dies, quibus ad vos cum qua poena venire consueverim scis vel scitis, ita ut imbecilla vestra vox vicum, in quo estis, repleret . . .' (CSCO 96. 7).

with a personal dispute between two incompatible individuals. The discord was inherent in the system. Women entered the Pachomian system, as far as we can discern from the sources, at a stage when this system was already established. There is no indication, either in the more or less symbolic account of Maria's arrival and subsequent foundation of a female community, or, more importantly, within the later rules and regulations, that the position of women was ever meant to be other than secondary and subordinate. The women followed a rule written for men. The entire economic structure of the Pachomian communities reflects the same subordination: like women within a household they were responsible for certain kinds of work and, beyond that, had to follow orders.

In essence, exactly the same is true for Shenoute and his monasteries. But, partly owing to the difference in sources available to us, the reality proved to be much more complex. One of the fundamental principles of Shenoute's ascetic model was equality, an equality which embraced not only the formerly rich and those who were poor, the educated and the non-educated, former slaves and those who were free, but also men and women. Many of his prescriptions attempted to ensure just this equality, both in the main monastery and in the *synagōgai*. Among those who lived in *synagōgai* there were, and had been from the beginning, women. Indeed, much of what Shenoute demanded of the mother was no different from his demands of other leaders of the junior branches. They as well were entirely dependent on the main monastery; they as well were required to inform Shenoute of everything they did, a request that was made 'not so that I might rule over you, but [simply as] I am guided by the love of God'.[68] They as well failed to comply.

But it was here that the equality ended. Whereas the other leaders could truly lead within the confines of their authority, this was not so for the mother. Her authority was further diminished by the fact that she was supervised and ruled by an intermediary. It is here that—from Shenoute's point of view—the notion of equality became 'unwieldy'.

If men and women were equal, then Tachom, that is to say the mother, should have had at least the same capacities and

---

[68] 'Non ac si in vos dominarer, sed amore Dei ductus' (CSCO 96. 7).

prerogatives as the leaders of the other *synagōgai*, if not more. Seeing that the mother of the female community was superior to and responsible for other mothers, *matres vicinarum*, in the same way that Shenoute was superior to other male communities, then Tachom and Shenoute should also have been equals, 'like father and mother'. Yet the mother was forced to subject herself completely to the authority not only of Shenoute but also of an another father, again in the name of equality. The balance between the postulate of equality on the one hand, and the reality of control and authority on the other was a difficult one to strike. Significantly, exactly the same tensions continued under Shenoute's sucessor, Besa. The frequency of female 'rebellion' (strife, disobedience, reluctance to disclose everything fully) indicates that the authority of the male superior was never so absolute as to be able to silence completely the well-founded demands for an equally significant role for mothers.[69] In other words, the struggle within the monastery reflects that in the outside world: what role to attribute to ascetically prominent women; where and how to limit their claims for authority which found its legitimization in the same normative body that was used to limit it. The result was constant tension.

The role and position of Shenoute and his impact on Egypt, that is on Coptic Christianity and Western monasticism (or rather his lack of impact on Western monasticism), deserve far more attention. It is worth considering, however, whether his attitude towards women, namely their strict equality with men, at least on a theoretical level, and the inevitable tensions caused by this postulate when exercised in practice, were among the factors that helped to single out Pachomius' model as the ideal to be emulated rather than Shenoute's. At any rate, in Egypt both men and women had a considerable variety of ascetic communities to

---

[69] Besa's writings also indicate that he indeed participates strongly in the supervision of the female communities; at least according to the sources, it is he, and not necessarily the mother concerned, who reprimands erring nuns, scolds others for lying, breaking their vows, etc. Again, a detailed examination of both Shenoute's and Besa's system for women remains a desideratum; cf. Besa, fr. 13 *To Aphthonia*, where he asks Aphthonia to report complaints to him or to the mother of her community (CSCO 158. 36–8); fr. 18 *To sinful nuns*, 'and you all together, let each woman obey your fathers in everything' (ibid. 48); fr. 20 *To Mary, mother of John, and Talou* (ibid. 52–5); fr. 21 *To nuns who are disrupting the community* (ibid. 55–8); fr. 39 *To a nun in charge in a convent* (ibid. 121–3).

choose from, all within the confines of 'orthodoxy',—that is, officially sanctioned, with leaders who were acknowledged by members of the ecclesiastical hierarchy. In contrast to Asia Minor, however, personal union between ascetics and the clergy was much less prominent. Almost no outstanding ascetic was also bishop or priest. Correspondingly, the spiritual guidance of the women was entrusted to lay ascetics; most leaders of monasteries were laics and often refused to co-operate with the ecclesiastical élite.

What emerges, therefore, are tensions not primarily between radical ascetics and the 'establishment' or between doctrinally divided members of essentially the same élite, but rather tensions between town and country, between urban areas and the *desertum*, between native Egyptians and the Graeco-Roman upper class; in short, the much debated tensions between the *koinē* and Alexandria.

10

'In the Desert and in the Countryside, in Towns or Villages': The *Historia Lausiaca* and the *Historia Monachorum*

When compared to Asia Minor the variety of ascetic practices in Egypt was even more bewildering and more individualistic, ranging from various ways of ascetic life within the village, via the solitary life in lesser or greater depths of the desert, to forms of semi-desert communities as represented by Pachomius and Shenoute. Even the communities, however strictly organized they were, performed experiments with individual ascetic practices, and these were often initiated by their very leaders. All experiments included women. Indeed, the variety of female ascetic practice seems if anything to have exceeded that of the men, but certain tendencies are evident.

The majority of ascetic women remained within the boundaries of the village and lived in organizational models that were once again variations on the theme of the family. Pachomius and Shenoute's female foundations were also in villages but combined the notion of the village with that of the desert perfectly: they were located in deserted villages or included in their very compound both village and desert. Women in Pachomius' system held a role resembling that of a 'mother' within a household. Shenoute, while allowing for a greater range of 'self-determination', adhered essentially to the same concept.

Women's theoretical equality as ascetics was readily accepted, yet any translation of that equality into an actual societal one was met with opposition. This dual standard evidently caused difficulties, and all parties concerned were well aware of the implications. Similar tensions between acceptance and even veneration of a woman's ascetic achievement and the impossibility of adequately translating these ideals into social practice arose also in

those forms of ascetic life that had moved to the margins of
society: the semi-anchorite and anchorite life in the desert.
Yet, in contrast to Asia Minor, in Egypt these tensions never
reached a level at which those marginal forms of life were condemned entirely, with all traces of an individual woman's extraordinary ascetic achievements being eradicated from our sources
as too revealing or too controversial. The great variety of ascetic
practices has clearly been preserved, even in those sources which
were not only 'orthodox', but which achieved a veritable best-
seller status: the *historiae monachorum*, travelogues and adven-
ture stories, whose particular success was to provide the Western
world with the much needed *exempla* of ascetic life.[1]

In 419/20 Palladius, by then bishop of Aspuna in Galatia but
better known by his former see of Helenopolis, wrote a chronicle
of his most formative years at the request of a certain Lausos,
Theodosius II's chamberlain: this was the *Historia Lausiaca*.[2]
Drawing on a variety of sources in addition to his own experiences
and encounters with the famous ascetics of Egypt and Palestine,
Palladius composed a 'compendium of lives and anecdotes of
ascetic saints', which, despite its 'fictional veneer', represents one
of the most important accounts of ascetic practices at the time,
both for its declared intent ('for the emulation and imitation of

---

[1] Rousseau, *Ascetics*, 92–5.

[2] Despite repeated criticism, the standard edition remains that by C. Butler,
The Lausiac History of Palladius, although, as demonstrated by R. Draguet
((ed.), *Les formes syriaques de la matière de l'Histoire Lausiaque* (CSCO 389–90,
398–9 (Scr. Syr. 169–70, 173–4); Louvain, 1978)), constant reference to the
older Syriac versions is necessary (CSCO Scr. Syr. 170, pp. 80*–83*); Bartelink
and Mohrmann, *La Storia Lausiaca*, 13–23; an Eng. trans. is available by R. T.
Meyer, *Palladius: The Lausiac History* (Ancient Christian Writers 34; London,
1965); D. F. Buck, 'The Structure of the Lausiac History', *Byzantion* 46 (1976),
292–307. Lausos is mentioned as the *praepositus sacri cubiculi* in *PLRE* ii, s.n.
'Lausos 1'. The *HL* is fraught with inaccuracies and contradictions regarding the
first half of Palladius' life, only in part explained by the *c.* 20 years that elapsed
between his stay in Egypt, 388–397/400 (*HL* 1 (Butler, ii)), and the composition
of the *HL*; for a chronology of Palladius' life see Gorce, *Géronte: Vie de Sainte
Mélanie*, 230 n. 1; Hunt, 'Palladius of Helenopolis', 458, 470 f.; id. 'St. Silvia of
Aquitaine: The Role of a Theodosian Pilgrim in the Society of East and West',
JThS 23 (1972), 351–73, 355 n. 4; Mohrmann and Leclercq, *Palladios: Dialogue
sur la vie de Jean Chrysostome*, i. 7–18; E. Preuschen, *Palladius und Rufinus: Ein
Beitrag zur Quellenkunde des ältesten Mönchtums* (Giessen, 1897), 233–46 (re-
viewed by Grützmacher, *Theologische Literaturzeitschrift* 23 (1898), 107).

those who wish to succeed in the heavenly way of life') and for the historical reality thus created.[3]

Palladius was neither the first nor the only author to describe the deeds of the famous ascetics. Some time after 395 an anonymous author wrote what purports to be the account of a journey of seven Palestinian ascetics from Lycopolis to Alexandria in search of the same famous Desert Fathers: the *Historia Monachorum in Aegypto*.[4] Both the *Historia Lausiaca* and the *Historia Monachorum* cover, to a certain extent, the same ground. What is more, although they are written from different angles, both works pursue the same aim: to present to their readers the widest possible range of ascetic ideals and models by relating 'the deeds of the Fathers, male and female,' performed 'in the desert and in the countryside . . . towns or villages . . . in desert-caves and in the most remote places'; 'for we are concerned not with the place where they settled, but rather it is their way of life that we seek.'[5]

---

[3] Quoted from Pall. *HL* (spurious) proem (Butler, ii. 3), and Hunt, 'Palladius of Helenopolis', 458 f.; W. Bousset, 'Zur Komposition der Historia Lausiaca', *ZNW* 21 (1922), 81–98; Buck, 'The Structure', 292–4; R. Draguet, 'L'Inauthenticité du prooemion de l'histoire Lausiaque', *Le Muséon* 69 (1946), 529–34; id. 'L'Histoire Lausiaque, une œuvre écrite dans l'ésprit d' Évagre', *RHE* 41 (1946), 321–5; Reitzenstein, *Historia Monachorum*, 154–61.

[4] As in the case of Butler's edition of the *HL*, the sole edition of the Greek text of the *HM*, by Festugière, *Historia Monachorum in Aegypto*, has received much criticism, but remains standard; in the following pages I use the English translation by N. Russel, *The Lives of the Desert-Fathers* (Cistercian Studies Series 34; Kalamazoo, 1980). Whether or not the *Historia Monachorum* describes an actual journey has long been the subject of debate; the work as we know it is again a compilation, using in part yet another history of the famous monks written by Timotheus of Alexandria, a text lost to us but still used by Sozomen (*HE* 6. 29. 2 (GCS 50. 279)). For a detailed discussion of the *HM*'s sources cf. in particular E. Schulz-Flügel (ed.), *Tyrannius Rufinus: Historia Monachorum sive De Vita Sanctorum Patrum* (Patristische Texte und Studien 34; Berlin, 1990), 5–17, 20–3; Schulz-Flügel doubts the authenticity of an actual journey, against B. Ward in the introd. to *Lives of the Desert-Fathers*, 3–6; Bousset, *Apophthegmata*, 72 f.; Butler, *The Lausiac History*, i. 7, 10–38, 198–203; Chitty, *The Desert*, 62 n. 42; P. Devos, 'Les Nombres dans l'Historia Monachorum in Aegypto', *AnBoll* 92 (1974), 97–108, here 97 n. 4; A. J. Festugière, 'Le Problème littéraire de l' "Historia Monachorum" ', *Hermes* 83 (1955), 257–84; id. *Historia Monachorum*, 1–133; Reitzenstein, *Historia Monachorum*, 1–4.

[5] *HM* pr. 10–11 (Festugière, 8); Pall. *HL* pr. (Butler, ii. 10, 15); Palladius' prologue echoes the Gospel of Luke. The question of each author's intended

Τῶν πατέρων διηγήματα, ἀρρένων τε καὶ θηλειῶν, 'the deeds of the Fathers, male and female'—Palladius does not use this expression accidentally. Most of his *exempla* lived in Egypt, and at least a third of the Egyptian saints were, to use Palladius' term, 'female fathers'. As already mentioned, he devotes an entire chapter to *γυναικῶν ἀνδρείων*, 'manly women . . . to whom God granted the capacity to fight struggles equal to those of men', and even a cursory reading of the chapter headings reinforces the impression that Palladius attempted indeed to present both male and female ascetics.[6] Here, the *Historia Monachorum* differs. The prologue is addressed to the 'pious brotherhood that lives on the Mount of Olives', and women are nowhere mentioned as a separate subject for discussion. Consequently, the chapters deal primarily with exemplary male Fathers, and all information regarding women is once again accidental, a 'side-effect' of the central theme.

According to Palladius, Paul the Simple, a disciple of St Antony, lived together with several other ascetics on Mount Pherme.[7] He distinguished himself from his fellow brothers by an astonishing capacity: 'he engaged in no work or business', but his ascetic labours consisted of three hundred prayers daily, and he would collect that many pebbles, hold them in his lap, and at each prayer cast out a pebble.' In other words, he prayed continuously.[8]

---

audience, particularly in the light of Rufinus' Latin translation of the *HM*, will be discussed elsewhere; cf. especially E. Magheri Cataluccio, *Il Lausaïkon di Palladio tra Semiotica e Storia* (Rome, 1984), 83–151.

[6] Pall. *HL* 41 (Butler, ii. 128). As Draguet's findings have shown (CSCO 390, Scr. Syr. 170, pp. 79*–80*, 82*), in composing the prologue, Palladius rewrote parts of another work addressed to a woman, but he took care to eliminate all obvious references to that work in his final Greek version. More importantly, though, the comparison with the Syriac texts demonstrates Palladius' conscious effort to address both men *and* women. The *HL* in Butler's edition comprises 71 chapters, 38 of which deal with Egypt, a reflection of Palladius' own biography.

[7] Pall. *HL* 20 (Butler, ii 62); *HL* 22 (ibid. 177) is dedicated to the same Paul the Simple; *HM* 24 (Festugière, 131) does not contain this story; Soz. *HE* 1. 13. 13–14 (GCS 50. 29); Bartelink, *La Storia Lausiaca*, 344 (n. 2 to *HL* 20); Guy, 'Le Centre monastique de Scété', *passim*; Heussi, *Ursprung*, 154–64; Reitzenstein, *Historia Monachorum*, 11–34; White, *The Monasteries of Wadi'n Natrun*, ii. 17–42.

[8] The topos of incessant prayer is by now a familiar one; 1 Thess. 17; Eph. 6: 18; 1 Tim. 5: 5; Acts 6: 4; 10: 2; 12: 5; Ath. *V. Ant.* 3 (PG 26. 845); F. Heiler, *Das Gebet: Eine religionsgeschichtliche und religionspsychologische Untersuchung*

However, as he confessed to the famous Macarius of Alexandria, his zeal was greatly diminished upon learning of a rival. A *parthenos* in a nearby village, 'who has practised asceticism for thirty years', surpassed him: she only ate on Saturdays and Sundays, filling the entire interim period of five days with seven hundred prayers upon each. The moral of the story is Macarius' consolation. He himself prays only one hundred times a day, supports himself through work, and eats a satisfying amount of food every day. However, his prayers are said with a 'pure heart' and he takes care never to be negligent. What counts is internal disposition, not numbers.

Two aspects here are noteworthy. First, during the second half of the fourth century a *parthenos* practised extreme fasting so as to be able to pray incessantly. As in Paul's case this prevented her from working, and it seems that she, like Paul, 'took nothing except what she ate'—a reference that to my mind implies reliance upon charity, if not begging. Secondly (and in contrast to Asia Minor), her behaviour is not condemned outright but criticized implicitly through its juxtaposition with the moderate regime practised by an acclaimed ascetic, a regime which not only includes regular eating habits, but also regular work.[9]

'Piamun was a virgin who lived with her mother spinning flax and eating only every other day at evening'[10]—a rather 'ordinary' routine for a virgin, which, however, gave Piamun extraordinary capacities. She 'was deemed worthy of the χαρίσματος προρρήσεων, the gift of prophecy', a gift she duly employed for the sake of her community. Once during the flood-season the well-armed oc-

(Munich, 1923⁵), 223 f.; M. J. Marx, 'Incessant Prayer in the Vita Antonii', *Studia Anselmiana* 38 (1956), 108–35; most numbers regarding age, amount of people, etc. mentioned by Palladius are ten- or hundred fold multiples of 3, 6, 10; i.e. 30, 60, 300, 600, etc.; cf. Devos, 'Les Nombres,' 97–108.

[9] Macarius of Alexandria lived roughly between 305 and 393/4; Pall. *HL* 18 (Butler, ii. 47); Soz. *HE* 3. 14 (GCS 50. 118); Hunt, 'Palladius of Helenopolis', 467 f.; the village could have been Nitria (El Barnugi); Palladius mentions no relatives or companions of this virgin. For the topos of work and its ascetic importance cf. also H. Dörries, 'Mönchtum und Arbeit', in W. Elliger (ed.), *Forschungen zur Kirchengeschichte und zur christlichen Kunst: Festschrift für J. Ficker* (Leipzig, 1931), 17–39; J. Frei, 'Die Stellung des alten Mönchtums zur Arbeit', *Erbe und Auftrag* 53 (1977), 332–6; H. Gülzow, 'Arbeit 4', in *TRE* iii. 624–6.

[10] Pall. *HL* 31 (Butler, ii. 86).

cupants of the neighbouring village threatened to attack Piamun's own in order to divert the vital water flow. An angel revealed the attack to Piamun, who in turn alerted the village elders. They, in desperation, begged Piamun to 'have mercy on the whole town' and to 'go out and make peace with them'. She refused to leave her abode, but transfixed the attackers on the spot by standing all night in prayer.

Piamun was clearly a 'holy woman', a force upon which the community had good reason to rely. Some aspects of her charismatic powers pre-date Christian times. Such village raids are well attested by papyrological and other evidence, and the transfixing of adversaries is an ancient legendary motif. Now the magic powers formerly possessed by the pagan priestesses—prophecy and transfixion—have been transferred to the Christian virgin. Significantly, Piamun alone amongst Palladius' *exempla* has the power of prophecy while remaining part of her village community. All others endowed with this charisma are desert anchorites, who follow the precedent set by the prophet Elias.[11]

In chapter 60 Palladius recalls an episode which occurred in Antinoe between 406 and 412/13.[12] One of Palladius' neighbours there was a virgin, who for sixty years, since she had 'left the world', had not emerged from her house, where she persevered in her asceticism together with her mother. This life of absolute

---

[11] The motif of transfixion, mostly combined with that of prophecy, found its way into Christian hagiography, cf. *HM* 6 and 8 (Festugière, 44, 56); and in particular Festugière, 'Lieux communs', 145–9, esp. 148; L. Bringmann, *Die Frau im ptolemäisch-kaiserzeitlichen Ägypten*, Diss. (Bonn, 1939), 75, 80; Reitzenstein, *Historia Monachorum*, 37 n. 3, on the prophetic gifts of Elias and his role. Attempts to divert water are described in *P. Lond.* 1246–8 (AD 345); *P. Cairo Pr.* 15–16; *P. Thead.* 20 mentions flood-guards; *CTh.* 9. 32. 1 (AD 409) (Mommsen-Meyer, i. 2, 485); R. S. Bagnall, 'Five Papyri on Fourth Century Money and Prices', *American Society of Papyrologists* 20 (1983), 1–8; Johnson and West, *Byzantine Egypt*, 9. Piamun is an Egyptian name, so this virgin may have been born pagan, around 320. R. S. Bagnall ('Religious Conversion', 107–12) classifies e.g. Poibammon as Christian because a martyr bore the same name; Wipszycka, 'Remarques sur les lettres privées', 203–21.

[12] While he was exiled there, Pall. *HL* 60 (Butler, ii. 154); this is Antinoe in the Thebaid, also known as Antinoopolis, modern Shēkh Abāda; Bartelink, *La Storia Lausiaca*, 390 (n. 1 to *HL* 58); Buck, 'The Structure', 304f.; Butler, *Lausiac History*, ii. 244; A. M. Malingrey, *Pallade: Dialogue sur la vie de Jean Chrysostome* (SC 341; Paris, 1988), 16.

seclusion had clearly ensured her sanctity. One night, the local martyr Colluthos—a figure who by virtue of his fate acts as a mediator between the divine and the human—revealed to her the hour of her approaching death. He invited her to celebrate the imminent reunion with her 'Master and . . . all the saints' by taking a meal at his sanctuary outside the town. The next day the virgin prepared bread, olives, and vegetables, left her home for the first time, and spent the day in prayer at the sanctuary. Having returned home, she made all final arrangements and instructed her mother (who was still alive!) to donate 'a book by Clement of Alexandria on the prophet Amos' to Palladius.[13] 'She died that night, without fever or delirium, but laid out for burial.'

The circumstances of the virgin's life conform exactly to the ideal norm, if indeed they do not surpass it, thus clearly ensuring the promised reward: her imminent death is announced by the local martyr, second-best only to an angel, and she is therefore able to leave this world not simply without any disfiguring struggle but perfectly arrayed and entirely ready to meet her master. A preannounced death, according to the conventions of hagiography, is a clear indication of the heroine's future angelic state. For Palladius this exemplary virgin had reached the highest degree of perfection.[14]

---

[13] Clement's book on Amos is lost but could have been a section of the *Hypotyposeis* (Eus. *HE* 6. 14. 1). Palladius would certainly have appreciated such a gift. A feature worth noting here is the virgin's literary interest. If Clement of Alexandria's book was only one among several, as is possible, this also indicates a certain economic status, as in the case of the virgin who had allegedly stolen books from her fellow heirs. The virgin and her mother seem to have owned their house; they were Palladius' neighbours, and may thus be counted among the *honoratiores* of their community.

[14] Colluthos is said to have died under Maximian (305–13). In his *Dial.* 11. 120–50 (SC 341. 224–8) Palladius relates a virtually identical story concerning the death of John Chrysostom, here announced by the martyr Basiliscos. Among the many examples of preannounced death are A. Sisoes 14 (Guy, 279); Ath. *V. Ant.* 89 (PG 26. 986 A); *VSM* 22–5; *HM* 1, 14, 17 (Festugière, 28, 95, 103); cf. in particular T. Baumeister, *Martyr Invictus: Der Martyrer als Sinnbild der Erlösung in der Legende und im Kult der frühen koptischen Kirche* (Forschungen zur Volkskunde 46; Münster, 1972), 109 for Colluthos, more generally 68–86, and *passim*; E. T. Bettencourt, 'L'idéal réligieux de S. Antoine', *Studia Anselmiana* 38 (1956), 45–65, esp. 57; Bieler, Θεῖος Ἀνήρ, 44–9; P. R. L. Brown, *The Cult of the Saints: Its Rise and Function in Latin Christianity* (Chicago, 1981), 1–22,

Palladius' primary intention was not to give a detailed description of organizational features. All three virgins discussed so far
were symbols, to demonstrate that internal attitude supersedes
external zeal, that true prayer achieves miracles, and that strict
adherence to the norm will guarantee eternal salvation. Nonethe-
less, organizational features transpire and are interesting simply
because they appear to be entirely self-explanatory and are
absolutely taken for granted. All three virgins lived within their
own village or town, at least two of them together with their
mothers, and all enjoyed a respected status locally.

A welcome insight into practical aspects of a *parthenos*' life,
this time in a village in the region of Hermoupolis (and an exact corroboration of our papyrological findings), is provided
by chapter 10 of the *Historia Monachorum*.[15] Here, a certain
presbyter Copres, 90 years old and the superior of a community
of fifty monks, reminisces about one of his elders, 'the first of the
monks in this place and also the first to devise the monastic
habit'. This Father, a desert ascetic called Patermouthius, had
had a rather unsavoury past: he belongs in the category of converted 'brigand chiefs and tomb-robbers', notorious for their
crimes.[16] One night, in the exercise of his then profession, Patermouthius 'attacked the *monastērion* of a woman who lived as a
virgin (παρθενευούσῃ), intending to rob it'. Having somehow managed to climb on to the roof, he failed to enter the 'inner chamber' and, worse, found himself trapped. Thus he had to remain
on the roof for the rest of the night. During a brief moment of
sleep, an apparition converted him to Christianity. Upon waking

69–85; Frank, *Angelikos Bios*, 9–10, 177–9, 199; E. Patlagean, 'Ancienne hagiographie byzantine et histoire sociale', *Annales ESC* 23 (1968), 106–26; Reitzenstein, *Des Athanasius Werk über das Leben des Antonius*, 29, 54 f.; B. Steidle,
'Homo Dei Antonius', *Studia Anselmiana* 38 (1956), 148–200, esp. 173–6, 198;
H. Uhlmann, 'Der heilige Colluthos', *Zeitschrift für Theologie und Kirche* 27
(1857), 264–84.

[15] *HM* 10 (Festugière, 76).

[16] Patermouthius—Rufinus translates 'nomine Pater Mutius'—is only known
from this account. The popular theme of the repentant robber has already been
mentioned above p. 258; cf. also Festugière, *Enquête*, 68 nn. 19, 20; Leipoldt,
Schenute, 94; for an interesting, though tangential aspect cf. G. J. M. Bartelink,
'Les Démons comme brigands', *VigChr* 21 (1967), 12–24. The incident must have
taken place at the beginning of the 4th cent.; Devos, 'Les Nombres', 101 f., 107 f.;
Russel, *The Lives*, 132 (nn. 7, 8 to *HM* 10), 20.

he found the virgin standing next to him and asked her for directions to the nearby church.

The description of the virgin's *monastērion* conforms exactly with our knowledge of private town-houses: sealed off towards the street with an inaccessible flat roof, it had at least two rooms, an outer and an inner one (τὸ ταμιεῖον). Obviously, Patermouthius did not associate the status of a virgin—if he knew at all that the occupant of the house was a *parthenos*—with poverty, rather with the contrary and probably rightly so. Clearly, the term *monastērion* is here used in its literal sense, a house where a woman practised the ascetic life as a *monachē*, alone, though she lived close to the church and its community of priests, who may have assisted her.[17]

Another *parthenos* called Alexandra had carried the notion of withdrawal and seclusion to its extreme: she immured herself in a tomb just outside Alexandria and 'never looked a woman or a man in the face'. Palladius, our source, learned about Alexandra shortly after his arrival in Alexandria, through Didymus the Blind. Alexandra had received through a window the supplies that were brought to her by her only link with the world—a servant-girl, who also discovered Alexandra's death ten years after her immurement. Melania the Elder had visited this virgin around 375 and had learned the secrets of her perseverance. Alexandra fought against *akēdia* by praying, spinning flax (just like Piamun), and by meditating upon the lives of her idols: the holy patriarchs, prophets, apostles, and martyrs.[18]

Others, as we have already seen, followed an approach which

[17] τὸ ταμιεῖον also means treasury, closet, or prayer-room, Matt. 6: 6; LSJ s.v. The Syriac text has a telling interpolation, 'and being unable to go into her house and plunder it, because the roofs of the house were as flat as the ground and they had no rain water pipes . . . for there is no rain in the Thebaid . . .'; Russel, *The Lives*, 160; Maehler, *Häuser und ihre Bewohner*, 120–2; Ward (*The Lives*, introd. 14–16, 21) assumes the priests to be monks; there is no indication of this in the text.

[18] Pall. *HL* 5 (Butler, ii. 21); Didymus the Blind lived *c.*313–98; J. Leipoldt, *Didymus der Blinde* (TU 29 NF 14; Leipzig, 1905), 4–8; for Melania the Elder's visit to Egypt in 374–5 cf. Jer. *Ep.* 4. 2 (CSEL 54. 20); F. X. Murphy, 'Melania the Elder, a biographical note', *Traditio* 5 (1947), 59–78. Another example of immurement is mentioned by A. Serapion 1 (Guy, 294), this time a repenting prostitute who is walled up in her cell by the *amma* of the monastery; Heussi, *Ursprung*, 209.

was diametrically opposed to Alexandra's complete seclusion: they rejected the world by abandoning all forms of settlement. Again, only a glimpse here and there, little more than Sarah's cryptic remarks, sheds some light on these women. Paphnutius, an accomplished ascetic, suddenly felt overwhelmed by doubts concerning the validity of the ascetic life *vis-à-vis* that of a layperson and requested divine enlightenment to support his case. Help from above was promptly forthcoming but did little at first to soothe his troubled soul.[19] Paphnutius was told to visit a fluteplayer in a nearby town. This flautist, 'a sinner, a drunkard, and a fornicator', not only had a disreputable profession, but furthermore a criminal past: he too had been the leader of a gang of brigands. Paphnutius' perseverance finally revealed one good deed. Once, in his days as a brigand, he had saved a ' "virgin of God" who was about to be raped by a gang of robbers, and at night led her back to the village'. What was a 'virgin of God' doing outside a village by herself?

Palladius' account of the Pachomian foundations affords a second glimpse.[20] One of the sisters in the female monastery was to all intents and purposes deranged. She appeared possessed by demons and was so repulsive to all that she was relegated to the kitchen, becoming the 'sponge of the monastery'. There, she performed the most menial tasks, never talked, was never seen eating, never complained. One day an angel appeared to the well-known Desert Father Piterum and said to him: 'Why do you think so much of yourself for being pious . . . ? Do you want

---

[19] Here is a very minor part in a story within a story which belongs to the genre of the 'Streitnovelle'. *HM* 14 (Festugière, 102); Paphnutius was a popular name: we know of several bishops, Soc. *HE* 1. 8. 11 (PG 67. 61); Ath. *Ep. Fest.* 19 (PG 26. 1430), and several monks, Paph. Cephalas, Pall. *HL* 46, 47 (Butler, ii. 134, 136, 224 n. 89); A. Paph., A. Matoes 10 (Guy, 264 ff., 191); Cass. *Conf.* 18. 15 (CSCL 13. 523). For the topos of ascetic competition cf. Festugière, 'Problèmes littéraires', 272–4; id. 'Lieux communs', 142–4; id. *Enquête*, 90 n. 1; R. Reitzenstein, *Hellenistische Wundererzählungen* (Leipzig, 1906) 75 f.; id. *Historia Monachorum*, 34–49; Russel, *The Lives*, 133 (n. 2 to *HM* 14); for the significant changes in the Latin translation of the chapter cf. Schulz-Flügel, *Tyrannius Rufinus*, 61 f.

[20] Pall. *HL* 32–4, here 34 (Butler, ii. 87–9); Bartelink, *La Storia Lausiaca*, 357 (n. 1 to *HL* 32); R. Draguet, 'Le Chapitre de l'Histoire Lausiaque sur les Tabennésiotes dérive-t-il d'une source copte?' *Le Muséon* 57 (1944), 53–146, no. 58 (1945), 15–95; F. Halkin, 'L'Histoire Lausiaque et les Vies grecques de S. Pachôme', *AnBoll* 48 (1930), 257–301.

to see someone more pious than yourself, a woman?' Piterum assented and was told to visit the monastery at Tabennesi. Once admitted, only after much deliberation and because he was well advanced in years, he demanded to see all the sisters. They assembled, he found one missing, asked again, and was told that they had one 'in the kitchen but she is "sale", [σαλὴν, deranged] (for this is what they call the mentally afflicted)'. Upon seeing her, Piterum exclaimed, 'you are the ones who are fools! This woman is "ammas" (thus with the name of "mother" do they call the women of highest spirituality (πνευματικάς), to both you and me.' The story comes to a surprising end: unable to bear her new honourable status, the *ammas* suddenly left the monastery: 'no one knew where she went and how she died.'[21]

Our primary concern here is not the notion of the 'religious fool', nor the fact that this downtrodden woman is seen as an ascetic who surpasses even such approved masters as Piterum himself—both aspects worthy of note.[22] What is interesting is the woman's end. No longer able to practise complete withdrawal within the confines of the monastery by humbling herself to a degree beneath contempt, she seems to have chosen a new and radical form of withdrawal: the life of a migrating ascetic, of a wandering virgin.

A certain Elias must have been one of the more prominent citizens of Athribis, a town in which he owned sizeable amounts of property. His personal wealth—and here he was in the company of many, as we have seen—did not prevent him from being an ascetic; but it was his ascetic inclination which prompted him to use his property in a slightly unusual manner.[23] 'Feeling com-

[21] Piterum cannot be otherwise identified, Butler, *The Lausiac History*, ii. 212; S. Hilpisch, 'Die Torheit um Christi Willen', *Zeitschrift für Aszese und Mystik* 6 (1931), 121–31; Heussi, *Ursprung*, 233–9; Reitzenstein, *Historia Monachorum*, 47–9; L. Rydén, *Bemerkungen zum Leben des Heiligen Narren Symeon von Leontios* (Uppsala, 1970), *passim*.

[22] It is hard to avoid speculating for which audience's benefit Palladius included this transformation of the quintessential housewife/maid, the 'sponge of the monastery', into an ascetic Cinderella, more admirable than a Desert Father; if we knew her name this fool (after all!) in the eyes of other women would probably have become the saint of all maids.

[23] Pall. *HL* 29 (Butler, ii. 84); this could be Atripe (Athribis) opposite Panopolis, the location of Shenoute's White Monastery; an alternative would be Athribis in the Delta; Bartelink, *La Storia Lausiaca*, 355 (n. 3 to *HL* 29). Butler

passion for those women who belonged to the order of ascetics . . .
he built a large monastery, where he collected those who wandered about (τὰς ἀλωμένας)'—over three hundred women. Elias'
foundation provided them with all amenities: medical care, household goods, and gardens. None the less, 'the women, having been
united there from many different ways of life, quarrelled continuously with each other. Since he had to listen to their arguments and act as a peacemaker', Elias decided to live among the
women. However, he was still young, and to be surrounded by
women was not without its difficulties. At some point he left for
the desert to purify himself and to regain his composure. His
prayers were answered, albeit more drastically than he had an-
ticipated. Three angels appeared and after having extracted Elias'
solemn promises that he would return to look after the women,
they castrated him with a razor. 'Not actually,' Palladius hastens
to add, 'but in a dream.' Successfully freed from temptations,
Elias returned to the monastery where he remained 'indoors in
a cell' for the following forty years, never again subjected to
'passions'.

After his death Elias was succeeded by Dorotheus, 'who had
grown old in a virtuous and active life'.[24] However, 'he could not
continue to live in this situation, in the heart of the monastery.'
He solved the problem by secluding himself in a chamber in the
attic and conducted all business through a window overlooking
the women's monastery, 'growing old in the upper storey. No
women came up to him, and he did not go down to them, for
there was no ladder.'

The facts conveyed by this chapter are as revealing as the way
in which Palladius presents them. Beyond doubt, a sizeable proportion of the women belonging to the τάγμα τῶν ἀσκητριῶν had

---

(*The Lausiac History*, ii. 204 n. 46) even suggests that Elias and Shenoute's
monasteries were identical. It is possible that Elias' foundation belongs to a
period when Shenoute's was not yet prominent—in any case, Palladius like all
other Greek sources omits Shenoute entirely. Other property-owning ascetics are
mentioned, e.g. in Ath. *V. Ant.* 2, 44, 47 (PG 26. 814 B, 908 B, 912 B); in a
Tebtunis papyrus edited by J. W. Barns ('A Fourth-Century Deacon's Petition
from Theadelphia', *SP* I (TU 63; Berlin, 1957), 3–9); also papyrus *SB* i. 5100; H.
Dressler, *The Usage of askeo and its Cognates in Greek Documents to 100 AD*
(Washington, DC, 1947) *passim*; Judge, 'The Earliest Use of Monachos', 76–89.

[24] Pall. *HL* 30 (Butler, ii. 86).

chosen perpetual 'wandering' as their ascetic practice. It was the harshness of this life 'in dispersion' which filled Elias (and perhaps others) with compassion and compelled him to look after them. The extent of his monastery reflects the numbers of those without a secure refuge; wandering ascetic women (ἀλωμέναι) constituted a significant minority.[25]

In relating the story of Elias, Palladius walks a tightrope. On the one hand, he never criticizes 'wandering' women, nor does he call their practice into question. On the other hand, he leaves little doubt that women should live within the security and safety of a community. The community in question was founded and guided by men. In Palladius' account, this arrangement, which might have given rise to criticism, is fully sanctioned by divine intervention. The format, as it were, of this intervention uses the purifying powers of the desert; but reinforces them by a physical act which has long given rise to 'ecclesiastical' controversy: castration. Here Palladius displays not only his loyalties to Origen but also his considerable diplomatic skill. Castration in Elias' case, and only in his case, is a divine grace: his institution clearly responds to a social need and is not only worthy of preservation, but of imitation. Thus, the source of potential disruption is simply and swiftly removed. At the same time, literal imitation of Elias' grace is discouraged: he is castrated only in a spiritual sense, in a dream; thus a literal repetition of this act, removing the external organs, will not guarantee the same result. Consequently, Dorotheus uses a different method.[26]

Palladius leaves no doubt that Elias' community, despite the roughness of its 'street-wise' inmates, was intended for 'homeless' ascetics and not simply for homeless women, and he thus con-

---

[25] ἀλύω means 'to wander, to roam about', LSJ s.v.

[26] The desert as a place of purification has already been discussed, cf. above, pp. 257–8, and e.g. Matt. 14: 13; Mark 6: 32; Luke 4: 42; Ath. *V. Ant.* 11 (PG 26. 856); H. Chadwick, 'Enkrateia', in *RAC* v. 357 f.; J. Gribomont, 'Eremo', in *DIP* iii. 1260–4; Guillaumont, 'La Conception du désert', 3–21. Palladius here joins the lengthy debate surrounding castration for ascetic reasons, based on Matt. 19:12; cf. e.g. Clem. Alex. *Strom.* 13. 91, 31. 11 (GCS 52 (15), 196, 238); Cass. *Conf.* 7. 2 (CSCL 13. 180); Pall. *HL* 38 (Butler, ii. 121); for voices condemning castration, beyond those mentioned in connection with Basil of Ancyra's *De virg.* (above, pp. 120–1), cf. e.g. J. Chrys. *Gal.* 5 (PG 61. 688 f.); id. *Hom. in Mt.* 19 (PG 58. 599); Brown, *The Body and Society*, 117, 140, 168 f.

firms our earlier findings.[27] He further leaves no doubt that the male founder and other brothers, presumably there to help, lived together with these women in a mixed community—there is nothing to prevent us from assuming that Dorotheus already lived in the monastery during Elias' lifetime.[28] Palladius clearly considered Elias and Dorotheus' model of an ascetic life worthy of imitation.

The examples discussed so far have led us from women who practised virginity alone or with their mothers in villages, leading a life of *stabilitas loci* and seclusion (even to the point of completely immuring themselves in a tomb), to those who chose perpetual *xeniteia*. Neither Palladius nor the author of the *Historia Monachorum* expressed judgements; clearly all these forms of life were acceptable, though, as illustrated by Elias, some were more practical than others. Elias also exemplifies another aspect, that of male and female ascetics living in close proximity, an aspect that brings us back to Paphnutius and his quest for ascetic competitors.

After his encounter with the flute-player, Paphnutius once again asked to be shown an ascetic rival. Now he is told to visit a certain πρωτοκωμήτης, or magistrate, of a neighbouring village in the Heracleopolite.[29] Surprised by the implicit comparison, Paphnutius soon discovers the magistrate's secret life: 'it is now thirty years since I separated from my wife. I slept with her for only three years and had three sons by her'—another example of *mariage blanc*, this time between two lay-persons, who otherwise never ceased to conduct their 'worldly' affairs.[30]

---

[27] A fact which has caused translators some difficulty; apparently wandering female ascetics could not have existed, therefore the translation is either 'to gather all those dispersed about into his monastery'; or 'those who had no secure refuge'; both possibilities are certainly historically accurate but do not offer a comprehensive explanation.

[28] Dorotheus is described as an 'old man' upon taking charge of the monastery, although he then guides it 'growing old'; this description of him as an 'old man' may be based on the topos *puer senex*, cf. Ch. 9 n. 27; Soz. *HE* 6. 29. 4 (GCS 50. 279); Giannarelli, *Tipologia femminile*, 41.

[29] *HM* 14 (Festugière, 105); for the position πρωτοκωμήτης cf. Festugière, *Enquête*, 93 n. 50; U. Wilcken and L. Mitteis, *Grundzüge und Chrestomathie der Papyrusurkunde*, i (Leipzig, 1912), 84; the following passage of the *HM* gives an interesting summary of a *prōtokōmētēs'* duties while implying the usual shortcomings of those holding this office.

[30] 1 Cor. 7: 38; cf. above, pp. 164, 185–7; Heussi, *Ursprung*, 22, 30; Reitzenstein, *Historia Monachorum*, 31.

Mariage blanc was also practised, albeit for a short time only, by Amoun, the founder of semi-anchorite life at Scetis.[31] The story of his life, told by the *Historia Monachorum*, Palladius, and Socrates, is interesting because of the variations contained in each of these accounts, all drawing upon the same source-tradition. According to the Greek version of the *Historia Monachorum*, Amoun, forced into marriage despite his ascetic inclinations, solved this conflict by proposing to his bride on the wedding-night that both should maintain their virginity.[32] She consented, but Amoun departed to the desert only a few days later. His wife exhorted all her servants to adopt the ascetic life and converted her house into a monastery. Rufinus altered the story slightly. In his version, the chaste marriage lasted until the death of the parents, and it is stated explicitly that the wife gathered many virgins around her, rather than simply encouraging all her servants, undoubtedly both male and female, to lead the ascetic life within her community.[33] In Palladius' version, the spiritual marriage lasts eighteen years rather than 'a few days'; he does not tell us anything about the fate of Amoun's wife, except that her husband visited her twice a year. Socrates' account corroborates that given by Palladius, with one exception. According to Socrates, both Amoun and his wife 'retired into the desert of Nitria, where they shared one common dwelling (ἀσκητήριον εἶχον κοινονόν), no longer having the distinction between male and female, being, as the Apostle says, "one in Christ"' (Gal. 3: 28). After some time the wife suggested that they both continue their ascetic practices in separate cells, and thus they spent the rest of their lives.[34]

Without going into a source-critical analysis, it is evident that Palladius and especially Socrates contain substantially different

---

[31] Amoun was Antony's contemporary; the story occurred therefore at the beginning of the 4th cent.; Bartelink, *La Storia Lausiaca*, 320 (n. 1 to *HL* 8). The village may have been Nitria, now El-Barnugi; Russel, *The Lives*, 137 (n. 3 to *HM* 22).

[32] *HM* 22 (Festugière, 128).

[33] Ruf. *HM* 30 (Schulz-Flügel, 375 f.).

[34] Pall. *HL* 8 (Butler, ii. 26); Soc. *HE* 4. 23 (PG 67. 509–11 B); Soz. *HE* 1. 14. 1–8 (GCS 50. 30) uses Palladius' account almost unaltered; Theod. *HE* 4. 12 (GCS 44. 232) attributes the same story to Pelagius.

information.[35] All sources agree upon the basic facts. Amoun and his wife begin their ascetic life in secrecy, in a spiritual marriage of varying duration. Upon Amoun's departure, or because of his wife's action, their chaste relationship is finally brought into the open. The result is most significant in the later version of Socrates: both embrace the eremitic life of the desert, at first in a common cell, then in separate cells side by side. In contrast, the account of the *Historia Monachorum* (intended initially for a Palestinian audience) represents the classic example of a family home transformed into an ascetic community, and thus men and women continue to live together. In the Greek version, this interpretation is only implied, but it is strengthened by Rufinus' apparent need to remove all ambiguities when introducing these models to the West: in his version, and here only, the sexes are clearly segregated.

All versions of the ascetic life chosen by Amoun's wife find, as we have already seen, their corroboration in other sources.[36] Socrates' account of men and women sharing a cell or living in close proximity in the desert is confirmed by Palladius' *Historia Lausiaca* itself—perhaps an indication that the common ascetic life of men and women as described in Socrates' dissenting version reflects an Eastern tradition, well known to an Eastern audience, but transmitted differently to the West.

Palladius' chapter 11 is devoted to Ammonius, one of the more famous desert ascetics who formed part of a group of intellectuals adhering to Origen's teachings. This group, called the 'Tall Brothers', played a decisive role in the Origenist controversy not only because they attracted men as famous as Evagrius and Palladius himself, but also because their contacts with Melania the Elder, Rufinus, John Chrysostom, and their circle spread the influence of the Origenistic monks to Alexandria, Jerusalem, Constantinople, and the West.[37] However, here this group is

[35] For the interrelation between the various sources cf. e.g. Reitzenstein, *Historia Monachorum*, 24–34, also 55.

[36] Cf. e.g. Clem. Alex. *Strom*. 3. 6. 45; 13. 92 (GCS 52 (15), 216, 238); Pall. *HL* 49 (Sisinnius) (Butler, ii. 143).

[37] Other members referred to by Pall. are at *HL* 21 (Eulogius), 38 (Evagrius), 58 (Diocles) (Butler, ii. 63, 116, 152); Epiph. *Haer*. 64 (2 GCS 31. 409 f.); O. Chadwick, *John Cassian: A Study in Primitive Monasticism* (Cambridge, 1968²), 24–6; Favale, 'Teofilo d'Alessandria', *Salesianum* 18 (1956), 498–535; A. J.

only relevant in so far as it adds weight to Socrates' version of Amoun's ascetic beginnings.[38]

This Ammonius, who was a disciple of Pambo, attained the heights of the love of God together with [three other brothers and] two sisters, ἅμα [τρισὶν ἀδελφοῖς ἑτέροις καὶ] δυσὶν ἀδελφαῖς. They went down to the desert, each making a μονή for themselves and keeping a distance from the others.

Ammonius was the group's leader; thus it is only reasonable to suppose that those with him (as Evagrius later on) shared his ascetic routine: for the body, only raw food with the exception of bread; for the intellect, memorizing not only the Old and New Testament, but also the writings of Origen, Didymus the Blind, Pierius, and Stephen, 'so the fathers of the desert testify'.[39] The arrangements within this famous and influential group were thus the same as those suggested by the papyrus transmitting Valeria's greetings to her daughters, as well as those recorded by Socrates for Amoun and his wife: men and women shared the life of desert ascetics, in body as well as in intellect.

From semi-anchorite communities of men and women to communities within villages and towns: both Palladius and the author of the *Historia Monachorum* went to considerable lengths to assure their readership that ascetic life flourished everywhere 'in the desert and in the countryside', and they promised to leave

Festugière, *Les Moines d'Orient*, i. (Paris, 1961), 77–91; Hunt, 'Palladius of Helenopolis'. 466–71.

[38] Pall. *HL* 11 (Butler, ii. 32); the same Ammonius is mentioned in the *HM* 20. 9 (Festugière, 121); Soc. *HE* 4. 23 (PG 67. 510); Soz. *HE* 6. 30. 5 (GCS 50. 285); A. Ammonius (Guy, 52); Bartelink, *La Storia Lausiaca*, 325 (n. 1 to *HL* 11); but the story of his exodus appears only in Palladius.

[39] The three brothers are omitted in several MSS, presumably owing to the later fate of the group, cf. Butler, *The Lausiac History*, ii. 32 (n. to ll. 16 and 17). Rousseau ('Blood-relationships', 136 f.) considers the sisters to be Ammonius' natural ones, which is a possibility, but not a compelling one. Whatever their relationship, the fact remains that women and men lived together as anchorites; Borias, 'Le Moine et sa famille', 82–91. For Ammonius' unusual fasting practices cf. Bartelink, *La Storia Lausiaca*, 326 (n. 29 to *HL* 11); Festugière, *Les Moines d'Orient*, i. 56–61; Frank, *Angelikos Bios*, 23–7; H. Musurillo, 'The Problem of Ascetical Fasting in the Greek Patristic Writers', *Traditio* 12 (1956), 1–64, here 24–35. For Didymus the Blind, Pierius, and Stephen cf. also Eus. *HE* 7. 32. 26–30 (Pierius); Jer. *Vir. ill.* 76 (Richardson, 41); Bartelink, *La Storia Lausiaca*, 326 (nn. 31, 32 to *HL* 11); Leipoldt, *Didymus der Blinde*, 6–8.

no one unmentioned 'in the cities, or in the villages'.[40] Owing to
the scope of his work, Palladius describes ascetic life within cities
and towns in greater detail than the pilgrims' travelogue. His
attention, beyond Alexandria itself, is concentrated on Antinoe,
one of his refuges in exile. By the time of his sojourn, c.410,
Antinoe had no less than twelve female monasteries.[41] One of
these, counting sixty virgins, was guided by Amma Talis, 'a
woman eighty years old in the ascetic life' and an exceptional
leader. Not only had she personally achieved such a degree of
apatheia that she could afford to touch Palladius' shoulder, she
also knew that her virgins loved her to the extent that locking the
front door had become unnecessary: their love imposed restraint
enough. One of Talis' virgins, Taor, was especially zealous. She
never accepted a new dress, veil, or sandals, to avoid ever having
to leave the monastery. She did not even join the rest of her companions for mass on Sundays. Thus Taor, who was also exceptionally beautiful, could work and pray without interruption.[42]

Talis' community is more interesting for what Palladius implies
rather than for what he tells us: seemingly virgins in other,
less ideally guided, communities did not always remain inside by
choice, so that there the 'lock in the hall of the monastery' was
intended not only to keep intruders out, but to keep sisters in.
Fittingly, Taor, the ideal disciple, excels in her refusal ever to
leave the premises. Apart from this detail, Palladius' information
confirms all other sources, except in regard to the community's
economic basis. Taor's refusal to go out even for new clothes
seems, uncharacteristically, to exclude textile work.[43] However,
the exact context in which a community such as Talis' has to be
placed is best described by the *Historia Monachorum*'s chapter
on Oxyrhynchus.[44]

'The city is so full of monasteries that the very walls resound

---

[40] *HM* pr. 10 (Festugière, 8); Pall. *HL* pr. (Butler, ii. 15).

[41] Pall. *HL* 59 (Butler, ii. 153); Palladius' other Egyptian refuge, Syene,
modern Aswan, is only mentioned in the prologue; cf. Pall. *Dial.* 20 (SC 341.
396); Maehler, *Häuser und ihre Bewohner*, 120–2.

[42] For the neglect of dress as ascetic practice cf. Frank, *Angelikos Bios*, 29 f.;
Judge, 'The Earliest Use', 86 n. 39; cf. also Pach. *Pr.* 81 (Veilleux, *Pachomian
Koinonia*, ii. 159); *P. Oxy.* xiv. 1774; *SB* iii. 7243.

[43] Sunday mass is also prescribed in the *Pseudo-Athanasian* c. 92 (Riedel and
Crum, *The Canons*, 58).

[44] *HM* 5, also pr. 10 (Festugière, 41, 7); Oxyrhynchus is modern Behnesa; H.
Kees, 'Oxyrhynchos', in *RE* xviii. 2043–6.

with the voices of monks. Other monasteries encircle it outside, so that the outer city forms another town alongside the inner.' Monks were everywhere. They outnumbered the secular citizens by far, residing in gate-towers, in porches, in former temples, and the capitol.[45] No place was safe from monastic dwellers; there were 'throngs of monks and nuns past counting'.

The effects of this monastic community on the daily life of the town must have been enormous: there were no less than twelve churches, and each monastery had its own oratory; the bishop celebrated mass constantly, even in the open; hospitality was offered everywhere; the magistrates distributed grain to needy strangers (perhaps to the occasional needy monk as well); and, of course, no pagan or heretic was within sight.[46]

How the town continued to function with such a considerable monastic community, even if described as positively as here, is hard to imagine. While numbers are not to be taken literally, there can be little doubt that the ascetic community in and around Oxyrhynchus was vast and counted significantly more women than men. Some of them lived in monasteries such as Talis', but many others clearly did not, inhabiting instead every public, and not so public, space available. In fact, the *Historia Monachorum* depicts an Oxyrhynchus which must have resembled early fourth-century Constantinople as described by Dagron: the monks 'forment une population mouvante installée dans les quartiers, autour des hospices, des martyria . . . dans la rue, à y sortir.' Though never made explicit in our sources, the droves of monks and virgins of every colour swarming everywhere inside the town and surrounding it like a second wall may well have caused resent-

---

[45] *Capitolium* normally stands for temple or even church; Oxyrhynchus had two; Festugière, *Enquête*, 38 n. 6; Russel, *The Lives*, 129 (n. 2 to *HM* 5). Five thousand monks lived within the city-walls, as many again surrounded it; the bishop of the town counted 10,000 monks and 20,000 virgins in his jurisdiction. The numbers, if applied to the town alone, are evidently contradictory, presumably the reason for Rufinus' omission of the figure of 5,000 for those within the walls; however, if jurisdiction beyond the city limits is implied they may be reconciled.

[46] Butler, *The Lausiac History*, ii. 209 f. with n. 54; Devos, 'Les Nombres', 100, 105–8; Festugière, *Enquête*, 39 n. 18, 40 n. 26; Russel, *The Lives*, 130 (n. 6 to *HM* 5); Wilcken, *Grundzüge und Chrestomathie*, 79 f.; Oxyrhynchus already had two churches in 300, and at least ten in the 6th cent.; Kees, 'Oxyrhynchos', *RE* xviii. 2043–6; oratories for monasteries are mentioned in *SBo* 27/G^1 32; Veilleux, *Pachomian Koinonia*, i. 272 (n. 2 to *SBo* 27).

ment, evoking once again the fifth-century scenario of bishops having to fight off large masses of roving monks, 'lacking all earthly possessions'.[47]

According to the *Historia Monachorum*, monasticism at Oxyrhynchus was flexible, and included a great variety of possible models. That such a flexibility in practice also meant flexibility in doctrine is explicitly denied: 'not one of the city's inhabitants is a heretic or a pagan', be they lay or ascetic; Rufinus adds, 'omnes catholici'. But such claims could easily suggest that in fact the contrary was the case: given the wide differences in orthopraxy there might well have been the same variety regarding orthodoxy.[48]

While it was not our purpose to discuss all the intricacies of both the *Historia Lausiaca* and the *Historia Monachorum*, both sources confirm and augment the information gained in previous discussions. Women are mentioned as practising ascetic life in villages and in the desert, alone, with their mothers, as partners in a *mariage blanc*, in communities, as anchorites, and as wandering ascetics. It is important to notice that neither property nor commerce was an obstacle to being a *parthenos*, the only title used for women apart from *ammas*. It is perhaps more important that virtually all communities referred to, with the exception of Amma Talis', included men who lived in close proximity to women. In fact, Palladius considers ascetics of both sexes as Fathers, and he, like Shenoute, Basil of Ancyra, and Gregory of Nyssa, characterizes ascetic women as having attained a male degree of virtue: they are 'gynaikai andreiai'.[49]

---

[47] Quotation from Dagron, *Naissance d'une capitale*, 513; Nilus, *De vol. paup.* (PG 79. 725–997); *Vie d' Alexandre l'Acémète*, 6–42, 48–50 (pp. 661–91, 696–9); Vööbus, *History of Asceticism*, ii. 185–96; *Callinici de Vita S. Hypatii Liber* in Festugière, *Les Moines d'Orient*, ii. 11–86.

[48] Interestingly, the same comment regarding the purity of faith in Oxyrhynchus is made by two local priests, Marcellinus and Faustinus, in a letter to Valentinian, Theodosius, and Arcadius: 'fidem catholicam inviolabiliter servare contendunt, ita ut se nullis haereticis nullisque praevaricatoribus per divina commisceant sacramenta', *Epistulae Imperatorum Pontificum Aliorum*, 2. 93 (ed. O. Günther (CSEL 35; Vienna, 1895) 33); the letter itself in fact refers to several doctrinally questionable inhabitants of Oxyrhynchus; cf. Jones, *The Later Roman Empire*, ii. 953; Festugière, *Enquête*, 39 n. 15. E. Schulz-Flügel (*Tyrannius Rufinus*, 57) assumes that Rufinus' insertion was caused by the fact that even the *arcanum* could be celebrated in the open, thus excluding *cathechumenoi*.

[49] Pall. *HL* 41 (Butler, ii. 128).

II

Athanasius of Alexandria and Urban
Asceticism

The previous discussions have made it abundantly clear that
ascetic life in Egypt was characterized by an extraordinary degree
of variety and, consequently, fluidity. Several models of ascetic
life coexisted and at times competed with each other. As in Asia
Minor, there were three distinct categories: ascetic life within
cities and towns, ascetic life in the isolation of the desert or the
countryside, and an ascetic life 'in between', in areas a little way
beyond the boundaries of the village or town though not in the
desert proper. The issue here is how our sources conceive of the
relationship between these forms, how they characterize their
relative merits and thus regulate them; and their perception of
these interrelations will in turn give us insights into the shaping of
asceticism in fourth-century Egypt.

So far, we have primarily discussed sources which either
originated in the *koine* and were representative of the genre of
ascetic life out of which they emerged, or were meant to 'export'
the Egyptian models to the remainder of the Empire. Now these
forms of ascetic life have to be integrated with those practised in
the city, in Alexandria, to render the picture more comprehensive. Of course, 'comprehensive' is a relative term; as in Asia
Minor, all that our sources permit is a case-study. Here, this will
take us back from the early fifth-century travelogues and histories
to the beginning of the fourth century and Athanasius of
Alexandria's writings to virgins.

The extent and nature of Athanasius of Alexandria's ascetic
writings has long been a matter of debate, but it is virtually
certain that he wrote at least two letters to ascetic women.
Indeed, the organizational features revealed in these letters correspond precisely to those prescribed in the *Pseudo-Athanasian*
and *Pseudo-Basilian Canons* discussed above (Chapter 7). The
two letters are known as the *Lettre aux Vierges* and the *Lettre à*

des vierges qui étaient allées prier à Jérusalem et étaient revenues.
Both were originally written in Greek and, although no specifi₵
date can be given, belong in all probability to the later period o⁷
Athanasius' life.[2]

[1] *S. Athanase. Lettres festales et pastorales en copte: Sur la virginité; La Lettre*
aux Vierges (= *LV*), ed. L. T. Lefort (CSCO 150, 151 (Scr. Copt. 19, 20);
Louvain, 1955), 73–99 (55–80), with quotations of the text by Shenoute, Apa
Mose, and Constantine of Assiout, 106–9 (85–7); this is a reissue of id. 'S.
Athanase: Sur la Virginité', *Le Muséon* 42 (1929), 197–274; *S. Athanase: Lettre à*
des vierges qui étaient allées prier à Jérusalem et qui étaient revenues (= *LVJer*),
ed. J. Lebon, in 'Athanasiana Syriaca 2', *Le Muséon* 41 (1928), 189–203. Jer.
(*Vir. ill.* 87 (Richardson, 45)) mentions that Athanasius wrote 'de virginitate . . .
plurimi'; the Coptic *History of the Church of Alexandria*, x (see *Storia della*
Chiesa di Alessandria, vol. i, ed. T. Orlandi (Testi e documenti per lo studio
dell'antichità 17; Milan, 1967), 52, 69; cf. also id. 'Ricerche su una storia
ecclesiastica alessandrina del IV secolo', *Vetera Christianorum* 11 (1974), 269–
312) likewise mentions an 'opus de virginitate'. These and other sources have
given rise to debates regarding the authenticity of Athanasius' writings *peri*
parthenias; cf. in particular M. Aubineau, 'Les Écrits de S. Athanase sur la
virginité', *RAM* 31 (1955), 140–71; C. U. Crimi, 'La paternità Atanasiana di un
testo *Ad Virgines*', *Le Muséon* 86 (1973), 521–4; L. Dossi, 'S. Ambrogio e S.
Atanasio nel De Virginibus', *Acme* 4 (1951), 246; Y.-M. Duval, 'La Problématique de la *Lettre aux Vierges* d'Athanase', *Le Muséon* 88 (1975), 405–33; id.
'L'originalité du *De virginibus* dans le mouvement ascétique occidental: Ambroise,
Cyprien, Athanase', in *Ambroise de Milan, XVIᵉ centenaire de son élection*
épiscopale (Études Augustiniennes; Paris, 1974), 9–66; T. Lefort, 'Athanase,
Ambrose et Chenoute sur la virginité', *Le Muséon* 48 (1935), 55–73, esp. 55–61.
The two works discussed in the following, the *LV* and the *LVJer*, are generally
regarded as authentic, though Orlandi ('Giustificazioni dell'encratismo', 365 f.)
continues to express doubts concerning the *LV*. The texts edited by J. Lebon ('Un
Logos peri Parthenias attribué à saint Athanase d'Alexandrie', in 'Athanasiana
Syriaca 1', *Le Muséon* 40 (1927), 205–48), R. P. Casey (*Der dem Athanasius*
zugeschriebene Traktat Peri Parthenias (Sitzungsberichte der Preussischen Akademie der Wissenschaften 33; Berlin, 1935), 1022–45), and E. v. d. Goltz (*Logos*
Soterias peri parthenias: Eine echte Schrift des Athanasius (TU 29, NF 14; Leipzig,
1905)) remain of dubious authenticity; cf. Riall, 'Athanasius of Alexandria',
app. vii, 385 f.; J. Roldanus, *Le Christ et l'homme dans la théologie d'Athanase*
d'Alexandrie: Étude de la conjonction de sa conception de l'homme avec sa
Christologie (Studies in the History of Christian Thought 4; Leiden, 1977²), 278 f.,
396–401; M. Tetz, 'Athanasius von Alexandrien', in *TRE* iv. 333–49, here 344.
[2] That is, the 350s to 370s. The notion of Athanasius as a Coptic author, based
on the widespread assumption that he spent much time among Coptic-speaking
monks, lacks evidence; Aubineau, 'Les Écrits de S. Athanase', 171; Lebon,
'Athanasiana Syriaca 2', 206–8; Lefort, 'S. Athanase: Sur la virginité', 210–12;
id. 'Athanase écrivain copte', *Le Muséon* 46 (1933), 1–33; Riall 'Athanasius
of Alexandria', app. iii, 358–62; Roldanus, *Le Christ et l'homme*, 278 n. 1,

Despite its intriguing title, the *Letter to the Virgins who went to Jerusalem to Pray and have Returned* has so far found very little scholarly attention; a fact which once again will have to excuse a certain degree of in-depth discussion.[3] The letter is directed to a group of virgins who have recently returned from a journey to Jerusalem, a pilgrimage to οἱ ἅγιοι τόποι, the 'holy places'. Their journey has been successful: tracing the principal events of Jesus' life as described by the Scriptures, they visited 'paradise' on earth and were loath to depart from the Holy Land, shedding 'des torrents de larmes amères'. Athanasius respects and shares those sentiments, but at the same time he offers a consolation which anticipates Gregory of Nyssa's later exhortation: one does not have to journey to Jerusalem to find paradise on earth. Indeed, the virgins are always in the Holy Land since whoever leads a life of sanctity carries Jerusalem inside him or herself. Thus, the virgins ought to dry their tears: as long as they remain pure, they will carry Christ within themselves and will preserve their own internal Holy Land.[4] This notion of a spiritual Jerusalem then leads to the central theme of the letter, transforming it into a veritable treatise *On Virginity*, on the correct method of achieving and preserving the purity that will guarantee the internal Holy Land.[5]

Athanasius' precepts to achieve correct virginal purity are in essence those which by now are all too familiar. The virgins addressed lived as a community, and the entire community, or at

399–401. Athanasius certainly contacted Coptic-speaking monks, cf. e.g. Ath. *Ap. c. Ar.* 6. 5 (*Athanasius Werk*, ii, ed. H. G. Opitz (Berlin, 1934), 92); Theod. *HE* 1. 2. 11 (GCS 44. 6 f.), and the extent and nature of this relationship will be discussed below.

[3] Aside from Lebon's critical remarks cf. also C. M. Badger, 'The New Man Created in God: Christology, Congregation and Asceticism in Athanasius of Alexandria', Diss. (Duke University, Durham, 1990), 258; the title is an addition by the scribe of the MS, Lebon, 'Athanasiana Syriaca 2', 210.

[4] *LVJer* (189–92); Eus. *HE* 4. 26. 13–14; id. *V. Const.* 3. 42 (GCS 7. 95); Elm, 'Perceptions of Jerusalem Pilgrimage', 219–21; Kötting, *Peregrinatio Religiosa*, 80–110; P. Thomsen, *Loca Sancta 1. Verzeichnis der im 1.–6. Jh. n. Chr. erwähnten Ortsnamen Palästinas* (Frankfurt, 1966²), *passim*; id. 'Untersuchungen zur ältesten Palästinaliteratur', *Zeitschrift des Deutschen Palästinavereins* 29 (1906), 101–32.

[5] The thematic difference has led to questions regarding the text's unity; Lebon, 'Athanasiana Syriaca 2', 211–12 argues convincingly in its favour.

least a substantial portion, had journeyed to Jerusalem. There
they stayed with συμπάρθενοι ('fellow virgins') in a female community which made a practice of offering hospitality to other
female ascetics—an interesting insight into the practical aspects
of Holy Land pilgrimage.

Athanasius' community lived under the guidance of an elder
mother assisted by several elder sisters, who had to be honoured
like the Lord himself, not as human beings, and obeyed without
murmuring. Equal respect was due to all fellow sisters, and pains
should be taken to avoid controversies, strife, and slander: even
if a fellow virgin has spoken evil against another, the victim ought
to remain silent, since she will be greatly rewarded in heaven.

External aspects of sanctity, though important, are only aids to
achieving the true aim: sanctity of spirit. Thus, the virgin must
never aim to please the world but concentrate on her virtues
without any distraction. She must eat only to sustain herself, not
for pleasure; take her baths not to enjoy but to calm herself,
avoiding by all means the use of perfume; she must walk without
letting her tunic trail and her feet dance, if possible not ever
greeting those she encounters on her way. Indeed, she must only
leave her house to walk to the church, covered so that no one
may see her face. The church is an oratory for divine education, a
sanatorium for the soul, and not a place for idle chatter. In
fact, silence and measured tones become a virgin under all circumstances. At the same time, she has to listen attentively to
'useful teachers' of divine doctrine; and must never lend her ears
to empty words.

'La vertu de la virginité n'est pas d'une seule sorte, mais
multiforme et variée.' It is the sanctity of a dove that the virgin
ought to imitate in order to be a fitting bride of Christ: domestic,
restrained, pure. It is to him that she has been promised; entirely
out of her own free will has she 'written that she will fight
the battle'. 'Aucune loi ne (l')exigeait, mais (ta) volonté (te)
conduisait': thus a fall is without excuse, a sin without remission.[6]

---

[6] *LVJer* 199; once the woman makes her decision, the transition from the old
to the new status in life is initiated by a solemn vow—in writing, thus predating
Shenoute's practice?—perhaps accompanied by a change of apparel. The letters
say nothing to indicate the actual manner in which this vow was professed. It does
not appear that the woman swore this vow in public or that there was any
congregational involvement; it seems to have been a private act.

'Indeed, it is better never to profess virginity than, having once made the profession, not to accomplish it perfectly' (Eccl. 5: 4). Therefore the virgin ought to avoid all contact with men other than priests and those who are qualified to give her instruction and spiritual profit.

Up to this point Athanasius' letter has followed a traditional line of instruction—albeit with his own particular nuances—characterizing in the process the life of a virgin in an urban community: seclusion is punctuated by visits to the baths and the church (and the occasional pilgrimage), while all other aspects of ascetic practice are observed under the guidance of a mother and elder sisters, with spiritual assistance given by members of the clergy and other men qualified to do so. It is in reference to these men that Athanasius embarks on a new, but again by now familiar, line of argument.[7]

As in Basil of Ancyra's treatise, some virgins are incapable of separating profitable instruction in doctrinal matters from the instructors; instead of listening to the divine words, they act vainly and laugh, made blind by desires of the flesh. Worse than that, others are not only incapable of distinguishing between good and bad when 'talking to men', they indeed dare to live with them. Of course, they profess that their cohabitation is 'de fraternité et d'amour spirituel', and that all are scrupulously observing their fasts, prayers, and continence.

Athanasius has no reason to doubt such affirmations but immediately points to all the shortcomings of these arrangements. Even if the virgin remains chaste, her cohabitation poses a constant threat to the man involved, potentially causing his downfall. Moreover, a virgin who lives with a man, even an ascetic, is no longer giving her undivided devotion to the Lord. If even a mortal husband rejects competition, how could the Lord tolerate such distractions? After all, the virgin made a promise, and she did so without the enforcement of the Law, because her state is above the Law. How can she renounce her celestial love for the sake of a dress, a roof over her head, and a piece of bread?

As far as the men are concerned, there ought to be no question but that such behaviour is intolerable. They would not dare to approach a married woman, but they do not think twice about

[7] *LVJer* 197 f.

placing a virgin below a married woman, making her the object
of scorn not only of her fellow virgins, but also of '[l]es femmes
mariées qui se sont éloignées de leurs maris pour la vie pure . . .'[8]
For all of this men offer the excuse that they do only 'le bien
pour Dieu, à cause du nom de vierge', supporting her materially.
Certainly, Athanasius points out, such a man's intentions may be
good, but his methods are flawed: instead of making a virgin into
his servant and companion, he ought simply to give her the
means for an ascetic life on her own. For a man who claims
to be a solitary ascetic (*monazontos*) cannot live together with a
woman; one plus one makes two, not one.

The pseudo-marriage of male and female ascetics was ubiquitous, once again prompted largely by the economic needs of the
women and the domestic advantages to be enjoyed by the men.[9]
And again, like Basil of Ancyra and the Cappadocian Fathers,
Athanasius never questions the intentions of the parties involved:
the men are bona fide ascetics and even doctrinal teachers, and
the virgins are virgins; what cannot be tolerated is the way in
which they cohabit. Yet Athanasius' sole practical suggestion for
addressing the economic dilemma is to exhort male ascetics to
give food and clothing to needy virgins without any expectations.

The organizational setting emerging from Athansius' second *Lettre
aux Vierges* differs only slightly insofar as some of the virgins
addressed still live within their own, natural, families.[10] The
exemplar guiding their day-to-day life is none other than Mary
herself. Like Mary, such a virgin is preoccupied only with God;
immersed in her prayers she is a constant source of amazement to
all members of her household; never querulous, never agitated,
she is always quiet and withdrawn in the meditation of the
Scriptures. She knows her duties: complete submission to God

---

[8] *LVJer* 202.

[9] i Cor 7: 3–38; Forlin Patrucco, 'Aspetti di vita familiare', 158–79; Giannarelli, *La tipologia femminile*, 88–94; E. Stauffer, 'Gameo', in *Theologisches
Wörterbuch zum Neuen Testament*, i (Stuttgart, 1957), 646–55.

[10] For the following cf. the excellent analysis by Duval, 'La Problématique de
la *Lettre aux Vierges*,' 405–33; the interpretation of *LV* is hampered by several
sizeable lacunae, of which only a small part has been reconstructed on the basis of
Shenoute's citations.

and to her parents, no communication whatsoever with male servants or other men. She only leaves the house to walk to church, accompanied by her parents, and to distribute the surplus of her labours to the poor; indeed, acts of charity (1 Tim. 9: 11) are one of her most beloved occupations.

Organizational features or the regulation of everyday activities are of an even more secondary nature in the *Lettre aux Vierges* than they were in the letter to those who returned from Jerusalem. There, concerns with the use of public baths, appropriate behaviour in church, and contacts with male ascetics figured prominently; here, though significant because of the role-model Mary, a virgin's daily life is not at all the focus.

Rather, Athanasius' theme is, again, the true nature of virginity. At the point where the extant text commences, he is in the process of delineating the relative position of marriage and virginity. If the durability of marriage has been defined by strict laws (Matt. 19: 6), then virginity, the union of the Word (*Λόγος*) with the virgin, has *a fortiori* to be immortal. Virginity has to be perpetual. Furthermore, while marriage is in accord with nature and with 'la lettre et . . . l'ésprit de la loi', virginity is above human nature and above the Law; it derives its approbation directly from the *Logos*, from Christ. In the same way that a man abandons mother and father for the sake of his wife (Matt. 19: 15), the virgin abandons humanity to resemble an angel. Although still within her family, she is no longer of that family: no longer bearing her parents' name, the virgin is a 'Daughter of Jerusalem'; her 'brother and fiancé' is Christ, represented on earth by the 'serviteur de votre fiancé', the bishop, Athanasius himself.

The reward of this new union is immortality. Virginity strives to become united in one spirit with the Lord (1 Cor. 6: 17). Therefore, as a mortal union generates mortal offspring, the union of the virgin with the Lord generates just and *immortal* thoughts.[11] Virginity thus lifts a human being above humanity, because the Lord himself came into the world, was made flesh through a virgin, and became human, and through this act 'la chose antérieurement difficile devint facile'—as demonstrated through the image and model, Mary. However, this by no means

---

[11] It is the absence of these 'just thoughts' which prevented the existence of true virginity among the 'Greeks and the barbarians'.

degrades marriage. Simply because virginity is better, marriage is not wrong. The Law has not recommended virginity for all precisely so that those who are not virgins can never be accused of disobeying a commandment. God's commandments form a unity, and they include various options so that we may be afforded a *free choice*. There is only one heavenly kingdom, and whoever obeys the Law he has chosen for himself will find himself in that kingdom: even if one star might be more splendid than another, all are still considered stars, and all stars form part of the same heaven.[12]

To recapitulate, the superior quality of virginity does not compromise that of marriage. Secondly, virginity's capacity to raise a mere mortal above humanity is a result of divine grace and not the 'product' of a mortal's own achievements. This divine grace, personified by analogy with the angel Gabriel, is bestowed upon a chosen few (Matt. 19: 17) and therefore precludes the existence of a divine commandment prescribing it for all. Because virginity is an act of grace, it has to be the result of the individual's free choice.

The stage is set. Virginity, in the final analysis, is above human nature and thus a result of divine grace, and marriage as well as other ways of life—including the consumption of meat and the right to wash oneself—are legitimate alternatives.[13] Armed with these basic principles, the virgins are ready for battle; now they may 'réfuter toutes les mauvaises idées des anciennes hérétiques et d'Hiéracas.'[14]

Athanasius' understanding of the nature of true virginity was far from uncontested. As the 'servant of your fiancé' and an 'elder' (presbyter?), he finds himself time and again confronted with the need to exhort his virgins 'not to change their *askēsis*

---

[12] Athanasius' argumentation is not entirely original, but embedded in a tradition shaped primarily by Methodius of Olympus (esp. *Symp.* 2. 1 (SC 95. 68–70)) and Origen, but also Basil of Ancyra; cf. H. Crouzel, *Virginité et mariage selon Origène* (Museum Lessianum 58; Paris, 1962), *passim*, esp. 111–16.

[13] Cf. Athanasius' reference to 1 Tim. 4: 1–3: 'The Spirit says expressly that in after time some will desert from the faith and give their minds to subversive doctrine. . . . They forbid marriage and inculcate abstinence from certain foods . . .'; for general features of Athanasius' ascetic teachings cf. below, and Gregg and Groh, *Early Arianism*, 131–59, 193 f.; Roldanus, *Le Christ et l'homme*, 277–348, esp. 303 f.

[14] Here the translation of *Le Muséon* 42, 249 is preferable.

into another one', not to become negligent and 'fallen'. In other words, far from being a simple exhortation, Athanasius' letter is also a defence against Hieracas and other heresies. Who were those 'hérétiques et apostats' and what did they teach?

HIERACAS AND HIS FOLLOWERS

The first place on Athanasius' list of heretics and apostates was held by Hieracas and with good reason, as the length of Athanasius' rebuttal indicates. As is so often the case, all we know of Hieracas stems from the pens of his adversaries, primarily the account given by Epiphanius in his *Panarion 67*. Contrary to many of Epiphanius' rather fictional descriptions, his account of Hieracas deserves greater credence, since it seems based on personal acquaintance, if not with the man himself, then at least with his work and his followers.[15]

Active from the end of the third until well into the fourth century, Hieracas was, according to Epiphanius, a remarkable character. A native Copt, he lived approximately one mile outside Leontopolis in his *monastērion* (ἐν τῷ μοναστηρίῳ αὐτοῦ), allegedly to the ripe old age of 90. Bilingual in Greek and Coptic, he not only knew the Old and New Testament by heart, but was well-versed in literature as well as in medicine, astrology, and magic.[16] He composed several (lost) works and earned his living as a calligrapher—in short, says Epiphanius, a highly erudite man. Though these abilities made him a well-known figure, it was not his erudition which had the greatest impact.[17]

For what, he asks, did the Word (*Logos*) come to make that was new? . . . If it was about the fear of God, the Law had that. If it was about marriage, the Scriptures preached about that. If it was about envy, greed, and injustice, the old covenant contained teachings about all of

---

[15] Epiph. *Haer.* 67 (3 GCS 37. 132–40); here in the translation by P. Amidon, *The Panarion of St. Epiphanius, Bishop of Salamis* (*Selected Passages*) (New York, 1990), 244–6; the *Vita Epiphanii*, 27 (PG 41. 57) depends here on the *Haer.*; A. v. Harnack, 'Hierakas und die Hierakiten', in *Realenzyklopädie für protestantische Theologie und Kirche* viii (Leipzig, 1900), 38–9; Heussi, *Ursprung*, 58–65.   [16] Cf. *LV* 66.

[17] ὀξὺς κατὰ πάντα τρόπον, Epiph. *Haer.* 67. 2–4 (3 GCS 37. 133, ll. 7–13); Badger, 'The New Man', 263 f.; Heussi (*Ursprung*, 58 n. 2) places his birth between 245 and 280, tending towards the earlier part (245–60), whereas his death must have occurred between 335 and 370; by 320 he was a well-known figure.

these. But this one thing he came to establish: to preach *enkrateia* in the world and to gather to himself chastity and *enkrateia*. For without these no one can live.

This fundamental concept was of profound consequence: to be a Christian was to be an ascetic. Marriage and the consumption of wine and meat, while appropriate for the times of the Old Testament, had become obsolete through Christ's incarnation. Thus, only a lifelong struggle for purity and ascetic perfection ensures salvation. On the basis of an allegorical interpretation of the Scriptures, Hieracas concluded that children could not be saved because they had no chance to fight the ascetic battle according to 2 Tim. 2: 5; and he rejected the resurrection of the body: only the purified soul could partake in the heavenly joys.[18]

Hieracas' rigorous teachings—before long associated with Manichaeism[19]—soon attracted a large following. Only 'virgins or monks or *enkrates* or widows' (παρθένος ἢ μονάζων ἢ ἐγκρατὴς ἢ χήρα) were admitted to his *synagōgai*, or communities.[20] Whereas Epiphanius never doubts Hieracas' genuine ascetic rigour, considers his Trinitarian doctrine orthodox, and criticizes only his allegorical method and his concept of the resurrection as Origenistic, he does not fail to accuse Hieracas' followers of various grave shortcomings.[21] Not only did they relax

---

[18] Epiph. *Haer.* 67. 1 (3 GCS 37. 133 l. 22–35 l. 1); contrary to Athanasius' accusations (*LV* 67) Hieracas did not condemn marriage, esp. that of the Patriarchs, outright.

[19] Presumably caused by his rejection of the resurrection of the body and the 'gifts of God' (Epiph. *Haer.* 67. 8 (3 GCS 37. 140 l. 7)); Hieracas' speculations concerning Melchisedek as well as his use of the apocryphal *Ascensio Isaiae* are also worth noting. The early Byzantine formulae of renunciation discussed by S. Lieu ('An Early Byzantine Formula for the Renunciation of Manichaeism: The Capita VII Contra Manichaeos of (Zacharias of Mytilene)', *JAC* 26 (1983), 152–218, esp. 197) mention Hieracas; F. Wisse, 'Gnosticism and Early Monasticism in Egypt', in B. Aland (ed.), *Gnosis: Festschrift für H. Jonas* (Göttingen, 1978), 431–40; Stroumsa, 'The Manichaean Challenge', 311.

[20] Heussi (*Ursprung*, 61–3) concludes that these *synagōgai* were occasional gatherings for divine service; but a permanent community seems more likely. Hieracas wrote ψαλμούς and νεωτερικούς (psalms and hymns) for these *synagōgai*, used in liturgical practices; Epiph. *Haer.* 67. 3 (3 GCS 37. 136 l. 12); one of these may have been identified by E. Peterson, 'Ein Fragment des Hierakas?', *Le Muséon* 60 (1947), 257–60.

[21] Interesting especially in the light of Arius' statement in his *Ep. ad Alex.* (= Ath. *De Decr. Nic. Syn.* 16 (Opitz, ii. 245 f.)), where he lists Hieracas next

their fast; but they lived with συνεισάκτους γυναῖκας, women who followed the same ascetic principles.[22]

The story sounds familiar. According to his adversaries, Hieracas was a man who had strayed outside the τοῦ Χριστοῦ πολιτεῖᾳ, a failing which worsened sharply among his followers and successors. Attempting to read beyond the condemnations, quite a different picture emerges. Potentially influenced by Origenistic or 'gnostic' teachings, Hieracas preached an ascetic rigorism based on the notion that asceticism was the *sine qua non* of salvation. The question is how his notion differed from the one that motivated an Antony, Amoun, Paphnutius, or any other ascetic who regarded as imperfect even the most exemplary Christian who failed to put into practice 'the one essential thing: the renunciation of marriage and worldly goods in favour of a hermit's life'.[23] Prima facie very little.

It was easy, as Athanasius did, to ridicule Hieracas' condemnation of marriage and to slander his followers for living hypocritically with *subintroductae*.[24] Yet it appears as if Hieracas and his followers, rather than being an aberration, in fact represent a strand of asceticism prevalent in all of Egypt. Indeed, they are attested around the end of the fourth century in the Arsinoite; at about the same time the patriarch of Alexandria ordered an anti-Hieracian purge in the monastery of Macarios.[25] As we have seen time and again, a stringently ascetic notion of Christianity was widespread and always included women who, as *parthenoi*, *enkrates*, and *chērai*, shared the lives of ascetic men

---

to Valentinus, Mani, and Sabellius as representatives of a flawed Christological doctrine; *Urk.* 6 (Opitz, iii. 12 f.) = Epiph. *Haer.* 69. 7 (3 GCS 37. 157–9); Duval, 'La Problématique de la *Lettre aux Vierges*', 424.

[22] Epiph. *Haer.* 67. 8 (3 GCS 37. 140 ll. 9–11).

[23] Wisse, 'Gnosticism and Early Monasticism', 434.

[24] *LV* 66–7; to summarize some of Athanasius' accusations: Hieracas' claim that marriage is bad because virginity is better parallels the argument that man is bad because the sun is better, clearly an absurdity (*LV* 66). Though Hieracas supports his views with Matt. 19: 12, he overlooks the fact that such passages were not intended as universal laws (*LV* 67). Furthermore, his prohibition of certain foods on principle is in clear contradiction to 1 Tim. 4: 1–3. In short, all Hieracas' teachings are pure vanity and hypocrisy (*LV* 69).

[25] According to the *HL* 19 (Macarius Alexandrinus = PG 34. 209) an ascetic in the Arsinoite seduced 300 faithful into becoming Hieracites, mentioned in

as a matter of course. To accuse Hieracas of hostility towards the body—the 'Manichaean' charge—is equally understandable: however, few of the stories told by the Fathers in the *Apophthegmata* suggest that they regarded the body as anything other than an instrument to be dominated and controlled to the point of extinction.

Hieracas, like most of the desert anchorites, had removed himself from the village and its community, that is from the direct influence of the Church and its clergy. This physical separation (accompanied by a theological separation, as indicated by his own psalms and hymns) caused conflicts; and here also Hieracas is the norm rather than the deviation. He was an Egyptian, a Coptic, and his followers, as is evident from Athanasius' harsh condemnation, seem to have resisted co-operation with the see of Alexandria.[26] But would he and his followers alone have merited such high-level condemnation as they now received through Athanasius if they had been, as Epiphanius implies, a relatively insignificant group? Clearly not. Hieracas, as Athanasius rightly points out, is a representative of ascetic practices shared by a substantial proportion of 'all the other heretics' and, as such, a serious threat well worth his attention. Who could those other heretics have been?

THE MELITIANS

'Melitius was a contemporary of the Hieracas mentioned above, flourished when he did, and comes next in order after him.'[27] Nowhere in Athanasius' letter to the virgins do we find even

Preuschen, *Palladius und Rufinus*, 124. This text has been rejected by Butler, *Lausiac History*, ii. 194 n. 28 = A 19; *Apopht.* 1490 B (Regnault (1976), 27–30) relates the same story of an Arsinoite monk attracted after many years of asceticism to Hieracas' teachings in connection with Macarius. For the purge cf. Evelyn White, *The Monasteries of Wādi'n Natrūn*, ii. 115 f.; Peterson, 'Ein Fragment', 259 f.; Wisse, 'Gnosticism and Early Monasticism', 438 f.

[26] Griggs, *Early Egyptian Christianity*, 83–92; contrary to J. Jarry, 'Le Manichéisme en Égypte byzantine', *Bulletin de l'institut français d'archéologie orientale* 66 (1968), 121–37, esp. 135 f.; cf. in particular Orlandi, 'Giustificazioni dell'encratismo', 341–68, esp. 344–9, 352–63.

[27] Epiph. *Haer.* 68 (3 GCS 37. 140–52) appears to be based on Melitian sources, esp. 68. 11 (ibid. 151); here 68. 1–3 (ibid. 140–3); Amidon, *Panarion*,

the slightest mention of the Melitians. Yet the severity of the Melitian threat to Athanasius' ecclesiastical power has long been a well-established fact. Already by 325, during the bishopric of Athanasius' predecessor and mentor, Alexander of Alexandria, Melitian bishops occupied more than half of all episcopal sees along the Nile as far south as Hermonthis. Unlike Hieracas and his followers, Melitians were also among the clergy of Alexandria itself. Beyond question, the *tagma* of Melitius, far from being a mere sect, was a veritable church of significant proportions, a true opposition with its own independent hierarchy, developed since 305/6. Thus the supremacy of the Alexandrian see was severely contested long before Athanasius' election: he inherited a heavy burden that overshadowed his career from its outset.[28] As it was, he had only succeeded under dramatic and slightly illegal circumstances, and against a majority of Melitian bishops;[29]

247–54. At the time of the 'Great Persecution' (304), a dispute arose between Peter, bishop of Alexandria, and Melitius, bishop of Lycopolis, concerning read-mission of the lapsed and other institutional and disciplinary matters. This dispute led eventually to Melitius' excommunication (306) and a formal schism. Even so, Melitius gathered an increasing following in Egypt and the Thebaid; F. H. Kettler, 'Der meletianische Streit in Ägypten', *ZNW* 35 (1936), 155–93, here 159–63, cf. also c. 12 of the council of Antioch, AD 328 (Mansi, ii. 1093); W. H. C. Frend, 'Athanasius as an Egyptian Christian Leader', *New College Bulletin* 8 (1974), 20–37 (repr. in id. *Religion Popular and Unpopular in the Early Christian Centuries* (London, 1976), here 28 f.); K. Müller, *Beiträge zur Geschichte der Verfassung der alten Kirche*, ii (Akademie der Preussischen Akademie der Wissenschaften, Phil.-hist. Kl. 3; Berlin, 1922), 12–17. On the spelling of Melitians cf. H. Hauben ('On the Melitians in P. Lond. VI 1914: The Problem of Papas Heraiscus', in *Proceedings of the Sixteenth Intern. Congress of Papyrology* (American Studies in Papyrology 23; Chicago, 1981), 447–56) 447 n. 1; E. Schwartz, 'Die Quellen über den melitianischen Streit', in *Gesammelte Schriften*, iii. 87–9.

[28] For a list of Melitian bishops cf. *Breviarium a Melitio datum Alexandro episcopo* = Ath. *Apol. sec.* 71 (Opitz, ii. 149); only 46% of all Egyptian sees were occupied by followers of Alexander of Alexandria, Peter's successor; S. T. Carroll, 'The Melitian Schism: Coptic Christianity and the Egyptian Church', Diss. (Oxford, Ohio, 1989), 114–20; Kettler, 'Der melitianische Streit', 156–71; A. Martin, 'Athanase et les Mélitiens (325–35)', in *Politique et Théologie chez Athanase d'Alexandrie, Actes du Colloque de Chantilly, 23ᵐᵉ–25ᵐᵉ Sept. 1973* (Théologie Historique 27; Paris, 1974), 32–61, here 32 f.

[29] Alexander and Melitius died in about 327/8 and were succeeded by Athanasius and John Arkhaph, bishop of Memphis. The clash between these personalities marks the second major breaking point in the schism; Eus. *V. Const.*

only six years later in 335, Melitian opposition forced him into exile to Trier.[30]

The Melitian Church was primarily Coptic. With the basis of its power firmly rooted along the Nile, it found a large number of its

2. 62, 3. 23 (GCS 7. 66, 88); *Urk.* 3 and 4 (Opitz, iii. 4–6); Soz. *HE* 2. 21. 1–2 (GCS 50. 76); Ath. *Chron.* (PG 26. 1351 B); id. *Apol. sec.* 59. 3 (Opitz, ii. 139); Epiph. *Haer.* 68. 5 (GCS 37. 145). The circumstances surrounding Athanasius' election will probably never be entirely clarified. It is clear, however, that Alexander designated Athanasius as his successor, contrary to current custom, and that his election was ratified by only six or seven bishops against *circa* 47; the Melitians also accused him of being less than the required age of 30 (Ath. *Apol. sec.* 6 (Opitz, ii. 92 n. 14)). Athanasius had informed Constantine of his appointment immediately, conveying a false impression of unanimity and harmony. Of course, the Melitians installed a counter-bishop, probably Heraiscos, and sent incessant missions of protest to Constantine accusing Athanasius of illegitimate ordination, high treason, and murder. Athanasius reacted with violence and repression; Ath. *Apol. sec.* 6. 4, 60–3 (Opitz, ii. 92, 140–3); Soc. *HE* 1. 27 (PG 67. 153, 157); Soz. *HE* 2. 17. 4, 25. 6 (GCS 50. 72, 84); Phil. *HE* 1. 9, 2. 11 (GCS 21. 10, 22); Nicaea c. 4 (Mansi, ii. 669); Girardet, *Kaisergericht und Bischofsgericht*, 54–65; Hauben, 'On the Melitians', 450–6; Martin, 'Athanase', 38–51; W. Telfer, 'Meletius of Lycopolis and Episcopal Succession in Egypt', *Harvard Theological Review* 48 (1955), 227–37; E. Schwartz, 'Von Nicäa bis Konstantins Tod', in id. *Gesammelte Schriften*, iii. 195–216.

[30] The Melitian cause benefited from Constantine's desire to ensure the unity of the Church on the occasion of his thirtieth anniversary as Augustus in 334/5; *Anon. Panegyrici Latini* 6 ⟨7⟩ (ed. Baehrens, 21, 3–6); Eus. *V. Const.* 4. 42 (GCS 7. 134); Ath. *Apol. sec.* 10. 1 (Opitz, ii. 95); Theod. *HE* 1. 29 (GCS 44. 83). At the time, only Athanasius' recalcitrance and incapacity to deal with the Melitian opposition seemed to prevent his aim; Ath. *Apol. sec.* 59–60 (Opitz, ii. 136–41); Gelasius 3. 15. 1 = *Urk.* 32 (Opitz, iii. 66); Soz. *HE* 2. 25. 1 (GCS 50. 84); Theod. *HE* 1. 28. 2–4 (GCS 44. 82). To solve these problems a council had been summoned to Caesarea, which Athanasius refused to attend, and a second council to Tyre which Athanasius could no longer ignore; Ath. *Apol. sec.* 71. 2, 86. 1 (Opitz, ii. 149, 164); *P. Lond.* vi. 1913 and 1914. In Tyre the Melitians carried the day, Athanasius was deposed and, despite his personal intervention with Constantine, exiled to Trier. Soz. *HE* 2. 25. 3–6 (GCS 50. 84); Ath. *Apol. sec.* 9, 86. 2–12 (Opitz, ii. 95, 164); L. Barnard, 'Athanasius and the Meletian Schism in Egypt', *Journal of Egyptian Archaeology* 59 (1973), 181–9; Frend, 'Athanasius as an Egyptian Christian Leader', 22 f.; Girardet, *Kaisergericht und Bischofsgericht*, 64–75; K. Holl, 'Die Bedeutung der neuveröffentlichten melitianischen Urkunden für die Kirchengeschichte', in *Gesammelte Aufsätze zur Kirchengeschichte*, ii (Tübingen, 1928; repr. Darmstadt, 1964), 283–97; Martin, 'Athanase', 50–2; P. Peeters, 'Comment S. Athanase s'enfuit de Tyre en 335?', in *Bulletin de l'Academie Royale Belgique, Cl. de Lettres* 30 (Brussels, 1946), 131–77; for a very detailed account of these years cf. Riall, 'Athanasius of Alexandria', 1–94.

supporters among Coptic ascetics. However, none of our literary sources indicated even the existence of Melitian ascetics until J. Bell published several papyri in 1924, which drastically altered our knowledge. Even before 334 the Melitian Church not only possessed its own clerical hierarchy, but had its own monastic *tagma* with fully organized communities.[31] These monasteries were mainly located in or very close to villages and towns. They were guided by a community of elders, who maintained close contact with the local clergy. For example, a certain Apa Pageus, one of the monks mentioned in *P. Lond.* vi. 1913, was at the same time a presbyter and responsible for a branch community in his village, Hipponon. When he is summoned to attend Constantine's council at Caesarea, he informs the 'elders' of the main community at Hathor that he has chosen a representative for his absence, and his choice has to be ratified by the main monastery.

The Melitian monks' involvement in the affairs of their local community is well documented. Monks interceded with financial aid for debtors, produced agricultural as well as other goods such as cloaks and shoes, and were actively involved in trade, as attested by the importance of the *oikonomos*. Links between monasteries were likewise close. Thus one renegade monk asked a certain Paieous to intervene on his behalf and to reconcile him with his own monastery, by writing κατὰ μονήν, 'around the houses'.[32]

The participation of women in Melitian monasticism is not absolutely certain, despite the occurrence of female names in the Melitian archive.[33] However, the widespread presence of

[31] *P. Lond.* vi. 1913–22; Bell, *Jews and Christians in Egypt*, 43–99 (reviewed by Holl, 'Die Bedeutung', 283–97); Judge, 'The Earliest Use', 84–9; A. Martin, 'Aux origines de l'Église copte: L'Implantation et le développement du christianisme en Égypte (I^e–IVe siècles)', *REA* 83 (1981), 35–56, here 45.

[32] *P. Lond.* vi. 1917; Judge, 'The Earliest Use', 85. Most of the letters published by Bell were addressed to or written by the same Apa Paieous, leader of a large and influential community near P-hator in the Upper Cynopolite *nomē*. Other communities existed in the Heracleopolite *nomē*, near Antaeopolis and near Hypselis; P. Barison, 'Ricerche sui monasteri dell' Egitto bizantino ed arabo secondo i documenti dei papiri greci', *Aegyptus* 18 (1938), 29–148, here 84; Hauben, 'On the Melitians', 447–56. Despite their geographic as well as chronological proximity, Melitian and Pachomian monasticism are two distinct phenomena; Heussi, *Ursprung*, 129–31; Martin, 'Athanase', 58–61.

[33] *P. Lond.* vi. 1922 may have been co-authored by a certain Bes; *P. Lond.* vi. 1920 l. 6 and vi. 1922 l. 13 refer to a certain Helena.

Melitians throughout Egypt and the urban character of their monasticism makes the presence of ascetic women among them highly likely.[34]

Athanasius, while expounding the vicissitudes of the comparatively obscure Hieracas at considerable length, as mentioned above, never once mentions Melitius or his monasticism in his *Lettre aux Vierges*. It is possible that by then the Melitians no longer had any impact. After 335 they soon lost the imperial favour and our knowledge becomes increasingly sparse.[35] Yet Melitian monasticism continued to exist well into the sixth century; thus to conclude that by the time of the *Lettre's* composition there was no longer a Melitian threat seems over-optimistic.[36] Athanasius probably wrote to virgins who lived in Alexandria itself. Since Melitians were concentrated in the *koinē*, especially around Memphis, he may simply not have felt the need to evoke this old spectre.[37] Further answers might emerge by reassessing the central themes of Athanasius' attack against Hieracas.

Hieracas, so Athanasius says, condemned marriage and the consumption of meat and wine because virginity and abstinence are better. This line of argument demonstrates that he is an ignoramus, concocting illogical arguments out of 'fables according to Greek Wisdom'. Quite evidently 'he is a stranger to our faith' . . . 'what Scripture has he read?'[38] The Melitian schism arose out of a rigoristic stance against those who had lapsed during the Diocletian Persecutions. Though we know nothing of their regime, it may not be too far-fetched to argue with Heussi that a similar rigoristic impetus may have informed their asceticism.[39] Not surprisingly, Athanasius condemns them elsewhere of crimes similar to those perpetrated by Hieracas: 'for the greater part, or rather the whole of them, have never had a religious education, nor are they acquainted with the sound faith

[34] Carroll ('Melitian Schism', 183 f.) presumes the presence of women and points to evidence from AD 512/13. A. H. Sayce ('Deux contrats grecs du Fayoum', *REG* 3 (1890), 131–44) cites contracts where monks sell monasteries to Melitian monks.

[35] John Arkhap was exiled in 336, Soz. *HE* 2. 31. 4 (GCS 50. 96); Ath. *Hist. Ar.* 50. 2 (PG 25. 753 c); Frend, 'Athanasius', 32; Martin, 'Athanase', 58; it is uncertain who actually occupied the see after 335/6.

[36] Martin, 'Athanase', 59–61.

[37] Hauben, 'The Melitians', 450, 455.

[38] *LV* 66; similar warnings in Ath. *Ep. ad Ammoun* (PG 26. 1169 f.).

[39] Heussi, *Ursprung*, 129 f.

in Christ, nor do they know at all what Christianity is.' In his Festal Letter 39 of 367, addressed to Theodore, the superior of the Pachomian *koinōnia*, and intended for distribution among his monks, Athanasius accuses Melitians of using apocryphal books, like the followers of Hieracas.[40]

In short, Melitians, like the followers of Hieracas, constituted a specific Coptic group with its own ascetic agenda, and it is conceivable that the true focus of Athanasius' attack against Hieracas was the Melitians.[41] That Athanasius remained for many years highly preoccupied by the Melitian opposition, both ecclesiastical and ascetic, becomes evident when examining yet another facet of the Melitian schism.

In 330, during the aftermath of Athanasius' election and faced with his increasing reluctance to allow them independent worship, a Melitian delegation went to Constantinople to petition the emperor for his support. Here they found an ally: the Homoian or 'Arian' bishop Eusebius of Nicomedia, who had presided at the council of Gangra which condemned Eustathius' followers. Eusebius and his group had by then won the support of the emperor and agreed to intercede on behalf of the Melitians, albeit on one condition: that they join forces with the supporters of Arius despite doctrinal differences. In fact, both groups, the Melitians and the followers of Arius, had one common foe, namely, Athanasius. Thus a fateful political alliance was forged: 'the Melitians, once pure in faith, mingled with the disciples of Arius.'[42]

---

[40] Ath. *Hist. Ar.* 78. 1 (Opitz, ii. 226); *Epist. Fest.* 39 (CSCO 151. 39); *Fest. Index*, 39 (*Histoire 'Acéphale' et Index Syriaque des Lettres festales d'Athanase d'Alexandrie*, ed. A. Martin and M. Albert (SC 317; Paris, 1985) 270); Eng. trans. by P. Schaff and H. Wace, *St. Athanasius: Selected Works and Letters* (Nicene and Post-Nicene Fathers of the Christian Church, 2nd ser., 4; Grand Rapids, 1891), 299, 551; cf. also the interesting passages in the *Ps.-Athanasian Canons* 11 and 12, forbidding Melitian songs (Riedel and Crum, *The Canons*, 23 f.); L. T. Lefort, 'Théodore de Tabennese et la lettre de s. Athanase sur le canon de la Bible', *Le Muséon* 29 (1910), 205–16. If Carroll's somewhat tenuous reconstruction of the Melitian interpretation of concepts of the Virgin Mary could be supported further, this might add another nuance to Athanasius' emphasis on Mariology in *LV*.

[41] Athanasius' reluctance to mention the Arians by name before the death of Constantine is a well-known fact; could the absence of 'Melitians' in the *LV* suggest an earlier date?

[42] Epiph. *Haer.* 68. 6 (3 GCS 37. 146); Ath. *Apol. sec.* 86 (Opitz, ii. 165); Soc.

ALEXANDER OF ALEXANDRIA AND ARIAN VIRGINS

After his diatribe against Hieracas and the other heretics, Athanasius launches into a long, unfortunately fragmented, passage based on the Song of Songs, where he exhorts the virgins again to defend their bridegroom against heretical attacks. Suddenly, however, Athanasius feigns incompetence to exalt the true merits of virginity adequately.[43] He therefore introduces his predecessor, Alexander of Alexandria, by recalling one of the latter's addresses to 'des vierges de votre espèce.'[44]

Alexander—the Holy Scriptures firmly clasped in his hands— once purportedly addressed some virgins as follows. Their fiancé is not a mortal being: he is God and God's only son, the Word, *Logos*, God's wisdom and his force. God and he are one and of the same substance; the Word exists with the Father and did not have its own beginning. The *Logos* is furthermore an excellent 'philanthropist': he became incarnate through the Virgin Mary. Yes, he took on a body, a created form, but solely to deliver this body and thus all believers from death. But, this does not mean that he became a mortal being: God has undergone before our eyes the vicissitudes of humanity, suffering human pain and hunger, sleeping, eating, and weeping. It is this God, the Son,

---

HE 1. 35 (PG 67. 169); Soz *HE* 2. 25 (GCS 50. 84–6); Eus. *V. Const.* 4. 42 (GCS 7. 134). Indeed, Athanasius represented his exile after 335 to Constantine as the result of a conspiracy by Melitians and Eusebians to reinstall Arianism, 'the vilest threat to Christianity'; Ath. *Apol. sec.* 27–8; 78. 1–2 (Opitz, ii. 107, 165). For the role of Eusebius cf. Ath. *De Syn.* 21 (PG 26. 718); E. Schwartz, 'Von Konstantins Tod bis Sardica', in *Gesammelte Schriften*, iii. 318–20; Girardet, *Kaisergericht*, 66–75; Martin, 'Athanase', 52–9; Schwartz, 'Von Nicäa bis Konstantins Tod', 247–57.

[43] The passage is quite Origenistic in character; Orig. *In Cant.* 1. 10; 2. 8, 15 (PG 13. 132, 193).

[44] *LV* 72–6; a well-known rhetorical device, which Athanasius uses repeatedly in the *Vita Antonii*; Duval, 'La Problématique de la *Lettre*', 426. This speech by Alexander, contrary to Lefort ('Athanase, Ambroise et Chenoute', 68), is probably not the one mentioned in Severus' *History of the Patriarchs of the Coptic Church of Alexandria*, 8 (trans. B. Evetts (Patrologia Orientalis I: 2, 4; Paris, 1907), 405); here, Severus quotes an incident related in a letter sent by Athanasius 'from his exile to certain virgins in the city of Alexandria': while Alexander was praying one night some virgins came asking to see him. They complained that some of their sisters fasted severely and refused to work. Alexander reassures them by emphasizing his own moderate regime.

who is the virgins' fiancé, brother, neighbour; the reason why they are called the 'Daughters of Jerusalem'.

But virgins must constantly guard against those who, jealous of their union, try to defy their fiancé by saying: 'The Word of God is a creation, drawn out of Nothingness and before it was engendered it did not exist.' And 'Christ is not truly God, . . . he is not of the same substance as God, . . . he is called the Word because he is God's messenger.' These words, so Alexander says, are uttered to corrupt innocent hearts and to deceive the simple-minded. Worse, they seek to separate the pure virgin from Christ's love by insinuating that their bond is with a human, and thus they degrade the vow of virginity.

In other words, Alexander's speech is nothing but the synopsis of Athanasius' treatise on *The Incarnation of the Word*, skilfully inserted in a line of argument that demonstrates the integral link between 'correct' virginity, incarnation, and the relationship between the Father and the Son—who are of one substance, *homoousios*. The supposed author of this speech leaves little doubt as to the true addressees of this veritable polemic: the Arians. Indeed, Athanasius could hardly have chosen a more authoritative figure than his predecessor, not only in the see of Alexandria, but also in the battle against the 'vilest of all heresies'.[45]

It was during Alexander's episcopate that the controversy between him and Arius first erupted.[46] Arius, born in Libya around 280, enters the historical scene only some thirty or so years later, as presbyter of an important church in the Alexandrian

---

[45] Cf. also Ath. *Or. 3 contra Ar.* (PG 26. 321–466); *Athanase d'Alexandrie: Sur l'incarnation du Verbe*, ed. Ch. Kannengiesser (SC 199; Paris, 1973); for controversial interpretations of the *De Incarnatione* cf. e.g. the discussion by J. Roldanus (*Le Christ et l'homme*, 12–22, 25–65, 107–23, 290 f., 317), and E. P. Meijering (*Athanasius: De Incarnatione Verbi* (Amsterdam, 1989), 11–21, and *passim*), who proposed an anti-Marcionite stance for *De Incar.*

[46] Alexander was bishop between 317 and 328; Ath. *Chron.* 1 (PG 26. 1351 B); Theod. *HE* 1. 2–4 (GCS 44. 6–9); Epiph. *Haer.* 69. 4 (3 GCS 37. 155); Kopecek, *History of Neo-Arianism*, i. 1–7; H. Kraft, 'Alexander', in *Kirchenväterlexikon* (Munich, 1966), 19; R. Williams, *Arius: Heresy and Tradition* (London, 1987), 32–41. Connections between Arius and Melitius cannot be established with certainty, cf. W. Telfer ('St. Peter of Alexandria and Arius' (Mélanges Paul Peeters I), *AnBoll* 67 (1949), 117–30) and R. Williams ('Arius and the Melitian Schism', *JThS* NS 37 (1986), 35–52).

district of Baucalis, where he enjoyed 'a high reputation as its spiritual director'.[47] In this capacity he taught a version of the relationship between Father and Son which diverged from that held by his bishop, Alexander. Around 318/19, their disagreement erupted into open conflict; Alexander accused Arius of Sabellianism and excommunicated him, a step which caused widespread resentment. In a later letter addressed to Bishop Alexander of Thessaloniki (or Constantinople) but intended for several bishops, Alexander describes this time as follows:[48]

They brought accusations against us before the courts, suborning as witnesses certain unprincipled women whom they seduced into error. On the other hand, they dishonoured Christianity by permitting their young girls (νεωτέραι) to ramble about the streets.

While here is not the place to discuss the history of Arius and his followers, this letter contains significant information regarding one particular aspect which will be the focus of the following: the role played by ascetic women in the Arian controversy.[49]

Who were those 'unprincipled women' and 'young girls'? The

[47] Epiph. *Haer.* 69. 1 (3 GCS 37. 152); E. W. Barnard, 'The Antecedents of Arius', *VigChr* 24 (1970), 172–88; E. Boularand, *L'Hérésie d'Arius et la foi de Nicée*, i. (Paris, 1972), 9–24; Kopecek, *History of Neo-Arianism*, i. 1–12; Williams, *Arius*, 29–32.

[48] *Urk.* 14 (Opitz, iii. 19–29); Theod. *HE* 1. 3 (GCS 44. 5 f.); Soz. *HE* 1. 15 (GCS 50. 32); Soc. *HE* 1. 6 (PG 67. 41–52); Boularand, *L'Hérésie*, 24–31; translation by Kopecek, *History of Neo-Arianism*, i. 5 f.

[49] Soc. *HE* 1. 5–7 (PG 67. 41–56); Soz. *HE* 1. 15–16 (GCS 50. 32–6); Theod. *HE* 1. 2, 4–6 (GCS 44. 5 f.); Ruf. *HE* 1. 1 (PL 21. 467). The state of research regarding Arianism is constantly in flux, and there is a vast bibliography; the following relies, in addition to the works already mentioned, primarily on H.-C. Brennecke, *Hilarius von Poitiers und die Bischofsopposition gegen Konstantius II: Untersuchungen zur dritten Phase des arianischen Streites (337–361)* (Patristische Texte und Untersuchungen 26; Berlin, 1984), esp. 1–64; R. Gregg (ed.), *Arianism: Historical and Theological Reassessments. Papers from the Ninth International Conference on Patristic Studies, Oxford, September 5–10, 1983* (Patristic Monograph Series 11; Philadelphia, 1985); R. Lorenz, *Arius judaizans? Untersuchungen zur dogmengeschichtlichen Einordnung des Arius* (Forschungen zur Kirchen-und Dogmengeschichte 31; Göttingen, 1980), 23–66; H.-I. Marrou, 'L'Arianisme comme phénomène alexandrin', in *Académie des Inscriptions et des Belles Lettres, Comptes Rendus* (Paris, 1973), 533–42 (repr. *Patristique et Humanisme* (Patristica Sorbonnensia 9; Paris, 1976)); T. E. Pollard, 'The Origins of Arianism', *JThS* 9 (1958), 103–11; A. M. Ritter, 'Arianismus', in *TRE* iii. 692–719; Simonetti, *La crisi ariana*, 26–33; Tetz, 'Athanasius von Alexandrien', 333–49; J. M. Wiles, 'In Defence of Arius', *JThS* 13 (1962), 339–47.

main theme of Alexander's letter is the methods employed by Arius and his followers to aggravate the disruption of the Church in Alexandria. Arius and his followers not only declared their own independence from the episcopal see, but were actively campaigning to gain support among other Alexandrian congregations. Further, and more importantly, they spread the conflict beyond the boundaries of the city: Arius solicited the support of his old friends Eusebius of Nicomedia and Eusebius of Caesarea, as well as that of his compatriots in Libya and the Pentapolis. However, Alexander's primary concern was the situation in Alexandria. And here these women become significant. After his condemnation of the Arians' use or abuse of 'unprincipled women', Alexander returns to them in paragraph 58 of the same letter, this time quoting directly from 2 Tim. 3: 6:

[The Arians] are deceivers, and propagate lies, and never adhere to the truth. They go about to different cities with no other intent than to deliver letters under the pretext of friendship and in the name of peace, and by hypocrisy and flattery to obtain other letters in return, in order to deceive a few *'silly women who are laden with sins'*.[50]

The Greek word γυναικάριον, the diminutive of γυνή, means simply 'little woman'. However, Alexander's characterization—loose, unprincipled, laden with sin—suggests a very specific type of women: prostitutes.[51] Alexander insinuates that the Arians went as far as to employ the services of common prostitutes to discredit the moral integrity of the orthodox clergy in a court of law—a fairly common stratagem used both by 'heretics' and 'orthodox' as the cases of Paul of Samosate, Eustathius of Antioch, and later on Athanasius himself attest.[52] It is certainly possible that the Arians did resort to this tactic. However, the true reason for

---

[50] *Urk.* 14. 5 and 58 (Opitz, iii. 20, 29).

[51] LSJ s.vv. γυναικάριον, and ἀτακτέω, 'unprincipled, irregular, disorderly'.

[52] It would be interesting to know more about the charges, but the sources offer no other information; Eus. *HE* 7. 30. 12; Soc. *HE* 1. 24 (PG 67. 144); Soz. *HE* 2. 25 (GCS 50. 85); Phil. *HE* 2. 7 (GCS 21. 19). A prostitute accused Eustathius of Antioch of illegitimate fatherhood; Paul had been accused of too close a contact with 'little women'; and a prostitute accused Athanasius in Tyre of bribery and fornication; H. Chadwick ('The Rise and Fall of Eustathius of Antioch', *JThS* 49 (1948), 27–35) maintains (p. 28) that all these accounts are pure legend. There seems to be no cause for such a conclusion; E. Schwartz, 'Das Antiochenische Synodalschreiben von 325', in *Gesammelte Schriften*, iii. 172–4; Simonetti, *La crisi ariana*, 104 f.

Alexander's concerns are not some real or imagined prostitutes, but a different type of woman.

According to Epiphanius, Arius was an old man by the time he 'departed from the true faith', but even so, he was

charming in his speech, and able to persuade and flatter souls. In no time therefore he managed to draw apart from the Church into a single group seven hundred virgins and, so the report goes, separated off seven presbyters and twelve deacons.

Epiphanius further states that Alexander not only excommunicated Arius, but 'with him was ejected a large crowd of virgins and other clerics whom he had defiled.'[53]

From the very beginning Arius' teachings enjoyed a great success not only among part of the Alexandrian clergy, but also, and quite significantly so, among the *parthenoi*.[54] To accuse an opponent and his teachings of appealing primarily to women is once again an oft-used stratagem: clearly, the opponent's doctrine is of such a volatile and feeble nature that it 'seduces' primarily those who are themselves volatile and feeble, women in other words.[55] Yet the situation in Alexandria appears to have posed a profound and serious threat; to accuse virgins of 'Arianism' was more than a mere rhetorical device. Both Alexander and Epiphanius leave little doubt that something about Arius and his teachings attracted women, *parthenoi* in particular, and influenced them in an intolerable fashion.[56]

One aspect may have been that Arius gave women, specifically ascetics, a greater role in public—perhaps in the form of a more serious involvement in doctrinal disputes. Alexander denounces two aspects in particular: the fact that Arians communicated with women through letters and other writings; and that Arians

---

[53] Epiph. *Haer.* 68. 4, 69, 3 (3 GCS 37. 144, 154); the translation of the phrase ὑπὸ ἕν (p. 154) is problematic; Amidon (*Panarion*, 256) translates 'into a single group'; 'into one place', 'at once', 'to draw away under the one', and even 'his teachings of the one' is also feasible.

[54] Though the number 700 is not to be taken literally, it nevertheless suggests large numbers.

[55] Cf. V. Burrus, 'The Heretical Woman as Symbol in Alexander, Athanasius, Epiphanius, and Jerome', *Harvard Theological Review* 84 (1991), 229–48, here 229–40.

[56] 'Through this', i.e. his teachings, he attracted the virgins; Epiph. *Haer.* 69. 3 (3 GCS 37. 154f.).

allowed their virgins 'to roam about the streets', that is, in *public* places, an activity through which they 'dishonour', literally 'tear to pieces', Christianity. Writing some twenty years after the outbreak of the controversy, Athanasius states that 'it is appropriate . . . to refute [Arians] . . . especially on account of the little women who are so readily deceived by them';[57] and complains: 'then they go to little women and address them in turn in these effeminate little words: "Did you have a son before you gave birth? Just as you did not, so too the Son of God did not exist before he was generated." '

Athanasius' *Lettre aux Vierges* is primarily a polemic against the lures of Arianism.[58] Athanasius does characterize Arius and his followers as representatives of the devil, but he does so on the basis of a succinct summary of Arian doctrines and their orthodox rebuttal in an address entirely directed to women. Would such elaboration have been necessary if the Arian heresy had truly 'no foundation'?—if the women attracted had simply been 'silly' and 'readily deceived'?

Unfortunately, we do not possess the means to reconstruct what may have attracted women to Arius' teachings. It is, however, evident that 'Arian' virgins existed from the very beginning.[59] It is equally evident that they continued to exist and to thrive at the time of Athanasius' letters so many decades later. Here, Athanasius had to defend his understanding of true virginity on at least two fronts: against a certain kind of Coptic asceticism, personified by Hieracas, but very likely practised by many others as well, the Melitians most prominent among them; and against Arianism. Both these different interpretations of asceticism posed a serious threat to Athanasius' audience. But in order to understand the true significance of this threat, it is necessary to focus on the nature of this audience.

---

[57] Ath. *Or. 1 contra Ar.* 1. 22, 23; 1. 26 (PG 26. 57, 59, 65).

[58] In fact, as mentioned above (n. 45), Alexander's speech agrees almost literally with passages from Athanasius' *Or. 3 contra Ar.* (PG 26. 321–466); Roldanus, *Le Christ et l'homme*, 317.

[59] Apparently this was a well-known fact, Jer. (*Ep.* 133, 4 *ad Ctesiphontem* (CSEL 56. 248) mentions 'Arrius, ut orbem caperet, sororem principis ante decepit' in an admittedly highly rhetorical account of the female companions of heretics.

ATHANASIUS AND ALEXANDRIAN ASCETICS

In 380, just installed in his new see of Constantinople, Gregory of Nazianzus introduced himself and his doctrinal position to the metropolitan audience by delivering a eulogy of an exemplary bishop, Athanasius of Alexandria. One part of this panegyric is dedicated to Athanasius' impact on monasticism. In a consciously stylized fashion, Gregory postulates that Athanasius' exiles were wonderfully transformed into benefits, thanks to his sojourn in the *phrontistēria*, the 'places of meditation', of the Egyptian ascetics.[60] These ascetics, according to Gregory, fall into two distinct categories: those who have completely renounced the world and live as hermits in solitude, μοναδικόν τε καὶ ἄμικτον; and those who obey the laws of charity, live in a community, τῇ κοινωνίᾳ, and combine the solitary life with that of the world, ἐρημικοί τε ὁμοῦ καὶ μιγάδες. During his sojourn Athanasius proved his true worth: in perfect imitation of Christ, he acted as a mediator and reconciled the eremitic life with that of the *koinōnia*, 'demonstrating that there is a priesthood which is a form of philosophical life and a philosophical life which also needs priestly ministry'.[61]

The choice of words, as well as the entire description of Athanasius' role as a mediator between the *bios praktikos* and the *bios theoretikos*, clearly reflects Gregory's own fundamental conflicts and bespeaks the specific concerns of Asia Minor. His description of Athanasius' monastic impact is in fact virtually identical to that which he attributed to Basil of Caesarea in his funeral oration only one year earlier. Yet we find again a clear distinction between ascetic life in the desert, as a hermit, and the one described as *migados* (mixed)—in community with others but involved in a life of *praxis*. Athanasius' contribution, like Basil's, was to have found a *via media*, combining both forms by adapting certain activities to a life of retreat and vice versa, πρᾶξιν ἡσυχίαν καὶ ἡσυχίαν ἔμπρακτον. Rather than disregarding this characterization as a mere rhetorical stylization, it might be worth while to investigate the potential meaning of *migados* in an Egyptian, or more precisely, Alexandrian context.

---

[60] Gr. Naz. *Or.* 21. 19 (SC 270. 148; for the date cf. 91 f.). For the following I am greatly indebted to the work of C. Badger, 'The New Man', 160–241.

[61] δεικνὺς ὅτι ἔστι καὶ ἱερωσύνη φιλόσοφος καὶ φιλοσοφία δεομένη μυσταγωγίας.

In the so-called *Epistula Ammonis*, the author, a certain Bishop Ammon, describes his choice of the ascetic life. At the age of 17 the just-converted youth 'heard the blessed pope Athanasius in church, proclaiming the life-style of the *monazontes* and *aeiparthenoi*, the 'ascetics' and the 'forever-virgins'.[62] Attracted by this life, Ammon chose it for himself, following at first 'a certain Theban monk in the city'. Before long he joined a Pachomian community, where his life was made easier by Theodore the Alexandrian, the superior of the so-called Greek house, who helped Ammon by translating for him. Theodore the Alexandrian's history virtually parallels that of Ammon. Also born a pagan, he converted at the age of 27, driven by the desire to become a monk. Athanasius made him a lector and 'arranged a place for him to live in the church, where he gave himself up to *askēsis*. He met no women at all, with the sole exception of his mother and his sister.' After twelve years of this life he became disenchanted with the *askēsis* of 'those who were in the church with him' and became a follower of Pachomius.[63]

Some of the *monazontes* and *aeiparthenoi* mentioned in Athanasius' sermon were not hermits in the desert but lived in Alexandria itself. As far as the virgins are concerned, we have already encountered them as early as 318/22. Unfortunately, our sources offer only the scantiest evidence for the immediately preceding decades. We only possess a Coptic fragment which purports to be a work of Alexander's predecessor Peter, and which mentions a 'virgin dedicated to the church'; and an account in Severus' *History of the Patriarchs of the Coptic Church* reminiscent of Athanasius' *Lettre aux Vierges*: Alexander received several virgins who complained about some of their fellow sisters' over-strict ascetic practice.[64] Information concerning male ascetics is as scarce. It is again Athanasius in his *Apology to Constantius* who indirectly confirms the ascetics' relevance as a force within

---

[62] *Ep. Am.* 2 (Goehring, 124).

[63] *SBo* 89–90; *G*[1] 94–5 has a much shorter account.

[64] Both sources are clearly influenced by hagiographical concerns. However, considering Alexander's own reference to Arian *neōterai*, stories about the Alexandrian bishops' involvement with *parthenoi* appear to have at least some historical basis; Severus, *History of the Patriarchs*, 8 (Patrologia Orientalis 1, 405); H. Koch, *Quellen zur Geschichte der Askese und des Mönchtums in der alten Kirche* (Tübingen, 1931), 38 f.; cf. above, n. 44.

the congregation: 'those who had been bishops from the time of Alexander, *monazontes* and *askētai*, were banished.'[65]

Even if attested only indirectly, ascetics, both male and female, already formed part of the Alexandrian congregation during the first two decades of the fourth century, certainly during Alexander's episcopate. When Athanasius enters the scene, our sources shed a clearer light. Athanasius himself, according to his *Apology against the Arians*, was considered by others a 'good, pious Christian, an ascetic, a genuine bishop'.[66] Theodore the Alexandrian joined certain *monazontes* and ascetics, who were closely aligned with the clergy, for several years before Pachomius' death in 346. In a conversation with Theodore about the value of their discipline, Pachomius describes these ascetics as 'the anchorites in Alexandria'.[67]

To gain closer insights into the life of these 'anchorites in Alexandria' and their relation to their counterparts in the desert, as represented by Antony the Great for example, we have to consult Palladius' *Historia Lausiaca*.[68]

Eulogius *monazōn*, a highly erudite man, had 'parted with the excitement of the world and disposed of everything', with the exception of an annuity since he could not work. Before long his solitary life began to bore him, and, since he did not want to join a community, he took on the care of a cripple. Fifteen years later the cripple revolted against the 'ascetic' life, crying for 'meat' and 'the crowds of the market-place'. Eulogius was greatly perplexed and consulted ἐκ γειτόνων ἀσκητάς ('the ascetics nearby'), who recommended a visit to 'the great one', Antony. He counselled both Eulogius and the cripple to return to their common cell, where they died soon thereafter.

In other words, the *monazontes* or ascetics in Alexandria either lived alone as 'anchorites' or in groups associated with the churches or as part of the clergy. Their ascetic regime was well known and scrutinized, as Theodore's disenchantment and Pachomius' subsequent enquiry attest, and they kept in touch

---

[65] Καὶ οἱ μὲν ἀπὸ Ἀλεξάνδρου ἐπίσκοποι, μονάζοντες καὶ ἀσκηταί, ἐχωρίσθησαν, Ath. *Apol. ad Const.* 28 (PG 25. 632).

[66] Ath. *Apol. c. Ar.* 6 (PG 25. 260).

[67] SBo 89.

[68] Pall. *HL* 21 (Butler, ii. 63).

with their desert counterparts, such as Antony and Pachomius.[69] For the virgins, a very similar picture emerges.

When exiled for the third time between 356 and 362 under Constantius—the same familiar from the Homoiousian ascendency and demise in 360—Athanasius is usually understood to have sought refuge, as for instance Gregory of Nazianzus has told us, among the Egyptian ascetics, that is, the Desert Fathers of Upper Egypt. However, there are other traditions which narrate these events differently. Palladius reports that Athanasius spent the entire six years in hiding with a virgin 'of exceptional beauty', who 'washed his feet and cared for all his bodily needs and his personal affairs, obtaining the loan of books for his use'. The *Festal Index* for the years 357 and 358 states that Athanasius was concealed in the city of Alexandria and was hunted by the authorities 'with much oppression, many being in danger on his account'. For the following year the *Index* reports that the 'prefect and *dux* Artemius, having entered a private house and a small cell in search of Athanasius the bishop, bitterly tortured Eudaemonis, a perpetual virgin.'[70]

At least at the beginning of this third flight into exile, Athanasius was helped by an Alexandrian virgin, perhaps called Eudaemonis, who lived by herself, had the means to support him, and subsequently paid dearly for defying imperial orders.

In a letter to Ecdicius, the prefect of Egypt, the emperor Julian bitterly decried Athanasius' success in baptizing 'Greek women of distinction'.[71] That many of the Alexandrian virgins were wealthy may not come as a surprise. Palladius mentions the sisters of the presbyter Isidor, who lived in a community with seventy other virgins. Palladius had met Isidor, then the head of the hospice for foreigners in Alexandria, in 388. Said to have

---

[69] Cf. also the Ps.-Athanasian c. 92 and Coptic 93 (Riedel and Crum, *The Canons*, 59, 139).

[70] Pall. *HL* 63 (Butler, ii. 158, and n. 112); *Fest. Index*, 28, 30, and 32 (SC 317. 257–61); Soz. *HE* 4. 10 (GCS 50. 150) mentions an initially faithful serving-woman, who eventually betrayed Athanasius' hideout; he managed to escape and she was tortured on his account; her masters had to flee the country; Badger, 'The New Man', 203–11.

[71] Julian, *Ep.* 112 [*Ep.* 6], *L'Empereur Julien: Œuvres complètes*, i.2, ed. J. Bidez (Paris, 1924), 192.

accompanied Athanasius to Rome, Isidor, and thus his sisters too, belonged to the upper echelons of Alexandrian society— another example of virgins with means.[72]

The emerging picture—of virgins who live alone, in a cell inside a house, side-by-side with others in communities, always involved in the affairs of the congregation, often in close association with its high-ranking clergy—confirms the prescriptions of the *Pseudo-Athanasian Canons* exactly: each house ought to have its own virgin, either a daughter or a suitable servant-girl; virgins may own and dispose of their property, and participate in the Eucharist, weddings, funerals, and birthday celebrations.[73] All the Alexandrian virgins belonged to a group of urban ascetics, the *tagma tōn monazontōn*. Some, like Alexandra in her tomb, perhaps Amma Theodora, the desert-dweller, and the group which eventually surrounded Amma Syncletica, lived just on the outskirts of the city; not yet part of the deep desert, they had, however, left the city itself behind—much like those numerous ascetics surrounding the town of Oxyrhynchus, as portrayed in the *Historia Monachorum*.

The *koinē*, or Egypt proper, knew perhaps even more diverse types of *migadoi* (ascetics living within an urban setting) than the metropolis itself; at least this is the impression given by the sources. Virtually all the ascetics mentioned in the papyri lived in villages or towns and were engaged in typical community activities: renting of property, payment of taxes, sale of produce, and so on. The earliest monk ever mentioned in the papyri, the famous 'Isaac monachos' of the *P. Coll. Youtie* 77, dating from 324, was a well-known and respected figure in his village of Karanis and associated with the local deacon Antonius.[74] The little we know about Melitian monasticism makes it clear that it was an urban or village phenomenon: Melitian monks were an important and influential part of their local community. Elias and his monastery for the 'wandering virgins' in Athribis, while not necessarily Melitian, also falls into a tradition of urban monasticism. Most of the virgins we have discussed lived in

---

[72] Pall. *HL* I (Butler, ii. 16); cf. Bartelink, *La Storia Lausiaca*, 309 n. 5, on Isidor's career.

[73] cc. 98, 99, 101, 102, 104 (Riedel and Crum, *The Canons*, 62–7).

[74] Judge, 'The Earliest Use', 72–4, 81–4.

villages, either alone or in small groups or in larger communities. Yet, importantly, the phenomenon is by no means
limited to women but constitutes a sizeable proportion of all
ascetic endeavours, be they conducted by men or women.

Indeed, even those who became the 'greats' of desert asceticism
often began their ascetic life in the village. Ammon, at least
according to some traditions, practised a widespread form of
urban asceticism before leaving for the desert: the spiritual marriage. Pachomius, according to the *Bohairic Life*, spent several
years as an ascetic engaged in charitable 'service of the sick in the
village', a form of asceticism seemingly fit for the clergy and the
so-called 'old men'. Only then did he join the 'holy old man
Palamon', who lived near a village. Antony's well-known first
stages of renunciation began within his own town. Only after this
initial phase did he move to the borders of the town, where he
began his *monērēs bios* under the guidance of an elder, who also
lived 'in a nearby village'.[75]

As soon as we reach the edges of the town or village, the
area between the settlement and the desert proper, the field is
dominated by 'old men'. Antony as well as Pachomius joined the
ranks of elders or *spoudaioi*, 'who had settled a little way from
the village, and who had become a model and example for
many'.[76] By the end of the third century, these 'old men' were
already a firmly established group. Women, in keeping with the
Historia Monachorum's account of Oxyrhynchus, are far less
prominently represented among those 'on the edge'. This may
well reflect precise intentions on the part of our sources: women
should stay within the village itself. But ascetic women did move
to the borders of villages, as well as into the desert. Arsenius'
'sisters' and the various virgins living with Desert Fathers fall into
this category; Amma Sarah lived in the desert 'near Pelusium',
the 'Father' of Bessarion appears to have lived somewhere in
between the deep desert and the inhabited areas, and there
are a number of examples whose actual dwelling-places remain
undefined. The deep desert itself, it seems, was truly out of
bounds for women; at least I have not come across any source
which directly and unmistakably places a woman in the *panerēmos*,

[75] *SBo* 8; Ath. *V. Ant.* 2–4 (PG 26. 841–5).

[76] *SBo* 8; Pachomius' place in the village was immediately occupied by another
old man.

two, three, or more days' walk away from human habitation. However, given the natural conditions of Egypt, this does not mean to say that the Desert Mothers or wandering virgins did not have to contend with actual desert life.

'The fundamental structure of Christianity in Egypt [is] . . . the constant and vital interplay between Christianity *as emerging from the cosmopolitan religiosity proper to the Hellenistic city of Alexandria* and Christianity *as bound to the spiritual landscape of the Nile valley*.'[77] Asceticism and its development is but one aspect of this 'constant and vital interplay', and while it is quite impossible to determine all the points where Egypt influenced Alexandria and vice versa, it has already become evident that the ascetics from both 'orbits' communicated with each other. However, there is a noticeable distinction between Pachomius' casual enquiry into the ascetic discipline of the 'anchorites in Alexandria' or Eulogius' alleged journey to the great Antony, and the direct involvement of a figure like Athanasius, so aptly described by Gregory as a mediator.[78] While I am not intending to provide an exhaustive answer, the question arises, of course, as to what Athanasius 'the mediator' truly accomplished, and more to the point, what his attempts at mediation reveal about his own position in Alexandria.

Athanasius' first exile, following the events at Tyre in 335, came to an end as a result of a general amnesty granted in 337 by the new ruler, Constantine II. Athanasius returned to Alexandria but was greeted by violent opposition, which had to be suppressed by government officials. The Homoian or 'Arian' party in Constantinople under the leadership of Eusebius of Nicomedia immediately used these incidents to file a complaint with the three emperors, flatly rejecting Athanasius' reinstatement. In 339

[77] C. Kannengiesser, 'Athanasius of Alexandria v. Arius: The Alexandrian Crisis', in Pearson and Goehring, *The Roots of Egyptian Christianity*, 204–15 (quotation 212), emphasis is the author's. Unfortunately, to my knowledge a comprehensive study on this complex subject is still outstanding, but cf. Krause, 'Das christliche Alexandrien und seine Beziehungen zum koptischen Ägypten', 53–62; A. Martin, 'L'Église et la khōra égyptienne au IVᵉ siècle', *Revue des Études Augustiniennes* 25 (1979), 3–26; ead. 'Les Premiers siècles du christianisme à Alexandrie: Essai de topographie religieuse (IIIᵉ–IVᵉ siècles)', *Revue des Études Augustiniennes* 30 (1984), 211–25.

[78] Gr. Naz. *Or.* 21. 18 (SC 270. 148).

they elected one of themselves, the Cappadocian Gregory, as the new Alexandrian bishop. Gregory's arrival, under imperial protection, gave rise to yet another wave of violence, described by Athanasius as follows:[79]

While the people . . . assembled in the churches, . . . Philagrius, who has long been a persecutor of the Church and its *parthenoi*, and is now Prefect of Egypt . . . and a fellow countryman of Gregory . . . , succeeded in gaining over the heathen multitude, with the Jews and disorderly persons, and . . . sent them . . . with swords and clubs into the churches to attack the people. . . . holy and undefiled virgins were being stripped naked and suffering treatment which is not to be named, and if they resisted they were in danger of their lives. *Monazontes* were being trampled under foot and perishing . . .

The violence continued and at Easter the following scenes ensued:

presbyters and laymen had their flesh torn, virgins were stripped of their veils, and led away to the tribunal of the governor; . . . the bread of the ministers ($\lambda \varepsilon \iota \tau o v \rho \gamma \tilde{\omega} v$) and *parthenoi* was intercepted. . . . Gregory . . . caused . . . the Governor publicly to scourge in one hour, four and thirty virgins, and married women, and men of rank, and cast them into prison.[80]

The day after Easter Athanasius fled to Rome 'after he had baptized many'. In the *Historia Arianorum* he once again describes these scenes, lamenting the number of *monazontes* scourged, *episkopoi* wounded, *parthenoi* beaten, 'while Gregory sat by with Balachius the Duke'.[81]

To say that Athanasius' account of these disturbances is tendentious is to state the obvious. Nevertheless, it is apparent that the 'Arian' or Homoian attack on his supporters centred on three distinct groups: men and women of rank and prominence, bishops, and the *tagma tōn monazontōn*, the male and female ascetics. Their property was confiscated, the financial contributions to the ascetics ceased: so is revealed a well-directed attempt to erode Athanasius' economic and political support. The targets of the 'Arian' attacks were not victims of random violence but

---

[79] Ath. *Ep. Encyc.* 3 (Opitz, ii. 172); Tetz, 'Athanasius', 337.
[80] Ath. *Ep. Encyc.* 4 (Opitz, ii. 173).
[81] *Fest. Index*, 11 (SC 317. 237); Ath. *Hist. Ar.* 12 (Opitz, ii. 189).

were chosen as the result of a clear strategy aimed at those
who were Athanasius' primary supporters, most prominently the
ascetics, male and in particular female. In other words, these
ascetics, the 'anchorites in Alexandria', were vital in the power
struggle between Athanasius and his 'Arian' opponents. All of
Athanasius' ascetic writings, his attempts to 'mediate' between
ascetics of various persuasions, and to establish contacts with
monastic groups, must be seen in the context of this vital conflict.

Yet, the significance of the ascetic support cannot simply be
explained by the fact that they were attacked. It does not follow
that ascetics should be singled out so clearly solely because they
supported Athanasius, unless another factor comes into play:
the two parties were vying for the same group of supporters.
Athanasius never explicitly mentions the possibility that 'Arians'
had *parthenoi* and *monazontes* of their own. Yet, as has already
become clear from our discussion of the *Lettre aux Vierges*, it is
more than likely that he had to fight for support among all
ascetics because he stood in direct competition with 'Arian' attempts to do the same. It is with this notion in mind, Athanasius'
position in the metropolis itself, that his relations with the ascetics
both in Alexandria and in Egypt have to be re-examined.

Athanasius' first venture into the ascetic heartland and his first
encounter with Egyptian monasticism occurred in 329/30, immediately after his ordination as bishop against an overwhelming
Melitian majority. He had embarked on this tour up the Nile
with the intention of giving 'comfort to the holy Church', pacifying
his opponents, and consolidating his support. Among the ascetics
he visited were the followers of Pachomius, who greeted their
guest and his entourage enthusiastically; and once Athanasius
was inside the monastery, Sarapion of Nitentori, the local bishop
and a prominent member of the entourage, suggested that he
ordain Pachomius to the priesthood, 'so that he should be set
over all the monks in my diocese'. Overhearing this exchange,
Pachomius disappeared at once and remained in hiding until
the bishop departed. Athanasius in response promised never to
ordain Pachomius but expressed his wish actually to meet the
monk—a meeting unlikely ever to have come to pass.[82]

---

[82] *Fest. Index*, 1 (SC 317. 229); *SBo* 28; as so aptly pointed out by C. Badger,
'The New Man', 194–7.

The *Lives* of Pachomius, in particular the *Bohairic Life*, accomplish quite a feat of diplomacy in recounting the incident. Rather than implying any actual confrontation between the two leaders or any attempt on Athanasius' side to ordain Pachomius by force and thus incorporate him and his ascetic model into the ecclesiastical framework, the *Lives* represent the events such that both sides accept the status quo—a relatively independent coexistence of both Pachomius' model and the Alexandrian see. Athanasius promises never to ordain Pachomius and Pachomius *in absentia* never rejects the opportunity of an actual meeting. In addition to neutralizing any potentially negative interpretations of the failed meeting, this account could reflect a conscious strategy on Athanasius' part. Instead of exercising force—as the Fathers in Asia Minor had done on several occasions—he seems to have been content to register absence of opposition. Pachomius was no Melitian and thus was permitted to follow his own course, as long as he did not interfere in Alexandria. Direct links between Athanasius and Pachomian monasticism did, of course, exist, though these connections were forged not with the founder himself, but at a much later stage with his successor Theodore.[83] The situation is not much different as far as Athanasius' personal relationship with Antony the Great is concerned.

In 337, the year in which Athanasius returned from his first exile, the *Festal Index* records that 'Antony the Great, "Father of the monks", came to Alexandria, and though he remained only two days, he marvelled at many things and healed many.'[84]

---

[83] Perhaps during Theodore's trips to Alexandria in *c*.345 and 346, as reported in *SBo* 96 / *G*[1] 109 and *SBo* 124–36 / *G*[1] 120, and in the *Ep. Amm.* 2 (Goehring, 124). It is not incidental that Ammon's *Letter*, written at the request of the Alexandrian bishop Theophilus, dealt with Theodore's relation to the metropolitan episcopate. Theodore was furthermore a recipient and promoter of Athanasius' *Festal Epistle* 39 regarding the unacceptability of certain writings (cf. above, n. 40); Badger, 'The New Man', 193–6, 203–8, 216–24. As has already been mentioned, Athanasius spent parts of his third exile from 356 to 362 among Egyptian monks, probably in a Pachomian community. *SBo* 185 and *G*[1] 137–8 mention Duke Artemius' search for Athanasius in the monastery at Phbow; connections between Athanasius and Pachomian groups are further supported by the *Ep. Amm.* 34 (Goehring, 155) and the *Fest. Index*, 35 (SC 317. 264). However, Badger ('The New Man', 222) maintains that no direct evidence proves that Athanasius ever set foot in a Pachomian monastery after 330.

[84] *Fest. Index*, 10 (SC 317. 237).

Antony's visit to Alexandria is well known, in particular because of the famous passage in the *Life of St Antony*. In Athanasius' version Antony had heard that the 'Arians falsely claimed that he held the same views as they'. He therefore 'came down from the mountain, and entering into Alexandria, he publicly renounced the Arians',[85] having been invited to do so by 'the bishops and all the brothers'. It is, however, by no means certain that Athanasius was among these bishops; he, indeed, may not yet have returned to Alexandria. What is certain is the fact that Antony's visit was instigated by and intended for the 'anchorites in the city', the urban ascetics. If Athanasius profited from his visit, he did so only indirectly.[86]

Relations between Antony and his Alexandrian counterparts are also attested elsewhere. Aside from Palladius' story involving Eulogius' visit to him, Antony's concern for the welfare of the 'anchorites in Alexandria' also emerges in the account of his encounter with one of the pro-Arian persecutors at the time of Bishop Gregory, the duke Balachius. Two different versions exist and, despite internal inconsistencies, both agree on one aspect: Antony's concern for the Alexandrian *monazontes*.[87] Duke Balachius was notorious for beating *parthenoi* and *monazontes*. These acts of cruelty prompted Antony to reproach Balachius and Bishop Gregory in a letter, though this was received with scorn. Shortly afterwards Balachius was killed by his own horse, an infamous death seen as caused by his infamous defiance of Antony's admonitions.

Another story reported by Sozomen is even more instructive. He writes that in response to Athanasius' first deposition in 335, the 'people of Alexandria' complained to the emperor Constantine.[88]

[85] Ath. *V. Ant.* 69–71 (PG 26. 942–4); trans. Gregg, *The Life of Antony*, 82.

[86] In fact, it is quite possible that Antony's visit was orchestrated instead by yet another Egyptian intermediary, Bishop Serapion of Thmuis, so M. Tetz, 'Athanasius und die Vita Antonii: Literarische und theologische Relationen', *ZNW* 73 (1982), 1–30, here 24. Martin (*Histoire 'Acéphale'*, 75 f.) assumes Athanasius' presence in Alexandria, but redates Antony's visit to 338; cf. also Heussi, *Ursprung*, 83.

[87] Ath. *Hist. Ar.* 14 (Opitz, ii. 189); id. *V. Ant.* 86 (PG 26. 964); Heussi, *Ursprung*, 98–100.

[88] Soz. *HE* 2. 31 (GCS 50. 96), emphasis mine; as already pointed out by Heussi (*Ursprung*, 91 f.), Sozomen's account is preferable to that of the *V. Ant.* 81 (PG 26. 956).

And Antony, the celebrated monk, wrote frequently to the emperor to entreat him to attach no credit to the insinuations of the Meletians . . . ; yet the emperor was not convinced. . . . He commanded *the clergy and the holy virgins* to remain quiet, and declared that he would not change his mind nor recall Athanasius.

Constantine's response clarifies the context of Antony's involvement. The people of Alexandria, but more specifically, the clergy and the *parthenoi* had started a campaign on behalf of the deposed Athanasius, for which they had sought and received the support of one of the most prominent ascetics, Antony. Thus, the connection was not primarily between Athanasius and Antony, but between Antony and those among the urban ascetics who supported Athanasius; it was they who orchestrated the letter-writing campaign in 335, and who invited Antony in 337/8. His visit might, of course, have increased Athanasius' ascetic power-base substantially. Athanasius takes great pains to emphasize that his return to Alexandria, at a time of intense struggle for superiority, was marked by a new wave of conversions to the *monērēs bios*, a wave apparently initiated by Antony's visit.[89]

If Athanasius' relationship with both Pachomius and Antony was rather more indirect than based on personal acquaintance, there is, of course, direct evidence linking Athanasius to monks outside Alexandria. Significantly, and in marked contrast to the general tenor of the *Apophthegmata*, many of the Egyptian ascetics that Athanasius knew personally were members of the clergy, more often than not recruited by the bishop himself. In his *Letter to Dracontius*, of 354 or 355, Athanasius eloquently scolds the recipient, an ascetic, for evading ordination: 'for if all were of the same mind as your present advisers, how would you have become a Christian, since there would be no bishops? Or if your successors are to inherit this state of mind, how will the Churches be able to hold together?' If he accepts ordination, Dracontius will not be alone. Many monks and superiors of monasteries before him, according to Athanasius, have already been ordained and are now fulfilling their pastoral duties, thus combining the 'philosophical life' with the *bios praktikos*. Athanasius then enumerates seven monks who are now bishops, most prominent among them Serapion, bishop of Thmuis.[90]

[89] Ath. *Hist. Ar.* 25 (Opitz, ii. 196); id. *V. Ant.* 88 (PG 26. 965).
[90] Ath. *Ep. ad Drac.*, esp. 4 and 7 (PG 25. 524–33, esp. 528 and 532);

Serapion, the author of the treatise *Against the Manichaeans* and the recipient of the dying Antony's sheepskin, may well have been the primary connection between Antony, the 'anchorites in the city', and Athanasius. He is also the recipient of several Athanasian letters. One letter concerning the death of Arius, written in 358 during Athanasius' third exile, is of particular interest.[91] Apparently, questions had arisen in Serapion's circle regarding not only Arius' death, but much more importantly, Arius' teachings and whether or not he had died in communion with the Church, that is, rehabilitated. Those surrounding Serapion were not the only Egyptian ascetics fascinated by Arius and his teachings. Others had already heard accounts of Arius' death, independently from Athanasius, and apparently from a much more dangerous source.

When Athanasius wrote to Serapion concerning Arius' death, he also wrote two letters to *monachoi*—in two cases asking the recipients to return the letters and not to copy or circulate them, a rather peculiar request.[92] What had happened? Arians were travelling around Egyptian monasteries, actively recruiting supporters. Whether these Arians were themselves ascetics, perhaps formerly Melitians, or Arian 'anchorites in the city' sent to recruit in Egyptian monasteries, remains, of course, entirely unclear. Their efforts fell on fertile ground: Athanasius could not simply send an open letter but replied only to the request of specific individuals who had contacted him because of these developments, and he did so with letters meant explicitly for private consumption. He was well aware of the threat and reacted accordingly: for a true ascetic merely to shun 'Arianism' is not enough. Even acquaintance with an avowed Arian, and

interesting also is Athanasius' characterization of monks and bishops in 9; for Serapion see Badger, 'The New Man', 214–16, and especially Tetz, 'Athanasius und die Vita Antonii', 8–19.

[91] Ath. *V. Ant.* 91 (PG 26. 972); id. *De morte Ar.* (Opitz, ii. 178–80); for the date of the letter cf. Tetz, 'Athanasius und die Vita Antonii', 12 f.; R. Draguet, 'Une lettre de Sérapion de Thmuis aux disciples d'Antoine (AD 356) en version syriaque et arménienne', *Le Muséon* 64 (1951), 1–25.

[92] Ath. *Ep. ad monachos*, 1 (Opitz, ii. 181 f.); id. *Ep. ad mon.* 2 (PG 26. 1185–8); it is interesting that Athanasius uses here the term *monachoi* rather than *monazontes*, the term he usually employs when speaking of Alexandrian ascetics. The letter headings may, however, not be original; Judge, 'The Earliest Use', 77.

with someone who claims not to be Arian but acts like one, is anathema.

Arians had something very attractive to offer to those involved in ascetic endeavours. As recent studies have shown, what can be reconstructed of Arius' teachings, especially those concerning salvation, may well support such an inherent attraction. To quote R. Gregg and D. Groh, 'the Arian scheme of *askēsis* proceeds from the axiomatic identification of Christ with creatures. . . . [Therefore,] Christ's election as a reward for his discipline . . . is within the reach of fellow creatures.'[93] Arius may have proposed spiritual identification of the believer with Christ the Son achieved through perfect ascetic practice; a highly attractive concept for those whose entire life was devoted to achieving *imitatio Christi*.

At any rate, Athanasius considers an ascetic's mere acquaintance with an Arian sympathizer dangerous enough to warrant an anathema. At the same time, during the period between 358 and 360, he issues a flurry of letters to ascetics in Egypt proper, coaxing some into becoming members of the clergy, dispelling rumours concerning Arius' death among others, and warning all against Arians. Another look at the situation in Alexandria at the time reveals that such activity was indeed called for.

Athanasius had returned to Alexandria in 346, after the death of Gregory and with imperial support from the West under Constans. Only seven years later Constans had been overthrown; one of Athanasius' staunchest supporters, Bishop Julius of Rome, had died; and Athanasius found himself once again isolated. The years between 353 and 356 were marked by constant attempts to apprehend him, and finally, in February of 356—as discussed above—he vanished from sight for the following six years. His supporters managed to hold the churches for four more months, until 'the Athanasians were ejected from the churches, and they were handed over to those who belonged to George', another Cappadocian and Homoian installed as bishop of Alexandria.[94] George arrived in Alexandria in 358, but was greeted by such

[93] As mentioned earlier, the state of research concerning Arianism is very much in flux; for the following cf. Gregg and Groh, *Early Arianism*, 142–4 (quotation 142); R. Gregg, 'The Centrality of Soteriology in Early Arianism', *American Theological Revue* 59 (1977), 260–78; Kopecek, *Neo-Arianism*, i. 4, 11; Stead, *Substance and Illusion*, *passim*; id. *Divine Substance, passim*.

[94] Ath. *Hist. Aceph.* 2. 2 (SC 317. 144).

violence that he had to depart until 361, leaving the control of the city to imperial officials.

A period of unprecedented struggle and violence ensued, culminating in the murder of Bishop George and the imperial representative. According to Athanasius, his followers were once more the target of attacks. Although the magnitude of the controversy far surpassed that of the year 339, the Arians again attacked the same group of people as two decades earlier. Virgins again were stripped and beaten, some were exiled to the Great Oasis, and others even suffered death. Under Duke Sebastianus, the pro-Arian authorities

[brought out from the houses] many virgins who condemned their impiety; others they insulted as they walked along the streets, and caused their heads to be uncovered by their young men. They also gave permission to *the females of their party* to insult whom they chose.

Who were the 'females of their party'? Perhaps simply Arian women, but most probably Arian virgins, in which case this is Athanasius' clearest and most outspoken indication of their existence.[95] On another occasion Count Heraclius enticed a mob to attack Athanasius' church on the pretext of 'the emperor's command'. Interestingly, only women, virtually all of them *parthenoi*, were present, because it was after the dismissal—an indication of liturgical activities carried out by these *parthenoi*?[96]

It was probably during this period, marked once again by intense struggles between Athanasius and the supporters of Arianism, with violent attacks against ascetics, and here in particular *parthenoi*, that Athanasius wrote his *Lettres aux Vierges*. During the same period he again actively solicited support among the ascetics in Egypt, not primarily among the Desert Fathers, but among those who were members of the clergy and resided in an urban context: the *migadoi*.

*

[95] Ath. *Hist. Ar.* 48, 58–63, 72 (Opitz, ii. 211, 215–18, 222); for a full account of the persecutions, id. *Apol. ad Const.* 27, 33 (PG 25. 629, 640)—27 repeats the story of virgins and women hiding in the cemetery; id. *Apol. de Fuga*, 6, 7 (Opitz, ii. 71 f.).

[96] *Parthenoi* and widows—like their deaconess counterparts in Asia Minor—presumably assisted the celebration in a variety of ways, most of them menial (guarding of doors etc.; see Ch. 5 above), but the fact that these women had just sat down could imply instructional or liturgical activities. Ath. *Hist. Ar.* 55 (Opitz, ii. 214).

The foregoing account did not set out to be an exhaustive description of Athanasius' relationship with asceticism and ascetics, and it has thus not addressed all the intricacies of doctrinal politics or attempted to clarify the complex web of interchanges between Alexandria and Egypt. Yet we have been able to observe certain mechanisms and identify certain alliances, which, combined with our findings in Asia Minor, are crucial for the making of asceticism.

The basis of Athanasius' influence in Alexandria itself, and thus one of the main guarantors for his ecclesiastical survival, were the ascetics. These ascetics, 'anchorites in the city' as Pachomius' *Bohairic Life* calls them, formed the *tagma tōn monazontōn*, consisting to a significant degree of women. Both male and female *parthenoi*—some of whom, again, cohabited—were at various times and in all ways (from appeals to the emperor to public harassments) actively involved in the political and doctrinal debates, despite the fact that Athanasius, much like every other Father of the Church before and after him, preached seclusion, solitude, and withdrawal from the world. All these virgins and ascetics were closely tied to their churches and their clergy; a sizeable number of the male *monazontes* were in fact members of the clergy themselves. Many virgins belonged to the upper echelons of society and could thus afford to provide financial benefits for their churches, but others were recipients of congregational support. Virgins did in some fashion participate in the celebration of the mass, and perhaps in certain liturgical activities.

Athanasius' opponents also relied on *parthenoi*. Perhaps in response to his personal charisma, perhaps as a result of his teachings, Arius and his followers likewise counted many ascetics among their supporters, again in particular women. Controversial from the beginning and virtually synonymous with all that is heretical—to the extent that Arianism became a catch-all phrase for all kinds of undesirable doctrinal positions—it is all but impossible to gain more precise, independent insights into the nature of asceticism as inspired by Arius, as we were able to do in the case of Homoiousians in Asia Minor. It is worth keeping in mind, though, that both the Homoian and the Homoiousian parties had for a long time formed the doctrinal majority in the Eastern Roman Empire, and that much of what can be reconstructed of their teachings has an Origenistic basis. All that has been attempted here is to demonstrate that Arian asceticism existed and was a vital force in Alexandria.

In times of intense doctrinal controversy, the charismatic nature of virginity, the great impact of these figures, 'temples of the Lord', clad in veils and sanctified by their way of life, revealed its true force: all sides needed ascetics, the cream of the Christian crop, to enhance the legitimacy of their standing, to add holiness to their quest. Despite the virtual absence of Arian sources, the magnitude of the struggle transpires easily, even through the pen of the ultimate victor, Athanasius. The repercussions of these struggles are magnified when we also consider his relationship to ascetics in Egypt: Athanasius' agenda when seeking contact with the Egyptian ascetic movement, especially with the great Desert Fathers, was dictated by the demands at home, by the necessity to gain and maintain the support of the ascetics, both male and female, in the city of Alexandria. Contrary to the impression given by many of the contemporary sources such as Gregory of Nazianzus (and certainly fostered by Athanasius himself), his involvement with the desert ascetics like Antony or Pachomius was indirect and facilitated by mediators such as Serapion of Thmuis or Theodore, not the result of an intense personal pursuit.

Athanasius was certainly in touch with the ascetics of Egypt. But the principal basis of his ascetic support in the *koinē* lay not with the true desert ascetics such as Pachomius, Ammon, even Antony, but with the *migadoi*, those 'who had withdrawn from the world', but, as in Asia Minor, remained in it by virtue of their life in towns and villages, and their membership in the clergy. It is among these ascetics that we find a significant proportion of bishops who had been ordained by Athanasius in person.

Athanasius' true concern, Alexandria, clearly shaped his dealings with Coptic asceticism. He was not primarily interested in Egypt for its own sake nor motivated by a desire to regulate and structure Egyptian asceticism—until and unless the Egyptian ascetics had an effect upon his urban ascetic support group. If indeed the targets behind his attacks on Hieracas in the *Lettre aux Vierges* were Melitians, or at least a Coptic monasticism aligned with the Melitians, this would support the point just made: aligned as they were with the Arians, Melitians could affect Athanasius' urban power-base, both inside Alexandria and along the Nile.

Athanasius' *Life of St Antony*, the ideal *exemplum* of the Desert Father and the model of eremitic life, was to shape the notion of asceticism for centuries to come. Palladius' *Historia Lausiaca* responded to a request made by a high-ranking court offical in Constantinople but soon reached best-seller status. The *Historia Monachorum* was written for a monastery in Jerusalem and translated into Latin by Rufinus of Aquileia, a member of one of the most influential ascetic circles in Jerusalem and Rome. Rufinus also translated Basil's Rule, and Rufinus' erstwhile friend Jerome that of Pachomius into Latin. Significantly, all these men, with the exception of Athanasius, belonged to a doctrinal faction that was later on attacked for its sympathies to the teachings of Origen, teachings which also influenced those of the Homoiousians or semi-Arians and the Homoians or Arians.[97]

Who was their audience? Not the Egyptian Desert Fathers, but an educated urban readership, among them ascetics. Thus, the transfer worked both ways. Athanasius used his interpretation of 'rural' Egyptian asceticism to control and organize inner-urban asceticism, and it was his modified form of pseudo-'rural' ascetic life, created in response to urban requirements, that was then exported to the West; but it was also reintroduced into the rural environment to control and organize the original, 'rural', ascetic movement according to its ideals. One tool employed in shaping monasticism in all its aspects, rural as well as urban, was orthodoxy: movements and forms of ascetic practice that did not fit the ideal, that could not be incorporated within the limits set by the *exempla*, were deemed heretical. Neither Rufinus nor Palladius nor Athanasius exalts virgins who have *become manly* in their external appearance as well as in inner virtue; or women who lived in the desert itself; or those who taught in public, that is, who taught men. Not one of them explicitly highlights, praises, or emphasizes the communal life of ascetic men and women either, unless it is sanctioned by special circumstances or divine interference. Here, however, the differences between an Eastern

---

[97] See Elm, 'Evagrius Ponticus' *Sententiae ad Virginem*', 97–120.

and a Western audience are most evident—certainly an aspect in need of further clarification.

Nevertheless, a great deal of the experimental vigour that characterized the life of women who participated in the ascetic movement transpires in our sources, even if much is condemned to remain in the shadows cast by emerging norms and institutions.

Conclusion

During the fourth century the Roman Empire underwent a transformation which is among the most decisive in the history of what was to become Europe in the West and Byzantium in the East. Inaugurated by Constantine's recognition of Christianity, and made manifest by Theodosius' famous edict defining orthodoxy for 'cunctos populos' in 380, the Roman Empire became the Christian Roman Empire. Neither Christianity nor the Roman Empire remained the same, and although the changes often consisted of little more than subtle rearrangements and reinterpretation of already existing concepts, structures, and institutions, yet they compounded into a fundamental and far-reaching metamorphosis.

By focusing on two regions within the Roman Empire where many of these transformations were played out, Asia Minor and Egypt, this study has sought to capture some of the dynamics at work in the formation of a new empire and a new Christianity through the prism of female asceticism and the processes of its institutionalization into what is commonly defined as monasticism. It has been my aim throughout to highlight and trace developments rather than to provide explanations. In closing, however, I would like to underline some considerations by way of both explanation and conclusion, and to suggest subjects for further investigation.

The making of asceticism did not occur in isolation. The development of both male and female asceticism and monasticism have to be understood in relation to each other, as well as in relation to a constantly changing environment. Asceticism is in essence a statement about the relationship between the body, the soul, and the human potential for salvation. Accordingly, every discussion of asceticism and its ideal realization is by implication a statement—to paraphrase Peter Brown—about the body, society, and the holy. In other words, the way in which the authors of our sources conceived of the organization of asceticism is intrinsically linked to their understanding of the relation between the supreme divinity, its mediation on earth, and the resulting political and social order. To reconstruct the processes leading to the organizational configuration of asceticism thus reveals prima-facie institutional developments, but it also reflects directly underlying intellectual (i.e. theological) notions and concurrent social and political concerns. While these observations might seem truisms, their stringent application has none the less yielded some striking results.

From the point of view of institutionalization, the emergence of organized ascetic communities for women in particular can be understood as a continuous interpretation and modification of the concept 'family'—more precisely, of the essentially aristocratic notion of the *familia*. According to our sources, this reinterpretation occurred in two seemingly diametrically opposite ways: either by a complete rupture with the family and its characteristics, e.g. as in the case of perpetual migration or extreme anchorite isolation, or by a continuous transformation of the family, which can be seen as a process of increasing movement away from the natural towards the ascetic family.

Thus, many women are described as embarking on their ascetic career by becoming virgin daughters, living in voluntary isolation amidst their extended natural *familiae*. The progressive 'conversion' of other family members then led to the formation of an ascetic household, comprising virgin widows as well as virgin mothers, which might then evolve, through the acceptance of non-related members, into a fully fledged ascetic community. These communities represent a new and specific organizational model: a monastery. It is, much like the aristocratic household, characterized by communal ownership of property, relative economic autarky, an individual normative system, an internal hierarchy often including slaves, voluntary yet obligatory affiliation, and continuity.

The organizational framework of the family is perceptible in all these ascetic adaptations. A woman's decision to become a 'virgin of God' is phrased in terms of an engagement and marriage to Christ; members of the clergy progressively adopt a role which can be seen as spiritual fatherhood, and the familial model also gives rise to other variations on the theme: the ascetic mother–daughter relationship, that of ascetic brothers and sisters, and the pseudo-marriage. Indeed, if the family was the original social model spawning ascetic variations, then this in itself would suffice to account for a finding which is otherwise surprising: the first ascetic communities consisted of men and women who lived together.

Beyond the merely organizational aspects, the discussions of the model 'family' in its ascetic interpretation has also revealed the specific normative intentions of the authors who formulated them. Both ascetic standpoints regarding the family, that of rupture as well as that of gradual transformation, existed contemporaneously, and they developed in constant interaction. This accounts for our perception of a wide variety of what I have called ascetic experiments. Yet, within this variety, the discussion of ascetic organizational models illustrates the fourth-century authors' preferences for some over others, and furthermore, the shifts in preference from existing models to new ones, following a distinct chronological sequence. Thus, models of complete rupture are prone to be characterized as 'heretical,' those of gradual transformation usually as 'orthodox.' However, within the 'orthodox' models, we have been able to observe a definite shift: an increasing amalgamation of ascetic structures with clerical roles, combined with a move away from models of symbiosis between male and female ascetics towards those where the sexes are segregated, paralleled by a rhetorical enhancement of rural models over urban ones.

It is at this juncture, the shift within an originally 'orthodox' model, that the nexus between the organization of female asceticism and of asceticism as such, the theological conceptualization of the relationship between the divine and the human, and the corresponding political order, emerges most clearly and becomes most crucial.

Gregory of Nyssa wrote his *Life of Macrina* within years of the edict in which Theodosius had encoded the new orthodoxy of his reign, subsequently endorsed by the synod of Constantinople: orthodoxy as embodied by Damasus of Rome and Peter of Alexandria. This new orthodoxy, Neo-Nicene, had been profoundly influenced not only by Athanasius, but also by Basil of Caesarea, Gregory of Nazianzus, and Gregory of Nyssa himself. These were the same men who significantly defined the organization and nature of asceticism: the earliest of the 'traditional' founder-figures of monasticism.

As this study has demonstrated, a fully fledged ascetic movement did, however, exist prior to Athanasius, Basil, the two Gregorys, and their followers. This movement possessed characteristics that allow it to be defined as 'monastic' in accordance with later definitions: there were settled communities with their own regulations, as well as normative texts elaborating the movement's intellectual, that is to say, doctrinal foundations. It originated primarily in urban centres or their direct vicinity, and was characterized by the symbiosis of men and women. In Asia Minor I have called this movement 'Homoiousian' or 'semi-Arian', in Egypt broadly speaking 'Arian'.[1] Since it has been my primary task here to establish this movement's very existence and organizational formation, I have largely refrained from discussing direct causal links between ascetic practice and doctrinal orientation. I do feel confident, however, in suggesting here not only that such links did indeed exist, but that the transformation or reform of ascetic and monastic organization through Basil and Athanasius coincided with a shift in the interpretation of the Trinity, and thus in the Christian world-view, predicated by the new demands of a Christianity increasingly enmeshed in political power.[2]

The Homoiousian or 'semi-Arian' as well as the so-called 'Arian' interpretation of the Trinity form part of an intellectual climate deeply grounded in the teachings of Origen and their interpretation by later theologians.[3] Central to Origen's teaching was the notion that the supreme divinity, the Father, was uncreated, a transcendental, perfect unity, yet at the same time the dynamic, ever present source of all being. All created beings originated from this primordial oneness, the Father, and were in essence

---

[1] Whereby I intend the 'doctrinal' terminology to imply adherence to a specific intellectual and theological climate, rather than to a well-defined sect.

[2] The nexus between theology and politics is, of course, no novelty; see e.g. the excellent study by G. Caspary, *Politics and Exegesis: Origen and the Two Swords* (Berkeley, 1979); however, the need for a discussion of the political implications of Origen's and his followers' thought, noted by Caspary (p. 125), remains pressing.

[3] I would like to thank Rebecca Lyman for allowing me to use her *Christology and Cosmology: Models of Divine Activity in Origen, Eusebius, and Athanasius* (Oxford, 1993) in proof. It has proved exceedingly helpful in the formulation of much of the following.

connected to the creator through their soul. The quintessential link between the uncreated Father and the creation was the Son, the incarnate *Logos*.

This 'constitutive relation' of created beings to the creator accounts for two central components of Origen's thought. On the one hand, it serves to explain the *de facto* diversity of the created world.[4] Despite its genesis out of primordial unity, creation is diverse. This is so because the soul's embodiment in matter results from and correlates to individual levels of decline, caused by the free will and the corresponding moral comportment of each individual. One's present physical condition is thus a result of one's individual choice. But, if choice can enmesh the soul more firmly within the created body, the individual's free will can also reverse this process: spiritual insight and continuous imitation of the incarnate Word, Jesus Christ, who alone has not fallen away from God, can effect the individual soul's return towards the original oneness, towards God.

Origen, like his Platonic predecessors, understood the created universe as a hierarchical system, in which the soul as participant in the original oneness occupied a higher position than the created matter of the body. However, rather than condemning the body as a prison, Origen viewed it as a means of enabling the soul to progress towards God; the body's very existence permitted the soul to rise above its limits by forcing it to struggle constantly with the boundaries set by the body's physicality. The body with its physical limitations was seen as transcendent, a passing stage through which the soul returned to its original, 'angelic' state: it is thus that 'angels become humans and humans angels'.[5]

Quite clearly, in such an understanding of the body sexual differentiation became all but superfluous. To imitate Jesus Christ was paramount to transcending boundaries set by the body, including the body's gender. To imitate the Word also negated whatever 'normal and physical constraints' were attached to gender.[6] Those who had reached the apex of such imitation in ascetic perfection, whether male or female, were no longer

---

[4] Lyman, *Christology*, 62.
[5] Orig. *In Matt.* 15. 27 (ed. E. Klostermann and E. Benz (GCS 10; Berlin, 1935–7), 429–30); Lyman, *Christology*, 49–63.
[6] Brown, *Body and Society*, 171.

subject to any of the strictures of this world; they 'have nothing through which they may be subject to Caesar'.[7]

Certainly the Homoiousian ascetic communities in Asia Minor and also a significant number of the communities in Egypt consisted of men and women who, 'like angels', practised ascetic perfection in common. Indeed, the symbiosis of male and female ascetics was the rule rather than the exception at the outset of the ascetic movement during the late third and early fourth century, and this symbiosis continued in various forms throughout the fourth century, though in an increasingly embattled position.

Nicaea heralded the dawn of a new understanding of the Trinity, and by implication of the order of the universe, an understanding that was the subject of intense debate and controversy for the next sixty years and more. Nicaea occurred within thirteen years of Christianity's acceptance as a legitimate religion, and it inaugurated a period that was to transform it into the religion of the Roman Empire. I would suggest that the concurrence of the breakdown of Origenistic axioms with the initial formation of a Christian Roman Empire is hardly coincidental. While here is not the place to explore this concurrence further, a very brief description of the principal tenets held by one of the major protagonists of the so-called Nicene notion of the Trinity, Athanasius, might highlight the direction in which notions of the body, society, and the holy were developing.

The notion that the incarnate Christ is not 'the culmination of pedagogical cosmology or [salvation] history, but rather the key to the salvation of all existence' is central to Athanasius' thought.[8] This emphasis on the centrality of the incarnate Christ is in no small part a response to Athanasius' own historical situation as bishop of Alexandria, and thus directly reflects his understanding and mastery of these circumstances: the emerging role of the bishop as 'architect of social and doctrinal unity, as well as the cosmopolitan representative of ecclesiastical and secular authority'.[9]

---

[7] Orig. *Com. Rom.* 9. 25 (PG 14. 1226); Caspary, *Politics and Exegesis*, 175.
[8] Lyman, *Christology*, 124; Ch. Kannengiesser, 'Athanasius of Alexandria and the Foundation of Traditional Christology', *Theological Studies* 34 (1973), 103–13, here 112.
[9] Lyman, *Christology*, 126.

In a move that might seem paradoxical given the nascent 'worldly' power of the bishop, and in significant contrast to Origen and some of his followers such as Eusebius, Athanasius argued that a profound division separates the created realm from the divine sphere. Like Origen, Athanasius saw the divine as a transcendental and eternal unity, but divinity, God, did not share any essence with the created order. Like Origen, Athanasius also posited that God was by nature eternally generative, but only within the divine essence. He thus transmitted all divinity to the Son and the Holy Spirit, not as a hierarchical sequence, but as his own self-expression. Anything outside the eternal oneness of the divine sphere was accidental; the sense of *creatio ex nihilo* became more intense. Thus the sole and fundamental division was that between created and uncreated being.

Such a concept of creation differs starkly from Origen's view of created beings existing in a world of free will, individual morality, and essential likeness to God. Athanasius saw all creation as inherently chaotic, unstable, and weak, and thus as necessarily alien to the stability and simplicity of the transcendent divinity. Free will was incapable of overcoming such essential weakness; the only salvation lay in incarnation. 'Creation remained in bondage . . . because it was external to God as created, and therefore needed to be transformed internally and essentially.'[10]

By distinguishing the creation of the Son from that of the cosmos, Athanasius enabled God to become, instead of the creator, the Father of Jesus Christ. Secondly, by emphasizing that the soul as well as the body as created were by nature weak and separate from God (and not just distinct from the divine through levels of decline), he significantly lowered the potential of an individual's free will. The connection between humans and the divine was now incarnation: solely through Christ's becoming flesh might the flesh become liberated from passion and instability, that is sin, and the mind become free.[11]

Ascetic practice thus no longer sought to transcend the body, but to transform it; a rigorously disciplined body was a direct sign of divine stability and therefore of sanctity. Becoming a true

---

[10] Despite the essential goodness of God's will, see Lyman, *Christology*, 136–9, quotation 139.

[11] Ath. *De Inc.* 4. 12–17 (SC 199. 156); Lyman, *Christology*, 254–7.

ascetic, an exemplar of sanctity, included both body and soul; it no longer signified the escape of the soul from the body as it progressed towards God. Thus, in sharply separating the entire created human, body and soul, from the divine, the body acquired a new significance. As the dramatic symbol of the sole saving force, the incarnate, embodied Son, the physical body itself became the locus of transformation and thus of salvation. As soon, however, as the body *qua* body acquires such a significance, then so do its external attributes, chief among them gender; and that includes the 'normal and physical constraints' associated with gender within society.

At a time when Christianity became more established, Athanasius posited a view of the world that was unstable and chaotic. While seemingly paradoxical, it was precisely the sharply deepened divide between chaos and stability, creation and creator, which stabilized the Church: if salvation depends on faith in the incarnation as the sole means to transform the physical body, and if faith is intrinsically linked to the Church, which is as separate from the secular world as the divine from creation, then physical perfection and ascetic transformation demand a turn away from the 'chaotic', unstable world towards the stable, structured society of the Church. The transforming power of asceticism, and for that matter of a truly Christian life, was thus no longer the heavenly journey of individuals through their free will, but became intrinsically linked to the Christian community, which alone allowed faith in the incarnation to become active through the correct interpretation of the Scriptures over and against 'false readings' practised by outsiders. Rather than free will effecting perfection of the soul, the primary agents enabling the physical body to be transformed were now grace, seen as an externally granted participation in divine power, and faith, understood as God's true revelation of the incarnate Son through Scripture interpreted correctly only within the Church. Thus, ascetic perfection through faith in the incarnation became collective; it transformed not only the ascetic's individual body, but this body in turn affirmed and symbolized the validity of the Christian community.

The expanding duality between creation and creator thus led to a heightened emphasis on the physical body as the means of salvation, which in turn intensified the emphasis on gender.

The more the body became the vehicle for salvation, the graver became the concerns regarding its fallibility and corruptibility, made manifest in its sexuality. Individual free will no longer had the same power and thus hopefulness it had carried in Origen's teachings. Now, increasingly, the weakness of the flesh could be countered solely through grace and faith as channelled through the Church, and in rigid maintenance of division and separation.

The consequences of this shift are perhaps most obvious in the writings of another, much later bishop and ecclesiastical leader, Ambrose of Milan. Like Athanasius, Ambrose understood the world as divided—between creator and creation, 'between Catholic and heretic, between Bible truth and "worldly" guess-work, Church and *saeculum*, soul and body. . . . To be a Catholic Christian means to keep these antitheses absolute: to admit "admixture" was to "pollute" one's own body and that of the Church.'[12] Virginity, the representation of the sexually 'unmixed' and hence unpolluted body of Christ, was thus for Ambrose the most powerful bulwark against any weakening of those absolutes and against corruption and sin. And nowhere did the steadfastness of the Church find a clearer symbol than in the sacred, pure body of a 'virgin of God'.

Views like this do not allow for the cohabitation of male and female ascetics. Of course, Ambrose was neither an Athanasius nor a Basil of Caesarea, a Gregory of Nazianzus or a Gregory of Nyssa. Many of Athanasius' views attest to his Origenistic roots, and the Cappadocians' high regard for Origen's teachings is common knowledge. The shift away from regarding the body and its gender as a passing stage to seeing it as a symbol of fallibility in need of transformation did not occur suddenly; nor did the maxim of ascetic life as necessarily segregated by gender take hold overnight. However, with Nicaea the theological course was set in a new direction, which took its institutional effect in due course. Thus, while Gregory of Nyssa portrayed his sister Macrina as a composite human being, the perfect saint, in whom all that is best in woman and man is fused, he nevertheless saw the true reason for the 'misery of the human condition' not in the fall of the soul into the body, as Origen had done, but in 'the plunge of

---

[12] For Ambrose see P. R. L. Brown's magisterial chapter, *Body and Society*, 341–65, quotation 347.

the human person, soul and body together, into the present fallen state of society'.[13] Macrina's virginal body in all its splendid transcendence of gender was no longer the body as a carrier of hope, but the 'garment of skin' perpetuating the vicissitudes of creation through sexuality.

Here, several points are worth reiterating. If I have elaborated on these theological concerns perhaps to a greater degree than may be expected in a conclusion, this is by no means to suggest that such shifts in the conceptualization of the universe are solely responsible for fundamental changes in institutionalization nor indeed can they be seen as distinct from secular concerns. I am not arguing that shifts in theology cause shifts in practice. Rather, shifts in the conceptualization of the universe respond to *de facto* shifts in society at large and reveal how contemporaries comprehend and evaluate these social shifts. Once made, however, shifts in the intellectual understanding can then, in turn, lead to a refashioning of society on a practical, institutional level that corresponds to new ways of understanding the relationship between the body, society, and the holy. Thus, rather than being one of cause and effect, the relationship between all these issues is one of continuous and constant interaction. Again, processes leading to institutionalization are a focal point which encapsulates the interaction of all these different levels—social, political, intellectual—most succinctly.

Although almost all the texts discussed in this study concern women and the ways in which they did or should have organized their ascetic lives, virtually all these texts were written by men and more often than not were also addressed to men. This by no means rules out that these texts do indeed reflect, to a certain extent, what ascetic women did and thought. Yet, in the first instance, most of our texts were written to delineate, evaluate, and elaborate male modes of action and self-perception via the rhetorical medium of the female. Texts such as the *Life of Macrina* were certainly intended to provide an exemplar for women aspiring to live as a 'virgin of God'. But the portrayal of Macrina was also Gregory's commentary on ways in which the newly

---

[13] Ibid. 291–304, quotation 301; V. Harrison, 'Male and Female in Cappadocian Theology', *JThS 41* (1990), 441–71; W. Völker, *Gregor von Nyssa als Mystiker* (Wiesbaden, 1955), 127.

emerging Christian Roman élite (and that means in particular the clergy) might understand its public, that is to say its political role: as a composite of and perfect synthesis between the male and the female, the familial and the ascetic, the public and the private.

At the same time, most of our sources stress the notion that 'monastic' asceticism is best practised in the countryside, far from the tumultuous city. The reasons for this increasing emphasis on the countryside, the *desertum*, as the proper place for ascetic perfection are manifold; but the fact remains that this ideal was presented to a primarily urban audience. The contrast between nature and the city was phrased in terms of a moral divide: the *desertum* appeared as the arena in which to battle against demons as well as a place of stability and tranquillity far removed from the world and in sharp contrast to the city as the centre of seduction and moral confusion. This divide could be interpreted purely allegorically, much like the notions about gender: the proper bearing of a Christian leader combined internal tranquillity with participation in the sole stable realm within the unstable city, the Church. It can also be seen, again like the notion of gender, as a *de facto* attempt to remove vocal ascetics from the urban decision-making process.

What entered the literary world, and thus history, as normative was an asceticism institutionalized *after* the shift; an asceticism predicated on notions of division between the divine and the created, between the stable and the unstable, between male and female, and between the *desertum* and the city.[14] It was an asceticism akin to notions established by Athanasius and others— notions that Theodosius had introduced to 'all his people'. It was this interpretation of asceticism, the 'monasticism', which, as captured and exemplified by the 'founder'-figures like Pachomius, Basil, and Augustine, became the normative ideal, and as such not only shaped historical perception but inevitably also history itself.

As a consequence and a testimony to the power of rhetoric, the initial phases of widespread experimentation and diversity were largely lost, either by simple omission as 'not adequate' or by being rewritten after condemnation as 'heretical'. Historiography

---

[14] Brown, *Body and Society*, 341–447.

likewise concentrated largely on the normative. Here, the investigation of female institutions has offered a counterpoint. The monastic organizations developing after 381 (and during the eventual breakdown of the Western part of the Roman Empire) prepared the way for the Benedictine rule, later the standard model, and in turn retroactively influenced what types of organizational model could be considered 'monastic'. These later rules encapsulated a specific, predominantly male, type of monastic organization, which found its most prominent representation in the Cistercian order. Female monastic life for the most part did not adhere to this norm. Most fourth-century female communities did not have daughter houses, they seldom formed part of a larger organization, and were mostly independent and highly flexible structures accommodating a variety of specific preconditions. This does not, however, mean that they did not exist *qua* institutions, nor that the writings addressed to them did not fulfil in practice the essential normative requirements of a rule.

To recapture some of the processes at work in the making of asceticism has at times required a painstakingly detailed account of many diverse sources. Only by listening very closely to our sources and their every nuance has it been possible to distinguish a wide variety of organizational models, of ways to achieve ascetic perfection along with a broader vision of the universe where the individual's free will could overcome the limits set by the body and its gender. It has also been possible to observe how this variety was slowly limited, while the broader concepts of individual perfection tightened into far more stringent views of Christian community and the role of men and women within it. Asceticism began as a method for men and women to transcend, as virgins of God, the limitations of humanity in relation to the divine. It slowly changed into a way for men as men and for women as women to symbolize the power of the Church to surpass human weakness. This coincided with the establishment of Christianity as the religion of the Roman Empire, and, not accidentally, with a decisive shift from God the eternal source of all being, manifest in the incarnate *Logos*, to God the Father, manifest in the Son. In the process the potential for human freedom as a road of ascent towards the divine became narrower for all ascetics; but for those who were not created in the image of a Father or a Son, it became increasingly all but closed. Historiography, in focusing on the eventual results of these gradual processes, and often anachronistically presupposing them for the earlier period, thus allowed the later results to be seen as being original, as if the ways of ascetic perfection which became the norm were indeed the only ones ever conceived as possible.

SELECT BIBLIOGRAPHY

PRIMARY SOURCES

Les Actes de Paul et ses lettres apocryphes, ed. L. Vouaux (Paris, 1922).

The Acts of the Christian Martyrs, ed. H. Musurillo (Oxford, 1972).

ALEXANDER OF LYCOPOLIS, *Contre la doctrine de Mani*, ed. A. Villey (Paris, 1985).

AMMIANUS MARCELLINUS, *Rerum Gestarum qui supersunt*, ed. and trans. J. C. Rolfe, 3 vols. (Loeb; London, 1935–40).

Anthologia graeca, ii, ed. H. Beckby (Munich, 1957).

The Apocrypha and Pseudepigrapha of the Old Testament in English, ii, ed. R. H. Charles (Oxford, 1913).

Apophthegmata Patrum, ed. J. B. Cotelier (PG 65. 71–440); Fr. trans. by J.-C. Guy, *Les Apophtegmes des Pères du Désert, série alphabétique* (Textes de Spiritualité Orientale 1; Begrolles, 1968); Eng. trans. by B. Ward, *The Sayings of the Desert Fathers* (Oxford, 1975).

—— *Les Sentences des Pères du Désert: Les Apophtegmes des Pères*, ed. L. Regnault (Solesmes, 1966).

—— *Les Sentences des Pères du Désert: Troisième recueil et tables*, ed. L. Regnault (Solesmes, 1976).

—— *Les Sentences des Pères du Désert: Nouveau recueil*, ed. L. Regnault (Solesmes, 1977).

ARISTOTLE, *Politics*, ed. and trans. H. Rackham (Loeb; London, repr. 1977).

ATHANASIUS OF ALEXANDRIA, *Apologia ad Constantium* (PG 25. 593–642).

—— 'Athanasiana Syriaca 1', ed. J. Lebon (*Le Muséon* 40 (1927), 205–48).

—— 'Athanasiana Syriaca 2': *S. Athanase: Lettre à des vierges qui étaient allées prier à Jérusaleme et qui étaient revenues* (= *LVJer*), ed. J. Lebon (*Le Muséon* 41 (1928), 189–203).

—— *Histoire 'Acéphale' et Index Syriaque des Lettres festales d'Athanase d'Alexandrie*, ed. A. Martin and M. Albert (SC 317; Paris, 1985).

—— *Historia Arianorum ad monachos* (PG 25. 691–796).

—— *Lettres festales et pastorales en copte: Sur la virginité; La Lettre aux Vierges* (= *LV*), ed. L. T. Lefort (CSCO 150, 151 (Scr. Copt. 19, 20); Louvain, 1955).

—— *Sur l'incarnation du Verbe*, ed. Ch. Kannengiesser (SC 199; Paris, 1973).

ATHANASIUS OF ALEXANDRIA, *Urkunden zur Geschichte des arianischen Streites*, ii–iii, ed. H. G. Opitz (Berlin–Leipzig, 1934–41).

—— *Vita Antonii* (PG 26. 835–976); earliest Lat. trans., ed. G. J. Bartelink and intr. by C. Mohrmann, *Vita di San Antonio* (Scrittori Greci e Latini, Vite dei Santi 1; Milan, 1974); Eng. trans. by R. C. Gregg and intr. by W. Clebsch, *The Life of Anthony and the Letter to Marcellinus* (The Classics of Western Spirituality; New York, 1980).

PSEUDO-ATHANASIUS, *The Canons of Athanasius of Alexandria*, ed. W. Riedel and W. Crum (London, 1904; repr. Amsterdam, 1973).

—— *Vita Sanctae Syncleticae* (PG 28. 1485–1558); Fr. trans. by O. Bernard, *La Vie de Sainte Synclétique; Discours de Salut à une vierge* (Spiritualité Orientale 9; Solesmes, 1972).

BASIL OF ANCYRA, *De Virginitate* (PG 30. 669–809).

—— *De Virginitate de Saint Basile (texte vieux-slave)*, ed. A. Vaillant (Paris, 1943).

BASIL OF CAESAREA, *Admonitio s. Basilii ad filium spiritualem*, ed. P. Lehmann (Sitzungsberichte der Bayrischen Akademie der Wissenschaften, phil.-hist. Klasse 7 (Munich, 1955–7), 3–63).

—— *Epistulae*:

Lettres, ed. Y. Courtonne, 3 vols. (Paris, 1957–66).

Le Lettere, i, ed. M. Forlin Patrucco (Corona Patrum 11; Turin, 1983).

Briefe zweiter Teil, ed. W. D. Hauschild (Stuttgart, 1973).

Eng. trans. R. J. Deferrari, *St. Basil: The Letters*, 4 vols. (Loeb; London, repr. 1986).

—— *Homilia dicta tempore famis et siccitatis* (PG 31. 304–28).

—— *Hom. X et XI de l'Hexaemeron: Sur l'origine de l'homme*, ed. A. Smets and M. van Esbroeck (SC 160; Paris, 1970).

—— *Homilia 22: Sermo de legendis libris gentilium. Ad adolescentes* (PG 31. 563–90) = *Aux jeunes gens sur la manière de tirer profit des lettres héleniques*, ed. F. Boulenger (Paris, 1965^2).

—— *Moralia* (PG 31. 692–869).

—— *The Philocalia of Origen: A Compilation of Selected Passages from Origen's Work made by St. Gregory of Nazianzus and St. Basil the Great*, Eng. trans. by G. Lewes (Edinburgh, 1911).

—— *Les Règles monastiques*, ed. L. Lebe (Maredsous, 1969).

—— *Les Règles morales et portrait du chrétien*, ed. L. Lebe (Maredsous, 1969).

—— *Regulae fusius tractatae* (*RF*); *Regulae brevius tractatae* (*RB*) (PG 31. 889–1320); Eng. trans. by W. K. L. Clarke, *The Ascetic Works of Saint Basil* (London, 1925); Ger. trans. by K. S. Frank, *Basilius von Caesarea: Die Mönchsregeln* (St Ottilien, 1981).

—— *Traité sur le Saint-Esprit*, ed. B. Pruche (SC 17*bis*; Paris, 1968^2).

PSEUDO-BASIL, *The Coptic Version of the Canons of St. Basil*, ed. W. Crum (Proceedings of the Society of Biblical Archaeology 26; London, 1904).

BENEDICT OF NURSIA, *Regula Benedicti*, ed. R. Hanslik (CSEL 75; Vienna, 1960).

BESA, *Letters and Sermons of Besa*, ed. K. H. Kuhn (CSCO 157, 158; Louvain, 1956).

—— *Sinuthii Vita Bohairice* (= *VShen*), ed. with Lat. trans. by H. Wiesmann (CSCO 129; Louvain, 1951); Eng. trans. by D. Bell, *Besa: The Life of Shenoute* (Cistercian Studies Series 73; Kalamazoo, 1983).

CALLINICUS, *Vita S. Hypatii*, ed. H. Usener (Leipzig, 1895); Fr. trans. by A. J. Festugière (*Les moines d'Orient*, ii (Paris, 1961), 11–86).

Canones apostolorum et conciliorum veterum selecti: Bibliotheca ecclesiastica, i, ed. H. T. Bruns (Berlin, 1839; repr. Turin, 1959).

CLEMENT, *Epistle 1 to the Corinthians* (PG 1. 201–328).

CLEMENT OF ALEXANDRIA, *Protrepticus und Paedagogus*, ed. O. Stählin (GCS 12; Leipzig, 1905).

—— *Stromata*, ed. O. Stählin, 2 vols. (GCS 15, 17; Leipzig, 1906, 1909).

PSEUDO-CLEMENT, *Homelien*, ed. B. Rehm (GCS 42; Berlin, 1953).

Corpus Juris Civilis: i, *Institutiones*, ed. P. Krüger; *Digesta*, ed. Th. Mommsen; ii, *Codex Justinianus*, ed. P. Krüger; iii, *Novellae*, ed. R. Schöll and W. Kroll (Berlin, 1959[12]).

CYPRIAN OF CARTHAGE, *Briefe und Schriften*, ed. G. Härtel (CSEL 3: 2; Vienna, 1871).

—— *Correspondance*, ed. L. de Bayard, 2 vols. (Paris, 1972[2]).

CYRIL OF SCYTHOPOLIS, *Das Leben des heiligen Euthymios*, ed. E. Schwartz (TU 49: 2; Leipzig, 1939).

Didascalia et Constitutiones Apostolorum, ed. F. X. Funk, 2 vols. (Paderborn, 1905; repr. Turin, 1970); Eng. trans. by R. H. Conolly, *Didascalia Apostolorum: The Syriac Version Translated and Accompanied by the Verona Fragments* (Oxford, 1929).

—— *Les Constitutions apostoliques*, ed. M. Metzger, 3 vols. (SC 320, 329, 336; Paris, 1985–7).

—— *La Didascalie des douze Apôtres*, ed. F. Nau (Ancienne littérature canonique syriaque 2; Paris, 1912[2]).

EGERIA, *Peregrinatio Aetheriae* = Éthérie: *Journal de voyage*, ed. H. Pétré (SC 21; Paris, 1948).

The So-called Egyptian Church-Order and Derived Documents, ed. R. H. Conolly (Texts and Studies 8: 4; Cambridge, 1916).

EPHREM OF NISIBIS, *Des heiligen Ephrems des Syrers Hymnen contra haereses*, ed. E. Beck (CSCO 169–70; Louvain, 1957).

EPIPHANIUS, *Ancoratus; Adversus Haereses* (*Panarion*), ed. K. Holl (GCS 25, 31, 37; Leipzig, 1915, 1922, 1933); Eng. trans. by P. Amidon,

The Panarion of St. Epiphanius, Bishop of Salamis (Selected Passages) (New York, 1990).

—— *Expositio fidei catholica* (GCS 37. 496–526).

EUNAPIUS, *Lives of the Philosophers and Sophists*, Eng. trans. by W. C. Wright (Loeb; London, 1922).

EUNOMIUS, *The Extant Works*, ed. R. P. Vaggione (Oxford, 1987).

EUSEBIUS OF CAESAREA, *Historia Ecclesiastica (HE)* = *Histoire ecclésiastique et les martyrs en Palestine*, ed. G. Bardy (SC 31, 41, 55, 73; Paris, 1952–60).

—— *Vita Constantini*, ed. I. Heikel (GCS 7; Leipzig, 1902); Eng. trans. by E. C. Richardson, *The Life of the Blessed Emperor Constantine* (Nicene and Post-Nicene Fathers of the Christian Church, 2nd ser., 1; Grand Rapids, 1961²), 481–559.

EUSEBIUS OF EMESA, *Homilia 7*, ed. É. M. Buytaert (Spicilegium sacrum Lovaniense 26; Louvain, 1953).

EVAGRIUS PONTICUS, *Euagrius Ponticus*, ed. W. Frankenberg (Abhandlungen der königlichen Gesellschaft der Wissenschaft zu Göttingen, phil.-hist. Kl., NF 13: 2; Berlin, 1912; repr. Nendeln, 1970); Ger. trans. of the letters by G. Bunge, *Briefe aus der Wüste* (Sophia 24; Trier, 1986).

—— *Nonnenspiegel und Mönchsspiegel*, ed. H. Gressmann (TU 39; Leipzig, 1913).

—— *Les six centuries des "Kephalaia Gnostica" d'Évagre le Pontique*, ed. A. Guillaumont (Patrologia Orientalia 28: 1; Paris, 1958).

—— *Traité Pratique ou Le Moine*, ed. A. and C. Guillaumont, 2 vols. (SC 170–1; Paris, 1971); Eng. trans. by J. E. Bamberger, *Evagrius Ponticus: The Praktikos; Chapters on Prayer* (Cistercian Studies Series 4; Kalamazoo, 1970).

Expositio totius mundi et gentium, ed. J. Rougé (SC 124; Paris, 1966).

GENNADIUS, *De viris illustribus*, ed. E. C. Richardson (TU 14; Leipzig, 1895).

GERONTIUS, *Vie de Sainte Mélanie*, ed. D. Gorce (SC 90; Paris, 1962).

GREGORY OF NAZIANZUS, *Carmen ad Olympiadem* (PG 37. 1542–9).

—— *Carmina de virtute 1a/1b*, ed. M. Kertsch and R. Palla (Graz, 1985).

—— *Discours 3–5*, ed. J. Bernardi (SC 309; Paris, 1983).

—— *Discours 20–3*, ed. J. Mossay (SC 270; Paris, 1980).

—— *Discours 27–31*, ed. P. Gallay (SC 250; Paris, 1978).

—— *Epistulae*:

Lettres, ed. with Fr. trans. by P. Gallay, 2 vols. (Paris, 1964).

Ger. trans. M. Wittig, *Briefe* (Bibliothek der griechischen Literatur 13; Stuttgart, 1981).

—— *Gegen die Putzsucht der Frauen*, ed. A. Knecht (Heidelberg, 1972).

—— *Oratio 43 in laudem Basilii Magni* (PG 36. 493–606); Fr. trans. by F. Boulenger, *Discours funèbres en honneur de son frère Césaire et de Basile de Césarée* (Textes et Documents 16; Paris, 1908); Eng. trans. by L. P. McCauley *et al.*, *Funeral Orations by St. Gregory Nazianzen and St. Ambrose* (Fathers of the Church 22; Washington, 1968²).

—— Σύνκρισις Βίων, ed. H. M. Werhahn (Klassisch-philologische Studien 15; Wiesbaden, 1953).

—— *Testamentum* (PG 37. 389–96).

—— *De Vita Sua*, ed. Ch. Jungck (Heidelberg, 1974).

GREGORY OF NYSSA, *De Virginitate = Traité de la virginité*, ed. M. Aubineau (SC 119; Paris, 1966).

—— *Epistulae*, ed. G. Pasquali (= *GN* viii.2; Leiden, 1959).

—— *Gregorii Nysseni Opera* (= *GN*), ed. W. Jaeger, 10 vols. (Leiden, 1952–90).

—— *In laudem fratris Basilii* (PG 46. 788–817).

—— *Vie de Moïse*, ed. J. Daniélou (SC 1*bis*; Paris, 1987⁴).

—— *Vita Sanctae Macrinae* (*VSM*) = *Vie de Sainte Macrine*, ed. P. Maraval (SC 178; Paris, 1971); Eng. trans. by V. W. Callahan, *Saint Gregory of Nyssa: Ascetical Works* (The Fathers of the Church: A New Translation 58; Washington, 1967).

HIPPOLYTUS, *Les Canons d'Hippolyte*, ed. R. G. Coquin (Patrologia Orientalis 31: 2; Paris, 1966).

—— *Die ältesten Quellen des orientalischen Kirchenrechts*, i, *Die Canones Hippolyti*, ed. H. Achelis (TU 6: 4; Leipzig, 1918).

—— *La Tradition apostolique, d'après les anciennes versions* (= *TA*), ed. B. Botte (SC 11*bis*; Paris, 1984²).

Historia Monachorum in Aegypto (= *HM*), ed. A. J. Festugière (Subsidia Hagiographica 34; Brussels, 1961²); Fr. trans. by id. *Enquête sur les Moines d'Égypte*; *Les Moines d'Orient*, iv.1 (Paris, 1964); both text and trans. repr. in Subsidia Hagiographica 53 (Brussels, 1971²); Eng. trans. by N. Russel, *The Lives of the Desert-Fathers* (Cistercian Studies Series 34; Kalamazoo, 1980).

IGNATIUS, *Letter to the Smyrnaeans; Letter to Polycarp* (PG 5. 708–28).

Inscriptions: Inscripti Antiquae Orae septentrionalis Ponti Euxini, ed. B. Latyschev (Societatis Archaeologicae Imperii Russi; St Petersburg, 1901).

—— *Inschriften griechischer Städte aus Kleinasien*, i, ed. R. Merkelbach, F. V. Dörner, and S. Sahin (Kommission für die Archäologische Erforschung Kleinasiens bei der österreichischen Akademie der Wissenschaften, Institut für Altertumskunde der Universität Köln; Bonn, 1972).

—— *Recueil des inscriptions grecques-chrétiennes d'Asie Mineure*, i, ed. H. Grégoire (Paris, 1922).

Inscriptions: Recueil des inscriptions grecques-chrétiennes d'Égypte, ed. G. Lefèbvre (Institut français d'archéologie orientale; Cairo, 1907).

Itinera Hierosolymitana saeculi III–VIII, ed. P. Geyer (CSEL 39; Vienna, 1898).

JEROME, *Apologie contre Rufin*, ed. P. Laradet (SC 303; Paris, 1983).

—— *Chronicon: Die Chronik des Hieronymus*, ed. R. Helm (GCS 47; Berlin, 1956²).

—— *Epistulae*, ed. I. Hilberg, 3 vols. (CSEL 54–6; Vienna, 1910).

—— *De viris illustribus*, ed. E. C. Richardson (TU 14; Leipzig, 1896).

JOHN CASSIAN, *Collationes* (PL 49. 481–1328).

—— *Institutions cénobitiques*, ed. J.-C. Guy (SC 109; Paris, 1965).

JOHN CHRYSOSTOM, *À une jeune veuve sur le mariage unique*, ed. B. Grillet (SC 138; Paris, 1968).

—— *Lettre d'exile à Olympias et à tous les fidèles*, ed. A. M. Malingrey (SC 103; Paris, 1964).

—— *Lettres à Olympias; Vie anonyme d'Olympias*, ed. A. M. Malingrey (SC 13*bis*; Paris, 1968).

—— *Sur La Vaine Gloire et l'éducation des enfants*, ed. A. M. Malingrey (SC 188; Paris, 1972).

JOHN OF EPHESUS, *Commentarii de beatis Orientalibus*, ed. with Eng. trans. by E. W. Brooks (Patrologia Orientalis 17–19; Paris, 1923–6); Lat. trans. by K. van Douwen and J. P. Land (Verslagen en Mededeelingen der K. Akademie van Wetenschappen, Aft. Letterkunde 18; Amsterdam, 1889).

JULIAN, *L'Empereur Julien. Œuvres complètes*: i, ed. J. Bidez (Paris, 1962²); ii.1, *Discours*, ed. G. Rochefort (Paris, 1963); ii.2, *Discours*, ed. C. Lacombrade (Paris, 1964).

Die Kirchenrechtsquellen des Patriarchats Alexandrien, ed. W. Riedel (Leipzig, 1900).

LACTANTIUS, *De la mort des persécuteurs*, ed. J. Moreau (SC 39; Paris, 1954).

LIBANIUS, *Opera*: x, *Epistulae*, ed. R. Foerster (Leipzig, 1920; repr. Hildesheim, 1963).

Liber Graduum, ed. M. Kmosko (Patrologia Syriaca 1: 3; Paris, 1926).

II Maccabees: A New Translation with Introduction and Commentary ed. J. Goldstein (New York, 1983).

METHODIUS, *Le Banquet*, ed. H. Musurillo (SC 95; Paris, 1963).

Monumenta Asiae Minoris Antiqua (= *MAMA*), ed. W. M. Calder and J. M. R. Cormack, 8 vols. (Publications of the American Society for Archeological Research in Asia Minor; Manchester, 1928–62).

MUSONIUS, *Reliquae*, ed. O. Hense (Leipzig, 1905).

Neutestamentliche Apokryphen, ii, ed. E. Hennecke and F. Schneemelcher (Tübingen, 1964³).

NILUS, *De voluntaria paupertate* (PG 79. 725–997).

Opuscula Graecorum veterum sententiosa et moralia, ed. J. C. Orellius, 2 vols. (Leipzig, 1819–21).

ORIGEN, *Commentarii in Psalmos* (PG 12. 1053–1685).

—— *Contra Celsum* (PG 11. 641–1632).

—— *Homélies sur S. Luc*, ed. H. Crouzel *et al.* (SC 87; Paris, 1962).

—— *In Canticum Canticorum* (PG 13. 61–216).

PACHOMIUS, *Die Briefe Pachoms: Griechischer Text der Handschrift W. 145 der Chester Beatty Library*, ed. H. Quecke (Textus Patristici et Liturgici 11; Regensburg, 1975).

—— *Histoire de saint Pacôme: Une redaction inédite des Ascetica*, ed. J. Bousquet and F. Nau (Patrologia Orientalia 4: 5; Paris, 1907).

—— *Pachomian Koinonia: The Lives, Rules and Other Writings of Saint Pachomius and his Disciples*, 3 vols.: i, *The Lives of Saint Pachomius and his Disciples*; ii, *Pachomian Chronicles and Rules*; iii, *Instructions, Letters, and Other Writings of Saint Pachomius and his Disciples*, Eng. trans. by A. Veilleux, intr. A. de Vogüé (Cistercian Studies Series 45–7; Kalamazoo, 1980–2).

—— *Pachomiana Latina: Règle et epîtres de s. Pachôme, epître de s. Théodore et 'Liber' de s. Orsiesius, Texte latin de s. Jerôme*, ed. A. Boon and L. T. Lefort (Bibliothèque de la *Revue d'Histoire Ecclésiastique* 7; Louvain, 1932); Fr. trans. by L. T. Lefort, *Œuvres de s. Pachôme et de ses disciples* (CSCO 160; Louvain, 1956).

—— *Vita Bohairice Scripta* (= *SBo*), ed. L. T. Lefort (CSCO 89; Louvain, 1953²); Fr. trans. by L. T. Lefort (CSCO 107; Louvain, 1936).

—— *Vita Copta de S. Pacomio*, ed. J. Gribomont and F. Moscatelli (Scritti Monastici NS 2; Padua, 1981); Fr. trans. by L. T. Lefort, *Les vies coptes de saint Pachôme et de ses premiers successeurs* (Bibliothèque du Muséon 16; Louvain, 1966²).

—— *Vitae Graecae* (= *G*), ed. F. Halkin (Subsidia Hagiographica 19; Brussels, 1932).

—— *La Vie latine de saint Pachôme traduite du grec par Denys le Petit*, ed. H. Cranenburg (Subsidia Hagiographica 46; Brussels, 1969).

—— *Vitae Sahidice Scriptae* (= *S*), ed. L. T. Lefort (CSCO 99–100; Louvain, 1952²).

PALLADIUS, *Dialogue sur la vie de Jean Chrysostome*, ed. A. M. Malingrey and P. Leclercq, 2 vols. (SC 341–2; Paris, 1988).

—— *The Lausiac History of Palladius* (= *HL*), ed. C. Butler, 2 vols. (Cambridge, 1898, 1904; repr. Hildesheim, 1967); It. trans. by G. J. Bartelink, intr. C. Mohrmann, *La Storia Lausiaca* (Scritti Greci e Latini, Vite dei Santi 2; Milan, 1974); Eng. trans. by R. T. Meyer, *The Lausiac History* (Ancient Christian Writers 34; London, 1965).

—— *Les Formes syriaques de la matière de l'Histoire Lausiaque*, ed. R.

Draguet (CSCO 389–90, 398–9 (Scr. Syr. 169–70, 173–4); Louvain 1978).

Patrum Nicaeanorum nomina latine, graece, coptice, syriace, arabice, armenice, ed. H. Gelzer, H. Hilgenfeld, and O. Cunze (Leipzig, 1897).

PHILO, *De Vita contemplativa*, ed. F. Daumas and P. Miquel (= vol. 29 of *Les Œuvres de Philon d'Alexandrie*, ed. R. Arnaldez; Paris, 1963).

PHILOSTORGIUS, *Historia Ecclesiastica = Kirchengeschichte mit dem Leber des Lucian von Antiochien und den Fragmenten eines arianischer Historiographen*, ed. J. Bidez and F. Winkelmann (GCS 21; Berlin 1972²).

PHILOSTRATUS, *Vita Apollonii*, i, ed. and trans. by F. C. Conybeare (Loeb; London, repr. 1989).

PLATO, *The Last Days of Socrates, The Apology, etc.*, trans. by M Tredennick (Loeb; London, 1954).

PLINY, *Letters and Panegyrics*, ii, trans. by B. Radice (Loeb; London, repr. 1976).

PLUTARCH, *Quaestiones Romanae*, ed. and trans. by F. C. Babbitt (Loeb London, repr. 1972).

—— *Vita Romuli* (*Plutarque: Vies*, i), ed. R. Flacelière (Paris, 1957).

RUFINUS, *Historia Ecclesiastica* (PL 21. 467–540).

—— *Historia Monachorum sive De Vita Sanctorum Patrum*, ed. E Schulz-Flügel (Patristische Texte und Studien 34; Berlin, 1990).

Sacrorum conciliorum nova et amplissima collectio (= Mansi), ed. J. D Mansi, 31 vols. (Florence–Venice, 1757–98); *Histoire des Conciles d'après les documents originaux*, ed. C. J. Hefele and H. Leclercq, 2 vols. (Paris, 1907); Eng. trans. (of Hefele) by W. R. Clark, *A History of the Christian Councils*, 2 vols. (Edinburgh, 1871).

SERAPION OF THMUIS, *Adversos Manichaeos*, ed. R. P. Casey (Harvard Theological Studies 15; Cambridge, 1931).

SEVERUS, *History of the Patriarchs of the Coptic Church of Alexandria*, ed. B. Evetts (Patrologia Orientalis 1: pts. 2 and 4; Paris, 1907).

SEXTUS, *The Sentences of Sextus*, ed. H. Chadwick (Texts and Studies 5 Cambridge, 1959).

SHENOUTE OF ATRIPE, *Vita et Opera Omnia*, ed. J. Leipoldt and W. C Crum (CSCO 41, 42, 73 (Scr. Copt. 1, 2, 5); Paris, 1908, 1913); Lat trans. by H. Wiesmann (CSCO, Scr. Copt. 96, 108, 129; Paris, 1931 1936, Louvain, 1951).

SOCRATES, *Historia Ecclesiastica* (PG 67; 9–842); Eng. trans. by A. C. Zenos, *Church History from A.D. 305–439* (Library of the Nicene and Post-Nicene Fathers 2: 2 (Grand Rapids, 1979²), 1–178).

SOZOMEN, *Historia Ecclesiastica = Kirchengeschichte*, ed. J. Bidez (GCS 50; Berlin, 1962); Eng. trans. by C. D. Hartrauft (Library of the Nicene and Post-Nicene Fathers, ibid. 179–427).

Storia della Chiesa di Alessandria, ed. T. Orlandi, 2 vols. (Testi e documenti per lo studio dell'antichità 17, 31; Milan, 1967).

STRABO, *Géographie 9*, ed. F. Lasserre (Paris, 1981).

Studia Pontica, ed. J. G. Anderson, F. Cumont, and H. Grégoire, 3 vols. (Brussels, 1903–10).

Synaxarium ecclesiae Constantinopolitanae, ed. H. Delehaye (Brussels, 1902).

Tabula Imperii Byzantini (= *TIB*), ii, *Kappadokien*, ed. F. Hild and M. Restle; iv, *Galatien und Lykaonien*, ed. K. Belke and M. Restle (Österreichische Akademie der Wissenschaften, phil.-hist. Kl. 149, 172; Vienna, 1981, 1984).

TERTULLIAN, *De Virginibus Velandis*, ed. E. Schulz-Flügel, Diss. (Göttingen, 1977).

Testamentum Domini nostri Jesu Christi (= *TD*), ed. I. E. Rahmani (Mainz, 1899).

THEODORET OF CYRRHUS, *Historia Ecclesiastica* = *Kirchengeschichte*, ed. L. Parmentier, and F. Scheidweiler (GCS 44; Berlin, 1954²).

—— *Historia Religiosa* = *Histoire des moines de Syrie*, ed. P. Canivet and A. Leroy-Molinghen, 2 vols. (SC 234, 257; Paris, 1974, 1979).

THEODOSIUS, *Theodosiani Libri XVI (Codex) cum constitutionibus Sirmondianis et leges novellae ad Theodosianum pertinentes* (= *CTh*), ed. T. Mommsen and P. Meyer, 2 vols. (Berlin; 1954²); Eng. trans. by C. Pharr, *The Theodosian Code and Novels and the Sirmondian Constitutions* (Princeton, NJ; 1969⁵).

Vie d'Alexandre l'Acémète, ed. E. De Stoop (Patrologia Orientalis 6: pt. 5, pp. 645–705; Paris, 1911).

Vie et récits de l'Abbé Daniel de Scété, ed. L. Clugnet (*Revue de l'Orient Chrétien* 5 (1900), 49–73).

Vita Sanctae Olympiadis diaconissae et narratio Sergiae de eiusdem translati, ed. H. Delehaye (*AnBoll* 15 (1896), 400–23; 16 (1897), 44–51); Fr. trans. by J. Bousquet, in *Revue de l'Orient Chrétien* 11 (1906), 225–50; Eng. trans. by E. A. Clark, *Jerome, Chrysostom, and Friends*, 107–57.

Vitae Monachorum, ed. E. Amélineau (Annales du Musée Guimet 25; Paris, 1894).

Vie et miracles de sainte Thècle, ed. G. Dagron (Subsidia Hagiographica 62; Brussels, 1978).

ZOSIMUS, *Historia Nova* (*Histoire Nouvelle*), ed. F. Paschoud, 3 vols. (Paris, 1978–89).

SECONDARY SOURCES

ACHELIS, H., *Virgines Subintroductae: Ein Beitrag zum VII. Kapitel des I. Korintherbriefes* (Leipzig, 1902).

ALAND, B. (ed.), *Gnosis: Festschrift für H. Jonas* (Göttingen, 1978).

ALBRECHT, R., *Das Leben der heiligen Makrina auf dem Hintergrund der Thekla-Traditionen* (Göttingen, 1986).

ALTANER, B., and STUIBER, A., *Patrologie: Leben, Schriften und Lehre der Kirchenväter* (Freiburg i.B., 1978).

AMAND DE MENDIETA, D., 'Essai d'une histoire critique des éditions générales grecques et gréco-latines de s. Basile de Césarée', *RBén* 52 (1940), 141–61; 53 (1941), 119–51; 54 (1942), 124–44; 56 (1945/6) 126–73.

—— *L'Ascèse monastique de S. Basile: Essai historique* (Maredsous. 1949).

—— 'La Virginité chez Eusèbe d'Émèse et l'ascétisme familial dans la première moitié du IVe siècle', *RHE* 50 (1955), 777–820.

—— 'The "Unwritten" and "Secret" Apostolic Tradition in the Theological Thought of Basil of Casearea', *Scottish Journal of Theology* Occasional Papers 13 (1965), 59–70.

—— and MOONS, M. CH., 'Une curieuse homélie grecque inédite sur la virginité adressée aux pères de famille', *RBén* 63 (1953), 18–69, 211–38.

AMÉLINEAU, E., *Monuments pour servir à l'histoire de l'Égypte chrétienne au IVe siècle: Histoire de St. Pakhôme et de ses communautes; Documents coptes et aràbes inédits* (Annales du Musée Guimet 17; Paris 1889).

ANDRESEN, C., *Die Kirchen der alten Christenheit* (Die Religionen der Menschheit 29, pts. 1 and 2; Stuttgart, 1971).

ANSON, J., 'The Female Transvestite in Early Monasticism: The Origin and Development of a Motif', *Viator* 5 (1974), 1–32.

ARIÈS, P., and DUBY, G. (eds.), *A History of Private Life*: i, *From Pagan Rome to Byzantium*, ed. P. Veyne (Cambridge, Mass., 1987).

ASPREGEN, K., *The Male Woman: A Feminine Ideal in the Early Church*, ed. R. Kieffer (Acta Universitatis Upsaliensis 4; Uppsala, 1990).

ATIYA, A. S., *A History of Eastern Christianity* (London, 1968).

AUBERT, J., *La Femme: Antiféminisme et Christianisme* (Paris, 1975).

AUBINEAU, M., 'Les Écrits de S. Athanase sur la virginité', *RAM* 31 (1955), 140–71.

BACHT, H., 'Pakhome—der große "Adler"', *Geist und Leben* 22 (1949) 367–82.

—— 'L'importance de l'idéal monastique de s. Pacôme pour l'histoire du monachisme chrétien', *RAM* 26 (1950), 308–26.

—— 'Antonius und Pachomius: Von der Anachorese zum Cönobitentum' in *Antonius Magnus Eremita* (Studia Anselmiana 38; Rome, 1956) 66–107.

—— 'Agrypnia: Die Motive des Schlafentzugs im frühen Mönchtum', in

G. Pflug, B. Eckart, and H. Friesenhahn (eds.), *Bibliothek-Buch-Geschichte: K. Köster zum 65. Geburtstag* (Frankfurt, 1977), 353–69.

BADGER, C. M., 'The New Man Created in God: Christology, Congregation and Asceticism in Athanasius of Alexandria' Diss. (Duke Univ.; Durham, NC, 1990).

BAER, R. A., *Philo's Use of the Categories Male and Female* (Arbeiten zur Literatur und Geschichte des Judentums 3; Leiden, 1970).

BAGNALL, R. S., 'P. Oxy. XVI 1905, SB V 7756 and Fourth-Century Taxation', *ZPE* 37 (1980), 185–96.

—— 'Religious Conversion and Onomastic Change in Early Byzantine Egypt', *Bulletin of the American Society of Papyrologists* 18 (1982), 105–24.

—— and SIJPESTEIJN, P. J., 'Currency in the Fourth Century and the Date of CPR V 26', *ZPE* 24 (1977), 111–24.

BAILEY, D. S., *The Man–Woman Relation in Christian Thought* (New York, 1959).

BALSDON, D., *Die Frau in der römischen Antike* (Munich, 1979).

BALTENSWEILER, H., *Die Ehe im Neuen Testament* (Zurich, 1967).

BARDENHEWER, O., *Geschichte der altkirchlichen Literatur*, iii (Freiburg i.B., 1923).

BARDY, G., *Saint Athanase (296–373)* (Paris, 1925).

—— 'L'Église et l'enseignement au IVᵉ siècle', *RevSR* 14 (1934), 525–49.

—— 'Macédonios et les Macédoniens', in *Dictionnaire de la Théologie Catholique*, ix (Paris, 1926), 1464–78.

BARISON, P., 'Ricerche sui monasteri dell'Egitto bizantino ed arabo secondo i documenti dei papiri greci', *Aegyptus* 18 (1938), 29–148.

BARLEA, O., *Die Weihe der Bischöfe, Presbyter und Diakone in vornicäaischer Zeit* (Munich, 1969).

BARNARD, E. W., 'The Antecedents of Arius', *VigChr* 24 (1970), 172–88.

—— 'Athanasius and the Meletian Schism in Egypt', *Journal of Egyptian Archeology* 59 (1973), 181–9.

BARNS, J., 'Shenute as an Historical Source', in *Actes du Xᵉᵐᵉ Congrès International des Papyrologes* (Warsaw, 1964), 151–9.

BARTELINK, G. J. M., 'Les Démons comme brigands', *VigChr* 21 (1967), 12–24.

BATTIFOL, P., 'Le *Peri Parthenias* du Pseudo-Athanase', *Römische Quartalschrift für christliche Alterthumskunde* 7 (1893), 275–86.

BAUMEISTER, TH., *Martyr Invictus: Der Märtyrer als Sinnbild der Erlösung in der Legende und im Kult der frühen koptischen Kirche* (Forschungen zur Volkskunde 46; Münster, 1972).

—— *Die Anfänge der Theologie des Martyriums* (Münsterische Beiträge zur Theologie 45; Münster, 1980).

BAUR, C., *Der heilige Johannes Chrysostomus und seine Zeit*, 2 vols.

(Munich, 1930); Eng. trans. by M. Gonzaga, *John Chrysostom and his Time*, 2 vols. (Westminster, Md., 1959–60).

BAYNES, N. H., 'Alexandria and Constantinople: A Study in Ecclesiastical Diplomacy', in id. *Byzantine Studies and Other Essays* (London, 1955), 97–115.

BECK, H. G., *Kirche und theologische Literatur im byzantinischen Reich* (*Handbuch der Altertumswissenschaften, Byzantinisches Handbuch* 12, 2, 1; Munich, 1959).

—— *Rede als Kunstwerk und Bekenntnis: Gregor von Nazianz* (Bayrische Akademie der Wissenschaften, hist.-phil. Klasse, Sitzungsberichte 4, Munich, 1977).

BELL, H. J., *Jews and Christians in Egypt: The Jewish Troubles in Alexandria and the Athanasian Controversy* (London, 1924; repr. New Haven, Conn., 1972).

BELLINI, E., 'La posizione dei monachi e dei vergini nella Chiesa secondo Gregorio Nazianzeno', *Scuola Cattolica* 99 (1971), 452–66.

BEN-DAVID, J., and NICHOLS CLARK, T. (eds.), *Culture and its Creators: Essays in Honor of Edward Shils* (Chicago, 1977).

BERNARDI, J., *La Prédication des Pères Cappadociens: Le prédicateur et son auditoire* (Paris, 1968).

BERNARDS, M., *Speculum Virginum: Geistigkeit und Seelenleben der Frau im Hochmittelalter* (Forschungen zur Volkskunde 36/8; Cologne, 1955).

BESSIÈRE, J., *La Tradition manuscrite de la correspondance de Saint Basile* (Oxford, 1923).

BIANCHI, U. (ed.), *La tradizione dell'enkrateia: Motivazioni ontologiche e protologiche. Atti del colloquio internazionale, Milano, 20–23 aprile 1982* (Rome, 1985).

BIDEZ, J., *Le Texte du prologue de Sozomène et de ses chapitres (VI, 28–34) sur les moines d'Égypte et de Palestine* (Berlin, 1935).

BIELER, L., Θεῖος Ἀνήρ: *Das Bild des göttlichen Menschen in Spätantike und Frühchristentum*, 2 vols. (Darmstadt, 1967²).

BIEZUNKA, I., *Études sur la condition juridique et sociale de la femme grecque en Égypte grécoromaine* (Lvov, 1939).

BIONDI, B., *Il diritto romano christiano*, 3 vols. (Milan, 1952–4).

—— *Il diritto romano* (Storia di Roma 20; Rome, 1957).

BLOND, G., 'Hérésie "encratite" vers la fin du IVᵉ siècle', *RSR* 32 (1944), 157–210.

BÖMER, F., *Untersuchungen über die Religion der Sklaven in Griechenland und Rom*, i (Abhandlungen der Akademie der Wissenschaften und der Literatur (Mainz) 7; Mainz, 1957; repr. in Forschungen zur Antiken Sklaverei 14: 1; Wiesbaden, 1981).

BONIS, K., 'Basilios von Caesarea und die Organisation der christlichen Kirche im vierten Jahrhundert', in J. Fedwick (ed.), *Basil of Caesarea. Christian, Humanist, Ascetic*, i. 281–335.

BONNEAU, D., *Le Fisc et le Nil: Incidences des irrégularités de la crue du Nil sur la fiscalité foncière dans l'Égypte grecque et romaine* (Publications de l'Institut de droit romain, NS 2; Paris, 1972).

BOPP, L., *Das Witwentum als organische Gliedschaft im Gemeinschaftsleben der alten Kirche* (Mannheim, 1965).

BORIAS, A., 'Le moine et sa famille (chez les Péres, Pachôme et Basile)', *Collectanea Cisterciensia* 40 (1978), 81–110, 195–217.

BOTTE, B., *La Tradition apostolique de saint Hippolyte: Essai de reconstitution* (Liturgiewissenschaftliche Quellen und Forschungen 39; Münster, 1963).

BOUDÉHOUX, J.-P., *Mariage et famille chez Clément d'Alexandrie* (Paris, 1970).

BOULARAND, E., *L'Hérésie d'Arius et la foi de Nicée*, 2 vols. (Paris, 1972–3).

BOUSSET, W., 'Zur Komposition der Historia Lausiaca', *ZNW* 21 (1922), 81–98.

—— *Apophthegmata, Studien zur Geschichte des ältesten Mönchtums* (Tübingen, 1923).

BOUYER, L., *La vie de s. Antoine* (Saint Wandrille, 1950; repr. Spiritualité Orientale 22; Bellefontaine, 1977).

BOWMAN, A. K., 'The Economy of Egypt in the Early Fourth Century', in *Imperial Revenue, Expediture and Monetary Policy in the Fourth Century AD: The Fifth Oxford Symposium on Coinage and Monetary History* (British Archaeological Reports, Int. Ser. 76; Oxford, 1980), 23–40.

—— *Egypt after the Pharaohs, 332 B.C.–642 A.D.: From Alexander to the Arab Conquest* (Berkeley, 1986).

BOYD, W. K., *The Ecclesiastical Edicts of the Theodosian Code* (Studies in History, Economics and Public Law 24: 2; New York, 1905), 3–70.

BRAKMANN, H., 'Alexandria und die Kanones des Hippolytus', *JAC* 22 (1979), 139–49.

BRAUNERT, H., *Die Binnenwanderung: Studien zur Sozialgeschichte Ägyptens in der Ptolemäer-und Kaiserzeit* (Bonner historische Forschungen 26; Bonn, 1964).

BRENNAN, B. R., 'Dating the Vita Antonii', *VigChr* 30 (1976), 52–4.

BRENNECKE, H.-C., *Hilarius von Poitiers und die Bischofsopposition gegen Konstantius II: Untersuchungen zur dritten Phase des arianischen Streites (337–361)* (Patristische Texte und Untersuchungen 26; Berlin, 1984).

—— *Studien zur Geschichte der Homöer: Der Osten bis zum Ende der homöischen Reichskirche* (Beiträge zur Historischen Theologie 73; Tübingen, 1988).

BRINGMANN, L., *Die Frau im ptolemäisch-kaiserzeitlichen Ägypten*, Diss. (Bonn, 1939).

BROCK, S., and ASHBROOK HARVEY, S. (eds.), *Holy Women of the Syrian Orient* (Berkeley, 1987).

BROWN, P. R. L., 'Saint Augustine's Attitude to Religious Coercion', *JRS* 54 (1964), 107–16.

—— 'The Rise and Function of the Holy Man in Late Antiquity', *JRS* 61 (1971), 80–101.

—— *The World of Late Antiquity, A.D. 150–750* (New York, 1971).

—— *The Cult of the Saints: Its Rise and Function in Latin Christianity* (Chicago, 1981).

—— 'The Saint as Exemplar in Late Antiquity', *Representations* 1 (1983), 1–25.

—— *The Body and Society: Men, Women, and Sexual Renunciation in Early Christianity* (New York, 1988).

BROX, N., 'Häresie', in *RAC* xiii. (Stuttgart, 1984), 284–97.

BÜCHLER, B., *Die Armut der Armen: Über den ursprünglichen Sinn der mönchischen Armut* (Munich, 1980).

BUCK, D. F., 'The Structure of the Lausiac History', *Byzantion* 46 (1976), 292–307.

BUDGE, E. A. WALLIS, *Coptic Apocrypha in the Dialect of Upper Egypt* (London, 1913).

BUGGE, J., *Virginitas: An Essay in the History of a Medieval Ideal* (Archives internationales d'histoire des idées, séries mineur 17; The Hague, 1975).

BURMESTER, O. H., 'On the Date and Authorship of the Arabic Synaxarium of the Coptic Church', *JThS* 39 (1938), 249–53.

BYNUM, C. WALKER, ' ". . . And Woman His Humanity": Female Imagery in the Religious Writing of the Later Middle Ages', in C. Walker Bynum, S. Harrell, and P. Richman (eds.), *Gender and Religion: On the Complexity of Symbols* (Boston, 1986), 257–88.

—— *Holy Feast and Holy Fast: The Religious Significance of Food to Medieval Women* (Berkeley, 1987).

—— *Fragmentation and Redemption: Essays on Gender and the Human Body in Medieval Religion* (New York, 1991).

CACITTI, R., 'L'etica sessuale nella canonistica del cristianesimo primitivo: Aspetti di istituzionalizzazione ecclesiastica nel III secolo', in R. Cantalamessa (ed.), *Etica sessuale e matrimonio nel cristianesimo delle origini*, 69–157.

CALDER, W. M., 'The Epigraphy of the Anatolian Heresies', in W. H. Buckler and W. M. Calder (eds.), *Anatolian Studies Presented to Sir W. M. Ramsay* (Manchester, 1923), 59–91.

—— 'The New Jerusalem of the Montanists', *Byzantion* 6 (1931), 421–5.

CAMELOT, T., *Virgines Christi: La virginité aux premiers siècles de l'Église* (Paris, 1944).

—— 'Les Traités "De Virginitate" au IVᵉ siècle', *EtCarm* 31 (1952), 273–92.

CAMERON, A., 'Neither Male nor Female', *GR* 27 (1980), 60–7.

—— and CAMERON A., 'Christianity and Tradition in the Historiography of the Later Roman Empire', *Classical Quarterly*, NS 14 (1964), 316–20.

—— and KUHRT A. (eds.), *Images of Women in Antiquity* (Detroit, 1983).

CAMPENHAUSEN, H. VON, *Die Idee des Martyriums in der frühen Kirche* (Göttingen, 1936).

—— 'Die asketische Heimatlosigkeit im altkirchlichen und frühmittelalterlichen Mönchtum', in id. *Tradition und Leben: Kräfte der Kirchengeschichte* (Tübingen, 1960), 290–7.

CANÉVET, M., 'Le "De instituto christiano" est-il de Grégoire de Nysse?', *REG* 82 (1969), 404–23.

CANTALAMESSA, R. (ed.), *Etica sessuale e matrimonio nel cristianesimo delle origini* (Studia Patristica Mediolanensia 5; Milan, 1976).

CARRIÉ, J. M., 'L'Égypte au IVᵉ siècle: Fiscalité, Économie, Société', in *Proceedings of the 16 Intern. Congress of Papyrology, New York 24–31 July 1980* (American Studies in Papyrology 23; Ann Arbor, 1981), 431–46.

CARROLL, S. T., 'The Melitian Schism: Coptic Christianity and the Egyptian Church' Diss. (Oxford, Oh., 1989).

CASEY, R. P., *Der dem Athanasius zugeschriebene Traktat "Peri Parthenias"* (Sitzungsberichte der Preussischen Akademie der Wissenschaften, phil.-hist. Kl. 33; Berlin, 1935), 1022–45.

CAVALLERA, F., 'Le "De Virginitate" de Basile d'Ancyre', *RHE* 6 (1905), 3–12.

CAVALLIN, A., *Studien zu den Briefen des hl. Basilius* (Lund, 1944).

CAVALLO, G., 'Libro e pubblico alla fine del mondo antico', in id. *Libri, editori e pubblico nel mondo antico* (Bari, 1975), 5–42.

CERETI, G., *Divorzio, nuove nozze e penitenza nella chiesa primitiva* (Bologna, 1977).

CHADWICK, H., 'Faith and Order at the Council of Nicaea: A Note on the Background of the Sixth Canon', *Harvard Theological Review* 53 (1960), 171–95.

CHADWICK, O., *John Cassian: A Study in Primitive Monasticism* (Cambridge, 1968²).

CHESNUT, G. F., *The First Christian Histories: Eusebius, Socrates, Sozomen, Theodoret and Evagrius* (Théologie historique 46; Paris, 1977).

CHITTY, D. J., 'A Note on the Chronology of the Pachomian Foundations', *SP* 2 (TU 64; Berlin, 1957), 379–85.

—— *The Desert a City: An Introduction to the Study of Egyptian and*

Palestinian Monasticism under the Christian Empire (Oxford, 1966).
CHODOROW, N., 'Family Structure and Feminine Personality', in M. Zimbalist Rosaldo and L. Lamphere (eds.), *Woman, Culture, and Society*, 43–66.

Christianisme et formes littéraires de l'Antiquité tardive en occident (Fondation Hardt, Entretiens sur l'antiquité classique 23; Paris, 1977).

CLARK, E. A., *Jerome, Chrysostom, and Friends* (New York, 1979).

—— *Ascetic Piety and Women's Faith: Essays on Late Ancient Christianity* (Studies in Women and Religion 20; Lewiston, 1986).

CLARKE, W. K. L., *St. Basil the Great: A Study in Monasticism* (Cambridge, 1913).

—— *The Life of Macrina* (London, 1916).

COLOMBAS, G. M., *El monacato primitivo*, 2 vols. (Madrid, 1974–5).

CONSOLINO, F. E., 'Modelli di santità femminile nelle più antiche Passioni romane', *Augustinianum* 24 (1984), 83–113.

—— 'Modelli di comportamento e modi di santificazione per l'aristocrazia femminile d'Occidente', in A. Gierdina (ed.), *Società romana e impero tardoantico*, i, *Istituzioni, ceti, economie* (Bari, 1986), 273–306.

CONSTABLE, G., 'Monachisme et pélerinage au Moyen Âge', *RH* 258 (1977), 3–27.

COOPER, K., 'Insinuations of Womanly Influence: An Aspect of the Christianization of the Roman Aristocracy', *JRS* 82 (1992), 150–64.

COURTONNE, Y., *Un témoin du IVe siècle oriental: Saint Basil et son temps d'après sa correspondance* (Paris, 1973).

COX, P., *Biography in Late Antiquity* (Berkeley, 1983).

CRACCO RUGGINI, L., 'I vescovi e il dinamismo sociale nel mondo cittadino di Basilio di Cesarea', in *Atti del Convegno internazionale su Basilio di Cesarea: La sua età e il Basilianesimo in Sicilia, Messina, 4–6 dicembre 1979* (Messina, 1983), 97–124.

CRAMER, J. A., *A Geographical and Historical Description of Asia Minor*, 2 vols. (Oxford, 1832; repr. Amsterdam, 1971).

CRIMI, C. U., 'La paternità Atanasiana di un testo *Ad Virgines*', *Le Muséon* 86 (1973), 521–4.

CROSS, F., and LIVINGSTONE, E. (eds.), *Oxford Dictionary of the Christian Church* (Oxford, 1974²).

CROUZEL, H., *Origène et la 'connaissance mystique'* (Museum Lessianum 56; Paris, 1961).

—— *Virginité et mariage selon Origène* (Museum Lessianum 58; Paris, 1962).

CRUM, W. E., *A Coptic Dictionary* (Oxford, 1939).

CURTIUS, E. R., *Europäische Literatur und lateinisches Mittelalter* (Bern and Munich, 1961³).

DAGRON, G., 'Les Moines et la ville: Le Monachisme à Constantinople jusqu'au Concile de Chalcédoine (451)', *Travaux et Mémoires* 4 (1970), 229–76.

—— *Naissance d'une capitale: Constantinople et ses institutions de 330 à 451* (Bibliothèque byzantine: Études 7; Paris, 1974).

—— 'Le Christianisme dans la ville byzantine', *DOP* 31 (1977), 3–25.

DALMAIS, J. H., 'Sacerdoce et monachisme dans L'Orient chrétien', *La Vie spirituelle* 79 (1948), 37–49.

D'ALVERNY, M.-TH., 'Comment les théologiens et les philosophes voient la femme', *Cahiers de civilisation médiévale* 20 (1977), 105–29.

DANIÉLOU, J., 'Grégoire de Nysse et le Messalianisme', *RSR* 48 (1960), 119–34.

—— 'Le Ministère des femmes dans l'Église ancienne', *La Maison-Dieu* 61 (1960), 70–96.

—— and MARROU, M., 'Le Mariage de Grégoire de Nysse et la chronologie de sa vie', *Revue des Études Augustiniennes* 2 (1956), 71–8.

DAVIES, J. G., 'Deacons, Deaconesses and the Minor Orders in the Patristic Period', *JEH* 14 (1963), 1–15.

DAVIES, S. L., *The Revolt of the Widows: The Social World of the Apocryphal Acts* (London, 1980).

DAVIS, S. (ed.), *Spoglio Lessicale Papirologico* (Milan, 1968).

DECHOW, J. F., 'Dogma and Mysticism in Early Christianity: Epiphanius of Cyprus and the Legacy of Origen', Diss. (Pennsylvania, 1975).

DELCOURT, M., 'Le Complexe de Diane dans l'hagiographie chrétienne', *RHR* 153 (1958), 1–33.

DELEHAYE, H., 'La Passion de S. Théodote d'Ancyre', *AnBoll* 22 (1903), 320–8.

—— *Les Légendes hagiographiques* (Subsidia Hagiographica 18; Brussels, 1927³).

—— 'Les Femmes stylites', *AnBoll* 27 (1908), 391–2.

—— *Les Passions des martyrs et les genres littéraires* (Brussels, 1966²).

DEMAROLLE, J. M., 'Les Femmes chrétiennes vue par Porphyre', *JAC* 13 (1970), 42–7.

DEMOUGEOT, E., *De l'unité à la division de l'empire romaine, 395–410* (Paris, 1951).

DENZLER, G., 'Autorität und Rezeption der Konzilsbeschlüsse in der Christenheit', *Concilium* 19 (1983), 507–11.

DEVOS, P., 'La Date du voyage d'Égérie', *AnBoll* 85 (1967), 165–94.

—— '"La Servante de Dieu" Poémenia d'après Pallade', *AnBoll* 87 (1969), 189–212.

—— 'Les Nombres dans l'*Historia Monachorum in Aegypto*', *AnBoll* 92 (1974), 97–108.

DIHLE, A., *Studien zur griechischen Biographie* (Abhandlungen der wissenschaftlichen Akademie in Göttingen, phil.-hist. Kl. 3: 37; Göttingen, 1956).

DINNEEN, L., *Titles of Address in Christian Greek Epistolography to 52*; *AD* (Washington, DC, 1929).

DÖLGER, F.-J., 'Nonna: Ein Kapitel über christliche Volksfrömmigkei' des 4. Jh.', *Antike und Christentum* 5 (1936), 44–75.

DÖRRIES, H., *Symeon von Mesopotamien: Die Überlieferung der mes salianischen "Makarios"-Schriften* (TU 55: 1; Leipzig, 1941).

—— *Die Vita Antonii als Geschichtsquelle* (Nachrichten der Akademie der Wissenschaften in Göttingen, phil.-hist. Kl. 14; Göttingen, 1949 repr. in id. *Wort und Stunde*, i. 145–224).

—— *De Spiritu Sancto: Ein Beitrag des Basilius zum Abschluß de. trinitarischen Dogmas* (Abhandlungen der Akademie der Wissen schaften in Göttingen, phil.-hist. Kl. 3: 39; Göttingen, 1965).

—— 'Urteil und Verurteilung. Kirche und Messalianer: Zum Umgang der Alten Kirche mit Häretikern', in id. *Wort und Stunde*, i. 335–51.

—— *Wort und Stunde: Gesammelte Studien zur Kirchengeschichte de: vierten Jahrhunderts*, 3 vols. (Göttingen, 1966).

—— 'Die Messalianer im Zeugnis ihrer Bestreiter: Zum Problem de: Enthusiasmus in der spätantiken Reichskirche', *Saeculum* 21 (1970) 213–27.

DOSSI, L., 'S. Ambrogio e S. Atanasio nel De Virginibus', *Acme ₄* (1951), 246.

DOUGLAS, M., *Purity and Danger* (London, 1966).

—— *How Institutions Think* (Syracuse, NY, 1986).

DRAGUET, R., 'Le Chapitre de l'Histoire Lausiaque sur les Tabennésiote: dérive-t-il d'une source copte?' *Le Muséon* 57 (1944), 53–146; 5₈ (1945), 15–95.

—— 'L'Inauthenticité du prooemion de l'Histoire Lausiaque', *Le Muséor* 59 (1946), 529–34.

—— 'L'Histoire Lausiaque: une œuvre écrite dans l'esprit d'Évagre' *RHE* 41 (1946), 321–64; 42 (1947), 5–49.

—— 'Une lettre de Sérapion de Thmuis aux disciples d'Antoine (AD 356 en version syriaque et arménienne', *Le Muséon* 64 (1951), 1–25.

DRESSLER, H., *The Usage of askeo and its Cognates in Greek Documents to 100 AD* (Washington, DC, 1947).

DUCHESNE, L. M. D., *Histoire ancienne de l'Église*, ii (Paris, 1910).

DUVAL, Y.-M., 'L'Originalité du De virginibus dans le mouvemen ascétique occidental: Ambroise, Cyprien, Athanase', in *Ambroise de Milan, XVIᵉ centenaire de son élection épiscopale* (Études Augustinien nes; Paris, 1974), 9–66.

—— 'La Problématique de la Lettre aux Vierges d'Athanase', *Le Muséor* 88 (1975), 405–33.

ELM, K., 'Die Stellung der Frau in Ordenswesen, Semireligiosentum und Häresie zur Zeit der Elisabeth', in id. (ed.), *Sankt Elisabeth: Fürstin,*

Dienerin, Heilige: Aufsätze, Dokumentation, Katalog (Sigmaringen, 1981), 7–28.

ELM, S., 'An Alleged Book-theft in Fourth Century Egypt: P. Lips. 43', *SP* 18 (1989), 209–15.

—— 'Perceptions of Jerusalem Pilgrimage as Reflected in Two Early Sources on Female Pilgrimage (3rd and 4th Century AD)', *SP* 20 (1989), 219–23.

—— 'The *Sententiae ad Virginem* by Evagrius Ponticus and the Problem of Early Monastic Rules', *Augustinianum* 30 (1990), 393–404.

—— 'Evagrius Ponticus' *Sententiae ad Virginem*', *DOP* 45 (1991), 97–120.

—— 'Vergini, vedove, diaconisse—alcune osservazioni sullo sviluppo dei cosidetti "ordini femminili" nel quarto secolo in Oriente', *Codex Aquilarensis* 5 (1991), 77–89.

—— 'Formen des Zusammenlebens männlicher und weiblicher Asketen im östlichen Mittelmeerraum während des vierten Jahrhunderts nach Christus,' in M. Parisse and K. Elm (eds.), *Doppelklöster und andere Formen der Symbiose männlicher und weiblicher Religiosen im Mittelalter* (Berliner Historische Studien 18: Ordensstudien 8; Berlin, 1992), 13–24.

EMMETT, A., 'Female Ascetics in the Greek Papyri', *JÖB* 32 (1982), 507–13.

—— 'An Early Fourth-century Female Monastic Community in Egypt?', in A. Moffat (ed.), *Maistor: Classical, Byzantine and Renaissance Studies for Robert Browning* (Byzantina Australiensia 5; Canberra, 1984), 77–83.

ENSSLIN, W., *Die Religionspolitik des Kaisers Theodosius des Großen* (Sitzungsberichte der Bayrischen Akademie der Wissenschaften, phil.-hist. Kl. 1953: 2; Munich, 1953).

EVELYN-WHITE, H. G., *The Monasteries of Wadi'n Natrun*, ii, *The History of Nitria and Scetis* (New York, 1932).

FABBRINI, F., *La manumissio in ecclesia* (Milan, 1965).

FABER, K. G., *Theorie der Geschichtswissenschaft* (Munich, 1982⁵).

FAIVRE, A., *Naissance d'une hiérarchie: Les Premières Étapes du cursus clérical* (Théologie historique 40; Paris, 1977).

FAVALE, A., 'Teofilo di Alessandria (352 c.–412)', *Salesianum* 18 (1956), 215–46, 498–535; 19 (1957), 34–83, 215–72.

FEDWICK, P. J., *The Church and Charisma of Leadership in Basil of Caesarea* (Studies and Texts 45; Toronto, 1979).

—— (ed.), *Basil of Caesarea: Christian, Humanist, Ascetic. A Sixteen-hundredth Anniversary Symposium*, 2 vols. (Toronto, 1981).

FELLECHNER, E. L., *Askese und Charitas bei den drei Kappadokiern*, Diss. (Heidelberg, 1979).

FELTEN, F. J., 'Herrschaft des Abtes', in F. Prinz and K. Bosl (eds.), *Herrschaft und Kirche: Beiträge zur Entstehung und Wirkungsweise episkopaler und monastischer Organisationsformen* (Monographien zur Geschichte des Mittelalters 33; Stuttgart, 1988), 147–296.

FERRARINI, A., 'Tradizioni orali nella Storia Ecclesiastica di Socrate Scolastico', *Studia Pataviana* 27 (1981), 29–54.

FESTUGIÈRE, A. J., *Hippocrate et l'Ancienne Médécine* (Paris, 1948).

—— 'Le Problème littéraire de l' "Historia Monachorum"', *Hermes* 83 (1955), 257–84.

—— *Antioche païenne et chrétienne: Libanius, Chrysostome et les moines de Syrie. Avec un commentaire archéologique sur l'Antiochikos par R. Mortin* (Bibliothèque des Écoles françaises d'Athènes et de Rome 194; Paris, 1959).

—— 'Lieux communs littéraires et thèmes de folk-lore dans l'hagiographie primitive', *Wiener Studien* 73 (1960), 123–52.

—— *Les Moines d'Orient*, 3 vols. (Paris, 1961–3).

FEUSI, I., *Das Institut der gottgeweihten Jungfrauen: Sein Fortleben im Mittelalter* (Fribourg, 1917).

FIEY, J. M., 'Cénobitisme féminin ancien dans les églises syriennes orientale et occidentale', *L'Orient syrien* 10 (1965), 281–306.

FIORENZA, E. S., 'Die Rolle der Frau in der urchristlichen Bewegung', *Concilium* 12 (1976), 3–9.

FLECK, L., *Entstehung und Entwicklung einer wissenschaftlichen Tatsache* (Basle, 1935); Eng. trans. by T. J. Trenn, *The Genesis and Development of a Scientific Fact* (Chicago, 1979).

FLOROVSKY, G., 'Theophilus of Alexandria and Apa Aphou of Pemdje', in S. Lieberman *et al.* (eds.), *H. A. Wolfson Jubilee Volume I* (American Academy for Jewish Research; Jerusalem, 1965), 275–310.

FONTAINE, J., and KANNENGIESSER, CH., (eds.), *Epektasis: Mélanges patristiques offerts au Cardinal J. Daniélou* (Beauchesne, 1972).

FORLIN PATRUCCO, M., 'Aspetti di vita familiare nel IV secolo negli scritti dei padri cappadoci', in R. Cantalamessa (ed.), *Etica sessuale e matrimonio nel cristianesimo delle origini*, 158–79.

—— 'Social Patronage and Political Mediation in the Activity of Basil of Caesarea', *SP* 17 (1982), 1102–7.

FOSS, C., 'Late Antique and Byzantine Ankara', *DOP* 31 (1977), 27–87.

—— 'Caesarea (Kayseri)' in J. Strayer (ed.), *Dictionary of the Middle Ages*, iii (New York, 1983), 9.

FOUCAULT, M., *The History of Sexuality*: i, *An Introduction*; iii, *The Care of the Self*, Eng. trans. by R. Hurley (New York, 1978, 1986).

FOX, M. M., *The Life and the Times of St. Basil the Great as Revealed in his Works* (The Catholic University of America, Patristic Studies 57; Washington, DC, 1939).

FRANCHI DE' CAVALIERI, P., *I Martirii di S. Teodoto e di S. Ariadne con un appendice sul testo originale del Martirio de S. Eleuterio* (StT 6; Rome, 1901).

—— *Note agiografiche I: Ancora del martirio di S. Ariadne* (StT 8; Rome, 1902).

FRANK, K. S., *Angelikos Bios: Begriffsanalytische und begriffsgeschichtliche Untersuchung zum 'engelgleichen Leben' im frühen Mönchtum* (Beiträge zur Geschichte des alten Mönchtums und des Benediktinerordens 26; Münster, 1964).

FRASER, N., *Unruly Practices: Power, Discourse, and Gender in Contemporary Social Theory* (Minneapolis, 1989).

FRAZEE, C. A., 'Anatolian Asceticism in the Fourth Century: Eustathios of Sebastea and Basil of Caesarea', *Catholic Historical Review* 66 (1980), 16–33.

FREI, J., 'Die Stellung des alten Mönchtums zur Arbeit', *Erbe und Auftrag* 53 (1977), 332–6.

FREIER, H., *Caput velare*, Diss. (Tübingen, 1963).

FRENCH, D. H., *Roman Roads and Milestones of Asia Minor*, i. *The Pilgrim's Road* (British Archaeological Reports 134; London, 1981).

FREND, W. H. C., 'Athanasius as an Egyptian Christian Leader', *New College Bulletin* 8 (1974), 20–37 repr. in id. *Religion Popular and Unpopular in the Early Christian Centuries* (London, 1976).

FROHNHOFER, H., 'Weibliche Diakone in der frühen Kirche', *Stimmen der Zeit* 204 (1986), 269–78.

GADAMER, H.-G., *Wahrheit und Methode: Grundzüge einer philosophischen Hermeneutik* (Tübingen, 1965[2]).

GAIN, B., *L'Église de Cappadoce au IVe siècle d'après la correspondance de Basile de Césarée (330–379)* (OrChrA 225; Rome, 1985).

GALLAY, P., *La Vie de Grégoire de Nazianze* (Lyons, 1943).

—— *Les Manuscrits des lettres de saint Grégoire de Nazianze* (Paris, 1957).

GARITTE, G., 'Un couvent de femmes au IIIe siècle? Note sur un passage de la vie grecque de S. Antoine', in *Scrinium Lovaniense: Mélanges historiques E. van Cauwenbergh* (Louvain, 1961), 150–9.

GARNSEY, P., *Social Status and Legal Privilege in the Roman Empire* (Oxford, 1970).

GASCON, J., 'P. Fouad. 87: Les Monastères pachômiens et l'état byzantin', *Bulletin de l'Institut Français d'Archéologie Orientale* 76 (1976), 157–84.

GAUDEMET, J., 'La Législation religieuse de Constantin', *Revue d'histoire de l'Église de France* 33 (1947), 38–41.

—— *L'Église dans l'Empire Romain (IVe–Ve siècles)* (Histoire du Droit et des Institutions de l'Église en Occident 3; Paris, 1958).

—— *La Formation du droit séculier et du droit de l'église aux IVe et Ve siècles* (Paris, 1979[2]).

GAUDEMET, J., 'Le Statut de la femme dans l'Empire romain'; 'Aspects sociologiques de la famille romaine'; 'Les Transformations de la vie familiale au Bas-Empire et l'influence du Christianisme'; repr. in id. *Études de droit romain*, iii (Pubblicazioni della Facoltà di Giurisprudenza della Università di Camerino 4: 3; Camerino, 1979), 225–310.

GEERTZ, C., 'Centers, Kings and Charisma: Reflections on the Symbolics of Power', in J. Ben-David and T. Nichols Clark (eds.), *Culture and its Creators*, 150–71.

GELZER, H., *Studien zur byzantinischen Verwaltung Ägyptens* (Leipzig, 1909).

GEORGHEAN, A. G., *The Attitude towards Labour in Early Christianity and Ancient Culture* (Washington, DC, 1945).

GEPPERT, F., *Die Quellen des Kirchenhistorikers Sokrates Scholastikus* (Leipzig, 1898).

GHEDINI, G., *Lettere cristiane dai papiri greci del III e IV secolo* (Milan, 1923).

GIANNARELLI, E., *La tipologia femminile nella biografia e nell'autobiografia cristiana del IV° secolo* (Istituto storico Italiano per il Medioevo: Studi Storici 127; Rome, 1980).

GIET, S., *Sasimes: Une méprise de Saint Basile* (Paris, 1941).

—— *Les Idées et l'action sociale de Saint Basile* (Paris, 1941).

—— 'S. Basile et le Concile de Constantinople de 360', *JThS* 6 (1955), 94–9.

—— 'Basile, était-il sénateur?', *RHE* 60 (1965), 424–44.

GILLIARD, F., 'The Social Origins of Bishops in the Fourth Century', Diss. (Berkeley, 1966).

GILLMANN, F., *Das Institut der Chorbischöfe im Orient: Historisch-kanonistische Studie* (Veröffentlichungen des kirchenhistorischen Seminars der Universität München 2: 1; Munich, 1903).

GIRARDET, K. M., *Kaisergericht und Bischofsgericht: Studien zu den Anfängen des Donatistenstreits (313–15) und zum Prozess des Athanasius von Alexandrien (328–46)* (Antiquitas 21; Bonn, 1975).

GIRON, N., *Légendes coptes* (Paris, 1907).

GOEHRING, J. E., *The Letter of Ammon and Pachomian Monasticism* (Patristische Texte und Studien 27; Berlin, 1988).

GOGGIN, TH. A., *The Times of St. Gregory of Nyssa as Reflected in the Letters and the Contra Eunomium* (Washington, DC, 1947).

GOLTZ, E. von der, *Logos Soterias peri parthenias: Eine echte Schrift des Athanasius* (TU 29, NF 14; Leipzig, 1905).

GOODY, J., 'Religion, Social Change and the Sociology of Conversion', in id. (ed.), *Changing Social Structure in Ghana* (London, 1975).

GORCE, D., *Les Voyages, l'hospitalité et le port des lettres dans le monde chrétien des IVᵉ et Vᵉ siècles* (Paris, 1925).

GOUGAUD, L., '*Mulierum consortia*: Étude sur le syneisaktisme chez les ascètes', *Erice* 9 (1921), 147–56.

GRAF, G., *Geschichte der christlichen arabischen Literatur*, i (Rome, 1944).

GRAILLOT, H., *Le Culte de Cybèle, mère des dieux, à Rome et dans l'Empire romain* (Paris, 1912).

GRANFIELD, P., and JUNGMANN, J. (eds.), *Kyriakon: Festschrift für J. Quasten*, 2 vols. (Münster, 1970–1).

GRANT, R. M., 'Theological Education at Alexandria', in B. A. Pearson and J. E. Goehring (eds.), *The Roots of Egyptian Christianity*, 178–89.

GREGG, R. C. (ed.), *Arianism: Historical and Theological Reassessments. Papers from the Ninth International Conference on Patristic Studies (Oxford, September 5–10, 1983)* (Patristic Monograph Series 11; Philadelphia, 1985).

—— and GROH, D. E., *Early Arianism: A View of Salvation* (Philadelphia, 1981).

GRÉGOIRE, H., and ORGELS, P., 'La Passion de S. Théodote, œuvre du Pseudo Nil, et son noyeau montaniste', *ByZ* 44 (1951), 165–84.

GRIBOMONT, J., *Histoire du texte des Ascétiques de saint Basile* (Bibliothèque du Muséon 32; Louvain, 1953).

—— 'Le Monachisme au IVᵉ siècle en Asie Mineure: De Gangres au Messalianisme', *SP* 2 (TU 64; Berlin, 1957), 400–15.

—— 'Eustathe le Philosophe et les voyages du jeune Basile de Césarée', *RHE* 54 (1959), 115–24.

—— 'Eustathe de Sébaste', in *DSp* iv.2 (Paris, 1961), 1708–12.

—— 'Le *De instituto christiano* et le Messalianisme de Grégoire de Nysse', *SP* 5 (1962), 312–22.

—— 'Le Dossier des origines du Messalianisme', in J. Fontaine and Ch. Kannengiesser (eds.), *Epektasis*, 611–25.

—— 'Basilio', in *DIP* (Rome, 1974), 1101–9.

—— 'Un aristocrate revolutionnaire, évêque et moine: Saint Basile', *Augustinianum* 17 (1977), 179–91.

—— 'Les Règles épistolaires de S. Basile: Lettres 173 et 22', *Antonianum* 54 (1979), 255–87.

—— 'Saint Basile et le monachisme enthousiaste', *Irénikon* 53 (1980), 123–44.

—— 'Le Panégyrique de la virginité, œuvre de jeunesse de Grégoire de Nysse', *RAM* 43 (1967), 249–66.

—— *Saint Basile: Évangile et Église*, 2 vols. (Spiritualité orientale 36–7; Bellefontaine, 1984).

GRIGGS, C. W., *Early Egyptian Christianity from its Origins to 451 C.E.* (Coptic Studies 2; Leiden, 1990).

GROTZ, J., *Die Entwicklung des Bußstufenwesens in der vornicänischen Kirche* (Freiburg i.B., 1955).

GRUNDMANN, H., *Religiöse Bewegungen im Mittelalter: Untersuchungen über die geschichtlichen Zusammenhänge zwischen der Ketzerei, den Bettelorden und der religiösen Frauenbewegung im 12. und 13. Jhd. und Über geschichtliche Grundlagen deutscher Mystik* (Hildesheim, 1961²).

GRYSON, R., *Les Origines du célibat ecclésiastique* (Recherches et Synthèses, Section d'histoire 2; Gembloux, 1970).

—— *Le Ministère des femmes dans l'Église ancienne* (Recherches et Synthèses, Section d'histoire 4; Gembloux, 1972).

—— 'L'Ordination des diaconesses d'après les constitutions apostoliques', *Mélanges de science religieuse* 31 (1974), 41–5.

—— 'L'Autorité des docteurs dans l'Église ancienne et médiévale', *Revue Théologique de Louvain* 13 (1982), 63–73.

GUILLAUMONT, A., 'Les Messaliens', *EtCarm* 31 (1952), 131–8.

—— *Les 'Képhalaia Gnostica' d'Évagre le Pontique et l'histoire de l'origénisme chez les Grecs et chez les Syriens* (Patristica Sorbonensia 5; Paris, 1962).

—— 'Le Site des "Cellia" (Basse Égypte)', *Revue archéologique* 2 (1964), 43–50.

—— 'Le Dépaysement comme forme d'ascèse, dans le monachisme ancien', *École Pratique des Hautes Études, Sciences religieuses* 76 (1968/9), 31–58.

—— 'Le Nom des "Agapètes"', *VigChr* 23 (1969), 30–7.

—— 'La Conception du désert chez les moines d'Égypte', *RHR* 183 (1975), 3–21.

—— 'Histoire des moines aux Kellia', *Orientalia Lovaniensia Periodica* 8 (1977), 187–202.

—— 'Les Fouilles françaises de Kellia, 1964–69', in R. Wilson (ed.), *The Future of Coptic Studies* (Leiden, 1978), 203–8.

—— 'Gnose et Monachisme: Exposé introductif', in J. Ries (ed.), *Gnosticisme et monde hellénistique. Actes du Colloque de Louvain-la-Neuve (11–14 mars 1980)* (Publ. de l'institut orientaliste de Louvain 27; Louvain-la-Neuve, 1982), 301–10.

GÜLZOW, H., *Christentum und Sklaverei in den ersten drei Jahrhunderten* (Bonn, 1969).

GUMMERUS, J., *Die homöusianische Partei bis zum Tode des Konstantius* (Leipzig, 1900).

GUY, J.-C., *Recherches sur la tradition grecque des Apophtegmata Patrum* (Subsidia Hagiographica 36; Brussels, 1962).

—— 'Le Centre monastique de Scété dans la littérature du Vᵉ siècle', *OrChrP* 30 (1964), 129–47.

—— *Paroles des anciens: Apophtegmes des Pères du Désert* (Collection des Points, Séries Sagesse 1; Paris, 1976).

GWATKIN, H. M., *Studies of Arianism* (Cambridge, 1900²).

HADJINICOLAOU-MARAVA, A., *Recherches sur la vie des esclaves dans le monde byzantine* (Collection de l'Institut Français d'Athènes 45; Athens, 1950).

HADOT, P., *Exercices spirituels et philosophie antique* (Études Augustiniennes; Paris, 1981), 59–74.

HAGEMANN, H. R., 'Die rechtliche Stellung der christlichen Wohltätigkeitsanstalten der östlichen Reichshälfte', *Revue internationale des droits de l'Antiquité* 3 (1956), 265–83.

HAGEMANN, W., 'Die rechtliche Stellung der Patriarchen von Alexandrien und Antiochien: Eine historische Untersuchung ausgehend vom Canon 6 des Konzils von Nizäa', *Ostkirchliche Studien* 13 (1964), 171–91.

HANSSENS, J. M., 'Nonnos, nonna et Nonnus, nonna', *OrChrP* 29 (1960), 29–41.

HARDY, E. R., *Christian Egypt: Church and People. Christianity and Nationalism in the Patriarchate of Alexandria* (New York, 1951).

HARNACK, A. VON, *Die Mission und die Ausbreitung des Christentums in den ersten drei Jahrhunderten*, 2 vols. (Leipzig, 1924[4]).

—— *Geschichte der altchristlichen Literatur bis Eusebius*, 2 vols. (Leipzig, 1958[4]).

HARRISON, V. F., 'Male and Female in Cappadocian Theology', *JThS* NS 41 (1990), 441–71.

HAUBEN, H., 'On the Melitians in P. Lond. VI (P. Jews) 1914: The Problem of Papas Heraiscus', in *Proceedings of the 16th International Congress of Papyrology, New York 24–31 July 1980* (American Studies in Papyrology 23; Chico, Calif., 1981), 447–56.

HAUSCHILD, W. D., *Die Pneumatomachen: Eine Untersuchung zur Dogmengeschichte des vierten Jahrhunderts*, Diss. (Hamburg, 1967).

—— *Gottes Geist und der Mensch: Studien zur frühchristlichen Pneumatologie* (Munich, 1972).

—— 'Eusthatius von Sebaste', in *TRE* x (Berlin, 1982), 547–50.

HAUSER-MEURY, M.-M., *Prosopographie zu den Schriften Gregors von Nazianz* (Theophania 13; Bonn, 1960).

HAUSHERR, I., 'L'Erreur fondamentale et la logique du messalianisme', *OrChrP* 1 (1935), 328–60.

—— *Direction Spirituelle en Orient autrefois* (OrChrA 144; Rome, 1955).

HECHENBACH, J., *De nuditate sacra sacrisque vinculis* (Giessen, 1911).

HEILER, F., *Das Gebet: Eine religionsgeschichtliche und religionspsychologische Untersuchung* (Munich, 1923[5]).

—— *Die Frau in den Religionen der Menschheit* (Theologische Bibliothek 33; Berlin, 1976).

HERRIN, J., 'In Search of Byzantine Women: Three Avenues of Approach', in A. Cameron and A. Kuhrt (eds.), *Images of Women in Antiquity*, 167–89.

HEUSSI, K., *Der Ursprung des Mönchtums* (Tübingen, 1936).

412   *Select Bibliography*

HEYNE, H., *Das Gleichnis von den klugen und törichten Jungfrauen: Eine literarisch-ikonographische Studie zur altchristlichen Zeit*, Diss. (Freiburg i.B.–Leipzig, 1922).

HILD, F., and RESTLE, M., *Das römische Straßensystem in Kappadokien* (Österreichische Akademie der Wissenschaften, phil.-hist. Kl. 131; Vienna, 1977).

HILPISCH, S., *Die Doppelklöster: Entstehung und Organisation* (Beiträge zur Geschichte des alten Mönchtums und des Benediktinerordens 1; Münster, 1928).

—— 'Die Torheit um Christi Willen', *Zeitschrift für Aszese und Mystik* 6 (1931), 121–31.

HOLL, K., *Enthusiasmus and Bußgewalt beim griechischen Mönchtum* (Leipzig, 1898).

—— *Amphilochius von Ikonium in seinem Verhältnis zu den großen Kappadoziern* (Tübingen, 1969²).

—— 'Die schriftstellerische Form des griechischen Heiligenlebens', *Neue Jahrbücher für das klassische Altertum, Geschichte und deutsche Literatur* 29 (1912), 406–27.

—— 'Die Bedeutung der neuveröffentlichten melitianischen Urkunden für die Kirchengeschichte', in id. *Gesammelte Aufsätze zur Kirchengeschichte*, ii (Tübingen, 1928; repr. Darmstadt, 1964), 283–97.

HOLLERICH, M. J., 'The Alexandrian Bishops and the Grain-trade: Ecclesiastical Commerce in Late Roman Egypt', *Journal of the Economic and Social History of the Orient* 25 (1982), 187–207.

HONIGMANN, E., *Patristic Studies* (StT 173; Rome, 1953).

HOPKINS, K., *Conquerors and Slaves* (Cambridge, 1978).

HORNSCHUH, M., 'Das Leben des Origenes und die Entstehung der alexandrinischen Schule', *ZKG* 71 (1960), 1–25, 193–214.

HORSLEY, G. H. (ed.), *New Documents Illustrating Early Christianity* (Macquarie University, 1981).

HUMBERTCLAUDE, P., *La Doctrine ascétique de saint Basile de Césarée* (Études de théologie historique; Paris, 1932).

HUNT, E. D., 'St. Silvia of Aquitaine: The Role of a Theodosian Pilgrim in the Society of East and West', *JThS* NS 23 (1972), 351–73.

—— 'Palladius of Helenopolis: A Party and its Supporters in the Church of the Late Fourth Century', *JThS* NS 24 (1973), 456–80.

—— *Holy Land Pilgrimage in the Later Roman Empire AD 312–460* (Oxford, 1982).

HURLEY, J., 'Did Paul Require Veils or the Silence of Women? A Consideration of 1 Cor 11: 2–16 and 1 Cor 14: 33b–36', *Westminster Theological Journal* 35 (1973), 190–220.

HUYGHE, R., *La Clôture des monialles des origines à la fin du XIIIe siècle: Étude historique et juridique* (Roubaix, 1944).

IANINI CUESTA, J., 'Dieta y Virginidad: Basilio de Ancira y san Gregorio di Nisa', *Miscelánea Comillas* 14 (1950), 187–97.

IMBERT, J., 'Réflexions sur le christianisme et l'esclavage en droit romain', *Revue internationale des droits de l'Antiquité* 2 (1949), 445–76.

JACOPI, G., 'Esplorazioni e studi in Paflagonia e Cappadocia', *Bollettino del Reale Istituto di Archeologia e Storia dell'Arte* 8 (Rome, 1937), 3–43.

JAEGER, W., *Das frühe Christentum und die griechische Bildung* (Berlin, 1963).

JERPHANION, G. DE, 'Ibora—Gazioura? Étude de géographie pontique', *Mélanges de la faculté orientale de l'université Saint Joseph* 5 (1911), 333–54.

JOANNOU, P., *La Législation impériale et la christianisation de l'Empire romain* (OrChrA 192; Rome, 1972).

—— and DENZLER, G., *Die Ostkirche und die Cathedra Petri* (Päpste und Papstum 3; Stuttgart, 1972).

JOHNSON, A., and WEST, L., *Byzantine Egypt: Economic Studies* (Princeton, NJ, 1949).

JONES, A. H. M., *The Later Roman Empire (284–602): A Social, Economic, and Administrative Survey*, ii (Oxford, 1964).

—— *The Cities of the Eastern Roman Provinces* (Oxford, 1971²).

—— 'Ancient Heresies: National or Social Movements', in *The Roman Economy: Studies in Ancient Economics and Administrative History* (Oxford, 1974), 308–29.

—— MARTINDALE, J. R., and MORRIS, J., *The Prosopography of the Later Roman Empire*, 2 vols. (Cambridge, 1971–80).

JONKERS, E., 'De l'influence du Christianisme sur la législation relative à l'esclavage dans l'antiquité', *Mnemosyne* (3rd. ser.) 1 (1933/4), 241–80.

JUDGE, E. A., 'The Earliest Use of Monachos for "Monk" (P. Coll. Youtie 77) and the Origins of Monasticism', *JAC* 20 (1977), 72–89.

—— 'Fourth-Century Monasticism in the Papyri', in *Proceedings of the 16th International Congress of Papyrology, New York 24–31 July 1980* (American Studies in Papyrology 23; Chico, Calif., 1981), 613–20.

—— and PICKERING, S. R., 'Papyrus Documentation of Church and Community in Egypt to the Mid-Fourth Century', *JAC* 20 (1977), 47–71.

KALSBACH, A., *Die altkirchliche Einrichtung der Diakonissen bis zu ihrem Erlöschen* (Römische Quartalschrift, suppl. 22; Freiburg i. B., 1926).

KANNENGIESSER, C. (ed.), *Politique et théologie chez Athanase d'Alexandrie: Actes du Colloque de Chantilly, 23–25 Sept. 1973* (Théologie Historique 27; Paris, 1974).

—— *Athanase d'Alexandrie: Évêque et écrivain* (Théologie historique 70; Paris, 1983).

—— 'Athanasius of Alexandria v. Arius: The Alexandrian Crisis', in

B. A. Pearson and J. E. Goehring (eds.), *The Roots of Egyptian Christianity*, 204–15.

KARAYANNOPOULOS, J., *Das Finanzwesen des frühbyzantinischen Staates* (Südosteuropäische Arbeiten 52; Munich, 1958).

—— 'Basil's Social Activity: Principles and Praxis', in J. P. Fedwick (ed.), *Basil of Caesarea*, i. 375–92.

KARTASCHOW, A., and WOLF, E., 'Die Entstehung der kaiserlichen Synodalgewalt unter Konstantin dem Großen: Ihre theologische Begründung und ihre kirchliche Rezeption,' in G. Ruhbach (ed.), *Die Kirche angesichts der konstantinischen Wende*, 149–86.

KASER, M., *Das römische Privatrecht*, ii, *Die nachkonstantinische Entwicklung* (*Handbuch der Altertumswissenschaften* 3. 3. 2; Munich, 1975²).

KASSER, R., *Kellia 1965: Topographie génerale, mensurations et fouilles aux Qouçour'Isa et aux Qouçour el-'Abid, mensurations aux Qouçour el-'Izeila* (Recherches suisses d'archéologie copte 1; Geneva, 1967).

KEIMER, I., 'L'Horreur des Égyptiens pour les démons du désert', *Bulletin de l'Institut d'Égypte* 26 (1944), 135–47.

KELLY, J. N. D., *Early Christian Doctrines* (London, 1968).

KETTLER, F. H., 'Der meletianische Streit in Ägypten', *ZNW* 35 (1936), 155–93.

KEYDELL, R., 'Die Unechtheit der Gregor von Nazianz zugeschriebenen *Exhortatio ad Virgines*', *ByZ* 43 (1950), 334–7.

KING, N. O., *The Emperor Theodosius and the Establishment of Christianity* (London, 1961).

KIRSTEN, E., 'Cappadocia', in *RAC* ii (Stuttgart, 1954), 861–91.

KLAWITER, F. C., 'The Role of Martyrdom and Persecution in Developing the Priestly Authority of Women in Early Christianity: A Case Study of Montanism', *Journal of American Academy of Religion* 44 (1976), 417–21.

KNOWLES, D., *From Pachomius to Ignatius: A Study in the Constitutional History of the Religious Orders* (The Sarum Lectures 1964/5; Oxford, 1966).

KOCH, H., '*Virgines Christi*: Das Gelübde der gottgeweihten Jungfrauen in den ersten drei Jahrhunderten' (TU 31; Leipzig, 1907), 59–112.

—— *Quellen zur Geschichte der Askese und des Mönchtums in der alten Kirche* (Tübingen, 1931).

—— *Virgo Eva, Virgo Maria: Neue Untersuchungen über die Lehre von der Jungfrauschaft und der Ehe Mariens in der ältesten Kirche* (Berlin, 1932).

KOENEN, L., 'Manichäische Mission und Klöster in Ägypten', in *Das römisch-byzantinische Ägypten: Akten des internationalen Symposions, 27–30 Sept. 1978 in Trier* (Aegyptiaca Treverensia 2; Mainz, 1983), 93–108.

KOPECEK, T. A., 'Social Class of the Cappadocian Fathers', *CH* 42 (1973), 453–66.

—— *A History of Neo-Arianism*, 2 vols. (Patristic Monograph Series 8; Philadelphia, 1979).

KOSKENNIEMI, H., *Studien zur Idee und Phraseologie des griechischen Briefes bis 400 n. Chr.* (Helsinki, 1956).

KÖTTING, B., *Peregrinatio Religiosa* (Münster, 1950).

—— and KAISER, B., 'Gelübde', in *RAC* ix (Stuttgart, 1976), 1055–99.

KRAUSE, M., 'Das christliche Alexandrien und seine Beziehungen zum koptischen Ägypten', in G. Grimm (ed.), *Alexandrien: Kulturbegegnungen dreier Jahrtausende im Schmelztiegel einer mediterranen Großstadt* (Aegyptiaca Treverensia 1; Mainz, 1981), 53–62.

KRETSCHMAR, G., 'Die Konzile der alten Kirche,' in H. J. Maqull (ed.), *Die Konzile der Christenheit* (Stuttgart, 1961), 13–74.

—— 'Ein Beitrag zur Frage nach dem Ursprung frühchristlicher Askese,' *Zeitschrift für Theologie und Kirche* 61 (1964), 27–64.

KÜBLER, B., 'Über das *Jus liberorum* der Frauen und die Vormundschaft der Mutter', *Zeitschrift der Savigny-Stiftung für Rechtsgeschichte, Röm. Abt.* 30 (1909), 154–83, 31 (1910), 176–9.

KUHN, K. H., 'A Fifth-century Abbot', *JThS* 5 (1954), 36–48, 174–87; 6 (1955), 35–48.

LABRIOLLE, P. DE, *La Crise Montaniste* (Paris, 1913).

—— 'Le "Mariage Spirituel" dans l'Antiquité Chrétienne', *RH* 137 (1921), 204–25.

LADEUZE, P., *Étude sur le cénobitisme Pakhômien pendant le IVe siècle et la première moitié du Ve* (Louvain–Paris, 1898; repr. Frankfurt, 1961).

LADNER, G., 'Homo Viator: Medieval Ideas on Alienation and Order', *Speculum* 42 (1967), 233–59.

LAEUCHLI, S., *Power and Sexuality: The Emergence of Canon Law at the Synod of Elvira* (Philadelphia, 1972).

LAKE, K. and CASEY, R., 'The Text of the De Virginitate of Athanasius', *Harvard Theological Review* 19 (1926), 173–90.

LALLEMAND, J., *L'Administration civile de l'Égypte de l'avènement de Dioclétien à la création du diocèse (284–382): Contribution à l'étude des rapports entre l'Égypte et l'Empire à la fin du IIIe et au IVe siècle* (Académie Royal de Belgique, Cl. des lettres, Mémoires 57: 2; Brussels, 1964).

LAMBERT, A., 'Apotactites et Apotaxamenes', in *DACL* i (Paris, 1903), 2604–26.

LAMPE, G. W. H., *A Patristic Greek Lexicon* (Oxford, 1961–8).

LANE FOX, R., *Pagans and Christians* (New York, 1987).

LAPORTE, J., *The Role of Women in Early Christianity* (Studies in Women and Religion 7; New York, 1982).

LA POTTERIE, I. DE, 'Mari d'une seule femme: Le sens théologique d'une formule Paulinienne', in *Paul de Tarse, Apôtre du notre temps* (Rome, 1979), 619–38.

LE BOULLUEC, A., *La Notion d'hérésie dans la littérature grecque (IIᵉ– IIIᵉ siècles)*, 2 vols. (Études Augustiniennes; Paris, 1985).

LECLERCQ, H., 'Ama', in *DACL* i (Paris, 1902), 1306–23.

—— 'Confréries', in *DACL* iii (Paris, 1914), 2553–60.

LECLERCQ, J., 'Pour l'histoire de l'expression "philosophie chrétienne"', *Mélanges de science religieuse* 9 (1952), 221–6.

LEDOYEN, H., 'Saint Basile dans la tradition monastique occidentale', *Irénikon* 53 (1980), 30–45.

LEFORT, L. T., 'Théodore de Tabennese et la lettre de s. Athanase sur le canon de la Bible', *Le Muséon* 29 (1910), 205–16.

—— 'S. Athanase: Sur la Virginité', *Le Muséon* 42 (1929), 197–274.

—— 'S. Athanase écrivain copte', *Le Muséon* 46 (1933), 1–33.

—— 'Athanase, Ambroise et Chenoute sur la virginité', *Le Muséon* 48 (1935), 55–73.

—— 'Les Premiers Monastères pachômiens: Exploration topographique', *Le Muséon* 52 (1939), 379–408.

—— 'Un nouveau "De virginitate" attribué à S. Athanase', *AnBoll* 67 (1949), 142–52.

LE GALL, J., 'Un critère de différenciation sociale: La Situation de la femme', in *Recherches sur les structures sociales dans l'Antiquité Classique. Colloque national du centre national de la recherche scientifique, Caen 25–26 avril 1969* (Paris, 1970), 275–86.

LEIPOLDT, J., *Schenute von Atripe und die Entstehung des national ägyptischen Christentums* (TU 25, NF 10; Leipzig, 1903).

—— *Didymus der Blinde von Alexandria* (TU 29, NF 14; Leipzig, 1905).

LELOIR, L., 'Infiltrations dualistes chez les Pères du Désert', in J. Ries (ed.), *Gnosticisme et monde hellénistique. Actes du Colloque de Louvain-la-Neuve (11–14 mars 1980)* (Publ. de l'institut orientaliste de Louvain 27; Louvain-la-Neuve, 1982), 327–36.

LEO, F., *Die griechisch-römische Biographie nach ihrer literarischen Form* (Leipzig, 1901).

LE QUIEN, M., *Oriens Christianus*, 3 vols. (Paris, 1740; repr. Graz, 1958).

LERNER, R. E., 'Beguines and Beghards', in J. Strayer (ed.), *Dictionary of the Middle Ages*, ii (New York, 1982), 157–62.

LEROY, J., 'La Tradition manuscrite du 'de virginitate' de Basile d'Ancyre', *OrChrP* 38 (1972), 194–208.

LIDELL, H. G., SCOTT, R., and JONES, H. S., *A Greek–English Lexicon* (Oxford, 1940⁹).

LIEBESCHUETZ, W., 'The Pagarchi: City and Imperial Administration in Byzantine Egypt', *Journal of Juristic Papyrology* 18 (1974), 163–8.

LIENHARD, J. T., 'St. Basil's "Asceticon Parvum" and the "Regula Benedicti"', *Studia Monastica* 22 (1980), 231–42.

LIEU, S., 'An Early Byzantine Formula for the Renunciation of Manichaeism: The Capita VII Contra Manichaeos of (Zacharias of Mytilene)', *JAC* 26 (1983), 152–218.

—— *Manichaeism in the Later Roman Empire and Medieval China* (Manchester, 1985).

LIGHTMAN, M., and ZEISEL, W., '*Univira*: An Example of Continuity and Change in Roman Society', *CH* 46 (1977), 19–32.

LOHSE, B., *Askese und Mönchtum in der Antike und in der alten Kirche* (Göttingen, 1969).

LOMBARDO, G., 'Il monachesimo basiliano', *Quaderni Medievali* 9 (1980), 217–22.

LOOFS, F., *Eustathius von Sebaste und die Chronologie der Basiliusbriefe: Eine patristische Studie* (Halle, 1898).

—— 'Makrina die Jüngere', in *Realenzyklopädie für Protestantische Theologie und Kirche*, xii (Leipzig, 1903), 93–4.

LORENZ, R., *Arius judaizans? Untersuchungen zur dogmengeschichtlichen Einordnung des Arius* (Forschungen zur Kirchen- und Dogmengeschichte 31; Göttingen, 1980).

LOZANOS, J. M., 'L'obbedienza: Problemi dottrinali e tentativi de soluzione', in G. Tamburrino (ed.), *Autorità e obbedienza nella vita religiosa* (Milan, 1978), 142–92.

LUHMANN, N., *Religious Dogmatics and the Evolution of Societies*, Eng. trans. by P. Beyer (Studies in Religion and Society 9; New York, 1984).

MACKINNON, C., *Toward a Feminist Theory of the State* (Cambridge, Mass., 1989).

MCLAUGHLIN, T. P., *Le Très Ancien Droit monastique de l'occident* (Ligugé, 1935).

MACLENNAN, H., *Oxyrhynchus: An Economic and Social Study* (Amsterdam, 1968).

MACMULLEN, R., 'Woman in Public in the Roman Empire', *Historia* 29 (1980), 208–18.

MCNAMARRA, J. A., *A New Song: Celibate Women in the First Three Christian Centuries* (New York, 1983).

—— 'Muffled Voices: The Lives of Consecrated Women in the Fourth Century', in J. A. Nichols and L. T. Shank (eds.), *Medieval Religious Women*, i, *Distant Echoes* (Cistercian Studies Series 71; Kalamazoo, 1984), 11–29.

MAEHLER, H., 'Häuser und ihre Bewohner im Fayum der Kaiserzeit', in G. Grimm, H. Heinen, and E. Winter (eds.), *Das römisch-byzantinische Ägypten: Akten des internationalen Symposions, 27–30*

Sept. 1978 in Trier (Aegyptiaca Treverensia 2; Mainz, 1983), 119–37.

MAGHERI CATALUCCIO, E., *Il Lausaïkon di Palladio tra Semiotica e Storia* (Rome, 1984).

MAGIE, D., *Roman Rule in Asia Minor* (Princeton, NJ, 1950).

MALINGREY, A. M., *Philosophia: Étude d'un groupe de mots dans la littérature grecque des présocratiques au IVᵉ siècle après J.C.* (Paris, 1961).

MALONE, E. E., 'The Monk and the Martyr', *Studia Anselmiana* 38 (1956), 201–28.

MARAVAL, P., 'Encore les frères et les sœurs de Grégoire de Nysse', *Revue d'histoire et philosophie religieuse* 60 (1980), 161–6.

MARKS, E., and DE COURTIVRON, I., *New French Feminism: An Anthology* (New York, 1981).

MARKUS, R. A., '*Coge intrare*: The Church and Political Power', in id. *Saeculum: History and Society in the Theology of Saint Augustine* (Cambridge, 1970), 133–53.

MARROU, H.-I., Μουσικὸς ᾿Ανήρ: *Étude sur les scènes de la vie intellectuelle figurant sur les monuments funéraires romaines* (Grenoble, 1938; repr. Rome, 1964).

—— *Histoire de l'éducation dans l'antiquité* (Paris, 1965⁶).

MARTIMORT, A. G., *Les Diaconesses: Essai historique* (Bibliotheca Ephemerides Liturgicae, Subsidia 24; Rome, 1982).

MARTIN, A., 'Athanase et les Mélitiens (325–335)', in *Politique et théologie chez Athanase d'Alexandrie: Actes du Colloque de Chantilly, 23–25 Sept. 1973* (Théologie Historique 27; Paris, 1974), 32–61.

—— 'L'Église et la khôra égyptienne au IVᵉ siècle', *Revue des Études Augustiniennes* 25 (1979), 3–26.

—— 'Aux origines de l'église copte: L'Implantation et le développement du christianisme en Égypte (Iᵉ–IVᵉ siècles)', *REA* 83 (1981), 35–56.

—— 'Les Premiers Siècles du christianisme à Alexandrie: Essai de topographie religieuse (IIIᵉ–IVᵉ siècles)', *Revue des Études Augustiniennes* 30 (1984), 211–25.

MARTROYE, F., 'Le Testament de St. Grégoire de Nazianze', *Mémoires de la Société Nationale des Antiquaires de France* 76 (1919–23), 219–63.

MARX, M. J., 'Incessant Prayer in the Vita Antonii', *Studia Anselmiana* 38 (1956), 108–35.

MATTHEWS, J., *Western Aristocracies and Imperial Court, AD 364–425* (Oxford, 1975).

—— *The Roman Empire of Ammianus* (Baltimore, 1989).

MAUSER, U. W., *Christ in the Wilderness: The Wilderness Theme in the Second Gospel and its Basis in the Biblical Tradition* (London, 1963).

MAY, G., 'Die Datierung der Rede "In suam ordinationem" des Gregor von Nyssa und die Verhandlungen mit den Pneumatomachen auf dem Konzil von Konstantinopel 381', *VigChr* 23 (1969), 38–57.
—— 'Basilios der Große und der römische Staat', in B. Moeller and G. Ruhbach (eds.), *Bleibendes im Wandel der Kirchengeschichte*, 47–70.
—— 'Die großen Kappadokier und die staatliche Kirchenpolitik von Valens bis Theodosius', in G. Ruhbach (ed.), *Die Kirche angesichts der konstantinischen Wende*, 322–37.
MAYER, J. (ed.), *Monumenta de viduis diaconissis virginibusque tractantia* (Florilegium Patristicum 42; Bonn, 1938).
MAZZA, M., 'Monachesimo basiliano: Modelli spirituali e tendenze economico-sociali nell'impero del IV° secolo', *Studi Storici* 21 (1980), 31–60.
MEIJERING, E. P., *Orthodoxy and Platonism in Athanasius: Synthesis or Antithesis* (Leiden, 1974).
MEINARDUS, O., 'A Study on the Canon Law of the Coptic Church', *Bulletin de la société de l'archéologie copte* 16 (1961–2), 231–42.
MEINHOLD, P., 'Pneumatomachoi', in *RE* xxi (Stuttgart, 1951), 1066–1101.
MENSBRUGGHE, A. VON DER, 'Prayer-time in Egyptian Monasticism (320–450)', *SP* 2 (TU 64; Berlin, 1957), 435–54.
MENTZU-MEIMARE, K., Ἡ παρουσία τῆς γυναίκας στίς ἡλλενικές ἐπιγραφές ἀπό τόν Δ μεχρί τόν Ι μ.Χ. αἰῶνα (*JÖB* 32: 2; Vienna, 1984).
MEREDITH, A., 'Asceticism—Christian and Greek', *JThS* NS 27 (1976), 312–32.
MESLIN, M., *Les Ariens d'occident (335–430)* (Patristica Sorbonensia 8; Paris, 1967).
METZ, R., *La Consécration des Vierges dans l'église romaine: Étude d'histoire de la liturgie* (Bibliothèque de l'Institut du Droit Canonique de l'Université de Strasbourg 4; Strasburg, 1954).
MEYENDORFF, J., 'Messalianism or Anti-Messalianism: A Fresh Look at the "Macarian" Problem', in P. Granfield and J. Jungmann (eds.), *Kyriakon*, ii. 585–90.
MILLAR, F., *The Emperor in the Roman World* (Ithaca, NY, 1977).
MILLER, T. S., *The Birth of the Hospital in the Byzantine Empire* (Baltimore, 1985).
MITCHELL, S., 'The Life of Saint Theodotus of Ancyra', *Anatolian Studies* 32 (1982), 93–113.
MOELLER, B., and RUHBACH, G. (eds.), *Bleibendes im Wandel der Kirchengeschichte* (Tübingen, 1973).
MOLLE, M. VAN, 'Confrontation entre les Règles et la littérature pachômienne posterieure', *Supplément de la Vie Spirituelle* 21 (1968), 394–424.

MOMIGLIANO, A., 'Pagan and Christian Historiography in the Fourth Century AD', in id. (ed.), *The Conflict between Paganism and Christianity in the Fourth Century* (Oxford, 1963), 1–16.

—— 'The Life of St. Macrina by Gregory of Nyssa', in J. W. Eadie and J. Ober (eds.), *The Craft of the Ancient Historian: Essays in Honor of C. G. Starr* (Lanham, Md., 1985), 443–58.

MONDINI, M., 'Lettere femminili nei papiri greco-egizi', *Studi della Scuola Papirologica* 2 (Milan, 1917), 29–50.

MONTET, P., *La Géographie de l'Égypte ancienne*, 2 vols. (Paris, 1956–61).

MOR, C. G., 'La manumissio in Ecclesia', *Rivista di Storia del Diritto Italiano* 1 (1928), 80–100.

MORRARD, F. E., 'Monachos, moine: Histoire du terme grec jusqu'au 4ᵉ siècle', *Freiburger Zeitschrift für Philosophie und Theologie* 20 (1973), 333–412.

—— 'Encore quelques réflexions sur Monachos', *VigChr* 34 (1980), 395–401.

MÜLLER, C. D., 'Athanasios von Alexandrien als koptischer Schriftsteller', *Kyrios* 14 (1974), 195–204.

MÜLLER, G. (ed.), *Lexikon Athanasianum* (Berlin, 1944–52).

MURPHY, F. X., 'Melania the Elder, a biographical note', *Traditio* 5 (1947), 59–78.

MUSURILLO, H., 'The Problem of Ascetical Fasting in the Greek Patristic Writers', *Traditio* 12 (1956), 1–64.

NAGEL, M., 'Lettre chrétienne sur papyrus (provenant de milieux sectaires du IVᵉ siècle?)', *ZPE* 18 (1975), 317–23.

NAGEL, P., *Motivierung der Askese in der Alten Kirche und der Ursprung des Mönchtums* (TU 95; Berlin, 1966).

—— 'Die Psalmoi Sarakoton des manichäischen Psalmenbuches', *Orientalistische Literaturzeitung* 62 (1967), 123–30.

NALDINI, M., *Il cristianesimo in Egitto* (Florence, 1968).

NESTLE, W., 'Die Haupteinwände des antiken Denkens gegen das Christentums', *ARW* 37 (1941/2), 51–100.

NIEDERWIMMER, K., *Askese und Mysterium: Über Ehe, Ehescheidung und Eheverzicht in den Anfängen christlichen Glaubens* (Göttingen, 1975).

NOCK, A. D., 'Eunuchs in Ancient Religion', in Z. Stewart (ed.), *Essays on Religion and the Ancient World*, i (Oxford, 1972), 7–15.

NORTON, C., 'Women Deacons in the Early Church', *The Modern Churchman* 26 (1936), 428–32.

OPITZ, H. G., 'Die Zeitfolge des arianischen Streites von den Anfängen bis zum Jahre 328', *ZNW* 33 (1934), 131–59.

OPPENHEIM, P., *Das Mönchskleid im christlichen Altertum* (Theologische Quartalschrift, Suppl. 28; Freiburg i.B., 1931).

ORLANDI, T. (ed.), *Storia della Chiesa di Alessandria*, i, *Da Pietro ad*

Atanasio (Testi e documenti per lo studio dell'antichità 17; Louvain, 1974).

—— 'Ricerche su una storia ecclesiastica alessandrina del IV secolo', *Vetera Christianorum* 11 (1974), 269–312.

—— 'Giustificazioni del'encratismo nei testi monastici copti del IV–V secolo', in U. Bianchi (ed.), *La tradizione dell'enkrateia*, 341–68.

—— 'Coptic Literature', in B. A. Pearson and J. E. Goehring (eds.), *The Roots of Egyptian Christianity*, 51–81.

OSTROGORSKY, G., *Geschichte des byzantinischen Staates* (*Handbuch der Altertumswissenschaften*, *Byzantinisches Handbuch* 1. 2; Munich, 1963³).

OTRANTO, G., 'Note sul sacerdozio femminile nell'antichità in margine a una testimonianza di Gelasio I', *Vetera Christianorum* 19 (1982), 341–60.

PARSONS, P. J., 'The Earliest Christian Letter?' (Miscellanea Papyrologica Florentina 7; Florence, 1980), 289.

PATLAGEAN, E., 'Ancienne hagiographie byzantine et histoire sociale', *Annales ESC* 23 (1968), 106–26.

—— 'L'Enfant et son avenir dans la famille byzantine (IVᵉ–XIIᵉ siècles)', *Annales de démographie historique* (1973), 85–93.

—— 'L'Histoire de la femme déguisée en moine et l'évolution de la sainteté féminine à Byzance', *Studi Medievali* 17 (1976), 597–623.

—— *Pauvreté économique et pauvreté sociale à Byzance (4ᵉ–7ᵉ siècles)* (Civilisations et Sociétés 48; Paris, 1977).

—— *Structure sociale, famille, chrétienté à Byzance (IV–XI siècles)* (London, 1981).

PEARSON, B. A., and GOEHRING, J. E. (eds.), *The Roots of Egyptian Christianity* (Studies in Antiquity and Christianity; Philadelphia, 1986).

PENCO, G., 'La vita ascetica come "filosofia" nell'antica tradizione monastica', *Studia Monastica* 2 (1960), 79–93.

—— 'Il monachesimo nel passaggio dal mondo antico a quello medievale', *Benedictina* 28 (1981), 47–64.

—— *Storia del monachesimo in Italia dalle origini alla fine del Medio Evo* (Tempi e figure 2a, Seria 31; Milan, 1981²).

PERLER, O., 'Das vierte Makkabäerbuch, Ignatius von Antiochien und die ältesten Märtyrerberichte', *Rivista di Archeologia Christiana* 25 (1949), 47–72.

PETERSON, E., 'Zum Messalianismus der Philippus-Akten', *Oriens Christianus* 29 (1932), 172–9.

—— 'Ein Fragment des Hierakas?', *Le Muséon* 60 (1947), 257–60.

PETITMENGIN, P., *Pélagie la Pénitente: Métamorphoses d'une légende*, 2 vols. (Études Augustiniennes; Paris, 1981).

PFISTER, J. E., 'A Biographical Note: The Brothers and Sisters of St. Gregory of Nyssa', *VigChr* 18 (1964), 108–13.

POLLARD, T. E., 'The Origins of Arianism', *JThS* 9 (1958), 103–11.

POMMEROY, S. B., *Goddesses, Whores, Wives and Slaves: Women in Classical Antiquity* (New York, 1975).

PREAUX, C., 'Monachisme et contre-culture', *Annuaire de l'Institut de Philologie et d'Histoire d'Orient et Slaves* 15 (1981), 65–78.

PREISIGKE, F., *Namenbuch* (Heidelberg, 1922).

PREUSCHEN, E., *Palladius und Rufinus: Ein Beitrag zur Quellenkunde des ältesten Mönchtums* (Giessen, 1897).

PUECH, A., *Histoire de la littérature grecque chrétien*, iii (Paris, 1930).

QUACQUARELLI, A., 'L'influenza spirituale del monachesimo femminile nell'età patristica', *Vetera Christianorum* 20 (1983), 9–23.

QUASTEN, J., *Musik und Gesang in den Kulturen der heidnischen Antike und christlichen Frühzeit* (Münster, 1930).

—— *Patrology*, 3 vols. (Utrecht, 1950–60).

QUISPEL, G., 'L'Évangile selon Thomas et les origines de l'ascèse chrétienne', in *Aspects du judéo-christianisme* (Travaux du Centre d'études supérieures spécialisé d'histoire des religions; Strasburg, 1965).

RADER, A., 'Christian Pre-monastic Forms of Asceticism: Syneisaktism, "Spiritual Marriage"', in W. Skudlarek (ed.), *The Continuing Quest for God, Monastic Spirituality in Tradition and Transition* (Collegeville, Minn., 1982), 80–7.

—— 'Early Christian Forms of Communal Spirituality: Women's Communities', ibid. 88–99.

RADFORD R. R., *Gregory of Nazianzus: Rhetor and Philosopher* (Oxford, 1969), 156–75.

—— (ed.), *Religion and Sexism: Images of Women in the Jewish and Christian Traditions* (New York, 1974).

RAMING, I., *Der Ausschluß der Frau vom priesterlichen Amt: Gottgewollte Tradition oder Diskriminierung? Eine rechtshistorisch-dogmatische Untersuchung der Grundlagen von Kanon 968 p. 1 des Codex Juris Canonici*, Diss. (Münster, 1973).

RAMSAY, W. M., *Cities and Bishoprics of Phrygia*, 2 vols. (Oxford, 1895–7).

—— *The Historical Geography of Asia Minor* (Royal Geographical Society, Supplementary Papers 4; London, 1890; repr. Amsterdam, 1962).

—— *Pauline and Other Studies* (London, 1906).

—— 'A Noble Anatolian Family of the Fourth Century', *Classical Review* 33 (1919), 1–9.

REITZENSTEIN, R., *Hellenistische Wundererzählungen* (Leipzig, 1906).

—— *Des Athanasius Werk über das Leben des Antonius* (Sitzungsberichte der Heidelberger Akademie der Wissenschaften, phil.-hist. Kl. 5; Heidelberg, 1914).

—— Historia Monachorum und Historia Lausiaca: Eine Studie zur Geschichte des Mönchtums und der frühchristlichen Begriffe Gnostiker und Pneumatiker (Göttingen, 1916).

RÉMONDON, R., 'L'Égypte et la suprême résistance au Christianisme (IIe–VIIe siècles)', Bulletin de l'institut français d'archéologie orientale 51 (1952), 63–78.

RIALL, R. A., 'Athanasius Bishop of Alexandria: The Politics of Spirituality', Diss. (Cincinnati, 1987).

RIES, J. (ed.), Gnosticisme et monde hellénistique. Actes du Colloque de Louvain-la-Neuve (11–14 mars 1980) (Publ. de l'institut orientaliste de Louvain 27; Louvain-la-Neuve, 1982).

RITTER, A. M., Das Konzil von Konstantinopel und sein Symbol: Studien zur Geschichte und Theologie des II. Ökumenischen Konzils (Forschungen zur Kirchen- und Dogmengeschichte 15; Göttingen, 1965).

ROBERT, L., Villes d'Asie Mineur: Études de géographie ancienne (Paris, 1962²).

—— Noms indigènes dans l'Asie Mineur gréco-romaine, i (Bibliothèque archéologique et historique de l'institut français d'archéologie d'Istanbul 13; Paris, 1963).

—— Hellenica, xiii (Paris, 1965).

—— À travers l'Asie Mineure: Poètes et prosateurs, monnaies greques, voyageurs et géographie (Paris, 1980).

ROBERTI, M., 'Patria potestas e paterna pietas', in Studi Albertoni, i (Milan, 1935), 257–70.

ROBINSON, J. A., The Philocalia of Origen (Cambridge, 1893).

ROLDANUS, J., Le Christ et l'homme dans la théologie d'Athanase d'Alexandrie: Étude de la conjonction de sa conception de l'homme avec sa Christologie (Studies in the History of Christian Thought 4; Leiden, 1977²).

ROSTOVTZEFF, M., The Social and Economic History of the Roman Empire, i, Eng. trans. by P. M. Fraser (Oxford, 1957²).

ROUGÉ, J., Recherches sur l'organisation du commerce maritime en Méditeranée sous l'Empire Romain (Paris, 1966).

—— 'La Législation de Théodose contre les hérétiques: Traduction du C.Th. 16. 5, 6–24', in J. Fontaine, and Ch. Kannengiesser (eds.), Epektasis, 635–49.

ROUILLARD, G., La Vie rurale dans l'empire byzantine (Paris, 1953).

ROUSELLE, A., Porneia: De la maîtrise du corps à la privation sensorielle (IIe–IVe siècles de l'ère chrétienne) (Paris, 1983).

ROUSSEAU, P., 'Blood-Relationship among Early Eastern Ascetics', JThS NS 23 (1972), 135–44; 25 (1974), 113.

—— Ascetics, Authority, and the Church in the Age of Jerome and Cassian (Oxford, 1978).

ROUSSEAU, P., *Pachomius: The Making of a Community in Fourth-Century Egypt* (Berkeley, 1985).

RUDBERG, S. Y., *Études sur la tradition manuscrite de saint Basile* (Lund, 1953).

RUHBACH, G. (ed.), *Die Kirche angesichts der konstantinischen Wende* (Darmstadt, 1976).

RUPPERT, F., *Das pachomianische Mönchtum und die Anfänge klösterlichen Gehorsams* (Münsterschwarzacher Studien 20; Münsterschwarzach, 1971).

RUSH, A., *Death and Burial in Christian Antiquity* (Catholic University of America Studies in Christian Antiquity 1; Washington, DC, 1941).

RYDÉN, L., *Bemerkungen zum Leben des Heiligen Narren Symeon von Leontios* (Uppsala, 1970).

SAUMAGNE, C., *Saint Cyprien, évêque de Carthage, 'pape' d'Afrique (248–58)* (Paris, 1975).

SCARVAGLIERI, G., 'Problematica sociologica dell'obbedienza', in G. Tamburrino (ed.), *Autorità e obbedienza nella vita religiosa* (Milan, 1978), 189–227.

SCHADEL, W., and WIEKEN, R. (eds.), *Early Christian Literature and the Classical Intellectual Tradition: In Honorem R. M. Grant* (Théologie Historique 53; Paris, 1979).

SCHIWIETZ, S., 'Geschichte und Organisation der pachomianischen Klöster im vierten Jahrhundert', *Archiv für katholisches Kirchenrecht* 81–3 (1901–3), 461–90, 631–49; 217–33, 454–75, 52–72.

SCHLADEBACH, J., *Basilius von Ancyra: Eine historisch-philosophische Studie*, Diss. (Leipzig, 1898).

SCHNEEMELCHER, W., 'Epiphanius von Salamis', in *RAC* v (Stuttgart, 1962), 909–27.

SCHWARTZ, E., 'Über die pseudoapostolischen Kirchenordunungen' (Schriften der wiss. Gesellschaft in Straßburg; Strasburg, 1910); repr. in *Gesammelte Schriften*, v (Berlin, 1963), 192–273.

—— 'Die Quellen über den melitianischen Streit: Zur Geschichte des Athanasius', in *Gesammelte Schriften*, iii (Berlin, 1959), 87–116.

—— 'Zur Kirchengeschichte des vierten Jahrhunderts', in *Gesammelte Schriften*, iv (Berlin, 1960), 1–110.

SCOTT, J. W., 'Gender: A Useful Category of Historical Analysis', *Amercian Historical Review* 91:5 (1986), 1053–75.

SEDGWICK, E. K., *Epistemology of the Closet* (Berkeley, 1990).

SÉGUY, J., 'Une sociologie des sociétés imaginées: Monachisme et utopie', *Annales ESC* 26 (1971), 328–54.

SERVAIS, E., and HAMBYE, F., 'Structure et signification: Problème de méthode en sociologie des organisations claustrales', *Social Compass* 18 (1971), 21–44.

SESTON, W., 'Remarques sur le rôle de la pensée d'Origène dans les origines du monachisme', *RHR* 108 (1933), 197–213.

SHILS, E., *Center and Periphery: Essays in Macrosociology* (Chicago, 1975).

SHISHA-HALEVY, A., 'Two New Shenoute-Texts from the British Library', *Orientalia*, NS 44 (1975), 149–85.

SIJPESTEIJN, P. J., 'Die "χωρὶς κυρίου χρηματίζουσα δικαίῳ τέκνων" in den Papyri', *Aegyptus* 45 (1965), 177–89.

SIMONETTI, M., *La crisi ariana nel IV secolo* (Studia Ephemeridis Augustinianum 11; Rome, 1975).

ŠPIDLÍK, T., *La Spiritualité de l'Orient chrétien* (OrChrA 206; Rome, 1978).

STAATS, R., 'Die Asketen aus Mesopotamien in der Rede des Gregor von Nyssa', *VigChr* 21 (1967), 167–79.

—— *Gregor von Nyssa und die Messalianer* (Patristische Texte und Studien 8; Berlin, 1968).

—— 'Die Datierung von "In suam ordinationem" des Gregor von Nyssa', *VigChr* 23 (1969), 58–9.

STEAD, C., *Substance and Illusion in the Christian Fathers* (London, 1985).

STEIDLE, B., 'Das Lachen im alten Mönchtum', *Benediktinische Monatsschrift* 20 (1938), 271–80.

—— '"Der Zweite" im Pachomiuskloster', *Benediktinische Monatsschrift* 24 (1948), 97–104, 174–9.

STEIN, E., *Histoire du Bas-Émpire*, i, *De l'état Romain à l'état Byzantin (284–476)* (Bruges, 1959).

STELZENBERGER, J., *Die Beziehung der frühchristlichen Sittenlehre zur Ethik der Stoa* (Munich, 1933).

STROBEL, A., 'Der Begriff des "Hauses" im griechischen und römischen Privatrecht', *ZNW* 56 (1965), 91–100.

—— *Das heilige Land der Montanisten: Eine religionsgeographische Untersuchung* (Religionsgeschichtliche Versuche und Vorarbeiten 37; Berlin, 1980).

STROUMSA, G. S., 'The Manichaean Challenge to Egyptian Christianity', in B. A. Pearson, and J. E. Goehring (eds.), *The Roots of Egyptian Christianity*, 307–19.

SYBEL, L. VON, 'Zur Synode von Elvira', *ZKG* 42 (1923), 243–7.

TAMBURRINO, P., 'L'incidenza delle correnti spirituali dell'Oriente sulle "Regula Benedicti"', *Benedictina* 28 (1981), 97–150.

TAUBENSCHLAG, R., *The Law of Greco-Roman Egypt in the Light of the Papyri, 332 BC–640 AD* (New York, 1944–8; repr. Warsaw, 1955).

—— 'La Compétence du Kyrios dans le droit greco-égyptien', in id. *Opera Minora*, ii (Warsaw, 1959), 353–77.

TEJA, R., *Organización economica y social de Capadocia en el siglo IV, según los padres Capadocios* (Acta Salmantina, Filosofia y Lectras 78; Salamanca, 1974).

—— 'Die römische Provinz Kappadokien in der Prinzipatszeit', in J. Vogt, and H. Temporini (eds.), *ANRW* 2. 7. 2 (Berlin, 1980), 1083–1124.

TELFER, W., 'St. Peter of Alexandria and Arius' (Mélanges Paul Peeters, i), *AnBoll* 67 (1949), 117–30.

—— 'Meletius of Lycopolis and Episcopal Succession in Egypt', *Harvard Theological Review* 48 (1955), 227–37.

TETZ, M., 'Arianismus', in *TRE* iii (Berlin, 1978), 692–719.

—— 'Athanasius von Alexandrien', in *TRE* iv (Berlin, 1979), 333–49.

—— 'Athanasius und die Vita Antonii: Literarische und theologische Relationen', *ZNW* 73 (1982), 1–30.

THEISSEN, G., 'Soziale Schichtung in der korinthischen Gemeinde', *Studien zur Soziologie des Urchristentums* (Wissenschaftliche Untersuchungen zum Neuen Testament 19; Tübingen, 1979), 238–45.

THÉLAMON, F., 'Modèles du monachisme oriental selon Rufin d'Aquilée', *Antichità Altoadriatiche* 12 (1977), 323–5.

—— *Païens et Chrétiens au IVe siècle: L'Apport de l'"Histoire ecclésiastique" de Rufin d'Aquilée* (Études Augustiniennes; Paris, 1981).

THIERRY, M., and THIERRY N., 'Les Enseignements historiques de l'archéologie Cappadocienne', *Travaux et Memoires* 8 (1981), 501–19.

THIERRY, N., 'Un problème de continuité ou de rupture: La Cappadoce entre Rome, Byzance, et les Arabes', *Comptes Rendus de l'Académie des Inscriptions et Belles-Lettres* (1977), 98–144.

—— 'Avanos-Vénasa, Cappadoce', in H. Ahrweiler (ed.), *Geographica Byzantina* (Byzantina Sorbonensia 3; Paris, 1981), 119–29.

THOMSEN, P., *Loca Sancta*, i, *Verzeichnis der im 1.–6. Jh. n. Chr. erwähnten Ortsnamen Palästinas* (Frankfurt, 1966²).

TIBILETTI, C., *Verginità e matrimonio in antichi scrittori cristiani* (Atti della Facoltà di Lettere e Filosofia di Macerata 2; Macerata, 1969), 10–217.

TIBILETTI, G., *Le lettere private nei papiri greci del III e IV secolo d. C. Tra paganesimo e cristianesimo* (Vita e Pensiero 15; Milan, 1979).

TILL, W., and LEIPOLDT, J., *Der koptische Text der Kirchenordnung Hippolyts* (TU 58; Berlin, 1954).

TILLEMONT, S. LENAIN DE, *Mémoires pour servir à l'histoire ecclésiastique des six premiers siècles*, 16 vols. (Paris, 1693–1712).

TIMBIE, J. A., 'Dualism and the Concept of Orthodoxy in the Thought of the Monks of Upper Egypt', Diss. (Philadelphia, 1979).

—— 'The State of Research on the Career of Shenoute of Atripe', in B. A. Pearson, and J. E. Goehring (eds.), *The Roots of Egyptian Christianity*, 258–70.

TREUCKER, B., *Politische und sozialgeschichtliche Studien zu den Basiliusbriefen* (Munich, 1961).

TURNER, E. G., *Greek Papyri: An Introduction* (London, 1980²).

TURNER, V., and TURNER, E., *Image and Pilgrimage in Christian Culture: Anthropological Perspectives* (New York, 1978).

VAGAGGINI, C., 'L'ordinazione delle diaconesse nella tradizione greca e bizantina', *OrChrP* 40 (1974), 145–89.

VAN BREMEN, R., 'Women and Wealth', in A. Cameron, and A. Kuhrt (eds.), *Images of Women in Antiquity*, 223–42.

VAN DAM, R., 'Emperor, Bishops, and Friends in Late Antique Cappadocia', *JThS* NS 37 (1986), 53–76.

VAN EIJK, T. H. C., 'Marriage and Virginity, Death and Immortality', in J. Fontaine, and Ch. Kannengiesser (eds.), *Epektasis*, 209–35.

VAN HAELST, J., 'Les Sources papyrologiques concernant l'Église en Égypte à l'époque de Constantin', in *Proceedings of the 12th International Congress of Papyrology, 13–17 August 1969* (American Studies in Papyrology 7; Toronto, 1970), 497–503.

VEILLEUX, A., *La Liturgie dans le cénobitisme pachômien au quatrième siècle* (Studia Anselmiana 57; Rome, 1968).

—— 'Monasticism and Gnosis', in B. A. Pearson, and J. E. Goehring (eds.), *The Roots of Egyptian Christianity*, 271–306.

VILLECOURT, L., 'La Date et l'origine des "Homélies spirituelles" attribuées à Macaire', *Comptes Rendus des séances de l'Académie des Inscriptions et Belles-Lettres* (1920), 250–8.

—— 'La Grande Lettre grecque de Macaire, ses formes textuelles et son milieu littéraire', *Revue de l'Orient Chrétien* 22 (1920/1), 29–56.

VILLER, M., and RAHNER, K., *Aszese und Mystik in der Väterzeit* (Freiburg i.B., 1939).

VINCENT, H., and ABEL, F. M., *Jérusalem: Recherches de topographie, d'archéologie et d'histoire*, 2 vols. (Paris, 1914, 1926).

VISCHER, L., *Basilius der Große: Untersuchungen zu einem Kirchenvater des vierten Jahrhunderts* (Basle, 1953).

VITEAU, J., 'L'Institution des Diacres et des Veuves', *RHE* 22 (1926), 513–37.

VIZMANOS, F. DE B., *Las Virgenes cristianas de la Iglesia primitiva* (Madrid, 1949).

VOGT, J., *Constantin der Grosse* (Munich, 1949).

VOGÜÉ, A. DE, 'Saint Pachôme d'après plusieurs études récentes', *RHE* 69 (1974), 245–53.

—— 'Le Nom du Superieur de monastère dans la Règle pachômienne: A propos d'un ouvrage récent', *Studia Monastica* 15 (1973), 17–22.

—— 'Les Grandes Règles de saint Basile: Un survol', *Collectanea Cisterciensia* 41 (1979), 201–26.

VÖLKER, W., *Das Vollkommenheitsideal des Origines* (Tübingen, 1931).

VOLTERRA, E., 'Les Femmes dans les "inscriptiones" des rescrits impériaux', in *Xenion: Festschrift für J. Zepos*, i (Athens–Freiburg i.B.–Cologne, 1973), 717–24.

VÖÖBUS, A., 'Die syrische Herkunft der Pseudo-Basilianischen Homilie über die Jungfräulichkeit', *Oriens Christianus* 40 (1956), 69–77.

—— *History of Asceticism in the Syrian Orient*, 2 vols. (CSCO 184, 197; Louvain, 1958, 1960).

WALLON, H., *Histoire de l'esclavage dans l'antiquité*, iii (Paris, 1879).

WEBER, M., *Economy and Society*, ed. G. Roth and C. Wittich, 3 vols. (i, Berkeley, 1978²; ii–iii, New York, 1968).

—— *Gesammelte Aufsätze zur Religionssoziologie*, i (Tübingen, 1972⁶).

WEINGARTEN, H., 'Der Ursprung des Mönchtums im nachkonstantinischen Zeitalter', *ZKG* 1 (1877), 1–35.

WERHAN, H. M., 'Dubia und Spuria unter den Gedichten Gregors von Nazianz', *SP* 7 (1966), 337–47.

WESTERMANN, W. L., *The Slave Systems of Greek and Roman Antiquity* (Memoirs of the American Philosophical Society 40; Philadelphia, 1955).

WHITTAKER, C. R., 'Inflation and the Economy in the Fourth Century AD', in *Imperial Revenue, Expenditure and Monetary Policy*, 1–22.

WILCKEN, U., and MITTEIS, L., *Grundzüge und Chrestomathie der Papyrusurkunde*, i (Leipzig, 1912).

WILES, J. M., 'In Defence of Arius', *JThS* 13 (1962), 339–47.

WILKINSON, J., *Egeria's Travels* (London, 1971).

—— *Jerusalem Pilgrims before the Crusades* (Warminster, 1977).

WILLIAMS, R., *Arius: Heresy and Tradition* (London, 1987).

WILPERT, J., *Die gottgeweihten Jungfrauen in den ersten Jahrhunderten der Kirche* (Freiburg i.B., 1892).

WINKELMANN, F., 'Einige Aspekte der Entwicklung der Begriffe Häresie und Schisma in der Spätantike', *Koinonia* 6 (1982), 89–109.

WIPSZYCKA, E., 'Les Confréries dans la vie religieuse de l'Égypte chrétienne', in *Proceedings of the 12th International Congress of Papyrology, 13–17 August 1969* (American Studies in Papyrology 7; Toronto, 1970), 511–25.

—— *Les Ressources et les activitiés économiques des églises en Égypte du IVᵉ au VIIIᵉ siècle* (Papyrologia Bruxellensia 10; Brussels, 1972).

—— 'Remarques sur les lettres privées chrétiennes des II–IV siècles', *Journal of Juristic Papyrology* 18 (1974), 203–21.

—— 'P. Berl. inv. 11860 A–B: Les Terres de la congrégation pachômienne dans une liste de payements pour les *apora*', in J. Bingen, G. Cambier, and G. Nachtergall (eds.), *Le Monde grec: Pensée, littérature, histoire, documents. Hommages à C. Preaux* (Brussels, 1975), 625–36.

WISSE, F., 'Gnosticism and Early Monasticism in Egypt', in B. Aland (ed.), *Gnosis*, 431–40.

WOLF, S., *Hypatia, die Philosophin von Alexandrien: Ihr Leben, Wirken und Lebensende nach den Quellenschriften dargestellt* (Vienna, 1879).

WULF, F., 'Die Stellung des Protestantismus zu Askese und Mönchtum in Geschichte und Gegenwart', in *Geistliches Leben in der heutigen Welt* (Freiburg i.B., 1960), 194–218.

WYSS, B., 'Gregor von Nazianz, ein griechischer-christlicher Dichter des 4. Jahrhunderts', *Museum Helveticum* 6 (1949), 177–210 (repr. in *Libelli* 53; Darmstadt, 1962).

YOUTIE, H. C., 'Short Texts on Papyri', *ZPE* 37 (1980), 211–29.

ZEHLER, F. E., *Kommentar zu den 'Mahnungen an die Jungfrauen' (carmen 1, 2, 2) Gregors von Nazianz*, Diss. (Münster, 1987).

ZELZER, K., 'Die Rufinusübersetzung der Basiliusregel im Spiegel ihrer ältesten Handschriften', in H. Bannert and J. Divjak (eds.), *Latinität und Kirche: Festschrift für R. Hanslik* (Vienna–Göttingen–Graz, 1977), 341–50.

ZIMBALIST ROSALDO, M., and LAMPHERE, L. (eds.), *Woman, Culture, and Society* (Stanford, Calif., 1974).

ZSCHARNACK, L., *Der Dienst der Frau in den ersten drei Jahrhunderten der christlichen Kirche* (Göttingen, 1902).

INDEX

INDEX OF PAPYRI USED

The papyri listed below represent those papyri explicitly cited in the text or notes. Papyri treated in secondary articles used in this study but not cited explicitly should be sought in the article cited.